CELL MOVEMENT

Volume 2

Kinesin, Dynein,
and Microtubule Dynamics

CELL MOVEMENT
Volume 2

Kinesin, Dynein,
and Microtubule Dynamics

Editors

Fred D. Warner
Syracuse University
Syracuse, New York

J. Richard McIntosh
University of Colorado
Boulder, Colorado

ALAN R. LISS, INC., NEW YORK

Address all Inquiries to the Publisher
Alan R. Liss, Inc., 41 East 11th Street, New York, NY 10003

Copyright © 1989 Alan R. Liss, Inc.

Printed in the United States of America

Library of Congress Cataloging-in-Publication Data

Cell movement / edited by Fred D. Warner, Peter Satir, Ian R. Gibbons.
   p.   cm.
  Includes bibliographies and index.
  Contents: v. 1. The dynein ATPases—v. 2. Kinesin, dynein, and microtubule dynamics /editors, Fred D. Warner, J. Richard McIntosh.
   ISBN 0-8451-4267-4 ISBN 0-8451-4296-8 (set)
   1. Cells—Motility. 2. Cytoplasmic streaming. 3. Dynein.
4. Kinesin. I. Warner, Fred D., 1943- . II. Satir, Peter.
III. Gibbons, Ian R.
   [DNLM: 1. Cell Movement.   QH 647 C3932]
QH647.C46 1988
574.87'64—dc19
DNLM/DLC   88-23027
for Library of Congress   CIP

Cover illustration.
   Platinum replica of two rotary shadowed, cytoplasmic dynein ATPase particles (left panel), and several kinesin ATPase molecules (right panel) prepared by rapid-freeze, deep-etch microscopy. Photographs by John E. Heuser. × 450,000. (See Chapter 17 by M.P. Sheetz.)

Designed by Jesse Sanchez

Contents

INTRODUCTION
Energy Transducing Proteins and Cell Movement

SECTION 1. Molecular Composition of Microtubules

Contributors

Richard Adams, Department of Cell Biology and Anatomy, Johns Hopkins University School of Medicine, Baltimore, MD 21205 **[3]**

Takao Arai, Institute of Basic Medical Sciences, University of Tsukuba, Tsukuba Science City, Ibaraki 305, Japan **[335]**

Tobias Baskin, Department of Botany, University of California, Berkeley, CA 94720 **[441]**

George S. Bloom, Department of Cell Biology and Anatomy, University of Texas Southwestern Medical Center, Dallas, TX 75235 **[321]**

Gary G. Borisy, Laboratory of Molecular Biology, University of Wisconsin, Madison, WI 53706 **[253]**

Scott T. Brady, Department of Cell Biology and Anatomy, University of Texas Southwestern Medical Center, Dallas, TX 75235 **[321]**

Beth Burnside, Department of Physiology-Anatomy, University of California, Berkeley, CA 94720 **[169]**

W. Zacheus Cande, Department of Botany, University of California, Berkeley, CA 94720 **[441]**

Stanley A. Cohn, Department of Molecular and Cellular Biology, National Jewish Center for Immunology and Respiratory Medicine, Denver, CO 80206 **[307]**

Susan K. Dutcher, Department of Molecular, Cellular, and Developmental Biology, University of Colorado, Boulder, CO 80309 **[83]**

Ursula Euteneuer, Department of Zoology, University of California, Berkeley, CA 94720 **[155]**

Susan P. Gilbert, Department of Molecular and Cell Biology, Pennsylvania State University, University Park, PA 16802 **[223]**

Lawrence S.B. Goldstein, Department of Cellular and Developmental Biology, Harvard University, Cambridge, MA 02138 **[233]**

Karen Greer, Department of Anatomy, University of Connecticut Health Science Center, Farmington, CT 06032 **[47]**

Thomas S. Hays, Department of Molecular, Cellular, and Developmental Biology, University of Colorado, Boulder, CO 80309 **[371]**

Nobutaka Hirokawa, Department of Anatomy and Cell Biology, University of Tokyo School of Medicine, Hongo, Tokyo 113, Japan **[383]**

Christopher Hogan, Department of Botany, University of California, Berkeley, CA 94720 **[441]**

Amie L. Ingold, Department of Molecular and Cellular Biology, National Jewish Center for Immunology and Respiratory Medicine, Denver, CO 80206 **[307]**

Ken Johnson, Department of Zoology, University of California, Berkeley, CA 94720 **[155]**

Michael P. Koonce, Department of Zoology, University of California, Berkeley, CA 94720 **[155]**

Philip L. Leopold, Department of Cell Biology and Anatomy, University of Texas Southwestern Medical Center, Dallas, TX 75235 **[321]**

Richard W. Linck, Department of Cell Biology and Neuroanatomy, University of Minnesota School of Medicine, Minneapolis, MN 55455 **[13,67]**

R. John Lye, Department of Molecular, Cellular, and Developmental Biology, University of Colorado, Boulder, CO 80309 **[141]**

Eckhard Mandelkow, Max-Planck-Unit for Structural Molecular Biology, c/o DESY, D-2000 Hamburg 52, Federal Republic of Germany **[23]**

Eva-Maria Mandelkow, Max-Planck-Unit for Structural Molecular Biology, c/o DESY, D-2000 Hamburg 52, Federal Republic of Germany **[23]**

Hirohisa Masuda, Department of Botany, University of California, Berkeley, CA 94720 **[441]**

The number in brackets is the opening page number of the contributor's article.

Gen Matsumoto, Analogue Information Section, Electrotechnical Laboratory, Tsukuba Science City, Ibaraki 305, Japan **[335]**

Kent L. McDonald, Department of Molecular, Cellular, and Developmental Biology, University of Colorado, Boulder, CO 80309 **[155,441]**

J. Richard McIntosh, Department of Molecular, Cellular, and Developmental Biology, University of Colorado, Boulder, CO 80309 **[371,403]**

Timothy J. Mitchison, Department of Pharmacology, University of California, San Francisco, CA 94143 **[421]**

Bryce M. Paschal, Cell Biology Group, Worcester Foundation for Experimental Biology, Shrewsbury, MA 01545 **[211]**

Curtis M. Pfarr, Department of Molecular, Cellular, and Developmental Biology, University of Colorado, Boulder, CO 80309 **[141]**

K. Kevin Pfister, Department of Cell Biology and Anatomy, University of Texas Southwestern Medical Center, Dallas, TX 75235 **[321]**

Thomas D. Pollard, Department of Cell Biology and Anatomy, Johns Hopkins University School of Medicine, Baltimore, MD 21205 **[3]**

Mary E. Porter, Department of Molecular, Cellular, and Developmental Biology, University of Colorado, Boulder, CO 80309 **[141]**

Melanie M. Pratt, Department of Anatomy and Cell Biology, University of Miami School of Medicine, Miami, FL 33101 **[115,125]**

Joel L. Rosenbaum, Department of Biology, Yale University, New Haven, CT 06511 **[47]**

E.D. Salmon, Department of Biology, University of North Carolina, Chapel Hill, NC 27599 **[431]**

Paul J. Sammak, Department of Physiology-Anatomy, University of California, Berkeley, CA 94720 **[253]**

Manfred Schliwa, Department of Zoology, University of California, Berkeley, CA 94720 **[155]**

Jonathan M. Scholey, Department of Molecular and Cellular Biology, National Jewish Center for Immunology and Respiratory Medicine, Denver, CO 80206 **[307]**

Trina A. Schroer, Department of Cell Biology and Physiology, Washington University School of Medicine, St. Louis, MO 63110 **[295]**

Michael P. Sheetz, Department of Cell Biology and Physiology, Washington University School of Medicine, St. Louis, MO 63110 **[277,295]**

Howard S. Shpetner, Cell Biology Group, Worcester Foundation for Experimental Biology, Shrewsbury, MA 01545 **[211]**

Roger D. Sloboda, Department of Biological Sciences, Dartmouth College, Hanover, NH 03755 **[205,223]**

Bohdan J. Soltys, Laboratory of Molecular Biology, University of Wisconsin, Madison, WI 53706 **[253]**

Walter Steffen, Department of Cell Biology and Neuroanatomy, University of Minnesota School of Medicine, Minneapolis, MN 55455 **[67]**

Judy Tong, Department of Zoology, University of California, Berkeley, CA 94720 **[155]**

Yoko Yano Toyoshima, Department of Biology, Ochanomizu University, Ohtsuka, Tokyo 112, Japan **[287]**

Shoichiro Tsukita, Department of Ultrastructural Research Section, Tokyo Metropolitan Institute of Medical Science, Honkomagome, Bunkyo-ku, Tokyo 113, Japan **[335]**

Ronald D. Vale, Cell Biology Program, Department of Pharmacology, University of California, San Francisco, CA 94143 **[287]**

Richard B. Vallee, Cell Biology Group, Worcester Foundation for Experimental Biology, Shrewsbury, MA 01545 **[211]**

Guy P.A. Vigers, Department of Molecular, Cellular, and Developmental Biology, University of Colorado, Boulder, CO 80309 **[371]**

Mark C. Wagner, Department of Cell Biology and Anatomy, University of Texas Southwestern Medical Center, Dallas, TX 75235 **[321]**

Linda Wordeman, Department of Botany, University of California, Berkeley, CA 94720 **[441]**

Preface

Kinesin, Dynein, and Microtubule Dynamics is the second volume of a two-part sequence that examines the biochemistry and cell biology of two groups of energy-transducing enzymes, the dynein and kinesin ATPases. The subject matter covered by this volume is more diverse than that of Volume 1 for several reasons. The material covered includes a characterization of two very different enzymes, kinesin and cytoplasmic dynein. Also included are articles describing types of microtubule-associated proteins which have no known motile function, but whose capacity to bind to microtubules and modulate their polymerization properties are likely to be important for microtubule dynamics and motility in vivo. Such molecules must be considered in a book on microtubule-mediated cell motility, because one of the characteristics of cytoplasmic microtubules and the processes they mediate is that the polymeric framework for motile action is labile, and both the assembly and disassembly of microtubules are often coupled to motile events. This volume also contains chapters on microtubule structure, on the organelles that govern the initiation of microtubule assembly, and on fruitful examples of microtubule-mediated motility where the absolute identity of the relevant force-coupled enzymes is not yet known. These subjects are all of obvious interest and importance in an analysis of microtubule-coupled cell movement.

The microtubule- and microfilament-dependent motility enzymes are responsible for movement in different directions, toward the plus (rapid assembly) or minus (slow assembly) ends of the linear polymer. As we assembled this volume, it became apparent that several terminologies were being used to describe this movement, but many of these (e.g., orthograde and retrograde in neurons) do not apply to all cell types. The confusion inherent in these terminologies can be moderated if the terms *plus-end* and *minus-end* are used by researchers to describe *the direction of movement of the enzyme along a track of filaments*, regardless of whether the enzyme is anchored to a vesicle, another filament, or a glass surface. Using this convention, dynein is a minus-end-directed motor while kinesin and myosin are both plus-end-directed motors. (A uniform terminology for the dynein ATPases and their subunits is presented in the preface to Volume 1, *The Dynein ATPases*).

Volume 2 is organized into five sections: 1) The molecular composition of microtubules, 2) cytoplasmic dynein ATPases, with particular attention to the forms of dynein and related ATPases that are found outside cilia or flagella, 3) cytoplasmic dynein ATPases, with particular attention to the dynamic behavior of microtubules and their accessory proteins, 4) kinesin-coupled particle translocation, and 5) the dynamic behavior of mitotic microtubules. Each section is begun by a *Perspective* chapter in which the editor of that section presents an overview of the subject under consideration, relating the material to other aspects of the field and of this series. The volume is introduced by a chapter from Richard Adams and Thomas D. Pollard in which they consider the features likely to be common to all of the motility enzymes including dynein, kinesin, and myosin-I.

The goal of this volume is not to be encyclopedic, but to assemble in one readily accessible place a set of articles that will reflect the current state of the field and the views of the major students of microtubule-mediated cell motility. In consequence of this goal, the volume also relates the diverse investigations that led to the discovery of the cytoplasmic forms of the microtubule-activated ATPases. The result is necessarily eclectic, but it is also timely, lively, informative, and interesting.

J. Richard McIntosh
April 1988

Acknowledgments

The editors are grateful for the expert editorial assistance of Jane H. McIlvain and Erika M. Robinson, whose patience, cooperation, and talent greatly assisted production of *Kinesin, Dynein, and Microtubule Dynamics.*

Contents of Volume 1
The Dynein ATPases

Fred D. Warner, Peter Satir, and Ian R. Gibbons, Editors

INTRODUCTION

Energy Transducing Proteins and Cell Movement

Chapter 1

Prediction of Common Properties of Particle Translocation Motors Through Comparison of Myosin-I, Cytoplasmic Dynein, and Kinesin

Richard Adams and Thomas D. Pollard

Prediction of Common Properties of Particle Translocation Motors Through Comparison of Myosin-I, Cytoplasmic Dynein, and Kinesin

Richard Adams and Thomas D. Pollard

Department of Cell Biology and Anatomy, Johns Hopkins University School of Medicine, Baltimore, Maryland 21205

The compartmentalization of the eukaryotic cell into various membranous organelles increases metabolic efficiency and sophistication but requires that the cell has a means of positioning and transporting these organelles within the cytoplasm for them to perform their allotted tasks. It has long been believed that these organelles are actively moved along the cytoskeleton, mediated by force-generating motors. We now have three proteins that have been identified as putative motors for organelles within the cytoplasm. Two of these are thought to move organelles along microtubules, the presumed substrate for long translocation within the cell; the third motor could move organelles along actin filaments. In comparing the characteristics of these enzymes in vitro and considering the requirements for the transport of organelles within the cell (widely studied in a number of cell types) we should now be able to make a number of predictions of properties not yet described for these motors and suggest future work to be done.

Two enzymes have been identified that interact with microtubules in vitro with properties expected of motors. The first to be discovered is an anterograde motor, kinesin (Vale et al., 1985a), first isolated from nervous tissue but since identified elsewhere. Subsequently a putative retrograde motor has been found, MAP 1C (Paschal and Vallee, 1987), which is a cytoplasmic dynein similar to the familiar cilliary dyneins. Together these two enzymes could provide bidirectional movement along microtubules. One actin-based organelle motor has been isolated, myosin-I. This enzyme resembles the catalytic amino-terminal portion of other myosins but does not polymerize to form filaments. It could move organelles along aligned actin filaments, possibly at the periphery of the cell, or be involved in whole cell motility and mechanics. These three motors are obviously different, but they have enough properties in common (Table 1–1) that their comparison should allow the prediction of further characteristics. Properties

TABLE 1–1.

	Dynein	Kinesin	Myosin-I
Sequence known	−	−	+
MgATPase activity stimulated by	Microtubules	Microtubules	Actin filaments
Enzyme activity regulated by			
Ca^{2+}	−	−	−
Phosphorylation	?	?	+
Translocation of			
Plastic beads		+	+
Polymer over glass	+	+	?
Organelles	?	+	+
Direction	Toward (−) end	Toward (+) end	Toward barbed (+) end
Binding to membranes	?	?	+
regulated by	?	?	?
Intracellular localization	?	Mitotic spindle	Plasma membrane and organelle membranes

that have been established to date to be common for the motors are as follows.

1. All of these motor proteins hydrolyze adenosine triphosphate (ATP) and use this energy to translocate the molecule and attached structures along a cytoskeletal polymer: either actin filaments or microtubules. Most of the attention has been given to microtubule-based particle movements, but since actin filaments are clearly the substrate in plant cells (for review, see Williamson, 1986) they are worthy of consideration as substrates for organelle translocation in animal cells as well.

2. Each motor moves unidirectionally over only one type of cytoskeletal polymer. Both + end (dynein) and − end (kinesin) motors are known for microtubules (Vale et al., 1985a; Paschal and Vallee, 1987), but only barbed + end motors (myosins) are known for actin filaments. There is no evidence for − end, actin-based motors. In theory they seem less probable than − end microtubule motors, since the often untethered − end of a single actin filament could not support the force generated by a moving organelle like the more rigid microtubules. This reservation is not conclusive. The fact that bundles of actin filaments probably possess sufficient rigidity should encourage a search for a − end actin-based motor.

3. The energy-transducing enzyme activity is coupled to interaction with the cytoskeletal polymer. This property was first discovered for myosins, and it seems that dyneins and kinesins behave much the same (for a comparison of myosin and dynein, see Johnson, 1985). Both myosin and kinesin have very low ATPase activity unless they interact with their substrate polymers. Dyneins have a higher basal level of Mg^{2+}ATPase activity that is stimulated to a lesser extent by microtubules (Johnson, 1985).

Given the extent of our knowledge of purified enzymes and our observations of organelle movements in living cells, we are able to predict further properties of these enzymes if they are, indeed, motors within the cell.

1. The motors must have the capacity to bind the transported particles. This is presumed in the cases of kinesin and cytoplasmic dynein based on in vitro motility of organelles in both the anterograde and retrograde directions (Vale et al., 1985b). In vitro reconstitution studies are eagerly awaited for purified enzymes and organelles. Below, we demonstrate binding of purified myosin-I to isolated membranes.

2. The activity of these particle motors

must be regulated in some way. Myosin-I is regulated by phosphorylation of the heavy chain (Maruta and Korn, 1977), so analogous enzymes should be sought for kinesin and cytoplasmic dynein. It seems likely that the binding to membranes is also regulated, but nothing has yet been learned about these interactions. It is clear that in the cell organelles can move bidirectionally. While they may persistently move in one direction for an enormous distance in an axon, they do have the ability to move in the counter direction and may be caused to do so experimentally (Smith, 1980). In other cells organelles can clearly be seen to undergo bidirectional movement. Once moving one way, translocation does appear to show persistence, suggesting that the possession of (presumably) two antagonistic motors does not result in zero net movement. The direction of intracellular movements in specialized pigmented cells are evidently controlled by intracellular concentrations of cyclic adenosine monophosphate (cAMP) (Rozdzial and Haimo, 1986). Such global control is not active in other cell types, but a similar local modulation of activity of the enzymes is expected.

Of the three classes of motor proteins, myosin-I is the best characterized biochemically (Table 1–1), but the least understood in terms of cell biology. While most of the recent interest in the field of intracellular particle movements has focused on microtubule-dependent motors, including kinesin and dynein, we have been investigating the possibility that myosin may be the motor for some organelle movements. The well-documented rapid movement of organelles along actin filament bundles in plants (for review, see Williamson, 1986) provides a strong biological basis for believing that myosin is associated with at least some such movements. Important questions include what sort of myosin is responsible for these movements and what processes in animal cells depend on these movements? We now believe that the single-headed myosin isozyme (myosin-I) is responsible for actin-based or-

ganelle movements and have begun to study the molecular basis for the interaction of this motor with cellular membranes.

Myosin-I was first discovered in *Acanthamoeba* (Pollard and Korn, 1973a). From the beginning it was realized that myosin-I is related to but distinct from the conventional myosin-II that had been found in muscle and nonmuscle cells. Like all other myosins, it binds reversibly to actin and has actin-activated ATPase activity (Pollard and Korn, 1973b). Unlike other myosins, it consists of a single heavy chain and does not polymerize into filaments.

The amino acid sequences deduced from genomic clones of *Acanthamoeba* (Jung et al., 1986) and bovine intestinal myosin-I (see below) (Hoshimaru and Nakanishi, 1987) explain the unique properties of myosin-I. The N-terminal region of the heavy chain is closely related to the heads of all other known myosins. The sequence of the C-terminal end of the heavy chain is incompatible with the formation of an α-helical coil (Figure 1–1). Hence, myosin-I has no tail and cannot form filaments.

Workers in Korn's laboratory have studied in detail the enzyme activity and functional domains of *Acanthamoeba* myosin-I (Fig. 1–1). The N-terminal 75 kDa domain has the ATPase activity and the ATP-sensitive actin-binding site (Lynch et al., 1986; Jung et al., 1987; Brzeska et al., 1988). The actin-activated ATPase activity requires phosphorylation of the heavy chain by a specific kinase (Maruta and Korn, 1977; Hammer et al., 1983). There is a second ATP-insensitive actin-binding site near the C-terminus (Lynch et al., 1986).

Myosin-I is not restricted to *Acanthamoeba*. It has subsequently been identified in other cells, including *Dictyostelium* (Cote et al., 1985), *Drosophila* rhabdomeres (Montell and Rubin, 1988), and bovine intestine (Hoshimaru and Nakanishi, 1987). The myosin-I family may also include the "110 k" actin-activated ATPase from the intestinal brush border (Collins and Borysenko, 1984; Conzelman and Mooseker, 1987) that forms a cross link from the actin

Myosin-I

Myosin-II

Fig. 1–1. Functional domains of myosin-I and myosin-II as revealed by biochemical studies (references are given in the text). Myosin-I has an N-terminal globular head, homologous to other myosins, containing an ATP-binding site and an ATP-sensitive actin-binding site. Unlike myosin-II and other myosins, the C terminus of myosin-I does not contain a self-associating, rod-like tail. Instead, myosin-I contains a second, ATP-insensitive actin-binding site. Removal of the C-terminal 30 kDa fragment of myosin-I does not abolish its ability to bind to membranes; we conclude, therefore, that the membrane-binding site of myosin-I is most likely located immediately C-terminal to the conserved globular head region.

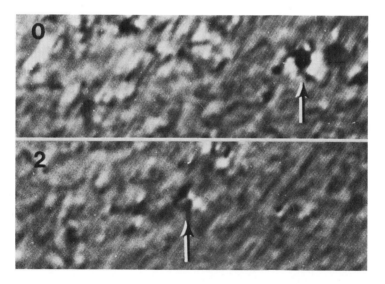

Fig. 1–2. Light micrographs taken at 2-min intervals of isolated *Acanthamoeba* organelles moving along the cortical actin bundles of *Nitella* (see Adams and Pollard, 1986). This is a phase contrast image with a background image continuously subtracted from the current image to contrast moving components. 0, zero minutes; 2, 2 min. 15,000×.

filament bundle to the overlying plasma membrane (Matsudaira and Burgess, 1979; Glenney and Weber, 1980). The 110 k ATPase differs from other myosin-Is in having up to four calmodulin molecules associated with the heavy chain (Coluccio and Bretscher, 1987) instead of light chains, although it should be noted that myosin light chains are related in part of their sequences to calmodulin (Kobayashi et al., 1988).

B A   B A

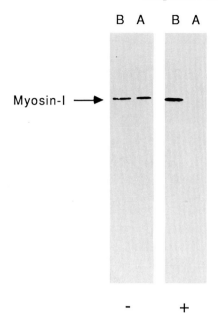

Myosin-I ➤

-           +

Fig. 1–3. Binding of purified *Acanthamoeba* myosin-I with NaOH-extracted membranes from *Acanthamoeba* organelles. Myosin-I was mixed with buffer with (+) or without (−) extracted membranes. Samples were taken of the mixture before centrifugation (B) and of the supernatant after centrifugation (A). The samples were run on a 7.5% Laemmli polyacrylamide gel, transferred to nitrocellulose, stained with a monoclonal antibody against myosin-I (M1.8), and visualized using a peroxidase-linked goat antimouse antibody. Myosin-I binds to and is pelleted with the extracted membranes.

The initial clue that myosin-I is responsible for organelle movements came from an in vitro motility assay (Adams and Pollard, 1986) based on *Nitella* actin bundles (Sheetz and Spudich, 1983). When crude extracts of *Acanthamoeba* were applied to *Nitella* actin bundles, some of the organelles bound to and moved along the actin filaments at a velocity of ~0.25 μm · sec^{-1} (Fig. 1–2). Antibody inhibition experiments suggested that myosin-I powered these movements. A monoclonal antibody that inhibited the actin-activated ATPase activity of myosin-I (Hagen et al., 1986) stopped the organelle movements along the *Nitella* actin. Several different antibodies that inhibit

the conventional two-headed myosin-II did not inhibit the organelle movements (Adams and Pollard, 1986) but did block the bulk contraction of gelled cytoplasmic extracts (Kiehart and Pollard, 1984). These movements were about 10 times faster than purified myosin-I–moved plastic beads in the same assay (Albanesi et al., 1985).

When the cytoplasmic extracts of *Acanthamoeba* were fractionated on a Percoll gradient, most of the myosin-II remained in the soluble fraction, but a large fraction of the myosin-I sedimented with various organelles (Adams and Pollard, 1986). About 20% sedimented near the bottom of the gradient together with the most dense organelles. These organelles could be recovered from the gradient and resume their movements along actin.

We have now investigated this association of myosin-I with membranes in detail. Removal of all of the myosin-1 from organelle membranes requires harsh conditions, such as 0.1 M NaOH. The stripped membranes retain their ability to bind myosin-I (Fig. 1–3), but do not bind myosin-II, muscle myosin subfragment-1, or other control proteins. In physiological ionic conditions, the K_d for the complex of myosin-IB with base-extracted membranes is about 140 nM, suggesting that substantial amounts of myosin-I may bind to membranes in the cell. Since neither muscle subfragment-1 nor the 30 kDa C-terminal chymotryptic fragment of *Acanthamoeba* myosin-IA binds to these membranes, we suspect that the membrane-binding site is located on the heavy chain somewhere between residues ~670 and ~920 (Fig. 1–1).

It is hoped that some indication of the role of myosin-I in the cell can be discerned from its intracellular distribution. This has been established only to the level of the light microscope at present. Published reports (Gadasi and Korn, 1980; Hagen et al., 1986) on the localization of myosin-I with fluorescent antibodies showed a general cytoplasmic distribution with some concentration near the plasma membrane. Closer examination of the intracellular distribution has re-

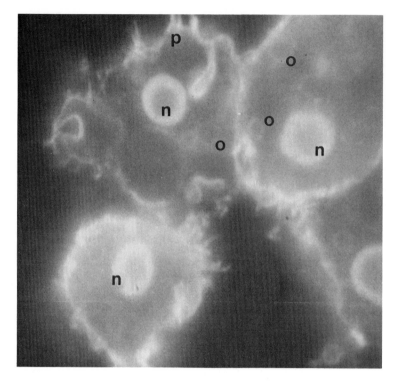

Fig. 1–4. Immunofluorescent localization of myosin-I in whole *Acanthamoeba.* Cells were fixed in 2% formaldehyde, extracted in acetone ($-20°C$), stained with a monoclonal antibody against myosin-I (M1.8), and visualized with a fluorescein-labeled goat antimouse antibody. The image was recorded with a SIT camera and enhanced with averaging and background subtraction. Antibody M1.8 also cross reacts with a low-M_r nuclear protein. n, Nucleus; p, plasma membrane; o, intracellular organelle. $3,600\times$.

vealed that myosin-I is also concentrated on the surface of a variety of organelles (Fig. 1–4). We await more precise localization in the electron microscope.

The physiological function of myosin-I–powered organelle movements is unknown, but we suggest that these movements may complement the microtubule-based, kinesin-powered (Kachar et al., 1987) organelle movements in *Acanthamoeba.* Like other myosins, myosin-I moves from the pointed end toward the barbed end of the actin filaments. Given the polarity of the actin filaments that are attached to the plasma membrane at their barbed ends (Pollard, 1975), this may emphasize movements of organelles toward the plasma membrane (Fig. 1–5), particularly in the vicinity of the

plasma membrane. A feature that appears to be in common with myosin-I and related proteins of other organisms is the association with microvilli (Matsudaira and Burgess, 1979) and the cell surface (Gadasi and Korn, 1980; Hagen et al., 1986). This may be taken as an indication that myosin-I may have a wider role in the organization and movement of the cell surface. Further, recent experiments with the experimental depletion of myosin-II in *Dictyostelium* (Knecht and Loomis, 1987; de Lozanne and Spudich, 1987) did not abolish cell motility. Myosin-I, known to exist in *Dictyostelium,* may be generating the tension required for cell motility.

We hope that the experience with myosin-I provides encouragement for those working

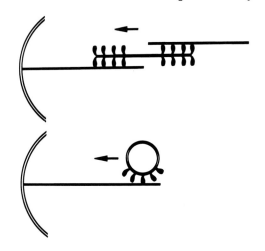

Fig. 1–5. By analogy to the force generated on a tethered actin filament by a conventional myosin filament, a vesicle coated with myosin-1 could be moved toward the plasma membrane along an actin filament bound by its + end.

on kinesin and cytoplasmic dynein to look for membrane-binding sites on stripped organelle membranes, for kinases that regulate enzyme activity, and for membrane association in situ with new optical methods and electron microscopy. Similarly, the existence of direction-specific microtubule-based motors suggests that it may be worth searching for a retrograde − end, actin-based motor. Major efforts are now required to learn how the cell uses these organelle-translocating motors and its other cytoskeletal proteins to give the complex temporal and spatial control needed for the cell to function. The muscle and axonemal paradigms may be useful in guiding these studies, but for organelle transport some complexity is likely to result from the need for local control of enzymatic activity and structural interactions.

ACKNOWLEDGMENTS

This work was supported by NIH research grant GM26338 to T.P. and a Muscular Dystrophy Association Postdoctoral Fellowship to R.A. The specimen shown in Figure 1–4 was prepared by L. Satterwhite.

REFERENCES

Adams, R.J., and T.D. Pollard (1986) Propulsion of organelles isolated from *Acanthamoeba* along actin filaments by myosin-I. Nature (Lond.) 322:754–756.

Albanesi, J.P., H. Fujisaki, J.A. Hammer, E.D. Korn, R. Jones, and M.P. Sheetz (1985) Monomeric *Acanthamoeba* myosins-1 support movement in vitro. J. Biol. Chem. 260:8649–8652.

Brzeska, H., T.J. Lynch, and E.D. Korn (1988) Localization of the actin-binding sites of *Acanthamoeba* myosin-IB and effect of limited proteolysis on its actin-activated Mg^{2+}-ATPase activity. J. Biol. Chem. 263:427–435.

Collins, J.H. and C.W. Borysenko (1984) The 110,000-dalton actin- and calmodulin-binding protein from intestinal brush border is a myosin-like ATPase. J. Biol. Chem. 259:14128–14135.

Coluccio, L.M. and A. Bretscher (1987) Calcium-regulated cooperative binding of the microvillar 110 K-calmodulin complex to F-actin: Formation of decorated filaments. J. Cell Biol. 105:325–533.

Conzelman, K.A., and M.S. Mooseker (1987) The 110-kD protein–calmodulin complex of the intestinal microvillus is an actin-activated Mg^{2+}-ATPase. J. Cell Biol. 105:313–324.

Cote, G.P., J.P. Albanesi, T. Ueno, J.A. Hammer, and E.D. Korn (1985) Purification from *Dictyostelium discoideum* of a low molecular-weight myosin that resembles myosin-I from *Acanthamoeba castellanii.* J. Biol. Chem. 260:4543–4546.

de Lozanne, A. and J.A. Spudich (1987) Disruption of the *Dictyostelium* myosin heavy chain gene by homologous recombination. Science 236:1086–1091.

Gadasi, H. and E.D. Korn (1980) Evidence for differential intracellular localization of the *Acanthamoeba* myosin isozymes. Nature (Lond.) 286:452–456.

Glenney, J.R. Jr., and K. Weber (1980) Calmodulin-binding proteins of the microfilaments present in isolated brush borders and microvilli of intestinal epithelial cells. J. Biol. Chem. 255:10551–10554.

Hagen, S.J., D.P. Kiehart, D.A. Kaiser and T.D. Pollard (1986) Characterization of monoclonal antibodies to *Acanthamoeba* myosin-I that cross-react with both myosin-II and low molecular-mass nuclear proteins. J. Cell Biol. 103:2121–2128.

Hammer, J.A., J.P. Albanesi, and E.D. Korn (1983) Purification and characterization of a myosin-I heavy chain kinase from *Acanthamoeba castellanii.* J. Biol Chem. 258:10168–10175.

Hoshimaru, M., and S. Nakanishi (1987) Identification of a new type of mammalian myosin heavy chain by molecular cloning. J. Biol. Chem. 262:14625–14632.

Johnson, K.A. (1985) Pathway of the microtubule-dynein ATPase and the structure of dynein: a comparison with actomyosin. Ann. Rev. Biophys. Biophys. Chem. 14:161–188.

Jung G., E.D. Korn, and J.A. Hammer (1987) The heavy chain of *Acanthamoeba* myosin-IB is a fusion of myosin-like and non-myosin-like sequences. Proc. Natl. Acad. Sci. U.S.A. 84:6720–6724.

Kachar, B., J.P. Albanesi, H. Fujisaki, and E.D. Korn (1987) Extensive purification from *Acanthamoeba castellanii* of a microtubule-dependent translocator with microtubule-activated Mg^{2+}-ATPase activity. J. Biol. Chem. 262:16180–16185.

Kiehart, D.P. and T.D. Pollard (1984) Inhibition of *Acanthamoeba* actomyosin-II ATPase activity and mechanochemical function by specific monoclonal antibodies. J. Cell Biol. 99:1014–1033.

Knecht, D.A. and W.F. Loomis (1987) Antisense RNA inactivation of myosin heavy chain gene expression in *Dictyostelium discoideum*. Science 236:1081–1086.

Kobayashi, T., T. Takagi, K. Konishi, Y. Hamada, M. Kawaguchi, and K. Kohama (1988) Amino acid sequence of the calcium-binding light chain of myosin from the lower eukaryote, *Physarum polycephalum*. J. Biol. Chem. 263:305–313.

Lynch, T.J., J.P. Albanesi, E.D. Korn, E.A. Robinson, B. Bowers, and H. Fujisaki (1986) ATPase activities and actin-binding properties of subfragments of *Acanthamoeba* myosin-IA. J. Biol. Chem. 261:17156–17162.

Murata, H., and E.D. Korn (1977) *Acanthamoeba* cofactor protein is a heavy-chain kinase required for actin-activation of the Mg^{2+}-ATPase activity of *Acanthamoeba* myosin-I. J. Biol. Chem. 252:8329–8332.

Matsudaira, P.T. and D.R. Burgess (1979) Identification and organization of the components in the isolated microvillus cytoskeleton. J. Cell Biol. 83:667–673.

Montell, C. and G.M. Rubin (1988) The *Drosophila ninaC* locus encodes two photoreceptor cell specific proteins with domains homologous to protein kinases and the myosin heavy chain head. Cell 52:757–772.

Paschal, B.M. and R.B. Vallee (1987) Retrograde transport by the microtubule-associated protein MAP 1C. Nature (Lond.) 330:181–183.

Pollard, T.D. (1975) Functional implications of the biochemical and structural properties of cytoplasmic contractile proteins. In S. Inoué and R.E. Stephens (eds). Molecules and Cell Movement. New York: Raven Press, pp. 259–285.

Pollard, T.D. and E.D. Korn (1973a) *Acanthamoeba* myosin. I. Isolation from *Acanthamoeba castellanii* of an enzyme similar to muscle myosin. J. Biol. Chem. 248:4682–4690.

Pollard, T.D. and E.D. Korn (1973b) *Acanthamoeba* myosin. II. Interaction with actin and with a new cofactor protein required for actin-activation of Mg^{2+}-ATPase activity. J. Biol. Chem. 248:4691–4697.

Rozdzial, M.M. and L.T. Haimo (1986) Bidirectional pigment granule movements of melanophores are regulated by protein phosphorylation and dephosphorylation. Cell 47:1061–1070.

Sheetz, M.P. and J.A. Spudich (1983) Movement of myosin-coated fluorescent beads on actin cables in vitro. Nature (Lond.) 303:31–35.

Smith, R.S. (1980) The short term accumulation of axonally transported organelles in the region of localized lesions of single myelinated axons. J. Neurocytol. 9:39–65.

Vale, R.D., T.S. Reese, and M.P. Sheetz (1985a) Identification of a novel force-generating protein, kinesin, involved in microtubule-based motility. Cell 42:39–50.

Vale, R.D., B.J. Schnapp, T. Mitchison, E. Steuer, T.S. Reese, and M.P. Sheetz (1985b) Different axoplasmic proteins generate movement in opposite directions along microtubules in vitro. Cell 43:623–632.

Williamson, R.E. (1986) Organelle movements along filaments and microtubules. Plant Physiol. 82:631–634.

SECTION

1

Molecular Composition of Microtubules

Edited by Richard W. Linck

PERSPECTIVE
Microtubule Structure and Function

Richard W. Linck

Department of Cell Biology and Neuroanatomy, University of Minnesota School of Medicine, Minneapolis,
Minnesota 55455

INTRODUCTION

Dynein and kinesin provide locomotive forces along microtubules, but by analogy to a railroad, the microtubules themselves are far more than simple, inert tracks. First, in most instances microtubules are functionally dynamic in either their assembly or bending properties (Dustin, 1984; Gibbons, 1981). Second, nearly 200 different polypeptides are associated with certain microtubule systems (Piperno et al., 1977), making them essentially subcompartments of the cell with a level of complexity between that of ribosomes and mitochondria. The chapters in this section deal with the microtubule itself, i.e., the structure, chemistry, and assembly of its subunit proteins, as well as genetic aspects of microtubule-organizing centers. The perspective presented here primarily concerns how various factors influence microtubule structure and, in turn, how the structure might influence microtubule function.

To begin, microtubules have a number of different functions and effective mechanisms, as summarized in Table 2–1. With regard to motility the mechanisms of

dynein-mediated sliding and bending have been well studied in cilia and flagella (Brokaw, 1972; Fox and Sale, 1987; Gibbons, 1981; Sale and Satir, 1977; Satir, 1968; Summers and Gibbons, 1971; Warner, 1976; Warner and Satir, 1974). Rapid advances have extended sliding-based motility by demonstrating that flagellar dynein and brain microtubule-associated protein (MAP) 1C (a dynein) can actively transport microtubules along glass surfaces (Paschal et al., 1987; Paschal and Vallee, 1987) and that kinesin can actively transport membrane-bound vesicles along microtubules (Vale et al., 1985a). The twisting and coiling associated with microtubule motility is not so well understood, but this behavior is readily apparent from studies of cilia, flagella, axostyles, and the manchette (Gibbons, 1975, 1981; McIntosh, 1973; McIntosh and Porter, 1967; Miki-Noumura and Kamiya, 1979; Mooseker and Tilney, 1973; Woodrum and Linck, 1980; Zobel, 1973). While straight sliding may not involve large changes in microtubule structure, bending and coiling necessarily require drastic conformational changes in the proteins forming the microtubule wall. Even without further

Cell Movement, Volume 2: Kinesin,
Dynein, and Microtubule Dynamics, pages 13–21
© 1989 Alan R. Liss, Inc.

TABLE 2–1. Reported Functions of Microtubules

Function	Effective Mechanism[a]
A. Motility	1. Translocation (sliding)
	2. Bending
	3. Coiling/twisting
	4. Polymerization (directional)
	5. Depolymerization (directional)
B. Architecture	6. Skeletal struts
	7. Subcellular compartmentalization
	8. Morphogenesis
C. Cybernetics	9. Mechanochemical sensory transduction (Chemical transport) (Information processing)

[a]Some of these mechanisms are interrelated, e.g., translocation is presumed to result from propagated signals, and in some cases bending accompanies sliding. Supporting references are given in the text.

evidence, it is hard to view these structural changes as being merely passive. On the one hand, conformational changes within the microtubule could regulate interaction with the force-generating enzymes, much as tropomyosin and troponin regulate actin-myosin interactions; on the other hand, structural changes could influence microtubule elasticity and thus contribute to the conversion of sliding to bending (cf., Brokaw, 1985; Summers and Gibbons, 1971; Warner, 1976).

In other microtubule-dependent events, such as mitosis, motility is coupled to microtubule assembly and disassembly (Dietz, 1972; Inoué and Sato, 1967; for review, see McIntosh, 1979). As reviewed elsewhere in these volumes, the very process of microtubule assembly/disassembly may provide the driving force for chromosome movement; alternatively, microtubule assembly/disassembly, may be secondary to some other force-generating event. While the mechanisms of microtubule-dependent chromosome movement have not been elucidated, it is fair to say that the problem may benefit

from renewed interest in the structure and biochemistry of novel microtubule proteins.

Microtubules also perform a variety of architectural functions. It is harder to categorize the architectural mechanisms, because microtubules are less well studied from this perspective and because these mechanisms cannot always be separated from those of motility. In Table 2–1 the mechanisms are divided, depending on whether the microtubules function as skeletal struts in the determination of cell shape, as determinants of subcellular compartmentalization, or as effectors of cell and tissue morphogenesis. These mechanisms are largely dependent on a variety of microtubule-associated bridges, and thus perhaps a more tenable subdivision will arise from further studies of the relevant proteins, similar to the subdivision of actin-associated proteins (Pollard and Cooper, 1986). The cytoskeletal role of microtubules is clearly exemplified by blood platelets and certain erythrocytes, whose discoid shapes are maintained by marginal bands of *coiled* microtubules (Behnke, 1970). More dynamic examples of the cytoskeleton occur in heliozoans, wherein the formation and retraction of transient axopodia are modulated by the assembly and disassembly, respectively, of a double spiral arrangement of microtubules (Tilney, 1971). In numerous other examples the patterns of interphase microtubule cytoskeletons are unique (Dustin, 1984; Weber and Osborn, 1979). These microtubule arrays are initiated by microtubule organizing centers (MTOCs) (for review, see Dutcher, Chapter 6). How such elaborate cell- and species-specific patterns are generated are not understood, but the number of protofilaments in microtubules and the nature of intertubule bridges and MTOCs are major factors (Tilney, 1971).

As polymers, microtubules have regular, periodic structure and are thus able to act as templates and determinants for subcellular compartmentalization. At the molecular level this feature is most clearly illustrated by the complex but regular arrangement of dynein arms, radial spokes, and nexin links in cilia and flagella (Amos et al., 1976; Gibbons, 1981; Warner, 1970) or comparable linkages in axostyles and axopodia of protozoa (McIntosh, 1973; McIntosh and Porter, 1967; Tilney, 1971). While the periodic arrangement of some of these microtubule-associated proteins ultimately serves a motility function, the regular structure of microtubules could also provide for the attachment of cellular enzymes and other proteins not directly coupled to motility. The general hypothesis that elements of the cytomatrix (actin, intermediate filaments, and microtubules) provide for subcellular compartmentalization of metabolic enzymes (cf. Master, 1984) awaits supporting evidence but is given credence by the observation that creatine phosphokinase appears to be associated with intermediate filaments (Eckert et al., 1980). A higher level of cellular organization is reflected in the association of other organelles, such as lysosomes and mitochondria, with microtubules (Ball and Singer, 1982; Collot et al., 1984; Hirokawa, 1982). In light of advances in our understanding of kinesin-dependent transport of membrane-bound organelles along microtubules, the microtubule–organelle association may be a reflection of a motility function; however, without trying to force the issue, such microtubule–organelle associations can be equally viewed as a means of compartmentalizing the cytoplasm. For the extensive role that microtubules play in morphogenesis, the reader is referred to Dustin (1984).

The final suggested function in the repertoire of microtubules is that of cybernetics, which most commonly involves sensory transduction. The basis for this idea derives from the fact that cilia are associated with chemosensory and mechanosensory cells (Barber, 1974; Dustin, 1984). Two principal mechanisms of sensory transduction have been suggested: 1) that ciliary microtubules generate and directly transmit chemical-electrical signals along their length and 2) that they act indirectly by mechanically deforming membranes and thereby inducing

ion flow through channels (Barber, 1974). In theory the propagation of bending waves along the ciliary axoneme implies that biochemical events must take place in a sequential fashion along the microtubule axis, e.g., a propagated cycle of dynein cross bridges (as suggested from the work of Tsukita et al., 1983) or a propagated regulatory mechanism. Such a propagated event may constitute a form of signal transduction, but other than theory there is no experimental evidence that microtubules so act. Experimental observations do support, however, the mechanism that a mechanical bend of the ciliary shaft indirectly transmits the original stimulus to the epithelial–nerve cell junction (Moran et al., 1977; Stommel, 1984; Stommel et al., 1980). Further speculation as to the function of microtubules has ranged from the suggestion that they transport ions and small molecules through their lumens (Slautterback, 1963) to the suggestion that they act as microprocessors (Hameroff and Watt, 1982). The evidence for these latter ideas is virtually non-existent, but their mention should stimulate further investigation rather than discourage it.

STRUCTURAL FACTORS INFLUENCING MICROTUBULE FUNCTION

Obviously, many factors are involved in regulating microtubule functions, but our perspective here will focus on *structural* parameters, i.e., the protein composition of microtubules, the structure of tubulin dimers, the tubulin lattice, the number of protofilaments, microtubule polarity, and microtubule length.

Microtubule Proteins and Intrinsic and Extrinsic MAPs

In discussing the composition and structure of microtubules, a distinction must be made between native microtubules and the polymers obtained by in vitro assembly methods. Native microtubules are most commonly composed of 13 protofilaments. The traditional view is that all 13 protofilaments are composed of tubulin, a concept that is reinforced by the observation that pure tu-bulin will polymerize in vitro into tubular structures, albeit with variable numbers of protofilaments, usually 14 (Pierson et al., 1978). A contrary view has been presented, based on evidence obtained from flagellar microtubules, suggesting that certain proto-filaments may be composed of non-tubulin proteins (Linck, 1982). Supporting argu-ments given for this hypothesis are 1) Any insoluble, non-tubulin protofilaments would be discarded during the assembly/disassem-bly cycles of tubulin purification, and 2) the polymerization of tubulin into tubular struc-tures reflects an inherent property of tubu-lin to form cylindrical sheets but does not prove that all native protofilaments are tu-bulin. With this caveat, more precise defini-tions of the terms *microtubule protein* and *microtubule-associated proteins (MAPs)* are needed. Accordingly, we suggest and define the terms *microtubule protein, in-trinsic MAPs* and *extrinsic MAPs;* this termi-nology may require modification as more information is obtained. *Microtubule pro-teins* are those that are capable of forming native microtubule protofilaments and that are presently known to include only tubulin. *Intrinsic MAPs* are those that do not form protofilaments but are incorporated with tubulin to form microtubules and can be solubilized only by disrupting the structural integrity of the microtubule. *Extrinsic MAPs* are generally those that can be removed from microtubules without disrupting the microtubule. Until they are better character-ized, we continue to refer to unspecified microtubule components as *MAPs* (see also Solomon, 1986; Vallee, 1986).

Axonemal dynein, kinesin, and the high-M_r brain MAPs 1 and 2 fall into the extrinsic category, since they can be salt-extracted from intact microtubules or can be reasso-ciated with preexisting microtubules (Amos, 1987; Gibbons, 1965; Vale et al., 1985a; Vallee, 1986). Several other MAPs have been described, but it is not yet clear into what category they fall: calmodulin and protein kinase components (cf. Dedman et al., 1979), chartins (Magendantz and Solomon,

1985), polypeptide IEF-51 (Kenney et al., 1988), stable-tubule-only polypeptides (STOPs) (Job et al., 1983; Margolis et al., 1986), tau (Cleveland et al., 1977a), and tektins (Linck and Stephens, 1987; see also Steffen and Linck, Chapter 5). It has only been possible to obtain some of these MAPs in a soluble form by depolymerizing or dis-rupting the microtubules, but in most cases this criterion is not sufficient to determine whether these components are intrinsic or extrinsic MAPs or are true microtubule pro-teins. Only the tektins (for review, see Stef-fen and Linck, Chapter 5) so far fulfill other criteria: Tektins are the last proteins to be solubilized from microtubules, they quanti-tatively remain associated with a two-pro-tofilament domain, and they appear to exist as filaments (possibly even as protofila-ments) in the microtubule wall (Linck et al., 1985).

Structure of Tubulin Dimers

Microtubules are primarily constructed of α- and β-tubulin subunits, which cross-linking studies have indicated exist as het-erodimer dimers in solution (Ludueña et al., 1977). Both the structure and chemistry of tubulin have been critically reviewed by Mandelkow and Mandelkow in Chapter 3 and by Greer and Rosenbaum in Chapter 4. In this perspective I wish to emphasize only certain points concerning how tubulin influ-ences microtubule structure and assembly.

Built into the structure of tubulin is the information to assemble into protofilaments in a polar fashion and to assemble laterally to form cylindrical sheets or tubules (Amos and Klug, 1974; Beese et al., 1987a; Mandelkow et al., 1986). Tubulin can be post-translationally modified, and, in addition, tubulin interacts with a variety of MAPs and other ligands, such as guanine nucleotide and tubulin-specific pharmacological compounds (e.g., colchicine and taxol); all of these modifica-tions and ligands affect tubulin assembly in vitro and in vivo. Mandelkow and Mandelkow (Chapter 3) offer an interesting explanation of how the guanine nucleotide-binding sites on the dimer could influence the assembly or stability of tubulin and the structural polarity of the microtubule; that model predicts which subunits (α or β) forms the minus and plus ends of microtubules.

Tubulin exists in several genetic and post-translationally modified isoforms, importantly, even within individual cells. This heterogeneity is sometimes related to functionally different tubulin systems, i.e., biochemical studies have shown that unique tubulin isoforms comprise different microtubule systems, including flagellar, mitotic, and more general cytoplasmic microtubules (Stephens, 1981; Suprenant et al., 1985; for review, see Silflow et al., 1987), and that another isoform occurs in certain membranes (Stephens, 1981, 1986). Nevertheless, considerable evidence indicates that products of a single tubulin gene may participate in many or all of the microtubule systems within a cell or organism (Fuller et al., 1987; Oakley and Morris, 1981; cf. Silflow et al., 1987); conversely, multiple genetic isoforms have been shown to coexist within individual microtubules (Lopata and Cleveland, 1987). Presumably, then, the post-translational modifications of tubulin far extend the limited number of tubulin isoforms provided by the genome. The microheterogeneity provided by post-translational modification has been studied by immunofluorescence microscopy (Bulinski et al., 1988). These studies have shown that an individual microtubule may be composed of a mixture of tyrosylated, non-tyrosylated, and acetylated (and presumably non-acetylated) tubulin. The function of such extraordinary chemical diversity within one microtubule is unclear (see Greer and Rosenbaum, Chapter 4), although the acetylation, detyrosylation, and phosphorylation of tubulin appears to be a property of relatively stable microtubules.

Tubulin Lattice

The tubulin lattice, i.e., the arrangement of tubulin dimers in the microtubule wall, will have major consequences on microtubule function, such as assembly, disassembly, stability, and interactions with effector MAPs. Two lattices were originally described, the A and B lattices, after the A and B subfibers of flagellar doublet microtubules (Amos and Klug, 1974). Several lines of evidence have since suggested that native singlet microtubules may be primarily composed of a B-lattice configuration and that tubulin may be assembled in vitro into cylinders composed of mixtures of the A- and B-lattices (Linck and Langevin, 1981; Mandelkow et al., 1977, 1986; McEwen and Edelstein, 1980; Woodrum and Linck, 1980). Microtubules composed of a B lattice would possess what has been called a *seam* formed by a stagger or discontinuity between certain protofilaments. A seam might take the form of two tubulin protofilaments laterally associated in an A-lattice configuration (see Fig. 3–3a in Mandelkow and Mandelkow, Chapter 3); a seam might also be constructed from one tubulin protofilament and one non-tubulin protofilament (see Linck and Langevin [1982] and related discussions above). Possible functions of such seams have been proposed and discussed elsewhere (Linck and Langevin, 1981); briefly, 1) seams may provide specific attachment sites for certain MAPs, 2) formation of the seam may be a key step in the nucleation of microtubule assembly, and 3) seams and MAPs may play a role in stabilizing microtubules.

The lattice may also be important in terms of the interaction of microtubules with dynein and kinesin. In cilia and flagella, the A-tubule of each doublet microtubule binds to one end of the dynein molecule (the A end), and this binding is adenosine triphosphate (ATP) independent (a physiologically stable connection); the other end of the dynein arm (the B end) binds to the B subfiber of the adjacent doublet tubule by an ATP-dependent process (a transient cross bridge); for relevant literature see Gibbons, 1965, 1975; Haimo et al., 1979; Porter and Johnson, 1983; Warner, 1976). The structural aspects of the microtubule recognized by dynein and kinesin are not known. It could be that dynein or kinesin, at either of their ends, recognizes a single α- or β-

tubulin subunit or a whole tubulin dimer; alternatively, the ATPase might bind to a pair of protofilaments with the appropriate subunit arrangement. In flagella, dynein binds by the A-end to only two points around the A-tubule, but the information specifying these exact points of association is not known. It could be that seams in the microtubule lattice dictate the dynein loci. Alternatively, and whether or not there are seams, the dynein loci could be determined by the organization of other MAPs around the microtubule or by the template structure of the basal body. These problems concerning the microtubule lattice and the structural interactions of microtubules with dynein and other MAPs await further study.

Number of Protofilaments

As is well known, microtubules of most cell types and species are composed of 13 protofilaments (pfs) (Ledbetter and Porter, 1964; Tilney et al., 1973); however, certain microtubules contain a different number of pfs. For example, nerve axons of the crayfish *Procambarus* have microtubules with 12 pfs, while adjacent glial cells have microtubules with the standard 13 (Burton et al., 1975). In the wild-type nematode *Caenorhabditis elegans* different types of microtubules contain 11, 13, or 15 pfs, but changes appear in specific sets of these microtubules in mutants with sensory defects (Chalfie and Thomson, 1982). What controls the number of pfs and how does the pf number affect microtubule function? The A-tubules of cilia and flagella have 13 pfs and are generated by a basal body, whose A-tubules also contain 13 pfs, clearly indicating a template function of basal bodies and centrioles in regulating pf number (Tilney et al., 1973). This phenomenon has been experimentally demonstrated by Scheele et al. (1982), who showed that flagellar axoneme A-tubules will nucleate the assembly of brain tubulin into 13 pf structures. Most cytoplasmic microtubules, however, are not nucleated directly by a centriolar template, and the regulatory mechanism of their pf numbers is unknown. Pf number is of course partly dependent on

the bond angles between tubulin protofilaments, but tubulin alone appears incapable of precisely specifying pf number, since pure tubulin polymerizes in vitro to form polymorphic structures with variable numbers of pfs, ranging from 9 to 16 with a mode of 14 (Linck and Langevin, 1981; Pierson et al., 1978). The possible effect of the high-M_r brain MAPs on microtubule structure has also been investigated, but these MAPs have not been found to regulate pf number (Scheele et al., 1982).

The effect of pf number is a critical factor in both the motility and architectural functions of microtubules. In highly ordered microtubule systems such as cilia, flagella, and axostyles, the azimuthal bond angle at which dynein arms bind to microtubules is of obvious importance to the stearic interactions between these components, and the number of pfs will directly affect that bond angle. The complex structural and chemical interactions required for axoneme motility would seem to have been a strong force in the evolution of the basal body, which generates the 9 + 2 axoneme and specifies the number of protofilaments. In a different system, that of the labile, spiral axonemes of heliozoans, the number of protofilaments must also be a factor in determining the bond angles of intermicrotubule bridges, which in turn govern the long-range order of the microtubule arrays (Tilney, 1971). Aside from the effects of pf number on architecture and motility, changes in the microtubule pf number also correlate with sensory defects in *Caenorhabditis* (Chalfie and Thomson, 1982); however, it is not known whether the change in pf number is directly related to the role of microtubules in mechanochemical transduction.

Microtubule Polarity

Microtubules are recognized to be polar structures; that is, their subunit proteins are oriented in the same direction along the tubule axis. The underlying polarity of the microtubule determines the directionality of force transmission by both orienting the attached force generators and influencing the direction of microtubule assembly and disassembly. Besides each microtubule having a given polarity, parallel microtubules within a functioning unit also have the same polarity; such microtubules are sometimes said to be "parallel" ($\Rightarrow$), in contrast to an antiparallel arrangement ($\leftrightarrows$).

Microtubule polarity is manifested in several ways. First, in cilia and flagella the assembly and elongation of the axoneme proceeds in vivo in a distal direction from the basal body template (cf., Dustin, 1984; Renaud and Swift, 1964; Witman, 1975). The uniform polarity of axonemal A-microtubules is clear from the orientation of the dynein arms (Gibbons, 1961) and radial spoke triplets (Warner and Satir, 1974); similarly, the uniform polarity of singlet microtubules in axostyles is evident from other structural considerations (Woodrum and Linck, 1980). In flagella the polarity of assembly was first observed in vitro by experiments showing that brain tubulin assembles preferentially onto the distal or plus ends of basal bodies and axonemal A-tubules and to a lesser extent onto the proximal or minus ends (Allen and Borisy, 1974; Bergen and Borisy, 1980; Rosenbaum et al., 1975).

For measuring the polarity of cytoplasmic microtubules two methods have been developed: 1) Haimo et al. (1979) found that flagellar dynein will reassociate with non-flagellar microtubules; and 2) Heidemann and McIntosh (1980) found that brain tubulin will assemble onto existing microtubules, forming curved arcs or hooks in cross section. In both methods the curvature of dynein arms and hooks indicates the absolute polarity by reference to cilia and flagella, where the plus end is distal (away from the center) and the minus end is proximal (toward the cell center). By these techniques it has since been found that most microtubules within a network have a uniform polarity. In each half of the meiotic or mitotic spindle, microtubules originating from the pole and from the kinetochores have the same relative polarity (Euteneuer and McIntosh, 1981a; Telzer and Haimo, 1981), with the distal or plus ends directed

away from the pole and toward the kinetochore. In melanophores, nerve axons, and heliozoan axopodia, microtubules are oriented with the plus end directed away from the cell body (Burton and Paige, 1981; for review, see Heidemann and Euteneuer, 1982). Microtubule polarity provides the underlying basis for determining the direction of force generation in mechanochemically coupled systems, many of which are considered in the ensuing sections of this volume.

Microtubule Length

Microtubule length is highly specified in certain organelles, and it is important in the architectural design and motility functions of microtubule systems. Individual microtubules are known to be as short as ~ 0.15 μm in the procentriole of *Allomyces arbusculus* (Renaud and Swift, 1964) or as long as 12 mm in the sperm tails of *Drosophila montana* (see Perotti, 1975). Even within a particular system, length is precisely governed. In cilia and flagella, the B subfibers terminate before the A-tubules, and the central pair tubules may be shorter or longer than the A-tubules, depending on species (Baccetti and Afzelius, 1976). In the axostyles of *Saccinobaculus,* microtubule lengths vary in a specific manner both within a single row and between different rows of microtubules (Woodrum and Linck, 1980). Furthermore, in the construction of the mitotic apparatus, e.g., in diatoms and PtK$_1$ cells, microtubule length in part defines the metaphase spindle morphology characteristic of each species, although microtubule lengths of course change during mitosis (McIntosh, 1979; Rieder, 1982).

What factors determine microtubule length? Although the pool of available subunits obviously influences the extent of microtubule elongation, evidence indicates that length is not specifically regulated by pure tubulin or by certain MAPs. In vitro purified brain tubulin and "partially purified tubulin" (i.e., recovered after one cycle of assembly disassembly) form tubule polymers that display wide variations in length

(Kuriyama and Miki-Noumura, 1975); however, in vivo microtubule lengths are precisely fixed, as noted above, even in the presence of excess pools of soluble tubulin (Inoué and Sato, 1967; Lefebvre and Rosenbaum, 1986; Rosenbaum et al., 1969). Furthermore, *Chlamydomonas* mutants have been characterized with short or long flagella, and the mutations do not map to tubulin genes (Barsel et al., 1988; Kuchka and Jarvik, 1987; Lefebvre and Rosenbaum, 1986). Clearly, then, other signal(s) or protein factor(s) must be responsible for length control.

One set of investigations has identified a possible mechanism of microtubule length control in sea urchin cilia. By pulse labeling deciliated sea urchin embryos, Stephens (1977) found that de novo synthesis of only two to three polypeptides was required for ciliary regeneration; all other axonemal polypeptides, including tubulin, were present in an excess pool. One of the required polypeptides, ~55 kDa, was made in a limited amount and was completely assembled into the cilium; additional synthesis of the 55 kDa polypeptide was required for subsequent cycles of ciliary regeneration. From these results Stephens (1977) postulated that the quantal synthesis of this component might be a factor controlling ciliary microtubule length. The 55 kDa polypeptide was originally identified as being a major constituent of Sarkosyl-insoluble protofilament ribbons of flagellar A-tubules (Linck, 1976), and has since been found to be biochemically and immunologically equivalent to one of the tektins (Linck and Stephens, 1987; Steffen and Linck, 1988; Stephens, 1987). Chapter 5 reviews additional evidence that tektins may be present in a variety of microtubule systems and may be regulators of microtubule length.

CONCLUSIONS

The function of microtubules depends to a large degree on their structure. This perspective has discussed several parameters of microtubule structure and how they might influence microtubule function, but there are many important outstanding problems. The full polypeptide composition of microtubules deserves greater attention, particularly with regard to the microtubule proteins, the intrinsic MAPs, and the extrinsic MAPs, as we have defined them here (see also Steffen and Linck, Chapter 5). Structural-chemical mapping of tubulin by biochemical and genetic methods is beginning to shed light on microtubule assembly and function (Mandelkow and Mandelkow, Chapter 3; Greer and Rosenbaum, Chapter 4), although further advances in crystallographic analysis are much needed. Evidence strongly suggests that microtubules are primarily dominated by a B-lattice arrangement of tubulin dimers, and such a structure has many exciting implications for microtubule assembly and function; however, further structural studies are required to define precisely the arrangement of tubulin and *other* possible microtubule proteins. The mechanism by which the cell specifies microtubule polarity is now partially understood: The inherent asymmetries of the tubulin monomers and dimers determine polarity within a microtubule (Mandekow and Mandelkow, Chapter 3), but the decision to orient microtubules rests with the MTOCs, most of which would appear to have the property of directing the initial orientation of tubulin dimers, possibly with α subunits oriented proximally and β subunits distally, as proposed by Mandelkow and Mandelkow (Chapter 3); however, kinetochores, if they truly nucleate microtubule assembly, would generate the opposite polarity. The number of protofilaments can be specified by the A-tubules of basal bodies and doublet tubules, which act as templates to nucleate 13-protofilament microtubules in vivo and in vitro; however, in vivo most microtubules are nucleated without an apparent structural template, and the mechanism for accurately specifying protofilament number is unknown. Each cell is also capable of specifying precise lengths of different microtubules within highly complex networks; the mechanism(s) of length control are not understood, but a possible explanation may be emerging (Steffen and Linck, Chapter 5). Finally, the ability of MTOCs (Dutcher, Chapter 6) not only to nucleate microtubules and specify their structure but also to provide three-dimensional spatial information within the cell offers challenges to biochemical, genetic, and structural approaches alike.

ACKNOWLEDGMENTS

This work was supported by United States Public Health Service grant GM35648 to R.W. Linck from the National Institute of General Medical Sciences.

Tubulin, Microtubules, and Oligomers: Molecular Structure and Implications for Assembly

Eckhard Mandelkow and Eva-Maria Mandelkow

Max-Planck-Unit for Structural Molecular Biology, % DESY, D-2000 Hamburg 52,
Federal Republic of Germany

INTRODUCTION

This review consists of two main parts. In the first, we summarize our current view of the structure of cytoplasmic tubulin, microtubules, and other assembly forms; in the second, we describe how different structures interact during microtubule assembly and disassembly. The analysis of microtubules and related structures may be subdivided on the basis of their hierarchy, ranging from the amino acid sequence of tubulin to protein domains, monomers (α or β), dimers (α–β), oligomers, microtubules or polymorphic assemblies, and finally to higher-order structures (microtubule bundles or networks). These levels of organization are usually studied by different methods; biochemistry dominates one end, X-ray diffraction and electron or light microscopy at the other. Various aspects of microtubule structure have been reviewed previously (Kirschner, 1978; Scheele and Borisy, 1979; Timasheff and Grisham, 1980; Amos, 1982; Correia and Williams, 1983; McKeithan and Rosenbaum, 1984; Dustin, 1984; Purich and Kristofferson, 1984; Cleveland and Sullivan,

1985; DeBrabander and DeMey, 1985; and other contributions to this volume). We will therefore recall only the main features and emphasize some recent results. Details on methods will be omitted; they can be found in the references.

STRUCTURE

Tubulin Monomers

Both tubulin chains (α- and β-tubulin, Fig. 3–1) have molecular weights around 50 kDa and consist of about 450 amino acid residues. Their sequences are known (Ponstingl et al., 1981; Krauhs et al., 1981; Valenzuela et al., 1981). They are about 40% homologous (60% when allowing for conservative substitutions). Tubulin has an average amino acid composition, an interesting feature being the highly acidic C-terminal 30–40 residues. A number of tubulin isoforms have been sequenced, all of which are highly homologous, with the notable exceptions of a variable C-terminal region (beyond residue 430) and a stretch near the N terminus between residues 33 and 59 (see review by

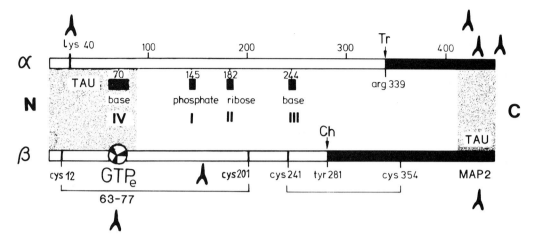

Fig. 3–1. Bar diagram representing the amino acid sequence of α and β tubulin. The solid and open parts show the C- and N-terminal domains, as defined by tryptic cleavage of α tubulin at arg339 and chymotryptic cleavage of β tubulin at tyr281. Shaded areas represent regions of high antigenicity when using isolated α or β monomers as antigens (α-specific antibodies near N terminus, β-specific ones near C terminus, cross reacting ones between corresponding domains of both chains). Regions I–IV show sites predicted to participate in nucleotide binding (conserved between α and β). Photo-cross-linked GTP is found in region IV (peptide 63–77); see Linse and Mandelkow, 1988). The inverted Ys are sites of monoclonal antibodies (Wehland et al., 1984; Breitling and Little, 1986; Grimm et al., 1987), one of which is near the acetylation site of α tubulin at lys40 (LeDizet and Piperno, 1987) and one near the phosphate binding loop of β tubulin (Hesse et al., 1987). MAP 2 and tau bind near the C terminus of β tubulin, tau also near the N terminus of α tubulin (Littauer et al., 1986). There are two pairs of closely spaced cysteines in β tubulin (Little and Ludueña, 1985, 1987).

Cleveland and Sullivan, 1985). It is interesting to note that a very high rate of homology exists between the N-terminal domain of β tubulin and the B subunit of chloroplast GAPDH, a protein apparently not related to microtubules (Cerff et al., 1986).

There is little direct evidence on the chain folding. Two pairs of cysteine residues of β-tubulin are in close proximity (cys241 and cys354, Little and Ludueña, 1985; cys12 and cys201 or 211, Little and Ludueña, 1987). Judging from circular dichroism, there is about 25% α helix and 47% β sheet (Lee et al., 1978). The X-ray fiber pattern suggests that α helices are distributed at various angles to the microtubule axis, whereas at least some β strands appear to be parallel to it (Mandelkow, 1986).

The shape of the monomer is known at about 2 nm resolution from electron microscopy of microtubules or various polymorphic forms combined with image recon-

struction (Amos and Klug, 1974; Amos and Baker, 1979; Tamm et al., 1979; Mandelkow et al., 1984) or X-ray fiber diffraction (E. Mandelkow et al., 1977; Beese et al., 1987a,b; Wais-Steider et al., 1987). The dimensions are about 4 nm (height), 3–5 nm (width), and 6–7 nm (radial extent). Both monomers are very similar, in agreement with the sequence homology. The image reconstructions show two peaks of density, recent X-ray data even three (Beese et al., 1987a). These could correspond to structural domains.

Chemical evidence for the domain structure comes from studies using limited proteolysis. The region around residue 300 is sensitive to a variety of proteases, suggesting two major domains comprising the N-terminal two-thirds and the C-terminal one-third of the molecule. For example, trypsin cleaves α tubulin at arg339, and chymotrypsin cleaves β tubulin at tyr281 (Mandelkow et al., 1985a). Another sensitive region is within 3–5 kDa of the C terminus (Serrano et al., 1984b; Sackett and Wolff, 1986). This region is on the outside of the microtubule wall since it binds microtubule-associated proteins (MAPs) and various antibodies (see below).

The comparison of tubulin with nucleotide binding proteins strongly suggests that the N-terminal domain is responsible for guanosine triphosphate (GTP) binding (Mandelkow et al., 1985a). There are three regions where tubulin is homologous with adenosine triphosphate (ATP) or dinucleotide binding proteins (see Fig. 3–1; I = residues 142–148, II = residues 180–183, III = residues 242–246) and another one (IV = residues 60–69), which tubulin shares with GTP-binding proteins (the numbering follows that of Krauhs et al. (1981) after alignment of α and β tubulin for optimal overall homology). The homologies suggest that regions I, II, and III are involved in the binding of phosphate, ribose, and base, respectively; region IV is also a candidate for base binding. The two predicted base binding sites can be distinguished by direct photo-cross linking of GTP to β tubulin and sequencing of the labeled peptide, showing that the guanine is cross-linked to the peptide 65–79, i.e., region IV (Linse and Mandelkow, 1988).

The homologies with nucleotide binding proteins suggest certain similarities in chain folding. As a rule, these proteins contain a central β-pleated sheet sandwiched between α helices (see Schulz and Schirmer, 1979). The nucleotides bind at turns where the chain exits from the C-terminal end of a β strand, switches around, and begins an α helix in a roughly opposite direction such that its dipole moment can compensate for the negative charges of the phosphates. In addition, there are some topological relationships between the β strands (e.g., sequence 3–1–2). This information can be used to construct hypothetical models of the base binding region of tubulin (see, e.g., Mandelkow et al., 1985b). However, in the absence of hard data such models should be

regarded with caution. One of the predicted sites (the cluster of glycines in region I) is directly comparable with the first of the three consensus sequences expected for GTP-binding proteins (see Dever et al., 1987), the second (DXXG) is absent. The third (NKXD) is also absent, but is adjacent to other homologous residues (region IV). From this position one would equate the stretch NKXD of G proteins with DLEP (69–72) of tubulin. Although they are different, they both have the hydrogen bonding capacity necessary to interact with the base, consistent with the observed base binding peptide. However, a problem remains in that region IV is upstream from region I rather than downstream as in the other G proteins. Thus the relationship between tubulin and nucleotide binding proteins remains ambiguous in spite of the observed homologies.

Both α and β tubulin bind GTP (see Jacobs et al., 1974). In the case of α tubulin, the binding is too tight to be measurable, and the dissociation of this "non-exchangeable" GTP correlates with protein denaturation. In the case of β tubulin, GTP and guanosine diphosphate (GDP) bind reversibly with dissociation constants of 22 and 61 nM (Zeeberg and Caplow, 1979). The nucleotide exchange is observed only with depolymerized tubulin dimers; microtubules or rings do not exchange and usually contain tightly bound GDP (Zeeberg et al., 1980), and the same holds true for oligomers smaller than rings (Mandelkow et al., 1988). The α and β monomers are nearly identical in the regions predicted to contribute to GTP binding, suggesting that the nucleotide binding pockets are very similar.

Several amino acid residues are targets for post-translational modifications and must therefore be located on the surface. Examples are the removal and attachment of the C-terminal tyrosine of α tubulin (Kumar and Flavin 1981; Gundersen et al., 1984), the acetylation of lysine 40 of α tubulin (L'Hernault and Rosenbaum, 1985a,b; LeDizet and Piperno, 1987), and the phosphorylation of α and/or β tubulin (Gard and Kirschner, 1985; Wandosell et al., 1986).

Finally, some structural information comes from the interaction between tubulin and other proteins, such as MAPs or antibodies. MAP 2 and tau bind near the C terminus of β tubulin (peptides 416–445), and tau also binds to N-terminal peptides of α tubulin (between residues 1 and 75; Littauer et al., 1986). The majority of antibodies bind near the C terminus, whose high antigenicity correlates with its high hydrophilicity and flexibility, the two criteria commonly used for predicting antigenic sites, another region of enhanced antigenicity is near the N terminus (Mandelkow et al., 1985b). The epitopes of several monoclonal antibodies have been mapped in these areas, e.g., near or at the C termini of α or β tubulin (Wehland et al., 1984; Breitling and Little, 1986), near residue 70 (Grimm et al., 1987) or 40 (LeDizet and Piperno, 1987) of α tubulin. These antibodies recognize both tubulin dimers and microtubules so that the epitopes must be exposed to the surface even in the polymer. Another antibody binding site is probably near the phosphate binding loop of β tubulin (region I in Fig. 3–1; Hesse et al., 1987).

Tubulin Dimers

Although from a structural point of view the monomer appears as the most prominent subunit, the functional subunit in assembly is the α–β heterodimer (Ludueña et al., 1977). The two monomers bind very tightly to one another (K_d below 1 μM; Detrich and Williams, 1978). The structural studies indicate that along a protofilament the monomers and the dimers associate head to tail. This implies that a microtubule has the same polarity as the monomers and dimers it consists of; the same holds true for most other assembly forms (except zinc-induced sheets; see Amos, 1982).

Some information on the arrangement of domains in dimers can be obtained from combining limited proteolysis with chemical cross linking (Kirchner and Mandelkow, 1985). The N-terminal domain of α tubulin interacts with the C-terminal domain of βtubulin, suggesting that these are responsi-

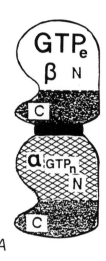

Fig. 3–2. Domain structure of tubulin dimers and protofilaments. **A:** Tubulin dimer. The intradimer bond is formed by the N-terminal domain of α tubulin (cross hatched, containing the non-exchangeable GTP_n) and the C-terminal domain of β tubulin (stippled); the solid region indicates the tight bond keeping the dimer together. Conversely, the interdimer bond (see Fig. 3–2B) involves the C-terminal domain of α tubulin (stippled) and the N-terminal domain of β tubulin (containing the exchangeable GTP_e; figure modified from Kirchner and Mandelkow, 1985). **B:** Model of the arrangement of domains in two protofilaments, shown nearly in register (as in the B lattice). The lower end has a crown of α monomers with their C-terminal domains exposed. The upper end has a crown of N-terminal β tubulin domains. A dimer associating onto the lower end must contribute its own GTP_e (tail polymerization). A dimer associating at the top is accepted by the GTP_e-bearing crown (left protofilament), and in turn it offers its own GTP_e to the next subunit (head polymerization). Thus every association event leads to the burial of the GTP involved inside the polymer, presumably it becomes hydrolyzed and non-exchangeable like the others further inside. GDP can replace GTP_e on dispersed dimers and presumably on the crown of exposed Nβ domains (hatched Nβ domains), thus modifying the assembly behavior (see text).

ble for the intradimer bonds (Fig. 3–2A). Conversely, the C-terminal domain of α tubulin and the N-terminal domain of β tubulin would be involved in the interdimer bonds formed during microtubule elongation.

These features are compatible with the

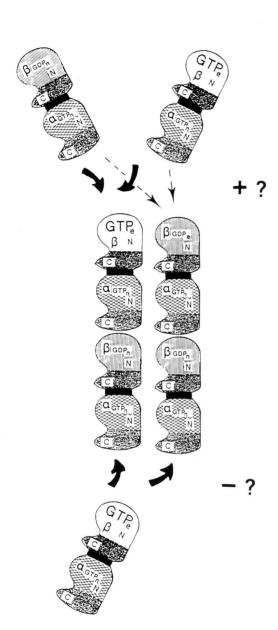

B

subunits but becomes non-exchangeable upon polymerization (GTP$_c$; Geahlen and Hayley, 1977; Mandelkow et al., 1985a; Nath and Himes, 1986). According to Figure 3–2B, this site would be exposed on a growing protofilament and become buried upon addition of a new subunit. On the other hand, α tubulin carries a GTP that is always non-exchangeable (GTP$_n$; judging by sequence homologies, this would also be on the N-terminal domain). Since this site is always buried, its function might be to keep the dimer tightly together.

The dimer model is consistent with a study of the tubulin-derived peptides that interact with tau. They are located near the N terminus of α tubulin and near the C terminus of β tubulin, compatible with their close juxtaposition (Littauer et al., 1986). The domain structure is also consistent with the observation that mutations in the N-terminal domain of β tubulin affect the polymerizability (Jung et al., 1987). Finally, the model explains the complementarity in antigenicity observed when polyclonal antibodies were raised against purified α or β tubulin (Mandelkow et al., 1985a). The α-specific antibodies were directed against the N-terminal domain of α tubulin whereas the β-specific ones recognized the C-terminal domain of β tubulin. In other words, the domains forming the interface between the two monomers in the dimer were the most antigenic ones if purified monomers were used as antigens. These antibodies inhibit microtubule assembly and cause depolymerization of preformed microtubules, both in vitro and in living cells, as might be expected from their binding near the interface (Füchtbauer et al., 1985); this is in contrast to most antibodies raised against whole tubulin dimer. The implications of the dimer structure for microtubule assembly kinetics will be discussed further below.

Microtubules

Microtubules are hollow cylinders whose inner and outer radii are about 8 and 13 nm (these numbers are only approximate, since the surface is rather corrugated; see E. Man-

known GTP-binding properties. The N-terminal domain of β tubulin binds the nucleotide that is exchangeable on dispersed

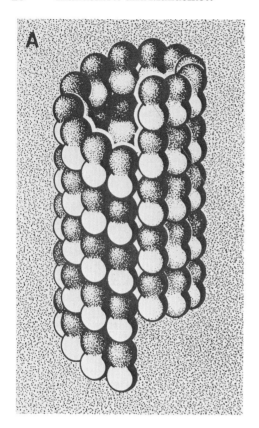

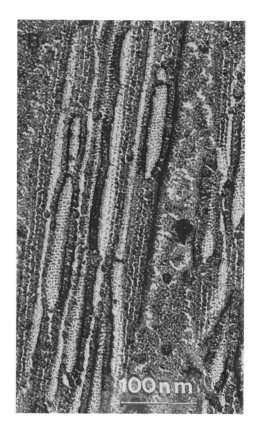

Fig. 3–3 A: Surface lattice of microtubules with 13 protofilaments. Each protofilament consists of an alternation of α tubulin (white) and β tubulin (stippled). The protofilaments are displaced by about 0.9 nm up relative to their right neighbor, thus generating the left-handed three-start helix of monomers. This arrangement requires some discontinuity in the helix, shown here as a "seam" between two protofilaments in front, where α and β monomers join laterally. The arrangement within the seam would be typical of the A lattice (see Amos and Klug, 1974). Note that this structure is not unique but serves as our current working model. **B:** Image of a freeze-etched and metal shadowed sample, offering a view into the inside of a particle and showing the striations of the three-start helix rising up to the right, consistent with a left-handed sense. (A and B reproduced from Mandelkow et al., 1986, with permission of the publisher.)

delkow et al., 1977; Beese et al., 1987a). The interaction between tubulin subunits determines the diameter of microtubules, but not their length. In vitro the length distribution is given by the kinetics of assembly and/or the number of nuclei (Gaskin et al., 1974; Johnson and Borisy, 1977; Kristofferson et al., 1980). In vivo the length is regulated by the interaction with other structures, e.g., with cellular nucleating centers, caps, or other microtubule proteins such as tektins (Stephens, 1977; DeBrabander et al., 1981; Brinkley, 1985; Steffen and Linck, 1988). Microtubules in cells usually contain 13 protofilaments (Tilney et al., 1973), although exceptions with more (or sometimes less) protofilaments are observed in cells. In vitro assembled microtubules often contain more than 13 protofilaments, but assembly onto seeds generates 13 (Scheele et al., 1982; Evans et al., 1985). The polar structure of microtubules implies that one end terminates with α-tubulin monomers, the other with β-tubulin monomers (Fig. 3–2B,

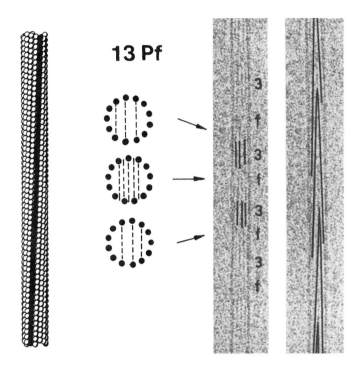

Fig. 3–4. Cryo-electron microscopy of unstained frozen-hydrated microtubules. The images on the right show a particle of 13 protofilaments. It reaveals the two edges as enhanced dark lines, where several protofilaments are viewed in superposition (note that the contrast is reversed relative to negative stain). Inside the edges, one can see regions with three weaker striations (labeled 3), corresponding to the superposition of microtubules from front and back. The possible superposition patterns are shown in the diagrams of the cross sections; they can be displaced slightly to the right or to the left of center, and they are separated by zones where the protofilaments are out or register (fuzzy; f). This means that the protofilaments have a slight supertwist, diagrammed on the left, where one protofilament is drawn dark. The supertwist also gives rise to a chevron pattern, which reveals the polarity of the microtubule (right; recognizable when glancing down the particle at a shallow angle).

3–3A). The relationship between these ends and the other indicators of microtubule polarity (hooks, dynein, assembly rate; see below) has not yet been determined directly. However, combining the dimer structure with kinetic arguments would suggest that the plus end has a crown of β monomers, as discussed below.

The protofilaments are nearly, but not exactly, parallel to the tubule axis, leading to a supertwist of microtubules. This can be detected by negative stain electron microscopy (Langford, 1980) but is revealed more clearly by cryoelectron microscopy of unstained microtubules (Mandelkow and Mandelkow, 1985; Fig. 3–4). The periodicity of the supertwist is variable, the minimum observed so far being about 2 μm. Microtubules with different degrees of twisting coexist; however, within a given microtubule, the supertwist is fairly constant. It allows one to determine the polarity of a microtubule (Fig. 3–4). The function of the supertwist and its variability is not known; it may simply reflect the inherent flexibility of microtubules, which would be needed, for example, in the sliding-bending transitions that underly flagellar motion (see Warner, 1979).

When discussing the arrangement of subunits in the microtubule wall, it is useful to distinguish between the monomer and dimer surface lattices (Fig. 3–3A). Monomers (α or β tubulin) are spaced 4 nm apart along the length of the protofilaments (giving rise to the set of 4-nm layer lines prominent in diffraction patterns from microtubules). Adjacent protofilaments are shifted by about 0.92 nm relative to one another. This generates a shallow helix (inclination about 10°) with 12-nm pitch (= 13 × 0.92 nm). Because of the 4-nm axial monomer repeat, three of the shallow helices are required to cover all monomers in the wall (12 nm = 3 × 4 nm; Fig. 3–3A). The combination of the 13 protofilaments and the three-start helix defines a variety of other possible helical families. Only a few of these are of physical relevance in that they connect adjacent monomers, for example, the 13-start (protofilaments), three-start, and 10-start family. The three-start helix is left-handed, the 10-start helix is right-handed, as determined by image reconstruction (Linck and Amos, 1974; Erickson, 1974) and confirmed by freeze fracturing (Mandelkow et al., 1986; Fig. 3–3B). Some reports showing apparently opposite handedness (e.g., Heuser and Kirschner, 1980; Schultheiss and Mandelkow, 1983) can be explained by experimental uncertainties.

The dimer lattice still represents a puzzle. Amos and Klug (1974) described the two principal possibilities where the dimers in adjacent protofilaments are shifted either by 4−0.92 = 3.18 nm or by 0.92 nm. Were there no difference between α and β tubulin, both would generate the same monomer lattice. However, when viewing along the three-start helix, the first case would lead to an alternation between α and β tubulin (α–β–α–β . . . as with the interaction between the "seam" protofilaments in Fig. 3–3A), while in the second case the monomers would be of the same kind (α–α–α . . . or β–β–β . . . all other protofilaments in Fig. 3–3A). Only the

first case would lead to complete helical symmetry of the microtubules; this lattice was proposed for flagellar A-tubules (hence the name A lattice). It has three helix families that connect adjacent dimers, the left-handed eight-start and right-handed five-start helices, and the 13-start "helix" corresponding to the protofilaments. A genetic (one-start) helix can be described but has no physical meaning. In the second case, proposed for flagellar B-tubules, the helical symmetry would have to be broken at least once around the circumference, e.g., at a seam. Since flagellar B-tubules do not form closed cylinders, this does not present a conceptual difficulty, but the idea of a closed microtubule (e.g., a cytoplasmic one) with incomplete helical symmetry seemed less appealing. The problem lies in the fact that all evidence obtained thus far for reassembled cytoplasmic or flagellar microtubule points to a B lattice (Mandelkow et al., 1977; Crepeau et al., 1978; Woodrum and Linck, 1980; McEwen and Edelstein, 1980; Linck and Langevin, 1981; Mandelkow et al., 1986), implying the presence of at least one discontinuity. It has been postulated that such a seam could represent the attachment site of some MAPs (e.g., tektin) and/or has a special function in the closure of a microtubule (Linck and Langevin, 1981, 1982; Linck et al., 1981; Steffen and Linck, 1988). Apart from the discontinuity, the prominent helix families of the B lattice are the left-handed three-start, the right-handed 10-start, and the 13-start (protofilaments) families. As in the A lattice, the genetic one-start helix is of no importance. Both lattices imply that microtubules cannot grow by elongation of a single helix, thus ruling out a simple linear or helical condensation scheme of the type assumed for actin (see Oosawa and Asakura, 1975). Rather, microtubules must be viewed as a two-dimensional array closed into a cylinder, such that several strands (protofilaments or one of the helices) grow simultaneously, involving both lateral and longitudinal interactions (see Voter and Erickson, 1984).

As was mentioned above, microtubules

possess a distinct polarity related to the polarity of the subunits. There are several structural and kinetic methods to establish the polarity. One structural method is the determination of subunit polarity by image processing of electron micrographs; however, the difference between "up" and "down" is weak at the subunit level, and the method does not lend itself to routine analysis (see Fig. 3–4). The second approach is based on the binding angle of dynein attached to microtubule walls (Allen and Borisy, 1974; Haimo et al., 1979); this is analogous to the arrowhead formation of myosin attached to actin filaments (Huxley, 1963). The most widely used method is based on the attachment of incomplete microtubule walls to complete microtubules (Mandelkow and Mandelkow, 1979; Heideman and McIntosh, 1980). In cross section, they form clockwise or anticlockwise hooks, depending on microtubule polarity. Using this approach, it was shown that parallel arrays of cytoplasmic microtubules usually have uniform polarities.

Given the structural polarity one may expect microtubules to be polar in a functional sense as well. This is borne out by assembly studies showing that the two ends of a microtubule grow at different rates. The fast-growing end, often termed the "plus" end, generally points away from nucleating sites; i.e., it is the distal end in flagella, pointing away from mitotic spindle poles in each half spindle or away from the nucleus in axons (Allen and Borisy, 1974; Binder et al., 1975; Heideman and McIntosh, 1980; Euteneuer and McIntosh, 1981a,b; Telzer and Haimo, 1981). Similarly, microtubule-based transport processes are related to the underlying structural polarity; for example, kinesin-based anterograde transport in axons takes place towards the plus end (Brady, 1985; Vale et al., 1985a), the retrograde transport induced by MAP 1C (a brain dynein; see Gibbons, 1987) proceeds towards the minus end (Paschal and Vallee, 1987), and dynein-induced motion is equivalent to retrograde transport (Sale and Satir, 1977). Some of the polarity criteria can be

related to one another. For example, hooks appear counterclockwise when looking at a microtubule cross section in the direction towards the plus end (Heideman and McIntosh, 1980). Thus, considering the two junctions that a flagellar B-tubule makes with the A-tubule, the hook polarity corresponds to the outer junction. Flagellar dynein projections are tilted towards the tip and slew clockwise when viewed towards the plus end.

It is not yet known which end corresponds to a terminal crown of α- or of β-tubulin subunits, or which of the major domains of tubulin are exposed at the two ends. Kinetic arguments suggest that the plus end should have a crown of β subunits. These questions become important when considering the mechanisms underlying the dynamic instability of microtubules (see below).

Polymorphic Assembly Forms

Tubulin assembly can lead to a surprisingly wide variety of polymorphic forms such as several types of rings (for review, see Scheele and Borisy, 1979; Voter and Erickson, 1979), sheets (Erickson, 1974), hoops (E.-M. Mandelkow et al., 1977), duplex tubules (Jacobs et al., 1975), double-walled microtubules (Erickson and Voter, 1976), twisted ribbons (Kirschner et al., 1975), vinblastin-induced spirals (Amos et al., 1984), halothane-induced macrotubules (Hinkley, 1976), or zinc-induced sheets (Tamm et al., 1979; Amos and Baker, 1979). Their common feature is that they are all made up of protofilaments; in other words, the longitudinal interaction between α–β heterodimers (8-nm repeat) is preserved. The variability resides in the lateral bonding between protofilaments and in the degree of protofilament coiling. In most cases, adjacent protofilaments have identical polarities, as in microtubules; zinc sheets are an exception in that their protofilaments have alternating polarities.

The polymorphic forms can be classified broadly into three groups. One of them is generated by poisoning of microtubules or

tubulin which alters the assembly properties, e.g., vinblastine, zinc, polycations, or
halothane. These forms represent non-
functional side branches of assembly. The
second group comprises aggregates such as
sheets, twisted ribbons, or hoops that appear
early along with microtubules in certain
assembly conditions and tend to disappear
with time. Based on the kinetics, they could
be viewed as assembly intermediates, but a
more likely interpretation is that they are
overshoot aggregates; i.e., they are formed
from functional tubulin with a slightly altered conformation. When they fall apart,
their subunits can be reused for microtubules (Mandelkow et al., 1983b). The third
group comprising rings and smaller oligomers also consists of functional subunits,
except that their conformation is antagonistic to microtubule formation because of altered solution conditions, e.g., low temperature or high GDP. These could be viewed as
inactive storage forms (Weisenberg and Rosenfeld, 1975).

The polymorphic assemblies have been
studied extensively (see review by Amos,
1982) since they used to be considered as
assembly intermediates of microtubules (for
a review of the models, see Kirschner,
1978). Most of these early hypotheses have
been abandoned; nevertheless, the polymorphic forms reveal building principles that are
important for microtubule assembly and disassembly (as discussed below). To illustrate
this, we consider two extreme cases. One is
a microtubule in which all protofilaments
are (nearly) straight; their lateral bonding
takes place with a curvature that leads to a
closed hollow cylinder of 25-nm diameter.
The other extreme is a ring consisting of a
tightly coiled protofilament, with a diameter
of about 35–40 nm. It is clear that protofilament coiling is not compatible with building a hollow cylinder. Thus the coiled protofilaments of rings must be straightened or
disassembled to be incorporated into a
microtubule. Conversely, if the protofilaments of a microtubule are induced to coil
up, the microtubule will fall apart. Thus the
degree of coiling is related to the assembly

competence of the protein. We may conveniently distinguish two main conformations
of the subunits, the "straight" one in which
protofilaments are capable of elongating and
associating into hollow cylinders and the
"coiled" one in which protofilaments can
still elongate but are restricted in their lateral bonding. The polymorphic forms may
be thought of as various compromises between the "straight" and "coiled" conformations. Rings, duplex microtubules, and vin-
blastin spirals show the tightest coiling;
macrotubules, twisted ribbons, or double-
walled microtubules are intermediate;
whereas zinc sheets or hoops have only a
very slight curvature. The conformations are
in turn controlled by solution parameters.
For example, conditions that destabilize
microtubules often lead to the coiled conformation observable as rings (e.g., low temperature, Ca^{2+}, or GDP; see Howard and
Timasheff, 1986), and microtubule assembly
conditions tend to straighten the protofilaments (e.g., high temperature, GTP). In this
view, the GTP hydrolysis following microtubule assembly would tend to destabilize the
microtubule because the bound GDP favors
the coiled conformation and thus puts the
tubule under tension.

Tubulin Oligomers

Oligomers of tubulin appear to play a
special role in microtubule assembly and/or
disassembly and thus require additional consideration. The term *oligomer* was first applied to closed rings consisting of about two
to three dozen tubulin molecules (reviewed
by Scheele and Borisy, 1979). Rings can form
either by a stoichiometric association between tubulin and MAPs (Vallee and Borisy,
1978) or by isodesmic self-assembly of pure
tubulin (Frigon and Timasheff, 1975; Howard and Timasheff, 1986). Electron microscopy showed that rings consist of one or
more concentric turns and may be stacked.
With regard to the association of dimers in
rings, three basic models have been advanced: the long axis of the dimers could
point along the circumference, radially, or
out of the plane. Only the first model is

compatible with X-ray data (Mandelkow et al., 1983a); it means that rings consist of coiled protofilaments.

Rings were initially considered as nucleating centers, since solutions rich in rings were particularly assembly-competent, and various assembly models were proposed depending on how the ring structure was related to the microtubule structure (reviewed by Kirschner, 1978; Scheele and Borisy, 1979). This role of rings was later called into question. It was shown that rings tended to disappear prior to microtubule assembly (Mandelkow et al., 1980; Spann et al., 1987), and in fact their persistence inhibited assembly (Murphy and Wallis, 1986). On the other hand, the assembly-promoting activity arises from the MAPs that are enriched in ring fractions of brain microtubule protein.

There are, however, tubulin oligomers smaller than rings. Some of these are unspecific aggregates resulting from tubulin's tendency to form disulfide cross links (Correia et al., 1987), but others are important in that they consist of functional protein and are somehow related to microtubule assembly. These oligomers share several properties with rings: They can be observed with pure tubulin (Bordas et al., 1983) but are stabilized by MAPs; they contain bound GDP, which is not readily exchanged (Mandelkow et al., 1988); and they consist of short stretches of coiled protofilaments, typically 50–100-nm-long (Fig. 3–5, 3–6B). The relationship between oligomers and microtubules can be demonstrated directly by rapid freezing of disassembling microtubules, followed by cryo-electron microscopy (Fig. 3–5). Oligomers are seen fraying out of microtubule ends; in a separate reaction, rings can be formed, presumably by association of several smaller oligomers (Mandelkow and Mandelkow, 1985) (indications of this behavior have been noted by several authors, e.g., Warner and Satir, 1973; Kirschner et al., 1974). In other words, there is an equilibrium between rings and smaller units, down to dimers, that is not dependent on GTP binding or hydrolysis and has a

different temperature dependence from that of microtubule assembly (Spann et al., 1987). For the purpose of this discussion, we will call an oligomer any short piece of protofilament irrespective of whether it coils into a closed ring.

Several possible roles have been proposed for small (nonring) oligomers. One is that they are involved in microtubule nucleation, as suggested by the concentration dependence of that process (Engelborghs et al., 1977; Carlier and Pantaloni, 1978; Voter and Erickson, 1984). The second is elongation, as judged from biphasic assembly kinetics in some conditions (Bayley et al., 1985; Weisenberg, 1980). A third view is that oligomers are the products of microtubule disassembly, as mentioned above (see also Kirschner et al., 1974). The first and second roles have been suggested by kinetic arguments; the third process is the only one for which there is direct structural evidence, and it also explains certain aspects of microtubule dynamics (i.e., oscillations) to be discussed below.

Microtubule-Associated Proteins

So far we have concentrated on the structure of tubulin and its assembly forms. The second component of microtubules consists of a large and growing number of proteins associated with microtubules in various ways, e.g., dynein, tektin, MAP 2, tau, and so forth (reviewed by Olmsted, 1986; and Linck, Chapter 2). Since these proteins are dealt with in detail elsewhere we will here only briefly touch upon a few questions related to the microtubule structure.

The distribution of dynein and other structures attached to microtubules in flagella is regularly linked to the structure of the underlying microtubule (e.g., periodicities are multiples of 8 nm), even though the symmetries of the components are different (Allen and Borisy, 1974; Linck et al., 1981; see Warner, 1979). By contrast, data on the arrangement of brain MAPs have been more difficult to obtain. In thin sections, MAP 2 appears as 15–40-nm projections from the microtubule surface (Herzog and Weber,

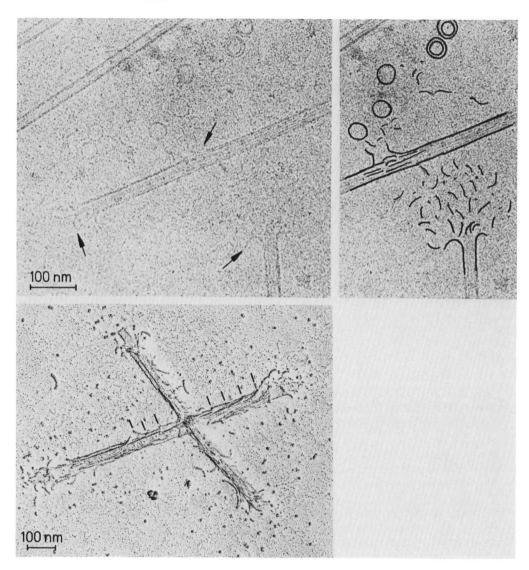

Fig. 3–5. Top left: Image of microtubules quench-frozen during disassembly. Oligomers are released from the ends and in some cases from the interior (arrows). These oligomers are coiled but not closed rings; these form at a later stage and can be seen in the background. **Top right:** Same view with contrast enhanced (note that the intrinsic contrast of frozen-hydrated samples is very weak). **Bottom:** Disassembling microtubules visualized by the glycerol-spray technique and metal shadowing. Coiled oligomers and dimers (small dots) are clearly seen. (Reproduced from Mandelkow and Mandelkow, 1985, with permission of the publisher.)

1978; Kim et al., 1979). However, rotary shadowing suggests a maximum length of the molecule between 100 and 160 nm (Voter and Erickson, 1982; Gottlieb and Murphy, 1985). Thus MAP 2 is a long thread-like molecule whose diameter is less than that of a coiled coil α helix such as the myosin rod. Judging by circular dichroism, the α helix content is very low (4%; Voter and Erickson, 1982), and nuclear magnetic resonance (NMR) suggests a high degree of flexibility (Woody et al., 1983). Most procedures of electron microscopy cause MAP 2 to collapse on the microtubule, giving it a knobby appearance (Zingsheim et al., 1979). In some conditions, an axial periodicity of about 32 nm has been observed (Amos, 1977; Kim et al., 1979). Assuming an A lattice for microtubules, Amos (1977) proposed a regular arrangement of MAP 2, with one MAP 2 molecule per 12 tubulin dimers, generating a 96-nm repeat. Axial repeats of 96 nm are also present in flagella (see Warner, 1979) and in a cytoplasmic microtubule–membrane complex (Murray, 1983); in these cases, the accessory proteins are attached only to one side of the microtubule rather than in a helical fashion.

Even fewer data are available on the arrangement of tau. This protein does not form projections on microtubules (Herzog and Weber, 1978; Zingsheim et al., 1979), suggesting a close attachment to the surface. The protein is also elongated (axial ratio 20:1) but has a low (12%) α-helix content (Cleveland et al., 1977). Studies of tau paracrystals reveal a surprising degree of elasticity (Lichtenberg et al., 1988), suggesting a possible function as a molecular "spring."

Like most proteins, MAPs probably consist of several domains, one of which binds to microtubules. Tubulin has its highest MAP-binding activity in its acidic C-terminal region. This holds true for MAP 2 and tau (Serrano et al., 1984a; Littauer et al., 1986) and probably for a variety of other cytoplasmic proteins that bind to microtubules but are not regarded as MAPs in the strict sense (e.g., GAPDH; Huitorel and Pantaloni, 1985). In the case of MAP 2 the microtubule binding domain lies within a 35-kDa fragment (Vallee, 1980), comprising about 30% of the length of the molecule near one of its ends (Gottlieb and Murphy, 1985). MAP 2 and tau bind to all polymorphic assembly forms of tubulin such that the fraction of unbound MAPs in solution is minor. In spite of the tight binding MAPs diffuse rather freely both along microtubules and through the cytoplasm (Scherson et al., 1984).

Many MAPs are capable of promoting assembly, but this cannot be generalized. Some MAPs copurify but do not stimulate assembly (Keller and Rebhun, 1982), and there are some microtubule-binding proteins that may not be related to microtubule function yet can induce bundles (e.g., GAPDH; Huitorel and Pantaloni, 1985). Some of the more interesting microtubule-binding proteins such as the motor protein kinesin do not copurify except in special conditions (Vale et al., 1985a; Brady, 1985).

On the whole, it seems fair to say that in spite of much work our knowledge on the arrangement and interactions of cytoplasmic MAPs is less than satisfactory. This may be due partly to their poor visibility in electron microscopy but also is due to the fact that their arrangement often is not periodic (for example, incomplete occupation of the available binding sites or floppiness of their protruding portions). A notable exception to this rule is a MAP decorating mitotic microtubules ("buttonin") whose surface lattice is clearly linked to that of the microtubule (Hirokawa and Hisanaga, 1987).

STRUCTURAL TRANSITIONS IN TUBULIN ASSEMBLY, DISASSEMBLY, AND OSCILLATIONS

In this section, we review briefly the development of microtubule assembly models, with emphasis on structural aspects. We finish with a discussion of microtubule oscillations since these are particularly useful for studying the interrelationship between the various tubulin assembly forms and their dependence on nucleotide binding and hydrolysis.

Development of Assembly Models

Numerous studies have dealt with the interactions between the subunits of microtubules during assembly and disassembly. Nevertheless, many aspects remain poorly understood, such as the pathway of nucleation or the structures of the elongating or disassembling species. In part this is due to the fact that assembly studies largely rely on

A

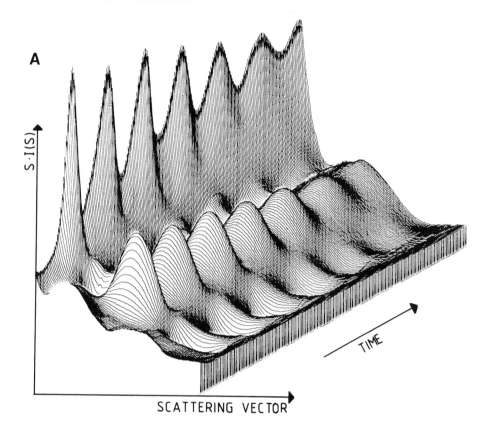

$S \cdot I(S)$

TIME

SCATTERING VECTOR

B

50 nm

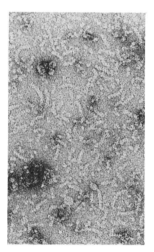

kinetic observations, which yield only limited structural information, whereas structural approaches tend to have poor time resolution. This means that the assembly theories rely to some extent on model-dependent interpretations of kinetic data and therefore are not unique; a given set of data can often be explained by very different models (for an illustration, see Pollard, 1986). One can distinguish several phases of theoretical concepts.

In the mid-1970s, the observation of various polymorphic forms (e.g., rings, sheets, twisted ribbons) led to their interpretation in terms of nucleating centers or at least intermediates in microtubule assembly. Depending on the structural interpretation of the initial states, various pathways of the early stages of assembly were devised (see review by Kirschner, 1978, and references therein). The early period of nucleation models came to an end when it was realized that the polymorphic forms were not absolutely necessary (see, e.g., Lee and Timasheff, 1975; Herzog and Weber, 1977), or that they disassembled before microtubule formation and thus were unlikely to be intermediates (Mandelkow et al., 1980). Regarding elongation, it was assumed that there was a reversible association between microtubule ends and subunits (α–β heterodimers) of the type $MT_n + S <—> MT_{n+1}$, which could be interpreted by the theory of linear or helical condensation (see Oosawa and Asakura, 1975) and led to equilibrium between polymers and a critical concentration of subunits at steady state (Gaskin et al., 1974; Bryan, 1976; Johnson and Borisy, 1977). Although GTP was known to promote assembly, its role was not directly incorporated into the models; i.e., the elongating unit was assumed to be tubulin-GTP.

In the late 1970s and early 1980s, following Wegner's analysis (1976) of the role of ATP in actin assembly, it was realized that because of the polarity the two ends behaved differently with respect to their interaction with subunits. Unequal rates of growth had been reported earlier with use of flagellar seeds defining polarity (Allen and Borisy, 1974; Binder et al., 1975). It was recognized that a difference between the ends persisted even at steady state because of the hydrolysis of GTP. This lead to the concept of treadmilling (Margolis and Wilson, 1978), in which on average one end gained subunits while the other one lost them, at constant overall length. The concept was appealing in that it seemed capable of explaining microtubule-based transport (e.g., in mitosis; Margolis and Wilson, 1981). However, the low efficiency of treadmilling in vitro (Bergen and Borisy, 1980) and its apparent absence in living cells (Wadsworth and Salmon, 1986; Soltys and Borisy,

Fig. 3–6. Microtubule oscillations monitored by X-ray scattering and electron microscopy. **A:** Time-resolved synchrotron X-ray scattering from a solution of oscillating microtubules, showing the X-ray intensity (z-axis) as a function of scattering angle (x-axis) and time (y-axis; 3 sec scan interval; for details, see Mandelkow et al., 1988; Lange et al., 1988). The central scatter **(left)** indicates overall assembly; the subsidiary maximum arises from microtubules. The initial temperature jump from 4°C to 37°C is at time 0. The periodicity of the fluctuations is about 2 min. The final state (after disappearance of the oscillations, not shown) is dominated by the scattering from oligomers. **B:** Electron micrographs of microtubules at different stages of oscillations. **Left:** Point of maximal assembly. One observes microtubules of normal appearance and oligomeric material in the background. **Center:** Disassembly phase. There is a noticeable increase in rod-like oligomers. Many microtubules appear broken. **Right:** Field of oligomers at an assembly minimum; typical lengths are between 20 and 100 nm, corresponding to three to 12 tubulin dimers. The longer oligomers clearly show the coiling characteristic of disassembled protofilament fragments that leads up to ring-like closure (see upper left). Complete rings are rare with purified tubulin but frequent with microtubule protein, presumably because of the stabilization of oligomers by MAPs.

1985) damped the interest in this phenomenon.

During that period, and until the present, there were comparatively few studies dealing with nucleation in vitro. It appears that cells control assembly by nucleating templates and by suppressing self-assembly (DeBrabander et al., 1981; see review by Brinkley, 1985); the templates also ensure a proper microtubule structure (Scheele et al., 1982; Evans et al., 1985). It became clear that in vitro a simple helical nucleation mechanism of the type proposed for actin (Oosawa and Asakura, 1975) was not applicable, essentially because a microtubule is neither a helix nor a linear chain but a two-dimensional polymer constrained to a cylindrical surface. This lead to models of two-dimensional or heterogeneous nucleation (Voter and Erickson, 1984) somewhat analogous to models proposed for the polymerization of sickle cell hemoglobin (Ferrone et al., 1985). This implied a reinterpretation of the polymorphic forms: rather than being assembly intermediates by themselves, they could be viewed as kinetic overshoot aggregates in which the structures of nucleating intermediates were preserved in an amplified form (this applies to sheets, hoops, and twisted ribbons; see Mandelkow et al., 1983b).

The role of GTP continued to be explored in more detail. Most workers agreed that GTP was necessary for nucleation and supported elongation; whether GDP supported elongation remained a matter of debate (see, e.g., Carlier and Pantaloni, 1978; Engelborghs and Van Houtte, 1981), but it seems clear now that at least a fraction of the assembled tubulin requires only GDP (Bayley and Manser, 1985; Lin and Hamel, 1987). There is also a general consensus that microtubules with bound GTP are more stable than after GTP hydrolysis, supported by the enhanced stability of microtubules assembled with nonhydrolyzable GTP analogues (Weisenberg and Deery, 1976). The opposite view was proposed on the basis of experiments showing that GTP hydrolysis lagged behind microtubule assembly, leading to the concept of a GTP "cap" at microtubule ends, which was interpreted at that time to be less stable than the GDP-containing interior (Bonne and Pantaloni, 1982; Carlier, 1982).

The mid-1980s until the present has been dominated by Mitchison and Kirschner's observation (1984a,b) that a steady population of microtubules showed a much more dynamic behavior than was previously envisioned. In other words, although a continuous exchange of subunits on microtubule ends was already implicit in earlier models, it was now realized that this could extend to many subunits, leading to distinct phases of growth and shrinkage of individual microtubules at a constant overall degree of polymerization. Shrinkage can lead to the complete loss of a microtubule (catastrophic disassembly; Mitchison and Kirschner, 1984a,b), although the more common case appears to be a partial shortening and subsequent recovery (tempered disassembly; Sammak et al., 1987). As in treadmilling, the two ends behave differently, the plus end being more dynamic (Horio and Hotani, 1986).

The basis for this phenomenon is still a matter of debate. One current model is based on the GTP cap hypothesis (see above), modified such that the microtubule cap with GTP subunits is now considered to be more (rather than less) stable than the interior (Carlier et al., 1984). This would allow the assumption that uncapped microtubules (with terminal GDP subunits) are unstable, thus explaining microtubule shrinkage. Several subsequent studies designed to test the hypothesis failed to demonstrate a GTP cap (Hamel et al., 1986; O'Brien et al., 1987; Schilstra et al., 1987). Thus, if a GTP cap exists, it is too small to be measurable. The GTP cap hypothesis is appealing in principle because it links the dynamic behavior of microtubules to the energy derived from GTP hydrolysis. However, in the absence of direct evidence alternative models should be considered as well.

Structures Participating in Microtubule Assembly and Disassembly: Dimers vs. Oligomers

The majority of assembly models, both old and new, are based on the assumption that microtubule ends grow by addition of subunits and shrink by release of subunits. There is strong kinetic evidence for this: Elongation depends on the concentration of microtubule ends and subunits, shortening depends on the number of ends (the actual rates depend in addition on the molecular rate constants and the length distributions, see Johnson and Borisy, 1977; Kristofferson et al., 1980). However, since the signals used for monitoring assembly (e.g., turbidity) are dominated by the contribution from microtubules, they contain little information on the nature of the assembling or disassembling unit. This has prompted several authors to search for species other than just subunits, such as oligomers. Here we briefly review some of the evidence.

Prenucleation events and nucleation. Considering the probable nonhelical structure of a microtubule wall (as discussed above), it is hard to imagine a mechanism based only on subunits. Evidence for the involvement of oligomers comes from the concentration dependence of nucleation (Engelborghs et al., 1977; Carlier and Pantaloni, 1978), and it seems likely that a limited longitudinal growth of protofilament pieces precedes their lateral association to form a closed wall (e.g., Voter and Erickson, 1984). These short fragments either may preexist (especially in the presence of MAPs) or they may be the first step in assembly. Tubulin rings are unlikely to be directly involved since they dissolve prior to assembly (prenucleation events; Mandelkow et al., 1980), and the kinetic and physicochemical properties of ring dissolution differ from those of microtubule nucleation (Spann et al., 1987). Distinct lateral aggregates of protofilament pieces may represent another intermediate step, as suggested by the prominence of protofilament triplets in

certain assembly conditions (Mandelkow et al., 1984).

Elongation. Once nucleation is completed, microtubule ends could grow by addition of subunits. This would lead to an exponential approach to steady state. However, one frequently finds biphasic assembly kinetics. This has been interpreted in terms of more than one species contributing to elongation at different rates (e.g., oligomers; Weisenberg, 1980; Pantaloni et al., 1981; Bayley et al., 1985; Burns and Islam, 1986). The analysis is complicated by the fact that light scattering is not a perfect measure of polymer growth; not only are early stages underrepresented (particles smaller than the wavelength of light), but higher-order aggregates (e.g., microtubule bundles) enhance the scattering without change in polymer mass. These and other effects could contribute to the deviation of assembly curves from an exponential approach to equilibrium. Growth by oligomers has also been inferred from their observation by native gel electrophoresis (Kravit et al., 1984), although the validity of the results is a matter of debate (Correia et al., 1987). Whatever the elongating unit, growth is likely to occur by linear elongation of protofilaments since there appears to be no continuous helix in the lattice that provides the necessary physical contact between subunits.

Disassembly. In principle, shortening could take place by release of subunits, and indeed subunits appear in solution after cold or dilution-induced disassembly of microtubules. However, several observations suggest that oligomers are the primary disassembly products, and that subunits are released by the subsequent breakdown of oligomers. Cryo-electron microscopy of disassembling microtubules embedded rapidly in amorphous ice shows short oligomers released from microtubule ends (Mandelkow and Mandelkow, 1985; Fig. 3–5); these can then either fall apart into subunits or anneal with each other into rings. Similarly, nucleotide exchange data show that the GDP found on tubulin rings is directly derived from microtubules, without an intervening subunit stage in which the nucleotide would become exchangeable (Zeeberg et al., 1980). The same holds true for the oligomers smaller than rings (Mandelkow et al., 1988). These data are consistent with earlier observations on disassembling microtubules made by negative stain electron microscopy (Kirschner et al., 1974). The lifetime of oligomeric breakdown products is short in standard assembly buffers, it increases with MAPs, and it becomes particularly noticeable in conditions favoring microtubule oscillations, as discussed below.

Mechanisms of Length Redistribution

Changes in length distributions have been observed with a variety of self-assembling biopolymers, including microtubules. They can be achieved by several mechanisms. The most obvious one is breakage; this can be an artefact in Ostwald-type viscosimetry or negative stain electron microscopy. However, it also occurs spontaneously, since the probability for breakage increases with polymer length and thus is influenced by the number of seeds (see Caspar, 1963). The reverse of breakage is annealing; it can be demonstrated by labeling different microtubule populations with specific antibodies and is prominent when the microtubules are short and their number concentration is high (Rothwell et al., 1987). A third mechanism is based on the subunit exchange from the ends, leading from a non-equilibrium length distribution (e.g., a spike distribution obtained by seeded assembly) to an equilibrium (exponential) distribution. A theoretical analysis has been given by Oosawa (1970), and the effect has been studied for microtubules by Kristofferson and Purich (1981). This redistribution is slow (hours) and would be expected even if polymerization were not coupled to nucleotide hydrolysis. Finally, the length distribution is strongly affected by dynamic instability, which can cause the simultaneous growth of some microtubules and disappearance of others (Mitchison and Kirschner, 1984a,b).

Implications of Tubulin Dimer Structure for Microtubule Assembly Models

We now return to the domain structure of tubulin (Fig. 3–2) and discuss possible implications for microtubule assembly models. Consider the two schemes printed below, showing three protofilaments roughly in a B-lattice configuration (adjacent protofilaments nearly in register, see Fig. 3–3). The first scheme shows tubulin dimers as a whole (Tub); in the second, we distinguish between the N- and C-terminal domains of α and β tubulin. The letters T ($=$GTP) and D ($=$GDP) represent the nucleotide attached to the subunit above it.

Scheme 1:

```
Plus end        Tub-Tub-Tub-Tub-Tub-Tub        Minus end
                  D   D   D   D   D
         Tub ↔ Tub-Tub-Tub-Tub-Tub-Tub ↔ Tub
          T       D   D   D   D   D   D       T
              Tub-Tub-Tub-Tub-Tub-Tub
                D   D   D   D   D   D
```

Scheme 2:

```
Plus end                                        Minus end
   NβCβ · NαCα-NβCβ · NαCα-NβCβ · NαCα-NβCβ · NαCα
    T           D           D           D
NβCβNαCα                                    NβCβNαCα
  ↔ NβCβ · NαCα-NβCβ · NαCα-NβCβ · NαCα-NβCβ · NαCα ↔
    T           D           D           D
   NβCβ·NαCα-NβCβ · NαCα-NβCβ · NαCα-NβCβ · NαCα
    T           D           D           D
```

In discussions on treadmilling, one usually assumes the model of scheme 1 (see Wegner, 1976; Margolis and Wilson, 1978; Bergen and Borisy, 1980). Here the polymer consists of tubulin subunits with bound GDP, and every incoming subunit carries its own GTP required for association (this is equivalent to tail polymerization in the sense defined by Alberts et al. [1983, p. 82] and applies to both ends). Because of structural polarity, the two ends (plus or minus) have different rate constants, and this leads to treadmilling or head-to-tail polymerization (in the sense defined by Wegner [1976], referring to the flux of subunits through the polymer at steady state). In this scheme, dissociation of subunits from the ends will reproduce the same type of polymer (both ends having crowns of tubulin-GDP, i.e., chemically identical species). One consequence is that, when the particle breaks or is cut, the new plus and minus ends have the same properties as the old ones, i.e., treadmilling in each particle would continue as before. Increasing the GDP in solution would merely reduce the assembly-competent pool of subunits (see Bayley and Martin, 1986) without affecting the polymer.

In scheme 2, we consider the domain structure in more detail. We still make the (oversimplified) assumption that only tubulin-GTP polymerizes, and that each association event causes the hydrolysis of one GTP (in agreement with the observed tight coupling of GTP hydrolysis; see Hamel et al., 1986; O'Brien et al., 1987; Schilstra et al., 1987). However, because of the dimer structure, the two ends are chemically distinct. The right end (considered to be minus for reasons given below) has a crown of Cα (= C-terminal domains of α tubulin). The incoming subunit contributes its own GTP for elongation (= tail polymerization); this GTP is hydrolyzed, buried inside the polymer, and presumably becomes as nonexchangeable as the other internal GDPs. This reaction is the same as in scheme 1. On the left end (plus), we have a crown of Nβ (= N-terminal domains of β tubulin). It carries a GTP ready to bind the *next* subunit; i.e., here we have head polymerization. As before, an association event causes the burial of the nucleotide that is responsible for it, again turning it into a non-exchangeable GDP. This scheme opens new reaction pathways. As long as GTP (and therefore tubulin-GTP) is in excess, the kinetic description of growth and treadmilling is the same as in scheme 1. However, GDP can now have two effects: It reduces the pool of tubulin-GTP (as above), and in addition it can chase the GTP on the crown of Nβ domains. Thus the

plus end could be selectively poisoned. This could lead to an increased off-rate of subunits and/or to a reduced on-rate of tubulin-GTP subunits at the plus end; i.e., the concentration required for recapping would be higher than the steady-state concentration in excess GTP (see Fig. 3–2B). Thus in the cell disassembly could be induced at the plus end by an increase in GDP without affecting the minus end, consistent with the observation of Gorbsky et al. (1987) of plus-end disassembly during mitosis. Moreover, when this microtubule is broken or cut, the new minus end would behave as the old one, but the new plus end would now have an exposed crown of Nβ domains with bound GDP and thus would be less stable than the old plus end. This would explain observations that a cut through microtubules assembled onto flagellar seeds leads to the rapid disassembly from the newly exposed plus end but not from the new minus end (Walker et al., 1988).

The relationship between domain structure and kinetics of assembly can be described in structural terms as follows: For the sake of argument, we imagine that the N-terminal domain of β tubulin with bound GTP (Nβ–GTP) is in a bonding conformation ("straight") and provides the glue between neighboring protofilaments, whereas Nβ–GDP is antibonding ("coiled") and disrupts protofilaments; other parts of the subunit, e.g., Nα–GTP, contribute to interprotofilament bonding. A subunit buried in the interior is surrounded by several neighbors whose mutual interaction largely compensates the unfavorable contribution of the Nβ–GDP domain, making the release of subunits from the interior very slow (although not impossible; see Mandelkow and Mandelkow, 1985). The situation is different at the ends where parts of the stabilizing bonds are unsaturated. On the minus end, the Nβ domains are buried in the polymer, whereas the terminal crown of α tubulin resists the disruption; the release of subunits is noticeable but still comparatively slow. However, the plus end needs a crown of Nβ domains largely saturated with GTP to keep the protofilaments together. If this GTP is hydrolyzed or exchanged with GDP, the protofilaments fray apart since there are no favorable bonding surfaces nearby; this leads to rapid unzipping and disassembly of the plus end. This could take place by release of single subunits, but the more general case seems to be the release of short stretches of protofilaments (oligomers); this is particularly evident during the oscillations (see below). This view is an alternative to the GTP cap model (see Carlier et al., 1984), which assumes a gradient of GTP hydrolysis into the interior of the polymer; in practice, both types of reaction could operate simultaneously. A final point concerns the number of protofilament ends with GTP necessary to keep the protofilaments glued together. Considering the structure of the microtubule end, it is unlikely that the rate constants vary linearly with the degree of saturation by GTP. Rather, there must be some cooperativity between protofilaments such that the stability decreases rather steeply once the number of terminal GTPs drops below some critical value. This is a unique feature of microtubules (compared to actin, say), and it is required to model the length oscillations of microtubules to be described below.

Microtubule Oscillations

The dynamic behavior of microtubules was initially deduced from the change of length distribution and number concentration at constant polymer mass (Mitchison and Kirschner, 1984a,b), and it was subsequently demonstrated on individual microtubules by light microscopy (Horio and Hotani, 1986). In these experiments, different microtubules behaved in an uncorrelated fashion. However, in certain conditions, it is possible to synchronize a whole population such that periodic assembly and disassembly can be observed in a bulk solution, giving rise to oscillations that can be monitored either by light scattering (Carlier et al., 1987b; Pirollet et al., 1987) or by X-ray scattering (Mandelkow et al., 1983b, 1988; Lange et al., 1988; see Fig. 3–6). The latter

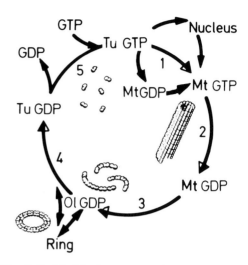

Fig. 3–7. Model of reaction cycle responsible for oscillations. Microtubules (MtGTP) are formed from active subunits (TuGTP; step 1); GTP is hydrolyzed upon assembly (MtGDP; step 2), leading to disassembly of microtubules into oligomers loaded with GDP (OlGDP), which transiently lock the subunits in an unpolymerizable state. When inactive subunits (TuGDP) are released from oligomers (step 4) they can be recharged to TuGTP (step 5), leading to the regrowth of microtubules and/or new nucleation. A side reaction is the dissolution of rings into oligomers and subunits (observed with microtubule protein just after the T jump and responsible for the undershoot; see Mandelkow et al., 1980). (Reproduced from Mandelkow et al., 1988, with permission of the publisher.)

method is particularly suitable for showing the relationship between subunits, oligomers, and microtubules. We will survey the main features and discuss them within the framework of the model shown in Figure 3–7. When assembly is initiated rapidly, e.g., by a fast temperature jump, at high protein concentration, and in certain assembly buffers, one observes the following structural transitions. 1) As soon as the temperature rises, the ring oligomers begin to disappear (prenucleation events), followed by rapid nucleation and elongation of microtubules. 2) The solution reaches an assembly maximum but then disassembles again, typically down to a level between 10% and 40% of the maximum. This event and the subsequent ones all take place while the temperature is maintained at 37°C. 3) After the assembly minimum, another round of assembly sets in, leading to a somewhat lower maximum than the first one, and so forth. 4) The oscillations continue for typically five to 15 cycles, with periodicities around 60–90 sec. 5) When the oscillations are damped out, the overall degree of polymerization is still high, with a pronounced contribution from microtubules. 6) After that the microtubules slowly disappear; the final state shows a scattering pattern typical of oligomers.

A detailed analysis of the scattering patterns shows that microtubules vary in antiphase with oligomers; i.e., the contribution from oligomers is highest at the minima of microtubule assembly. This can be demonstrated by electron microscopy of solutions taken at different time points during the oscillations (Fig. 3–6): During the disassembly phase, microtubules are seen to release oligomers from their ends, and they show numerous breakpoints. At the minima, oligomers are abundant, as well as at the final equilibrium.

Analysis of the protein-bound nucleotide reveals the following features. Oscillations require GTP hydrolysis (no oscillations are observed with non-hydrolyzable GTP analogs). The maxima of protein-bound GTP coincide roughly with the minima of microtubule assembly, and conversely a maximum of GDP is bound at the maximum of assembly. Finally, nucleotide exchange studies show that GTP is exchangeable only on subunits, and neither on microtubules nor on oligomers.

These data are consistent with the model of Figure 3–7. Tubulin with bound GTP is assembly-competent (step 1); during the first round this will involve nucleation, but in later assembly phases the existing microtubules may serve as seeds. The bound GTP becomes hydrolyzed during microtubule assembly (step 2); in principle this destabilizes microtubules, but the destabilization does not become effective as long as the pool of polymerizable subunits is high. When this

drops to some critical value the destabilization becomes noticeable, and microtubules disassemble into oligomers (step 3). The feature important for oscillations is step 4, the release of subunits from oligomers. In standard assembly conditions this event is fast; i.e., the oligomers are short-lived, so that the subunits are released, quickly exchange their bound GDP with GTP from the solution, and thus become assembly-competent again within a few seconds (see Engelborghs and Eccleston, 1982). However, in oscillation conditions (depending on salts, MAPs, phosphorylation, etc.; see Mandelkow et al., 1988) the oligomers become more stable; they have GDP bound and cannot exchange it for GTP, so this species remains incompetent for assembly. Polymerizability is regained only by the slow release of subunits from the oligomers. The subunits are reactivated by GTP from the solution, and when they reach a critical level they can rescue shrinking microtubules and re-initiate growth. In other words, oligomers act as a buffer of tubulin, thus regulating the level of active subunits. In this model, the equilibrium between oligomers and their association into rings is a side reaction that is not directly related to microtubule assembly or disassembly.

Several implications of the model should be noted. One is that only tubulin-GTP is competent to form microtubules, but not oligomers. This appears adequate for the elongation phase, but it leaves open the question of what kind of oligomers, if any, are involved in nucleation. Conversely, oligomers are regarded as inactive storage aggregates of tubulin-GDP, generated during microtubule disassembly. Second, if one assumes that disassembling microtubules are largely devoid of GTP, tubulin-GTP must be able to stop disassembly once the concentration is high enough, implying that tubulin-GTP would add to microtubule ends with bound GDP. Computer modelling shows that this could be achieved by cooperative interactions at microtubule ends, thus circumventing the need for a GTP cap. In addition, or alternatively, disassembling microtubules could depolymerize completely (i.e., show catastrophic disassembly), and new nucleation could take place. Third, oscillations are expected only when oligomers become sufficiently long-lived, compared with the other steps in the cycle; otherwise one would expect a simple approach to steady state. Finally, GTP exchange is assumed to take place rapidly on tubulin subunits, but neither on oligomers nor on microtubules, with the possible exception of the crown of Nβ domains. It is clear, however, that the model is incomplete and needs further refinement; for example, it does not address the questions of microtubule breakage during disassembly or the different reactivities of the plus and minus ends.

The model presented here differs in several respects from that of Carlier et al. (1987a,b). The main difference is the introduction of oligomers as the primary breakdown products of microtubules. Both models assume some rate-limiting step following microtubule disassembly. Carlier et al. (1987a,b) postulate a slow exchange of GTP on tubulin, which is difficult to reconcile with other experimental evidence (see, e.g., Engelborghs and Eccleston, 1982). Also, we assume that disassembling microtubule ends can be elongated even when they have bound GDP if only the tubulin-GTP concentration becomes high enough. These issues will have to be clarified by future studies.

The study of oscillations is useful in that it allows one to define conditions that are conducive to dynamic instability. In vitro they are generated by combining two types of solution variables (Lange et al., 1988): 1) agents that favor tubulin assembly in general, i.e., into microtubules or oligomers, and that can be thought of as stabilizing the longitudinal bonds along protofilaments; examples are Mg^{2+}, glycerol, dimethyl sulfoxide, and others; 2) agents that preferentially disrupt microtubules while still allowing the formation of oligomers, e.g., by favoring the "coiled" conformation; examples are high salt or Ca^{2+}. The joint effect is that the protein released from disassembling microtubules is transiently trapped in inactive oligomers, thus delaying the regeneration of active subunits. Since oscillations are the result of two antagonistic effectors, they can be achieved in a wide variety of conditions, some of which could be operational within living cells.

A final point concerns the synchronization. In vitro this is achieved by a rapid stimultaneous nucleation, leading to the coordinated behavior of the microtubules. This would suggest that chemical signalling is important for oscillations in bulk solution (analogous to the chemical signalling that controls oscillations of glycolytic enzymes; see Markus and Hess, 1984). However, microtubules can oscillate independently of one another (Horio and Hotani, 1986) so that synchronization of the whole solution is not absolutely necessary. In this case, one can still model oscillations of individual microtubules by considering the restricted diffusion of the reacting species, especially oligomers and microtubules (analogous to models used to explain pattern generation, see Glansdorff and Prigogine, 1971). Thus the behavior of microtubule ends could be controlled by their microenvironment. This would explain the unsynchronized dynamic behavior of microtubules in cells.

CONCLUSIONS

We have surveyed the current knowledge of the structure of tubulin, microtubules, and other assembly forms and have tried to emphasize some relationships between structure and assembly. Unfortunately, some of the most important data are lacking. Regarding the primary structures, only the sequences of tubulin and its isoforms (reviewed by Cleveland and Sullivan, 1985) and one type of MAP (tau; see Lee et al., 1988) are known so far; several others are expected in the near future (N. Cowan; T. Seebeck; K. Kosik; personal communications). Even worse, none of the proteins of interest have been solved to atomic resolution by X-ray crystallography. The low-resolution structures obtained by image reconstruction or X-ray fiber diffraction have been useful in clarifying the arrangements of subunits, but in most cases they cannot be linked to the available chemical data. This means that much of the discussion on structure, interactions between proteins, assembly mechanisms, influence of drugs, etc., is speculative, and there appears to be a discrepancy between the great amount of work performed on these problems and the interpretability of the results. These problems will persist as long as the three-dimensional structures of microtubule proteins remain unknown.

ACKNOWLEDGMENTS

This work is supported by the Bundesministerium für Forschung und Technologie (grant 05-180MP-BO) and the Deutsche Forschungsgemeinschaft (grant MA 563/2).

Post-Translational Modifications of Tubulin

Karen Greer and Joel L. Rosenbaum

Department of Biology, Yale University, New Haven, Connecticut 06511

INTRODUCTION

Regulation of the formation and breakdown of microtubule-containing structures is essential to all eukaryotic cells. In every cell, assembly of the mitotic spindle must be controlled precisely and coordinated with other cell processes to maintain the accuracy of cell division. The microtubules that course throughout the interphase cell are major determinants of cell shape. Control over cytoskeletal assembly and structure provides specialized asymmetric cell forms, such as neuronal processes and flagella. In these organelles, the microtubules are not only structural elements but also interact with proteins such as kinesin (Vale, 1987) and dynein (Johnson, 1985) to produce movement.

The problem of assembly is complex, since cells contain not one but a number of microtubule-containing structures. Each is distinct not only in form but also in stability. Stability of a microtubule array means not only how long the array persists in the cell, but how resistant its component microtubules are to experimental depolymerization induced by cold, hydrostatic pressure, or tubulin-binding drugs (Behnke and Forer, 1967). By both these criteria, cilia and flagella are composed of very stable microtubules. Most but not all interphase microtubules are labile in the presence of cold or tubulin-binding drugs (for review, see Raff, 1979). The microtubules that are formed during mitosis are of both kinds. The kinetochore and astral microtubules formed at metaphase disappear in anaphase and are labile to depolymerizing treatments. In contrast, the centrosomal or "interpolar" microtubules persist throughout telophase and are more resistant to depolymerizing treatments (Brinkley and Cartwright, 1971, 1975).

Two major ideas have been the basis for current concepts of the mechanisms of differential microtubule formation in the cell. The first describes differential assembly as resulting directly from the polymerization properties of tubulin and has its conceptual origins in the hypothesis of Inoué that a dynamic equilibrium exists between assembled spindle microtubules, assembled microtubules of other organelles, and an unpolymerized pool (Inoué and Sato, 1967). It is apparent from the differences in stability between various microtubules that some microtubules can readily lose or gain subunits from the pool of unpolymerized subunits surrounding them and are thus in a state of dynamic equilibrium with unpolymerized dimer in solution. Others are, by some means, isolated from these interactions and are thus more stable. In the case of the mitotic microtubules described above, the exchange of subunits between microtubules and the solution can be visualized with the aid of fluorescently labeled tubulin subunits, and the rates of turnover have been shown to be greatest in the microtubules most sensitive to depolymerization by cold or drugs (Salmon et al., 1984; Saxton and McIntosh, 1987). "Dynamic equilibrium" of monomers and polymers in solution has also provided a conceptual basis for the study of microtubule polymerization and depolymerization in vitro, as in the nucleated condensation model of Johnson and Borisy (1977). From increasingly detailed observation of microtubule behavior, it is now known that this equilibrium between monomer and polymer is actually a complex steady state maintained by the input of energy from the hydrolysis of guanosine triphosphate (GTP) that accompanies microtubule assembly. For example, the demonstration in vitro of "treadmilling" (movement of labeled subunits from one end of a microtubule to another) by Margolis and Wilson (1978) implies that the free subunit concentration sufficient to prevent disassembly can differ at opposite ends of a microtubule, as proposed by Wegner (1976), a situation impossible for an equilibrium polymer (see Terry and Purich, 1982). This difference may explain the significance of microtubule-organizing centers in the formation of microtubule arrays in vivo. If a microtubule has one end (requiring the higher tubulin concentration to prevent disassembly) stabilized by association with a microtubule-organizing center, depolymerization of that microtubule will occur only when the tubulin concentration is below that required to maintain the other end (Kirschner, 1980). Even more complex steady-state behavior, in which some microtubules grow at steady

state while others are shrinking, has been observed. One proposed explanation of these phenomena depends on the relation between the rates of GTP hydrolysis and microtubule assembly. Since hydrolysis of GTP can lag behind assembly, microtubules can have at their ends tubulin with bound GTP; these microtubules are predicted to be more resistant to depolymerization than tubulin with bound guanosine diphosphate (GDP) (Hill and Carlier, 1983; Hill and Chen 1984). Thus, at any time, stable polymers with "GTP caps" could coexist with, or be converted to, unstable polymers that have lost their tubulin-GTP ends by depolymerization or hydrolysis of GTP to GDP (Mitchison and Kirschner, 1984a,b). Kirschner and Mitichison (1986) describe the potential of this "dynamic instability" model, which allows profound variation in assembly and stability of microtubules in a cell, to provide mechanisms for regulation and differentiation of cytoskeletal structure. Recent in vitro and in vivo data (Kristofferson et al., 1986; Schulze and Kirschner, 1986; Gorbsky et al., 1987; Sammak et al., 1987) demonstrate the rapid turnover of microtubule subunits predicted by this model of microtubule dynamics but suggest that shrinking microtubules may frequently be "rescued" and resume growth, as was seen with single microtubules in vitro by Horio and Hotani (1986). If "dynamic instability" characterizes the behavior of microtubules in vivo, then the events that stabilize particular microtubules are crucial to determining the pattern of microtubule assembly in the cell (Kirschner and Mitichison, 1986).

The second set of ideas put forth to explain differential microtubule assembly is based on heterogeneity of the ensemble of proteins that make up the assembled polymer. Microtubule protein purified from neuronal tissue by cycles of polymerization and depolymerization consists of the major structural protein, tubulin, as well as microtubule-associated proteins (MAPs) (Sloboda et al., 1975; for reviews, see Vallee and Bloom, 1984; Olmsted, 1986). Some of these associated proteins promote in vitro assembly when added to purified tubulin (Wein-garten et al., 1975; Sloboda et al., 1976; Binder and Rosenbaum, 1978) and have been shown to interact with calmodulin (Lee and Wolff, 1982, 1984) and protein kinases (Vallee et al., 1981; Murthy and Flavin, 1983; Burns et al., 1984), regulatory proteins that affect microtubule assembly in vitro (for review, see McKeithan and Rosen-baum, 1984). Variation of the proteins asso-ciated with tubulin in different microtubule-based structures, or modification of their properties by interaction with regulatory elements, may allow differential microtu-bule assembly and stability in the cell. For example, the high-M_r MAPs (Matus and Rie-derer, 1986) and a group of MAPs known as the tau proteins (Fellous et al., 1986) un-dergo complex changes in relative abun-dance during development of mammalian brain.

Heterogeneity of tubulin itself has also been proposed as a basis for variations in microtubule assembly and function (Fulton and Simpson, 1976). When electrophoretic analysis first resolved two forms of the tubu-lin subunit (Renaud et al., 1968), it was proposed that these corresponded to differ-ent subfibers of the flagellar outer doublet microtubules (Stephens, 1970). These two forms are now known to be α and β tubulin, which appear in equimolar amounts in all microtubules (Olmsted et al., 1971). It has been shown that tubulin from a single organ-ism (Field et al., 1984; Kemphues et al., 1979; Raff et al., 1982; Burland et al., 1984; McKeithan and Rosenbaum, 1981; McKei-than et al., 1983; Russel and Gull, 1984) or a single cell (Gozes and Sweadner, 1981) can display numerous electrophoretic variants of both α and β tubulin. In most eukaryotes, tubulin is encoded by multigene families. Thus, some of the variability in isoforms (tubulin molecules that are detectably dif-ferent by two-dimensional gel or other ana-lytic methods) is due to the presence of different tubulin isotypes (gene products that differ in amino acid sequence). By mu-tational analysis, some of the variants have been assigned to single genes (Schatz et al., 1986; Kemphues et al., 1982; Cabral et al., 1980; May et al., 1985). In the higher eu-karyotes, tubulin genes are expressed in a tissue-specific fashion. These complex pat-terns of tubulin gene expression are de-scribed in the recent review by Cleveland and Sullivan (1985) and in a shorter discus-sion by Cleveland (1987). It is clear that heterogeneity of tubulin genes can be used by an organism to regulate the number and proportions of tubulin isotypes available in the cell. It is difficult to demonstrate, how-ever, that any gene encodes a tubulin spe-cific for a particular microtubule-containing structure. A mutatation of a testis-specific β-tubulin gene in *Drosophila* results in a tubulin molecule that, when incorporated into cellular microtubules, forms distinctly aberrant microtubules. This has been used to show that a single gene product partici-pates in the formation of many, and perhaps all, of the cellular microtubules observed in the testis (Fuller et al., 1987). The composi-tion of microtubules in several cell types from mouse (Lewis et al., 1987) and from chicken (Lopata and Cleveland, 1987) has been examined by the use of isotype-specific antisera. These experiments have shown that each of several tubulin gene products, if expressed in that cell, can be found in all its microtubules. Transfection of mouse cells with foreign genes (Bond et al., 1986) and disruption of yeast tubulin genes (Schatz et al., 1986; Adachi et al., 1986) also demon-strate the ability, if not the necessity, of a single gene product to be assembled into all microtubule-containing structures in these cells. Although these experiments have ex-amined a wide range of cell types, there are specialized microtubule arrays that have not been included and may require a particular tubulin (J.C. Bulinski, personal communica-tion). Therefore, these experiments do not exclude the possibility that a single tubulin gene product can usually form, or function more efficiently in, a particular organelle. It seems, however, that the existence of tubu-lin multigene families is not the sole expla-nation for the diversity of microtubule struc-ture, or vice versa.

Post-translational modifications of tubulin not only create tubulin variation additional to that encoded in the genome but are also processes that in principle can be slowed, accelerated, or reversed to generate rapid changes in the population of tubulin forms in the cell. In the models of microtubule dynamics described above, one of the effects of GTP binding and hydrolysis is to establish a heterogeneity among microtubules. Thus this reversible alteration of the tubulin molecule may lead to differential microtubule assembly or stability. Recently, evidence has been accumulating that some direct covalent modifications of tubulin have a similar role in regulating microtubule differentiation by generating microtubules that vary in the types and amounts of modified tubulin they contain. The remainder of this review focuses on these modifications and the evidence that they participate in the process of cytoskeletal differentiation. Tubulin is known to be post-translationally modified in several ways, but only for phosphorylation, tyrosination, and acetylation is there evidence relating the modification of tubulin to particular microtubule arrays. Other modifications are less well characterized at present. For example, a large shift in the isoelectric point of α tubulin in cold-insoluble microtubules occurs during axonal transport. This has been attributed to post-translational modification, but the chemical moeity that is added or removed has not yet been identified (Brady et al., 1984). In other cases, tubulin is modified in vitro, for example, by adenosine diphosphate (ADP) ribosylation or proteolysis, but little is known about the occurrence or significance of the corresponding modification in vivo. The literature has recently been reviewed in detail by Purich and Scaife (1985).

COVALENT PHOSPHORYLATION OF TUBULIN

Besides the phosphate groups of the guanine nucleotides non-covalently associated with tubulin, phosphate groups may also be found associated with tubulin by direct co-valent linkage to serine residues. This was first reported by Eipper (1974), who analyzed the incorporation of $^{32}PO_4$ into β tubulin in rat brain slices. Other in vivo labeling studies with $^{32}PO_4$ failed to detect labeled tubulin in brain microtubule protein (Sloboda et al., 1975; Rappaport et al., 1976), but recently Gard and Kirschner (1985) showed a substantial and reproducible increase in in vivo phosphorylation of tubulin during differentiation of neuroblastoma cells.

The phosphorylation of β tubulin in neuroblastoma cells appears to be correlated with the assembly state of microtubules. Neuroblastoma cells respond to serum starvation by extension of neurite processes, which resemble axons and contain large numbers of microtubules. During this extension, the amount of PO_4 in β tubulin increases about fourfold. In vivo labeling of cells with ^{35}S shows that a β-tubulin isoform (β_2) appears at the expense of a slightly more basic isoform (β_1), suggesting that β_1 is the precursor of the phosphorylated β_2. The correlation of assembly state and β-tubulin phosphorylation in vivo is also apparent from the effect of drugs affecting the assembly of microtubules. Cells treated with taxol, which promotes microtubule assembly, show a dramatic increase in the level of β-tubulin phosphorylation, although there is no effect on the morphology of the neuroblastoma cells. Conversely, colchicine, which depolymerizes microtubules and causes retraction of the neurite processes, reverses the accumulation of phosphorylated β tubulin that accompanies neurite extension (Gard and Kirschner, 1985).

The reversible phosphorylation of β tubulin indicates that neural cells posess enzymes capable of phosphorylating and dephosphorylating β tubulin and suggests that these enzymes may be investigated in vitro. Phosphorylation of tubulin has been demonstrated a number of times in vitro, and these kinase activities fall into two classes. The first class includes kinase activities stimulated by the presence of cyclic adenosine monophosphate (cAMP). These phosphorylate MAPs at least as efficiently, and often much more efficiently, than they phosphorylate tubulin (Sloboda et al., 1975; Jameson et al., 1980). A second class includes kinase activities that are insensitive to inhibitors of cAMP-dependent protein kinases and are stimulated by the presence of Ca^{2+} and calmodulin (Burke and DeLorenzo, 1981). These enzymes also add more phosphate to MAPs than to tubulin, but are less specific than the cAMP-dependent tubulin kinases (Goldenring et al., 1983; Wandosell et al., 1986; Vallano and DeLorenzo, 1986). The fact that Ca^{2+} activates a tubulin kinase may explain why tubulin phosphorylation is absent in experiments (Sloboda et al., 1975; Rappaport et al., 1976) using microtubule assembly buffers containing EGTA. Phosphorylation of tubulin by the Ca^{2+}-calmodulin-dependent kinase inhibits its self-assembly (Wandosell et al., 1986). Hargreaves et al. (1987) have shown that this phosphorylated tubulin interacts much more strongly than unphosphorylated tubulin with artificial membranes. Peptide mapping of tubulin phosphorylated by this kinase shows that multiple phosphate groups are added to the C-terminal end of the molecule (Wandosell et al., 1986), a domain of the molecule known to be essential for normal microtubule assembly (Serrano et al., 1984b).

Both cAMP- and Ca^{2+}, calmodulin-dependent tubulin kinases prefer adenosine triphosphate (ATP) over GTP as the phosphate donor, although microtubule protein can be phosphorylated at the expense of GTP when the enzyme dinucleotide kinase, which catalyzes the reaction GTP + AMP ↔ ATP + GMP, is present (Jacobs and Huitorel, 1979). There is a substantial literature concerning the effects of ATP on some of the in vitro assembly properties of microtubule proteins (see, e.g., Margolis and Wilson, 1979; Burns and Islam, 1986). Some of these changes ultimately may be shown to result from the phosphorylation of microtubule proteins, including not only tubulin but the high-M_r MAPs. Phosphorylation of MAP 2 has already been correlated with effects on in

vitro assembly (Jameson and Caplow, 1981; Burns et al., 1984).

Despite the extensive work on phosphorylation of microtubule proteins in vitro, there is some reason to believe that the tubulin kinase responsible for β-tubulin phosphorylation in vivo is not one of those described above. The correlation of β-tubulin phosphorylation in neuroblastoma cells with microtubule assembly in vivo suggests the existence of a tubulin kinase that preferentially phosphorylates the polymer or a tubulin phosphatase that preferentially dephosphorylates unassembled tubulin (Gard and Kirschner, 1985). In vitro none of the enzyme activities described above have yet been shown to be affected by the tubulin polymerization state. There is also the problem of substrate specificity. The large amount of phosphate added to MAP 2 by these kinase activities in vitro could result from the large number of available phosphorylation sites on MAP 2. It is more difficult to explain why these kinases phosphorylate α and β tubulin in vitro to the same extent (Wandosell et al., 1986; Ikeda and Steiner, 1979; Goldenring et al., 1983), even though α tubulin is not phosphorylated in vivo (Eipper, 1974; Sloboda et al., 1975; Ikeda and Steiner, 1979; Gard and Kirschner, 1985). Recently, it has been shown that the phosphorylation of tubulin by casein kinase II in vitro results in phosphorylation of a single isoform of β tubulin. Identification and localization of the phosphorylated residue by amino acid analysis and peptide mapping show that tubulin phosphorylated in vitro by casein kinase II and tubulin phosphorylated in vivo are both phosphorylated on a serine residue(s) in the carboxy terminus of the molecule (Serrano et al., 1987).

TYROSINATION AND DETYROSINATION OF TUBULIN

Tubulin–Tyrosine Ligase and Tubulin Carboxypeptidase

The discovery that α tubulin is post-translationally modified by the addition of tyrosine was made by Barra et al., (1973), who were studying the incorporation of labeled amino acids by brain homogenates. They found that levo-3,4-dihydroxyphenyl-alanine (L-DOPA), phenylalanine, and especially tyrosine were incorporated into protein (Rodriguez et al., 1975) and that this process required ATP but not protein synthesis (Barra et al. 1973). The single protein that incorporated tyrosine by this process was soon found to be α tubulin (Barra et al., 1974). Later, an enzyme activity that removes the carboxy-terminal tyrosine from α-tubulin was found (Hallak et al., 1977, Argaraña et al., 1980). Both the enzyme responsible for adding the C-terminal tyrosine (tubulin–tyrosine ligase; TTL) and the enzyme that removes the C-terminal tyrosine from newly synthesized protein (tubulin carboxypeptidase; TCP) have been identified and have been characterized with the aid of assays that provide exogenous brain tubulin as a substrate and measure the incorporation or release of radioactive tyrosine (Raybin and Flavin, 1977a; Murofushi, 1980; Argaraña et al. 1980; Martensen, 1982).

Since most α-tubulin genes encode a C-terminal tyrosine, tubulin that is a substrate for TTL usually has already served as a substrate for TCP. Recently, sequence data has revealed that a few α-tubulin genes encode tubulins lacking the terminal tyrosine. Some of these are sufficiently divergent from most α tubulins that their products may not be recognized as a substrate by TTL and thus would not participate in cyclic tyrosination. Whether there is a relation between the expression of these genes and previous reports of "non-substrate" tubulin (Nath and Flavin, 1979) remains to be determined. A tubulin product ending in the usually penultimate amino acid glutamate (e.g., the mouse α-4 gene sequenced by Villasante et al., 1986) has the same carboxy-terminal sequence as enzymatically detyrosinated tubulin, which may be significant if detyrosinated tubulin has special functions in the cell.

The enzyme TTL has been found in a large

number of organisms, including both vertebrates (Preston et al., 1979) and invertebrates (Kobayashi and Matsumoto, 1982). Among mammalian tissues, expression of TTL is highest in brain and muscle tissue, especially early in development (Deanin and Gordon, 1976). In chickens, the levels of TTL in the brain are higher in 12–18-day embryos than in 1-week-old chicks, and the TTL levels in embryonic muscle peak at 12–14 days (Deanin et al., 1977). The levels of TTL have also been reported to change during the cell cycle in Chinese hamster ovary (CHO) cells (Forrest and Klevecz, 1978). In each of these cases, the claim can be made that the peak in enzyme activity coincides with a period of rapid cytoskeletal remodeling. Less is known about the distribution of the enzyme responsible for removing the tyrosine from tubulin. This enzyme is present in brain extracts (Argaraña et al., 1980; Martensen, 1982) and is distinct from TTL. Its pattern of sensitivty to inhibitors also distiguishes it from carboxypeptidase A, a pancreatic enzyme that can utilize tubulin as a substrate (Hallak et al., 1977; Arce et al., 1978).

The two enzymes show marked differences in their utilization of unpolymerized tubulin and microtubules as substrates. For TTL, tubulin dimer appears to be the preferred substrate. Drugs that inhibit microtubule polymerization, including colchicine, podophyllotoxin, and vinblastine, do not inhibit tyrosination of tubulin in vitro (Arce et al., 1975; Thompson et al., 1979; Nath and Flavin, 1978). Arce et al. (1978) labeled an equilibrium mixture of tubulin dimer and polymer with radioactive tyrosine in vitro and then separated dimer from polymer by filtration. Most of the label was found on tubulin dimers, and all the tyrosine incorporated into microtubules could be accounted for by exchange with labeled dimers during the reaction. Recent evidence obtained with enzyme purified by immunoaffinity chromatography suggests that the enzyme binds to a site composed of residues from both the α and β subunits of tubulin (Wehland and Weber, 1987a). This site, like one of the two sites on tubulin for GTP binding, may be rendered inaccessible by polymerization. In contrast, detyrosination of tubulin by brain homogenates is strongly inhibited by colchicine and other drugs that inhibit microtubule polymerization (Kumar and Flavin, 1981). The release of tyrosine from prelabeled tubulin occurs when tubulin is allowed to polymerize. Buffer conditions that favor polymerization of microtubules also favor tyrosine release (Hallak et al., 1977). When tyrosinated microtubules are separated from dimers (Arce et al., 1978), the loss is greater from microtubules than from dimers.

The preferential tyrosination of dimers and detyrosination of polymers suggest that tyrosinated subunits join a polymer, become detyrosinated while the subunit is within a microtubule, and become tyrosinated only when the microtubule depolymerizes and the subunits enter the dimer pool. Were this the case, the exchange kinetics of tyrosine from steady-state microtubules in vitro would resemble those of labeled GTP, which can be exchanged only when a subunit is in solution. In experiments almost identical in design to those of Margolis and Wilson (1978, 1981) using GTP, polymers with a non-random distribution of radioactive tyrosine were prepared by pulse-labeling microtubules. The kinetics of label loss during a subsequent chase are strikingly similar to those seen for GTP (Deanin et al., 1980). The half-life of the tyrosine label, however, is much less than that of GTP (Margolis and Wilson, 1981). This suggests that tyrosine loss precedes loss of the subunit from the microtubule. Recent evidence obtained using antibodies to tyrosinated and detyrosinated tubulin (see below) also indicates that detyrosination occurs while subunits are within the microtubule.

Because of the differing activities of the two enzymes on polymerized tubulin, it appears that the microtubule assembly cycle and the cycle of tyrosine loss and gain are in some way related. If tyrosinated and detyrosinated tubulin or microtubules differ in function, then this would provide a means of

coupling tyrosination to the dynamics of the microtubule. Thompson (1982) speculates that progressive detyrosination of subunits while in the polymer, in conjuction with treadmilling, would produce a polymer with a gradient of tyrosination from one end to the other, but the author does not assign a specific purpose for the polarity thus generated. Alternatively, Burns (1987) envisions a model in which only tyrosinated dimers can assemble into microtubules, and the proportions of tyrosinated and detyrosinated dimers regulate the assembly competence of the tubulin pool. These models imply that there should be some difference between tyrosinated and detyrosinated tubulin or microtubules of different tyrosination states. Despite the relation between the state of polymerization and the activities of the two enzymes, however, changes in the proportion of tyrosinated tubulin do not seem to affect the behavior of tubulin in the in vitro assembly reactions so far studied (Raybin and Flavin, 1977b; Arce et al., 1978).

Tyrosinated and Detyrosinated Tubulin

In the absence of clear in vitro evidence for functional differences between tyrosinated and detyrosinated tubulin, other methods, which examine the rate of tyrosine incorporation into α tubulin or the distribution of tyrosinated and detyrosinated tubulin within cells, have been used to determine whether the activities of the two enzymes in vivo lead to differential distribution of tyrosinated and detyrosinated tubulin.

The activity of tubulin tyrosine ligase in vivo is usually measured by the uptake of radioactive tyrosine into tubulin in the presence of protein synthesis inhibitors (Raybin and Flavin, 1977b; Thompson, 1977; Nath and Flavin, 1979; Nath et al., 1981). Tyrosination of α tubulin in cultured muscle cells is so rapid that it represents 95% of tyrosine incorporated into α tubulin *without* protein synthesis inhibitors, as measured by the difference between radioactive tyrosine incorporated into α tubulin compared with β tubulin. This indicates that tyrosination in vivo is cyclical, since the rate of post-translational addition of tyrosine is much greater than the rate of new tubulin synthesis (Thompson et al., 1979). Since most newly synthesized tubulin is already tyrosinated, however, incorporation of tyrosine in vivo is not necessarily an indication of the amount or distribution of tyrosinated tubulin. Ratios of tyrosinated to total tubulin have been measured either by direct examination of tubulin C-terminal amino acids or by measuring the amount of tyrosine released by treatment of the tubulin with pancreatic carboxypeptidase. The findings can, to some extent, be related to levels of TTL found in cell extracts (see above). Tubulin from chick embryos (Rodriguez and Borisy, 1978) or newborn rats (Barra et al., 1980) contains more terminal tyrosine than tubulin from older animals. An increase in tyrosinated tubulin accompanies neurite outgrowth in a neuroblastoma cell line (Nath and Flavin, 1979) and the stimulation of chemotaxis in polymorphonuclear leukocytes (Nath et al., 1981). In the case of developing rat brain, it appears that the fraction of soluble tyrosinated tubulin is nearly twice that of the microtubules, but, in the adult, tyrosination of monomer and polymer is about the same (Rodriguez and Borisy, 1979).

A more powerful method of assaying the state of tubulin tyrosination became available with the preparation of antibodies specific to either tyrosinated or detyrosinated tubulin. Gundersen et al. (1984) prepared polyclonal antibodies directed against the in vitro-synthesized C-terminal peptides of tyrosinated and detyrosinated α tubulin. These antibodies are known as anti-Tyr and anti-Glu, and the epitopes they recognize are designated Tyr–tubulin (containing a C-terminal tyrosine, or tyrosinated) and Glu–tubulin (lacking a C-terminal tyrosine and thus containing glutamic acid as the C-terminal residue, or detyrosinated). Specificity was demonstrated by immunoassays using the two synthetic peptides. Also, tubulin or microtubules treated with pancreatic carboxypeptidase A, and thus completely detyrosinated, bound only the anti-Glu antibody. Recently, Wehland and Weber (1987b) used synthetic peptides corresponding to the C-terminal ends of tyrosinated and detyrosinated α tubulin to elicit monoclonal antibodies specific for the two forms of α tubulin.

In addition, a monoclonal antibody called YL1/2 raised against yeast α tubulin by Kilmartin et al. (1982) has been shown by Wehland et al. (1983b) to react specifically with tyrosinated α tubulin. Although this antibody was elicited with the entire α-tubulin molecule, the epitope is the C-terminal peptide of tyrosinated tubulin (Wehland et al., 1986). Remarkable cytoskeletal disruptions can be induced by microinjection of YL1/2 into cultured cells. Normally, in these cells, the microtubules radiate from a microtubule-organizing center in the center of the cell, where the Golgi apparatus is also located. In the presence of the drug taxol, bundles of microtubules form near the cell periphery. Fragments of the Golgi apparatus are found in association with these bundles. Injection with YL1/2 disrupts the association of the Golgi with the microtubules in both normal and taxol-treated calls, while injection with a monoclonal anti-α-tubulin antibody not specific for tyrosinated tubulin has no effect (Wehland et al., 1983a). Injections of larger quantities of the antibody disrupt mitosis, cell translocation, and saltatory motion of intracellular particles as well as inducing the formation of large bundles of microtubules. In the latter experiment, the results were not compared with injections of equivalent amounts of an antibody against all α tubulin (Wehland and Willingham, 1983). The effects of YL1/2 show that a region of α tubulin modified by tyrosination is essential to microtubule function, but do not yield any information on the roles of tyrosinated and non-tyrosinated tubulin.

Antibodies specific for tyrosinated and detyrosinated α tubulin have been used to determine the extent of tyrosination of different kinds of microtubules in various cells and the spatial and temporal organization of the two forms of microtubules. Specifically, they have been used to analyze 1) the distribution of Glu– and Tyr–tubulin in the interphase cytoskeleton, including localization of the two forms within a single microtubule; 2) the distribution of Glu– and Tyr–tubulin in specialized arrays of microtubules; and 3) the changes with time in the ratios of Tyr– and Glu–tubulin within microtubule-containing structures. These results show that tubulin detyrosination is correlated with the assembly and differentiation of particular structures within many types of cells, from microorganisms to mammalian neurons.

The cytoskeletal microtubules of all cultured cells that have been examined give similar patterns of immunofluorescent staining: Most of the microtubules in the interphase cytoskeleton stain with the anti-Tyr antibody; the relatively few microtubules that stain with the anti-Glu antibody are distributed throughout the cytoskeleton, among the more numerous Tyr microtubules. In the interphase cytoskeleton of most cells, the Tyr microtubules are so much more numerous than the Glu microtubules that it is difficult to discern the difference in staining pattern between antibodies against Tyr–tubulin and total tubulin. The Glu-staining microtubules usually have a characteristic "sinuous" appearance (Gundersen et al., 1984; Geuens et al., 1986, Wehland and Weber, 1987b). It is in fact remarkable that Glu and Tyr microtubules are found in such proximity in the cytoplasm. Any mechanism that explains the differences in degree of tyrosination of microtubules must explain how an enzyme can substantially detyrosinate one microtubule and not those immediately adjacent to it (Gundersen et al., 1984).

Since microtubules containing mostly tyrosinated tubulin can coexist in the cytoplasm with microtubules containing mostly detyrosinated tubulin, the question arises: to what extent do Tyr– and Glu–tubulins exist in the same microtubules? By immunofluorescent staining with both the anti-Tyr and anti-Glu antibodies, Gundersen et al. (1984) found single microtubules that could react

with *both* anti-Glu and anti-Tyr antibodies as well as microtubules that stained exclusively with one antibody or the other. This finding was confirmed by localization of the Glu and Tyr epitopes with the resolution of electron microscopy (Geuens et al., 1986) The latter study used the anti-Glu antibody and YL1/2, with secondary antibodies coupled to two sizes of small gold particles. The increased resolution of the electron microscopy technique showed that various microtubules bind different proportions of Glu and Tyr antibodies, ranging from 11% to 70%. It appears that, in some microtubules, one epitope is present at levels too low to be detected by immunofluorescence. In some cases, long segments of a single microtubule can be visualized. The proportion of Tyr– to Glu–tubulin does not appear to change along the length of these microtubules. The absence of any gradient of modification is significant for those models where the process of modification is related to the displacement of tubulin subunits within the microtubule, i.e., treadmilling (Geuens et al., 1986; Gundersen and Bulinski, 1986b).

Given the lack of evidence that different tubulin genes can specify particular microtubule structures (Cleveland, 1987), there is considerable interest in the idea that post-translational modifications can give rise to functionally different tubulins or microtubules. The anti-Glu and anti-Tyr antibodies have now been used to examine the distribution of tyrosinated and detyrosinated microtubules within a number of specialized microtubule-containing structures.

Many of the most prominent and specialized microtubule-containing structures in cells are the most extensively modified. Flagella and cillia contain a high proportion of detyrosinated tubulin (Gundersen and Bulinski, 1986b; Schneider et al., 1987). When the antibodies raised to synthetic peptides are used, flagella and centrioles react much more strongly with anti-Glu than do cytoskeletal microtubules. The neural processes of spinal cord explant cells also stain intensely with anti-Glu. Thus, microtubules in flagella and these neuronal processes contain more detyrosinated (Glu) tubulin than most other interphase microtubules, most of which stain weakly or not at all with anti-Glu (Gundersen et al., 1984; Gundersen and Bulinski 1986b). A single organelle may differ in its degree of detyrosination depending on the cell type in which it is located. For example, the marginal bands of toad erythrocytes do not appear to be detyrosinated at all, whereas the marginal bands of chicken and human platlets react strongly with the anti-Glu antibody. Tyrosination, then, is not required to specify the structure of this particular organelle (Gundersen and Bulinski, 1986b). When immunofluorescence of fixed cells is used to visualize the distribution of modified tubulin, the unpolymerized tubulin in the cells is usually extracted and thus is unavailable for analysis. The tyrosination state of tubulin in the soluble pool is significant if, as was suggested by Burns (1987), only tyrosinated tubulin is assembly-competent in vivo (Gundersen and Bulinski, 1987). Gundersen and Bulinski (1986b) analyzed the ratio of tyrosinated to detyrosinated tubulin in extracts from a number of cell types. These extracts, prepared by detergent lysis of whole cells, contain the total cell tubulin. Extracts of cells containing structures such as neuronal processes or cilia have more detyrosinated tubulin than extracts of cultured cells, which is consistent with the high content of detyrosinated tubulin in these stable structures. Glu–tubulin in cell extracts is derived from microtubules containing Glu–tubulin, as demonstrated by the composition of extracts from cells containing a marginal band. Immunoblots of extracts from cells where the marginal band stains with anti-Glu antibody (see above) show the presence of Glu–tubulin. No Glu–tubulin is detected in toad erythrocytes, where the marginal band is not visualized by anti-Glu immunofluoresce. In summary, this study showed that the ratio of tyrosinated to detyrosinated tubulin for the whole cell is correlated with the amount of detyrosinated tubulin polymerized into microtubules. Recently the tyrosination states of polymerized and unpolymerized tubulin in cultured cells were analyzed by immunoblotting. In the TC-7 cell line, little or no Glu–tubulin was found in the soluble tubulin fraction. The authors conclude that detyrosinated tubulin, once released from disassembled microtubules, is efficiently retyrosinated by TTL (Gundersen et al., 1987). Complete tyrosination of subunits in the soluble pool has recently been demonstrated in vivo by observing the retyrosination of detyrosinated tubulin after microinjection into cells (Webster et al., 1987). Earlier results showing detyrosinated tubulin in the monomeric pool (Rodriguez and Borisy, 1979) could have resulted from differences in the methods of analysis or artifactual presence of Glu–tubulin in the soluble fraction because of depolymerization of microtubules containing Glu–tubulin during the extraction process (Webster et al., 1987). They may, however, indicate that various cell types differ in the levels of detyrosinated tubulin in their unpolymerized pools as well as in their microtubule assemblies.

The microtubules of the mitotic spindle show a pattern of tubulin detyrosination that not only is specific to particular microtubules but also changes with time. Throughout prophase, metaphase, and anaphase, the pattern of anti-Tyr immunofluorescence resembles the total microtubule distribution. The pattern of anti-Glu staining, besides being less intense, is also more restricted in distribution. Although some anti-Glu staining is seen in the half-spindles at metaphase, anti-Glu staining is not visible in the astral fibers nor near the cell equator. When the interzonal microtubules form at anaphase, they do not stain with the anti-Glu antibody. As the cells progress into telophase, the interzonal microtubules become the midbody (Brinkley and Cartwright, 1971). The midbody stains brightly with the anti-Glu antibody and retains its anti-Glu staining through telophase, whereas the new cytoplasmic microtubules that form in the daughter cells show no reaction at all with anti-Glu (Gundersen and Bulinski, 1986a).

Geuens et al. (1986) report that all classes

of microtubules in metaphase possess almost equal amounts of Glu–tubulin, as determined by electron microscopy using gold-conjugated anti-Tyr and anti-Glu antibodies. They contend that, with immunofluorescence staining, the greater density of microtubules in the half-spindle allows anti-Glu microtubules to be visualized there, while binding of the anti-Glu antibody to less closely packed astral fibers goes undetected. The more distinct differences in immunofluorescent localization seen in anaphase and telophase have not yet been analyzed by electron microscopy.

Two interesting points can be made about the restricted distribution of Glu–tubulin in the mitotic spindle. First, as Geuens et al. (1986) remind us, no MAP so far studied has the same distribution seen for Glu microtubules in the mitotic spindle. Differential association of MAPs based on tyrosination state may still be a possibility—if some MAP were *excluded* from Glu microtubules, the distribution might appear so similar to that of total tubulin that it would be undetectable without simultaneously localizing Glu microtubules. Immunofluorescent localization of calmodulin has been shown to resemble the pattern of anti-Glu staining (Andersen et al., 1978; Welsh et al., 1979; DeMey et al., 1980), but this may result from the effect described above, in which staining of spindle-associated proteins is brightest in areas of high microtubule density. Second, the recognition of some microtubules by the anti-Glu antibody changes with time, as is shown by the behavior of the interzonal microtubules that become the midbody in telophase. This suggests that the accumulation of post-translationally modified tubulin may be correlated with the age of the microtubule. Further evidence suggesting this possibility is given by immunofluorescence of tissue culture cells after treatment with various drugs. Nocodazole, cold, and colcemid reversibly depolymerize cellular microtubules. When cells are released from these treatments, reassembly of the microtubule array occurs, requiring less than 5 min for cold-depolymerized microtubules and about 50 min for colcemid-depolymerized microtubules. Regardless of the depolymerizing agent used, none of the microtubules formed react with the Glu antibody until about 25 min after reassembly is complete (Gundersen et al., 1987).

The microtubule-containing structures of microorganisms often display a remarkable degree of organization and exhibit dramatic changes related to the life cycle. Here, the pattern of tubulin protein in the whole cell, or in a cellular fraction containing a particular microtubule array, may be amenable to two-dimensional gel analysis. In some cases, the relation of certain tubulin isoforms to tubulin genes is known (Burland et al., 1984; Silflow et al., 1985; May et al., 1985; Birkett et al., 1985a,b) Thus the study of tubulin post-translational modifications in microorganisms is especially informative.

In the case of trypanosomes, tubulin from the subpellicular microtubules and the flagella, as well as unpolymerized tubulin, has been isolated and analyzed (Sherwin et al., 1987). Tyrosinated tubulin was detected in all the trypanosomal microtubule arrays enumerated above and in unpolymerized tubulin. Two-dimensional gels of each of these subcellular fractions probed with YL1/2 display an α-tubulin pattern indistinguishable from that of the total tubulin in that fraction as visualized by Coomassie blue staining or an antibody to total α tubulin. Thus all the microtubule arrays in the cell contain some Tyr–tubulin, and it appears that no isotype in the trypanosome is excluded from tyrosination.

The most remarkable feature of tubulin tyrosination in trypanosomes is its relation to the cell cycle as visualized by immunofluorescence. An antibody that recognizes both forms of α tubulin shows bright fluorescence throughout the cell body because of the subpellicular microtubules that run the length of the cell. Staining of microtubules by YL1/2 (an anti-Tyr antibody) is localized to the microtubules in the posterior one-third of the cell body. The single flagellum of the trypanosome in interphase does not stain with YL1/2. One of the early events in cell division is the emergence and growth of a second, "daughter" flagellum from one of the basal bodies. This daughter flagellum stains brilliantly with YL1/2, so at this time there are two flagella, one (the daughter) that reacts with YL1/2 and thus contains tyrosinated tubulin and another (the original) that does not stain and thus must contain detyrosinated tubulin. Shortly after the daughter flagellum reaches full length, the basal bodies separate. At that time, the flagella and the posterior region of the cell body lose their reactivity with YL1/2. This very weak staining persisits through nuclear division and cytokinesis. Even though there is a point in the cell cycle at which the fluorescence of all other microtubule-containing structures is lost, the basal bodies stain brightly with anti-Tyr antibodies at all times during the cell cycle. This study did not present any data using an antibody either to detyrosinated or to total α tubulin. These antibodies would have shown some of the cellular microtubules from the time of separation of basal bodies to the reappearance of tyrosinated microtubules in the daughter cells. The decrease in tyrosinated tubulin in the cell body with time, and especially the behavior of the growing flagella, suggests a correlation between persistence of microtubules through time and an increase in their post-translational loss of tyrosine (Sherwin et al., 1987).

In *Physarum* the tyrosination state of α tubulin from the amoebal and plasmodial stages of the life cycle has been determined by two-dimensional immunoblotting with the antibody YL1/2 (Birkett et al., 1985a). A curious feature of these immunoblots is that YL1/2 recognizes the three α-tubulin isoforms found in the amoebal cytoplasm but not an isoform of α tubulin found only in plasmodia. It does, however, recognize one of the two β-tubulin isoforms, also plasmodiaspecific. Since the epitope of the YL1/2 antibody is the C-terminus of α tubulin, with its terminal tyrosine, this pattern of antibody reactivity might signify an exchange of sequences between the plasmodial α- and β-tubulin genes. The nucleotide sequences of one of the *Physarum* tubulin genes encodes a polypeptide that is divergent from other known α tubulins and lacks a C-terminal tyrosine (Monteiro and Cox, 1987). If this tubulin gene is sufficiently divergent, TTL may not be able to recognize its product as a substrate, and tubulin encoded by this gene would never by tyrosinated. -Tubulin genes that encode C-terminal ends that are divergent and do not end with tyrosine have also been discovered in mouse (Villasante et al., 1986), chicken (Pratt et al., 1987), *Drosophila* (Theurkauf et al., 1986), and yeast (Schatz et al., 1986). Some of these encode phenylalanine, an alternative substrate for TTL (Arce et al., 1975). If members of this group of genes are indeed TTL substrates of varying affinity, they may ultimately be useful in elucidating the function of cyclic tyrosination in vivo.

The distribution of tyrosinated tubulin in brain tissue and neural cells in culture conforms to the patterns seen thus far—limited distribution of detyrosinated tubulin and an increase in detyrosined tubulin in certain microtubule arrays with time. In neuroblastoma cells, differentiation results in the accumulation of Glu microtubules in the extended neurite cell processes (Wehland and Weber, 1987b). Sections taken from immature rat brains have been examined using the antibody YL1/2, which stains most cell structures recognized by an antibody to total tubulin. The molecular layer of brain contains axons (parallel fibers), dendrites and cell bodies (of Purkinje cells), and glial cells. In this layer, the reaction with YL1/2 is lost by the parallel fibers but is retained by all non-axonal structures as the cells develop and begin to form synapses with each other (Cumming et al., 1984a). All parts of the axon of the sciatic nerve as well as all parts of retinal ganglion cells beyond the cell body contain detyrosinated tubulin. There is no apparent gradient of detyrosination along the length of the axon. Apparently, detyrosination in the axon occurs at or near the time tubulin enters the axon and does not depend on extensive treadmilling or on axonal transport (Burgoyne and Norman, 1986).

ACETYLATION OF α TUBULIN

In a number of microorganisms, including *Crithidia, Trypanosoma, Chlamydomonas,* and *Polytomella,* the major α tubulin in the flagella appears as a distinct isoform on two-dimensional gels (Russel et al., 1984; Schneider et al., 1987; McKeithan et al., 1983; McKeithan and Rosenbaum, 1981). The absence of this specific isoform in the in vitro translation products of *Chlamydomonas* and *Polytomella* RNA first suggested that this flagellar α tubulin might arise from post-translational modification (McKeithan et al., 1983). Pulse-chase in vivo labeling with ^{35}S, which demonstrated a precursor-product relationship between the major cytoplasmic α tubulin (α_1) and the more acidic flagellar α tubulin (α_3), lent support to the idea that the flagellar-specific isoform is not directly encoded by the α-tubulin genes (McKeithan et al., 1983; Green and Dove, 1984; Russel and Gull, 1984). The nature of the modification was determined by labeling of *Chlamydomonas* cells with ^{3}H-acetate in the presence of cycloheximide. Only α_3 tubulin was labeled, and the labeled amino acid was identified as ε-acetyl-lysine (L'Hernault and Rosenbaum, 1983, 1985a). The major α tubulin of the flagella and subpellicular microtubules of *Trypanosoma* can also be specifically labeled in this way and presumably is similarly modified (Schneider et al., 1987).

The relation between acetylation and flagellar assembly has been explored in detail in *Chlamydomonas.* Conversion of cytoplasmic α_1 tubulin to flagellar α_3 tubulin occurs during flagellar outgrowth. If regeneration of flagella is blocked by colchicine, new flagellar proteins are synthesized (Lefebvre et al., 1978), but the acetylated α_3 tubulin does not appear (Brunke et al., 1982; L'Hernault and Rosenbaum, 1982). When *Chlamydomonas* resorbs its flagella, proteins from the disassembled flagella return to the cell body. α_3 Tubulin from the resorbed flagella found in the cell body is deacetylated to α_1 (L'Hernault and Rosenbaum, 1985b). The correlation between

axonemal assembly and tubulin acetylation can also be seen within the flagellum. The axoneme, which contains all the assembled tubulin, can be isolated from the rest of the flagellar proteins, including unassembled tubulin (Witman et al., 1972). The major form in the assembled axoneme is acetylated α_3 tubulin, but its unacetylated precursor (α_1) predominates in the unassembled fraction. This provides two pieces of information: Not all the tubulin in the flagella is acetylated, only that that is assembled; also, acetylation of α_1 tubulin occurs at or shortly after the time of assembly. If acetylation occurred much before assembly of the tubulin subunit at the distal tip of the axoneme, the unassembled tubulin would contain a sizable fraction of α_3 tubulin, and the same reasoning implies that acetylation does not lag far behind assembly. Microtubule assembly in vivo is not dependent on acetylation, however, since there are assembled microtubules in the *Chlamydomonas* cytoplasm, where the major form of α tubulin is the unacetylated α_1 (L'Hernault and Rosenbaum, 1983). A more dramatic demonstration of the lack of acetylation of cytoplasmic microtubules is seen in *Polytomella,* which has hundreds of intracellular microtubules that can be separated from the soluble pool of cytoplasmic tubulin. The major α tubulin in both the microtubules and the soluble pool is the unacetylated α_1 (McKeithan and Rosenbaum, 1981). From these observations, it can be seen that, although acetylation is correlated with assembled microtubules in the flagella, neither all flagellar nor all assembled tubulin is acetylated.

The enzyme responsible for α-tubulin acetylation has been isolated from *Chlamydomonas* flagella and characterized (Greer et al., 1985; Maruta et al., 1986). This enzyme specifically acetylates α tubulin from mammalian brain as well as from *Chlamydomonas.* Acetylation in vitro results in addition of an acetyl group to the ε-amino group of lysine, just as on α tubulin in vivo (Greer, 1988). Unlike C-terminal tyrosination, this acetylation of lysine is not unique to tubulin, since it occurs on histones (Doenecke and Gallwitz, 1982), but histones are a poor substrate for the tubulin acetyltransferase. This substrate specificity distinguises it from any other known acetyltransferase. Polymerized tubulin is acetylated more readily than the dimer, and colchicine, which inhibits assembly of brain microtubule protein, also inhibits tubulin acetylation in vitro (Maruta et al., 1986).

Following the biochemical demonstration of acetylation of α tubulin in the flagellum, an antibody that recognizes flagellar but not cytoplasmic α tubulin from sea urchin and *Chlamydomonas* was isolated and was shown to be specific for acetylated tubulin. The antibody recognizes α tubulin derived from the cytoplasm of these organisms only after the lysine residues have been acetylated with acetic anhydride in vitro (Piperno and Fuller, 1985). Using this antibody, Piperno and Fuller showed that axonemes from a number of species, including *Chlamydomonas, Tetrahymena, Drosophila,* and human, contain acetylated tubulin. Fractionation of sea urchin axonemes showed that the microtubules of the central pair, which differ in structure and stability from the outer doublets, contain the same proportions of acetylated α tubulin as the outer doublets. The antibody was also used to help determine which lysine in axonemal α tubulin is acetylated. After proteolytic digestion of α tubulin from *Chlamydomonas* axonemes, the peptide recognized by the antibody was sequenced. This peptide contained acetyllysine in the residue corresponding to lysine-40 in the α-tubulin molecule. The sequence around lysine-40 is conserved in most α-tubulin genes, but some encode products that do not have lysine at that position. There is considerable overlap between the α tubulins that lack lysine-40 and those that have unusual C termini. Thus there may be α-tubulin gene products that participate neither in detyrosination and tyrosination nor in acetylation (LeDizet and Piperno, 1987).

In addition, a number of non-flagellar microtubules are also visualized by this antibody. These include the subpellicular microtubule array of *Trypanosoma* and the basal bodies of *Chlamydomonas* (Schneider et al., 1987; LeDizet and Piperno, 1986). The staining by this antibody of a subset of microtubules in interphase tissue culture cells is similar to the pattern seen using an antibody to detyrosinated tubulin. This distribution of acetylated tubulin in interphase cells has been confirmed by another, independently isolated, antibody raised against sea urchin axonemes (Thompson et al., 1984) that recently was shown also to be specific for acetylated α tubulin (Grant et al., 1986).

Specific structures stained by antibodies to acetylated α tubulin in most cells include centrioles and primary cilia (Thompson et al., 1984; Piperno et al., 1987). Primary cilia have nine outer doublets identical to those found in flagella, but lack other flagellar structures such as central pair microtubules, nexin links, dynein arms, and radial spokes (for review, see Poole et al., 1985). In some cells, microtubules of the mitotic spindle have been shown to be acetylated. During mitosis, kinetochores, microtubules in the polar regions, and continuous fibers all appear to react with the antibody. The midbodies are also stained (Piperno et al., 1987). Curiously, none of the microtubules of the cell line PtK$_2$ stain with either of the antibodies specific to acetylated α tubulin. Tubulin extracted from PtK$_2$ cells and chemically acetylated in vitro is recognized, suggesting that PtK$_2$ cells, rather than having acetylated tubulin that is not recognized by the antibodies, actually lack detectable levels of acetylated tubulin (Piperno et al., 1987). These cells also possess the enzymes responsible for the acetylation of α tubulin, since acetylated α tubulin appears in these cells after injection of the cells with antibodies against acetylated α tubulin, which presumably blocks access to α tubulin by deacetylases (Grant et al., 1987).

Like detyrosinated tubulin in trypanosomes, the acetylated tubulin in *Physarum* shows striking changes related to the cell cycle. *Physarum* has three distinct stages in its life cycle—the unicellular amoeba, the multinucleate plasmodium, and the unicellular and non-proliferating flagellate. In the flagellate, the microtubules of the flagellum are acetylated, as is the extensive cone of cytoplasmic microtubules radiating from the basal body. In the amoeba, acetylated tubulin can be detected only during mitosis. The mitotic spindle of the amoeba contains some acetylated tubulin in and near the centrioles, but the mitotic spindle of the plasmodium has none. Since the plasmodium contains no other microtubule-containing structures, despite its expression of plasmodial-specific tubulin isotypes, the plasmodium is devoid of acetylated microtubules. Analysis of two-dimensional gels probed with various antibodies, including one specific to acetylated tubulin, reveals that one antibody specific for *Physarum* α tubulin recognizes only *unacetylated* tubulins. This antibody recognizes almost all the microtubules in ameobal and plasmodial cells, including the interphase microtubules and the entire mitotic spindle (Diggins and Dove, 1987; Sasse et al., 1987).

The existence of endogenous acetylase activity in brain microtubule protein (Greer et al., 1985) suggests that brain tissue contains acetylated α tubulin. This has recently been confirmed by Cambray-Deakin and Burgoyne (1987), using an antibody specific to acetylated α tubulin. In mature rat brain, acetylated tubulin was found in parallel fibers (axons) and was absent from dendrites and from cells without neuronal processes. The authors compare these results to their earlier study localizing detyrosinated α tubulin and find a remarkable degree of overlap between the two modifications in adult brain. In the developing rat cerebellum, parallel fibers contain acetylated tubulin at all stages of development. Since staining with anti-Tyr antibodies is not lost until about the time of synapse formation (Cumming et al., 1984a), this suggests that accumulation of modified tubulin in the parallel fibers continues at least until this stage of development. Cerebellar granule cells, which give rise to the parallel fibers, can be grown in culture. The cell bodies and neurite processes of these cells stain with antibodies both for acetylated and for tyrosinated tubulin. It is possible that, in vivo, acetylation occurs when the axonal process is formed, but that detyrosination requires formation of appropriate synapses, which do not form in culture (Cumming et al., 1984b). Further investigation of these cells may help elucidate the role of tubulin acetylation and detyrosination, as well as the relationship of these two processes, in determining cytoskeletal structures.

Studies using antibodies specific to acetylated tubulin have shown that within the array of interphase microtubules, the most stable microtubules are acetylated. The subset of cytoplasmic microtubules that are acetylated appears to have enhanced stability to colchicine or colchemid. When *Chlamydomonas* cells are treated with colchicine (LeDizet and Piperno, 1986), or when tissue culture cells are treated with nocodazole or colcemid (Piperno et al., 1987; Thompson et al., 1984), most of the cytoplasmic microtubules depolymerize. All the microtubules that are left after 1–2 hr in the drug react with an antibody against acetylated tubulin. Disassembly of the cytoskeleton by cold or hypotonic medium, however, does not preferentially spare acetylated microtubules (Thompson et al., 1984; LeDizet and Piperno, 1986; Piperno et al., 1987).

Extended treatment of cultured cells with taxol results in the formation of large microtubule bundles. These microtubules stain intensely with an antibody to acetylated tubulin. Quantitiative immunoassays show that the amount of α tubulin in taxol-treated cells is about one and one-half times that of untreated cells, but the amount of acetylated tubulin in taxol-treated cells increases almost fourfold. The increase in acetylated tubulin is reversed upon removal of taxol and restoration of the normal cytoskeleton (Piperno et al., 1987). Thus stabilization of microtubules increases their content of acetylated tubulin. It is, therefore, surprising that taxol *inhibits* acetylation in vitro (Maruta et al., 1986). There is evidence that the taxol binding site is at a region of the tubulin molecule crucial to acetylation, since the epitope recognized by one of the antibodies specific for acetylated tubulin is masked in the presence of taxol. After fixation, the epitope is once again accessible to the antibody (Thompson et al., 1984). It is not obvious, however, why binding of taxol would interfere with acetylation in vitro but not in vivo. Perhaps taxol binds at a different time relative to microtubule assembly or with a different stoichiometry in vivo than in vitro.

Treatment of cells with drugs that depolymerize microtubules provides evidence that acetylation does not occur immediately upon assembly. Depolymerization of cytoplasmic microtubules by cold, colchicine, or nocodazole is rapidly reversible. Double-labeling with antibodies for acetylated and for total tubulin shows that, whereas the cytoskeleton appears completely reassembled 3 min after nocodazole removal, only short segments of microtubules are acetylated. When cells with cytoskeletons depolymerized by colchicine are prepared for double-labeling as rapidly as possible after the drug is removed, a small aster of microtubules containing no acetylated tubulin is apparent in the center of the cells. After cells are released from cold treatment, the first acetylated microtubules appear in the centrosphere after about 10 min (Thompson et al., 1984; Piperno et al., 1987). Thus tubulin acetylation appears to occur after microtubule polymerization and may be significant not in the assembly process per se but in some later event, such as the binding of MAPs or microtubule stabilization.

In summary, the pattern of tubulin acetylation in a number of cell types has been determined by two-dimensional gel analysis and cytochemical studies using antibodies specific to acetylated tubulin. These findings, together with the study of tubulin acetylation in vitro, provide enough information to exclude some of the simplest explanations for the role of acetylation. Acetylation does not affect assembly of brain microtubule protein nor its disassembly by cold in vitro (Maruta et al., 1986). There-

fore, it does not appear to change the assembly characteristics of purified tubulin dimers. The function of acetylation does not appear to be limited to some aspect of flagellar assembly, such as facilitating the formation of outer doublets or the binding of flagellar accessory proteins, since acetylated tubulin is not limited to flagella. In general, however, the microtubules that become acetylated are microtubules that are especially stable to drug treatment or are within stable microtubule arrays, such as axonemes, midbodies, and centrioles.

SIGNIFICANCE OF TUBULIN POST-TRANSLATIONAL MODIFICATIONS

Microtubules in which the tubulin has been post-translationally modified appear to be a subset of cellular microtubules. The evidence presented above indicates that, in many cases, there is extensive overlap within this subset among detyrosinated and acetylated microtubules. Flagella, basal bodies and centrioles from a number of cells contain, almost without exception, high levels of both detyrosinated (Gundersen and Bulinski, 1986a,b; Sherwin et al., 1987) and acetylated (Piperno and Fuller, 1985; LeDizet and Piperno, 1986; Schneider et al., 1987; Diggins and Dove, 1987; Sasse et al., 1987; Shea and Walsh, 1987) tubulin. Phosphorylated β tubulin appears to be located in axons and neurite processes (Ikeda and Steiner, 1979; Gard and Kirschner, 1985), sites where acetylated and detyrosinated tubulin have been found (Cambray-Deakin and Burgoyne, 1987; Cumming et al., 1984a; Gundersen and Bulinski, 1986b; Wehland and Weber, 1987b; Black and Keyser, 1987; Edde et al., 1987). In interphase cells, the subsets of microtubules stained by antibodies to detyrosinated and acetylated microtubules resemble each other in number and morphology (Gundersen et al., 1984; Wehland and Weber, 1987b; Thompson et al., 1984; Piperno et al., 1987). In vitro studies of the enzymes responsible for detyrosinating and acetylating tubulin indicate that both these enzymes prefer polymerized tubulin as a substrate and that the rate of tubulin modification is not dependent on the number of microtubule ends (Arce et al., 1978; Arce and Barra, 1985; Kumar and Flavin, 1981; Maruta et al., 1986). From the distribution of phosphorylated tubulin, the same preference for polymerized tubulin has been inferred for the kinase that generates the phosphorylated β tubulin seen by Gard and Kirschner (1985). These observations indicate that the way in which subsets of microtubules become post-translationally modified may be similar for these three modifications and that the modifications may serve similar functions in the cell. In the following discussion, the three covalent modifications of tubulin will be considered together.

Because cilia, flagella, and the highly ordered subpellicular microtubules of *Trypanosoma* contain acetylated tubulin (Piperno and Fuller, 1985; Schneider et al., 1987), and because acetylation was first discovered in conjunction with flagellar assembly (L'Hernault and Rosenbaum, 1983), it was once thought that acetylation and other modifications might specify a particular microtubule structure, such as outer doublets, or possibly facilitate the arrangement of microtubules into parallel arrays (Sasse et al., 1987; Wehland et al., 1983a). The wide variety of microtubules found to carry each of the modifications suggests that none of these modifications is limited to microtubules of a particular morphology nor to microtubule arrays of a particular geometry.

Although modification does not seem to be associated with any particular spatial properties of microtubules, there is, for each of the modifications, a strong correlation with microtubule stability. Axonemes, basal bodies, and the microtubules of the axons (Burgoyne et al., 1982; Gray et al., 1982) are examples of stable microtubule arrays and have been found to contain detyrosinated or acetylated tubulin. In some cases, the level of tubulin modification in stable microtubules has been seen to increase with the age of the microtubule, for example, in the flagella of trypanosomes (Sherwin et al., 1987) and in the axonal microtubules of the cere-

bellum (Cumming et al., 1984a; Cambray-Deakin and Burgoyne, 1987). Recent studies of microtubule dynamics in vivo have confirmed the correlation between stability and modification. After injection of biotin-conjugated tubulin into living cells, this labeled tubulin exchanges with tubulin in the cellular microtubules. A nonfluorescent antibody to the biotinylated tubulin can be used to block the binding of fluorescent antitubulin antibodies to the exchanged subunits. This procedure selectively shows stable microtubules. By double-labeling with this method together with antibodies to post-translationally modified tubulin, Kirchner and coworkers found that there is extensive congruence between detyrosinated, acetylated, and stable microtubules (Schulze and Kirschner, 1986; Schulze et al., 1987).

A number of explanations can be proposed for the correlation between tubulin modification and microtubule stability. Some of these postulate direct effects of tubulin modification on the rate of assembly or the molecular composition of the assembling microtubule. Others suggest that the modification plays some role in the processes by which microtubules become differentiated after assembly.

Post-translational modification could alter the assembly properties of tubulin or the structure of the microtubules assembled from modified tubulin, so that the stability of the polymer is enhanced. If modification altered the assembly properties of tubulin, then one would expect this difference between modified and unmodified tubulin to be detectable in vitro. Brain tubulin that has been enzymatically detyrosinated (Raybin and Flavin, 1977b) or acetylated (Maruta et al., 1986) has not yet been shown to differ from untreated tubulin in any assembly or disassembly experiments. Injection of enzymatically detyrosinated tubulin into tissue culture cells reveals no differences between its localization in the cell and that of untreated brain tubulin (Webster et al., 1987). Furthermore, after all the microtubules in a permeabilized cell are detyrosinated by treatment with carboxypeptidase A, only a few microtubules display the enhanced resistance to nocodazole depolymerization that is characteristic of microtubules containing modified tubulin (Khawaja et al., 1988).

Even if modification did not alter the polymerization of tubulin itself, it could still increase the stability of the polymer by facilitating the binding of MAPs. The localization of modified tubulin in the brain may be useful in determining which, if any, MAPs are preferentially associated with modified tubulin, since the most extensively studied examples of differential MAP distribution are in neural cells and tissue. No studies directed at colocalization of MAPs and modified tubulin have yet been reported, although inspection of the literature suggests some intriguing possibilities. For example, the tau proteins are localized to axons (Binder et al., 1985), which contain modified tubulin (Cumming et al., 1984a; Cambray-Deakin and Burgoyne, 1987). Also, the complement of high-M_r MAPs and tau proteins changes with development, with the mature isotypes appearing at about the time that post-translational modifications of tubulin occur (Matus and Riederer, 1986; Fellous et al., 1986).

In the investigation of the association of MAPs with modified microtubules, it may be essential to remember that a single modification of tubulin could facilitate the binding of more than one MAP. The MAP(s) associated with a single form of modified tubulin would then be determined by which of these MAPs is present in the vicinity of each microtubule at the time of its assembly. In this case, it would be impossible to find that any form of modified tubulin is invariably associated with a single MAP.

Other proposed functions for tubulin modification are based on the idea that the modification of tubulin does not change the assembly or binding properties of the modified microtubule but plays an indirect role in regulating the formation, stability, and organization of microtubule-containing organelles. For example, if the cell was able to control the process of modification by regulating the activity of modifying enzymes, then it would be possible to have a common pool of tubulin subunits, from which all microtubules could assemble. The level of modification of the tubulin subunits of microtubules formed at different times would then depend on the levels of modifying enzymes present. These different subsets of microtubules might be differentially stabilized, for example, by binding different MAPs (McKeithan et al., 1983). This implies that modification occurs at or after assembly and would be reversed when modified tubulin subunits reenter the dimer pool after microtubule disassembly. This has been shown to occur during axonemal assembly and disassembly in *Chlamydomonas* (L'Hernault and Rosenbaum, 1985b; McKeithan and Rosenbaum, 1981). Conversion of detyrosinated tubulin injected into cells occurs in a pattern that suggests that the tubulin is retyrosinated after the subunits are released into the dimer pool by turnover of the microtubules in the interphase cytoskeleton (Webster et al., 1987). The lag in appearance of modified tubulin on newly formed microtubules (Gundersen et al., 1987; Sherwin et al., 1987; Thompson et al., 1984; Piperno et al., 1987) and the preference of the modifying enzymes for polymerized tubulin (Kumar and Flavin, 1981; Maruta et al., 1986) are evidence that tubulin modification occurs after assembly in other cells.

The observation that microtubules must persist for some time to be modified suggests the possibility that microtubules are not stable because of their modification but are modified because of their stability (Kirschner and Mitchison, 1986). If modifications occur after assembly and increase with time, then stable microtubules, regardless of the mechanism of stabilization, would be demarcated by the accumulation of post-translational modifications with age. The necessity of differentiating stable microtubules is apparent if, as suggested by the "dynamic instability" model of microtubule dynamics, all microtubules have some finite probability of losing their GTP cap and then depolymerizing (Mitchison and Kirschner, 1984b).

In this case, a nucleation center such as a centriole or basal body will always have microtubules associated with it, but individual microtubules will depolymerize and be replaced by others (Mitchison and Kirschner, 1984a). Over time, a large number of microtubule configurations will exist, and only those microtubules protected from depolymerization will persist. The rapid turnover of microtubules in vivo (Schulze and Kirschner, 1986; Sammak et al., 1987) lends support to the idea that most cellular microtubules are prone to depolymerization. If the more stable microtubules have become modified, they are now differentiated from the majority of the microtubules. Furthermore, events at the end of the microtubule that determined its stability during and shortly after assembly have now influenced the structure of the microtubule along its entire length. From the numerous microtubules associated with a microtubule-organizing center, the particular microtubules that have persisted for some time can be identified by their modifications and may then become permanently stabilized (Schulze and Kirschner, 1986; Kirschner and Mitchison, 1986).

The role of post-translational modifications as indicators of microtubule age is attractive in that it is consistent with the present evidence that modification, although correlated with stable microtubules, appears to be "a consequence, not a cause," of that stability (Gundersen et al., 1984). Even this explanation, however, answers only a few of the questions raised by tubulin modification. Although there is no evidence that modification per se stabilizes the microtubule, any other explanation raises the question of what actually does enhance the stability of modified microtubules. Any explanation for the role of acetylation of tubulin will have to account for the two cell lines from *Potorous tridactylis* that lack acetylated tubulin (Thompson et al., 1984; Piperno et al., 1987) even though tubulin acetyltransferase is present in these cells (Grant et al., 1987). Even more perplexing is the puzzle posed by the few tubulin genes that do not encode a C-terminal tyrosine (Monteiro and Cox, 1987; Pratt et al., 1987; Schatz et al., 1986; Villasante et al., 1986; Theurkauf et al., 1986). Recent analysis of acetylated tubulin has determined that some of these genes also lack the lysine residue where *Chlamydomonas* tubulin is acetylated (LeDizet and Piperno, 1987). Whether expression of these tubulins is part of the mechanisms by which modified tubulin is restricted to certain microtubules remains to be determined. It may soon be possible to answer some of these questions by adding genetic methods to the study of tubulin modification and its role in the processes by which a single protein forms a diversity of cellular structures.

ACKNOWLEDGMENTS

The authors thank Drs. J. Chloë Bulinski and Richard Linck for their helpful comments on the manuscript.

K. Greer was a predoctoral trainee on the United States Public Health Service grant GM07223. Her present address is: Department of Anatomy, University of Connecticut Health Center, Farmington, CT 06020. This article is taken from a dissertation submitted to fulfill in part the requirements for the degree of Doctor of Philosophy in Yale University.

NOTE ADDED IN PROOF

Recent work provides additional evidence that modification of microtubules by acetylation or detyrosination correlates with the stability of the microtubules, and that this stability may be due to the binding of MAPs to the walls of the microtubules. Work by H. Kim and L. Binder (unpublished results) shows that during temperature-induced cycles of assembly/disassembly of brain microtubules, more than 80% of the acetylated tubulin is associated with the cold-stable fraction. Although treatment with calcium releases a significant proportion of the tubulin from this cold-insoluble fraction, all of the detectable acetylated tubulin remains with the cold- and calcium-insoluble fraction. It is possible that the proteins shown by Margolis et al. (1986a) to confer cold stability on temperature-cycled brain microtubules do so because they only bind to the walls of microtubules containing acetylated α-tubulin. A recent report by Sale et al. (1988) also demonstrates this increase in the proportion of acetylated α-tubulin in cold-stable fractions during temperature-dependent microtubule assembly/disassembly. Since microtubules enriched in acetylated α-tubulin are not preferentially stable in vivo, Sale et al. favor the idea that acetylated α-tubulin associates with MAPs present in the pellet of microtubules formed in vitro and they are thus stabilized.

In other recent work, Sherwin and Gull (unpublished results), working on trypano-somes, have demonstrated that during cell division new microtubules are assembled in between the old ones in the cytoskeleton. The assembling ends of these microtubules contain tyrosinated α-tubulin, whereas the remaining portions of these same microtubules are detyrosinated (glu) as determined by gold antibody labeling of negatively stained preparations. Interestingly, it appears as if detyrosination of α-tubulin may be correlated with the formation of cross-bridges between neighboring microtubules. It is possible that the assembling tyrosinated ends are more labile, in part due to the lack of cross-bridging via MAPs, whereas the detyrosinated portions of the microtubule, assembled earlier, are more stable, due in part to their cross-bridging by MAPs.

Tektins in Ciliary and Flagellar Microtubules and Their Association With Other Cytoskeletal Systems

Walter Steffen and Richard W. Linck

Department of Cell Biology and Neuroanatomy, University of Minnesota School of Medicine, Minneapolis, Minnesota 55455

INTRODUCTION

In the past several years a novel set of proteins, called *tektins,* have been described that appear to form longitudinal filaments in the walls of ciliary and flagellar microtubules and that have several properties in common with intermediate filament proteins. In this chapter we review work concerning the organization of tektins in ciliary and flagellar microtubules and basal bodies, we provide evidence for the existence of tektin-like proteins in several microtubule and intermediate filament systems of mammalian cells and, finally, we discuss the possible biological functions of tektins.

TEKTINS IN CILIARY AND FLAGELLAR MICROTUBULES

Fractionation of Axonemes and Characterization of Tektins

Ciliary and flagellar axonemes from sea urchin sperm, molluscan gills, or *Chlamydomonas* can be fractionated in a variety of ways. Incubation of demembranated axonemes in a buffer with low-ionic strength results in preparations containing doublet microtubules and remnants of central pair microtubules (Gibbons, 1965). The doublet microtubules can then be separated and treated in ways that selectively solubilize the B-subfibers, yielding intact A-subfiber microtubules (Linck, 1973; Stephens, 1970; Witman et al., 1972a). Alternatively, axonemal microtubules can be fractionated by Sarkosyl treatment into ribbons of approximately three protofilaments (Linck, 1976; Meza et al., 1972; Witman et al., 1972a,b); the polypeptide composition of the Sarkosyl ribbons will be discussed in detail below. Finally, extraction of axonemal microtubules with 0.5% Sarkosyl/2 M urea yields a preparation of filaments 2–6 nm in diameter, free of tubulin, and composed principally of a set of three proteins, called *tektins* (Linck et al., 1982; Linck and Langevin, 1982) (see Figs. 5–1, 5–2).

To date, three flagellar tektins have been characterized most thoroughly from the sea urchin *Strongylocentrotus purpuratus* (Beese, 1984; Linck and Langevin, 1982;

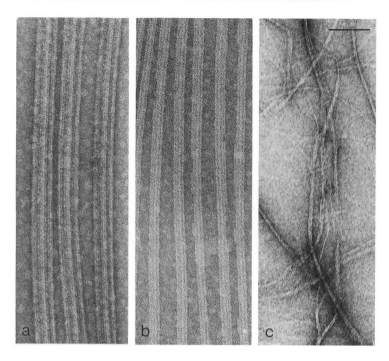

Fig. 5–1. Negative stain electron micrographs of **a:** axonemal doublet microtubules, **b:** 0.5% Sarkosyl-insoluble protofilament ribbons, and **c:** 0.5% Sarkosyl/2 M urea-insoluble tektin filaments isolated from *Strongylocentrotus purpuratus* flagellar axonemes. Bar = 100 nm.

Linck and Stephens, 1987). Their apparent molecular masses, as determined by sodium dodecyl sulfate (SDS) polyacrylamide gel electrophoresis (PAGE), are 47 k Da, 51 kDa, and 55 kDa (Fig. 5–2, lane 1). The tektins and α and β tubulin have been electrophoretically purified by SDS-PAGE and compared by high-resolution two-dimensional tryptic peptide mapping and amino acid analysis. Tryptic peptide mapping reveals a 63–67% coincidence in the number and position of peptides of the 51 kD tektin as compared with the 47 kDa and 55 kDa tektins, and a >70% coincidence between the 47 kDa and 55 kDa tektins; none of the tektins, however, bears any significant degree of similarity with either α or β tubulin. By amino acid analysis the tektins are strikingly similar to each other but differ significantly from the tubulins. The tektins can also be separated from each other and from tubulin by reverse-phase high-performance liquid chromatography (HPLC) on an acetonitrile gradient; they elute in the order of 51kDa/55kDa/47kDa, corresponding to their relative hydrophobicities as predicted from their amino acid compositions. These results have demonstrated that the tektins are related but distinctly different polypeptides and that they are not tubulin variants (Linck and Stephens, 1987). In separate studies tektin filament preparations have been shown to yield strong α-type X-ray patterns (Beese, 1984) and to possess ~70% α helix, as measured by circular dichroism (Linck and Langevin, 1982). The observed α-helical structure correlates well with the low proline content of the tektins.

Tektins from two sea urchins, *Lytechinus pictus* (L.p.) and *S. purpuratus* (S.p.), have been compared and studied by immunological methods. From both species filaments 2–6 nm in diameter and composed of ~2-nm subfibrils can be isolated by extraction of axonemal microtubules with 0.5% Sarkosyl/2 M urea (Linck et al., 1987). In

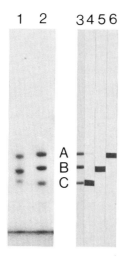

1 2 3 4 5 6

Fig. 5–2. M_r comparison of tektins from *S. purpuratus,* S.p. **(lane 1)** and *Lytechinus pictus,* L.p. **(lane 2)** by SDS-PAGE and immunoblot specificities of antibodies against tektins (antitektins). Lane 1: The major polypeptide bands (from top to bottom) are (S.p.) tektin A = 55 kDa, (S.p.) tektin B = 51 kDa, and (S.p.) tektin C = 47 kDa. Lane 2: (L.p.) tektin A = 56–57 kDa, (L.p.) tektin B = 51–52 kDa, and (L.p.) tektin C = 46 kDa. Nitrocellulose blots of *L. pictus* tektins from lane 3 were stained with affinity-purified anti-(L.p.) tektin C **(lane 4)**, anti-(L.p.) tektin B **(lane 5)**, and anti-(L.p.) tektin A **(lane 6)**. Note that the antitektins are primarily monospecific, and only antitektin C cross reacts weakly with tektin A. A full characterization of these antitektins has been reported elsewhere (Linck et al., 1987).

each case the filaments are composed of three equimolar tektins, but the apparent M_rs for the tektins differ slightly between species (Fig. 5–2, lanes 1, 2). Because of these differences and for simplicity we refer to them as tektin A, B, and C, in decreasing order of M_r. Each tektin from both species has been purified to homogeneity by preparative SDS-PAGE and used to raise polyclonal antibodies, i.e., antitektins (Linck et al., 1987). The antitektins from *L. pictus* and from *S. purpuratus* were affinity purified, using *L. pictus* tektin filaments denatured by SDS as the affinity probe. The specificity and cross reactivity of the *L. pictus* antitektins are shown in Figure 5–2, lanes 4–6. Within a species antitektin A and antitektin B are

TABLE 5–1. Comparative M_rs and Immunological Relatedness of Tektins

Tentative Tektin designation	Apparent M_r (kDa)[a]	
	L. pictus	*S. purpuratus*
A	56–57	55
B	51–52	51
C	46	47

The tektins are arranged in three groups, A, B, and C, in descending order of apparent M_r. Antibodies against each tektin (antitektins) are primarily monospecific. Antitektins from one species strongly cross react with only the same tektin type in the other species; thus, the tektins are categorized by similarities in M_r and immunological cross reactivities. Note that antitektin C cross reacts weakly with tektin A both within the same species (see Fig. 5–2) and between species (data not shown). (Reproduced from Steffen and Linck, 1988, with permission of the publisher.)
[a]Based on comparative SDS-PAGE (Laemmli, 1970).

primarily monospecific for their respective antigens, whereas antitektin C cross reacts slightly with tektin A and, to a lesser extent, with tektin B. Between species the same pattern of specificity and cross reactivity was observed, i.e., anti-(L.p.) tektins cross react in an identical manner with *S. purpuratus* tektins, and vice versa, indicating that each tektin in one species is related to its counterpart in the other species. Thus, on the basis of their M_r similarities and immunological relatedness, the tektins are grouped, as shown in Table 5–1. In a different study monoclonal antibodies have been raised that specifically recognize each of the three tektins from *S. purpuratus* (Chang and Piperno, 1987). Since the tektins could migrate differently, depending on grades of SDS, such as with tubulin (Bibring et al., 1976), it is not yet known whether our order of tektins corresponds to that described by Chang and Piperno (1987).

Biochemical Localization of Tektins in Microtubules

The tektins appear to be localized within a specific domain of the ciliary and flagellar microtubule wall. Extraction of sea urchin sperm flagellar microtubules with 0.5% Sarkosyl solubilizes a significant fraction of

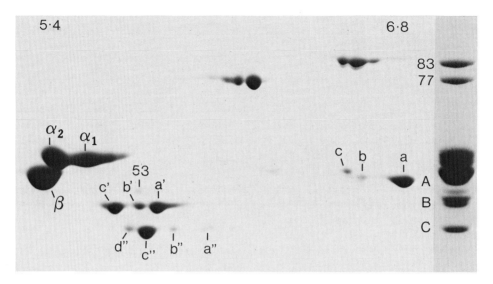

Fig. 5–3. One-dimensional SDS-PAGE **(right)** and two-dimensional isoelectric focusing SDS-PAGE **(left)** of *S. purpuratus* Sarkosyl ribbons stained with Serva blue. Protofilament ribbons were prepared from 0.5% Sarkosyl extraction of doublet microtubules. pI range is shown along the top, and actual values have been given by Linck et al. (1987). Polypeptide band A separates into three polypeptide spots (a, b, and c); polypeptide band B also separates into three polypeptide spots (a', b', and c') and polypeptide band C separates into four polypeptide spots (a'', b'', c'', and d''). Note that α tubulin splits into two spots (α₁ and α₂). Two-dimensional IEF/SDS-PAGE analysis of purified tektin filaments reveals a composition of only a, b, c / a', b' / a'', b'', c'', d''. (Reproduced from Linck et al., 1987, with permission of the publisher.)

the tubulin and yields a preparation consisting entirely of two to four protofilaments (Fig. 5–1b). The polypeptide composition of this resistant protofilament-ribbon fraction is shown in Figure 5–3; by the criterion of one-dimensional SDS-PAGE the principal components of the protofilament (pf) ribbons are tubulin, the 47, 51, and 55 kDa tektins, and a 77/83 kDa polypeptide pair. Earlier biochemical studies suggested that the 77/83 kDa polypeptides and those now known to be tektins are specifically associated with the pf ribbon (Linck, 1976). Immunochemical analyses have since verified that the proteins recognized by antitektins A, B, and C reside exclusively in the insoluble pf ribbon fraction (Chang, 1987; Stephens et al., 1987).

Using the monospecific, polyclonal antitektins described earlier, we have examined more closely the composition of Sarkosyl-resistant protofilament ribbons from *S. purpuratus* flagella by two-dimensional immunoblot analysis (Fig. 5–3, only protein staining shown). Antitektin A recognizes only the main 55 kDa spot a and adjacent spots b and c; typically, no other polypeptides are stained. Antitektin B specifically stains the two 51 kDa spots a' and b', but not spot c'. Antitektin C stains four 47 kDa polypeptides (a'', b'', c'', and d'') and cross reacts with the principal 55 kDa spot a. The antitektins did not recognize the other major polypeptides in this preparation, i.e., tubulins or the 77/83 kDa polypeptide pair. These results raise the question of whether the various polypeptide spots recognized by the antibodies are tektin isoforms, modified tektins, or unrelated protein contaminants and also whether certain other spots (e.g., c') are immunologically distinct tektins. Indeed, the cross reaction of each anti-echinoderm tektin with multiple polypeptides in molluscan ciliary microtubules suggests a higher degree of complexity among the tektins (Linck et al., 1987; Stephens et al., 1987).

Structural Organization of Tektins in Microtubules

The structural organization of tektins in the pf ribbon and the locus of the pf ribbons in the microtubules are not precisely known. Electron microscopic observations of partially fractionated axonemal microtubules originally suggested a model in which the three-protofilament ribbon forms a portion of the A-tubule wall in the region where it contacts with the inner B-tubule junction (Linck, 1976). Subsequent evidence also suggests that central pair singlet microtubules may also possess tektins and a relatively resistant pf-ribbon domain (vide infra). More recent investigations have verified and delineated this model.

Immuno–light microscopic (LM) and immuno–electron microscopic (EM) studies provided the first demonstration that tektins were integral components of the flagellar A-tubules and more specifically of the pf ribbons (Linck et al., 1985). For these studies polyclonal antibodies were raised against "non-denatured tektin filaments" (filaments obtained by extraction with 0.5% Sarkosyl/ 2 M urea, composed of the three equimolar tektins, and having high α-helical content) and affinity purified. By immunoblotting, the antibodies specifically stain the three tektin bands on SDS-PAGE immunoblots of whole axonemes. The antibodies, or antitektins, stain the axonemes and basal body regions of methanol-fixed sperm by immunofluorescence microscopy, and they also label isolated tektin filaments, as seen by indirect immunogold negative stain EM. Curiously, these particular antitektins do not uniformly label native A-microtubules attached to carbon film; however, if the microtubules attached to the grid surface are extracted with Sarkosyl–urea to solubilize the tubulin, filaments become apparent that do label with the antitektins. Finally, the antitektins label thin fibrils that project from the ends of microtubules and pf ribbons. In sum, these results imply that the antigenic sites for these particular tektins are arranged in the native microtubule such that they are masked by tubulin and/or other associated proteins. Furthermore, the results tend to suggest that the tektins exist as filaments oriented longitudinally in the microtubule wall. Additional immuno-EM studies with a monoclonal antibody raised against tektin filament preparations have revealed a 48-nm axial periodicity. Such a spacing indexes with the 96-nm fundamental repeat of axonemes and is a multiple of six 8-nm tubulin dimers (Amos et al., 1986). These findings provide a structural basis for the probable interaction of tektin with tubulin.

Since the above studies were done with polyclonal antibodies directed against a mixed population of tektins, it was not possible to determine whether each tektin was present in every axonemal microtubule or to determine which tektins might be present in basal bodies. For these reasons we have employed the monospecific antibodies prepared against each purified tektin (Linck et al., 1987; Steffen and Linck, 1988). In the following experiments we examined the antitektin and antitubulin staining of *L. pictus* sperm tails, which have the unusual property of splaying into discrete axonemal microtubules, held together at their base by the basal body (Steffen and Linck, 1988). Antitubulin staining of such preparations (Fig. 5–4a) reveals nine filaments with lengths identical to the native sperm tail. This pattern would clearly seem to originate from the staining of all nine doublet tubules and their A-tubule extensions; the central pair singlet microtubules appear to have been lost as a result of specimen preparation. Staining with each of the antitektins shows an identical pattern, i.e., nine filaments (Fig. 5–4b). If each antitektin is truly monospecific, these results would suggest that each doublet microtubule and its A-tubule extension contains all three tektins. Furthermore, both antitubulin and all antitektins stain the basal body, with the antitektin staining being particularly intense.

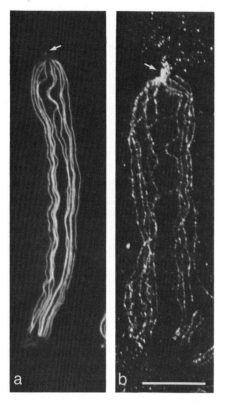

Fig. 5–4. Immunofluorescence microscopy of splayed sperm tails of *L. pictus*. Labeling of the splayed axonemes with a polyclonal antitubulin **(a)** revealed a pattern of nine filaments with lengths identical to that of intact sperm tails. These nine filaments, i.e., the nine outer doublet microtubules and A-tubule extensions, merge at one end in a dot-like structure (arrows). Based on the location in the sperm and labeling with antitubulin, these dots represent basal bodies. All three antitektins also stained the basal bodies and the nine microtubules along their length **(b)**. When applied at the same concentrations, antitektins A, B, and C (10–20 μg/ml) produced essentially identical staining intensities. The punctuated staining, as seen with anti-(L.p.) tektin B (b), may result from a partial masking of tektin by tubulin. Compared with the staining of basal bodies with antitubulin, the labeling with antitektin is much more intense. Bar = 10 μm.

Using a different species, the bat star *Patiria miniata*, it was possible to preserve partially the central pair singlet microtubules, as judged by antitubulin staining (Steffen and Linck, 1988). In this case, a faint but respectable staining of the central tubules can be observed with antitektin C, suggesting the presence of an immunologically related tektin in these tubules. Previous studies of other species have noted that each central singlet microtubule decomposes to leave a relatively stable ribbon of approximately four protofilaments, analogous to those obtained by Sarkosyl extraction of doublet tubules (Linck and Langevin, 1981, 1982). It is possible that this pf ribbon is correlated with the apparent existence of tektins in the central singlet tubules.

EVIDENCE FOR TEKTINS IN NON-FLAGELLAR CYTOSKELETAL STRUCTURES

Given the reasonably well characterized presence of tektins in microtubules of echinoderm and molluscan cilia, flagella, and possibly basal bodies, we were naturally interested in determining whether tektins might also be present in centrioles and microtubules of non-flagellar origin and in higher organisms. Furthermore, we wanted to study in more detail the apparent similarities between tektins and intermediate filament proteins. We review here previously published studies with monoclonal antibodies and also report here our novel results (Steffen and Linck, 1987) with the monospecific polyclonal antitektins described above (Linck et al., 1987; Steffen and Linck, 1988). To reiterate, our antibodies against either *L. pictus* or *S. purpuratus* were affinity purified using *L. pictus* tektin filaments.

To look for antibody cross reactivity, particular care must be taken to obtain a specific signal. Two types of antibodies can be employed, monoclonal and polyclonal. Because a monoclonal antibody recognizes a single epitope, such an antibody is not always able to differ between two non-homologous polypeptides. Several monoclonal antibodies are known to cross react with non-homologous proteins (Wehland et al., 1984). In contrast, a detectable cross reaction with unrelated polypeptides is less likely when affinity-purified polyclonal antibodies are used. Even then, there is a chance of an unspecific cross reaction via the Fc portion (Hansson et al., 1984).

Antitektin Staining of Microtubule Structures in Mammalian Cells

Centrioles and centrosomes. To study these organelles, we investigated the following cell lines: CHO (Chinese hamster ovary), GF (gerbil fibroma), HeLa (human cervical epithelioid carcinoma), IM (Indian mundjac skin), LLC-PK$_1$ (pig kidney epithelia), and 3T3 (mouse embryonic fibroblast). In all these cell lines at least one of the antitektins (antitektin A, B, or C) stained dot-like structures either juxtanuclear and in the center of microtubule asters or at spindle poles (Fig. 5–5). The data revealed from the different cells are summarized in Table 5–2. The staining patterns can be divided into two groups: staining of centrioles and staining of centrosomes. In interphase cells of CHO, HeLa, and LLC-PK$_1$, some antitektins stain paired dots. The number of the dots is cell cycle-dependent. Number, size, and localization of these dot-like structures indicate that they corresponded to centrioles (see also Fig 5–6). In 3T3, CHO, GF, and IM cells antitektins stain larger structures or areas about 1 μm in diameter. The size of these structures clearly differs from the size of the stained centrioles. Based on these observations it is assumed that the staining pattern corresponded to centrosomes. The centrosomes appear as either single areas or areas composed of several smaller dots, depending on the antitektin and on the cell line used. With immunofluorescence, however, it is not possible to decide whether the centrioles are also stained or whether only pericentriolar material is stained.

As a control, the specific staining can be eliminated by preabsorbing each antitektin with its respective purified tektin. Furthermore, staining with Fab fragments prepared from each antitektin yields similar images (Fig. 5–5a,b), eliminating the possibility of an Fc-specific interaction with intermediate filament-like proteins (Hansson et al., 1984).

Midbody. Besides the centriole/centro-some staining, immunofluorescence staining with certain antitektins also reveals a staining of the midbody region, in 3T3 and CHO cells recognized by antitektin A, in HeLa cells by antitektin C, and in LLC-PK$_1$ cells by all three antitektins. The staining pattern in all these cell types is more or less alike, independent of the antitektin used; however, the intensity of the staining is different between those cells. By far the strongest staining is obtained in CHO cells; therefore, these cells will be used to make more detailed descriptions of the change of immunofluorescence pattern during the formation of the midbody. The different types of pattern are shown in Figure 5–6. In late anaphase, when the chromosomes have almost reached the spindle poles, the first immunofluorescence staining can be observed in the equator region; it appears as a diffuse area with filamentous material aligned parallel to the cell axis. The filamentous structure and parallel alignment of the staining pattern becomes more obvious in early telophase. With on-going telophase the filaments appear to shorten and move closer together until they form a continuously stained midbody. In a later stage the staining of the midbody is equally divided perpendicular to the cell axis. Before the daughter cells are totally separated, the staining gradually decreases.

Mitotic spindle. In three of the cell lines studied, immunofluorescence reveals a staining of the spindle area: with antitektin B in CHO cells, with antitektin C in HeLa cells, and with antitektins A and C in LLC-PK$_1$ cells (Fig. 5–7). The fluorescence of the spindles appears diffuse and occasionally fibrous, with slightly higher intensities at the spindle poles. This staining can be observed from prometaphase until early anaphase.

Cross Reaction of Antitektins With Intermediate Filaments and Nuclear Envelopes

Intermediate filaments. When the tektins were first described, similarities between them and intermediate filament (IF) proteins were noted (Linck, 1982; Linck et

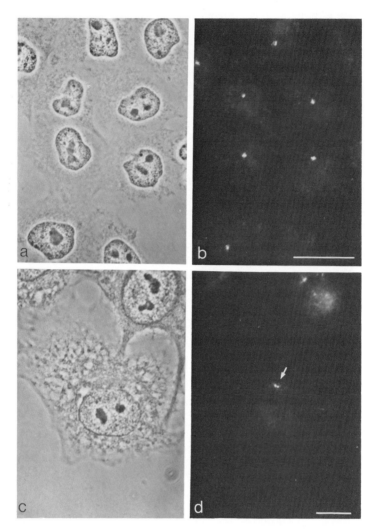

Fig. 5–5. Immunofluorescence staining of centrioles and centrosomes in Triton X-100–extracted mammalian cells. **a:** Phase contrast image of methanol-fixed CHO cells in interphase. **b:** Same cell as in a stained with Fab fragments of anti-(L.p.) tektin B, showing juxtanuclear dots. **c:** Phase contrast image of a methanol-fixed HeLa cell in interphase. **d:** Same cell as in c stained with anti-(L.p.) tektin C, showing a pair of dots closely associated with the nucleus. These dots appear in the centers of aster-like microtubule arrays of interphase cells and at the spindle poles of mitotic cells (see Fig. 5–6 and Steffen & Linck, 1988). Because of their location, small size, and normally paired appearance, we conclude that the dots in HeLa cells correspond to centrioles. The staining in CHO cells is somewhat ambiguous. By immunofluorescence microscopy it not clear whether the staining corresponds to centrioles or to centrosomes. Bar = 10 μm.

al., 1982; Linck and Langevin, 1982). Since then, the list of physicochemical properties that these two groups of proteins share has grown. Tektins and IF proteins are relatively insoluble; e.g., they are solubilized by urea above 5 M. Tektins and most IF proteins occupy an M_r range from 46,000 to about 60,000 and a pI range from 5.8 to 7.0. The amino acid compositions of tektins are remarkably similar to those of IF proteins (cf.,

TABLE 5–2. Immunofluorescence Antitektin Staining of Centrioles Versus Centrosomes in Different Mammalian Cells

Cells	Centriole staining						Centrosome staining					
	A		B		C		A		B		C	
	L.p.	S. p.	L.p.	S.p.	L.p.	S.p.	L.p.	S.p.	L.p.	S.p.	L.p.	S.p.
3T3	−	−	−	−	−	−	−	−	+	−	+	−
CHO	+	?	−	?	+	?	−	?	+	?	−	?
GF	−	−	−	−	−	−	+	+	+	+	−	−
HeLa	+	−	−	−	−	−	−	−	−	−	−	−
IM	−	−	−	−	−	−	−	−	+	−	−	−
LLC-PK₁	+	+	+	+	+	+	−	−	−	−	−	−

+, Staining; −, no staining; ?, not determined. In some cell lines, when an anti-(L.p.) tektin revealed staining, the equivalent anti-(S.p.) tektin did not. A possible reason for this observation might be that both sets of antibodies were affinity purified with tektins from *L. pictus*. The antibodies against tektins from *L. pictus* and from *S. purpuratus* could recognize different epitopes on centriolar/centrosomal proteins. During affinity purification only those centriolar/centrosomal-specific *S. purpuratus* antitektins that recognize an epitope in common also with *L. pictus* tektins remain in the antibody fraction.

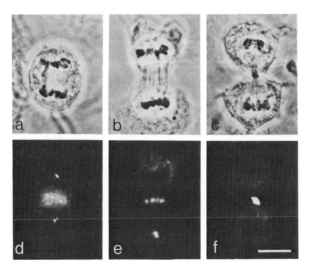

Fig. 5–6. Immunofluorescence staining of CHO cells with anti-(L.p.) tektin C during the formation of the midbody. **a–c:** Phase contrast images. **d–f:** Immunofluorescence images. a,d: Late anaphase. b,e: Early telophase. c,f: Late telophase. Anti-(L.p.) tektin C recognized a component during the formation of the midbody. The component could first be recognized in late anaphase as a diffuse staining in the equator region (d), which soon became aligned in bundles parallel to the cell axis (d,e). During telophase these bundles became shorter, merged together, and finally formed plates perpendicular to the cell axis (f). Note that anti-(L.p.) tektin C also labeled the centrioles. Bar = 10 μm.

Linck and Stephens, 1987); the amino acid sequences of the tektins are not yet known but are under investigation. Both sets of proteins have high α-helical contents (Linck and Langevin, 1982), and filaments composed of these proteins yield strong α-type X-ray patterns (Beese, 1984; Fraser et al., 1972). Tektin filaments appear to be composed of 2-nm subfibrils similar to the 2-nm coiled-coil formations of IF protein subunits (cf., Amos et al., 1986; Linck and Langevin, 1982; Linck et al., 1985; Steinert et al., 1985). Finally, tektins and IF proteins have certain structural similarities, as indicated by immu-

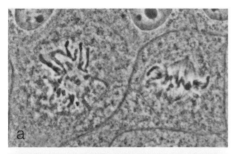
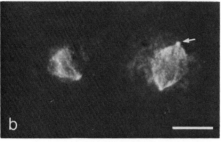

Fig. 5–7. Immunofluorescence staining of the spindle in LLC-PK$_1$ cells. **a:** Phase contrast image of prometaphase and metaphase LLC-PK$_1$ cells. **b:** Same cells labeled with anti-(S.p.) tektin C showing a diffuse staining of the spindle fibers. Note that the antitektin also reacted with the spindle poles (arrow). Bar = 10 μm.

nological cross reactivities, which we will now discuss.

Amos et al. (1986) initially found that a monoclonal antibody, IFA, which is known to recognize most, if not all, IF proteins (Pruss et al., 1981), appeared to cross react with tektins A and B and more weakly with C; however, since this reaction was observed on immunoblots of purified tektins but not whole axonemal protein, the conclusions were not definitive.

In the converse experiment, Chang and Piperno (1987) showed that a monoclonal antibody specific for the lower 46 kDa flagellar tektin from *S. purpuratus* cross reacts with IFs and IF proteins. By immunofluorescence microscopy this monoclonal antibody stains vimentin-like IF patterns in BHK-21 cells and striated patterns in chick embryo myotubes; on one-dimensional immunoblots the antibody cross reacts with a 55 kDa

polypeptide band, which corresponds to desmin and vimentin.

For conclusions regarding the immunological relatedness of proteins, polyclonal antibodies generally provide a more rigorous basis of comparison than do monoclonal antibodies. For this reason we have investigated the cross reaction of our affinity-purified, polyclonal antitektins with mammalian IFs and IF proteins. A cross reaction with intermediate filament-like proteins can be observed in two cell lines (HeLa and LLC-PK$_1$). Both cell lines are epithelial. In HeLa cells anti-(L.p.) tektin B stains filaments or bundles of filaments (Fig. 5–8a,b). The filaments are distributed more or less evenly throughout the cytoplasm. No major focal point exists. The staining pattern is virtually identical to the staining pattern obtained with an antikeratin. After treatment with 0.12 μg/ml colcemid for 4 hr, the filaments are located closer to the nucleus, forming a cage (data not shown).

Anti-(L.p.) tektin B also recognizes a filamentous network in LLC-PK$_1$ cells; however, the staining pattern differs from that in HeLa cells (Fig. 5–8c,d). In many cells the filaments form focal points. The filament pattern is, however, not identical to the microtubule pattern obtained with an antitubulin. In cells forming a continuous monolayer the highest density of filaments can be observed at the edges of the outermost cells.

As suggested by immunofluorescence data, anti-(L.p.) tektin B appears to cross react with keratin filaments. On SDS-PAGE blots of whole HeLa cells anti-(L.p.) tektin B stains a polypeptide band of approximately 54 kDa (Fig. 5–9, lanes 1, 2). The same band was detected in immunoblots of 0.5% Triton X-100–extracted cells, as well as in immunoblots of 0.5% Sarkosyl/2 M urea–extracted cells (data not shown). In one-dimensional SDS PAGE of Sarkosyl-urea–extracted cells the 54 kDa protein is one of the major components. By SDS-PAGE immunoblot a polyclonal antikeratin (Polyscience, Warrington, PA) stained three bands of about 54, 59, and 68 kDa (data not shown). The 54 kDa band is the same as that stained by

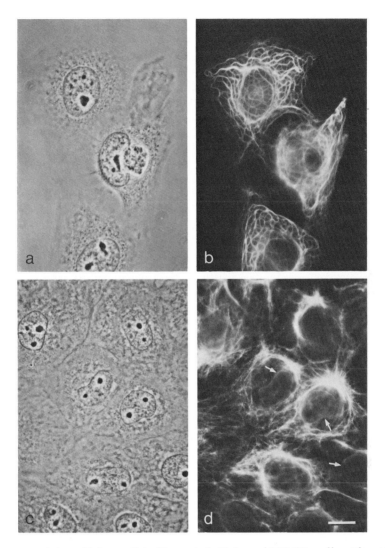

Fig. 5–8. Immunostaining of intermediate filaments in HeLa and LLC-PK₁ cells with anti(L.p.) tektin B. **a:** Phase contrast image of HeLa cells. **b:** Immunofluorescence staining revealing a typical keratin-like pattern. **c:** Phase contrast image of LLC-PK₁ cells. **d:** Immunofluorescence staining of intermediate filaments. Antitektin B also cross reacted in these cells with the nuclear envelope (arrows). Bar = 10 μm.

anti(L.p.) tektin B. In SDS-PAGE immunoblots of LLC-PK₁ cells anti-(L.p.) tektin B recognizes a polypeptide band of approximately 55 kD (Fig. 5–9, lanes 3,4).

Nuclear envelope.. Chang and Piperno (1987) developed a set of monoclonal antibodies against flagellar tektins from *S. purpuratus*. The monoclonal antibody to their tektin C cross reacts in immunoblots with nuclear lamins A and C from rat hepatocytes, and by immunofluorescence microscopy this antibody stains the nuclear envelopes of BHK-21 cells and chick embryo myocytes.

We find that our own polyclonal anti-(L.p.) tektin B stains the nuclear envelope in LLC-PK₁ cells (Fig. 5–8d), and anti-(L.p.) tektin C appears to stain the nuclear envelope in gerbil fibroma cells (data not shown)

1 2 3 4

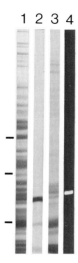

Fig. 5–9. SDS-PAGE immunoblot staining. **Lane 1:** Serva blue staining of a preparation of whole HeLa cells. **Lane 2:** Immunoblot staining of a similar preparation with anti(L.p.) tektin B, revealing a strong reaction with an ~54 kD polypeptide and a weak reaction with an ~43 kD polypeptide (4-chloro-1-naphthol was used to visualize the peroxidase-conjugated secondary antibody). **Lane 3:** Ponceau S staining of a nitrocellulose replica of a Triton X-100–extracted, spindle-enriched fraction of LLC-PK$_1$ cells. **Lane 4:** The identical blot was used to stain with anti-(L.p.) tektin B. The antitektin recognized an ~55 kDa polypeptide. To visualize the peroxidase-conjugated secondary antibody, Luminol/Luciferin was used as a substrate (Laing, 1986). Bars on the left hand side indicate M$_r$ markers (from bottom to top) 43, 66, and 116 kDa.

and in chick embryo neurons (Edson et al., 1987). The staining can be observed wherever an envelope is present. The intensity of the staining of the envelope surface in gerbil fibroma cells is not homogeneous, however, with the surface of the envelope being divided into areas of higher and lower intensity of fluorescence. Because of the possible anomalous migration of tektins in different grades of SDS (discussed earlier), we cannot yet be certain whether the tektin C studied by Chang and Piperno is the same as our tektin C; however, our agreement on the cross reactivity of antitektin C with nuclear envelopes would suggest a similarity be-

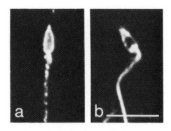

Fig. 5–10. Immunofluorescence of sea urchin sperm stained with antitektins. **a:** *L. pictus* sperm stained with affinity-purified anti-(L.p.) tektin B. **b:** *S. purpuratus* sperm stained with anti-(S.p.) tektin B (antiserum). In both cases antitektin B stained the sperm head envelope. Bar = 10 μm.

tween nuclear lamins A and C and the lower molecular mass, ~46−47 kDa tektin (C) from *S. purpuratus.*

Antitektin staining of sperm head envelope. A possible nuclear envelope staining can also be observed in sea urchin sperm. Previous results with antibodies directed against the mixed tektins (Amos et al., 1985) indicated a staining of the periphery of the sperm head. We have now found that antibodies to tektin B appear to stain in a specific fashion the outline of the sperm head or nuclear envelope (Fig. 5−10); in some cases this staining is as intense as that of the flagellum. At the light microscope level we refer to this region as the *sperm head envelope.* Such staining is seen with anti-(L.p.) tektin B that was affinity purified with *L. pictus* tektins and with non-affinity-purified anti-(S.p.) tektin B, but not with anti-(S.p.) tektin B that was affinity purified with *L. pictus* tektins. Presumably, the cross reacting antibodies are retained by homologous species affinity probes, but are not retained by heterologous species probes. The staining of the sperm head may be relevant to the cross reaction between antitektins and the nuclear lamin proteins. All antitektins also stain the acrosome regions, and antitektin C stains areas coincident with the mitochondria.

SUMMARY: THE POSSIBLE FUNCTIONS OF TEKTINS

We will now discuss current evidence for the relatedness of tektins and then consider the function of these proteins and their possible presence in the cytoplasm.

Relatedness of the Tektins

The three tektins so far characterized form a set of polypeptides possibly related to each other in their primary structure. Evidence supporting this hypothesis includes 1) overall similarities in the amino acid compositions and tryptic peptide maps of all three tektins (Linck and Stephens, 1987); 2) peptide map similarities between tektins B and C, based on limited cleavage with *Staphylococcus aureus* V8 protease (Linck and Langevin, 1982); and 3) the immunological cross reactivities described here, namely, recognition of tektin A by antitektin C (Fig. 5–2). To reinforce the latter point, the antitektin C recognition of tektin A is observed both within each species and between two species of sea urchins. The immunoblots of sea urchin flagella and molluscan cilia (Linck et al., 1987; Stephens et al., 1987) could be interpreted to suggest that there are more than three tektins, but we cannot yet exclude the possibility that the immunological cross reactions are the results of minute contaminants in the preparation of our tektins as immunogen and/or as affinity probes.

A Structural Model for Tektins in Ciliary and Flagellar Microtubules

While there is no direct proof of the structural organization of the tektins in ciliary and flagellar microtubules, the sum of available evidence supports a model in which the tektin subunits are associated to form linear, α-helical coils or fibrils (2 nm diameter), which may supercoil to form filaments of larger diameter (e.g., 6 nm); these tektin fibrils/filaments may lie between the grooves of the tubulin protofilaments, or, alternatively, they may actually form certain protofilaments of the A-microtubule, as previously proposed (Linck, 1982; Linck and Langevin, 1982; Amos et al., 1986). As noted earlier, the measured and predicted α-helical structure of the tektins may provide for a structural interaction be-

tween tektins and tubulin (Amos et al., 1986). The presence of tektins may be important to the assembly and function of the outer doublet microtubules; however, the presence of stable ribbons and possibly tektins in the central pair singlet microtubules suggests that the tektins are not specific to doublet tubules and that they may have a more fundamental role in microtubules. We will review these possible functions later in this chapter.

Relationship of Tektins to Intermediate Filament Proteins

The tektins are strikingly similar to IF proteins in terms of their structural chemical properties, including their relative insolubility in 5 M urea (Lazarides, 1980; Linck and Langevin, 1982), range of molecular weights (46–60 kDa), range of isoelectric points (6.0–6.8), amino acid compositions, high α-helical content and α-type X-ray patterns, and association into filaments with a basic 2-nm subfibrillar organization and with apparent axial repeats of 48 nm (cf., Amos et al., 1986; Beese, 1984; Geisler and Weber, 1980; Linck et al., 1987; Linck and Langevin, 1982; Linck and Stephens, 1987; Steinert et al., 1985). Nucleotide sequencing of cDNA probes of tektins is in progress, and the results so far indicate that tektin A is similar to keratins and nuclear lamins; nevertheless, the degree of similarity is weak (J.M. Norrander and R.W., Linck, unpublished observations).

Tektins and IF proteins also show immunological similarities. Chang and Piperno (1987) reported that one monoclonal antibody specific for *S. purpuratus* tektin C cross reacts with mammalian desmin and vimentin; a second monoclonal antibody specific for *S. purpuratus* tektin C cross reacts with nuclear lamins A and C, which have primary sequence homology with IF proteins (Fisher et al., 1986; McKeon et al., 1986). Our results indicate that affinity-purified, polyclonal antitektin B recognizes a keratin-like pattern in HeLa cells by immunofluorescence. In immunoblots antitektin B recognizes a 55 kDa polypeptide in LLC-PK$_1$

cells and a 54 kDa polypeptide from HeLa cells with the same molecular weight as a human keratin (Fig. 5–9). These polypeptides are major components in preparation of intermediate filaments and their M_rs and pIs are similar to those of keratins 7 and 8 (W. Steffen and R.W. Linck, unpublished data; cf. Quinlan et al., 1985). A further report that a polyclonal antidesmin (DAKO) cross reacts with tektin C (Chang and Piperno, 1987) has not been substantiated (cf., Linck et al., 1987). The antidesmin/tektin result was obtained using an unpurified antibody (antisera) against desmin and might have arisen from preimmune activity; it is not possible, however, to obtain preimmune serum from DAKO for testing. In the course of our work, we have found several rabbits to be preimmune to both tektins and IF proteins; thus we have been careful to avoid using such rabbits and have further affinity purified our antibodies. The *bona fide* immunological similarities between tektins and IF proteins could be explained on the basis of the molecular structure of the IF protein subunit, constructed from an evolutionarily conserved α-helical core domain (of approximately 37 kDa) and variable IF-specific terminal domains (Steinert et al., 1985). If tektins are related in the same way, the polyclonal antibodies would appear to be primarily directed against variable domains, and certain monoclonal antibodies would be directed against epitopes in the conserved regions. In this regard, Chang and Piperno (1987) have noted that their monoclonal antibodies recognize proteolytically resistant domains of tektins of appropriate sizes to correspond to the α-helical domains of IF proteins. Nethertheless, until the primary sequences of tektins are determined, the evolutionary homology of tektins and IF proteins remains uncertain.

The actual biological functions of IFs have not been clearly determined. Certainly one set of functions appears to be cytoskeletal, i.e., a generalized role in the determination of cell shape and spatial organization within the cell (Lazarides, 1980). While the molecular basis for the tektin–IF similarities remains to be elucidated, present evidence suggests that flagellar tektins may serve as a model system to provide insights into IF function.

Structure and Function of Tektins in Cilia and Flagella

Our results above demonstrate that all three tektins are present throughout the length of each axonemal doublet microtubule and its A-tubule extension and that all three antitektins recognize tektin-like proteins in basal bodies and centrioles. The presence of tektins in these organelles might correlate with unique features that these microtubule systems have in common, i.e., a high degree of stability and species-specific length (Wheatley, 1982).

In terms of stability, Behnke and Forer (1967) divided microtubules into four classes: A-tubules of axonemal doublet microtubules with high stability, followed by B-tubules of axonemal doublet microtubules, followed by central pair microtubules, followed by cytoplasmic microtubules. The stability is surely controlled by factors that influence the assembly–disassembly kinetics of microtubules. Detailed fractionation experiments of sea urchin sperm flagella confirmed the high stability of doublet microtubules, especially of A-tubules (Linck, 1973; Stephens, 1970; Witman et al., 1972a). Furthermore, LM and EM studies have indicated that tektins, which contribute up to 12% of the mass of A-tubules, are part of the wall of these microtubules (Amos et al., 1986; Linck et al., 1985; Linck and Langevin, 1982). As previously mentioned, tektins are similar to intermediate filaments in terms of their biochemical and biophysical properties. Intermediate filaments are known to contribute to a large extent to the stability of the cell shape (Lazarides, 1980). It can therefore be speculated that tektins might also contribute to the stability of the organelles of which they are part. The question now is: How might they provide such a function? Because tektins, along with tubulin, are the major components of the Sarkosyl-resistant protofilament ribbons, they very likely interact directly with tubulin. In protofilament ribbons Linck and Langevin (1982) observed a 96-nm helical repeat with respect to the tektin–tubulin complex. In addition, a 48-nm repeat was obtained with a monoclonal antibody in tektin filament preparations (Amos et al., 1986). Based on these findings, a structure of the tektin filaments was proposed (Linck and Langevin, 1982; Amos et al., 1986) that closely matches the lattice of tubulin subunits (Amos et al., 1986; Amos and Klug, 1974; Grimstone and Klug, 1966; Mandelkow et al., 1986; Wais-Steider et al., 1987). The proposed interaction between tektin and tubulin could directly affect microtubule stability. Certain classes of cytoplasmic microtubules also reveal a greater stability to drugs, cold, and Ca^{2+} treatment, i.e., certain spindle microtubules and midbody microtubules (e.g., Brinkley and Cartwright, 1975). The cross reaction of our polyclonal antitektins with centrioles, midbody, and spindle indicates the presence of tektins or tektin-related polypeptides in these structures. It is not known whether tektin-related polypeptides are integral parts of cytoplasmic microtubules, but as such they could very well influence the stability of midbody and spindle microtubules.

A special feature of axonemal microtubules is their species-specific length. Immunofluorescence microscopy has now revealed that tektins are present along the entire length of axonemal doublet microtubules and their A-tubule extensions. Stephens (1977) demonstrated that in ciliary axonemes of sea urchin embryos from *S. purpuratus* one component, component 20, which corresponds to tektin A in *S. purpuratus* sperm axonemes (Stephens et al., 1987), is synthesized *de novo* in a limited amount. This observation, together with our finding that tektin A is present along the length of axonemal microtubules, is consistent with Stephen's hypothesis that component 20 (tektin A) is involved in length determination of these microtubules.

Evidence for Tektin-Like Proteins Associated With Cytoplasmic Microtubules

Since A- and B-tubules of the triplet microtubules in centrioles serve as a template for axonemal doublet microtubules, and since tektins are present in the A-tubules of axonemal doublet microtubules, it is not surprising to find a cross reaction of the antitektins with centrioles. The staining of basal bodies and centrioles with affinity-purified antitektins and Fab fragments provides evidence that these microtubule organelles contain tektins.

Three observations substantiate a tektin-like component in the spindle. 1) Chang (1987) was able to demonstrate that a monoclonal antibody raised against tektins recognizes a component of ~48 kDa in a 1% Sarkosyl-insoluble fraction of isolated mitotic spindles from sea urchins. 2) In a different set of experiments, isolated sea urchin spindles, extracted free of tubulin, still retain their spindle shape (Hays and Salmon, 1983; Rebhun and Palazzo, 1986, 1987). A polypeptide of 55 kDa appears to be the major component of such a preparation. The amino acid composition of the spindle matrix component is similar to that of intermediate filaments (Rebhun and Palazzo, 1987) and, therefore, similar to that of tektins, indicating a possible relationship to tektin filaments. 3) Last but not least, the suggestion of a spindle tektin is supported by our observation that polyclonal antitektins stain the mitotic spindle apparatus in several mammalian cell lines (Fig. 5–7).

ACKNOWLEDGMENTS

This work was supported by United States Public Health Service grant GM35648 to R. W. Linck from the National Institute of General Medical Sciences.

Genetic Analysis of Microtubule Organizing Centers

Susan K. Dutcher

*Department of Molecular, Cellular, and Developmental Biology,
University of Colorado, Boulder, Colorado 80309*

INTRODUCTION

Microtubule organizing centers are defined by their ability to nucleate microtubule growth, and they appear to play a role in the regulation of the assembly, organization, and distribution of microtubules in eukaryotic cells. During the course of the cell cycle, these organelles undergo a variety of changes in form and in number. While there may be a number of minor microtubule organizing centers, this chapter will consider only the major microtubule organizing center, corpuscular sites of assembly called *centrosomes*. In higher organisms, the centrosome consists of the pericentriolar cloud and a pair of centrioles. In lower eukaryotes, the centrosome often lacks a centriole and appears as an amorphous region in electron micrographs. The ability of the microtubule organizing center to organize microtubules is primarily a property of the pericentriolar material and not of the centrioles themselves (Berns and Richardson, 1977; Picket-Heaps, 1971; Debec et al., 1982), although the centrioles do initiate flagellar axonemes and primary cilia. Numerous reviews have been written about the

structure and the behavior of microtubule organizing centers (Fulton, 1971: Peterson and Berns, 1980; Wheatley, 1982; McIntosh, 1983; Brinkley, 1985). In this chapter, I will concentrate on the behavior of the microtubule organizing centers of the yeast *Saccharomyces cerevisiae* and of the alga *Chlamydomonas reinhardtii.*

Most of the information that has been garnered about the microtubule organizing centers of eukaryotic cells has come from light and electron microscopic studies. The behavior and the structure of this organelle has been described in many organisms. Berns and Richardson (1977) have attempted to delineate the function by laser ablation experiments, which involve a small number of cells and cell types and are extremely harsh on the cells. Recently, genetic and molecular analyses of this organelle have become possible. Genetics in combination with molecular biology make it possible to eliminate single polypeptide components of a process and to determine the resulting phenotype. In this chapter, mutants that appear to affect the microtubule organizing centers of *Saccharomyces* and *Chlamydomonas* are discussed.

**Cell Movement, Volume 2: Kinesin,
Dynein, and Microtubule Dynamics, pages 83–94**
© **1989 Alan R. Liss, Inc.**

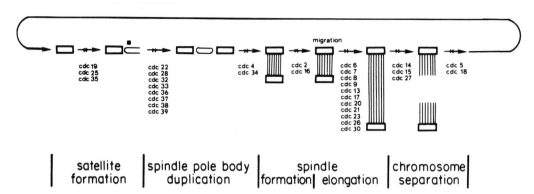

Fig. 6–1. The events of the mitotic spindle pole cycle in *Saccharomyces cerevisiae* as illustrated by cell division cycle (*cdc*) mutants. The morphology of the spindle pole body and the associated microtubules for the different mutants at 36° C. Seven different phenotypes can be observed. Three mutants arrest with a single spindle pole body and no satellite. Eight mutants arrest with a single spindle pole body and a satellite. Two mutants arrest in G_1 with a duplicated spindle pole body and no intracellular spindle. Two mutants arrest with an intranuclear spindle that fails to migrate. Eleven mutants arrest with a short intracellular spindle. Three mutants arrest with an elongated spindle. Two mutants arrest during telophase. (Adapted from Byers and Goetsch, 1974, with permission of the publisher.)

MICROTUBULE ORGANIZING CENTERS OF *SACCHAROMYCES CEREVISIAE*

In many fungi, which include both the budding and fission yeast, the microtubule organizing center is an electron-dense, amorphous structure that is embedded in the nuclear membrane (Robinow and Marak, 1966; Peterson and Ris, 1976; Byers and Goetsch, 1974). These structures are known as *spindle pole bodies* (Kubai, 1975). They serve as the poles of the mitotic and the meiotic spindles (Robinow and Marek, 1966) and appear to organize microtubules in the cytoplasm (Byers and Goetsch, 1975; Kilmartin and Adams, 1984). Microtubules extend perpendicularly from the inner face of the spindle pole body into the nucleus and from the outer face into the cytoplasm. The nuclear envelope of *Saccharomyces* remains intact during both mitotic and meiotic divisions; these inward microtubules make up the intranuclear spindle. The spindle pole body cycle is illustrated in Figure 6–1. In early G_1 of the cell cycle the spindle pole body is present as a single structure. The first recognizable change is the appearance of densely staining material, which resembles the spindle pole body in its

staining properties, on the cytoplasmic surface of the surrounding nuclear envelope. This adjacent nuclear envelope is stained differentially from the rest of the nuclear envelope and has been termed the *half-bridge* (Byers and Goetsch, 1975). This satellite stays on the cytoplasmic surface until a new spindle pole body is formed; concurrently the satellite disappears. The new spindle pole body, which is the same size as the pre-existing one, lies next to the old one in the plane of the nuclear envelope. No intermediates in the duplication process have been observed by electron microscopy (Byers, 1981).

With respect to other cellular events, the spindle pole bodies are duplicated in cells that have initiated the emergence of a new daughter cell or bud and have initiated chromosomal DNA replication (Byers and Goetsch, 1974). The duplicated spindle pole bodies remain together until the daughter cell has reached about one-third the size of the mother cell; the two microtubule organizing centers separate, and an intranuclear spindle is formed. No intermediates have been observed by electron microscopy in the formation of the intranuclear spindle, which suggests this process is either rapid or unstable to fixation conditions.

The cytoplasmic microtubules that emanate from the spindle pole body are found in the vicinity of small 30–40-nm vesicles that accumulate at the site of bud emergence (Matile et al., 1969; Byers and Goetsch, 1975). It has been postulated that these microtubules may play a role in the migration and localization of these vesicles to the bud site. During the process of conjugation between cells of the opposite mating type, the migration of the two nuclei in the newly fused zygote toward each other may be directed by the cytoplasmic microtubules of the spindle pole body (Byers and Goetsch, 1975).

Examination of yeast cells by immunofluoresence using a monoclonal antibody that recognizes α-tubulin, Kilmartin and Adams (1984) demonstrated many of the same features that were observed by electron microscopy. One feature of the cytoplasmic microtubules was clarified. A large bundle of microtubules emanates from both spindle pole bodies after duplication, and one bundle of these microtubules extends to, or into, the bud.

Preparations enriched in spindle pole bodies can be made by using the spindle pole body as a site for the initiation of polymerization of purified tubulin (Kilmartin and Fogg, 1982). No biochemical characterization of these preparations has been reported.

MUTANTS THAT AFFECT THE FUNCTION OF THE SPINDLE POLE BODY

CDC31

Mutations in the *CDC31* locus were originally defined by temperature-sensitive alleles that arrest progress through the cell cycle. Phenotypically, the mutants arrest as large double cells (Hartwell et al., 1974). Most cell cycle mutants with this arrest phenotype have completed DNA replication and have duplicated the spindle pole body to form an intranuclear mitotic spindle (Byers

and Goetsch, 1974). By electron microscopy *cdc31* mutants have not duplicated the spindle pole body, but have a single large spindle pole body. A unipolar spindle is frequently formed (Byers, 1981). Chromosome segregation is aberrant; one of the daughter cells receives both chromosomal complements, and the other cell does not receive any chromosomes. Thus, the ploidy of the cell is doubled by a shift to the restrictive temperature (Schild et al., 1981).

The *CDC31* locus has been isolated by complementation of the temperature-sensitive lethal phenotype (Baum et al., 1986). Comparisons of the opening reading frame in the *CDC31* gene show significant homology with calmodulin and other members of the calcium-binding protein family. The opening reading frame codes for a highly acidic polypeptide with an apparent M_r 18,700. Recently, Baum and Byers (personal communication) have shown that the polypeptide encoded by the *CDC31* gene has calcium-binding activity. These results suggest that duplication of the microtubule organizing center of yeast may be regulated by changes in the calcium concentrations in the cell. There is no evidence that the gene product of the *CDC31* locus is a component of the spindle pole body.

KAR1

Mutations at the *KAR1* locus have two phenotypes. Some alleles define an essential function for the *KAR1* locus; these mutations are either conditional or nonconditional lethals (Rose and Fink, 1987). In addition, there is an allele that has no effect on viability, but affects the completion of nuclear fusion or karyogamy during the process of conjugation (Conde and Fink, 1976). Some of the temperature-sensitive conditional lethal alleles have a weak karyogamy phenotype (Rose and Fink, 1987).

Based on the genetic behavior of the *kar1-1* allele, it was postulated that the gene product of this locus may be a component of the spindle pole body (Fink and Conde, 1976; Dutcher and Hartwell, 1983). The rationale for this argument was based on the unusual dominance that the mutant allele exhibited. The *kar1-1* mutation is recessive for the karyogamy defect in mating between diploid cells that are heterozygous for the mutation; karyogamy occurs with normal proficiency. However, each parental nucleus must contribute one wild-type allele for successful karyogamy; zygotes formed between a homozygous wild-type cell and a homozygous mutant cell do not complete nuclear fusion. This "nuclear dominance" was shown to be the result of the requirement for the wild-type gene product prior to cytoplasmic fusion (Dutcher and Hartwell, 1983). The prerequisite for the Kar$^+$ gene product prior to cytoplasmic fusion is consistent with a role in the assembly of the spindle pole body or in its regulation.

The *KAR1* gene has been isolated by complementation of the karyogamy defect. The gene contains an open reading frame that corresponds to a polypeptide with an apparent M_r 53,000. Disruption of the *KAR1* gene and overproduction of the wild-type *KAR1* gene produce the same phenotype; cells fail to duplicate the spindle pole body and fail to complete the cell cycle (Rose and Fink, 1987). It is not known if the Kar gene product is a subunit of the spindle pole body.

SPA1

This locus was isolated by screening a yeast λ-gt11 library with a human autoimmune serum that recognizes the centrosome in human cells (Tuffanelli et al., 1983). The *SPA1* locus encodes a polypeptide with an apparent M_r 56,000. This polypeptide is localized to the nuclear envelope and is overproduced in mutant strains that make extra spindle pole bodies, which suggests that the Spa gene product may be a component of the spindle pole body (M. Snyder and R. Davis, manuscript in preparation).

Disruption mutations in the *SPA1* locus show poor viability at 30°C and do not grow at 37°C. These mutants also show a karyogamy defect that is phenotypically similar to the defect exhibited by the *kar1* mutations. In addition, there is an elevated rate of chromosome loss in the mutant strain

and an abnormal number of nuclei (M. Snyder and R. Davis, manuscript in preparation).

Other Mutants

There are a large number of temperature-sensitive mutants (*cdc* mutants) that arrest the development of the spindle pole body throughout the cell division cycle (Pringle and Hartwell, 1980). The effect of many of these mutants on the spindle pole body may be indirect. That is, the spindle pole body cycle may be dependent on the completion of other cell division cycle events that do not occur in the mutants. The failure to complete other requirements may block the progress of the spindle pole body cycle without directly affecting the spindle pole body itself; one goal is to understand which of the mutants may be affecting the spindle pole body directly.

One phenotype that might be expected of a microtubule organizing center mutant would be defects in mitotic chromosome segregation. Many of the *cdc* mutants, as well as other mutants, affect the fidelity of chromosome segregation (DiNardo et al., 1984; Holm et al., 1985; Hartwell and Smith, 1985; Meeks-Wagner et al., 1986). For example, mutants in DNA ligase (Hartwell and Smith, 1985) or in topoisomerase II (L. Hartwell, personal communication) give a decrease in the fidelity of chromosome segregation. Consequently, the observation that mutants affect chromosome loss per se is not sufficient evidence for a role in the assembly or function of the microtubule organizing center. The application of molecular biology may be the clearest way to deciphering whether a gene product is directly affecting the spindle pole body.

An example of an interesting mutation that may affect spindle pole bodies is *NDC1* (Thomas and Botstein, 1986). This mutation is a cold-sensitive conditional lethal; at each cell division one of the cells receives all of the chromosomal DNA complement and the other cell fails to receive any chromosomal DNA. The cell that received DNA is the mother or daughter with equal probability. Unlike *cdc31* mutants, *ndc1* cells form a bipolar spindle at the restrictive temperature. Thomas and Botstein have postulated that the defect in the *NDC1* mutant may be in the failure of the spindle pole body to form attachment sites for the segregation of chromosomes to both poles of the mitotic and meiosis II spindles. Equally likely is their model that *NDC1* affects the chromosomes rather than the spindle pole body. No molecular analysis has been performed on *NDC1*.

MICROTUBULE ORGANIZING CENTERS OF *CHLAMYDOMONAS REINHARDTII*

In *Chlamydomonas,* the major microtubule organizing center is the flagellar apparatus. This structure consists of two basal bodies that are located at right angles to one another. Each basal body consists of nine triplet microtubules in a characteristic 9 + 0 organization. This structural motif is found also in centrioles and basal bodies of higher eukaryotes (Brinkley, 1985). Although these basal bodies resemble centrioles in morphology and in location, the convention in algae has been to call them *basal bodies.*

The two basal bodies are connected by a system of fibers known as *striated fibers.* There is a distal fiber and two proximal fibers, for which *proximal* refers to the end nearest the nucleus. In interphase cells each of the basal bodies is elaborated by a transition zone and by a flagellar axoneme. It is in the transition zone that the triplet microtubules of the basal body become the doublet microtubules of the axoneme. During most of interphase, a probasal body is attached at the proximal end of each of the full-length basal bodies by two thin filaments (Ringo, 1967; Gould, 1975). A probasal body is an annulus of nine triplet microtubules. The timing of the formation of these probasal bodies is not known. In addition, another fiber connects the basal bodies to the nucleus (see section on *VFL* mutants).

As the cell begins mitosis, there are a number of changes in the flagellar apparatus (Fig. 6–2). First, the flagellar axonemes and

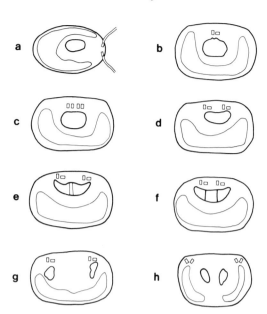

Fig. 6–2. The events of the basal body cycle in *Chlamydomonas reinhardtii.* **a:** Interphase. **b:** Preprophase; protoplast rotates 90° within the cell wall. **c:** Preprophase; basal body replication. **d:** Prophase. Basal bodies move to the poles. **e:** Metaphase. **f:** Anaphase. **g:** Late telophase; the interzonal spindle degenerates and phycoplast begins to form. **h:** Late cytokinesis; two daughter cells begin to reestablish interphase organization within mother cell wall. (Adapted from Triemer and Brown, 1974, with permission of the publisher.)

the transition zones are reabsorbed into the cell (Cavalier-Smith, 1974), the cytoplasmic microtubules disassemble (Le Dizet and Piperno, 1986; Holmes and Dutcher, manuscript in preparation), and the striated fibers disappear. Each of the pair of basal bodies comes to lie parallel to one another, and the probasal bodies elongate. The two new basal bodies rotate and come to lie parallel to the existing ones (Triemer and Brown, 1974). At the beginning of prophase one pair of basal bodies moves toward each mitotic pole. It is not clear whether the microtubules of the mitotic spindle emanate from the region surrounding the basal body and pass through the fenestrated nuclear envelope (Johnson and Porter, 1968; Coss, 1974) or begin in the nuclear envelope (Triemer and Brown,

1974). The mitotic spindle is crescent shaped; the basal bodies remain near the cell membrane (Triemer and Brown, 1974; Holmes and Dutcher, manuscript in preparation). At telophase each pair of basal bodies moves to the anterior end of the cell, where they reestablish the flagellar apparatus.

During mitosis the protoplast within the cell wall rotates about 90°. The exact timing of this event is not clear but may occur in preprophase (Triemer and Brown, 1974). Cytokinesis begins with furrowing of the membrane at the anterior end of the cell between the basal bodies; the formation of the cleavage furrow coincides with the formation of a band of microtubules that runs perpendicular to the spindle (Cavalier-Smith, 1974; Johnson and Porter, 1968). The role of these microtubules in cytokinesis is not known.

Most of the cytoplasmic microtubules of an interphase *Chlamydomonas* cell emanate from the basal body region. There are two distinct classes of cytoplasmic microtubules. The first class is composed of four rootlet microtubules. They radiate from the basal body complex in a cruciate pattern. Two of the rootlet microtubules consist of two microtubules, and the other two microtubules consist of four microtubules (Goodenough and Weiss, 1978). These microtubules may be directly attached to the basal bodies and remain attached to the basal bodies during gentle lysis procedures (Gould, 1975; Wright et al., 1985). These microtubules are similar to axonemal microtubules in that they are stable to standard depolymerization conditions and stain differently with osmium (Gould, 1975). The second class of microtubules is similar to cytoplasmic microtubules in other organisms. These microtubules are not attached to the basal bodies; the exact location of the ends of these microtubules is not clear.

MUTANTS THAT AFFECT THE FUNCTION OF THE MICROTUBULE ORGANIZING CENTER

VFL

There are three loci in *Chlamydomonas* that alter the number of basal bodies (Wright et al., 1983, 1985; Adams et al., 1985). The mutants have the phenotype of variable numbers of flagella and variable numbers of basal bodies. Mutants at *VFL1* and *VFL3* have associated cytokinesis phenotypes, which may be responsible for the inaccurate segregation of the basal bodies. Mutants at the *VFL2* locus are not associated with a cytokinesis defect. In many algae there is a calcium-dependent contractile fiber that runs from the basal bodies to the nucleus (Salisbury and Floyd, 1978; Salisbury et al., 1984). Immunofluoresence of wild-type *Chlamydomonas* cells was performed using an antibody raised against an M_r 20,000 polypeptide from the flagellar rootlet of *Tetraselmes*. The antibody recognizes two polypeptides that have different isoelectric points; they appear to bind to calcium ions, and one component is a phosphoprotein (Salisbury et al., 1984). The immunofluoresence shows a fiber that extends between the basal bodies and the nucleus. This staining pattern is missing in *VFL2* mutants (Wright et al., 1983, 1985). Wright et al. suggest that this fiber may function in localization and segregation of the basal bodies during the cell cycle.

UNI

There are five mutants that affect the structure of the basal bodies; they were recognized because they failed to assemble one of the two flagella (Huang et al., 1983; Dutcher, 1986). The basal body that lacks a flagellum in these mutants fails to assemble the transition zone. The basal body that contains a flagellum possess additional material that resembles transition zone material in its staining pattern; this material is assembled into a nonuniform arrangement. These mutants are intriguing in that it is always the flagellum opposite of the eyespot that is always assembled. This observation suggests that the two basal bodies differ from one another. A positional difference between the two basal bodies may be related to a difference in their generational age. A similar difference has been observed for centrioles of animal cells as well as other algal cells

(Vorobjev and Chentosov, 1982). The gene products of these loci are not known.

PF10

The mutation at this locus affects flagellar movement (Lewin, 1954; Dutcher, Gibbons, and Inwood, in press). The *pf10-1* allele is a conditional mutation. Under low light intensity, the strain is immotile. This mutant assembles flagella, but the flagella have an abnormal waveform. However, under increased light intensities the immotility is suppressed (Dutcher, Gibbons, and Inwood, in press). Therefore, the restrictive condition is low light (1,000 ergs/cm^2 sec) and the permissive condition is high light (4,000 ergs/cm^2 sec). This conditional phenotype suggests that the effect of the mutant product can be modulated (Dutcher, Gibbons, and Inwood, in press).

Vegetatively dividing diploids that are heterozygous for the *pf10* mutation are motile since the mutation is recessive to the wild-type allele (Dutcher, 1986). However, the mutant exhibits an unusual behavior in newly formed zygotes. Rescue of the swimming defect is not observed in newly formed heterozygous diploid dikaryons. The defect is not rescued by the presence of wild-type cytoplasm in the newly formed zygotes despite the fact that there is a large pool of flagellar axonemal polypeptides (Dutcher, 1986). This behavior is similar to the nuclear dominance observed for the *kar1-1* allele. Because two of the flagella remain wild-type and two remain mutant, it seems likely that the defect is not in the flagellar axoneme but elsewhere within the cell. A likely location for the defect is within the microtubule organizing center.

Biochemical analysis of preparations enriched in isolated basal bodies from the *pf10* mutant shows the absence of two polypeptides of apparent M_r 65,000 that are present in similar preparations from wild-type cells. It is not known if either of these is the gene product of the *PF10* locus (Dutcher, 1986). There is also a decrease in the amount of one axonemal polypeptide with an apparent M_r 220,000 in *pf10* axonemes (Inwood, 1985).

Studies are underway to address this question.

Other Mutants

The mutations *uni1* to *uni5* and *pf10* share the property that they map to a newly defined linkage group in *Chlamydomonas*. It has been referred to as the *UNI linkage group* (Ramanis and Luck, 1986) or as *linkage group XIX* (Dutcher, 1986). Mutants in this linkage group share a number of properties. All of the mutants affect microtubule-based functions. The mutations fall into three phenotypic classes. The classes include mutations that affect flagellar assembly or length, that affect flagellar function, and that confer resistance to the antimicrotubule drug amiprophos-methyl (Morejohn and Fosket, 1984; Bajer and Mole-Bajer, 1986). Second, many of these mutants show the unusual dominance behavior illustrated above for *pf10*, which suggests that they are not acting primarily at the level of the flagellar axoneme. This linkage group also has a circular genetic map and unusual temperature sensitivity with regard to recombination frequencies (Ramanis and Luck, 1986; Dutcher, 1986).

Currently, there are more than 20 loci that have been mapped to this linkage group. Mutants that affect flagellar assembly fall into 8 complementation groups that include *uni1* to *uni5*, which have the phenotype of one flagellum rather than two flagella; 8 *fla* loci, which are temperature-sensitive flagellar assembly mutants; *fla11*, *pf7*, and *pf8*, which assemble short flagella; *sun1*, *sun3*, and *sun5*, which are suppressors of the Uni phenotype; and *enh1*, which enhances the Uni phenotype (McVittie, 1974; Adams et al., 1982; Huang et al., 1983; Dutcher, 1986). The *sun* and *enh* mutants have no apparent phenotype in a wild-type background. Mutants that affect flagellar function include *pf10* (Dutcher, Gibbons, and Inwood, in press) and *pf29* (Ramanis and Luck, 1986). A single locus with 20 independent alleles confers resistance to amiprophos-methyl, oryzalin, and butamiphos (James et al., 1988). Cell division is arrested in *Chlamydo-*

monas by these herbicides. Mutants at the *APM1* locus are recessive and interact with mutants at a second unlinked, recessive locus, *APM2*. Haploid strains that contain both *apm1* and *apm2* mutations are inviable. Diploids that are heterozygous at both recessive loci are resistant to the drugs. The mutants are dominant enhancers of one another (Lindsley and Grell, 1985). *Dominant enhancers* are defined as the absence of complementation between different loci. Mutations that are dominant enhancers of one another may be explained by proteins that interact directly with one another (Hays et al., manuscript submitted) or by the accumulation of slightly deleterious phenotypes. The cause of the dominant enhancer phenotype of the *apm1* and *apm2* mutations is not known (James et al., 1988). These drugs alter the microtubule integrity in *Haemanthus* and other plants (Morejohn and Fosket, 1984; Bajer and Mole-Bajer, 1986), but the mode of action is not known.

All of the phenotypes of mutants on linkage group XIX suggest that the loci on this linkage group may be related to functions of both microtubules and basal bodies of the *Chlamydomonas* cell (Dutcher, 1986). If this hypothesis is correct, then defining the range of phenotypes conferred by mutations on linkage group XIX would serve as a useful model system for understanding the role of centrioles and basal bodies in eukaryotic cells. The majority of loci that have been identified affect flagellar assembly and function. To ascertain the extent of phenotypes conferred by mutants on this linkage group, we have begun to use an approach that is routinely used in organisms such as *Drosophila* and *Caenorhabditis*.

DELETION ANALYSIS IN
CHLAMYDOMONAS REINHARDTII

A locus can best be studied genetically by generating new alleles. A general strategy for the isolation of new alleles is to construct a diploid organism that is heterozygous for a mutation of interest. If the mutation is recessive, then the genetic screen is for appear-

ance of the mutant phenotype. If the mutation is dominant, then the genetic screen is for the appearance of the wild-type phenotype. The mutant phenotype could arise by creating new alleles, by dominant mutations at other loci, by mitotic recombination, or by dominant enhancers. Each of these possibilities can be identified by standard genetic techniques.

A region of a chromosome can be studied by similar approaches with the caveat that the mutations that are generated are generally chromosomal aberrations such as deletions. Once a deletion of a region is obtained and the deletion has a phenotype, it is possible to saturate the region with point mutations. These new mutations can then be analyzed. This technique was adapted to study the phenotypes of deletions and new point mutations on linkage group XIX. We have developed screens for identifying new alleles and deletions in heterozygous diploids and methods to analyze them.

The ability to isolate and to analyze new alleles and deletions in an organism has two requirements. Diploid organisms must be scorable for the phenotype of interest, and these organisms must be able to enter the meiotic sexual cycle so that the mutants can be analyzed genetically. *Chlamydomonas* can be propagated mitotically both as a haploid and as a diploid (Ebersold, 1967). Diploid cells are produced from a small percentage of the successful conjugations between haploid cells of opposite mating-type or by polyethylene glycol-mediated fusion (Matagne et al., 1979). These diploid cells cannot be induced to reenter the meiotic cycle as diploid cells (Fig. 6–3). However, these cells can enter the meiotic cycle by an indirect method; cells heterozygous at the mating-type locus can mate with cells of the plus mating type. The zygotic cells entering meiosis are either triploid or tetraploid depending on the ploidy of the mating-type plus parent. If the meiotic cells are triploid, then the progeny that are produced are aneuploid, and less than 20% of the aneuploid progeny survive (Dutcher and Gibbons, 1988). If the meiotic cells are

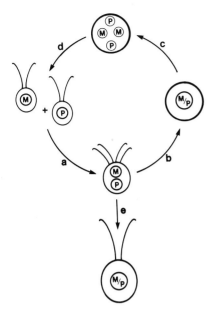

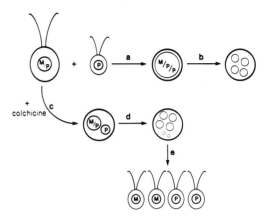

Fig. 6–4. Inhibition of nuclear fusion in *Chlamydomonas.* **a:** Formation of quadriflagellated cells between a diploid strain and a haploid strain produces a triploid zygote. **b:** These zygotes enter meiosis but produce predominantly aneuploid, inviable progeny. **c:** Inhibition of nuclear fusion between the diploid and haploid nuclei by addition of colchicine produces a binucleated zygote. **d:** Binucleated zygotes produce six meiotic products. Four of the products arise from the diploid parental nucleus, and two of the products arise from the haploid parental nucleus. **e:** Only the meiotic products from the diploid nucleus produce viable progeny, and normal segregation is observed.

Fig. 6–3. Life cycle of *Chlamydomonas reinhardtii.* **a:** Haploid cells that have been arrested in G_1 of the cell cycle will mate with cells of the opposite mating type (plus [P] and minus [M]) to form zygotes. **b:** Quadriflagellate zygotes will complete nuclear fusion, the flagella are reabsorbed into the cell body, and a thick zygotic wall is made. **c:** Zygotic cells undergo maturation to become competent to enter into meiosis. **d:** Cells will undergo meiosis in 18–24 hr after induction by light and fresh nutrients to form four meiotic spores that can be isolated and analyzed. These progeny can divide mitotically. **e:** Quadriflagellated cells can escape meiosis and become mitotic diploid cells that divide mitotically and can conjugate as mating-type minus cells.

tetraploid, then the progeny are diploid and the survival frequency is about 90%. In either case, analysis of new mutations that are generated in the diploid organism is difficult. This type of analysis can be facilitated by a method that allows diploid cells to enter the meiotic cycle.

Meiotic Analysis of Diploid Strains in *Chlamydomonas*

The formation of triploid cells following conjugation of diploid and haploid strains requires cytoplasmic fusion followed by nuclear fusion. If nuclear fusion is inhibited, it is

possible to recover haploid meiotic progeny from a vegetatively growing diploid strain (Fig. 6–4). The inhibition of nuclear fusion was accomplished by the addition of microtubule-binding drugs to gametic cultures of haploid and diploid cells. Addition of colchicine, oryzalin, and amiprophos-methyl inhibited nuclear fusion in 19–70% of the zygotes formed between haploid and diploid parents, depending on the exact treatment (Dutcher, 1988). The rationale of this treatment is that addition of microtubule-depolymerizing drugs will inhibit nuclear migration (Chambers, 1939; Zimmerman and Zimmerman, 1967; Longo and Anderson, 1968, 1969; Delgado and Conde, 1984), and the failure of the nuclei to achieve the proper orientation with respect to one another inhibits nuclear fusion. Inhibition of fusion between the haploid and diploid nuclei in the newly formed zygotes produces

TABLE 6–1. Behavior of Spores From Nuclear Fusion Blocked Zygotes

Test	Markers analyzed	P1 × P2[a]	H × D12
Independent assortment[b]	*ani1–sr1*	15:13:51	10:12:39
Recombination	*ani1–spr1*	54:0:25	49:0:12
Viability in crosses to haploids[c]	NA	94 ± 2.2	92 ± 1.2

[a]P1 and P2 are haploid strains and are the parents off diploid D12. H is a wild-type haploid strain. The cross of P1 and P2 is performed in the absence of colchicine, and the cross of H and D12 is performed in the presence of colchicine.

[b]Ratio of parental ditypes:nonparental ditypes:tetratypes.

[c]Percentage of viable spores based on 450 tetrads for P1 × P2 and based on 720 tetrads for H × D12 in which progeny were crossed to wild-type cells (137c).

NA: not applicable.

TABLE 6–2. Alleles and Phenotypes of *fla10*

Isolate name	Allele	No. of tetrand[a]	Flagellar phenotype[b]
dd224	*fla10-1*	NA[c]	Temperature sensitive
DEO 7	*fla10-2*	16	Nonconditional
DEO 14	*fla10-3*	14	Nonconditional
DEO 15	*fla10-4*	22	Temperature sensitive
DEO 16	*fla10-5*	34	Temperature sensitive
DBDE 13	*fla10-6*	15	Temperature sensitive
DBDE 15	*fla10-7*	12	Nonconditional
DBDE 18	*fla10-8*	17	Temperature sensitive
DEB 7	*fla10-9*	12	Temperature sensitive
DEB 7.1	*fla10-10*	14	Nonconditional
DEB 14	*fla10-11*	19	Temperature sensitive
DEB 22	*fla10-12*	20	Nonconditional

[a]Number of tetrads analyzed from cross of mutagenized diploid parent by a haploid tester (137c) in the presence of colchicine (Dutcher, 1988).

[b]Phenotype of newly isolated haploid mutant when recovered from the diploid parental strain.

[c]Not applicable.

six-spored meiotic asci (Dutcher, 1988). Four of these spores are products of two meiotic divisions of the diploid parent. The genetic markers in these spores show independent assortment, levels of recombination, and viability similar to products produced by a meiosis between the two haploid parents of the diploid (Table 6–1). By all criteria examined, these four spores were haploid products and were not aneuploid or diploid. The remaining two spores are abnormally small; they are less than one-fifth the diameter of the other four spores; these spores fail to germinate. The most reasonable explanation is that these spores are produced from the products of a meiosis I division of the haploid nucleus. They would be expected to be aneuploid and inviable (Dutcher, 1988). These results in *Chlamydomonas* suggest that cytoplasmic microtubules play an important role in the process of nuclear fusion.

Isolation of New Alleles of *FLA10*

A diploid strain heterozygous for the *fla10-1* mutation was constructed and is designated *Q1-4*. The homozygous *fla10/fla10* diploid strain assembles functional flagella at 21° C but fails to assemble flagella at 32° C. The heterozygous strain assembles flagella at both 21° C and 32° C, which indicates that the mutation is recessive to the wild-type allele. Q1-4 was mutagenized with diepoxybutane, diepoxyoctane, or dibutadiene diepoxide. The mutagen diepoxybutane generates deletions and chromosomal rearrangements in *Drosophila* (Reardon et al., 1987); however, in *S. cerevisiae* no deletion mutations were recovered (J. Boeke and R. Zerat, personal communication). These mutagens were chosen with the intent of generating amorphic or null alleles that could be used to ascertain whether this gene was required for processes other than flagellar assembly. The screen was designed to obtain strains that fail to assemble flagella at 32° C, but are motile at 21° C. This phenotype can occur by changes in the wild-type allele of the diploid strain. Twelve strains were obtained in this screen (Table 6–2).

The phenotypes of diploid strains that were aflagellate at 32° C and flagellated at 21° C were analyzed by temperature-shift experiments. Liquid cultures were grown at 21° C and then shifted to 32° C. The fraction of cells with flagella was monitored by light microscopy at 0, 1, 3, 5, 8, and 24 hr after the shift to 32° C. Several differences were ob-

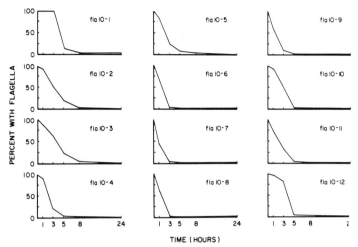

Fig. 6–5. Kinetics of flagellar loss in heteroallelic *fla10* diploids. All of the strains contain the *fla10* allele and a second allele, which is designated in the right corner of each graph. The y axis shows the percentage of flagellated cells; the x-axis shows the time of incubation at 32° C.

served among the newly isolated strains and between these strains and a homozygous *fla10-1/fla10-1* diploid strain. Cultures of *fla10-1* homozygotes are 95% aflagellate by 5 hr, and the loss of flagella is very rapid. The new isolates, which carry *fla10-1* and a new *fla10* allele become aflagellate with different kinetics (Fig. 6–5). One group becomes aflagellate after 5 hr, a second group becomes aflagellate after 8 hr, and a final isolate requires more than 8 hr to become 95% aflagellate. There is no correlation between the severity of the alleles as haploids and their kinetics of flagellar loss (see below). Both nonconditional alleles and temperature-sensitive alleles fall into these two classes (Table 6–2). These differences suggest that the mutagenized diploid strains contain new alleles and are not homozygous for the *fla10-1* allele via a mitotic recombination event.

Each of the strains was analyzed meiotically. Three different phenotypes were observed among the meiotic progeny. Six of the new alleles were temperature sensitive; they assemble flagella at 21° C but not at 32° C. Four of the new alleles were nonconditional alleles; they failed to assemble flagella at any temperature from 16° C to 32° C.

The final allele showed two phenotypes. The *fla10-5* allele was temperature sensitive for flagellar assembly and showed a growth defect. Each of the new alleles was shown to be the result of a single mutation by crossing the isolates to a wild-type parent. For each isolate, we observed two mutant and two wild-type spores in an average of 34 tetrads examined. For the aflagellate strains, we used the method of Pasquale and Goodenough (1987) to achieve mating. To verify that each isolate was a new mutation at the *FLA10* locus, we crossed each isolate to a *fla10-1* strain. For each isolate, we observed four mutant spores in an average of 46 tetrads examined (Table 6–3). Therefore, the screen has identified 12 new alleles at the *FLA10* locus.

One of the new alleles showed a growth defect. This strain has a doubling time of 29 hr compared with 8 hr for the *fla10-1* allele at 21° C. The flagellar assembly defect and the growth defect cosegregated in 46 tetrads. The growth defect appears to map to the *FLA10* locus. In addition, the growth defect is recessive to the wild-type *FLA10* allele and is complemented by three different *fla10* alleles at the permissive and the restrictive temperature (Table 6–4). Be-

TABLE 6–3. Segregation of New Alleles of *fla10*

Isolate name	Allele	No. of tetrands × 137c[a]	No. of tetrands × *FLA10-1*[b]
DEO 7	*fla10-2*	35[c]	48
DEO 14	*fla10-3*	37[c]	52
DEO 15	*fla10-4*	31	41
DEO 16	*fla10-5*	39	46
DBDE 13	*fla10-6*	32	47
DBDE 15	*fla10-7*	32[c]	44
DBDE 18	*fla10-8*	29	43
DEB 7	*fla10-9*	32	39
DEB7.1	*fla10-10*	44[c]	49
DEB 14	*fla10-11*	33	51
DEB 22	*fla10-12*	29	47

[a]All crosses produced two mutant and two wild-type spores. This result indicates that a single mutation is responsible for the flagellar assembly defect.
[b]All crosses produced four mutant spores. This result indicates that the mutant phenotype is tightly linked to the *FLA10* locus.
[c]Matings were accomplished in the presence of dibutyryl cAMP and isobutylmethylxanthine (Pasquale and Goodenough, 1987).

TABLE 6–4. Complementation Tests of Diploids With *fla10-5*

Parent	Flagellar Assembly	Growth
FLA10	+	+
fla10-1	−	+
fla10-4	−	+
fla10-8	−	+

cause the cells with the *fla10-5* mutation grow at a reduced rate, spontaneous revertants that increase the growth rate can be easily isolated. Several independent revertants are isolated and examined. In at least one of these revertants, both the growth defect and the flagellar assembly defect have been reverted. In meiotic crosses, the reversion event is closely linked to the original defect based on 35 tetrads.

The growth defect and the flagellar assembly defect appear to be consequences of a mutation in the same locus based on the cosegregation of the phenotypes and on the coreversion of the phenotypes. This mutation as well as alleles at the *APM1* locus (James et al., 1988) suggests that linkage group XIX carries loci that affect processes beyond flagellar assembly and function and supports the hypotheses that other microtubule-based functions are encoded on linkage group XIX and that these functions can be disrupted by mutations on this linkage group. This approach will be useful for fully defining the extent of functions performed by microtubule organizing centers.

CONCLUSIONS

Genetic and molecular biological techniques are just beginning to be applied to the study of microtubule organizing centers. Currently, it is hard to predict what new information will be reaped from the combination of these approaches. It does seem clear that the ability to inactivate single components of these structures may elucidate the assembly and function of them in the future.

ACKNOWLEDGMENTS

I thank Jeff Holmes for many useful discussions and Chris Sappenfield for help with the isolation of new alleles of *fla10*. I thank Gary and Benjamin Stormo for their patience. In addition, I thank Peter Baum, Jef Boeke, Breck Byers, Lee Hartwell, Mike Synder, and Ron Zerat for communicating data before publication.

The work has been supported by grants from the National Institutes of Health and from The Searle Scholars Program/Chicago Community Trust.

Bibliography 1, Chapters 2-6

Adachi, Y., T. Toda, O. Niwa, and M. Yanagida (1986) Differential expressions of essential and non-essential α-tubulin genes in *Schizosaccharomyces pombe*. Mol. Cell Biol. 6:2168–2178.

Adams, G.M.W., B. Huang, and D.J.L. Luck (1982) Temperature-sensitive, assembly defective flagellar mutants of *Chlamydomonas reinhardtii*. Genetics 100:579–586.

Adams, G.M.W., R.L. Wright, and J.W. Jarvick (1985) Defective temporal and spatial control of flagellar assembly in a mutant of *Chlamydomonas reinhardtii* with variable flagellar number. J. Cell Biol. 100:955–964.

Alberts, B., D. Bray, J. Lewis, M. Raff, K. Roberts, and J. Watson (1983) Molecular Biology of the Cell. New York: Garland Publishing Co.

Allen, C., and G.G. Borisy (1974) Structural polarity and directional growth of microtubules of *Chlamydomonas* flagella. J. Mol. Biol. 90:381–402.

Amos, L.A. (1977) Arrangement of high molecular weight associated proteins on purified mammalian brain microtubules. J. Cell Biol. 72:642–654.

Amos, L.A. (1982) Tubulin and associated proteins. In J.R. Harris (ed): Electron Microscopy of Proteins. London: Academic Press, pp. 207–250.

Amos, L.A. (1987) Kinesin from pig brain studied by electron microscopy. J. Cell Sci. 87:105–111.

Amos, W.B., Amos, L.A. and Linck, R.W. (1985): Proteins closely similar to flagellar tektins are detected in cilia but not in cytoplasmic microtubules, Cell Motil. 5:239–249.

Amos, L.A., and T.S. Baker (1979) The three-dimensional structure of tubulin protofilaments. Nature 279:607–612.

Amos, L.A., J.S. Jubb, R. Henderson, and G.P.A. Vigers (1984) Arrangement of protofilaments in two forms of tubulin crystal induced by vinblastine. J. Mol. Biol. 178:711–729.

Amos, L.A., and A. Klug (1974) Arrangement of subunits in flagellar microtubules. J. Cell Sci. 14:523–549.

Amos, L.A., R.W. Linck, and A. Klug (1976) Molecular structure of flagellar microtubules. In R. Goldman, T. Pollard, and J.L. Rosenbaum (eds): Cell Motility, Book C. Cold Spring Harbor, New York: Cold Spring Harbor Laboratory pp. 847–867.

Amos, W.B., L.A. Amos, and R.W. Linck (1986) Studies of tektin filaments from flagellar microtubules by immunoelectron microscopy. J. Cell Sci. Suppl. 5:55–68.

Andersen, B., M. Osborn, and K. Weber (1978) Specific visualization of the distribution of the calcium dependent regulatory protein of cyclic phosphodiesterase (modulator protein) in tissue culture cells by immunofluorescence microscopy: Mitosis and intracellular bridge. Cytobiologie 17:354–364.

Arce, C.A., and H.S. Barra (1985) Release of C-terminal tyrosine from tubulin and microtubules at steady state. Biochem. J. 226:311–317.

Arce, C.A., M.E. Hallak, J.A. Rodriguez, H.S. Barra, and R. Caputto (1978) Capability of tubulin and microtubules to incorporate and to release tyrosine and phenylalanine and the effect of the incorporation of these amino acids on tubulin assembly. J. Neurochem. 31:205–210.

Arce, C.A., J.A. Rodriguez, H.S. Barra, and R. Caputto (1975) Incorporation of L-tyrosine, L-phenylalanine and L-3.4 dihydroxyphenylalanine as single units into rat brain tubulin. Eur. J. Biochem. 59:145–149.

Argaraña, C.E., H.S. Barra, and R. Caputto (1980) Tubulinyl-tyrosine carboxypeptidase from chicken brain: Properties and partial purification. J. Neurochem. 34:114–118.

Baccetti, B., and B.A. Afzelius (1976) The Biology of the Sperm Cell. New York: S. Karger, p. 254.

Bajer, A.S., and J. Mole-Bajer (1986) Drugs with colchicine-like effects that specifically disassemble plant but not animal microtubules. In D. Soifer (ed): Dynamic Aspects of Microtubule Biology. New York: New York Academy of Sciences, pp. 767–784.

Ball, E.H., and S.J. Singer (1982) Mitochondria are associated with microtubules and not with intermediate filaments in cultured fibroblasts. Proc. Natl. Acad. Sci. USA 79:123–126.

Ballowitz, E. (1888) Untersuchungen über die Strukturen der Spermatozoen. Arch. Mikrosk. Anat. 32:401–473.

Barber, V.C. (1974) Cilia in sense organs. In M.A. Sleigh (ed): Cilia and Flagella. New York: Academic Press, pp. 403–433.

Barra, H.S., C.A. Arce, and R. Caputto (1980) Total tubulin and its amino-acylated and non-amino-acylated forms during the development of rat brain. Eur. J. Biochem. 109:439–446.

Barra, H.S., C.A. Arce, J.A. Rodriguez, and R. Caputto (1974) Some common properties of the protein that incorporates tyrosine as a single unit and the microtubule proteins. Biochem. Biophys. Res. Commun. 60:1384–1390.

Barra, H.S., J.A. Rodriguez, C.A. Arce, and R. Caputto (1973) A soluble preparation from rat brain that incorporates into its own proteins [^{14}C]-arginine by a ribonuclease-sensitive system and [^{14}C]-tyrosine by a ribonuclease-insensitive system. J. Neurochem. 20:97–108.

Barsel, S.E., D.E. Wexler, and P.A. Lefebvre (1988) Genetic analysis of long-flagella mutants of Chlamydomonas reinhardtii. Genetics 118:637–648.

Baum, P., C. Furlong, and B. Byers (1986) Yeast gene required for spindle pole body duplication: Homology of its product with Ca^{2+}-binding proteins. Proc. Natl. Acad. Sci. USA 83:5512–5516.

Bayley, P.M., F.M. Butler, D.C. Clark, E.J. Manser, and S.R. Martin (1985) The assembly of microtubule protein in vitro: The kinetic role of MAP-containing fragments in microtubule elongation. Biochem. J. 227:439–455.

Bayley, P.M., and E.J. Manser (1985) Assembly of microtubules from nucleotide- depleted tubulin. Nature 318:683–685.

Bayley, P.M., and S.R. Martin (1986) Inhibition of microtubule elongation by GDP. Biochem. Biophys. Res. Commun. 137:351–358.

Beese, L. (1984) Microtubule Structure: An Analysis by X-ray Diffraction. Ph.D. thesis, Brandeis University.

Beese, L., G. Stubbs, and C. Cohen (1987a) Microtubule structure at 18Å resolution. J. Mol. Biol. 194:257–264.

Beese, L., G. Stubbs, J. Thomas, and C. Cohen (1987b) Structure of microtubules with reduced hydration: comparison of results from X-ray diffraction and electron microscopy. J. Mol. Biol.196:575–580.

Behnke, O. (1970) Microtubules in disk-shaped blood cells. Int. Rev. Exp. Patho. 9:1–92.

Behnke, O., and A. Forer (1967) Evidence for four classes of microtubules in individual cells. J. Cell Sci. 2:169–192.

Bergen, L.G., and G.G. Borisy (1980) Head-to-tail polymerization of microtubules in vitro. J. Cell Biol. 84:141–150.

Berns, M., and M.S. Richardson (1977) Continuation of mitosis after selective laser microbeam irradiation of the centriolar region. J. Cell Biol. 75:977–982.

Bibring, T., J. Baxandall, S. Denslow, and B. Walker (1976) Heterogeneity of the alpha subunit of tubulin and the variability of tubulin within a single organism. J. Cell Biol. 69:301–312.

Binder, L.I., W.L. Dentler, and J.L. Rosenbaum (1975) Assembly of chick brain tubulin onto flagellar axonemes of Chlamydomonas and sea urchin sperm. Proc. Natl. Acad. Sci. USA 72:1122–1126.

Binder, L.I., A. Frankfurter, and L.I. Rebhun (1985) The distribution of tau in the mammalian central nervous system. J. Cell Biol. 101:1371–1378.

Binder, L.I., and J.L. Rosenbaum (1978) The in vitro assembly of flagellar outer doublet tubulin. J. Cell Biol. 79:500–515.

Birkett, C., K.E. Foster, L. Johnson, and K. Gull (1985a) Use of monoclonal antibodies to analyse the expression of a multi-tubulin family. FEBS Lett. 187:211–218.

Birkett, C.R., K.E. Foster, and K. Gull (1985b) Evolution and patterns of expression of the *Physarum* multi-tubulin family analysed by the use of monoclonal antibodies. In W.E. Timerlake (ed): Molecular Genetics of Filamentous Fungi. New York: Alan R. Liss, Inc., pp. 265–275.

Black, M.M., and P. Keyser (1987) Acetylation of α-tubulin in cultured neurons and the induction of tubulin acetylation in PC12 cells by treatment with nerve growth factor. J. Neurosci. 7:1815–1833.

Bond, J.F., J.L. Fridovich-Keil, L. Pillus, R.C. Mulligan, and F. Solomon (1986) A chicken-yeast chimeric β-tubulin protein is incorporated into mouse microtubules in vivo. Cell 44:461–468.

Bonne, D., and D. Pantaloni (1982) Mechanism of tubulin assembly: GTP hydrolysis decreases the rate of microtubule depolymerization. Biochemistry 21:1075–1081.

Bordas, J., E.-M. Mandelkow, and E. Mandelkow (1983) Stages of tubulin assembly and disassembly studied by time-resolved synchrotron X-ray scattering. J. Mol. Biol. 164:89–135.

Brady, S.T. (1985) A novel brain ATPase with properties expected for the fast axonal transport motor. Nature 317:73–75.

Brady, S.T., M. Tytell, and R.J. Lasek (1984) Axonal tubulin and axonal microtubules: Biochemical evidence for cold stability. J. Cell Biol. 99:1716–1724.

Breitling, F., and M. Little (1986) Carboxy-terminal regions on the surface of tubulin and microtubules. Epitope localization of YOL1/34, DM1A and DM1B. J. Mol. Biol. 189:367–370.

Brinkley, B.R. (1985) Microtubule organizing centers. Annu. Rev. Cell Biol. 1:145–172.

Brinkley, B.R., and J. Cartwright (1971) Ultrastructural analysis of mitotic spindle elongation of mammalian cells in vitro: Direct microtubule counts. J. Cell Biol. 50:416–431.

Brinkley, B.R., and J. Cartwright (1975) Cold-labile and cold-stable microtubules in the mitotic spindle of mammalian cells. Ann. N.Y. Acad. Sci. 253:428–439.

Brokaw, C.J. (1972) Flagellar movement: A sliding filament model. Science 174:455–462.

Brokaw, C.J. (1985) Computer simulation of flagellar movement. VI. Simple curvature-controlled models are incompletely specified. Biophys. J. 48:633–642.

Brunke, K.J., P.S. Collis, and D.P. Weeks (1982) Post-translational modification of tubulin dependent on organelle assembly. Nature 297:516–518.

Bryan, J. (1976) A quantitative analysis of microtubule elongation. J. Cell Biol. 71:749–767.

Bulinski, J.C., J.E. Richards, and G. Piperno (1988) Posttranslational modifications of α-tubulin: Detyrosylation and acetylation differentiate populations of interphase microtubules in cultured cells. J. Cell Biol. 106:1213–1220.

Burgoyne, R.D., E.G. Gray, K. Sullivan, and J. Barron (1982) Depolymerization of dendritic microtubules following incubation of cortical slices. Neurosci. Lett. 31:81–85.

Burgoyne, R.D., and K.M. Norman (1986) α-Tubulin is not detyrosinated during axonal transport. Brain Res. 381:113–120.

Burke, B.E., and R.J. DeLorenzo (1981) Ca^{2+} and calmodulin-stimulated endogenous phosphorylation of neurotubulin. Proc. Natl. Acad. Sci. USA 78:991–995.

Burland, T.G., R. Gull, T. Schedl, R.S. Boston, and W.F. Dove (1984) Cell type-dependent expression of tubulins in *Physarum*. J. Cell Biol. 97:1852–1859.

Burns, R. (1987) Tubulin's terminal tyrosine. Nature 327:103–104.

Burns, R.G., and K. Islam (1986) Modulation of the kinetic parameters of microtubule assembly by MAP-2 phosphorylation, the GTP/GDP occupancy of oligomers, and the tubulin tyrosylation status. Ann. N.Y. Acad. Sci. 466:340–356.

Burns, R.G., K. Islam, and R. Chapman (1984) The multiple phosphorylation of the microtubule-associated protein MAP 2 controls the MAP 2 tubulin interaction. Eur. J. Biochem. 141:609–615.

Burton, P.R., R.E. Hinkley, and G.B. Pierson (1975) Tannic acid-stained microtubules with 12, 13, and 15 protofilaments. J. Cell Biol. 65:227–233.

Burton, P.R., and J.L. Paige (1981) Polarity of axoplasmic microtubules in the olfactory nerve of the frog. Proc. Natl. Acad. Sci. USA 78:3269–3273.

Byers, B. (1981) Multiple roles of the spindle pole bodies in the life cycle of *Saccharomyces cerevisiae*. In D. Von Wettstein, J. Friis, M. Kielland-Brandt, and A. Stenderup (eds): Molecular Genetics in Yeast. Copenhagen: Monksgaard Press, pp. 119–131.

Byers, B., and L. Goetsch (1974) Duplication of spindle plaques and integration of the yeast cell cycle. Cold Spring Harbor Symp. Quant. Biol. 38:123–131.

Byers, B., and L. Goetsch (1975) Behavior of spindles and spindle plaques in the cell cycle and conjugation of *Saccharomyces cerevisiae*. J. Bacteriol. 124:511–523.

Cabral, F., M.E. Sobel, and M.M. Gottesman (1980) CHO mutants resistant to colchicine, colcemid or griseofulvin have an altered β-tubulin. Cell 20:29–36.

Cambray-Deakin, M.A., and R.D. Burgoyne (1987) Posttranslational modification of α-tubulin: Acetylated and deacetylated forms in axons of rat cerebellum. J. Cell Biol. 104:1569–1574.

Carlier, M.F. (1982) Guanosine-5'-triphosphate hydrolysis and tubulin polymerization. Mol. Cell Biochem. 47:97–113.

Carlier, M.F., D. Didry, and D. Pantaloni (1987a) Microtubule elongation and guanosine 5'-triphosphate hydrolysis. Biochemistry 26:4428–4437.

Carlier, M.F., T. Hill, and Y.D. Chen (1984) Interference of GTP hydrolysis in the mechanism of microtubule assembly. Proc. Natl. Acad. Sci. USA 81:771–775.

Carlier, M.F., R. Melki, D. Pantaloni, T.L. Hill, and Y. Chen (1987b) Synchronous oscillations in microtubule polymerization. Proc. Natl. Acad. Sci. USA 84:5257–5261.

Carlier, M.F., and D. Pantaloni (1978) Kinetic analysis of cooperativity in tubulin polymerization in the presence of guanosine di- or triphosphate nucleotides. Biochemistry 17:1908–1915.

Caspar, D.L.D. (1963) Assembly and stability of the tobacco mosaic virus particle. Adv. Protein Chem. 18:37–121.

Cavalier-Smith, T. (1974) Basal body and flagellar development during the vegetative cell cycle and the sexual cycle of Chlamydomonas reinhardtii. J. Cell Sci. 16:529–556.

Cerff, R., J. Hundrieser, and R. Friedrich (1986) Subunit B of chloroplast glyceraldehyde-3-phosphate dehydrogenase is related to β-tubulin. Mol. Gen. Genet. 204:44–51.

Chalfie, M., and J.N. Thomson (1982) Structural and functional diversity in the neuronal microtubules of Caenorhabditis elegans. J. Cell Biol. 93:15–23.

Chambers, E.L. (1939) The movement of the egg nucleus in relation to the sperm aster in the echinoderm egg. J. Exp. Biol. 16:409–429.

Chang, X.-J. (1987) Flagellar Tektins: Location in the Axoneme and Homology to Subunits of Intermediate Filaments. Ph.D. Thesis, Rockefeller University, New York.

Chang, X.-J., and G. Piperno (1987) Cross-reactivity of antibodies specific for flagellar tektin and intermediate filament subunits. J. Cell Biol. 104:1563–1568.

Chen, Y., and T.L. Hill (1985) Monte Carlo study of the GTP cap in a five-start helix model of a microtubule. Proc. Natl. Acad. Sci. USA 82:1131–1135.

Cleveland, D.W. (1987) The multitubulin hypothesis revisited: What have we learned? J. Cell Biol. 104:381–383.

Cleveland, D.W., S.-Y. Hwo, and M.W. Kirschner (1977a) Purification of tau, a microtubule-associated protein that induces assembly of microtubules from purified tubulin. J. Mol. Biol. 116:207–225.

Cleveland, D.W., S.-Y. Hwo, and M.W. Kirschner (1977b) Physical and chemical properties of purified tau factor and the role of tau in microtubule assembly. J. Mol. Biol. 116:227–247.

Cleveland, D.W., and K.F. Sullivan (1985) Molecular biology and genetics of tubulin. Annu. Rev. Biochem. 54:331–365.

Collot, M., D. Louvard, and S.J. Singer (1984) Lysosomes are associated with microtubules and not with intermediate filaments in cultured fibroblasts. Proc. Natl. Acad. Sci. USA 81:788–792.

Conde, J., and G.R. Fink (1976) A mutant of Saccharomyces cerevisiae defective for nuclear fusion. Proc. Natl. Acad. Sci. USA 73:3651–3655.

Correia, J.J., M.K. Welch, and R.C. Williams (1987) Evidence for the spontaneous formation of disulfide crosslinked aggregates of tubulin during nondenaturing electrophoresis. Arch. Biochem. Biophys. 255:244–253.

Correia, J.J., and R.C. Williams (1983) Mechanisms of assembly and disassembly of microtubules. Annu. Rev. Biophys. Bioeng. 12:211–235.

Coss, R.A. (1974) Mitosis in Chlamydomonas reinhardtii: Basal bodies and mitotic apparatus. J. Cell Biol. 63:325–329.

Crepeau, R.H., B. McEwen, and S.J. Edelstein (1978) Differences in alpha and beta polypeptide chains of tubulin resolved by electron microscopy with image reconstruction. Proc. Natl. Acad. Sci. USA 75:5006–5010.

Cumming, R., R.D. Burgoyne, and N.A. Lytton (1984a) Immunocytochemical demonstration of α-tubulin modification during axonal maturation in the cerebellar cortex. J. Cell Biol. 98:347–351.

Cumming, R., R.D. Burgoyne, and N.A. Lytton (1984b) Immunofluorescence distribution of α-tubulin, β-tubulin and microtubule-associated protein 2 during in vitro maturation of cerebellar neurones. Neuroscience 12:775–782.

Deanin, G.G., and M.W. Gordon (1976) The distribution of tyrosyltubulin ligase in brain and other tissues. Biochem. Biophys. Res. Commun. 71:676–683.

Deanin, G.G., S.F. Preston, R.K. Hanson, and M.W. Gordon (1980) On the mechanism of turnover of the carboxy-terminal tyrosine of the α-chain of tubulin. Eur. J. Biochem. 109:207–216.

Deanin, G.G., W.C. Thompson, and M.W. Gordon (1977) Tyrosyltubulin ligase activity in brain, skeletal muscle, and liver of the developing chick. Dev. Biol. 57:230–233.

Debec, A., A. Szollosi, and D. Szollosi (1982) A *Drosophila melanogaster* cell line lacking centrioles. Biol. Cell 44:133–138.

DeBrabander, M., and J. DeMey (1985) Microtubules and Microtubule Inhibitors. Amsterdam: Elsevier.

DeBrabander, M., G. Geuens, R. Nuydens, R. Willebrords, and J. DeMey (1981) Taxol induces the assembly of free microtubules in living cells and blocks the organizing capacity of centrosomes and kinetochores. Proc. Natl. Acad. Sci. USA 78:5608–5612.

Dedman, J.R., B.R. Brinkley, and A.R. Means (1979) Regulation of microfilaments and microtubules by calcium and cyclic AMP. In P. Greengard and G.A. Robison (eds): Advances in Cyclic Nucleotide Research, Vol. 11. New York: Raven Press, pp. 131–174.

Delgado, M.A., and J. Conde (1984) Benomyl prevents nuclear fusion in *Saccharomyces cerevisiae*. Mol. Gen. Genet. 193:188–189.

DeMey, J., M. Moeremans, G. Geuens, R. Nuydens, H. Van Belle, and M. DeBrabander (1980) Immunocytochemical evidence for the association of calmodulin with microtubules of the mitotic apparatus. In M. DeBrabander and J. DeMey (eds): Microtubules and Microtubule Inhibitors. Amsterdam: Elsevier/North Holland Biomedical, pp. 227–241.

Detrich, H.W., and R.C. Williams (1978) Reversible dissociation of the α-β dimer of tubulin from bovine brain. Biochemistry 17:3900–3907.

Dever, T.E., M.J. Glynias, and W.C. Merrick (1987) GTP-binding domain: Three consensus sequence elements with distinct spacing. Proc. Natl. Acad. Sci. USA 84:1814–1818.

Dietz, R. (1972) Die Assembly-Hypothese der Chromosomenbewegung und die Veranderung der Spindellange wahrend der Anaphase I in Spermatocyten von *Pales ferruginea*. Chromosoma 38:11–76.

Diggins, M.A., and W.F. Dove (1987) Distribution of acetylated α-tubulin in *Physarum polycephalum*. J. Cell Biol. 104:303–309.

DiNardo, S., K. Voelkel, and R. Sternglanz (1984) DNA topoisomerase II mutant of *Saccharomyces cerevisiae*: Topoisomerase II is required for segregation of daughter molecules at the termination of DNA replication. Proc. Natl. Acad. Sci. USA 81:2616–2620.

Doenecke, D., and D. Gallwitz (1982) Acetylation of histones in nucleosomes. Mol. Cell Biochem. 44:113–128.

Dustin, P. (1984) Microtubules. New York: Springer-Verlag, p. 482.

Dutcher, S.K. (1986) The genetic properties of linkage group XIX. In R.B. Wickner, A. Hinneabusch, A.M. Lambowitz, and A. Hollaender, I.C. Gunsalus (eds): Extrachromosomal Elements in Lower Eukaryotes. New York: Plenum Publishing Corp., pp. 303–325.

Dutcher, S.K. (1988) Nuclear fusion-defective phenocopies in *Chlamydomonas reinhardtii*: Mating type functions for meiosis can act through the cytoplasm. Proc. Natl. Acad. Sci. USA 85:3946–3950.

Dutcher, S.K., and W. Gibbons (1988) Isolation and characterization of dominant tunicamycin resistance mutations in *Chlamydomonas reinhardtii*. J. Phycol. 24:230–236.

Dutcher, S.K., W. Gibbons, and W.B. Inwood (1988) A genetic analysis of suppressors of the *PF10* Mutation in *Chlamydomonas reinhardtii*. Genetics, (in press).

Dutcher, S.K., and L.H. Hartwell (1983) Genes that act before conjugation to prepare the *Saccharomyces cerevisiae* nucleus for caryogamy. Cell 33:203–210.

Ebersold, W.T. (1967) *Chlamydomonas reinhardtii*. Heterozygous diploid strains. Science 157:446–449.

Eckert, B.S., S.J. Koons, A.W. Schantz, and C.R. Zobel (1980) Association of creatine phosphokinase with the cytoskeleton of cultured mammalian cells. J. Cell Biol. 86:1–5.

Edde, B., B. DeNechaud, P. Denoulet, and F. Gros (1987) Control of isotubulin expression during neuronal differentiation of mouse neuroblastoma and teratocarcinoma lines. Dev. Biol. 123:549–558.

Edson, K.J., R.W. Linck, and P. Letourneau (1987) Evidence for the presence of tektin-like proteins in the chick nervous system. J. Cell Biol. 105:316a.

Eichenlaub-Ritter, U., and A. Ruthmann (1982) Evidence for three "classes" of microtubules in the interpolar space of the mitotic micronucleus of a ciliate and the participation of the nuclear envelope in conferring stability to microtubules. Chromosoma 85:687–702.

Eipper, B.A. (1974) Properties of rat brain tubulin. J. Biol. Chem. 249:1407–1416.

Engelborghs, Y., L.C.M. DeMaeyer, and N. Overbergh (1977) A kinetic analysis of the assembly of microtubules in vitro. FEBS Lett. 80:81–85.

Engelborghs, Y., and J. Eccleston (1982) Fluorescence stopped-flow study of the binding of S6-GTP to tubulin. FEBS Lett. 141:78–81.

Engelborghs, Y., and A. Van Houtte (1981) Temperature jump relaxation study of microtubule elongation in the presence of GTP/GDP mixtures. Biophys. Chem. 14:195–202.

Erickson, H.P. (1974) Microtubule surface lattice and subunit structure and observations on reassembly. J. Cell Biol. 60:153–167.

Erickson, H.P., and W.A. Voter (1976) Polycation-induced assembly of purified tubulin. Proc. Natl. Acad. Sci. USA 73:2813–2817.

Euteneuer, U., and J.R. McIntosh (1981a) Structural polarity of kinetochore microtubules in PtK1 cells. J. Cell Biol. 89:338–345.

Euteneuer, U., and J.R. McIntosh (1981b) Polarity of some motility-related microtubules. Proc. Natl. Acad. Sci. USA 78:372–376.

Evans, L., T.J. Mitchison, and M.W. Kirschner (1985) Influence of the centrosome on the structure of nucleated microtubules. J. Cell Biol. 100:1185–1191.

Fellous, A., R. Ohayon, J.C. Mazie, F. Rosa, R.F. Lalueña, and V. Prasad (1986) Tau micro-heterogeneity: An immunological approach with monoclonal antibodies. Ann. N.Y. Acad. Sci. 466:240–256.

Ferrone, F.A., J. Hofrichter, and W.A. Eaton (1985) Kinetics of sickle hemoglobin polymerization. II. A double nucleation mechanism. J. Mol. Biol. 183:611–631.

Field, D.J., R.A. Collins, and J.C. Lee (1984) Heterogeneity of vertebrate brain tubulins. Proc. Natl. Acad. Sci. USA 81:4041–4045.

Fink, G.R., and J. Conde (1976) Studies on *kar1*, a gene required for nuclear fusion in yeast. In B.R. Brinkley and K.R. Porter (eds): International Cell Biology 1976–1977. New York: Rockefeller University Press, pp. 414–419.

Fisher, D.Z., N. Chaudhary, and G. Blobel (1986) cDNA sequencing of nuclear lamins A and C reveals primary and secondary structural homology to intermediate filament proteins. Proc. Natl. Acad. Sci. USA 83:6450–6454.

Forrest, G.L., and R.R. Klevecz (1978) Tyrosyltubulin ligase and colchicine binding activity in synchronized Chinese hamster cells. J. Cell Biol. 78:441–450.

Fox, L.A., and W.S. Sale (1987) Direction of force generated by the inner row of dynein arms on flagellar microtubules. J. Cell Biol. 105:1781–1787.

Fraser, R.D.B., T.P. MacRae, and G.E. Rogers (1972) Keratins: Their Composition, Structure and Biosynthesis. Springfield, IL: Charles C. Thomas.

Frigon, R.P., and S.N. Timasheff (1975) Magnesium-induced self-association of calf brain tubulin. II. Thermodynamics. Biochemistry 14:4567–4573.

Füchtbauer, A., M. Herrmann, E.-M. Mandelkow, and B. Jockusch (1985) Disruption of microtubules in living cells and in cell models by high affinity antibodies to β-tubulin. EMBO J. 4:2807–2814.

Fuller, M.T., J.H. Caulton, J.A. Hutchens, T.C. Kaufman, and E.C. Raff (1987) Genetic analysis of microtubule structure: A β-tubulin mutation causes the formation of aberrant microtubules in vivo and in vitro. J. Cell Biol. 104:385–394.

Fulton, C. (1971) Centrioles. In J. Reinert and H. Ursprung (eds): Origin and Continuity of Cell Organelles. New York: Springer-Verlag, pp. 170–221.

Fulton, C., and P.A. Simpson (1976) Selective synthesis and utilization of flagellar tubulin. In R. Goldman, T. Pollard, and J. Rosenbaum (eds): Cell Motility. Cold Spring Harbor, NY: Cold Spring Harbor Laboratory, pp. 987–1005.

Gard, D.L., and M.W. Kirschner (1985) A polymer-dependent increase in phosphorylation of β-tubulin accompanies differentiation of a mouse neuroblastoma cell line. J. Cell Biol. 100:764–774.

Gaskin, F., C.R. Cantor, and M.L. Shelanski (1974) Turbidimetric studies of the in vitro assembly and disassembly of porcine neurotubules. J. Mol. Biol. 89:737–758.

Geahlen, R.L., and B.E. Haley (1977) Interactions of a photoaffinity analog of GTP with the proteins of microtubules. Proc. Natl. Acad. Sci. USA 74:4375–4377.

Geisler, N., and K. Weber (1980) Purification of smooth-muscle desmin and a protein-chemical comparison of desmins from chicken gizzard and hog stomach. Eur. J. Biochem. 111:425–433.

Geuens, G., G.G. Gunderson, R. Nuydens, F. Cornelissen, J.C. Bulinski, and M. DeBrabander (1986) Ultrastructural colocalization of tyrosinated and detyrosinated α-tubulin in interphase and mitotic cells. J. Cell Biol. 103:1883–1893.

Gibbons, I.R. (1961) Structural asymmetry in cilia and flagella. Nature 190:1128–1129.

Gibbons, I.R. (1965) Chemical dissection of cilia. Arch. Biol. (Liege) 76:317–352.

Gibbons, I.R. (1975) The molecular basis of flagellar motility in sea urchin spermatozoa. In S. Inoué and R.E. Stephens (eds): Molecules and Cell Movement. New York: Raven Press, pp. 207–232.

Gibbons, I.R. (1981) Cilia and flagella of eukaryotes. J. Cell Biol. 91:107s–124s.

Gibbons, I.R. (1987) New jobs for dynein ATPases. Nature 330:600.

Gibbons, I.R., and A.V. Grimstone (1960) On flagellar structure in certain flagellates. J. Biophys. Biochem. Cytol. 7:697–716.

Glansdorff, P., and I. Prigogine (1971) Thermodynamic Theory of Structure, Stability and Fluctuations. New York: Wiley Interscience.

Goldenring, J.R., B. Gonzalez, J.S. McGuire, and R.J. DeLorenzo (1983) Purification and characterization of a calmodulin-dependent kinase from rat brain cytosol able to phosphorylate tubulin and microtubule-associated proteins. J. Biol. Chem. 258:12632–12640.

Goodenough, U.W., and R.L. Weiss (1978) Interrelationships between microtubules, a striated fiber, and the gametic mating structures of *Chlamydomonas reinhardtii*. J. Cell Biol. 76:430–438.

Gorbsky, G.J., P.J. Sammak, and G.G. Borisy (1987) Chromosomes move poleward in anaphase along stationary microtubules that coordinately disassemble. J. Cell Biol. 104:9–18.

Gottlieb, R.A., and D.B. Murphy (1985) Analysis of the microtubule-binding domain of MAP 2. J. Cell Biol. 101:1782–1789.

Gould, R.R. (1975) The basal bodies of *Chlamydomonas reinhardtii*. Formation from probasal bodies, isolation and partial characterization. J. Cell Biol. 65:65–74.

Gozes, I., and K.J. Sweadner (1981) Multiple tubulin forms are expressed by a single neurone. Nature 294:477–480.

Grant, J.R., K.L. Darrow, and W.C. Thompson (1986) The acetylation state of cytoplasmic microtubules defines their stability to drug-induced polymerization. J. Cell Biol. 103:132a.

Grant, J.R., K.L. Darrow, and W.C. Thompson (1987) A microinjection study of the dynamics of acetylation and deacetylation of microtubules in PtK2 cells. J. Cell Biol. 105:119a.

Gray, E.G., L.E. Westrum, R.D. Burgoyne, and J. Barron (1982) Synaptic organization and neuron microtubule distribution. Cell Tissue Res. 226:579–588.

Green, L.L., and W.F. Dove (1984) Tubulin proteins and RNA during the myxamoeba–flagellate transformation of *Physarum polycephalum*. Mol. Cell Biol. 4:1706–1711.

Greer, K. (1988) α-Tubulin Acetyltransferase in *Chlamydomonas* Flagella. Ph.D. Thesis, Yale University.

Greer, K., H. Maruta, S.W. L'Hernault, and J.L. Rosenbaum (1985) α-Tubulin acetylase activity in isolated *Chlamydomonas* flagella. J. Cell Biol. 101:2081–2084.

Grimm, M., F. Breitling, and M. Little (1987) Location of the epitope for the α-tubulin monoclonal antibody TU-01. Biochim. Biophys. Acta 914:83–88.

Grimstone, A.V., and A. Klug (1966) Observations on the substructure of flagellar fibers. J. Cell Sci. 1:351–362.

Gundersen, G.G., and J.C. Bulinski (1986a) Microtubule arrays in differentiated cells contain elevated levels of a post-translationally modified form of tubulin. Eur. J. Cell Biol. 42:288–294.

Gundersen, G.G., and J.C. Bulinski (1986b) Distribution of tyrosinated and nontyrosinated α-tubulin during mitosis. J. Cell Biol. 102:1118–1126.

Gundersen, G.G., and J.C. Bulinski (1987) A function for tubulin tyrosination. Nature 238:676.

Gundersen, G.G., M.H. Kalnoski, and J.C. Bulinski (1984) Distinct populations of microtubules: Tyrosinated and nontyrosinated α-tubulin are distributed differently in vivo. Cell 38:779–789.

Gundersen, G.G., S. Khawaja, and J.C. Bulinski (1987) Post polymerization detyrosination of α-tubulin: A mechanism for subcellular differentiation of microtubules. J. Cell Biol. 105:251–264.

Haimo, L.T., B.R. Telzer, and J.L. Rosenbaum (1979) Dynein binds to and crossbridges cytoplasmic microtubules. Proc. Natl. Acad. Sci. USA 76:5759–5763.

Hallak, M.E., J.A. Rodriguez, H.S. Barra, and R. Caputto (1977) Release of tyrosine from tyrosinated tubulin: Some common factors that affect this process and the assembly of tubulin. FEBS Lett. 73:147–152.

Hamel, E., J.K. Batra, A.B. Huang, and C.M. Lin (1986) Effects of pH on tubulin–nucleotide interactions. Arch. Biochem. Biophys. 245:316–330.

Hameroff, S.R., and R.C. Watt (1982) Information processing in microtubules. J. Theor. Biol. 98:549–561.

Hansson, G.K., G.A. Starkebaum, E.P. Benditt, and S.M. Schwartz (1984) Fc-mediated binding of IgG to vimentin-type intermediate filaments in vascular endothelial cells. Proc. Natl. Acad. Sci. USA 81:3103–3107.

Hargreaves, A.J., F. Wandosell, and J. Avila (1987) Phosphorylation of tubulin enhances its interaction with membranes. Nature 323:827–828.

Hartwell, L.H., R.K. Mortimer, J. Culotti, and M. Culotti (1974) Genetic control of the cell division cycle in yeast. V. Genetic analysis of cdc mutations. Genetics 74:267–286.

Hartwell, L.H., and D. Smith (1985) Altered fidelity of chromosome metabolism in cell cycle mutants of *Saccharomyces cerevisiae*. Genetics 110:381–395.

Hays, T.S., and E.D. Salmon (1983) A non-microtubular component of sea urchin isolated spindles. J. Cell Biol. 97:44a.

Heidemann, S.R., and U. Euteneuer (1982) Microtubule polarity determination based on conditions for tubulin assembly. Methods Cell Biol. 207–216.

Heidemann, S.R., and J.R. McIntosh (1980) Visualisation of the structural polarity of microtubules. Nature 286:517–519.

Herzog, W., and K. Weber (1977) In vitro assembly of pure tubulin into microtubules in the absence of microtubule-associated proteins and glycerol. Proc. Natl. Acad. Sci. USA 74:1860–1864.

Herzog, W., and K. Weber (1978) Fractionation of brain microtubule-associated proteins. Isolation of two different proteins which stimulate tubulin polymerisation in vitro. Eur. J. Biochem. 92:1–8.

Hesse, J., M. Thierauf, and H. Ponstingl (1987) Tubulin sequence region B155–174 is involved in binding exchangeable GTP. J. Biol. Chem. 262:15472–15475.

Heuser, J.E., and M.W. Kirschner (1980) Filament organization revealed in platinum replicas of freeze-dried cytoskeletons. J. Cell Biol. 86:212–234.

Hill, T., and Y.D. Chen (1984) Phase changes at the end of a microtubule with a GTP cap. Proc. Natl. Acad. Sci. USA 81:5772–5776.

Hill, T.L., and M.F. Carlier (1983) Steady-state theory of the interference of GTP hydrolysis in the mechanism of microtubule assembly. Proc. Natl. Acad. Sci. USA 80:7234–7238.

Hinkley, R.E. (1976) Microtubule-macrotubule transformations induced by volatile anaesthetics. J. Ultrastruct. Res. 57:237–250.

Hirokawa, N. (1982) Cross-linker system between neurofilaments, microtubules, and membranous organelles in frog axons revealed by the quick-freeze, deep-etching method. J. Cell Biol. 94:129–142.

Hirokawa, N., and S. Hisanaga (1987) Buttonin, a unique button-shaped microtubule-associated protein (75 kD) that decorates spindle microtubule surface hexagonally. J. Cell Biol. 104:1553–1561.

Holm, C.A., T. Goto, J.C. Wang, and D. Botstein (1985) DNA topoisomerase II is required at the time of mitosis in yeast. Cell 41:553–563.

Horio, T., and H. Hotani (1986) Visualization of the dynamic instability of individual microtubules by dark-field microscopy. Nature 321:605–607.

Howard, W.D., and S.N. Timasheff (1986) GDP state of tubulin: Stabilization of double rings. Biochemistry 25:8292–8300.

Huang, B., Z. Ramanis, S.K. Dutcher, and D.J.L. Luck (1983) Uniflagellar mutants of Chlamydomonas: evidence for the role of basal bodies in the transmission of positional information. Cell 29:745–753.

Huitorel, P., and D. Pantaloni (1985) Bundling of microtubules by glyceraldehyde-3-phosphate dehydrogenase and its modulation by ATP. Eur. J. Biochem. 150:265–269.

Huxley, H.E. (1963) Electron microscope studies on the structure of native and synthetic protein filaments from striated muscle. J. Mol. Biol. 7:281–308.

Ikeda, Y., and M. Steiner (1979) Phosphorylation and protein kinase activity of platelet tubulin. J. Biol. Chem. 254:66–74.

Inoué, S., and H. Sato (1967) Cell motility by labile association of molecules. J. Gen. Physiol. 50:259–277.

Inwood, W.B. (1985) A reversion analysis of an abnormal swimming mutation in Chlamydomonas reinhardtt. Ph.D. Thesis, University of Colorado, Boulder.

Jacobs, M., P.M. Bennett, and M.J. Dickens (1975) An outer component of microtubules. Nature 257:707–709.

Jacobs, M., and P. Huitorel (1979) Tubulin-associated nucleoside diphosphokinase. Eur. J. Biochem. 99:613–622.

Jacobs, M., H. Smith, and E.W. Taylor (1974) Tubulin: Nucleotide binding and enzyme activity. J. Mol. Biol. 89:455–468.

James, S.W., L.P.W. Ranum, C. Siflow, and P.A. Lefebvre (1988) Mutants resistant to anti-microtubule herbicides map to a locus on the uni linkage group in Chlamydomonas reinhardtii. Genetics 118:141–147.

Jameson, L., and M. Caplow (1981) Modification of microtubule steady-state dynamics by phosphorylation of the microtubule-associated proteins. Proc. Natl. Acad. Sci. USA 78:3413–3417.

Jameson, L., T. Frey, B.F. Dalldorf, and M. Caplow (1980) Inhibition of microtubule assembly by phosphorylation of microtubule-associated proteins. Biochemistry 19:2472–2479.

Job, D., C.T. Rauch, E.H. Fischer, and R.L. Margolis (1983) Regulation of microtubule cold stability by calmodulin-dependent and independent phosphorylation. Proc. Natl. Acad. Sci. USA 80:3894–3898.

Johnson, K.A. (1985) Pathway of the microtubule-dynein ATPase and the structure of dynein: A comparison with actomyosin. Annu. Rev. Biophys. Biophys. Chem. 14:161–188.

Johnson, K.A., and G.G. Borisy (1977) Kinetic analysis of microtubule self-assembly in vitro. J. Mol. Biol. 117:1–31.

Johnson, U.G., and K.R. Porter (1968) Fine structure of cell division in Chlamydomonas reinhardtii. Basal bodies and microtubules. J. Cell Biol. 38:403–425.

Jung, M.K., P.W. Dunne, I.H. Suen, and B.R. Oakley (1987) Sequence alterations in β-tubulin mutations of Aspergillus nidulans. J. Cell Biol. 105:277a.

Khawaja, S., G.G. Gundersen, and J.C. Bulinski (1988) Enhanced stability of microtubules enriched in detyrosinated tubulin is not a direct function of detyrosination level. J. Cell Biol. 106:141–149.

Keller, T., and L.I. Rebhun (1982) *Strongylocentrotus purpuratus* spindle tubulin. I. Characterization of polymerization and depolymerization in vitro. J. Cell Biol. 93:788–796.

Kemphues, K.F., T.C. Kaufman, R.A. Raff, and E.C. Raff (1982) The testis-specific β-tubulin subunit in *Drosophila melanogaster* has multiple functions in spermatogenesis. Cell 31:655–670.

Kemphues, K.J., R.A. Raff, T.C. Kaufman, and E.C. Raff (1979) Mutation in a structural gene for a β-tubulin specific to testis in *Drosophila melanogaster*. 76:3991–3995.

Kenney, D.M., L.D. Weiss, and R.W. Linck (1988) A novel microtubule protein in the marginal band of human blood platelets. J. Biol. Chem. 263:1432–1438.

Kilmartin, J.V., and A.E.M. Adams (1984) Structural rearrangements of tubulin and actin during the cell cycle of the yeast *Saccharomyces*. J. Cell Biol. 98:922–933.

Kilmartin, J.V., and J. Fogg (1982) Partial purification of yeast spindle pole bodies. In P. Cappuccinelli and N.R. Morris (eds): Microtubules in Microorganisms. New York: Marcel Dekker, Inc., pp. 157–170.

Kilmartin, J.V., B. Wright, and C. Milstein (1982) Rat monoclonal antitubulin antibodies derived by using a new non-secreting rat cell line. J. Cell Biol. 93:576–582.

Kim, H., L.I. Binder, and J.L. Rosenbaum (1979) The periodic association of MAP 2 with brain microtubules in vitro. J. Cell Biol. 80:266–276.

Kirchner, K., and E. Mandelkow (1985) Tubulin domains responsible for assembly of dimers and protofilaments. EMBO J. 4:2397–2402.

Kirschner, M.W. (1978) Microtubule assembly and nucleation. Int. Rev. Cytol. 54:1–71.

Kirschner, M.W. (1980) Implications of treadmilling for the stability and polarity of actin and tubulin polymers in vivo. J. Cell Biol. 86:330–334.

Kirschner, M.W., L.S. Honig, and R.C. Williams (1975) Quantitative electron microscopy of microtubule assembly in vitro. J. Mol. Biol. 99:263–276.

Kirschner, M.W., and T.J. Mitchison (1986) Beyond self-assembly: From microtubules to morphogensis. Cell 45:329–342.

Kirschner, M.W., R.C. Williams, M. Weingarten, and J. Gerhart (1974) Microtubules from mammalian brain: Some properties of their depolymerization products and a proposed mechanism of assembly and disassembly. Proc. Natl. Acad. Sci. USA 71:1159–1163.

Kobayashi, T., and G. Matsumoto (1982) Cytoplasmic tubulin from squid nerve fully retains C-terminal tyrosine. J. Biochem. 92:647–652.

Krauhs, E., M. Little, T. Kempf, R. Hofer-Warbinek, W. Ade, and H. Ponstingl (1981) Complete amino acid sequence of β-tubulin from porcine brain. Proc. Natl. Acad. Sci. USA 78:4156–4160.

Kravit, N.G., C.S. Regula, and R.D. Berlin (1984) A reevaluation of the structure of purified tubulin in solution: Evidence for the prevalence of oligomers over dimers at room temperature. J. Cell Biol. 99:188–198.

Kristofferson, D., T.L. Karr, and D.L. Purich (1980) Dynamics of linear protein polymer disassembly. J. Biol. Chem. 255:8567–8572.

Kristofferson, D., T.J. Mitchison, and M.W. Kirschner (1986) Direct observation of steady-state microtubule dynamics. J. Cell Biol. 102:1007–1019.

Kristofferson, D., and D.L. Purich (1981) Time scale of microtubule length redistribution. Arch. Biochem. Biophys. 211:222–226.

Kubai, D. (1975) The evolution of the mitotic spindle. Int. Rev. Cytol. 43:167–227.

Kuchka, M.R., and J.W. Jarvik (1987) Short flagellar mutants of *Chlamydomonas reinhardtii*. Genetics 115:685–691.

Kumar, N., and M. Flavin (1981) Preferential action of a brain detyrosylating carboxypeptidase on polymerized tubulin. J. Biol. Chem. 256:7678–7686.

Kuriyama, R., and T. Miki-Noumura (1975) Light-microscopic observations of individual microtubules reconstituted from brain tubulin. J. Cell Sci. 19:607–620.

Laemmli, U.K. (1970) Cleavage of structural proteins during the assembly of the head of bacteriophage T4. Nature (London) 227:680–685.

Laing, P. (1986) Luminescent visualization of antigens on blots. J. Immunol. Methods 92:161–165.

Lange, G., Mandelkow, E.-M., Jagla, A. and Mandelkow, E. (1988). Tubulin oligomers and microtubule oscillations. Eur. J. Biochem., (in press).

Langford, G.M. (1980) Arrangement of subunits in microtubules with 14 protofilaments. J. Cell Biol. 87:521–526.

Lazarides, E. (1980) Intermediate filaments as mechanical integrators of cellular space. Nature 283:249–256.

Ledbetter, M.C., and K.R. Porter (1964) The morphology of microtubules. Science 144:872–874.

LeDizet, M., and G. Piperno (1986) Cytoplasmic microtubules containing acetylated α-tubulin in *Chlamydomonas reinhardtii*: Spatial arrangement and properties. J. Cell Biol. 103:13–22.

LeDizet, M., and G. Piperno (1987) Identification of an acetylation site of *Chlamydomonas* α-tubulin. Proc. Natl. Acad. Sci. USA 84:5720–5724.

Lee, G., N. Cowan, and M.W. Kirschner (1988) The primary structure and heterogeneity of tau protein from mouse brain. Science 239:285–288.

Lee, J.C., D. Corfman, R.P. Frigon, and S.N. Timasheff (1978) Conformation study of calf brain tubulin. Arch. Biochem. Biophys. 185:4–14.

Lee, J.C., and S.N. Timasheff (1975) The reconstitution of microtubules from purified calf brain tubulin. Biochemistry 14:5183–5187.

Lee, Y.C., and J. Wolff (1982) Two opposing effects of calmodulin on microtubule assembly depend on the presence of microtubule-associated proteins. J. Cell Biol. 257:6306–6310.

Lee, Y.C., and J. Wolff (1984) Calmodulin binds to both microtubule-associated protein 2 and tau proteins. J. Biol. Chem. 259:1226–1230.

Lefebvre, P.A., S.A. Nordstrom, J.E. Moulder, and J.L. Rosenbaum (1978) Flagellar elongation and shortening in *Chlamydomonas*. IV. Effect of flagellar detachment, regeneration and resorption on the induction of flagellar protein synthesis. J. Cell Biol. 78:8–27.

Lefebvre, P.A., and J.L. Rosenbaum (1986) Regulation of the synthesis and assembly of ciliary and flagellar proteins during regeneration. Annu. Rev. Cell Biol. 2:517–546.

Lewin, R.A. (1954) Mutants of *Chlamydomonas moewussii* with impaired motility. J. Gen. Microbiol. 11:358–363.

Lewis, S.A., W. Gu, and N.J. Cowan (1987) Free intermingling of mammalian β-tubulin isotypes among functionally distinct microtubules. Cell 49:539–548.

L'Hernault, S.W., and J.L. Rosenbaum (1982) Reversible post-translational modification of α-tubulin is coupled to flagellar assembly and disassembly in *Chlamydomonas*. J. Cell Biol. 95:342a.

L'Hernault, S.W., and J.L. Rosenbaum (1983) *Chlamydomonas* α-tubulin is posttranslationally modified in the flagella during flagellar assembly. J. Cell Biol. 97:258–263.

L'Hernault, SW., and J.L. Rosenbaum (1985a) *Chlamydomonas* α-tubulin is posttranslationally modified by acetylation on the ε-amino group of a lysine. Biochemistry 24:463–478.

L'Hernault, S.W., and J.L. Rosenbaum (1985b) Reversal of the posttranslational modification of *Chlamydomonas* flagellar α-tubulin occurs during flagellar resorption. J. Cell Biol. 100:457–462.

Lichtenberg, B., Mandelkow, E.-M., Hagestedt, T. and Mandelkow, E. (1988). Structure and elasticity of microtubule-associated protein tau. Nature 334, 359–362.

Lin, C.M., and E. Hamel (1987) Interrelationships of tubulin-GDP and tubulin-GTP in microtubule assembly. Biochemistry 26:7173–7182.

Linck, R.W. (1973) Chemical and structural differences between cilia and flagella from the lamellibranch mollusc *Aequipectens irradians*. J. Cell Sci. 12:951–981.

Linck, R.W. (1976) Flagellar doublet microtubules: Fractionation of minor components and α-tubulin from specific regions of the α-tubule. J. Cell Sci. 20:405–439.

Linck, R.W. (1982) The structure of microtubules. Ann. N.Y. Acad. Sci. 383:98- 121.

Linck, R.W., D.F. Albertini, D.M. Kenney, and G.L. Langevin (1982) Tektin filaments: Chemically unique filaments of sperm flagellar microtubules. Cell Motil. Suppl. 1:127–132.

Linck, R.W., and L.A. Amos (1974) The hands of helical lattices in flagellar doublet microtubules. J. Cell Sci. 14:551–559.

Linck, R.W., L.A. Amos, and W.B. Amos (1985) Localization of tektin filaments in microtubules of sea urchin sperm flagella by immunoelectron microscopy. J. Cell Biol. 100:126–135.

Linck, R.W., M.J. Goggin, and J.M. Norrander (1986) Cell and molecular biology of tektins from ciliary and flagellar microtubules. J. Cell Biol. 103:280a.

Linck, R.W., M.J. Goggin, J.M. Norrander, and W. Steffen (1987) Characterization of antibodies as probes for structural and biochemical studies from ciliary and flagellar microtubules. J. Cell Sci. 88:453–466.

Linck, R.W., and G.L. Langevin (1981) Reassembly of flagellar B(αβ) tubulin into singlet microtubules: Consequences for cytoplasmic microtubule structure and assembly. J. Cell Biol. 89:323–337.

Linck, R.W., and G.L. Langevin (1982) Structure and chemical composition of insoluble filamentous components of sperm flagellar microtubules. J. Cell Sci. 58:1–22.

Linck, R.W., G.D. Olson, and G.L. Langevin (1981) Arrangement of tubulin subunits and microtubule-associated proteins in the central-pair microtubule apparatus of squid sperm flagella. J. Cell Biol. 89:309–322.

Linck, R.W., and R.E. Stephens (1987) Biochemical characterization of tektins from sperm flagellar doublet microtubules. J. Cell Biol. 104:1069–1075.

Lindsley, D., and G. Zimm (1985) The genome of *Drosophila melanogaster*. Dros. Inf. Ser. 62:100–103.

Linse, K., and E.-M. Mandelkow (1988) The GTP binding peptide of tubulin. J. Biol. Chem (in press).

Littauer, U.Z., D. Giveon, M. Thierauf, I. Ginzburg, and H. Ponstingl (1986) Common and distinct tubulin binding sites for microtubule-associated proteins. Proc. Natl. Acad. Sci. USA 83:7162–7166.

Little, M., and R.F. Ludueña (1985) Structural differences between brain β1- and β2-tubulins: Implications for microtubule assembly and colchicine binding. EMBO J 4:51–56.

Little, M., and R.F. Ludueña (1987) Location of two cysteines in brain β1-tubulin that can be cross-linked after removal of exchangeable GTP. Biochim. Biophys. Acta 912:28–33.

Longo, F.J., and E. Anderson (1968) The fine structure of pronuclear development and fusion in the sea urchin *Arbacia punctulata*. J. Cell Biol. 39:339–368.

Longo, F.J., and E. Anderson (1969) Cytological aspects of fertilization in the lamellibranch, *Mytilus edulis*. II. Development of the pronucleus and the association of the maternally and paternally derived chromosomes. J. Exp. Zool. 172:95–103.

Lopata, M.A., and D.W. Cleveland (1987) In vivo microtubules are copolymers of available β-tubulin isotypes: Localization of each of six vertebrate β-tubulin isotypes using polyclonal antibodies elicited by synthetic peptide antigens. J. Cell Biol. 105:1707–1720.

Ludueña, R.F., E.M. Shooter, and L. Wilson (1977) Structure of the tubulin dimer. J. Biol. Chem. 252:7006–7014.

Magendantz, M., and F. Solomon (1985) Analyzing the components of microtubules: Antibodies against chartins, associated proteins from cultured cells. Proc. Natl. Acad. Sci. USA 82:6581–6585.

Mandelkow, E. (1986) X-ray diffraction of cytoskeletal fibers. Methods Enzymol. 134:633–657.

Mandelkow, E., E.-M. Mandelkow, and J. Bordas (1983a) Structure of tubulin rings studied by X-ray scattering using synchrotron radiation. J. Mol. Biol. 167:179–196.

Mandelkow, E., E.-M. Mandelkow, and J. Bordas (1983b) Synchrotron radiation as a tool for studying microtubule self-assembly. TIBS 8:374–377.

Mandelkow, E., R. Schultheiss, and E.-M. Mandelkow (1984) Assembly and three-dimensional reconstruction of tubulin hoops. J. Mol. Biol. 177:507–529.

Mandelkow, E., J. Thomas, and C. Cohen (1977) Microtubule structure at low resolution by X-ray diffraction. Proc. Natl. Acad. Sci. USA 74:3370–3374.

Mandelkow, E.-M., A. Harmsen, E. Mandelkow, and J. Bordas (1980) X-ray kinetic studies of microtubule assembly using synchrotron radiation. Nature 287:595–599.

Mandelkow, E.-M., M. Herrmann, and U. Rühl (1985a) Tubulin domains probed by subunit-specific antibodies and limited proteolysis. J. Mol. Biol. 185:311–327.

Mandelkow, E.-M., K. Kirschner, and E. Mandelkow (1985b) Domains, antigenicity, and substructure of tubulin. In M. DeBrabander and J. DeMey (eds): Microtubules and Microtubule Inhibitors 1985. Amsterdam: Elsevier, pp. 31–47.

Mandelkow, E.-M., G. Lange, A. Jagla, U. Spann, and E. Mandelkow (1988) Non-equilibrium states and autonomous oscillations in microtubule assembly observed by time-resolved X-ray scattering. EMBO J. (in press).

Mandelkow, E.-M., and E. Mandelkow (1979) Junctions between microtubule walls. J. Mol. Biol. 129:135–148.

Mandelkow, E.-M., and E. Mandelkow (1985) Unstained microtubules studied by cryo-electron microscopy: Substructure, supertwist, and disassembly. J. Mol. Biol. 181:123–135.

Mandelkow, E.-M., E. Mandelkow, P.N.T. Unwin, and C. Cohen (1977) Tubulin hoops. Nature 265:655–657.

Mandelkow, E.-M., R. Schultheiss, R. Rapp, M. Müller, and E. Mandelkow (1986) On the surface lattice of microtubules: Helix starts, protofilament number, seam, and handedness. J. Cell Biol. 102:1067–1073.

Margolis, R.L., D. Job, M. Fabion, and C.T. Rauch (1986a): Sliding of STOP proteins on microtubules: a model system for diffusion-dependent microtubule motility. Ann. N.Y. Acad. Sci. 466:306–321.

Margolis, R.L., C.T. Rauch, and D. Job (1986b) Purification and assay of a 145-kDa protein (STOP$_{145}$) with microtubule-stabilizing and motility behavior. Proc. Natl. Acad. Sci. USA 83:639–643.

Margolis, R.L., and L. Wilson (1978) Opposite end assembly and disassembly of microtubules at steady state in vitro. Cell 13:1–8.

Margolis, R.L., and L. Wilson (1979) Regulation of the microtubule steady state in vitro by ATP. Cell 18:673–679.

Margolis, R.L., and L. Wilson (1981) Microtubule treadmills—possible molecular machinery. Nature 293:705–711.

Markus, M., and B. Hess (1984) Transitions between oscillatory modes in a glycolytic model system. Proc. Natl. Acad. Sci. USA 81:4394–4398.

Martensen, T. (1982) Preparation of brain tyrosinotubulin carboxy-peptidase. Methods Cell Biol. 24:265–269.

Maruta, H., K. Greer, and J.L. Rosenbaum (1986) The acetylation of α-tubulin and its relationship to the assembly and disassembly of microtubules. J. Cell Biol. 103:571–579.

Master, C. (1984) Interactions between glycolytic enzymes and components of the cytomatrix. J. Cell Biol. 99:222s–225s.

Matagne, R.F., R. Deltour, and L. Ledoux (1979) Somatic fusion between cell wall mutants of *Chlamydomonas reinhardtii*. Nature 278:344–346.

Matile, P., H. Moor, and C.F. Robinow (1969) Yeast cytology. In A.H. Rose and J.S. Harrison (eds): The Yeasts. New York: Academic Press, pp. 219–302.

Matus, A., and B. Riederer (1986) Microtubule-associated proteins in the developing brain. Ann. N.Y. Acad. Sci. 466:167–179.

May, G.S., J. Gambino, J.A. Weatherbee, and N.R. Morris (1985) Identification and functional analysis of β-tubulin genes by site-specific integrative transformation in *Aspergillus nidulans*. J. Cell Biol. 101:712–719.

McEwen, B., and S. Edelstein (1980) Evidence for a mixed lattice in microtubules reassembled in vitro. J. Mol. Biol. 139:123–145.

McIntosh, J.R. (1973) The axostyle of *Saccinobaculus*. II. Motion of the microtubule bundle and a structural comparison of straight and bent axostyles. J. Cell Biol. 56:324–339.

McIntosh, J.R. (1979) Cell division. In K. Roberts and J.S. Hyams (eds): Microtubules. New York: Academic Press, pp. 381–441.

McIntosh, J.R. (1983) The centrosome as an organizer of the cytoskeleton. Mod. Cell Biol. 2:115–142.

McIntosh, J.R., and K.R. Porter (1967) Microtubules in the spermatids of the domestic fowl. J. Cell Biol. 35:153–173.

McKeithan, T.W., P.A. Lefebvre, C.D. Silflow, and J.L. Rosenbaum (1983) Multiple forms of tubulin in *Polytomella* and *Chlamydomonas*: Evidence for a precursor of α-tubulin. J. Cell Biol. 96:1056–1063.

McKeithan, T.W., and J.L. Rosenbaum (1981) Multiple forms of tubulin in the cytoskeletal and flagellar microtubules of *Polytomella*. J. Cell Biol. 91:352–360.

McKeithan, T.W., and J.L. Rosenbaum (1984) The biochemistry of microtubules: A review. Cell Muscle Motil. 5:255–288.

McKeon, F.D., M.W. Kirschner, and D. Caput (1986) Homologies in both primary and secondary structure between nuclear envelope and intermediate filament proteins. Nature 319:463–468.

McVittie, A. (1974) Genetic studies on flagellum mutants of *Chlamydomonas reinhardtii*. Genet. Res. 19:157–164.

Meeks-Wagner, D., J.S. Wood, B. Garvick, and L.H. Hartwell (1986) Isolation of two genes that affect mitotic chromosome transmission in *Saccharomyces cerevisiae*. Cell 44:53–63.

Meza, I., B. Huang, and J. Bryan (1972) Chemical heterogeneity of protofilaments forming the outer doublets from sea urchin flagella. Exp. Cell Res. 74:535–540.

Miki-Noumura, T., and R. Kamiya (1979) Conformational change in the outer doublet microtubules from sea urchin sperm flagella. J. Cell Biol. 81:355–360.

Mitchison, T.J., and M.W. Kirschner (1984a) Microtubule assembly nucleated by isolated centrosomes. Nature 312:232–237.

Mitchison, T.J., and M.W. Kirschner (1984b) Dynamic instability of microtubule growth. Nature 312:237–242.

Monteiro, M.J., and R.A. Cox (1987) Primary structure of an α-tubulin gene of *Physarum polycephalum*. J. Mol. Biol. 193:427–438.

Mooseker, M.S., and L.G. Tilney (1973) Isolation and reactivation of the axostyle. Evidence for a dynein-like ATPase in the axostyle. J. Cell Biol. 56:12–26.

Moran, D.T., F.J. Varela, and J.C. Rowley III (1977) Evidence for active role of cilia in sensory transduction. Proc. Natl. Acad. Sci. USA 74:793–797.

Morejohn, L.C., and D.E. Fosket (1984) Inhibition of plant microtubule polymerization in vitro by the phosphoric amide herbicide amiprophos-methyl. Science 224:874–876.

Murofushi, H. (1980) Purification and characterization of tubulin-tyrosine ligase from porcine brain. J. Biochem. 87:979–984.

Murphy, D.B., and K.T. Wallis (1986) Erythrocyte microtubule assembly in vitro: Tubulin oligomers limit the rate of microtubule self-assembly. J. Biol. Chem. 261:2319–2324.

Murray, J.M. (1983) Three-dimensional structure of a membrane-microtubule complex. J. Cell Biol. 98:283–295.

Murthy, A.S., and M. Flavin (1983) Microtubule assembly using the microtubule associated protein MAP-2 prepared in defined states of phosphorylation with protein kinase and phosphatase. Eur. J. Biochem. 137:37–46.

Nath, J., and M. Flavin (1978) A structural difference between cytoplasmic and membrane-bound tubulin of brain. FEBS Lett. 95:335–338.

Nath, J., and M. Flavin (1979) Tubulin tyrosylation in vivo and changes accompanying differentiation of cultured neuroblastoma-glioma hybrid cells. J. Biol. Chem. 254:11505–11510.

Nath, J., M. Flavin, and E. Schiffman (1981) Stimulation of tubulin tyrosylation in rabbit leukocytes evoked by the chemoattractant formyl-methionyl-leucyl-phenylalanine. J. Cell Biol. 91:232–239.

Nath, J.P., and R.H. Himes (1986) Localization of the exchangeable nucleotide binding domain in β-tubulin. Biochem. Biophys. Res. Commun. 135:1135–1143.

Oakley, B.R., and N.R. Morris (1981) A β-tubulin mutation in *Aspergillus nidulans* that blocks microtubule function without blocking assembly. Cell 24:837–845.

O'Brien, E.T., W.A. Voter, and H.P. Erickson (1987) GTP hydrolysis during microtubule assembly. Cell 24:837–845.

Olmsted, J.B. (1986) Microtubule-associated proteins. Annu. Rev. Cell Biol. 2:421–457.

Olmsted, J.B., G.B. Witman, K. Carlson, and J.L. Rosenbaum (1971) Comparison of the microtubule protein of neuroblastoma cells, brain and *Chlamydomonas* flagella. Proc. Natl. Acad. Sci. USA 68:2273–2277.

Oosawa, F. (1970) Size distribution of protein polymers. J. Theor. Biol. 27:69–86.

Oosawa, F., and S. Asakura (1975) Thermodynamics of the Polymerisation of Protein. London: Academic Press.

Pantaloni, D., M.F. Carlier, C. Simon, and G. Batelier (1981) Mechanism of tubulin assembly: Role of rings in the nucleation process and of associated proteins in the stabilization of microtubules. Biochemistry 20:4709–4716.

Paschal, B.M., S.M. King, A.G. Moss, C.A. Collins, R.B. Vallee, and G.B. Witman (1987) Isolated flagellar outer arm dynein translocates brain microtubules in vitro. Nature 330:672–674.

Paschal, B.M., and R.B. Vallee (1987) Retrograde transport by the microtubule-associated protein MAP 1C. Nature 330:181–183.

Pasquale, S.M., and U.W. Goodenough (1987) Cyclic AMP functions as a primary sexual signal in gametes of *Chlamydomonas reinhardtii*. J. Cell Biol. 105:2279–2292.

Perotti, M.E. (1975) Ultrastructural aspects of fertilization in *Drosophila*. In B.A. Afzelius (ed): The Functional Anatomy of the Spermatozoan. New York: Pergamon Press, pp. 57–68.

Peterson, J.B., and H. Ris (1976) Electron microscopic study of the spindle and chromosome movement in the yeast *Saccharomyces cerevisiae*. J. Cell Sci. 22:219–242.

Peterson, S.P., and M.W. Berns (1980) The centriolar complex. Int. Rev. Cytol. 64:81–106.

Pickett-Heaps, J.D. (1971) The autonomy of the centriole: Fact or fallacy? Cytobios 3:205–214.

Pierson, G.B., P.R. Burton, and R.H. Himes (1978) Alteration in numbers of protofilaments in microtubules assembled in vitro. J. Cell Biol. 76:223–228.

Piperno, G., and M.T. Fuller (1985) Monoclonal antibodies specific for an acetylated form of α-tubulin recognize the antigen in cilia and flagella from a variety of organisms. J. Cell Biol. 101:2085–2094.

Piperno, G., B. Huang, and D.J.L. Luck (1977) Two-dimensional analysis of flagellar proteins from wild-type and paralyzed mutants of *Chlamydomonas reinhardtii*. Proc. Natl. Acad. Sci. USA 74:1600–1604.

Piperno, G., M. LeDizet, and X.-J. Chang (1987) Microtubules containing acetylated α-tubulin in mammalian cells in culture. J. Cell Biol. 104:289–302.

Pirollet, F., D. Job, R.L. Margolis, and J.R. Garel (1987) An oscillatory mode for microtubule assembly. EMBO J. 6:3247–3252.

Pollard, T.D. (1986) Rate constants for the reaction of ATP- and ADP-actin with the ends of actin filaments. J. Cell Biol. 103:2747–2754.

Pollard, T.D., and J.A. Cooper (1986) Actin and actin-binding proteins. A critical evaluation of mechanisms and functions. Annu. Rev. Biochem. 55:987–1035.

Ponstingl, H., E. Krauhs, M. Little, and T. Kempf (1981) Complete amino acid sequence of α-tubulin from porcine brain. Proc. Natl. Acad. Sci. USA 78:2757–2761.

Poole, C.A., M.H. Flint, and B.W. Beaumont (1985) Analysis of the morphology and function of primary cilia in connective tissue: A cellular cybernetic probe? Cell Motil. 5:175–193.

Porter, M.E., and K.A. Johnson (1983) Characterization of the ATP-sensitive binding of *Tetrahymena* 30S dynein to bovine brain microtubules. J. Biol. Chem. 258:6575–6581.

Pratt, L.F., S. Okamura, and D.W. Cleveland (1987) A divergent testis-specific α-tubulin isotype that does not contain a coded C-terminal tyrosine. Mol. Cell Biol. 7:552–555.

Preston, S.F., G.G. Deanin, R.K. Hanson, and M.W. Gordon (1979) The phylogenetic distribution of tubulin tyrosine ligase. J. Mol. Evol. 13:233–244.

Pringle, J.R., and L.H. Hartwell (1981) The *Saccharomyces cerevisiae* cell cycle. In J.N. Strathern, E.W. Jones, and J.R. Broach (eds): The Molecular Biology of the Yeast *Saccharomyces*, vol. I. Cold Spring Harbor, New York: Cold Spring Harbor Laboratory, pp. 97–142.

Pruss, R.M., R. Mirsley, M.C. Raff, R. Thorpe, A.J. Dowding, and B.H. Anderton (1981) All classes of intermediate filaments share a common antigenic determinant defined by a monoclonal antibody. Cell 27:419–428.

Purich, D.L., and D. Kristofferson (1984) Microtubule assembly: A review of progress, principles, and perspectives. Adv. Protein Chem. 36:133–212.

Purich, D.L., and R.M. Scaife (1985) Microtubule cytoskeletal proteins as targets for covalent interconverting enzymes. Curr. Top. Cell. Regul. 27:107–116.

Quinlan, R.A., D.L. Schiller, M. Hatzfeld, T. Achtstätter, R. Moll, J.L. Jorcano, T.M. Magin, and W.W. Franke (1985) Pattern of expression and organization of cytokeratin intermediate filaments. Ann. N.Y. Acad. Sci. 455:282–306.

Raff, E.C. (1979) The control of microtubule assembly in vivo. Int. Rev. Cytol. 59:1–96.

Raff, E.C., M.T. Fuller, T.C. Kaufman, K.J. Kemphues, J.E. Rudolph, and R.A. Raff (1982) Regulation of tubulin gene expression during embryogenesis in Drosophila melanogaster. Cell 28:33–40.

Ramanis, Z., and D.J.L. Luck (1986) Loci affecting flagellar assembly and function map to an unusual linkage group in Chlamydomonas reinhardtii. Proc. Natl. Acad. Sci. USA 83:423–426.

Rappaport, L., J.F. Leterrier, A. Virian, and J. Nunez (1976) Phosphorylation of microtubule-associated proteins. Eur. J. Biochem. 62:539–549.

Raybin, D., and M. Flavin (1977a) Enzyme which specifically adds tyrosine to the α-chain of tubulin. Biochemistry 16:2189–2194.

Raybin, D., and M. Flavin (1977b) Modification of tubulin by tyrosylation in cells and extracts and its effects on assembly in vitro. J. Cell Biol. 73:492–504.

Reardon, J.T., C.A. Liljestrand-Golden, R.L. Dusenbery, and P.D. Smith (1987) Molecular analysis of diepoxybutane-induced mutation at the rosy locus of Drosophila melanogaster. Genetics 115:323–331.

Rebhun, L.I., and R.E. Palazzo (1986) Isolated spindle matrix. J. Cell Biol. 103:411a.

Rebhun, L.I., and R.E. Palazzo (1987) A 55 kD protein in sea urchin and clam spindles. J. Cell Biol. 105:283a.

Renaud, F.L., A.J. Rowe, and I.R. Gibbons (1968) Some properties of the protein forming the outer fibers of cilia. J. Cell Biol. 36:79–90.

Renaud, F.L., and H. Swift (1964) The development of basal bodies and flagella in Allomyces arbusculus. J. Cell Biol. 23:339–354.

Rieder, C.L. (1982) The formation, structure, and composition of the mammalian kinetochore and kinetochore fiber. Int. Rev. Cytol. 79:1–58.

Ringo, D.L. (1967) Flagellar motion and fine structure of the flagellar apparatus in Chlamydomonas reinhardtii. J. Cell Biol. 33:543–571.

Robinow, C.F., and J. Marek (1966) A fiber apparatus in the nucleus of the yeast cell. J. Cell Biol. 29:129–151.

Rodriguez, J., H.S. Barra, C.A. Arce, M.E. Hallak, and R. Caputto (1975) The reciprocal exclusion by L-dopa (L-3,4-dihydroxyphenylalanine) and L-tyrosine of their incorporation as single units into a soluble rat brain protein. Biochem. J. 149:115–121.

Rodriguez, J.A., and G.G. Borisy (1978) Modification of the C-terminus of brain tubulin during development. Biochem. Biophys. Res. Commun. 83:579–586.

Rodriguez, J.A., and G.G. Borisy (1979) Tyrosination state of free tubulin subunits and tubulin disassembled from microtubules of rat brain. Biochem. Biophys. Res. Commun. 89:893–899.

Rose, M.D., and G.R. Fink (1987) KAR1, a gene required for function of both intranuclear and extranuclear microtubules in yeast. Cell 48:1047–1060.

Rosenbaum, J.L., L.I. Binder, S. Granett, W.L. Dentler, W. Snell, R. Sloboda, and L. Haimo (1975) Directionality and rate of assembly of chick brain tubulin onto pieces of neurotubules, flagellar axonemes, and basal bodies. Ann. N.Y. Acad. Sci. 253:147–177.

Rosenbaum, J.L., J.E. Moulder, and D.L. Ringo (1969) Flagella elongation and shortening in Chlamydomonas. The use of cycloheximide and colchicine to study the synthesis and assembly of flagellar proteins. J. Cell Biol. 41:600–619.

Rothwell, S.W., W.A. Grasser, H.N. Baker, and D.B. Murphy (1987) The relative contributions of polymer annealing and subunit exchange to microtubule dynamics in vitro. J. Cell Biol. 105:863–874.

Russel, D.G., and K. Gull (1984) Flagellar regeneration of the trypanosome Crithidia fasciculata involves post-translational modification of cytoplasmic α-tubulin. Mol. Cell Biol. 4:1182–1185.

Russel, D.G., D. Miller, and K. Gull (1984) Tubulin heterogeneity in the trypanosome Crithidia fasciculata. Mol. Cell Biol. 4:779–790.

Sackett, D.L., and J. Wolff (1986) Proteolysis of tubulin and the substructure of the tubulin dimer. J. Biol. Chem. 261:9070–9076.

Sale, W.S., J.C. Besharse, and G. Piperno (1988) Distribution of acetylated α-tubulin in retina and in in vitro-assembled microtubules. Cell Motility and the Cytoskeleton 9:243–253.

Sale, W.S., and P. Satir (1977) Direction of active sliding of microtubules in Tetrahymena cilia. Proc. Natl. Acad. Sci. USA 74:2045–2049.

Salisbury, J.L., A. Baron, B. Surek, and M. Melkonian (1984) Striated flagellar roots: Isolation and partial characterization of a calcium-modulated contractile organelle. J. Cell Biol. 99:962–970.

Salisbury, J.L., and G.L. Floyd (1978) Calcium-induced contraction of the rhizoplast of a quadriflagellate green alga. Science 202:975–977.

Salmon, E.D., R.J. Leslie, and W.M. Saxton (1984) Spindle microtubule dynamics in sea urchin embryos. Analysis using fluorescein-labeled tubulin and measurements of fluorescence redistribution after laser photobleaching. J. Cell Biol. 99:2165–2174.

Sammak, P.J., G.J. Gorbsky, and G.G. Borisy (1987) Microtubule dynamics in vivo: A test of mechanisms of turnover. J. Cell Biol. 104:395–405.

Sasse, R., M.C.P. Glyn, C.R. Birkett, and K. Gull (1987) Acetylated α-tubulin in *Physarum:* Immunological characterization of the isotype and its usage in particular microtubule organelles. J. Cell Biol. 104:41–49.

Satir, P. (1968) Studies on cilia. III. Further studies on the cilium tip and a "sliding filament" model of ciliary motility. J. Cell Biol. 39:77–94.

Saxton, W.M., and J.R. Mcintosh (1987) Interzone microtubule behavior in late anaphase and telophase spindles. J. Cell Biol. 105:875–886.

Schatz, P.J., L. Pillus, P. Grisafi, F. Solomon, and D. Botstein (1986) Two functional α-tubulin genes of the yeast *Saccharomyces cerevisiae* encode divergent proteins. Mol. Cell Biol. 6:3711–3721.

Scheele, R.B., L.G. Bergen, and G.G. Borisy (1982) Control of the structural fidelity of microtubules by initiation sites. J. Mol. Biol. 154:485–500.

Scheele, R.B., and G.G. Borisy (1979) In vitro assembly of microtubules. In K. Roberts and J.S. Hyams (eds): Microtubules. New York: Academic Press, pp. 217–254.

Scherson, T., T.E. Kreis, J. Schlessinger, U.Z. Littauer, G.G. Borisy, and B. Geiger (1984) Dynamic interactions of fluorescently labeled microtubule-associated proteins in living cells. J. Cell Biol. 99:425–434.

Schild, D., H.N. Ananthaswamy, and R.K. Mortimer (1981) An endomitotic effect of a cell cycle mutation of *Saccharomyces cerevisiae.* Genetics 97:551–562.

Schilstra, M.J., S.R. Martin, and P.M. Bayley (1987) On the relationship between nucleotide hydrolysis and microtubule assembly: Studies with a GTP-regenerating system. Biochem. Biophys. Res. Commun. 147:588–595.

Schneider, A., T. Sherwin, R. Sasse, D.G. Russell, K. Gull, and T. Seebeck (1987) Subpellicular and flagellar microtubules of *Trypanosoma brucei brucei* contain the same α-tubulin isoforms. J. Cell Biol. 104:431–438.

Schultheiss, R., and E. Mandelkow (1983) Three-dimensional reconstruction of tubulin sheets and re-investigation of microtubule surface lattice. J. Mol. Biol. 170:471–496.

Schulz, G.E., and R.H. Schirmer (1979) Principles of Protein Structure. Heidelberg: Springer Verlag.

Schulze, E., D. Asai, J.C. Bulinski, and M.W. Kirschner (1987) Posttranslationalmodification and microtubule stability. J. Cell Biol. 105:2167–2177.

Schulze, E., and M.W. Kirschner (1986) Microtubule dynamics in interphase cells. J. Cell Biol. 102:1020–1031.

Serrano, L., J. Avila, and R.B. Maccioni (1984a) Controlled proteolysis of tubulin by subtilisin: Localization of the site for MAP 2 interaction. Biochemistry 23:4675–4681.

Serrano, L., J. DeLaTorre, R.B. Maccioni, and J. Avila (1984b) Involvement of the carboxyl-terminal domain of tubulin in the regulation of its assembly. Proc. Natl. Acad. Sci. USA 81:5989–5993.

Serrano, L., L. Diaz-Nido, F. Wandosell, and J. Avila (1987) Tubulin phosphorylation by casein kinase II is similar to that found in vivo. J. Cell Biol. 105:1731–1740.

Shea, D.K., and C.J. Walsh (1987) mRNAs for α- and β-tubulin and flagellar calmodulin are among those coordinately regulated when *Naegleria gruberi* amebae differentiate into flagellates. J. Cell Biol. 105:1303–1309.

Sherwin, T., A. Schneider, R. Sasse, T. Seebeck, and K. Gull (1987) Distinct localization and cell cycle dependence of COOH terminally tyrosylated α- tubulin in microtubules of *Trypanosoma brucei brucei.* J. Cell Biol. 104:439–446.

Silflow, C.D., R.L. Chisholm, T.W. Conner, and L.P.W. Ranum (1985) The two α-tubulin genes of *Chlamydomonas reinhardtii* code for slightly different proteins. Mol. Cell Biol. 5:2389–2398.

Silflow, C.D., D.G. Oppenheimer, S.D. Kopczak, S.E. Ploense, S.R. Ludwig, N. Haas, and D.P. Snustad (1987) Plant tubulin genes: Structure and differential expression during development. Dev. Genet. 8:435–460.

Slautterback, D.B. (1963) Cytoplasmic microtubules. I. Hydra. J. Cell Biol. 18:367–388.

Sloboda, R.D., WL. Dentler, and J.L. Rosenbaum (1976) Microtubule-associated proteins and the stimulation of tubulin assembly in vitro. Biochemistry 15:4497–4505.

Sloboda, R.D., S.A. Rudolph, J.L. Rosenbaum, and P. Greengard (1975) Cyclic AMP-dependent endogenous phosphorylation of a microtubule-associated protein. Proc. Natl. Acad. Sci. USA 72:177–181.

Soifer, D. (1986) Dynamic aspects of microtubule biology. Ann. N.Y. Acad. Sci. 466:1–978.

Solomon, F. (1986) What might MAPs do? Results of an in situ analysis. Ann. N.Y. Acad. Sci. 466:322–327.

Soltys, B.J., and G.G. Borisy (1985) Polymerization of tubulin in vivo: Direct evidence for assembly onto microtubule ends and from centrosomes. J. Cell Biol. 100:1682–1689.

Sorokin, S.P. (1968) Reconstructions of centriole formation and ciliogenesis in mammalian lungs. J. Cell Sci. 3:207–230.

Spann, U., W. Renner, E.-M. Mandelkow, J. Bordas, and E. Mandelkow (1987) Tubulin oligomers and microtubule assembly studied by time-resolved X-ray scattering: Separation of prenucleation and nucleation events. Biochemistry 26:1123–1132.

Steffen, W., and R.W. Linck (1987) Tektin-like polypeptides in cultured mammalian cells. J. Cell Biol. 105:123a.

Steffen, W., and R.W. Linck (1988) Evidence for tektins in centrioles and axonemal microtubules. Proc. Natl. Acad. Sci. USA 85:2643–2647.

Steinert, P.M., A.C. Steven, and D.R. Roop (1985) The molecular biology of intermediate filaments. Cell 42:411–419.

Stephens, R.E. (1970) Thermal fractionation of outer doublet microtubules into A and B-subfiber components: α- and β-tubulin. J. Mol. Biol. 47:353–363.

Stephens, R.E. (1977) Differential protein synthesis and utilization during cilia formation in sea urchin embryos. Dev. Biol. 61:311–329.

Stephens, R.E. (1981) Chemical differences distinguish ciliary membrane and axonemal tubulins. Biochemistry 20:4716–4723.

Stephens, R.E. (1986) Membrane tubulin. Biol. Cell 57:95–110.

Stephens, R.E., S. Oleszko-Szuts, and R.W. Linck (1987) Retention of ciliary superstructure after removal of tubulin. J. Cell Biol. 105:95a.

Stommel, E.W. (1984) Calcium regenerative potentials in Mytilus edulis gill abfrontal ciliated epithelial cells. J. Comp. Physiol. 155A: 445–456.

Stommel, E.W., R.E. Stephens, and D.L. Alkon (1980) Motile statocyst cilia transmit rather than directly transduce mechanical stimuli. J. Cell Biol. 87:652–662.

Summers, K.E., and I.R. Gibbons (1971) Adenosine triphosphate-induced sliding of tubules in trypsin-treated flagella of sea urchin sperm. Proc. Natl. Acad. Sci. USA 68:3092–3096.

Suprenant, K.A., E. Hays, E. LeCluyse, and W.L. Dentler (1985) Multiple forms of tubulin in the cilia and cytoplasm of Tetrahymena thermophila. Proc. Natl. Acad. Sci. USA 82:6908–6912.

Tamm, L.K., R.H. Crepeau, and S.J. Edelstein (1979) Three-dimensional reconstruction of tubulin in zinc-induced sheets. J. Mol. Biol. 130:473–492.

Telzer, B.R., and L.T. Haimo (1981) Decoration of spindle microtubules with dynein: Evidence for uniform polarity. J. Cell Biol. 89:373–378.

Terry, B.K., and D.L. Purich (1982) Nucleotide-dependent enzymes associated with microtubule systems. Adv. Enzymol. 53:113–161.

Theurkauf, W.E., H. Baum, J. Bo, and P.C. Wensink (1986) Tissue-specific and constitutive α-tubulin genes of Drosophila melanogaster code for structurally distinct proteins. Proc. Natl. Acad. Sci. USA 83:8477–8481.

Thomas, J.H., and D. Botstein (1986) A gene required for the separation of chromosomes on the spindle apparatus in yeast. Cell 44:65–76.

Thompson, W.C. (1977) Post-translational addition of tyrosine to α-tubulin in vivo in intact brain and in myogenic cells in culture. FEBS Lett. 80:9–13.

Thompson, W.C. (1982) The cyclic tyrosination/detyrosination of α-tubulin. Meth. Cell Biol. 24:235–255.

Thompson, W.C. (1986) Segregation of an antigenically unique subset of α-tubulin subunits into cold-stable microtubules during in vitro microtubule assembly. Ann. N.Y. Acad. Sci. 466:660–663.

Thompson, W.C., D.J. Asai, and D.H. Carney (1984) Heterogeneity among microtubules of the cytoplasmic microtubule complex detected by a monoclonal antibody to α-tubulin. J. Cell Biol. 98:1017–1025.

Thompson, W.C., G.G. Deanin, and M.W. Gordon (1979) Intact microtubules are required for rapid turnover of carboxyl-terminal tyrosine of α-tubulin in cultured cells. Proc. Natl. Acad. Sci. USA 76:1318–1322.

Tilney, L.G. (1971) How microtubule patterns are generated. The relative importance of nucleation and bridging of microtubules in the formation of the axoneme of Raphidiophrys. J. Cell Biol. 51:837–854.

Tilney, L.G., J. Bryan, D.J. Bush, F. Fujiwara, M.S. Mooseker, D.R. Murphy, and D.H. Snyder (1973) Microtubules: Evidence for 13 protofilaments. J. Cell Biol. 59:267–275.

Timasheff, S.N., and L.M. Grisham (1980) In vitro assembly of cytoplasmic microtubules. Ann. Rev. Biochem. 49:565–591.

Triemer, R.E., and R.M. Brown (1974) Cell division in Chlamydomonas moewusii. J. Phycol. 10:419–433.

Tsukita, S., S. Tsukita, J. Usukura, and H. Ishikawa (1983) ATP-dependent structural changes of the outer dynein arm in Tetrahymena cilia: A freeze-etch replica study. J. Cell Biol. 96:1480–1485.

Tucker, J.B. (1979) Spatial organization of microtubules. In K. Roberts and J. S. Hyams (eds): Microtubules. New York: Academic Press, pp. 315–357.

Tuffanelli, D.L., F. McKeon, D.M. Kleinsmith, T.K. Burham, and M. Kirschner (1983) Anticentromere and anticentriole antibodies in the scleroderma spectrum. Arch Dermatol 119:560–566.

Vale, R.D. (1987) Intracellular transport using microtubule-based motors. Annu. Rev. Cell Biol. 3:347–378.

Vale, R.D., T.S. Reese, and M.P. Sheetz (1985a) Identification of a novel force-generating protein, kinesin, involved in microtubule-based motility. Cell 42:39–50.

Vale, R.D., B.J. Schnapp, T.S. Reese, and M.P. Sheetz (1985b) Organelle, bead, and microtubule translocations promoted by soluble factors from squid giant axon. Cell 40:559–569.

Valenzuela, P., M. Quiroga, J. Zaldivar, W.J. Rutter, M.W. Kirschner, and D.W. Cleveland (1981) Nucleotide and corresponding amino acid sequences encoded by α and β tubulin mRNAs. Nature 289:650–655.

Vallano, M.L., and R.J. DeLorenzo (1986) Separation of microtubule-associated cAMP and calmodulin-dependent kinases that phosphorylate MAP 2. Ann. N.Y. Acad. Sci. 466:453–456.

Vallee, R.B. (1980) Structure and phosphorylation of microtubule-associated protein 2 (MAP 2). Proc. Natl. Acad. Sci. USA 77:3206–3210.

Vallee, R.B. (1986) The contractile apparatus and the cytoskeleton. Methods Enzymol. 134.

Vallee, R.B., and G.S. Bloom (1984) High molecular weight microtubule associated proteins. Mod. Cell Biol. 3:21–75.

Vallee, R.B., G.S. Bloom, and F.C. Luca (1986) Differential structure and distribution of the high molecular weight microtubule-associated proteins, MAP 1 and MAP 2. Ann. N.Y. Acad. Sci. 466:134–144.

Vallee, R.B., and G.G. Borisy (1978) The non-tubulin component of microtubule protein oligomers. Effect on self-association and hydrodynamic properties. J. Biol. Chem. 253:2834–2845.

Vallee, R.B., M.J. DiBartolomeis, and W.E. Theurkauf (1981) A protein kinase bound to the projection portion of MAP 2 (microtubule-associated protein 2). J. Cell Biol. 90:568–576.

Villasante, A., D. Wang, P. Dobner, P. Dolph, S.A. Lewis, and N.J. Cowan (1986) Six mouse α-tubulin mRNAs encode five distinct isotypes: Testis-specific expression of two sister genes. Mol. Cell Biol. 6:2409–2419.

Vorobjev, I.A., and Y.S. Chentosov (1982) Centrioles in the cell cycle. J. Cell Biol. 93:938–949.

Voter, W.A., and H.P. Erickson (1979) Tubulin rings: Curved filaments with limited flexibility and two modes of association. J. Supramol. Struct. 10:419–431.

Voter, W.A., and H.P. Erickson (1982) Electron microscopy of MAP 2 (microtubule-associated protein 2). J. Ultrastruct. Res. 80:374–382.

Voter, W.A., and H.P. Erickson (1984) The kinetics of microtubule assembly: Evidence for a two-stage nucleation mechanism. J. Biol. Chem. 259:10430–10438.

Wadsworth, P., and E.D. Salmon (1986) Analysis of the treadmilling model during metaphase of mitosis using fluorescence redistribution after photobleaching. J. Cell Biol. 102:1032–1038.

Wais-Steider, C., N.S. White, D.S. Gilbert, and P.M. Eagles (1987) X-ray diffraction patterns from microtubules and neurofilaments in axoplasm. J. Mol. Biol. 197:205–218.

Wandosell, F., L. Serrano, M.A. Hernandez, and J. Avila (1986) Phosphorylation of tubulin by a calmodulin-dependent protein kinase. J. Biol. Chem. 261:10332–10339.

Warner, F.D. (1970) New observations on flagellar fine structure. The relationship between matrix structure and the microtubule component of the axoneme. J. Cell Biol. 47:159–182.

Warner, F.D. (1976) Cross-bridge mechanisms in ciliary motility. The sliding–bending conversion. In R. Goldman, T. Pollard, and J. Rosenbaum (eds): Cell Motility, Book C. Cold Spring Harbor, New York: Cold Spring Harbor Laboratory, pp. 891–914.

Warner, F.D. (1979) Microtubule sliding and regulated motion. In K. Roberts and J.S. Hyams (eds): Microtubules. New York: Academic Press, pp. 359–380.

Warner, F.D., and P. Satir (1973) The substructure of ciliary microtubules. J. Cell Sci. 12:313–326.

Warner, F.D., and P. Satir (1974) The structural basis of ciliary bend formation. Radial spoke positional changes accompanying microtubule sliding. J. Cell Biol. 63:35–63.

Weber, K., and M. Osborn (1979) Intracellular display of microtubular structures revealed by indirect immunofluorescence microscopy. In K. Roberts and J.S. Hyams (eds): Microtubules. New York: Academic Press, pp. 279–313.

Webster, D.R., G.G. Gundersen, J.C. Bulinski, and G.G. Borisy (1987) Assembly and turnover of detyrosinated tubulin in vivo. J. Cell Biol. 105:265–276.

Wegner, A. (1976) Head-to-tail polymerization of actin. J. Mol. Biol. 108:139–150.

Wehland, J., M. Henkart, R. Klausner, and I.V. Sandoval (1983) Role of microtubules in the distribution of the Golgi apparatus: Effect of taxol and microinjected anti-α-tubulin antibodies. Proc. Natl. Acad. Sci. USA 80:4286–4290.

Wehland, J., H.C. Schoeder, and K. Weber (1984) Amino acid sequence requirements in the epitope recognized by the α-tubulin-specific rat monoclonal antibody YL 1/2. EMBO J. 3:1295–1300.

Wehland, J., H.C. Schroder, and K. Weber (1986) Contribution of microtubules to cellular physiology: Microinjection of well-characterized monoclonal antibodies into cultured cells. Ann. N.Y. Acad. Sci. 466:609–621.

Wehland, J., and K. Weber (1987a) Tubulin-tyrosine ligase has a binding site on β-tubulin: A two-domain structure of the enzyme. J. Cell Biol. 104:1059-1067.

Wehland, J., and K. Weber (1987b) Turnover of the carboxy-terminal tyrosine of α-tubulin and means of reaching elevated levels of detyrosination in living cells. J. Cell Sci. 88:185–203.

Wehland, J., and M.C. Willingham (1983a) A rat monoclonal antibody reacting specifically with the tyrosylated form of α-tubulin. II. Effects on cell movement, organization of microtubules, and intermediate filaments, and arrangement of Golgi elements. J. Cell Biol. 97:1476–1490.

Wehland, J., M.C. Willingham, and I.V. Sandoval (1983b) A rat monoclonal antibody reacting specifically with the tyrosylated form of α-tubulin. I. Biochemical characterization, effects on microtubule polymerization in vitro, and microtubule polymerization and organization in vivo. J. Cell Biol. 97:1467–1475.

Weingarten, M.D., A.H. Lockwood, S.-Y. Hwo, and M.W. Kirschner (1975) A protein factor essential for microtubule assembly. Proc. Natl. Acad. Sci. USA 72:1858–1862.

Weisenberg, R.C. (1980) Role of co-operative interactions, microtubule-associated proteins and guanosine triphosphate in microtubule assembly: A model. J. Mol. Biol. 139:660–677.

Weisenberg, R.C., and W.J. Deery (1976) Role of nucleotide hydrolysis in microtubule assembly. Nature 263:792–793.

Weisenberg, R.C., and A. Rosenfeld (1975) Role of intermediates in microtubule assembly in vivo and in vitro. Ann. N.Y. Acad. Sci. 253:78–89.

Welsh, M.J., J.R. Dedman, B.R. Brinkley, and A.R. Means (1979) Tubulin and calmodulin: Effects of microtubule and microfilament inhibitors on localization in the mitotic apparatus. J. Cell Biol. 81:624–634.

Wheatley, D.N. (1982) The Centriole, a Central Enigma of Cell Biology. New York: Elsevier Biomedical Press.

Witman, G.B. (1975) The site of in vivo assembly of flagellar microtubules. Ann. N.Y. Acad. Sci. 253:178–191.

Witman, G.B., K. Carlson, J. Berliner, and J.L. Rosenbaum (1972a) Chlamydomonas flagella. I. Isolation and electrophoretic analysis of microtubules, matrix, membranes, and mastigonemes. J. Cell Biol. 54:507–539.

Witman, G.B., K. Carlson, and J.L. Rosenbaum (1972b) Chlamydomonas flagella. II. The distribution of tubulins 1 and 2 in the outer doublet microtubules. J. Cell Biol. 54:540–555.

Woodrum, D.T., and R.W. Linck (1980) Structural basis of motility in the microtubule axostyle: Implications for cytoplasmic microtubule structure and function. J. Cell Biol. 87:404–414.

Woody, R.W., G.C.K. Roberts, D.C. Clark, and P.M. Bayley (1983) Proton NMR evidence for flexibility in microtubule-associated proteins and microtubule protein oligomers. FEBS Lett. 141:181–184.

Wright, R.L., B. Chojnacki, and J.W. Jarvik (1983) Abnormal basal body number, location, and orientation in a striated fiber defective mutant of Chlamydomonas reinhardtii. J. Cell Biol. 96:1697–1707.

Wright, R.L., J. Salisbury, and J.W. Jarvik (1985) A nucleus-basal body connector in Chlamydomonas reinhardtii that may function in basal body localization and segregation. J. Cell Biol. 101:1903–1912.

Zeeberg, B., and M. Caplow (1979) Determination of free and bound microtubular protein and guanine nucleotide under equilibrium conditions. Biochemistry 18:3880–3886.

Zeeberg, B., J. Cheek, and M. Caplow (1980) Exchange of tubulin dimer into rings in microtubule assembly-disassembly. Biochemistry 19:5078–5086.

Zimmerman, A.M., and S. Zimmerman (1967) Action of colcemid in sea urchin eggs. J. Cell Biol. 34:483–488.

Zingsheim, H.P., W. Herzog, and K. Weber (1979) Differences in surface morphology of microtubules reconstituted from pure brain tubulin using two different microtubule-associated proteins: The high molecular weight MAP 2 proteins and tau proteins. Eur. J. Cell Biol. 19:175–183.

Zobel, C.R. (1973) Effect of solution composition and proteolysis on the conformation of axonemal components. J. Cell Biol. 59:573–594.

SECTION 2

The Dynein ATPases, Part 1: Cytoplasmic Forms of Dynein

Edited by Melanie M. Pratt

PERSPECTIVE
Cytoplasmic Dynein and Related Adenosine Triphosphatases

Melanie M. Pratt

*Department of Anatomy and Cell Biology, University of Miami School of Medicine,
Miami, Florida 33101*

INTRODUCTION

Ciliary and flagellar axonemes might be described as the fundamental microtubule-based machines, powered by adenosine triphosphate (ATP) and driven by dynein motors. From the time that microtubules were seen as ubiquitous components of cells (Porter, 1966), it was postulated that they might be involved in analagous forms of non-axonemal motility and that microtubule-associated ATPases similar to axonemal dynein might act as force generators. Since 1968, and especially in the last 10 years, evidence has accumulated that supports the existence of non-axonemal dyneins, usually referred to as *cytoplasmic dynein*. The chapters in this section review these data and analyze the information with respect to the function of dynein-like enzymes in several forms of non-axonemal cell motility.

Chromosome movement, vesicle transport, and cell shape changes, now known to be microtubule-based movements, were recognized as critical to normal cell function years before any cytoskeletal components had been identified. Descriptions of chromosome movements and an appreciation of their vital importance in cell replication and heredity appear as early as 1878 (Flemming, 1878; see Mazia et al., 1965). Similarly, intracellular transport of organelles (for review, see Rebhun, 1972; Schliwa, 1984) and cell shape changes, primarily during embryogenesis, were described and analyzed nearly 100 years ago (Davenport, 1895). The impetus to study the mechanochemistry of these forms of motility came not from an esoteric interest in microtubules or dynein, since neither were known at the time, but rather from a basic understanding that these processes were fundamental to normal cell function and growth. Faults in the machinery responsible for chromosome movement may lead to errors in the distribution of genetic material during cell division. Furthermore, an understanding of mitotic machinery might allow us to arrest the uncontrolled division of tumor cells. Vesicle transport in nerve axons is one of the most conspicuous examples of organelle movement, and impaired vesicle movement would have profound effects on nerve growth and regeneration and may explain some forms of distal neuropathy. Cell shape changes are critical to normal development of a variety of embryos, particularly in the formation of muscle cells and the neural tube, so much so that malfunction of the system causing shape changes could engender a variety of developmental abnormalities.

It is now clear that chromosome movement, vesicle transport, and cell shape changes depend on a framework of microtubules (for discussion, see Dustin, 1984). Electron microscopy has revealed intimate associations between chromosomes (Mazia et al., 1965; Zimmerman and Forer, 1981; Inoué, 1981b) or transported organelles (Allen, 1975; for review, see Rebhun, 1972; Grafstein and Forman, 1980; Schliwa, 1984; Miller and Lasek, 1985) and microtubules, and analysis of microtubule distributions implicates intertubule sliding as part of the mechanism of shape change in several cell types (Byers and Porter, 1964; Burnside, 1971; Karfunkel, 1971; Warren, 1974; Warren and Burnside, 1978). In each of these systems, if microtubules are disrupted, movement ceases. In addition, all these motility systems require energy and use ATP as the chemical power source (Adams, 1982; Stearns and Ochs, 1982; Forman, 1982; Forman et al., 1983a; Pratt, 1984; Gilson et al., 1986; Rozdzial and Haimo, 1986a). In their dependence on microtubules and on ATP, then, these systems are analagous to axonemal motility, and a logical extension of this analogy is to postulate the existence of cytoplasmic forms of dynein that serve as a motor.

The authors of each chapter in this section have investigated this hypothesis and either have identified molecules that can be classified as dyneins and that may serve as motors for non-axonemal microtubule-based cell movement or have demonstrated that certain motile processes have the characteristics of dynein-driven systems. This section contains descriptions of three dyneins de-

rived from non-axonemal sources and analyses of two other systems that may well employ dyneins as force generators for vesicle movement and cell elongation. In light of the rapid expansion of information concerning the molecular bases of microtubule translocation, the remainder of this chapter focuses on some of the theoretical considerations common to all investigations of cytoplasmic dynein function as well as the more practical matters surrounding the classification of molecules as dynein ATPases.

CLASSIFICATION AND TERMINOLOGY FOR CYTOPLASMIC FORMS OF DYNEIN

In their descriptive analyses of dynein ATPases and related proteins, the chapters in this section describe characteristics that can be used to classify cytoplasmic microtubule-associated motors as dyneins. It is important to realize, however, that at this time the definition is necessarily broad and is continually evolving. The same is true, although to a lesser degree, of axonemal dynein, for which the definition has evolved over 20 years and continues to change as new forms of the molecule are isolated and characterized using new experimental techniques (Bell et al., 1982).

Axonemal dynein is now recognized as a group of isoenzymes that includes the inner and outer arms of cilia and flagella from a wide range of sources (Gibbons, 1982; Bell et al., 1982). The criteria that distinguish axonemal dynein from other ATPases can be grouped in three categories: enzymatic, physical/structural, and functional. The ciliary and flagellar dyneins from different sources, however, exhibit a range of properties within each category. In 1982, Gibbons formulated a definition that provided basic criteria for identifying dyneins. Enzymatically, these proteins have ATPase activity with "a moderately high degree of specificity for ATP as a substrate and a divalent cation requirement that can be satisfied by either Mg^{2+} or Ca^{2+}." Physically, dyneins have "sedimentation coefficients in the range of 10S–30S [and] . . . one or more very large polypeptide subunits with apparent molecular weights in the range of 300,000–350,000." Functionally, these enzymes "occur in motile intracellular systems based on microtubules, where they play a major role in the transduction of the chemical energy provided by ATP hydrolysis into mechanical work."

In recent years, three other criteria for classifying dyneins have become available. First, new electron microscopic methods have revealed unique structural features of axonemal dynein (Johnson and Wall, 1983; Goodenough and Heuser, 1984; Goodenough et al., 1987). In addition, it has been shown that the dynein heavy chains are susceptible to specific cleavage at the active site in the presence of ATP, vanadate, and ultraviolet light (Lee-Eiford et al., 1986; Gibbons et al., 1987). It appears that this assay may become diagnostic for dynein polypeptides (see Lye, Chapter 9). Finally, the work of Sale and colleagues has demonstrated that axonemal dyneins generate movement in only one direction with respect to intrinsic microtubule polarity, and they have suggested that this criterion may also serve to identify dynein ATPases (Sale and Satir, 1977; Fox and Sale, 1987).

All the molecules identified as dyneins in the following chapters were identified based on comparisons to axonemal dyneins, and they all satisfy criteria in several categories; hence, it seems reasonable to adopt these axonemal dynein criteria for use in identifying new cytoplasmic (non-axonemal) ATPases as dyneins. Considering the differences between axonemal and non-axonemal motility discussed below, cytoplasmic motors can be expected to differ somewhat from axonemal criteria and, as Gibbons (1982) has pointed out, these differences are likely to correspond to differences in function.

At the time that non-axonemal forms of dynein were first reported, their lack of functional and structural identity to axonemal forms posed problems concerning terminology. Most investigators chose to use the term *dynein-like* until some strict bio-

chemical criteria, for example, peptide mapping, proved the protein in question to be identical to an authentic dynein. Given the fundamental similarities that are now apparent between axonemal and non-axonemal forms of dynein, it seems appropriate that all these ATPases be called by the name dynein. Because the term "cytoplasmic" dynein is widely understood to refer to non-axonemal forms of the enzyme (although the axoneme is, of course, formally part of the cytoplasm), we propose to use the modifier for forms of the enzyme that are identified in locations other than the axoneme. The use of other modifiers that delineate source (egg, brain, HeLa, etc.) can be used further to distinguish cytoplasmic dyneins one from another.

MODELS AND THEORETICAL CONSIDERATIONS

Two different motors, dynein and kinesin, serve as models for force production in microtubule-based systems. Although both of these proteins use ATP as a chemical source of energy, they differ substantially in enzymatic, physical, and functional properties (for review, see Schnapp and Reese, 1986; Amos, 1987). Until the identification of kinesin in 1985 (Vale et al., 1985a), dynein-mediated axonemal movement was the sole model for microtubule-based motility, so most investigators had been looking for cytoplasmic forms of dynein. The identification of kinesin was unanticipated and illustrates the importance of having a functional assay that relates to the cellular function being investigated. The properties of the movements dictate certain characteristics of the motor protein, and an investigation into possible functions of a cytoplasmic dynein must begin with an analysis of the motile system being studied. In particular, three properties of axonemal and non-axonemal motility stand out as critical in defining the necessary characteristics of a cytoplasmic motor protein. First, because microtubules have an intrinsic polarity, the criterion of *direction of movement* is important. Second, because different movements

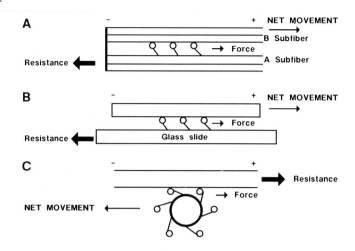

Fig. 7–1. Direction of dynein-generated movement with respect to microtubule polarity. Dynein always generates force toward the plus end of the microtubule with which it has nucleotide dependent interaction. **A:** In an axoneme, where movement toward the microtubule minus ends is resisted by attachments at the base, net tubule movement is toward the plus end. **B:** Dynein attached to glass does not generate enough force to move the coverslip, but added microtubules in solution are subject to little resistance, and, again, net movement is toward the microtubule plus end. **C:** In dynein-mediated organelle transport, the prediction is that microtubules are partially anchored so that they resist sliding toward their plus ends, and thus net movement would be of the dynein-decorated organelle toward the microtubule minus end.

display different rates, *power requirements* must be considered. Third, because axonemal dyneins interact only with microtubules, whereas cytoplasmic dyneins may associate with other organelles, the *molecular structure* of the ligand binding sites may be an issue.

Direction of Movement

Chromosome movement, vesicle transport, and cell elongation all occur in two directions along groups of oriented cytoplasmic microtubules (for reviews and discussion, see Zimmerman and Forer, 1981; Schliwa, 1984; Dustin, 1984). The issue of directionality with regard to the motor arose with two critical discoveries, first, the demonstration that the microtubules within a given cytoplasmic array are all of the same polarity (Euteneuer and McIntosh, 1980, 1981; Telzer and Haimo, 1981; Heidemann and McIntosh, 1980; Burton and Paige, 1981) and, second, the direct observation of organelle movement in two directions along a single microtubule (Schnapp et al., 1985;

Allen et al., 1985; Koonce and Schliwa, 1985). Microtubules have intrinsic structural polarity that derives from the kinetics of polymer assembly. The two ends, which can be distinguished morphologically in the presence of exogenous tubulin (Heidemann and McIntosh, 1980) or dynein (Haimo, 1982), are referred to as *plus* and *minus* (Allen and Borisy, 1974), reflecting their kinetic tendency to add or lose tubulin subunits. The discovery that movement could occur in both directions on a single microtubule, therefore, makes it clear that directionality has to be a property of the motor or motors driving motility (Schliwa, 1984). The two basic types of models suggested are 1) two different motors working in concert but each generating movement in only one direction and 2) a single motor that can generate movement in either direction, presumably controlled by some regulatory system.

Considerable attention has been focused on the fact that the two motors, kinesin and dynein, can generate movements toward opposite microtubule ends. Kinesin, interacting with microtubules via a nucleotide-dependent binding site, moves toward the microtubule plus end (Vale et al., 1985a,b; Porter et al., 1987b). Any other structure to which the kinesin is attached (a vesicle or an inert bead) also moves toward the microtubule plus ends, unless the structure is too big to be moved, as when the kinesin is attached to a glass coverslip. In this case, the microtubule moves across the glass in the opposite direction, toward the minus end (Vale et al., 1985a,b; Porter et al., 1987b). Using nerve axons as a reference, kinesin has been called an anterograde translocator, because microtubule plus ends are found at the distal (synaptic) region of nerve axons (Burton and Paige, 1981). Thus motors that transport structures to which they are attached toward microtubule plus ends in other cell types are sometimes referred to as anterograde motors.

In axonemes, dynein interacting with a B subfiber via an ATP-dependent binding site drives that microtubule doublet toward its plus end. The dynein molecule effectively moves toward the minus end of that microtubule (Sale and Satir, 1977; Fox and Sale, 1987), and, were it not for constraints at the base of the axoneme, the A subfiber to which the dynein is stably attached would also move toward its minus end (Fig. 7–1A). Thus the B (ATP-dependent) end of a dynein molecule walks along microtubules toward their minus ends, and structures stably attached to the dynein (at the A end) but free to move are also translocated to the minus end (Fig. 7–1C). Again, if this structure is too big to be moved, the microtubule moves instead (Paschal et al., 1987a), this time toward its plus end (Paschal and Vallee, 1987; Vale and Toyoshima, 1988) (Fig. 7–1B). Relative to microtubule polarity, dynein movement is opposite to kinesin movement, so, continuing the analogy to the nerve system, dynein has been called a *retrograde translocator*.

Three of the cytoplasmic forms of dynein are retrograde translocators by this definition. When bound to a glass coverslip, the

HeLa (Lye, Chapter 9), *Caenorhabditis elegans* (Lye, Chapter 9), and brain (Paschal and Vallee, 1987; Vallee, Chapter 13) dyneins each mediate gliding of microtubules toward plus ends (though perhaps not exclusively, as discussed below). Since kinesin is also present in these systems, it is possible that these two proteins are responsible for bidirectional organelle transport. In this regard, the results of Lye et al. (1987; also, Chapter 9) are especially interesting. Using pieces of axonemes onto which free microtubules had been polymerized at the plus end, these investigators observed that the gliding induced by either the *C. elegans* or the HeLa dynein was opposite to that predicted for dynein (Lye et al., 1987; also, Chapter 9). This unexpected result was later determined to be due to in part to anomolies of the tubule polymerization off of the axonemal seeds, and the Hela and *C. elegans* proteins have now been found to mediate microtubule gliding with the direction expected for dynein. In analyzing the results, however, these investigators observed that a mixture of kinesin and dynein isolated from either of these two sources generated gliding of the decorated axonemes in the direction opposite that of either dynein alone. These data clearly suggest that the two enzymes interact and affect the motility generating properties of one another.

There is evidence from several systems that two different classes of motors coexist and provide for microtubule-based movement in opposite directions, but, in most of these, only one motility protein has been identified. Vale and coworkers (1985a) have shown that nerve cells contain kinesin as the anterograde transporter, as well as an unidentified retrograde motor with some characteristics in common with dynein. In both erythrophores and melanophores, a dynein-like ATPase appears to mediate organelle movement toward the cell center consistent with the predicted polarity (Clark and Rosenbaum, 1982; Beckerle and Porter, 1982; Rozdzial and Haimo, 1986a). Pigment granule aggregation is blocked by inhibitors of dynein ATPase activity (Beckerle and Porter,

1982; Clark and Rosenbaum, 1982), and a high-M_r polypeptide has been identified in melanoma that cross reacts with antidynein antibodies (Ogawa et al., 1987). Dispersion of pigment in the opposite direction does not appear to be dynein-mediated, although it is an ATP-dependent process (Rozdzial and Haimo, 1986a,b). Instead, dispersion requires phosphorylation of an M_r 57,000 protein, and there is evidence that phosphorylation alone may be sufficient to generate granule movement toward the cell periphery (Rozdzial and Haimo, 1986a,b). Finally, in the sea urchin egg, where cytoplasmic dyneins have been identified and characterized (Pratt, Chapter 8; Lye Chapter 9), retrograde-type movements have not been analyzed, but anterograde-type motility appears to be kinesin-mediated (Pryer et al., 1986a; Porter et al., 1987b).

Although dynein in trypsin-treated axonemes (Sale and Satir, 1977; Fox and Sale, 1987) and isolated, purified kinesin generate unidirectional movement (Vale et al., 1985a; Porter et al., 1987b), we cannot rule out the possibility that control mechanisms in vivo affect these motors so that they can generate movement in both directions (Lye et al., 1987). In particular, dynein has been shown to be a complex molecule comprising two or three ATPases (Tang et al., 1982; Shimizu and Johnson, 1983; Pratt, 1986a), and it is conceivable that the subunits are regulated such that each can generate movement in one direction.

Some systems provide evidence that single motors can generate bidirectional movement. With the fresh water amoeba *Reticulomyxa*, Euteneuer and her colleagues have identified a motor that appears to mediate organelle translocation in both directions along microtubules (Koonce and Schliwa, 1985; Euteneuer et al., Chapter 10). Direction of movement appears to be controlled by phosphorylation (Koonce and Schliwa, 1986a; Euteneuer et al., 1988) but is opposite to that seen in melanophores. In *Reticulomyxa*, phosphorylation induces organelle movement toward the cell center. The putative motor has some characteristics in com-

mon with dynein and may provide evidence to support the idea that dynein-like motors can mediate bidirectional transport. In addition, Gilbert and Sloboda (1986) have prepared a vesicle fraction from squid giant axon that translocates in both directions, although no control mechanism has been identified. Some evidence suggests that the motility is generated by a high-M_r protein with some similarity to microtubule-associated protein (MAP 2) and some to dynein (Sloboda, Chapter 14; Pratt, 1986a).

Rates of Movement and Power Requirements

Observed rates of axonemal and non-axonemal microtubule-based movements vary over several hundred-fold (Table 7–1). In flagellar axonemes having either one and two sets of dynein arms, microtubules slide at rates of 8–10 and 14–20 μm/sec, respectively (Yano and Miki-Noumura, 1980; Fox and Sale, 1987). In contrast, chromosomes move at a rate of 1–5 μm/min, hundreds of times slower (Nicklas, 1975). Rates of organelle transport, cell shape change, and in vitro microtubule gliding occur between these two extremes. Retinal cone elongation proceeds at about 2 μm/min (Burnside et al., 1982), similar to chromosome movement, perhaps implicating microtubule sliding as a mechanism in the latter. Pigment granule transport in melanophores (Schliwa, 1984) and organelle transport in sea urchin eggs (Rebhun, 1972; Pryer et al., 1986a) and squid axon (Allen et al., 1982; Brady et al., 1982) occur at 0.5–2 μm/sec, and microtubules glide at these rates in the presence of either the *C. elegans* (Lye, Chapter 9) or bovine brain dynein (Paschal and Vallee, 1987; Paschal et al., 1987b). These movements are six orders of magnitude faster than chromosome movement but still slower than axonemal microtubule sliding rates. In erythrophores and *Reticulomyxa*, organelle translocation rates up to 25 μm/sec have been reported (Euteneuer, Chapter 10; Schliwa, 1984) similar to rates of microtubule sliding in axonemes.

Several mechanisms can be envisioned by

TABLE 7–1. Directionality and Rates of Some Forms of Microtubule-Based Motility

Cell type or organism	Movement	Direction[a]	Rate	Reference
Sea urchin sperm flagella	Axonemal outer doublet sliding	−	8–20 μm/sec	Fox and Sale, 1987
Various	Anaphase chromosome movement	−	1–5 μm/min	Zimmerman and Forer, 1981
Teleost fish	Retinal cone elongation	?	2 μm/min	Burnside et al., 1982
Melanophores Sea urchin eggs Squid giant axon	Pigment granule or other organelle translocation	+ and −	0.5–2 μm/sec	See text
Erythrophores *Reticulomyxa*	Pigment granule or other organelle translocation in vivo	+ and −	10–20 μm/sec	Schliwa, 1984
Reticulomyxa	In vitro movement of 320 kDa protein-coated beads	+ and −	8 μm/sec	Euteneuer, Chapter 10
C. elegans Bovine brain	Microtubule gliding on glass	−	0.5–2 μm/sec	See text

[a]Direction indicates translocation of the motor and the structure to which it is attached relative to intrinsic microtubule polarity: +, toward microtubule plus end; −, toward microtubule minus end.

which cytoplasmic dyneins could generate movements of such widely differing speeds. If the loads vary substantially in each system, then an identical motor working with the same efficiency would generate movements of differing rates. However, if we assume that the loads or resistance to movement are approximately equal, then the power requirements of each of these classes of motility are quite different. In this case, the movements may utilize different motors with varying rate-limiting steps in their mechanochemical cycles. Alternatively, the same motor could be acting in each form of movement but could be slowed by some governor of force production. The rates of movement also could be regulated by the absolute number of force generators at work, although axonemal microtubule sliding rates suggest that only interactions between two parallel rows of arms can influence sliding rates, not the absolute number of arms working in a single row (Gibbons and Gibbons, 1973; Yano and Miki-Nomoura, 1981; Okagaki and Kamiya, 1986).

All the cytoplasmic dynein ATPases appear to be similar, but data concerning loads and forces for non-axonemal microtubule-based movements are scant. Nicklas (1982)

has analyzed the forces generated during chromosome movement and calculated that cytoplasmic dynein ATPase would meet the power requirements better than either kinesin or myosin. However, coupling ratios between ATP hydrolysis and movement need to be determined for chromosome movement, microtubule gliding, and vesicle transport. In the latter two cases, it would also be useful to determine levels of force production similar to those obtained for axonemal microtubule sliding (Kamimura and Takahashi, 1981). These measurements are possible, although not simple to obtain, using the in vitro microtubule gliding assays recently developed (Vale et al., 1985a–d; Paschal et al., 1987a; Vale and Toyoshima, 1988).

There is no clear biochemical evidence for a governor or molecular gear that could modulate dynein force production, but one characteristic of dynein could allow for the generation of multiple rates of movement. Both flagellar dynein and cytoplasmic dynein can be isolated in latent-activity forms (Gibbons and Fronk, 1979; Lye, Chapter 9; Pratt, Chapter 8). The latent activity is typically demonstrated on the basis of ATPase stimulation by low concentrations of Triton

X-100. Though this treatment is hardly physiological, it indicates that the enzyme can manifest at least two activity states and suggests that regulation may take place via an hydrophobic site on the dynein molecule.

In retinal cones, cyclic adenosine monophosphate (cAMP) has been shown to regulate cell elongation (Gilson et al., 1986; Burnside, Chapter 11). In cone cells, movement is generated via intermicrotubule sliding, which is sensitive to dynein ATPase inhibitors and so is analagous to axonemal movement. Gilson et al. (1986) have pointed out that the requirement for a cAMP-dependent event in initiation of retinal cell elongation resembles cAMP-dependent activation of axonemal motility in sperm (Brokaw, 1982; Morisawa and Okuno, 1982; Murofushi et al., 1982; Tash and Means, 1982; Sale, 1985). In both cases, phosphorylation of regulatory components in implicated, suggesting another possible mechanism for controlling cytoplasmic dynein activity and force generation.

Molecular Structure and Binding Sites

Within the last 5 years, the use of scanning transmission electron microscopy (STEM) and the development of new techniques for observing the structures of single protein molecules in shadowed metal replicas have revealed that axonemal dyneins possess a characteristic morphology (Johnson and Wall, 1983; Goodenough et al., 1987). The structure of the outer row dynein arms from *Chlamydomonas* (Witman et al., 1983), *Tetrathymena* (Johnson and Wall, 1983), and sea urchin sperm tails (Sale et al., 1985) consists of two or three globular heads, each connected by an individual stem to a common base. The shapes and dimensions of dynein molecules from different sources are so similar that this morphology now constitutes one criterion for identifying dynein ATPases. Among cytoplasmic dyneins, only the brain molecule has been examined using STEM (Vallee et al., 1988). Structurally, brain dynein is nearly identical to the two-headed sperm flagellar dynein.

Two binding sites for interaction with other molecules have been identified for axonemal dyneins (Bell and Gibbons, 1982; Haimo and Fenton, 1984). Both these sites specifically associate with microtubules but by different molecular mechanisms. Microtubule–dynein interaction at one site is nucleotide (ATP)-dependent, and the other site is ionically controlled (Mitchell and Warner, 1981; Warner and McIlvain, 1982). Mass measurements made in the STEM have shown that each of the globular heads comprises a single dynein heavy chain (Johnson and Wall, 1983; Witman et al., 1983). The head end, therefore, contains the enzymatic active site and, presumably, the ATP-dependent microtubule binding site. The morphology of dynein–microtubule complexes suggests that the ionic binding site is found near the base of the molecule (for review, see Goodenough and Heuser, 1984). Isolated cytoplasmic dyneins possess two similar bonding sites (Pratt, Chapter 8), as evidenced most strikingly by their induction of microtubule bundling (Hollenbeck et al., 1984; Hollenbeck and Chapman, 1986; Lye, Chapter 9).

Functional differences between axonemal and cytoplasmic dynein, however, suggest that some structural differences may be found. Axonemal dynein generates movement solely via interaction with microtubules. Intermicrotubule sliding, such as that observed in *Reticulomyxa* (Koonce et al., 1987; Euteneuer, Chapter 10) and teleost retinal cones (Warren and Burnside, 1978; Burnside, Chapter 11), is only one form of non-axonemal, tubule-associated motility. In the cytoplasm, microtubule-based movements often involve translocation of other cellular organelles. It is reasonable to predict, therefore, that cytoplasmic dynein may have additional or altered binding sites for transported organelles, such as chromosomes, vesicles, or mitochondria, and there is some evidence to support this conjecture. Sea urchin egg dynein appears to associate with vesicular organelles (Pratt, Chapter 8), and two different high-M_r proteins from squid giant axon, each with some characteristics of a dynein-like motor (Pratt, 1986c, also, Chapter 8; Gilbert and Sloboda, 1986), have been shown to mediate microtubule–vesicle interactions. In *Reticulomyxa*, the 320 kDa dynein-like protein mediates organelle movement along microtubules and, therefore, must interact with both structures (Euteneuer, Chapter 10). Vallee et al. (Chapter 13) have suggested that the different intermediate and light chains characteristic of cytoplasmic vs. axonemal forms of the enzyme are good candidates as unique binding sites for cytoplasmic organelles. The demonstration that axonemal dyneins bind cellular organelles, a possibility that has not been tested, would obviate the postulated unique binding sites on cytoplasmic forms of the enzyme.

CURRENT AND FUTURE CHALLENGES

The field of cytoplasmic dynein research is very young. The last 5 years have seen a furor over the discovery and identification of proposed new motors for non-axonemal, microtubule-based motility. The future will undoubtedly see detailed characterizations of these proteins as well as the identification and isolation of new ones. Although none of the proteins described in the following chapters completely satisfies the dynein ATPase criteria assembled for axonemal dynein, they all show significant dynein character. Detailed comparisons of these proteins to axonemal dynein and to each other are found in the following chapters and are summarized in Table 7–2. In analyzing relationships between axonemal and cytoplasmic dyneins, many investigators have suggested that the non-axonemal form of the enzyme is likely to be the evolutionary predecessor to the axonemal form. For example, the high-M_r microtubule-binding ATPases in *Reticulomyxa* and *C. elegans* may well represent primitive forms of dynein.

In terms of characterizing dynein-like proteins, the immediate emphasis will probably be on correlation of in vivo and in vitro data.

It is critical to determine the relevance of microtubule gliding on glass to cellular motility and to identify the physiological binding sites of putative motor enzymes. Another crucial issue is that of motor modulation, primarily in terms of rate.

Studies of the molecular structure of cytoplasmic dynein and related enzymes are likely to yield useful information about the relationships of these molecules both to axonemal dynein and to each other, and about mechanisms of movement. Electron microscopic techniques for studying molecular structures of isolated proteins are ready to be applied to any putative motor that can be purified. As they are currently being used, these methods provide sufficient resolution to distinguish dynein from other macromolecules and a rigorous means of classifying microtubule-associated ATPases as dynein (Johnson and Wall, 1983; Witman et al., 1983; Goodenough and Heuser, 1984; Sale et al., 1985; Goodenough et al., 1987; Vallee et al., 1988). In combination with biochemical data, structural information will also aid in the identification of regulatory subunits and microtubule, organelle, and ATP binding domains.

The use of molecular cloning techniques will be important in analyzing the presence of dynein-like molecules in a wide variety of cell types. Williams et al. (1986) have reported the cloning of a portion of a dynein heavy chain gene from *Chlamydomonas*. Other clones will no doubt be available soon, and these nucleic acid probes, as well as antibody probes, can be used to identify and clone dynein genes from other cells. Comparisons of the nucleotide sequences for cytoplasmic and axonemal dyneins will permit assessment of the relationships between these proteins. In addition, newly identified motor proteins can be compared to known dyneins using determined and predicted amino acid sequences. This kind of sequence data will permit us to identify unequivocally cytoplasmic dyneins and related ATPases.

TABLE 7–2. Dynein-Like Characteristics of Related Non-Axonemal ATPases

		Enzymatic				Physical			Functional	
		Mg²⁺ or Ca²⁺	Inhibitors[b]				High-M_r	UV[d]	ATP-dependent	MT[e]
ATPase	Reference[a]	Activated	Vanadate	EHNA*	NEM**	S value	chains	cleavage	MT-association	motility
Axonemal dynein	1	Yes	Yes	Yes	Yes	10–14[c]	Yes	Yes	Yes	Yes
Sea urchin egg dynein	2	Yes	Yes	Yes	No	18–21 12–14	Yes	Yes	Yes	N.D.
C. elegans dynein	3	Yes	Yes	N.D.	Yes	19–20 20	Yes	Yes	Yes	Yes
Reticulomyxa 320 kDa protein	4	Yes	Yes	No	N.D.	23–24	Yes	Yes	Yes	Yes
MAP 1C brain dynein	5	Yes	Yes	N.D.	Yes	20	Yes	Yes	Yes	Yes
Spinal nerve HMW4	6	Yes	Yes	No	N.D.	19	Yes	N.D.	Yes	N.D.

[a]References: 1, Volume 1, this series; 2, Pratt, Chapter 8; 3, Lye, Chapter 9; 4, Euteneuer et al., 1988; 5, Paschal et al., 1987a; 6, Hollenbeck and Chapman, 1986.

[b]Inhibitor concentrations are 1–100 μM vanadate, 1–5 mM EHNA, 1–2 mM NEM.

[c]Various S values reported for flagellar and egg dynein reflect a range reported for different isotypes from different species.

[d]UV cleavage occurs only in the presence of ATP and vanadate (see Lye, Chapter 9).

[e]MT motility denotes either intermicrotubule sliding, microtubule gliding on glass, or motor-coated bead translocation.

*Erythro-9-2,3,-hydroxynonyl adenine.

**N-ethylmaleimide.

Dyneins in Sea Urchin Eggs and Nerve Tissue

Melanie M. Pratt

Department of Anatomy and Cell Biology, University of Miami School of Medicine, Miami, Florida 33101

INTRODUCTION

In his first description of dynein isolated from *Tetrahymena* cilia, Gibbons (1965) noted that the enzyme showed distinct similarity to an ATPase found in isolated mitotic spindles (Mazia, 1961). Since that report, the use of this analogy has resupinated, and it is now ciliary (and flagellar) dyneins that serve as standards for comparison of mitotic and other cytoplasmically derived ATPases. The reason for this inversion is that the relatively greater abundance and ease of preparation have made axonemal dyneins more amenable to study, and more information has been obtained about them than is presently available for the cytoplasmic enzyme.

In studying the molecular mechanisms of microtubule-associated movements, our laboratory has relied heavily on the model provided by axonemal motility. Although other possibilities exist, we see it as essential to examine the hypothesis that a cytoplasmic form of dynein is the mechanochemical transducer for some forms of non-axonemal, microtubule-based motility. Our approach has been first to determine whether dynein ATPase can be isolated from non-axonemal sources and then to assess homology of this putative dynein with the flagellar and ciliary enzymes. We have also asked whether dynein is present in non-axonemal locations associated with microtubule-based motility. Two cell types have been examined in some detail, and this discussion will focus on the identification, purification, and characterization of dynein from the sea urchin egg and on the search for dynein-like ATPase in nerve tissue. In this chapter, the term *egg dynein* is defined as dynein that can be isolated from sea urchin eggs, *cytoplasmic dynein* is used as a more general term to refer to the family of dynein-like molecules that are non-axonemal in origin, and *axonemal dynein* is used to denote the dyneins isolated from cilia and flagella. Egg dynein is, by these criteria, one member of the group of cytoplasmic dyneins.

The cytoplasm may contain multiple isoforms of dynein, which differ in physical structure and developmental expression. The data reviewed here suggest that these isoforms may be distinguished by polypeptide composition, solubility, localization, and microtubule association. The challenge is to determine the specific functions of these cytoplasmic dyneins.

Cell Movement, Volume 2: Kinesin,
Dynein, and Microtubule Dynamics, pages 125–140

SEA URCHIN EGG
CYTOPLASMIC DYNEIN

Identification and Purification of Egg Dynein

Identification of dynein-like ATPase in unfertilized sea urchin eggs. The first report of dynein-like activity in sea urchin eggs was that of Weisenberg and Taylor (1968). They began their study in search of a mitotic ATPase that might power chromosome movement and concluded that, although dynein-like activity was associated with the mitotic apparatus (MA), much more of the same activity was found in other regions of the zygote as well as in the unfertilized egg. Because sea urchin eggs were available in sufficient quantities for biochemical studies and because sperm flagellar dynein could be easily prepared as a standard, we began to refine and extend the initial observations of Weisenberg and Taylor (1968) some 10 years after the initial report (Pratt, 1980).

Velocity sedimentation on sucrose density gradients was used to fractionate a 100,000g supernatant of sea urchin eggs, and, by several criteria, the ATPase activity that appeared in a single peak was found to be very similar to flagellar axonemal dynein. These similarities included cosedimentation at 14S and comigration on sodium dodecyl sulfate (SDS)-polyacrylamide gels of two protein bands in the egg 14S peak with the two flagellar dynein heavy chains. Furthermore, the egg ATPase exhibited the unique enzymatic properties that characterize dyneins (Pratt, 1980; also, see below). Although this egg ATPase was clearly dynein-like, there were concerns about some of its properties. First, the polypeptides that comigrated with flagellar heavy chains appeared to contain bound carbohydrate (as judged by staining with Schiff reagent after periodic acid treatment). This result was unexpected in that the enzyme was thought to be a "soluble" protein, and it also cast doubt on the relative mobilities of the proteins on SDS gels. Second, the egg dynein polypeptides comprised some 2–4% of total egg protein, a surprisingly large fraction. Finally, there was no direct evidence that the ATPase activity was in fact associated with the high-M_r polypeptides because of heterogeneity in the sucrose density gradient peak. Therefore, further characterization required more extensive purification of the enzyme.

Purification of egg dynein. Hisanaga and Sakai (1983) first reported a preparation of dynein from eggs of the sea urchin *Hemicentrotus pulcherrimus* that was homogeneous in polypeptide composition. Their purification protocol, a modification of one they had presented earlier (Hisanaga and Sakai, 1980), included gel filtration, hydroxylapatite and affinity column chromatography of a 100,000g supernatant of an egg extract, followed by sucrose density gradient centrifugation. The crucial innovation was their use of a calmodulin (CaM) affinity column to which egg dynein bound in a calcium-dependent manner.

Three different classes of purification protocols are typically used to prepare sea urchin egg dynein. The first (Table 8–1, Fig. 8–1), used in our laboratory (Pratt, 1986b), is a modification of the Hisanaga and Sakai (1983) procedure and relies on ion-exchange and calmodulin-affinity chromatography and a final sucrose density gradient fractionation. The second procedure employs gel filtration and ion exchange column chromatography along with a final sucrose gradient (Scholey et al., 1984; Porter et al., 1988). The third procedure utilizes microtubule affinity (Hollenbeck et al., 1984; Scholey et al., 1984; Asai and Wilson, 1985) that is sometimes combined with sucrose density gradient centrifugation. The column chromatography procedures (both plus and minus calmodulin-affinity) produce the purest enzyme preparations in quantities sufficient for detailed characterization, but all the methods accomplish substantial enrichment of high-M_r polypeptides and Mg^{2+} ATPase activity having the characteristics of dyneins. The preparations that have been analyzed in some detail and that are discussed below are described in Table 8–2.

TABLE 8–1. Purification of Egg Dynein*

Purification step[a]	Protein (mg)	Activity[b] (units)	Specific Activity (units/mg)	Yield (% units)	Purification[c] (-fold)
Whole egg homogenate (WE)	5,825.0	9.95	0.0017		
55% ammonium SO$_4$ precipitate (55AS)	793.8	5.12	0.013	51.5	7.6
DEAE-Sephacel pool (DE)	34.5	2.10	0.061	21.1	35.9
CaM-affinity pool (CaM)	2.3	0.26	0.114	2.6	67.1
Sucrose gradient pool (SDGC)	0.21	0.04	0.198	0.21	116.0

*See Pratt (1986b), for details.

[a]The entire egg homogenate and ammonium sulfate precipitate were assayed. Column and SDGC pools refer to pooled fractions from the peak containing ATPase activity.

[b]One unit of dynein activity releases 1 μmole inorganic phosphate per minute.

[c]-Fold purification refers to increase in specific activity.

Characterization of Egg Dynein: Homology With Flagellar Dynein

Enzymatic activity, molecular forms, and ATP binding. Enzymatically, egg dynein exhibits the unique properties of nucleotide hydrolysis that characterize axonemal dyneins, including high substrate specificity for ATP, nearly equal activation by Mg^{2+} and Ca^{2+} ions, stimulation of Mg^{2+} ATPase activity by up to 0.5 M NaCl or KCl, broad pH optima ranging between 6 and 8, and a lack of ATPase activity in the presence of EDTA at high salt concentration. The K_m for ATP of the egg enzyme falls in the range of 45–110 μM, depending on the purity of the preparation and the conditions of the assay (Hisanaga and Sakai, 1983; Hollenbeck et al., 1984; Penningroth et al., 1985). These values agree with the K_m values for ATP reported for sperm flagellar dynein (Gibbons and Fronk, 1972, 1979), although it should be noted that much lower values have been determined for *Tetrahymena* ciliary dynein (Shimizu, 1981). Like axonemal dyneins, egg dynein Mg^{2+} ATPase activity is inhibited by vanadate anions (Gibbons et al., 1978), and by erythro-9-2,3,hydroxylnonyl adenine (EHNA) (Penningroth et al., 1982).

The enzymatic differences between egg and flagellar dynein are primarily a matter of degree. Egg enzyme preparations of purity comparable to sperm flagellar dynein consistently show lower Mg^{2+} ATPase activities

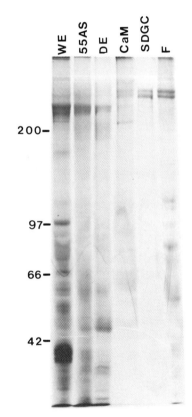

Fig. 8–1. Protein composition of fractions during purification of sea urchin egg dynein. Fractions, as designated and defined in Table 8–1, were analyzed on 5–10% polyacrylamide gels containing a 2–8 M urea gradient, using the discontinuous buffer system of Laemmli (1970). The positions of flagellar (F) dynein bands and of molecular weight markers are indicated.

TABLE 8–2. Comparison of Isolated Egg Dyneins

Species[c]	Purification protocol	S value	Specific activity[a]	MT association[b]	Designation	Reference
S. purpuratus	Chromatography	13S	0.2	M Yes	Egg dynein	Pratt et al., 1984;
S. droebachiensis	and SDGC[c]			F N.D.[d]		Pratt, 1986b
H. pulcherrimus	Chromatography and SDGC	12.3S	0.5	M Yes F Yes	Cytoplasmic dynein of sea urchin eggs	Hisanaga and Sakai, 1983, 1986
L. pictus	A Microtubule	20S	0.05	M Yes	High-M$_r$ MAP	Scholey et al.,
S. purpuratus	affinity	12S		F N.D.	ATPase	1984; Porter et al., 1988
S. droebachiensis	B Chromatography	20S	0.15	M No F No	Column-purified ATPase	Lye, Chapter 9
S. purpuratus	Microtubule affinity or SDGC	20S	0.15 0.57	M Yes F N.D.	20S Mg^{2+} ATPase	Asai and Wilson, 1985

[a]Specific activity (μmoles phosphate/mg/min).
[b]Microtubule association: M, repolymerized microtubules; F, flagellar outer doublet tubules.
[c]Sucrose density gradient centrifugation.
[d]N.D., not determined.
[e]Genera: S, *Stronglocentrotus*; H, *Hemicentrotus*; h, *hytechinus*.

under identical ionic and nucleotide conditions (Pratt, 1980; Pratt et al., 1984; Scholey et al., 1984; Asai and Wilson, 1985; Penningroth et al., 1985). In addition, egg dynein is somewhat less specific for ATP, cleaving other nucleotides at up to 40% of the ATP hydrolysis rate (Pratt et al., 1984; Penningroth et al., 1985), and is less sensitive to inhibition by vanadate (Pratt et al., 1984; Penningroth et al., 1985; Asai and Wilson, 1985). Finally, it has been shown that both egg and flagellar dynein Mg^{2+} ATPase can be stimulated by Triton X-100 and by Ca^{2+}-calmodulin (Hisanaga and Pratt, 1984), and the flagellar enzyme is always stimulated to a greater degree than the egg dynein (Hisanaga and Pratt, 1984).

Different investigators, using velocity sedimentation analysis, have identified two macromolecular forms of egg dynein having sedimentation coefficients of 10S–14S (Hisanaga and Sakai, 1983, 1986; Pratt, 1980, 1986b; Scholey et al., 1984; Penningroth et al., 1985) and 20S–23S (Hisanaga and Sakai, 1983, 1986; Asai and Wilson, 1985; Collins and Vallee, 1986a). These ATPases are comparable in size to the two forms reported for solubilized axonemal dyneins from *Tetrahy-*

mena cilia (Mitchell and Warner, 1981; Johnson and Wall, 1983) and the outer arm dynein of *Chlamydomonas* flagella (Piperno and Luck, 1979; Pfister et al., 1982) and sea urchin sperm flagella (Gibbons and Fronk, 1979; Tang et al., 1982; Sale et al., 1985; Fox and Sale, 1987). Each of the *Tetrahymena* forms is composed of different sets of heavy, intermediate, and light chains, and they make up different arm structures (Mabuchi and Shimizu, 1974), but, in *Chalmydomonas* and sperm outer arm, the smaller dynein forms are made up of some of the subunits of the larger forms (Pfister et al., 1982; Tang et al., 1982; Sale et al., 1985; Goodenough et al., 1987). In the case of egg dynein, Collins and Vallee (1986a) reported that the two forms of the enzyme do not appear to be interconvertible. Instead, the larger form predominates when purification takes place in very-low-ionic-strength buffers, whereas addition of greater than 0.1 M salt favors isolation of the smaller form. Foltz and Asai (1988), however, found that the large form could be converted to the small form by addition of 0.5 M salt but that breakdown to a smaller form required more time that previous workers had allowed. On

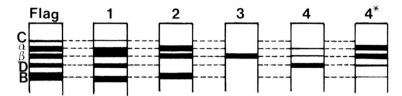

Fig. 8–2. Schematic drawing of the high-M_r polypeptides of several sea urchin egg dynein preparations. Bands were drawn as they would appear on high-resolution polyacrylamide gels when compared with a sperm flagellar axoneme standard (Flag). Only preparations that have been analyzed for comigration with axonemal standards are shown, at the position of the axonemal heavy chain with which they were reported to comigrate. Each fraction was originally run on a slightly different gel system, so their comigration with each other is not yet proved. The preparations are as follows: 1, ion-exchange and calmodulin-affinity chromatography, followed by sucrose-density gradient centrifugation (SDGC) (Pratt, 1986b); 2, SDGC or ATP-dependent microtubule affinity (Asai and Wilson, 1985); 3, gel filtration, hydroxyapatite, and CaM-affinity chromatography followed by SDGC (Hisanaga and Sakai, 1983); 4, ATP elution of taxol-assembled microtubules (Scholey et al., 1984; Porter et al., 1988); 4*, purification from the microtubule-depleted supernatant in 4 by gel filtration and ion-exchange chromatography followed by SDGC (Scholey et al., 1984; Porter et al., 1988).

the other hand, Hisanaga and Sakai (1986) found that, for some but not all species of sea urchins, the larger form can be observed only in the presence of 0.5 M KCl and furthermore that addition of salt to the smaller form (isolated in the presence of 0.05 M KCl) causes conversion to the larger form. Porter et al. (1988) have also demonstrated direct interconversion of a 20S form of egg dynein to 10S–12S upon stimulation of ATPase activity in the presence of 0.1% Triton X-100.

Direct observation of cytoplasmic dynein molecules in the electron microscope may help to clarify the relationship between 12S–14S and 20S forms of egg dynein. Hisanaga and Hirokawa (1987) have shown that the 12S form is an asymmetric molecule consisting of a single globular head and a filamentous stalk. The egg dynein resembles one half of the two-headed 21S sperm flagellar dynein (Sale et al., 1985). The heads of axonemal dynein molecules can be distinguished on the basis of shape (Goodenough and Heuser, 1984; Sale et al., 1985), and, since the 12S egg dynein has a distinctive pear-shaped head, it should be possible to determine, by morphological observation, whether it composes a part of the 20S molecular form. The 20S egg dynein has not yet been examined ultrastructurally, but a 20S cytoplasmic dynein from bovine brain is a two-headed molecule (Vallee et al., 1987, 1988).

All the molecular forms of egg dynein isolated are composed in part of high-molecular-mass polypeptides. In most cases, the bands have the same relative mobilities on SDS–PAGE as one or more flagellar dynein heavy chains. In Figure 8–2, the compositions of several egg dynein preparations are diagrammed, based on their published comigration with axonemal polypeptides. We have used the axonemal designations C, α, β, D, and B (Gibbons et al., 1976) to name these bands, although functional equivalence is not addressed or implied by this terminology. It is particularly interesting to note that each of the egg dynein purification protocols produces a slightly different constellation of these high-molecular-mass bands (Pratt, 1986a). Some variations in heavy chain composition may be due to species differences and different purification protocols, but it is also possible that they reflect the isolation of different forms of egg dynein. In any case, it is important to point out that, in the more highly purified preparations, none of the egg dynein polypeptides appear to contain bound carbohydrate (Hisanaga and Sakai, 1983; Pratt et al., 1984), so their comigration with axonemal bands is no longer in question (see above).

The relative molecular masses reported for the egg high-M_r polypeptides range from 295,000 to 385,000 (Hisanaga and Sakai, 1983; Pratt, 1984; Scholey et al., 1984; Penningroth et al., 1985), but, because of the lack of M_r standards in this range, these numbers are probably no more reliable than those previously reported for axonemal heavy chains. Gibbons et al. (1987) have recently estimated the M_r of sperm flagellar outer arm polypeptides at approximately 428,000 by adding the masses of two discreet fragments obtained after ultraviolet (UV) cleavage. This value is in better agreement with the mass determined by other methods (Bell, 1983; Johnson and Wall, 1983). Because of the comigration of the egg and flagellar chains on SDS–PAGE, values of 400,000 are likely to be good estimates for the egg high-molecular-mass bands. In addition, Porter et al. (1988) have recently demonstrated UV cleavage of the egg dynein heavy chains, and the fragments are approximately the same size as the flagellar products. Nearly all the egg dynein preparations also contain polypeptides of lower M_r, which, by analogy to flagellar dynein, may be intermediate and light chains of the active enzyme, but none of them have been positively identified.

Analysis of each preparation of egg dynein has provided good evidence that the Mg^{2+} ATPase activity is associated with the heavy chain polypeptides, and, where a heavy chain has been purified to homogeneity, this conclusion is unequivocal (Hisanaga and Sakai, 1983). As is shown in Figure 8–2, however, most egg dyneins contain more than one heavy chain, as well as a number of lower-M_r bands. To determine which of these polypeptides contained the enzyme active site, we identified the ATP-binding species in one form of egg dynein (Pratt, 1986a). Using a photoaffinity analog of ATP, 8-azido-ATP ($8\text{-}N_3\text{ATP}$), we found that two of the egg dynein heavy chains bound the analog specifically (Fig. 8–3a). The smaller of the two polypeptides binds nearly five times as much $8\text{-}N_3\text{ATP}$ as the larger one. Two flagellar dynein polypeptides having the same relative mobility on SDS gels also bound the analog, but in approximately equal amounts. The results suggest that differences between egg and axonemal dynein hydrolysis rates and sensitivity to inhibitors may result from different relative activities of two separate catalytic subunits within each enzyme.

Peptide mapping and antibody cross reactivity. The homologies of egg and flagellar dyneins were further analyzed at a molecular level by comparing the one-dimensional peptide maps of three of the heavy chains (Pratt, 1986a). Two of these comparative maps are shown in Figure 8–3b. Using either *Staphylococcus* V8 protease or α-chymotrypsin to digest the proteins, corresponding egg and flagellar polypeptides appeared to be more than 85% homologous. This is greater than the approximate 75% homology that occurs between different flagellar heavy chains (Pratt, 1986a). By these criteria egg and flagellar dynein subunits again show substantial similarity as well as some significant differences. It is particularly interesting to note that the smallest of the chains (those having unequal ATP binding) display the most dissimilar peptide maps (Fig. 8–3b) (Pratt, 1986a).

Immunological cross reactivity has been used to demonstrate homology between egg and axonemal dyneins, but these analyses have also revealed some differences in molecular structure. Both polyclonal and monoclonal antibodies to flagellar heavy chains recognize comigrating polypeptides in enriched and purified preparations of egg dynein (Piperno, 1984; Asai et al., 1986; Porter et al., 1988). Some of these antiflagellar dynein (anti-FD) antibodies also cross react with ciliary dynein heavy chains. Piperno (1984) has shown that several monoclonal antibodies against flagellar dynein heavy and intermediate chains recognize antigens in the fertilized sea urchin egg. Asai (1986) has prepared polyclonal and monoclonal (Asai et al., 1986) antibodies against the egg 20S Mg^{2+} ATPase. Neither of these antibodies recognizes any flagellar antigens; however, the polyclonal antiserum reacts with a sea

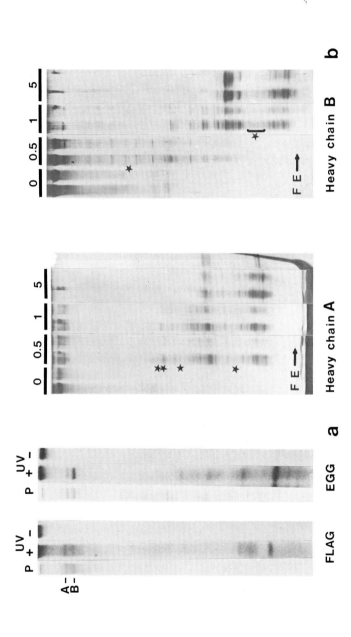

Fig. 8–3. ATP-binding and peptide map comparisons of egg and flagellar dynein. **a:** Purified egg and flagellar dynein proteins (P) were incubated with $[\alpha\text{-}^{32}P]8\text{-}N_3ATP$ in the presence (+) and absence (−) of UV light and then fractionated on polyacrylamide gels. The two lanes at right in each group are autoradiograms showing ATP-binding polypeptides. **b:** Flagellar and egg heavy chains A or B were loaded in alternating lanes across a peptide mapping gel and overlaid with varying amounts of *Staphylococcus* V8 protease as indicated at the top of the lanes in nanograms. The last lane in the map of heavy chain A contains 1 μg V8 protease alone. Stars designate peptides unique to the flagellar chain (for details, see Pratt, 1986a).

urchin embryonic ciliary heavy chain. We have used polyacrylamide gel-purified egg dynein heavy chains as antigens and produced an anti-egg dynein (anti-ED) serum, which shows no cross reactivity with ciliary or flagellar polypeptides (Pratt et al., 1986, 1988). It is interesting that polyclonal antisera can distinguish between egg and flagellar dynein, given the substantial homology of the proteins as deduced from peptide mapping (Pratt, 1986a). Taken together, the antibody data support the conclusions from ATP-binding and peptide map comparisons that egg and axonemal dynein polypeptides are homologous but also have unique regions. In addition, there is some evidence that these antisera are able to distinguish different isoforms of egg dynein. Porter et al. (1988) have found that an antiflagellar dynein antibody cross reacts with a soluble form of egg dynein, but not with a dynein-like polypeptide (of slightly lower molecular weight than the soluble form) that binds to microtubules. In addition, some antibodies recognize dynein associated with the mitotic apparatus, but not forms extracted from whole eggs, and vice versa (see below).

Microtubule association. One important characteristic of dynein is association with microtubules. Axonemal dyneins have two microtubule binding sites within the axoneme, one ATP-sensitive and one ATP-insensitive, and both of these can also be demonstrated for in vitro dynein binding to repolymerized singlet microtubules (Haimo et al., 1979; Warner and McIlvain, 1982; Porter and Johnson, 1983). Egg dynein also binds to microtubules in vitro, and the available data support the assumption of two classes of microtubule binding sites, one ATP-sensitive and one ATP-insensitive, although the functional implications of the binding are not yet clear.

Hisanaga and Sakai (1983) reported that approximately one-third of the purified 14S egg dynein ATPase bound to outer doublet microtubules, and all the bound material could be removed by treatment with 0.5 M KCl, suggesting interaction via the nucleotide-insensitive site. In addition, we have

used the alloaffinity procedure described by Nasr and Satir (1985) to demonstrate microtubule binding by a partially purified preparation of 14S egg dynein and have detected only ATP-insensitive binding (unpublished observation). Using less purified egg extracts as starting material, Scholey, Porter, and coworkers (Scholey et al., 1984; Porter et al., 1988) demonstrated that dynein-like ATPase cosedimented with taxol-polymerized microtubules. A portion of the pelleted ATPase activity was released upon incubation with 5 mM ATP (considerably higher than the micromolar levels that released functional axonemal dynein polypeptides), and another fraction could be extracted with high-salt treatment. The egg dynein activity extracted with ATP and has a sedimentation coefficient of 20S (Porter et al., 1988).

Asai and Wilson (1985) have reported that microtubule affinity and ATP-dependent release can be used to purify egg dynein. High-molecular-mass polypeptides were enriched in the ATP-released material and were found to comigrate with the heavy chains found in a 20S form of the egg enzyme. The S value of the ATP-eluted dynein, however, was not directly measured (Asai and Wilson, 1985). Hollenbeck et al. (1984) also reported ATP-sensitive binding of egg dynein-like ATPase and high-molecular-mass polypeptides to microtubules. Only 25–35% of the bound ATPase activity was released by treatment with 2 mM ATP, however, indicating that much of the binding is ATP-insensitive. These data suggest that this egg enzyme has two microtubule binding sites, a conclusion supported by the fact that the ATP-released material could bundle microtubules, as seen by dark-field and electron microscopy. The functional significance of egg-dynein-microtubule interactions has yet to be demonstrated. For example, upon rebinding to outer doublet microtubules, both sperm flagellar and *Tetrahymena* ciliary dynein ATPase activity is activated (Gibbons and Fronk, 1979; Warner and Mitchell, 1980), and microtubule sliding and flagellar beating are restored (Gibbons and Gibbons, 1979). In contrast, there have been no reports of activation of egg dynein ATPase upon binding to microtubules and no demonstration of in vitro motility. In addition, there has not yet been a detailed study of the kinetics of egg dynein binding to microtubules or of the relevance of nucleotide specificity.

Localization of Egg Dynein

Dynein has been localized in unfertilized eggs and early embryos by two different techniques. In one type of study, various cell fractions and organelles have been isolated and assayed for the presence of egg dynein ATPase activity and high-M_r polypeptides. Other studies have utilized the antibodies described above to localize dynein by immunocytochemistry. In addition, the two techniques have been combined to identify egg dynein antigens in isolated cellular fractions. There is good evidence to suggest that, in addition to a large soluble pool, dynein is associated with the egg cortex, the first metaphase mitotic apparatus, and vesicular organelles (see below). Some of the data are contradictory, however, so the unequivocal localization of egg dynein remains an open question.

Dynein in the egg cortex. Myosin is present in the sea urchin egg cortex and plays a role in contractile ring function (Mabuchi and Okuno, 1977; Kiehart et al., 1982), but egg dynein also appears to be a cortical component and appears to make up more of the ATPase activity found in this region than myosin. Looking for an enzyme that might provide the energy for the cortical contraction responsible for cleavage of fertilized sea urchin eggs, Miki (1963a) measured the bulk ATPase activity in isolated cortices from embryos of various developmental stages. Interestingly, she found that enzyme activity peaked at metaphase and decreased as cleavage proceeded. Mabuchi (1973) later examined the enzymatic properties of the cortical ATPase and concluded that it was clearly more dynein-like than myosin-like. Immunoprecipitation (Kobayashi et al., 1978) and immunostaining with both anti-FD and anti-ED antibodies have

confirmed the cortical localization of egg dynein both before and after fertilization (Mohri et al., 1976; Asai, 1986; Pratt et al., 1986). In addition, we have preliminary evidence, obtained from immunostained frozen sections of eggs, that a portion of the cortical reaction is due to dynein found on the surfaces of the cortical granules (see below) (Pratt et al., 1988). Presumably, this dynein would also be found on the inner side of the plasma membrane after the cortical granules are discharged at fertilization and on the few granules that remain in the fertilized egg.

Dynein in the mitotic spindle. A variety of experimental evidence has suggested that dynein is associated with the MA. Mazia et al. (1961) and Miki (1963b) first described the properties of an ATPase activity associated with isolated mitotic spindles, but both of these studies were done prior to the identification of dynein ATPase by Gibbons and Rowe (1965). Since then, other investigators have reported that dynein-like ATPase activity and, in some cases, high-M_r polypeptides are associated with the isolated sea urchin MA (Weisenberg and Taylor, 1968; Pratt et al., 1980). In addition, several of the anti-FD antibodies mentioned above immunofluorescently stain the MA both in the egg and after isolation (Mohri et al., 1976; Yoshida et al., 1985), and Hirokawa et al. (1985) report that another monoclonal antibody raised against a sperm flagellar dynein heavy chain specifically binds to a microtubule-associated antigen as assayed by immuno–electron microscopy. Consistent with these results, the monoclonal antibodies against sea urchin sperm axonemal dyneins described by Piperno (1984) detect an enrichment of dynein in isolated mitotic spindles.

Other data, in particular immunolocalization using anti-ED antibodies, are inconsistent with the hypothesis that dynein plays a role in the MA. Asai (1986) has shown that the anti-20S Mg^{2+} ATPase does not stain the mitotic spindle in first-metaphase sea urchin embryos. We have confirmed this result using our anti-ED antibody and further have shown by immunostaining of Western blots (of SDS-gel fractionated proteins) and dot blots (of native proteins) that the egg dynein antiserum does not react with any MA proteins (Pratt et al., 1988). Leslie et al. (1986) have recently described the preparation of mitotic cytoskeletons composed of the cortices and mitotic apparatus from fertilized eggs of the sea urchin *Strongylocentrotus franciscanus*. Our anti-ED antibody stains the cortices but not the spindles in these preparations, and the antigen remains associated with the cytoskeleton after cold extraction of several mitotic components, in particular tubulin (Leslie and Pratt, unpublished results). Resolution of these conflicting data will require more investigation, but we believe it is significant that all the antibodies that localize dynein in the MA were prepared against the axonemal enzymes. Since axonemal dyneins are characterized by tight association with outer doublet microtubules, it is possible that these antibodies recognize epitopes that play a role in microtubule binding. In contrast, the anti-EDs were prepared against soluble forms of the enzyme which, as discussed above, do not exhibit substantial binding to microtubules. These antibodies may not, therefore, recognize microtubule-bound mitotic forms of dynein. In any case, the different antibodies appear to distinguish separate forms of dynein that exist in distinct spatial distributions within the egg and that may perform separate functions.

Dynein association with vesicular organelles. Immunostaining of whole eggs and frozen sections of eggs using our anti-ED antibody revealed antigen localization not only in the cortex, as described, but also throughout the egg. The fluorescence pattern appeared as myriad circular outlines, as if a vesicular network were being recognized (Pratt et al., 1988). To analyze this distribution, we modified the cell fractionation protocols of Vale et al. (1985a) and Pryer et al. (1986) to produce soluble and organelle fractions from unfertilized sea urchin eggs (Fig. 8–4a), which were then probed with the anti-ED antibody. The antigen was found to be enriched in the organelle fractions (Fig. 8–4b), whereas soluble fractions equivalent to the starting material for our egg dynein preparation contained the antigen but at a reduced percentage of total protein over the level found in organelles (Pratt et al., 1986, 1988). Negative stain immuno–electron microscopy confirmed that the antigen was associated with the surface of vesicular components (Fig. 8–4c), and immunological analysis of egg fractions obtained by a different procedure (Oberdorf et al., 1986) showed enhanced antigen association with mitochondria and microsomes. These data are particularly interesting in relation to the association of both mitochondria (for review, see Dustin, 1984) and the endoplasmic reticulum (Terasaki and Fugiwara, 1986) with microtubule pathways.

Possible Functions of Egg Dynein

Cytoplasmic dynein-like proteins have been postulated to provide the force for all cell movements that depend on microtubules, including mitotic chromosome movement, vesicle and organelle transport, and cell shape changes. There is evidence that chemical inhibitors of dynein ATPase slow or stop chromosome movement in lysed mammalian cell models (Cande and Wolniak, 1978) and in isolated yeast spindles (Cande and McDonald, 1986), and immunofluorescent antibodies against flagellar dynein stain the mammalian mitotic apparatus (Yoshida et al., 1985; see Pratt, 1984, for a review of dynein ATPases in mitotic spindles). The data discussed above suggest that dynein is also localized in sea urchin mitotic spindles; however, there is no evidence that this protein is the same egg dynein that we have defined. In addition, there is as yet no direct test for dynein function in the sea urchin MA. The data do not support a role for egg dynein per se in chromosome movement, although we cannot rule out the possibility that some form of cytoplasmic dynein contributes to mitotic motility.

Many investigators have suggested a role for dynein in vesicle transport. Pryer et al. (1986) have specifically studied vesicle transport in sea urchin egg extracts and concluded that movement in only one direction appeared to be mediated by kinesin. Membranated organelles in eggs, however, move in two directions (for review, see Rebhun, 1972). The polarity of dynein-mediated movement (Sale and Satir, 1977; Fox and Sale, 1987) would support organelle transport toward microtubule minus ends, in the direction opposite to kinesin, were the dynein associated in an ATP-insensitive manner with organelles (as opposed to the microtubules). As discussed above, we have found that egg dynein is present on the surfaces of isolated egg vesicles in the presence or absence of ATP (Pratt et al., 1986, 1988), but we have not yet examined the microtubule-binding or motile properties of these vesicles.

Another possible role for egg dynein is as a storage form for ciliary dynein. Prior to hatching, each cell in the sea urchin blastula forms a cilium, and large pools of ciliary proteins including dynein are present in the embryo at the time of ciliogenesis (Auclair and Seigel, 1966; Stephens, 1972, 1977). It has been suggested, therefore, that egg dynein may be a precursor of the ciliary enzyme (Weisenberg and Taylor, 1968; Pratt, 1980; Asai et al., 1986; Asai, 1986), but, in fact, there has been no demonstration that a ciliary dynein pool exists in the *unfertilized egg*. Investigation of whether egg dynein serves as a stored precursor of ciliary dynein has been limited to comparisons of egg and ciliary enzyme composition, immunoreactivity, and developmental expression (Stephens, 1972, 1977; Pratt, 1980; Asai et al., 1986; Asai, 1986). Interpretation of these data is complicated. First, it is at present impossible to distinguish chemically between ciliary dynein, egg dynein that may serve as a ciliary precursor, and egg dynein that may serve a non-axonemal function in the egg. Second, isolated egg dynein (and perhaps ciliary dynein) prepared by any of the published procedures represents only a fraction of the total dynein in the egg, so that, in assessing homology by immunochemical or mapping techniques, only a subset of the

egg enzyme is being considered. Thus, the only meaningful data are those that would demonstrate clear non-identity of an egg-derived dynein and a cilia-derived dynein. Currently available data suggest that some ciliary dynein is stored in the unfertilized egg and some is synthesized after fertilization. The ciliary precursor in the egg may be part of that isolated as egg dynein, but the lack of 100% identity leaves open the possibility that some egg dynein is not destined for ciliary incorporation. The precursor question can be seen, therefore, as a distinct issue but one related to the central challenge to demonstrate directly a non-axonemal function for egg dynein.

Multiple Forms of Dynein in Eggs

The preceeding discussion makes it clear that the information concerning egg dynein characteristics, localization, and function are varied and at times contradictory. Investigators in this field agree that sea urchin eggs contain a dynein-like protein that is similar but not identical to axonemal forms of the enzyme. The concensus goes no further, and each investigator has produced and interpreted data to support a different polypeptide conformation, cellular distribution, and functional role of egg dynein. Some of the differences can be attributed to species variation and to unique purification and assay protocols. It is also possible, however, that each investigator is assaying a different subset of the total dynein in eggs.

The variation in published observations can be explained by hypothesizing that sea urchin eggs contain multiple isoforms of dynein. The data suggest that these isoforms include, but may not be limited to, the following: a readily soluble form, some of which can bind to microtubules; a vesicle-associated form; and a form destined to be incorporated into embryonic cilia. At the time of first metaphase, following fertilization, a mitotic form is also seen. This mitotic isoform may arise by modification of the soluble form, possibly involving activation of the molecules previously incapable of microtubule binding or by new protein synthesis.

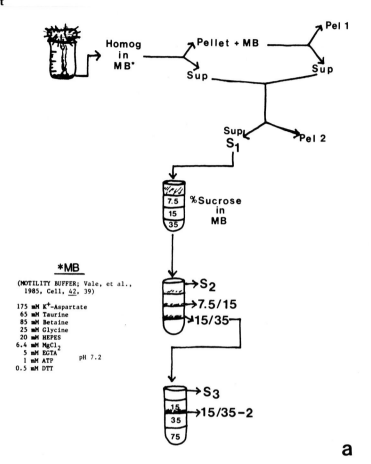

*MB

(MOTILITY BUFFER; Vale, et al.,
1985, Cell, 42, 39)

175 mM K+-Aspartate
 65 mM Taurine
 85 mM Betaine
 25 mM Glycine
 20 mM HEPES
6.4 mM MgCl2
  5 mM EGTA   pH 7.2
  1 mM ATP
0.5 mM DTT

a

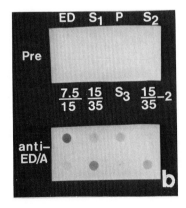

b

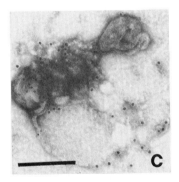

c

The multi-isoform hypothesis is not yet substantiated for egg dynein, but there are several good examples of this concept among other cytoskeletal proteins. Tubulin isoforms have been described in a wide variety of species, and, in some cases, the different forms of tubulin are encoded by separate genes (Cleveland et al., 1980; for review, see Cleveland, 1987). There are also examples where tubulin isoforms arise by post-translational modifications, including acetylation (1 'Hernault and Rosenbaum, 1985) or tyrosylation (Barra et al., 1974; Gunderson et al., 1984). Importantly, it has been discerned that different tubulins make up separate subsets of microtubules within cells and may carry out unique functions (Cleveland et al., 1980; Piperno et al., 1987; Gunderson et al., 1987). Similarly, it is possible that different dynein isoforms carry out separate and specific functions at different sites within a single cell.

DYNEIN-LIKE ATPASES IN NERVE TISSUES

In the search for cytoplasmic forms of dynein, nerve tissue was an obvious source because it was known as a rich source of microtubules, most of which were found in nerve axons, and there was a wealth of published data to show that organelle movement, like fast axonal transport, was a microtubule-dependent process (for review, see Dustin, 1984). The concept that dynein functions in association with axonal microtubules has become even more appealing with the identification of kinesin which plays a role in vesicle movement in the direction corresponding to anterograde transport (Vale et al., 1985b). Dynein could generate movement in the opposite direction (based on demonstrated polarity of axonemal microtubule sliding; Sale and Satir, 1977; Fox and Sale, 1987) and so is one candidate for a "retrograde" motor (Vale et al., 1985b). Dynein has recently been identified in brain tissue by Paschal, Vallee, and coworkers (1987); however, it is soluble, whereas the motor is presumably vesicle-associated. The following section discusses early reports of dynein-like enzymes in brain and squid giant axon, and data suggesting that other high-molecular-mass polypeptides and ATPases are associated with axoplasmic vesicles.

ATPase Activity in Brain and Nerve

In 1974, two sets of investigators reported the identification of dynein-like ATPase and microtubule-associated Mg^{2+} ATPase activity in brain tissue (Burns and Pollard, 1974; Gaskin et al., 1974). Both investigators also noted, however, that the enzyme activity did not appear to purify with the high-M_r polypeptides, but instead was associated with a large macromolecular species that in one case was suggested to be vesicular (Gaskin et al., 1974). The Elegant work of Murphy and his coworkers (1983a,b) revealed that this ATPase activity is associated with membrane vesicles that fortuitously copurify with microtubules even after several cycles of assembly. Enzyme activity is associated with

---

Fig. 8–4. Preparation of organelles from sea urchin eggs and immunoassay for dynein-like proteins. **a:** Eggs were homogenized in motility buffer (MB), centrifuged at 10,000 rpm for 5 min, and then reextracted with MB. The resulting supernatants were pooled and fractionated on a step gradient. The pool from the 15–35 interface was diluted and refractionated on another gradient. Samples were collected and named as indicated. **b:** Fractions prepared as shown in a were dotted onto nitrocellulose (250 ng protein/dot). Specific egg dynein antigens were assayed by incubation with preimmune or anti-egg dynein A (anti-ED/A) antisera followed by a goat-anti-rabbit IgG antibody coupled to horseradish peroxidase. Secondary antibody was visualized by incubation with 4-chloro-2-naphthol and hydrogen peroxide. **c:** Egg dynein was visualized on isolated vesicles by negative stain immuno–electron microscopy (Rothwell et al., 1985). Isolated organelles from the 15–35 interface were fixed lightly, placed on copper grids, and incubated with the anti-ED/A and a secondary antibody coupled to colloidal gold. The complex was visualized by staining with 1.5% uranyl acetate. Scale bar = 200 nm.

polypeptides of 50,000 Da and is similar to the F_1 mitochondrial ATPase. The high-molecular-mass polypeptides identified by Burns and Pollard (1974) and by Gaskin et al. (1974) were undoubtably the microtubule-associated proteins (MAPs) 1 and 2, which have since been characterized (Vallee et al., 1986; for review, see Soifer, 1986). It is one of these MAPs, MAP 1C, that Paschal and coworkers (1987) have identified as dynein.

A major and clear disadvantage in using brain as a source for isolation of axonal transport ATPases is the complexity of the tissue. For this reason, many researchers turned to peripheral nerve tissue, with the result that Mg^{2+}—Ca^{2+} ATPases were identified in cat and frog nerve (Khan and Ochs, 1974; Hammerschlag and Bobinski, 1981). Sheckett and Lasek (1982) later described what appeared to be the same ATPase isolated from squid giant axon. This preparation has the great advantage that pure axoplasm is used as the starting material, and thus the axonal localization of the enzyme activity is confirmed. In each of these three reports, the ATPase activity was found in a particulate fraction, and the investigators proposed its association with the axonal cytoskeleton. It is equally possible however, as pointed out by Sheckett and Lasek (1982), that the enzyme is associated with a vesicle fraction. Significantly, this enzyme does not have the characteristics of the F_1-like ATPase described by Murphy et al. (1983a,b). Instead, the ATPase activity shows some similarity to dynein, although direct comparisons have not been made. None of the nerve ATPases was purifed to homogeneity, but the cleanest preparation was that of Sheckett and Lasek (1982), who found that the ATPase activity was associated with a polypeptide of M_r over 200,000.

We have recently identified a Mg^{2+} ATPase activity in squid axons (Pratt, 1986c), which we believe is identical to that described by Sheckett and Lasek (1982). This activity is found in a preparation of axoplasmic vesicles and shows enzymology similar though not identical to that of dynein. We had been trying for some time to isolate dynein from axoplasm but found that most of the ATPase activity was insoluble. We, therefore, adopted a new strategy of using taxol-stabilized microtubules as an affinity substrate to identify microtubule-binding proteins, which resulted in the isolation of stable complexes of microtubules and axoplasmic vesicles. These microtubule-vesicle complexes contained a defined subset of axoplasmic proteins, which were shown by fractionation studies to be vesicle-associated (Pratt, 1986c; also see Fig. 8–5). Significantly, the complexes had ATPase activity and contained a substantial amount of an high-molecular-mass protein (3), which comigrated with a flagellar dynein heavy chain (Fig. 8–5). Another large protein (2) was found to associate with the microtubule–vesicle complexes but only in the presence of nucleotide. This second protein is the one described by Gilbert and Sloboda (1986; Sloboda, Chapter 14) as a MAP 2-like protein that binds ATP. Significantly, protein 3, which comigrates with dynein, did not bind ATP in their assays. All these vesicle-associated ATPases and ATP-binding proteins are possible motors for retrograde transport, or might even play a role in anterograde vesicle movement, but further careful analysis is necessary. The possible relationship between these proteins and dynein is especially intriguing now that we have evidence for egg dynein association with sea urchin vesicles (see above).

Using a different purification strategy, including ATP-induced release of microtubule-associated proteins and subsequent sucrose-density gradient fractionation, Hollenbeck and Chapman (1986) identified a high-M_r protein with ATPase activity from bovine spinal nerve roots. This protein appears to be different from any of those discussed above. It is associated with microtubules but can be solubilized with ATP, in contrast to the vesicle-associated ATPase, which partially copurifies with microtubules but requires dichloromethane or detergent for solubilization (Murphy et al., 1983a,b). Although the enzymatic activity is activated by Mg^{2+} ions, it shows unique ionic and inhibitor sensitiv-

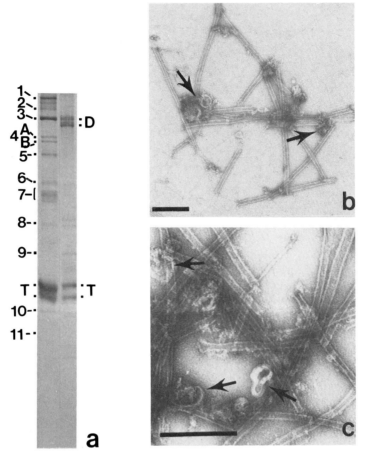

Fig. 8–5. Protein composition and ultrastructure of microtubule-vesicle complexes (MtVC) from squid giant axon. Complexes were prepared by incubating taxol-stabilized squid brain microtubules with disrupted axoplasm and then collecting the tubules through a 50% sucrose cushion (Pratt, 1986c). **a:** The polypeptide profile of the MtVC was compared with that of flagellar axonemes on gradient polyacrylamide gels. Consistent components of the MtVC are indicated by number at the left. The positions of dynein (D) and tubulin (T) are also marked. **b** and **c:** Negative stain electron microscopy showing the MtVC at low (B) and high (C) magnifications. Arrows indicate prominent vesicular components. Scale bars = 250 nm.

ities when compared to the Mg^{2+} ATPases, the F_1-like ATPase, and dynein. In addition, this protein can induce microtubule bundling, suggesting that it has two tubulin binding sites rather than a strong vesicle binding domain.

CONCLUSIONS

The concept of non-axonemal dynein ATPases has been a subject of conjecture for over 20 years. It is now clear that true dynein can be isolated from several non-axonemal sources, including sea urchin egg and bovine brain. Furthermore, at least some of the egg dynein can associate with non-axonemal cytoplasmic microtubules and with motile organelles. An important and immediate challenge in the characterization of egg dynein is to demonstrate that the non-axonemal enzyme can produce force and movement in association with cytoplasmic microtubules. One experimental approach is to construct in vitro motility systems similar to the ones described by Vale and coworkers (1985a,b) and by Pryer et al. (1986), which have been used successfully to demonstrate the motile properties of brain dynein (Paschal et al., 1987a, 1987b). Another is to make specific anti-dynein probes that inhibit ATPase activity and to analyze their effects on cytoplasmic motility, in the way that other workers have tested the role of myosin ATPase in intracellular movement (Mabuchi and Okuno, 1977; Kiehart et al., 1982).

Another immediate goal in the analysis of cytoplasmic dynein function is the identification and characterization of the enzyme from sources other than echinoderm eggs and bovine brain. Recent advances have made it practical to use the power of molecular biology to address this issue. Improvements in nucleic acid biochemistry have made possible the cloning of larger genes, including MAP 2 at 250,000 Da (Goldstein et al., 1986) and spectrin at 240,000 Da (Birkenmeier et al., 1985). In addition, there are now several excellent dynein antibodies that can be used to screen cDNA libraries in expression vectors. Moreover, a part of a *Chlamydomonas* dynein heavy chain gene has been cloned (Williams et al., 1986), proving the feasibility of this approach and providing a probe for future cloning endeavors.

The information available about egg dynein preparation, characterization, and localization provides a foundation for the further study of this enzyme and of cytoplasmic dyneins in general. Biochemical comparisons of egg dynein with axonemal dynein have shown that the two are similar but have significantly unique properties. With improved purification procedures and immunological and nucleic acid probes, it is now possible to compare egg and axonemal dyneins morphologically, to determine the relationships between different isoforms of cytoplasmic dynein, and to analyze the presence of cytoplasmic dynein in other cell types.

ACKNOWLEDGMENTS

The author thanks Barbara Schroeder, Bruce Crise, and Aline Betancourt for technical assistance with much of the work discussed here; Teri Butler for providing the samples appearing in Figure 1; and George Shelton for photographic work. David Asai, Leah Haimo, Peter Hollenbeck, Steve Penningroth, Gianni Piperno, Mary Porter, Nancy Pryer, and Pat Wadsworth provided reprints and in some cases preprints to help in preparing this review. I am also grateful to my colleagues Win Sale, Mary Porter, Nelson Barton, and David Burgess for many stimulating discussions. Special thanks go to Win Sale for several critical readings of the manuscript and many incorporated suggestions and to Fred Warner for editorial assistance.

CHAPTER

9

Cytoplasmic Dynein and Microtubule Translocators

R. John Lye, Curtis M. Pfarr, and Mary E. Porter

Department of Molecular, Cellular, and Developmental Biology, University of Colorado, Boulder, Colorado 80309

INTRODUCTION

Many types of intracellular movement depend on microtubules, but the molecular basis of force production for these movements is not well understood. In some instances, e.g., chromosome motion during anaphase, motility is closely coupled to the assembly and disassembly of the microtubules themselves (Inoué and Sato, 1967). Other forms of motility, such as the beating of cilia and flagella, utilize the sliding of microtubules relative to one another to achieve movement (Satir, 1968; Summers and Gibbons, 1971). Still other forms of intracellular motility, such as fast axonal transport, depend on the interaction of microtubules with some additional components, such as the membrane of a vesicle (Allen et al., 1985; Brady et al., 1985; Gilbert et al., 1985; Schnapp et al., 1985; Vale et al., 1985a,b). Thus far, two families of microtubule-associated motors have been identified: dynein and kinesin. An important theme in current research is to identify the role that each type of motor plays in microtubule-mediated motility.

The dynein adenosine triphosphatases (ATPases) were first identified as the large, multisubunit enzymes that form the inner and outer arms of eukaryotic cilia and flagella (reviewed in Gibbons, 1965; Luck, 1984). These enzymes couple a chemical cycle of ATP binding and hydrolysis to a mechanical cycle of microtubule cross bridging and release (reviewed in Johnson, 1985). In the axoneme, the dynein arm that is bound to the A subfiber "walks" toward the proximal or "minus" end of the adjacent B subfiber; thus the B subfiber is pushed toward the tip of the axoneme, with its distal or "plus" end leading (Sale and Satir, 1977; Fox and Sale, 1987).

Kinesins have recently been identified in extracts of squid axoplasm (Vale et al., 1985c) and in some non-neuronal tissues (Scholey et al., 1985; Vale et al., 1985c). This enzyme may be distinguished from the dynein ATPase of cilia and flagella by functional, structural, and pharmacological criteria (Vale et al., 1985c). In vitro, kinesin "walks" over microtubules toward their "plus" ends and thereby induces the gliding of microtubules, with their minus ends leading. Kinesin-coated beads move toward the plus end of the microtubules with which they associate (Vale et al., 1985d; Pryer et al., 1986; Porter et al., 1987d). Since microtubules in nerve axons are oriented with their plus ends at the nerve terminal (Burton and Paige, 1981; Heidemann et al., 1981), kinesin in neuronal tissue is thought to act as an anterograde vesicle motor.

A unidirectional motor like kinesin cannot account for the bidirectional movements of organelles and particles seen both in vivo and in vitro (Brady et al., 1985; Vale et al., 1985a,b,d; Gilbert et al., 1985; Pryer et al., 1986). Furthermore, pharmacological and immunological studies of particle movements in vitro have indicated the presence of additional mechanochemical factors that move vesicles or beads over microtubules in the direction opposite to that induced by kinesin (Vale et al., 1985d; Koonce and Schliwa, 1986a; see minireview, this section). Since microtubule sliding and bidirectional motility are features of many types of microtubule movements both in vivo and in vitro, and since the polarity of action of flagellar dynein is opposite to that of kinesin, several investigators have sought a cytoplasmic motor analogous to the dynein ATPase that might serve as a retrograde or minus-end-directed microtubule-associated motor.

The search for a cytoplasmic dynein has met with mixed results in different systems. For the most part, analyses of mammalian cell lines and brain tissues have produced equivocal evidence (Zieve and McIntosh, 1981; Murphy et al., 1983b; Yoshida et al., 1985). On the other hand, several investigators have identified a dynein-like ATPase activity in extracts of unfertilized sea urchin eggs (Weisenberg and Taylor, 1968; Pratt, 1980; Hisanaga and Sakai, 1980, 1983; Scholey et al., 1984; Hollenbeck et al., 1984; Asai and Wilson, 1985; Penningroth et al., 1985; Pratt, Chapters 7, 8). Many workers have proposed a mitotic function for this enzyme (Mohri et al., 1976; Pratt, 1980; Pratt et al., 1980; Hirokawa et al., 1985). However, sea urchin eggs also assemble large numbers of embryonic cilia at the late blastula stage of development (Stephens, 1972, 1977; Kimura, 1977), so it is possible that the cytoplasmic dynein is present in the sea urchin egg simply as a ciliary precursor.

In this chapter, we review data on the structure and function of the cytoplasmic dynein activity present in sea urchin eggs. We also describe a new approach for the identification of dynein-like polypeptides and present evidence for the existence of novel, dynein-like microtubule translocators in several cell types in which they are unlikely to serve simply as axonemal dynein precursors.

CYTOPLASMIC DYNEIN IN SEA URCHIN EGGS

Cytoplasmic dynein has been identified in sea urchin eggs as a vanadate-sensitive ATPase activity that copurified with high-M_r polypeptides (Weisenberg and Taylor, 1968; Pratt, 1980; Hisanaga and Sakai, 1980, 1983; Hisanaga and Pratt, 1984; Pratt et al., 1984; Hollenbeck et al., 1984; Scholey et al., 1984; Asai and Wilson, 1985; Penningroth et al., 1985). The detailed characteristics of the different preparations are, however, highly variable (see Pratt, Chapter 7, for review). For example, it has been unclear whether the cytoplasmic dynein activity is a single enzyme or exists in multiple isoforms. Since sea urchin 21S flagellar dynein is easily dissociated into 10S–12S subunits (Tang et al., 1982), it is possible that the 12S species identified by most laboratories (Weisenberg and Taylor, 1968; Pratt, 1980; Hisanaga and Sakai, 1983; Scholey et al., 1984; Penningroth et al., 1985) is a breakdown product of the 20S species (Asai and Wilson, 1985). Alternatively, the different subunits may represent distinct isoforms, such as those associated with inner and outer arms on flagellar doublet microtubules (Piperno and Luck, 1979, 1981). In addition, the polypeptide composition of the cytoplasmic dynein preparation varies with each report. This variability may be due, in part, to the existence of multiple dynein isoforms, or it may result simply from differences in purification technique (see Pratt, Chapter 7, for review).

The uncertainty over polypeptide composition has inevitably clouded the interpretation of data concerning the binding of cytoplasmic dynein to microtubules. Several laboratories have reported the copelleting of a dynein-like ATPase activity and high-M_r polypeptides with either endogenous or exogenous microtubules (Hisanaga and Sakai, 1983; Scholey et al., 1984; Hollenbeck et al., 1984; Asai and Wilson, 1985). However, the amount of dynein-like ATPase activity recovered from the microtubules was fairly low (Hollenbeck et al., 1984; Scholey et al., 1984). Furthermore, recent studies on the enzymatic characteristics of the microtubule-associated ATPase have indicated that sea urchin microtubules also contain ATPase activities distinct from cytoplasmic dynein (Collins and Vallee, 1986b; Dinenberg et al., 1986; Porter et al., 1988).

Another unresolved issue is the relationship of cytoplasmic dynein to the axonemal precursors of embryonic cilia (Stephens, 1972, 1977; Kimura, 1977). Comparative peptide mapping data indicated that homologies exist between cytoplasmic and flagellar dynein heavy chains (Pratt, 1986a), but immunological evidence has been equivocal. For example, antibodies prepared against flagellar dynein have been reported to cross react with preparations of cytoplasmic dynein (Asai and Wilson, 1982; Asai et al., 1985) and to recognize related antigens in isolated mitotic apparatus (Mohri et al., 1976; Sakai et al., 1976; Piperno, 1984; Hisanaga et al., 1987). On the other hand, antibodies prepared against cytoplasmic dyneins have been shown to cross react with embryonic cilia in one case (Asai, 1986) and cytoplasmic vesicles in another (Pratt, 1986c) but have failed to stain the mitotic spindle (Asai, 1986; Pratt, 1986c).

Thus, in spite of intense study, it remains uncertain whether sea urchin cytoplasmic dynein is a single enzyme, what its polypeptide composition is, and whether it is related to axonemal components or functions elsewhere in the cytoplasm. With these questions in mind, we set out to reinvestigate the nature and location of cytoplasmic dynein in unfertilized sea urchin eggs (Porter et al., 1988).

ONE FORM OF CYTOPLASMIC DYNEIN IN SEA URCHIN EGGS IS IMMUNOLOGICALLY RELATED TO FLAGELLAR AND CILIARY DYNEINS

We have approached the study of the egg dynein ATPases with a combination of biochemical and immunological techniques. First, we have prepared polyclonal antibodies against the sea urchin sperm flagellar dynein A band (containing both the α and β heavy chains) and have used blot affinity-purified antibodies (Olmsted, 1981) to follow the distribution of dynein-related polypeptides throughout a variety of fractionation protocols (Porter et al., 1988). Second, we have correlated these data with the distribution of dynein-like ATPase activity in the different egg fractions. Our results indicate that homogenization of sea urchin eggs in an isotonic buffer, followed by differential centrifugation, releases dynein-related antigens into a soluble cytoplasmic extract (Porter et al., 1988). Following microtubule polymerization, induced by the addition of taxol and guanosine triphosphate (GTP) to the egg extracts, and differential centrifugation to collect the microtubules (Vallee and Bloom, 1983; Scholey et al., 1984), over 90% of the dynein-related antigens and ATPase activity remains in the microtubule-depleted egg extract. This activity can be further purified via column chromatography and sucrose density gradient centrifugation to yield a peak of ATPase activity cosedimenting at 20S with high-M_r polypeptides. The enzymatic characteristics of this preparation are virtually identical to those described for flagellar dynein (e.g., broad pH optimum, strict requirement for divalent cations, high degree of specificity for ATP, and inhibition by micromolar levels of sodium vanadate), in agreement with data obtained by others (Hisanaga and Sakai, 1983; Pratt et al., 1984; Scholey et al., 1984; Hollenbeck et al., 1984; Asai and Wilson, 1985). The soluble enzyme can also be

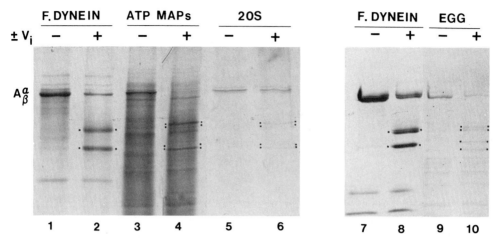

Fig. 9–1. Vanadate-sensitized UV cleavage of heavy chain polypeptides prepared from sea urchin sperm flagella and sea urchin egg cytoplasm. The following fractions were irradiated for 10 min at 365 nm in the presence of 10 mM MgATP ± 100 μM sodium vanadate and then analyzed by SDS-PAGE on 5–15% polyacrylamide gradient gels. Only the high-M_r region (>100,000 kDa) of the gel is shown. **Lanes 1,2:** Sea urchin sperm flagellar 21S dynein containing the α and β heavy chains. **Lanes 3, 4:** A 10-mM MgATP extract of sea urchin egg microtubules. **Lanes 5,6:** The 20S peak following sucrose density gradient centrifugation of the ATP MAPs. In a separate experiment, the following samples were irradiated in the presence of 1 mM MgATP plus/minus 10 μM sodium vanadate: **Lanes 7,8:** Sea urchin sperm flagellar 21S dynein (α and β). **Lanes 9,10:** Sea urchin cytoplasmic dynein prepared from microtubule-depleted egg extracts.

activated up to fivefold by preincubation with 0.1% Triton X-100, thereby displaying the "latent" activity described for flagellar dynein by Gibbons and Fronk (1979) and for egg dynein by Asai and Wilson (1985). Sedimentation in the presence of 0.1% Triton X-100 shifts the peak of ATPase activity and high-M_r polypeptides to approximately 10S–12S (Porter et al., 1988). These data suggest that the soluble 20S cytoplasmic dynein activity is similar to latent activity 21S dynein from sperm flagella (Tang et al., 1982).

High-resolution sodium dodecyl sulfate-polyacrylamide gel electrophoresis (SDS-PAGE) has indicated that our most highly purified preparations of the soluble cytoplasmic dynein are composed of two or three heavy chain polypeptides depending on the gel system used for analysis. These polypeptides comigrate with the A band heavy chain polypeptides (containing both the α and β chains) of both embryonic cilia and flagellar dynein. Furthermore, the purified egg and ciliary dynein polypeptides cross react on immunoblots with our antibodies against the flagellar dynein A band polypeptides. Ultraviolet (UV) irradiation of purified cytoplasmic dynein in the presence of MgATP and vanadate induces the specific cleavage of the dynein heavy chains into peptide fragments (see below), which approximately comigrate with the cleavage products of the flagellar dynein A-band (Fig. 9–1, lanes 7–10). Finally, immunolocalization studies have indicated that, although dynein-related antigens can be detected on immunoblots of isolated mitotic apparatus, these antigens are not concentrated in the mitotic apparatus above the background staining of the cytoplasm (Porter and Grissom, unpublished observations). Our results demonstrate that these cytoplasmic dynein polypeptides are closely related to ciliary and flagellar dynein polypeptides and are consistent with the hypothesis (Weisenberg and Taylor, 1968; Asai, 1986) that the soluble cytoplasmic dynein in sea urchin eggs is part of a precursor pool for ciliogenesis (Porter et al., 1988).

DYNEIN-LIKE POLYPEPTIDES IN SEA URCHIN EGGS THAT ARE IMMUNOLOGICALLY UNRELATED TO THE FLAGELLAR DYNEIN HEAVY CHAINS (α AND β)

Dynein-like ATPase activity has also been described in association with high-M_r polypeptides in preparations of taxol-assembled microtubules (Scholey et al., 1984). Closer examination of these preparations has indicated, however, that the taxol-assembled microtubules from sea urchin eggs contain a complex mixture of ATPase activities and multiple high-M_r polypeptides (Dinenberg et al., 1986; Collins and Vallee, 1986b; Porter et al., 1988). Dynein-related polypeptides and ATPase activity are only minor components of these preparations (Porter et al., 1988).

Although taxol-assembled microtubules contain relatively small amounts of the soluble cytoplasmic dynein polypeptides, these preparations do contain a distinct high-M_r polypeptide, previously designated HMr-3 by Scholey et al. (1984). HMr-3 has several dynein-like characteristics: 1) Its association with microtubules is ATP-sensitive; 2) it sediments at 20S on sucrose density gradients (Porter et al., 1988); and 3) it is susceptible to cleavage by UV irradiation in the presence of vanadate (Porter et al., 1988) (Figs. 9–1, 9–2). The HMr-3 polypeptide can, however, be distinguished from both flagellar dynein and the soluble cytoplasmic dynein on the basis of its weak cross reactivity with antiflagellar dynein antibodies, its heavy chain composition on high-resolution gels, its low specific activity ATPase, and its pattern of vanadate-sensitized UV cleavage products (Porter et al., 1988). These results suggest that HMr-3 may represent a dynein-like polypeptide that is distinct from the pool of ciliary dynein precursors. If so, then we might expect to find microtubule-associated polypeptides (MAPs) analogous to HMr-3 in other cell types that do not assemble cilia or flagella, and recent evidence suggests that this is the case.

VANADATE-SENSITIZED UV CLEAVAGE AS A PROBE FOR DYNEIN-LIKE POLYPEPTIDES

Recent studies by Gibbons and colleagues have suggested that the vanadate-sensitized UV cleavage reaction of the dynein heavy chains may be a specific probe for the presence of dynein-like ATP binding sites in other polypeptides (Lee-Eiford et al., 1986; Gibbons et al., 1987; Gibbons and Gibbons, 1987). We have now tested the specificity of the UV cleavage reaction with other vanadate-sensitive ATPases and have observed no detectable cleavage under our conditions with these test enzymes: bovine brain kinesin (with or without microtubules), rabbit skeletal muscle myosin, and dog kidney Na^+, K^+-ATPase (Porter et al., 1987b) (see Fig. 9–3). We have also tested a number of MAPs, including the sea urchin egg MAPs HMr-1 and HMr-2 and bovine brain MAP 2. We have found these polypeptides to be resistant to vanadate-sensitized UV cleavage under our conditions. These data suggest that the vanadate-sensitized UV cleavage reaction may be a specific probe for the presence of dynein-like ATP binding domains in non-axonemal polypeptides. We have now found a number of high-M_r, ATP-sensitive, MAPs that are susceptible to vanadate-induced UV cleavage (see Fig. 9–2). These include the sea urchin MAP HMr-3 (Porter et al., 1988); the *Caenorhabditis elegans* microtubule translocator (Lye et al., 1987); and related polypeptides prepared from extracts of mammalian brain (Paschal et al., 1987; Porter et al., 1987b), *Drosophila* embryos (Porter et al., 1987c), and mammalian tissue culture cells (Pfarr and McIntosh, unpublished results) (see Fig. 9–2). The function and interrelationships of these polypeptides is the subject of current investigation.

Dynein-like polypeptides have also been identified in various cell extracts by other laboratories. Pallini and coworkers (1983) identified dynein-like cytidine-triphosphatases (CTPases) in extracts of mammalian brain, tissue culture cells, and insect eggs.

A.

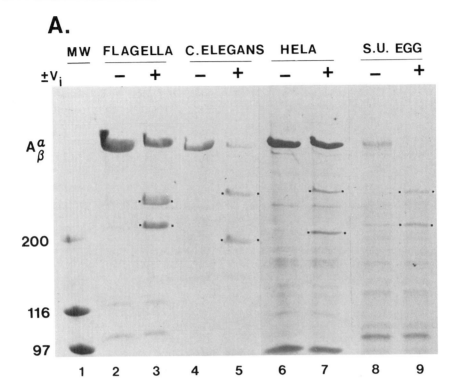

B.

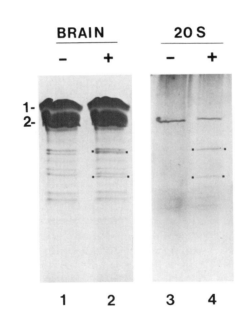

A.

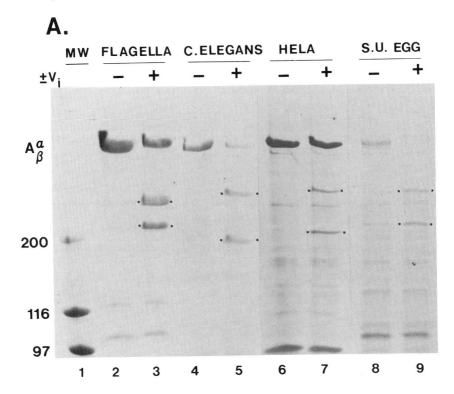

B.

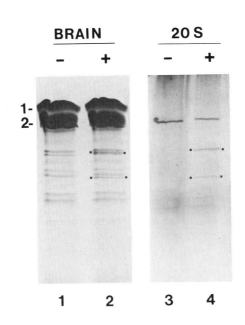

These enzymes shared similar high-M_r polypeptides and sedimented at 19S on sucrose density gradients. High-M_r polypeptides that display ATP-sensitive microtubule binding have also been found in extracts of squid axoplasm (Gilbert and Sloboda, 1986; Pratt, 1986a) and bovine spinal cord (Hollenbeck and Chapman, 1986). The spinal cord polypeptide, designated HMW-4, was capable of bundling microtubules in vitro as assayed by dark-field light microscopy (Hollenbeck and Chapman, 1986). Whether any of these dynein-like polypeptides is susceptible to vanadate-induced UV cleavage remains to be determined.

A DYNEIN-LIKE MICROTUBULE TRANSLOCATOR FROM *C. ELEGANS*

The studies on cytoplasmic dyneins described above share a common limitation: They have been conducted on extracts from ciliated organisms. As such, it is difficult to know whether the dynein-like molecules identified correspond to soluble precursors of axonemal structures or to cytoplasmic enzymes with a function outside the axoneme. Most animals contain cilia or flagella at some stage of development or in some organ. Sea urchins are ciliated at the late blastula stage, insect sperm are flagellated, mammals contain cilia and flagella in various organs, and many tissue culture cells contain a primary cilium. In addition, cells in continuous culture often express genes from tissues other than their tissue of origin. For these reasons, we have chosen to look for dynein-like molecules in an organism that is not ciliated at any stage of its life cycle. The nematode *C. elegans* does not form motile cilia; the sperm are ameboid (Nelson et al., 1982), and neither the embryos, the intestines, nor the gonads are ciliated (Chitwood and Chitwood, 1974). Although the touch sensory neurons contain doublet microtubules (Ward et al., 1975), these microtubules are not arranged as in an axoneme and appear to be structural rather than motile. We have recently purified from *C. elegans* a dynein-like protein that is therefore unlikely to be of axonemal origin (Lye et al., 1987).

Using a modification of the taxol-dependent purification method of Vallee (1982), we have prepared microtubules from extracts of gravid *C. elegans* adults. This procedure utilizes the microtubules that polymerize from the endogenous tubulin as an affinity matrix for collecting microtubule binding proteins. The microtubules and their associated polypeptides are collected by differential centrifugation through a sucrose cushion. When the pellet is analyzed by SDS-PAGE, the predominant polypeptides are α and β tubulin, but there are several other proteins whose sedimentation depends on the presence of the assembled microtubules (Lye et al., 1987). Most prominent among these is a polypeptide of

Fig. 9–2. Vanadate-sensitized UV cleavage of high-M_r MAPs prepared from different organisms: **A:** The following fractions were irradiated for 30 min at 365 nm in the presence of 1 mM MgATP ± 10 μM sodium vanadate. **Lanes 2,3:** Sea urchin sperm flagellar 21S dynein (α and β). **Lanes 4,5:** Purified, high-M_r microtubule translocator prepared from *C. elegans.* **Lanes 6,7:** Partially purified, high-M_r MAP from HeLa cell extracts. **Lanes 7,8:** An ATP extract of sea urchin egg microtubules (similar to lanes 3 and 4 in Fig. 9–1). **Lane 1** contains molecular weight markers. Lanes 6 and 7 were stained with silver nitrate; the remainder were stained with Coomassie brilliant blue. **B:** A crude MgATP extract of twice-cycled bovine brain microtubules containing MAPs 1 and 2 was irradiated in the absence (**lane 1**) or the presence (**lane 2**) of 100 μM sodium vanadate for 30 min. The majority of the MAP 1 and MAP 2 heavy chains was unaffected by the UV irradiation. However, trace amounts of two new peptide fragments were detected in the sample containing vanadate (lane 2). The crude MgATP extract was then subjected to sucrose density gradient centrifugation and separated into multiple MAP-containing species. The MAP fractions sedimenting at 20S and at 7S were then retested for their sensitivity to vanadate-induced UV cleavage. Only the 20S material, shown in **lanes 3** and **4,** was sensitive to UV induced cleavage in the presence of MgATP and vanadate (lane 4).

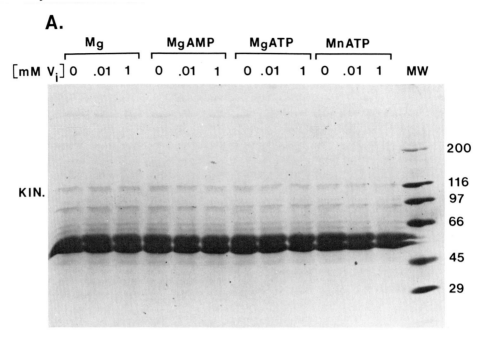

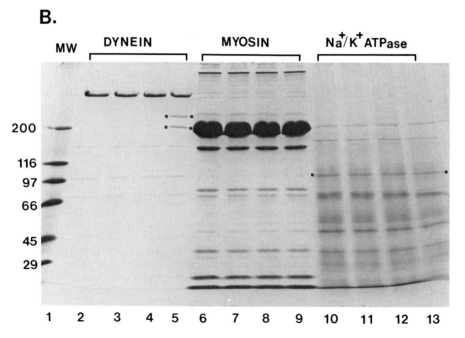

Fig. 9–3. Vanadate-induced UV cleavage is a specific probe for dynein-like ATPases. **A:** Bovine brain kinesin (kindly provided by Bonnie Neighbors) was incubated in the presence of taxol-assembled phosphocellulose purified tubulin under different conditions as indicated and UV irradiated for 30 min at 0°C. The irradiated samples were then analyzed by SDS-PAGE. No cleavage of the kinesin 120 kDa polypeptide was observed under the conditions tested. **B:** Sea urchin flagellar dynein, rabbit skeletal muscle myosin, and dog kidney Na^+, K^+-ATPase were tested for their sensitivity to vanadate-induced UV cleavage. Each enzyme was UV irradiated for 30 min at 0°C under the following conditions: buffer alone **(lanes 2, 6, 10)**, buffer + 1 mM MgATP **(lanes 3, 7, 11)**, buffer + 10 μM vanadate **(lanes 4, 8, 12)**, buffer + 1 mM MgATP + 10 μM vanadate **(lanes 5, 9, 13)**. Only the dynein heavy chain was cleaved in the presence of MgATP and sodium vanadate.

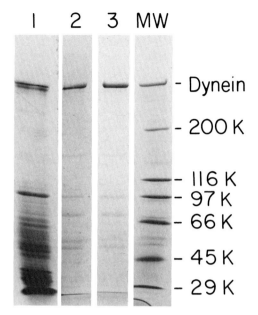

Fig. 9–4. Stages in the purification of the microtubule translocator from *C. elegans*. Fractions taken during the purification of the microtubule translocator were analyzed on a 4–11% SDS-polyacrylamide gradient gel. **Lane 1** is the supernatant that remains after microtubules have been incubated in buffer containing 10 mM MgATP and 100 mM NaCl, followed by centrifugation to pellet the microtubules. **Lane 2** is the pooled fractions from a 5–20% sucrose density gradient that contain microtubule translocating activity. **Lane 3** is the fraction from a DEAE-Sephadex column that contains the peak of the microtubule translocating activity. In each case, a peak of ATPase activity copurifies with the peak of the motility inducing activity. **Lane MW** contains Sigma high-M_r markers plus sea urchin sperm flagellar 21S dynein (α and β).

$M_r \sim 400$ kDa, which coelectrophoreses with the heavy chains of either sea urchin or *Tetrahymena* axonemal dynein. The binding of this polypeptide to microtubules is sensitive to the concentration of ATP in the extract. If either hexokinase (and glucose) or apyrase is added during microtubule assembly, thereby reducing the concentration of endogenous ATP, the amount of the 400 kDa polypeptide that pellets is in-

creased approximately tenfold. The microtubule pellet may then be washed in buffer to remove loosely bound proteins and any residual hexokinase or apyrase without significant loss of the bound, dynein-like polypeptide. When the washed microtubules are then incubated in buffer supplemented with 10 mM MgATP and 100 mM NaCl, almost all of the 400 kDa polypeptide is extracted from the microtubules.

The ATP-extractable material contains a dynein-like ATPase activity. If the ATP-extractable proteins are concentrated and separated on a 5–20% sucrose density gradient, a major fraction of this ATPase activity cosediments with the peak of the 400 kDa polypeptide at $\sim$ 20S. If the peak of the 400 kDa polypeptide from the sucrose gradient is loaded onto an anion-exchange column and eluted with a step gradient of KCl, the ATPase activity continues to copurify with the 400 kDa polypeptide. Since this ATPase activity copurifies with the 400 kDa polypeptide through three different separatory procedures (microtubule affinity, sucrose density sedimentation, and ion-exchange chromatography; see Fig. 9–4), the protein that contains the 400 kDa polypeptide is likely to be an ATPase.

We have used the video-enhanced microscopic assay that was employed to identify kinesin in squid axoplasm and sea urchin extracts and have detected microtubule gliding activity in crude preparations of the nematode 400 kDa polypeptide. The MgATP extract prepared from nematode taxol-assembled microtubules supports the translocation of taxol-stabilized microtubules in vitro. This translocator activity cosediments on sucrose gradients at 20S with both the peak of the 400 kDa polypeptide and the major peak of the ATPase activity; none of the other fractions from the gradient contains motility-inducing activity. The fractions from the ion-exchange column that contain both the 400 kDa polypeptide and the ATPase activity are also able to support microtubule translocation; none of the other fractions supports microtubule gliding. Therefore, as well as being an ATPase, the protein that contains the 400 kDa polypeptide is likely to be involved in microtubule-based movement.

Although both the ATPase and the microtubule translocating activities copurify with the 400 kDa polypeptide through the three steps of purification, and the 400 kDa polypeptide is the major component of the active fractions, it is possible that these activities are due to other components that fortuitously copurify with the 400 kDa polypeptide. To address this question, and to determine whether the ATPase is dynein-like, we have examined the concentrations of various reagents required to inhibit both the ATPase activity and the motility. The ATPase is 50% inhibited by N-ethylmaleimide (NEM) at concentrations >1 mM and by sodium ortho-vanadate at concentrations >10 μM. These values are comparable to the concentrations that inhibit flagellar dynein ATPases (Gibbons et al., 1978). The motility is blocked by NEM concentrations >1 mM and by vanadate concentrations >5 μM.

Flagellar dynein possesses a "latent" activity ATPase that is stimulated by treatment with the non-ionic detergent Triton X-100 (Gibbons and Fronk, 1979). The detergent-treated dynein is, however, unable to restore the beat frequency of salt-extracted axonemes in reconstitution experiments (Gibbons and Gibbons, 1979). If the purified nematode ATPase is treated with 0.2% Triton X-100, its ATPase activity is enhanced by 50%. However, detergent treatment of the nematode enzyme has an adverse effect on microtubule translocation; initially translocation is slowed, whereas incubations of several hours abolish activity altogether. Control preparations incubated in parallel but without detergent are still active.

As described above, the vanadate-sensitized UV cleavage reaction may be diagnostic for dynein-like ATP binding sites. If the nematode protein is UV irradiated in the presence of ATP and vanadate, the 400 kDa heavy chain is cleaved to produce two cleavage products (Fig. 9–2). After UV irradiation, the nematode protein is unable to translocate microtubules. This loss of activity is not due simply to the UV irradiation, because control preparations in which the vanadate has been reduced with norepinephrine (Gibbons et al., 1978) before irradiation continue to support microtubule translocation (Lye et al., 1987). In sum, the responses of the ATPase activity and the motility-inducing activity to vanadate, NEM, Triton, and vanadate-sensitized UV cleavage suggest that both activities are caused by the same protein, and that this protein is dynein-like.

The nematode protein is clearly different from kinesin, even though it shares the ability to translocate microtubules in vitro. Kinesin sediments on sucrose gradients at 9.5S rather than 20S (Porter et al., 1987a). The heavy chain of kinesin has an M_r of 115–135 kDa (depending on the species), rather than the 400 kDa heavy chain of the nematode protein (Vale et al., 1985c; Scholey et al., 1985). Although hexokinase and apyrase are equally effective at promoting the binding of the nematode protein to microtubules, the binding of kinesin to microtubules is enhanced far more by apyrase than by hexokinase (Cohn et al., 1987). Kinesin-induced motility is much less sensitive than the nematode protein to inhibition by NEM and vanadate (Vale et al., 1985a), and it is relatively insensitive to Triton X-100 (Porter et al., 1987a). The motility induced by the nematode protein is much less sensitive to the non-hydrolyzable ATP analogue AMP-PNP than is kinesin-induced motility. As previously described, kinesin is not cleaved by UV light under the conditions that are used to cleave flagellar dynein (Porter et al., 1987b) (see Fig. 9–3). Kinesin can utilize GTP, and to a limited extent Inosine-Triphosphate (ITP) (Vale et al., 1985c; Porter et al., 1987a), whereas only ATP supports motility induced by the nematode protein. The rate of movement produced by the nematode protein is ~2 μm/sec with saturating ATP, whereas kinesin moves microtubules at ~0.6 μm/sec under similar conditions (Vale et al., 1985c; Cohn et al., 1987; Porter et al., 1987a). We conclude that the nematode *C. elegans* contains a dynein-like microtubule translocator that is clearly distinct from kinesin and is unlikely to be of axonemal origin.

A DYNEIN-LIKE TRANSLOCATOR IN HELA CELLS

The HeLa cell is a useful system for the study of microtubule translocating proteins. Since this cell line is derived from a single, non-neuronal cell type, one can seek microtubule-based motor proteins that are distinct from the axonal transport factors present in more complex tissues. Such microtubule translocators are excellent candidates for components of a general intracellular transport system or of the mitotic spindle.

Although kinesin has been found and partially characterized in HeLa cells (Pfarr, unpublished results), evidence for the presence of a dynein-like polypeptide in tissue culture cells has been equivocal. Antibodies against bovine flagellar dynein have failed to identify dynein-like polypeptides in one case (Zieve and McIntosh, 1981), and antibodies against sea urchin flagellar dynein stained the mitotic spindle of PtK$_2$ cells in another (Yoshida et al., 1985). Biochemical data have indicated that HeLa cells contain a dynein-like polypeptide that is distinct from the flagellar isoforms. For instance, Pallini et al. (1983) identified a MAP that comigrated with the heavy chain of flagellar dynein and exhibited nucleoside triphosphatase activity. This activity was distinct from flagellar dynein phosphatase activity in that it exhibited a high rate of CTP hydrolysis.

We have used the vanadate-sensitized UV cleavage reaction (Lee-Eiford et al., 1986; Gibbons et al., 1987) as a probe for dynein-like proteins in HeLa cells and have identified a MAP of 420 kDa that is cleaved into fragments of 230 and 190 kDa (see Fig. 9–2). This 420 kDa MAP is present at low concentration in preparations of taxol-stabilized microtubules made by a modification of the procedure of Vallee (1982). Attempts at increasing the binding of this protein to microtubules through the depletion of ATP by addition of either apyrase or hexokinase

and glucose (Lye et al., 1987) have proved ineffective. Addition of purified taxol-stabilized microtubules to crude cytosolic extracts has also failed to increase the yield of the 420 kDa MAP in microtubule pellets. These results suggested either that the protein was in an inactive, low-affinity state or that other cellular components were inhibiting binding.

Since most of the cytoplasmic dynein activity in sea urchin eggs also exhibits weak affinity for microtubules, an effort was made to adapt schemes used for the purification of egg dynein to the HeLa cell system (Hollenbeck et al., 1984; Porter et al., 1988). Briefly, a high-speed (100,000g) cytosolic extract of HeLa cells was precipitated by addition of 55% ammonium sulfate, resuspended, and fractionated by gel filtration chromatography. High-M_r polypeptides eluting near the void volume were tested for their ability to bind microtubules and for their susceptibility to vanadate-induced UV cleavage. Polypeptides of about 420 and 75 kDa could be distinguished in this mixture by their ATP-sensitive binding to microtubules. The ATP-extracted 420 kDa peptide is cleaved in the presence of MgATP, vanadate ions, and UV light into fragments identical in size to those detected in our earlier microtubule preparations. These results indicated that our modified purification protocol increased the yield of the UV-cleavable polypeptide.

This ATP extract was capable of inducing microtubule gliding in vitro (Pfarr and McIntosh, unpublished results). However, neither the crude cytosolic extract nor the gel filtration fraction from which the activity was purified would support motility in vitro. Microtubule gliding in the presence of the HeLa translocator required MgATP. The rate of gliding was temperature-dependent; at 24°C, microtubules moved across a glass surface at a rate of 1.5 $\pm$ 0.3 μm/sec, whereas, at 37°C, microtubules glided at ~4 μm/sec. Gliding activity was inhibited by 5 μM vanadate but was insensitive to equimolar AMP-PNP and ATP.

Even though the rate of gliding induced by the HeLa translocator was approximately three times the rate reported for kinesin (Vale et al., 1985c), the possibility that the gliding resulted from contaminating HeLa kinesin was explored. Immunoblots of the gel filtration fractions and the corresponding ATP extracts of microtubules probed with polyclonal antibodies to brain kinesin (Neighbors et al., 1988) indicated the presence of low levels of kinesin. However, when the ATP extract was fractionated by 5–20% sucrose density gradient centrifugation, the microtubule gliding activity sedimented at about 20S, whereas kinesin sedimented at about 10S (Porter et al., 1987a; Paschal and Vallee, 1987). Only the 10S fraction was able to bind antibodies to kinesin, indicating that the sucrose gradient achieved an effective separation of kinesin and the translocator activity. The 10S fraction was, however, not able to support motility, presumably because the kinesin was present in very low concentration, as confirmed by silver-stained polyacrylamide gels. The peak motility-inducing fractions at 20S also contained the highest concentration of the 420 and 75 kDa polypeptides.

When the 20S sucrose gradient fractions were incubated with taxol-stabilized microtubules in the absence of ATP, the mixture formed large bundles of microtubules as seen with dark-field microscopy. Upon addition of 1 mM ATP, these bundles dissociated, but the bundles could be reformed by depleting the added ATP through the addition of apyrase. This ATP-sensitive bundling activity is similar to activities described in preparations from sea urchin eggs (Hollenbeck et al., 1984) and from bovine spinal cord (Hollenbeck and Chapman, 1986).

We have investigated the role of the 420 kDa polypeptide in both microtubule bundling and gliding, using the UV-cleavage reaction as a probe. In the presence of 25 μM sodium vanadate, 1 mM MgATP, and UV light, the HeLa 420 kDa polypeptide is cleaved nearly to completion in 45 min (Pfarr and McIntosh, unpublished results). This cleavage reaction can be blocked by addition of norepinephrine, which reduces, and thereby inactivates, the vanadate ions

(Gibbons et al., 1978). When norepinephrine was added before irradiation, the 420 kDa polypeptide remained intact and was able to support both microtubule bundling and gliding. When norepinephrine was added after irradiation, the 420 kDa polypeptide was cleaved, and the mixture became incapable of bundling or moving microtubules. Thus the cleavage of the 420 kDa polypeptide correlated with a loss of both in vitro gliding activity and ATP-sensitive bundling activity.

In summary, we have isolated a microtubule translocator from HeLa cells that is distinct from kinesin and displays several dynein-like properties. We are currently investigating the distribution and function of this dynein-like motor in the cell.

POLARITY OF MOVEMENT ON MICROTUBULES

Since microtubules have an intrinsic structural polarity and are distributed in the cell in polarized arrays, one must identify the direction of movement induced by each motor protein relative to the microtubule over which it moves. Two approaches have been used to visualize polarized movement along microtubules. The first is the observation of the motion of latex beads over microtubules of known polarity (Vale et al., 1985c). Crude extracts from squid axoplasm (Vale et al., 1985c), sea urchin eggs (Pryer et al., 1986), *Acanthamoeba* (Kachar et al., 1987), and *Reticulomyxa* (Koonce et al., 1986) all induced bidirectional bead movement. This assay has also been used to analyze partially purified motor proteins; it revealed unidirectional movement for both kinesin (Vale et al., 1985b; Porter et al., 1987a) and the *Acanthamoeba* translocator (Kachar et al., 1987).

The second method for observing polarized movements relative to microtubules is to allow decorated axonemes to glide across a glass surface to which a motor protein has been adsorbed (Pryer et al., 1986; Paschal and Vallee, 1987). The axonemes were demembranated and extracted with high salt to remove the outer dynein arms; then they were incubated with microtubule protein below its critical concentration for self-assembly. Growth off the ends of the axonemes resulted in "tufts" of singlet microtubules. Microtubule growth was asymmetric, with faster polymerization at the plus end (by definition) (Allen and Borisy, 1974; Binder et al., 1975). By determining whether the tuft at the plus end was leading or trailing as the axoneme moved, one could determine the polarity of microtubule movement. This approach has worked well for the characterization of kinesin (Pryer et al., 1986; Porter et al., 1987a; Paschal and Vallee, 1987), but, when it was applied to the characterization of movement induced by the dynein-like motors from nematodes or HeLa cells, some interesting anomalies arose.

When axonemes decorated predominantly with tufts at one end were added to a drop of nematode translocator protein pre-adsorbed to a glass coverslip, the axonemes consistently moved with their tufts trailing (Lye et al., 1987). Similar results were obtained with the HeLa translocator (Pfarr, unpublished observations). This polarity of movement appeared to be the same as that reported for kinesin (Vale et al., 1985a; Pryer et al., 1986; Porter et al., 1987a), suggesting that the HeLa and nematode motors were "walking" toward the plus end of the microtubule. However, when preparations of kinesin and the HeLa or nematode motors were mixed together, the axonemes moved with their "tufts" leading. Since both kinesin and the dynein-like proteins by themselves induced movement of decorated axonemes with their tufts trailing, a mixture of kinesin and a dynein-like motor was expected to move axonemes in the same direction. We are currently investigating the mechanisms for this apparent reversal of axoneme movement, but the need for an unambiguous polarity assay became evident.

To circumvent the complexities inherent in using microtubule-decorated axonemes, we have used whole sperm, which were demembranated and high salt extracted by a modification of the procedure of Gibbons (1985). These extracted sperm are translocated across a glass surface in the presence of kinesin or dynein-like motors from HeLa or the nematode. With this assay, we have determined that the polarity of both the HeLa and the nematode proteins is opposite that of kinesin; both dynein-like motors "walk" toward the minus end of the microtubule. Kinesin from either sea urchin or bovine brain moves the sperm with their heads leading, whereas both the HeLa and nematode motors move the sperm with their heads trailing.

Recently, Paschal and Vallee (1987) reported polarized microtubule gliding induced by MAP 1C, a dynein-like microtubule translocator from bovine brain (Paschal et al., 1987b). They used splayed *Chlamydomonas* axonemes to demonstrate that MAP 1C, like both the HeLa and the nematode motor proteins, walks toward the minus end of the microtubule. Thus all the known dynein-like motor proteins, including flagellar dynein (Sale and Satir, 1977; Fox and Sale, 1987), move microtubules with their minus ends trailing.

SUMMARY AND CONCLUSIONS

Cytoplasmic dyneins have now been identified in a variety of cells and tissues. Some cell types, such as the unfertilized sea urchin egg, contain at least two dynein isoforms (Porter et al., 1988). One of these isoforms is probably part of the precursor pool for ciliogenesis (Weisenberg and Taylor, 1968; Asai, 1986; Porter et al., 1988), but the second isoform (HMr-3) may be a truly cytoplasmic enzyme. Other cells and tissues (the nematode *C. elegans,* mammalian brain, and HeLa cells) also contain dynein-like microtubule translocators (Lye et al., 1987; Paschal et al., 1987b; Pfarr and McIntosh, unpublished results). These cell types do not assemble motile cilia or flagella, so these dynein-like polypeptides are unlikely to be involved in axonemal motility. All these preparations share structural and functional characteristics that identify them as dyneins.

First, all are large particles ($\sim$20S) that contain heavy chain polypeptides, which are susceptible to vanadate-induced UV cleavage. Second, all exhibit a dynein-like ATPase activity and the ability to "walk" over microtubules toward their minus ends. The cytoplasmic dyneins can, however, be distinguished from the flagellar dyneins both antigenically (Asai, 1986; Porter et al., 1988) and by the size of their vanadate-sensitized UV cleavage products (Figs. 9–1, 9–2). These results suggest that the dyneins make up a family containing both flagellar and cytoplasmic isoforms. This situation is reminiscent of myosin, which exists in both muscle and non-muscle forms (Harrington and Rogers, 1984).

Although the cytoplasmic dyneins described here share homology at their ATP binding sites, as demonstrated by their vanadate-sensitized UV cleavage, other domains of these translocators may be more heterogenous. Such heterogeneity might reflect differences in the functions of these cytoplasmic dyneins. To determine the in vivo functions of these enzymes, it will be necessary to develop specific probes for the various members of the dynein family. Such specific probes, in conjunction with the rapid development of functional in vitro models for spindle elongation (Cande and McDonald, 1985, 1986), organelle transport (Koonce and Schliwa, 1986a,b; Rozdzial and Haimo, 1986b; Allen et al., 1985; Brady et al., 1985; Vale et al., 1985a–d; Pryer et al., 1986; Gilbert et al., 1985) and other microtubule based movements (Koonce et al., 1987; see Euteneuer, Chapter 10), may enable workers in the field to characterize the various functions of these enzymes and perhaps to identify additional motor proteins involved in microtubule-based motility.

ACKNOWLEDGMENTS

We thank Dr. M. Suffness (N.C.I.) for providing the taxol used in part of this work. We especially thank Dr. J.R. McIntosh for many helpful discussions and numerous useful comments on the manuscript.

In Vitro Analysis of Cytoplasmic Organelle Transport

Ursula Euteneuer, Ken Johnson, Michael P. Koonce, Kent L. McDonald, Judy Tong, and Manfred Schliwa

Department of Zoology, University of California, Berkeley, California 94720; Department of Molecular, Cellular, and Developmental Biology, University of Colorado, Boulder, Colorado 80309 (K.L.M)

INTRODUCTION

Intracellular transport of membrane-bound organelles is one of the most conspicuous features of all eukaryotic cells, although it is expressed to different degrees in different cell types. The best known and most dramatic examples of this cellular activity include the movement of food vacuoles and "particles" along the filopodial networks of certain protists, first described more than 150 years ago (Dujardin, 1835), the transport of vesicular organelles along neurites (reviewed in Grafstein and Forman, 1980), and the movement of pigment granules in chromatophores (reviewed in Schliwa and Euteneuer, 1983). This form of intracellular motility is distinguished from cytoplasmic streaming in that organelles move independently of one another and can pass each other even in very close proximity without disturbing each other's pathway. Because organelles may switch erratically from periods of quiescence to sudden translatory activity and even may reverse their direction of movement intermittently, it is also often referred to as "saltatory" movement (Rebhun, 1972). It was suggested early

on that organelle movements are not autonomous but are generated by interactions with some other system in the cytoplasm (Ballowitz, 1914). Because the characteristics of organelle saltations have much in common with phenomena that occur in the mitotic spindle, it was proposed that fibers similar to those seen in spindles and asters may be involved (Rebhun, 1963), although, at the time this suggestion was made, no evidence for the extensive deployment of such fibers in the cytoplasm was available. With the discovery of microtubules as components of the spindle as well as the cytoplasm, this notion gained credibility (Porter, 1966). In the years that followed, observations on a wide variety of cell types established a spatial relationship between the orientation of microtubules and the pathways of organelle movements (see, e.g., Bikle et al., 1966; Freed and Lebowitz, 1970), and further suggested a causal link based on the finding that the experimentally induced microtubule degradation leads to cessation of this form of motility (summarized in Schliwa, 1984). Since, however, all these studies were performed on intact cells, they did not resolve the question whether

Cell Movement, Volume 2: Kinesin, Dynein, and Microtubule Dynamics, pages 155–167

microtubules are directly involved (e.g., by exerting a sliding or shear force on the particles), or whether they merely act as guidelines for the force-generating action of a microtubule-independent motor, such as actomyosin. What was lacking were more direct, biochemical approaches, including the identification, isolation, characterization, and in vitro reconstitution of the molecular components of the transport machinery. Thanks to the development of procedures for the high-resolution analysis of living cells, including the visualization of organelle movements along single microtubules (Allen et al., 1981; Inoué, 1981a), in combination with convenient functional assays for motility, such in vitro studies are now possible. Their review is one of the purposes of these volumes.

A potentially powerful link between studies on intact cells and biochemical analyses of isolated components is provided by permeabilized, reactivatable cells. Lysed cells, or "cell models" (Hoffmann-Berling, 1954), reduce the biochemical complexity of the system, allow the application of compounds and proteins that normally do not cross the cell membrane, and offer the possibility of selective extraction and characterization of the components that make up the force-generating machinery. Cell models were instrumental in dissecting the force-generating and regulatory components of muscle cells and ciliary axonemes and thus have helped us to understand the molecular mechanisms of contraction and ciliary beat. The success with permeabilized models of these two systems is due in large part to the fact that their components are arranged in stable, highly ordered arrays. The molecular machinery that drives organelle movements, on the other hand, appears to be less organized and more labile; therefore, the development of in vitro models for the study of organelle movements did not appear feasible initially. However, work done during the past 5 years demonstrates that, in cells made permeable to certain molecules, organelle movements arrested due to the loss of metabolites can be reactivated by the addition of exogenous adenosine triphosphate (ATP) (e.g., Adams, 1982; Forman, 1982; Clark and Rosenbaum, 1982; Rozdzial and Haimo, 1986a). What is more, it has been possible to break open a cell completely, to separate the motile machinery from extraneous material, and to reconstitute certain forms of microtubule-dependent movements in vitro (Brady et al., 1982; Allen et al., 1985; Vale et al., 1985a,b; Gilbert et al., 1985; Gilbert and Sloboda, 1986). Several aspects of these experiments are dealt with elsewhere in this volume.

This chapter summarizes studies on the reactivation of organelle movements in a promising model system, the giant amoeba *Reticulomyxa,* and experiments aimed at reconstituting motility in vitro. The relationship of a molecular candidate responsible for force generation in this system to other microtubule-dependent motors is discussed. Possible mechanisms for the regulation of the direction of movement are also considered.

THE MODEL SYSTEM

A few years ago, we discovered an unusual organism on the sides and bottom of a freshwater aquarium in our laboratory (Schliwa et al., 1984b). The organism, which has now been taken into culture in Petri dishes, was identified as the giant amoeba *Reticulomyxa* (Nauss, 1949). This polymorphic cell possesses a central cell body composed of a system of interconnected veins 10–50 μm in diameter and a peripheral, highly anastomosing feeding network of fine cytoplasmic strands that may extend for several centimeters from the cell body and may cover an area of several hundred square millimeters (Fig. 10–1). This still somewhat enigmatic protozoan exhibits the most prolific form of intracellular organelle transport we have ever encountered. Whereas the strands of the cell body are characterized by multistriate, countercurrent streaming, the reticulate peripheral network displays rapid, bidirectional movements of myriads of organelles at rates of up to 25 μm/sec. The mere phenomenology of transport in the network suggested that this amoeba might serve as a good model system for its study. During the past few years, we have laid the groundwork to turn it into a useful model system for the study of the mechanism and regulation of microtubule-associated motility using three lines of inquiry: 1) morphological characterization of the network and the filamentous components of the transport machinery, 2) analysis of some of the physiological characteristics of organelle movements using a reactivatable model system, and 3) identification and initial biochemical characterization of a molecular candidate for the microtubule-dependent motor.

MORPHOLOGY

Immunofluorescence microscopy with monoclonal antibodies against *Reticulomyxa* tubulin and actin (U. Euteneuer, unpublished data) show the strands of the peripheral network to contain parallel arrays of both microtubules and actin filaments (Koonce et al., 1986) (Fig. 10–2). Many of the finest threads (diameter 50–100 nm) harbor just a single microtubule, yet they show a superimposable actin staining pattern (Fig. 10–3). This feature demands superb coordination on the part of the cell during network extension and argues that both fiber systems are laid down simultaneously. As yet we have no clue how this precise colocalization is achieved and what its functional significance is. Experiments in which networks labeled with rhodamine-phalloidin and visualized with a low-light-level video camera were reactivated with ATP suggest that actin might be involved in the rapid retraction of the network towards the cell body (K. Johnson, M. Koonce, and M. Schliwa, unpublished observations). Initial speculations that actin participates in organelle transport could not be confirmed; fragmentation with gelsolin does not perturb either reactivated movement per se or its directionality (see next section).

By correlating light and electron microscopic observations of the same strands, organelles were shown to be able to move

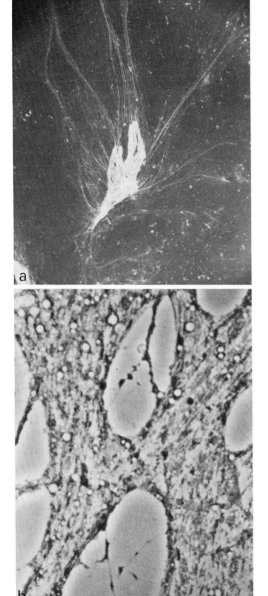

Fig. 10–1. a: Overview of a typical single organism of *Reticulomyxa* showing the central cell body and the system of thick reticulopodial strands extending from it. ×4.8. **b:** Phase-contrast micrograph of a small portion of the peripheral network in which the reticulopodial strands have flattened onto the glass surface. The striated appearance of the cytoplasm is caused by massive arrays of cytoplasmic microtubules. The phase-dense granules are mitochondria, virtually all of which are in constant, rapid motion. ×486.

Fig. 10–2. Immunofluorescence micrograph of the periphery of a reticulopodial network stained with a monoclonal antibody against *Reticulomyxa* tubulin. The bundled arrays of microtubules spread into fan-shaped sheets at the periphery of the advancing reticulopodium. × 1,070.

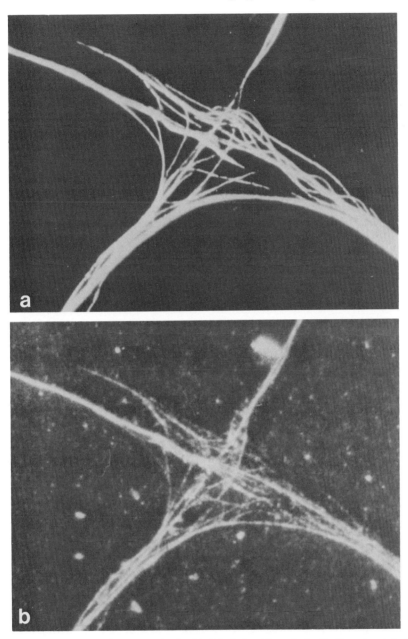

Fig. 10–3. A small portion of the network, double-labeled with antitubulin for microtubules **(a)** and rhodamine-phalloidin for actin **(b)**. The two staining patterns are almost completely superimposable. × 3,200.

bidirectionally in processes that contain single microtubules (Koonce and Schliwa, 1985). Similar observations in other cell types both in vivo (Hayden and Allen, 1984) and in vitro (Allen et al., 1985; Vale et al., 1985b) helped establish that this is an important feature of organelle transport. Since the microtubule is known to have an intrinsic molecular polarity, organelle movement cannot be explained by simply invoking one unidirectional force-generating enzyme, such as myosin or dynein, both of which generate a power stroke in only one direction along a polar fiber (Huxley, 1969; Sale and Satir, 1977; Fox and Sale, 1987).

The close association of microtubules and actin filaments is confirmed by electron microscopy, which demonstrates the two fibers to form mixed bundles parallel to the long axis of the reticulopodial threads (Fig. 10–4). Presumably, the two are linked to one another by an as yet unidentified class of cross linkers (Koonce et al., 1986).

PHYSIOLOGY

To facilitate a physiological characterization of the transport system in *Reticulomyxa*, efforts were undertaken to develop a demembranated cell model in which organelle transport could be reactivated under controlled in vitro conditions. Experiments with different lysis conditions have led to the identification of a simple buffer solution that affords complete removal of the plasmalemma while stabilizing the underlying linear arrays of microtubules and actin filaments and maintaining the attachment of organelles to these fibers (Fig. 10–5). The buffer consists of 50% PHEM buffer (60 mM PIPES, 25 mM HEPES, 10 mM EGTA, 2 mM $MgCl_2$; Schliwa and van Blerkom, 1981) supplemented with 5% hexylene glycol, 1 mM orthovanadate, and 0.15% Brij 58 (Koonce and Schliwa, 1986a). When strands or flattened sheets of the reticulopodial network are lysed in this solution, rinsed with buffer, and supplied with ATP, organelles resume in vivo-like bidirectional motility at rates of up to 20 μm/sec. The lysed model is very stable. Although organelles tend to detach from their linear cytoskeletal tracks after some time, some are still seen to move along them as much as 30 min after reactivation was initiated. In addition, lysed preparations can be left in buffer for at least 1 hr, but, upon addition of ATP (minimum concentration required is 10 μM), reactivated motility is indistinguishable from that of freshly lysed preparations.

To test whether actin filaments are involved in organelle movement, lysed preparations were incubated with plasma gelsolin (kindly provided by Drs. Robert Ezzell and Helen Yin) in the presence of 20 μM free calcium, a concentration that does not affect microtubule integrity or organelle attachment. After 10 min, no intact actin filaments are detected by fluorescence microscopy with rhodamine-phalloidin or a monoclonal antibody against amoeba actin, yet, upon addition of ATP, bidirectional organelle movement is reactivated. Thus organelle transport appears to be strictly microtubule-dependent.

A number of inhibitors known to interfere with dynein-mediated axonemal motility were tested for their effects on reactivated organelle movements. Orthovanadate, which inhibits dynein at 1–5 μM (Gibbons et al., 1978) and MAP 1C at 10–50 μM (Paschal and Vallee, 1987), was found to block movements at concentrations of 100 μM or more. Vanadate did not inhibit motility at all at concentrations up to 25 μM. Erythro-9[3-(2-hydroxynonyl)]adenine (EHNA), another potent inhibitor of dynein in vitro (Penningroth et al., 1982), was ineffective at concentrations as high as 5 mM, whereas N-ethylmaleimide (NEM) blocked movement at a concentration of 2 mM. This "inhibitor profile" of reactivated organelle movements clearly differs from that of other microtubule-associated ATPases. In particular, there is no selective inhibition of retrograde movement with vanadate or NEM, a feature that may distinguish putative anterograde from retrograde motors in the squid giant axon (Vale et al., 1985b; see, however, Brady 1987, for a different view). Reactivated motility is strictly ATP-dependent. Other nucleoside triphosphates or non-hydrolyzable analogs of ATP are ineffective. Thus the *Reticulomyxa* motor is different in certain respects from axonemal dynein and from other recently identified microtubule-dependent motors, such as kinesin (Vale et al., 1985a), MAP 1C (Paschal et al., 1987b; Paschal and Vallee, 1987), and a 400 kDa protein present in *Caenorhabditis elegans* eggs (Lye et al., 1987).

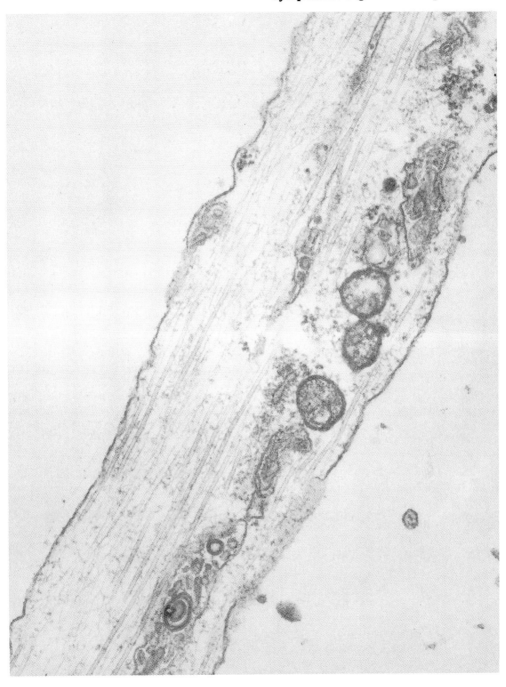

Fig. 10–4. Thin section of a reticulopodial strand, showing the parallel, intermingled arrays of microtubules and 6-nm filaments. ×6,000.

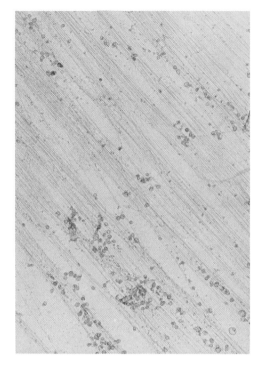

Fig. 10–5. Whole-mount preparation of the flattened portion of a lysed reticulopodial network as seen in the high-voltage electron microscope after critical-point drying. Many organelles are still associated with the long, parallel arrays of microtubules. ×2,340.

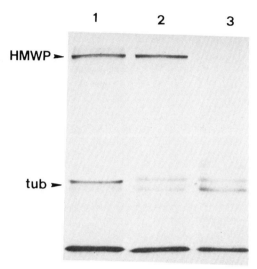

Fig. 10–6. Autoradiograph of a 7.5% SDS polyacrylamide gel demonstrating the cosedimentation of a high-M_r polypeptide (HMWP) with microtubules in the absence of ATP. *Reticulomyxa* amoebae were metabolically labeled with ^{35}S-methionine for 2 days. A cytoplasmic extract of these cells was mixed with taxol-stabilized, DEAE-cellulose-purified bovine brain microtubules in the presence of added hexokinase (0.1 mg/ml) and glucose (10 mM) to deplete the pool of ATP. **Lane 1:** Microtubule pellet in the absence of ATP. **Lane 2:** Material released from the pelleted microtubules by 5 mM ATP. **Lane 3:** Microtubule pellet in the presence of 5 mM ATP (no hexokinase added). tub, Tubulin.

Molecular Identity of the Motor

ATP-dependent binding to microtubules is an important diagnostic criterion for a molecule involved in microtubule-dependent motility. Based on the finding that a nonhydrolyzable analog of ATP, 5'-adenylylimidodiphosphate (AMP-PNP) will promote the binding of vesicles to microtubules in extruded squid axoplasm (Lasek and Brady, 1985), several groups have used AMP-PNP-dependent cosedimentation with microtubules as an initial step in the identification of putative organelle motors (Brady, 1985; Vale et al., 1985a; Scholey et al., 1985). This technique has not been successful in the *Reticulomyxa* system and neither AMP-PNP, tripolyphosphate (an AMP-PNP substitute; Kuznetsov and Gelfand, 1986), nor vanadate enhance the binding of any *Reticu-*

lomyxa polypeptide to microtubules (Figs. 10–6, 10–7). It is only the complete depletion of ATP that promotes the specific binding of a high-M_r polypeptide (HMWP) from *Reticulomyxa* extracts to microtubules (Euteneuer et al., 1988). This is analogous to the microtubule-dependent motor in *C. elegans* egg extracts, whose binding to microtubules is enhanced far more by ATP depletion than by AMP-PNP (Lye, Chapter 9). The microtubule binding of kinesin-like polypeptides in several cell types, on the other hand, is enhanced by AMP-PNP even if ATP is still present (Brady, 1985; Scholey et al., 1985; Vale et al., 1985a).

The *Reticulomyxa* polypeptide that binds to microtubules in the absence of ATP has a

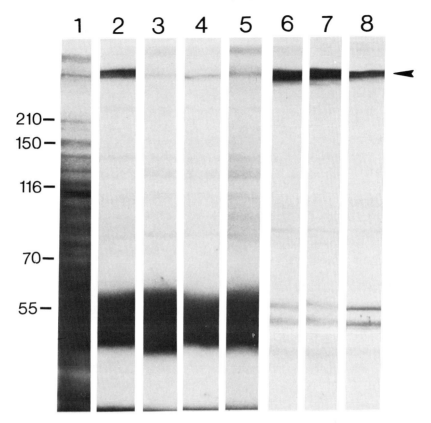

Fig. 10–7. Binding to, and release from, phosphocellulose column-purified, taxol-stabilized bovine brain microtubules of *Reticulomyxa* polypeptides under various experimental conditions. **Lane 1:** *Reticulomyxa* cytoplasmic extract. **Lane 2:** Microtubule pellet in the absence of ATP (with added hexokinase and glucose). **Lane 3:** Microtubule pellet in the presence of 10 mM AMP-PNP plus 0.5 mM ATP. **Lane 4:** Microtubule pellet in the presence of 2.5 mM tripolyphosphate plus 0.5 mM ATP. **Lane 5:** Microtubule pellet in the presence of 0.5 mM ATP. **Lane 6:** Material released with 5 mM ATP from microtubules prepared as in lane 2. **Lane 7:** Material released with 0.4 M NaCl in the presence of 5 mM ATP. **Lane 8:** Material released with 0.4 M NaCl alone. The HMWP does not bind to microtubules in the presence of AMP-PNP, tripolyphosphate, or ATP. The HMWP binds to microtubules in the absence of ATP and is effectively released from the microtubules with ATP and/or high salt. Molecular weight markers are indicated on the right. The HMWP is denoted by an arrowhead.

subunit M_r of >400 kDa and in polyacrylamide gels runs between MAP 1 and MAP 2 of bovine brain microtubule protein. It can be released from microtubules with ATP (Figs. 10–6, 10–7), strengthening the notion that it is a good candidate for a microtubule-dependent motor in *Reticulomyxa*. AMP-PNP or pyrophosphate is ineffective in dissociating this protein from microtubules. No other polypeptides of *Reticulomyxa* cell extracts showed a similar ATP-dependent binding to, and release from, microtubules. ATP-eluted fractions from microtubule pellets in which the HMWP constitutes about 90% of the non-tubulin components possess an ATPase activity of >0.1 µmole/min/mg protein. This ATPase activity is significantly inhibited by 100 µM vanadate, reduced by EHNA and unaffected by azide. It is only slightly enhanced (about 20%) in the presence of microtubules.

Sucrose gradients (5–30%) of the ATP-eluted fractions in which the HMWP constitutes 80–90% of the non-tubulin material show the peak of the HMWP and the ATPase activity to cofractionate at a sedimentation coefficient of 20–23S (Euteneuer et al., 1988). When polystyrene beads are incubated in these sucrose gradient fractions and added to lysed microtubule networks of *Reticulomyxa* stripped of endogenous organelles by 1% Triton X-100, the fractions that contain both the peak of the HMWP and the ATPase activity will cause bead movement along the microtubules at average rates of 3.6 μm/sec (up to 7.5 μm/sec). Other fractions of the gradient did not produce any movement. This observation, coupled with the finding that the inhibitor profile of the HMWP ATPase resembles that of reactivated organelle movements suggests that the HMWP is a component of the *Reticulomyxa* organelle motor. Unexpectedly, bead movement is bidirectional. In this respect, the *Reticulomyxa* motor differs significantly from kinesin-like factors, which produce unidirectional motility directed towards the "plus" ends of microtubules (Vale et al., 1985a), or MAP 1C, which effects movement in a direction opposite that of kinesin (Paschal and Vallee, 1987). The *Reticulomyxa* HMWP shares with axonemal dynein heavy chains a susceptibility to cleavage at a single site upon irradiation with UV light in the presence of vanadate and ATP (Lee-Eiford et al., 1986; Gibbons et al., 1987). This treatment yields two large polypeptides with molecular masses of about 200 and 240 kDa when compared with striated muscle myosin and erythrocyte spectrin (Fig. 10–8). Similar treatments have been found to cleave the 400 kDa protein in *C. elegans* extracts (Lye et al., 1987) and MAP 1C (Paschal et al., 1987b). UV-induced cleavage may turn out to be a useful diagnostic tool for the identification of dynein-like proteins. If so, then the *Reticulomyxa* HMWP can be considered a cytoplasmic form of dynein.

DIRECTIONALITY

If kinesin and the dynein-like MAP 1C are indeed involved in powering organelle

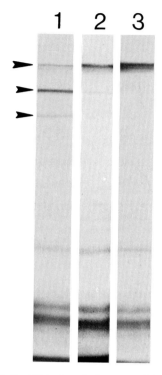

Fig. 10–8. UV-induced cleavage of the HMWP in the presence of vanadate and ATP. **Lane 1:** Release material exposed to 254 nm UV light in the presence of 100 μM ATP and 100 μM vanadate for 60 min on ice. **Lane 2:** Sample treated as in lane 1 except that no vanadate was present. Some unspecific cleavage seems to have occurred. **Lane 3:** Untreated sample. Small arrowheads mark the positions of the fragments. A 6% polyacrylamide gel was used.

movements in neurons, which to date is a speculation yet to be supported by experimental evidence, then it is reasonable to assume that the former might be responsible for movement away from the cell body, whereas the latter drives movements in the opposite direction. The direction of movement would thus be specified by the type of molecule associated with an organelle. In *Reticulomyxa* organelles can move in both directions along a single microtubule, and reversals in the direction of movement are quite frequent. If the HMWP turns out to be the only microtubule motor, how can it support movement in both directions along microtubules, and how is the direction of movement specified and controlled? Based on work with extracts of the squid giant axon, Vale et al. (1985b) suggest that two different motors power transport in opposite directions: Kinesin appears to be involved in anterograde movement, whereas an as yet unidentified factor is responsible for transport in the retrograde direction. Thus the direction of movement would be under fairly rigid control, consistent with the fact that, in intact axons, certain types of organelles tend to move in one direction only (Tsukita and Ishikawa, 1981; Allen et al., 1982). In *Reticulomyxa,* changes in the direction of movement of organelles or beads are not uncommon, suggesting that directionality is less tightly controlled and/or that the regulatory system is more flexible. In a search for modulators of directionality, our attention was turned to protein kinases. When lysed networks of *Reticulomyxa* are incubated with a cyclic adenosine monophosphate (cAMP)-dependent protein kinase in the presence of cAMP and ATPγS, rinsed, and reactivated with ATP, >95% of the organelles are seen to move towards the cell body, i.e., in the retrograde direction (Koonce and Schliwa, 1986b). This effect is phosphorylation-dependent, because it is not observed if one of the three components is omitted, and it can be inhibited with the "kinase inhibitor protein." A calcium/calmodulin-dependent kinase isolated from brain tissue (kindly provided by H. Schulman) does not produce unidirectional motility. Actin is not involved either; its fragmentation by gelsolin does not alter the effect of the cAMP-dependent protein kinase.

The observation of kinase-mediated unidirectional organelle movement is intriguing and merits further study. The involvement of a kinase would offer a flexible biochemical mechanism for the regulation of the direction of organelle transport. It is unclear whether this effect is the result of mere inhibition of anterograde movement or its reversal. The distinction between these two possibilities is not purely academic; it may allow us to distinguish between two different biological control mechanisms. In the

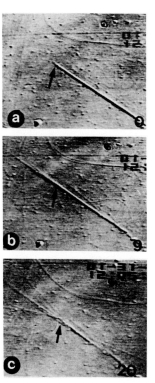

Fig. 10–9. Video sequence of microtubule sliding in a cut *Reticulomyxa* microtubule bundle before (**a**) and after (**b,c**) ATP addition. The numbers in the lower right hand corner are the time (in seconds) after ATP addition. Arrows denote the original position of the end of the microtubule bundle. × 1,000.

first case, inhibition of movement in one direction, the control mechanism would be a simple on–off switch for anterograde movement. The direction of movement would be "controlled" only in the sense that it is specified in an unalterable fashion. A reversal in the direction of anterogradely moving particles, on the other hand, suggests that the motor/regulator is endowed with the potential to alter the direction of movement and as such appears to represent a more sophisticated control mechanism, perhaps in the form of a macromolecular switch.

It is intriguing that the direction of cAMP-induced organelle movements in the lysed model is opposite that of cAMP-induced pigment granule movements in chromatophores. cAMP has long been known to be involved in triggering granule dispersion, i.e., movement away from the cell center (see summary by Bagnara and Hadley, 1973). In chromatophores, too, cAMP appears to act as a second messenger in a protein kinase regulatory system. For example, pigment dispersion in xanthophores has been shown to coincide with the phosphorylation of a 57 kDa granule-associated polypeptide (Lynch et al., 1986a,b). Rozdzial and Haimo (1986a) showed that, in permeabilized scale melanophores, dispersion not only coincides with but actually requires phosphorylation of a 57 kDa polypeptide. In this cell system, thiophosphorylation by ATPγS alone may be sufficient to bring about dispersion (anterograde movement), whereas ATPγS is incapable of eliciting motility in the *Reticulomyxa* lysed model. The identity of the 57 kDa polypeptide is unknown. It might be a regulatory molecule or a component of the organelle motor. Since the regulatory subunits of most cAMP-dependent kinases are in the 55−60 kDa range, and since these subunits can be autophosphorylated, the possibility that the 57 kDa polypeptide represents the autophosphorylated regulatory subunit has to be considered as well.

MICROTUBULE DYNAMICS

In addition to bidirectional organelle movements, reactivated models of *Reticulomyxa* also show prominent motility within the microtubule bundles (Koonce and Schliwa, 1986a). The extent of this activity ranges from moderate looping-out of microtubules from larger bundles, to extensive and sometimes vigorous splaying and bending that leads to the formation of three-dimensional networks of what appear to be single microtubules. To test whether this striking behavior might be produced by sliding forces generated within the microtubule bundles, analogous to the shear forces that power bending of axonemes, an experimental model was devised in which this phenomenon could be studied under more controlled conditions. Lysed networks were cut with a fine glass needle to generate 20−50-μm-long segments of microtubule bundles with "free" ends. Any intermicrotubule sliding that might occur within these bundles would then be translated into active telescoping instead of splaying or passive looping (Koonce et al., 1987). Following removal of the majority of organelles by a rinse with Triton X-100, addition of ATP to these bundle segments will indeed cause microtubule sliding in a manner reminiscent of trypsin-treated flagellar axonemes (Fig. 10−9; see Summers and Gibbons, 1971). In 84 of 95 (88%) bundle ends recorded by video microscopy, microtubules are seen to protrude from both ends at rates of up to 10 μm/sec, increasing the bundle length up to three-fold. Frequently microtubules are completely ejected from a bundle and float free in solution. Neither the ejected microtubules nor the bundles themselves are ever found to glide across the coverslip, as has been reported for other cell systems (Allen et al., 1985; Vale et al., 1985b; Lye et al., 1987). As with organelle movements, microtubule telescoping is independent of intact actin filaments, and sliding shows similar sensitivities to vanadate, EHNA, and NEM. It is, therefore, not possible to state whether microtubule sliding and organelle movements are brought about by the same motor or by different motors with similar sensitivities to these compounds.

Microtubule sliding adds a new dimension to the dynamics of the reticulopodial network. It readily explains the dramatic ATP-induced splaying and bending of microtubule bundles in the lysed model, and it is likely to contribute to in vivo network dynamics, such as extension, zipping, branching, and fusion of reticulopodial strands (Koonce et al., 1986; see also Travis et al., 1983, for a description of similar phenomena in the foraminiferan *Allogromia*). Since microtubule sliding is superimposed on organelle transport, it might also enhance rapid movement of some of the organelles due to a "piggyback" effect: An organelle may move along a microtubule, which in turn slides past another microtubule.

In addition to ciliary and flagellar axonemes, force generation by microtubule-associated ATPases most likely powers the bending of protozoan axostyles (see Heuser, 1986, and references therein) and is believed to contribute to the elongation of the mitotic spindle in anaphase (McIntosh et al., 1969; Cande and McDonald, 1985). Certain other examples of extensive cell shape changes, such as the elongation of myoblasts (Warren, 1974), lens cells (Byers and Porter, 1964), neural ectoderm (Karfunkel, 1971), and teleost retinal cones (Burnside and Nagle, 1983) all seem to require coordinated microtubule behavior and have been proposed to involve force generation derived from microtubule sliding. In these cells, just as in *Reticulomyxa* networks, microtubules are not as highly organized as in axonemes or axostyles. The demonstration of sliding between *Reticulomyxa* microtubules lends support to the idea that cell elongation in these systems may be brought about by a similar force-generating mechanism. Further support comes from the recent finding that an ATPase from bovine spinal cord (Hollenbeck and Chapman, 1986) or a set of polypeptides present in sea urchin eggs (Hollenbeck et al., 1984) causes ATP-dependent microtubule bundling in vitro. Microtubule sliding has not been reported, however, in these two systems. The relationship of these and other high-M_r polypeptides commonly referred to as cytoplasmic dynein (Pratt et al., 1984; Scholey et al., 1985; Pratt, 1986c) to the *Reticulomyxa* organelle and/or microtubule motor remains to be established.

CHAPTER
11

Microtubule Sliding and the Generation of Force for Cell Shape Change

Beth Burnside

Department of Physiology-Anatomy, University of California, Berkeley, California 94720

INTRODUCTION

At the time of their discovery, one of the first functions attributed to microtubules was a role in the establishment and maintenance of cell shape (Porter, 1966). Subsequent observations have linked microtubules with cell shape changes in many cell types (Snyder and McIntosh, 1976; Stephens and Edds, 1976; Hyams and Stebbings, 1981; Sakai et al., 1982). This correlation of microtubules with cell shape has primarily been drawn from two observations: 1) during elongation of cells or cell projections microtubules appear with their long axes parallel to the axis of elongation; and 2) disrupting microtubules with relatively specific inhibitors blocks elongation and/or causes loss of asymmetric shape. As many have noted, these observations do not prove that microtubules participate directly in generating the motive force for cell shape change. Microtubules could merely provide the structural reinforcement necessary to maintain asymmetries established by microtubule-independent force-generating mechanisms.

Recent observations drawn from several cell types, however, strongly suggest that microtubules can participate directly in mo-

tive force production for cell shape changes. Two postulated mechanisms for direct microtubule participation in cell shape change have received the most attention: 1) elongation of microtubules by assembly of subunits onto their ends (Inoué and Sato, 1967; Kirschner and Mitchison, 1986) and 2) inter-microtubule sliding powered by motors consisting of mechanochemical bridges, as observed in the dynein–microtubule interactions of cilia and flagella (Satir, 1982). This chapter focuses on the roles of microtubule sliding in cell shape change.

The evidence is increasingly compelling that microtubule-associated motors are not restricted to cilia and flagella but are ubiquitous. Such evidence includes the identification of microtubule-associated organelle "translocators" in brain and in other tissues (Scholey et al., 1985; Vale et al., 1985a–c; Vale, Chapter 18) and the identification of dynein-like ATPases in non-ciliated cells (Pratt, Chapter 8). For example, the microtubule-associated protein MAP 1C from brain has recently been shown to be a dynein-like ATPase capable of producing movement of isolated microtubules (Paschal et al., 1987b).

Although microtubule interactions with

specific motors could affect cell shape by a variety of mechanisms, for example, by directed displacement of cytoplasmic constituents, much evidence suggests that motor-driven intermicrotubule sliding plays a contributory role in specific examples of cell shape change (see earlier discussions by Hyams and Stebbings, 1981; Satir, 1982). Intermicrotubule sliding between cytoplasmic microtubules has recently been directly demonstrated in the slime amoeba *Reticulomyxa* (Koonce et al., 1987; Euteneuer, Chapter 10). In isolated, demembranated fragments of the amoeba's cytoplasmic projections, microtubules undergo adenosine triphosphate (ATP)-dependent sliding disintegration, thereby lengthening the fragment. This reactivated movement resembles the sliding disintegration of trypsin-digested flagellar axonemes (Summers and Gibbons, 1971).

Possible roles of microtubule assembly in cell shape determination have recently been thoughtfully considered by Kirschner and Mitchison (1986) and by Hill (1981). Though assembly mechanisms clearly influence cell shape, it is difficult to prove that assembly per se provides motive force for movement. Since *any* microtubule-dependent, force-producing mechanism would require the prior assembly of microtubules in the appropriate location to produce movement, it is difficult to separate experimentally the need for temporal and spatial control of microtubule assembly from the actual force-producing events. Thus, microtubule assembly is likely to be required whether or not it contributes to force production.

EVIDENCE FOR MICROTUBULE SLIDING IN CELL SHAPE CHANGE

Several early studies suggested that microtubule sliding might play on important role in both cytoplasmic and ciliary motility. One of the first was the suggestion from McIntosh and Porter (1967) that nuclear elongation in chicken spermatids was mediated by a helical array of microtubules found surrounding the nucleus as it elongates from a sphere to a slender cylinder. They proposed that cross bridges mediated sliding between microtubules of adjacent gyres of the helix. This sliding would maintain the pitch of the helix while simultaneously decreasing the diameter and increasing the overall length of the helix, thereby elongating the nucleus (and the cell). Faint cross bridges observed between the adjacent microtubules of the helices were postulated to be mechanochemical motors responsible for producing sliding. Recent inhibitor studies of isolated spermatids in culture indicate that disruption of the microtubules of the helix blocks nuclear elongation (Abe and Uno, 1984).

Roles for microtubule sliding have been suggested for several other types of microtubule-based movement, such as the elongation of the mitotic spindle (McIntosh et al., 1969; cf. Cande, Chapter 28) and the undulatory movements of the microtubular axostyles of flagellates (McIntosh, 1973; Mooseker and Tilney, 1973). Reactivated motility of detergent-isolated flagellate axostyles was shown to resemble that of demembranated axonemes from cilia and flagella in that isolated axostyles could be reactivated with ATP, contained an ATPase with dynein-like characteristics, and contained high-M_r polypeptides that comigrated with dynein polypeptides from scallop cilia (Mooseker and Tilney, 1973; Bloodgood, 1975). Intermicrotubule cross bridges located either within or between microtubule rows have been proposed by different workers to be the mechanochemical cross bridges responsible for force production (Mooseker and Tilney, 1973; McIntosh, 1973; Bloodgood, 1975; Woodrum and Linck, 1980; Heuser, 1987).

Sliding microtubules may be involved in diverse types of cell shape changes, ranging from the elongation of vertebrate myogenic cells (Warren, 1974) to the body elongation of ciliates (Huang and Pitelka, 1973; Huang and Mazia, 1975). For example, on the basis of morphological studies, Huang and Pitelka (1973) proposed that body elongation in the ciliate *Stentor* results from the relative slid-

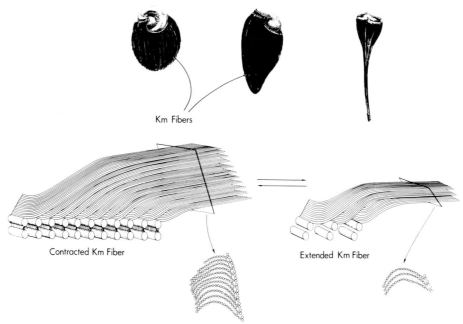

Km Fibers

Contracted Km Fiber

Extended Km Fiber

Fig. 11–1. Body elongation in the ciliate *Stentor*. Huang and Pitelka (1973) noted that elongation is accompanied by decreased overlap of the stacked microtubule ribbons of the Km fibers and proposed that bridges between microtubules of adjacent ribbons act as motors to produce elongation by microtubule sliding.

ing of the parallel, overlapping microtubule ribbons of the Km fibers (Fig. 1). They proposed that the Km microtubule ribbons telescope together passively during contraction and then elongate by active microtubule sliding to decrease overlap of the ribbons. Intertubule bridges observed between microtubules of adjacent ribbons were postulated to function like dynein arms to produce sliding between microtubule ribbons (Fig. 11–1). Recently Matsuoka and Shigenaka (1985) showed that elongation in a ciliate with similar dramatic length changes (*Blepharisma*) appears not to depend on Km fiber microtubules but rather on nearby vacuole-associated microtubules that are also aligned longitudinally. Colchicine treatment disrupts the latter microtubules but not those of the Km fibers and simultaneously blocks body elongation. Since the vacuole-associated microtubules bundle during elongation, Matsuoka and Shigenaka suggest that elongation is produced by slid-

ing of the vacuolar rather than the Km microtubules.

A particularly favorable system for studying the role of microtubules in cell elongation has been provided by the teleost retinal cone. Several years ago, Warren and Burnside (1978) provided initial morphological evidence for force production by intermicrotubule sliding in the extensive cell elongation that takes place in these cones during dark adaptation (Figs. 11–2, 11–3). They showed that cone elongation was microtubule dependent, and they estimated from microtubule counts at different cone lengths that there was no net assembly of microtubules as the cones elongated. Subsequent studies involving a variety of experimental approaches (to be summarized below) have all turned out to be consistent with the suggested role for microtubule sliding. The teleost cone is now one of the most extensively studied examples of cell elongation, and it provides some of the strongest evi-

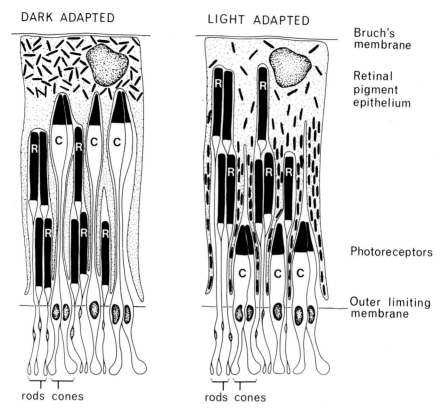

Fig. 11–2. Retinomotor movements of photoreceptors and retinal pigment epithelium (RPE) in a teleost fish (drawn from the green sunfish *Lepomis cyanellus*). In the light, cones (C) contract and rods (R) elongate to bury their outer segments in the dispersed screening pigment of the RPE. In the dark, movements are reversed: Cones elongate, rods contract, and pigment granules aggregate to the base of the RPE cell. These movements position cones first in line for light reception in the light and rods first in line in the dark. Photoreceptors are attached to the supporting glial cells of the retina at the outer limiting membrane. (Reproduced from Burnside and Nagle, 1983, with permission of the publisher.)

dence available for participation of dynein-like microtubule motors in metazoan cell shape change. Therefore, the remainder of this chapter will describe in some detail what is known about cone elongation and will relate this system to others that exhibit microtubule-dependent movement.

TELEOST RETINAL CONE ELONGATION
The System

In lower vertebrates, retinal photoreceptors change shape in response to changes in light conditions (Fig. 11–2) (Burnside and Nagle, 1983; Burnside and Dearry, 1986). In the dark, cones elongate and rods contract, whereas in the light, cones contract and rods elongate. These retinomotor movements ensure that the appropriate receptor type is positioned first in line for optimal vision in bright or dim light (cones are bright-light and rods dim-light receptors). Occurring in animals with fixed pupils, these movements serve the functions provided by pupillary movements in mammals.

The extent of cone shape change may be quite dramatic. In the green sunfish (*Lepomis cyanellus*), cones elongate as much as 100 μm in the dark (Burnside et al., 1982a). These movements are mediated by

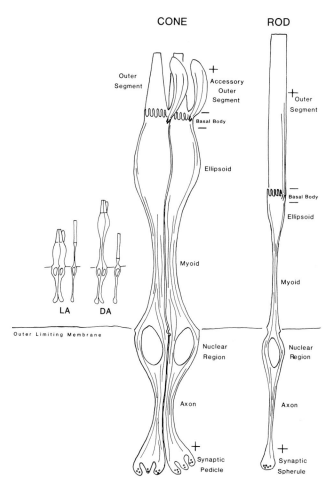

Fig. 11–3. The microtubule cytoskeletons of teleost cones and rods. All cytoplasmic microtubules, including those in the motile myoid region, are oriented with parallel polarity, with their plus (+) ends toward the photoreceptor synapse and their minus (−) ends toward the outer segment. Therefore, any microtubule sliding in the myoid during elongation would have to occur between microtubules of parallel polarity orientation. The only apparent candidate for a microtubule organizing center is the basal body of the connecting cilium of the outer segment. LA indicates light-adapted and DA, dark-adapted retino motor positions of the photoceptors. (Reproduced from Troutt and Burnside, 1987, with permission of the publisher.)

the cell's slender, neck-like myoid region, which contains abundant axially oriented microfilaments and microtubules (100–300, depending on myoid length) (Fig. 11–3). Inhibitor studies with colchicine, nocadazole, and cytochalasins indicate that cone elongation is microtubule dependent and actin independent, while cone contraction is actin dependent and microtubule independent (Burnside, 1976; Warren and Burnside, 1978; Burnside et al., 1983). Neither microtubules nor actin filaments are required for maintenance of the elongated or contracted state in situ in the retina; thus both elongation and contraction are active motile processes. Thus separate deployment of actin and microtubule "machinery" provides enormous advantages for the experimental dissection of force-producing mechanisms and their regulation.

Teleost cones provide several other advantages for studying cell movement. Although the proximal regions of cones are attached to neighboring cells of the retina, the motile myoid region of the cone lies free in the subretinal space, a glycosaminoglycan-filled (and hence well-lubricated) potential space between the retina and the retinal pigment epithelium (Fig. 11–2). Thus we may consider aspects of force production for cone movement without the complicating variables concerned with attachment and detachment from neighboring cells or substrate. We can obtain cone myoid elongation in isolated intact retinas in culture, where the parallel alignment and concerted movement of thousands of cones greatly facilitates morphometric analysis of cone position and microtubule distribution changes during elongation. Since the rate of cone elongation is slow, like that of spindle elongation or chromosome movement (1–2 μm/min over a period of 30–60 min) (Gilson et al., 1986), experimental intervention is easily achieved. We are now able to elicit cone myoid elongation in isolated whole cones, in detached fragments of cones containing only the inner and outer segments (CIS-COS), and as will be described in detail below, in lysed cell motile models (Burnside et al., 1983; Gilson et al., 1986; Dearry and Burnside, 1986).

Reactivated Elongation in Lysed Cone Models

Using retinas of the green sunfish we have developed motile models of teleost cones that retain their ability to move after permeabilization with the detergent Brij-58 (Burnside et al., 1982b). Detergent treatment extracts much of the cone's soluble cytoplasmic constituents and allows penetration of even high-M_r molecules like myosin subfragment-1 (approximately 100 kDa), while leaving the motile machinery functionally intact (Fig. 11–4) (Porrello et al., 1983). These models can be induced to undergo ATP-dependent elongation or contraction depending on the composition of the media in which they are reactivated (Porrello and Burnside, 1984; Gilson et al.,

1986). When cone models are incubated in reactivation media containing high cyclic adenosine monophosphate (cAMP; $>10^{-6}$ M) and low Ca^{2+} ($<10^{-7}$ M) cone myoids elongate 15–20 μm (Fig. 11–5) (Gilson et al., 1986). Incubation in reactivation media containing high Ca^{2+} ($>10^{-7}$ M) and low cAMP ($<10^{-6}$ M) produces cone contraction (Porrello and Burnside, 1984). Thus we may activate either microtubule-dependent elongation or actin-dependent contraction in lysed cone models by varying only the cAMP and Ca^{2+} concentrations.

Lysed cone models undergo linear reactivated elongation at approximately 2 μm/min in reactivation media containing 1 mM ATP, 1 mM cAMP, and 10^{-8} M Ca^{2+} (Fig. 11–5) (Gilson et al., 1986). Reactivated elongation is initiated in cones already partially elongated (myoid lengths 15–25 μm) and continues for 15–20 μm to a final length of 30–45 μm. Although the extent of reactivated cone elongation is less than that found in vivo, it is similar to that observed in isolated intact retinas in culture (Fig. 11–5). In reactivation media containing 1 mM ATP and 1 mM cAMP, the elongation rate is faster than that observed in cultured intact retinas and is equivalent to the fastest rates we have observed in vivo. Thus both rate and extent of elongation in the models compares favorably with that in intact cells, indicating that the microtubule elongation machinery retains its functional organization after lysis. If the lysis step is omitted or if ATP or cAMP is omitted from the reactivation medium, no more than 5 μm of elongation is observed. Also, no elongation occurs if lysis and reactivation are initiated in retinas with fully contracted cones; thus models appear to be able to sustain, but not to initiate, elongation. Perhaps it is necessary to assemble sufficient microtubule machinery before lysis to permit reactivated elongation to occur (see below).

cAMP is required in addition to ATP for activation of cone elongation. This activation role for cAMP in cones resembles that described for activation of ciliary and flagellar motility (cf. Garbers and Kopf, 1980; Muro-

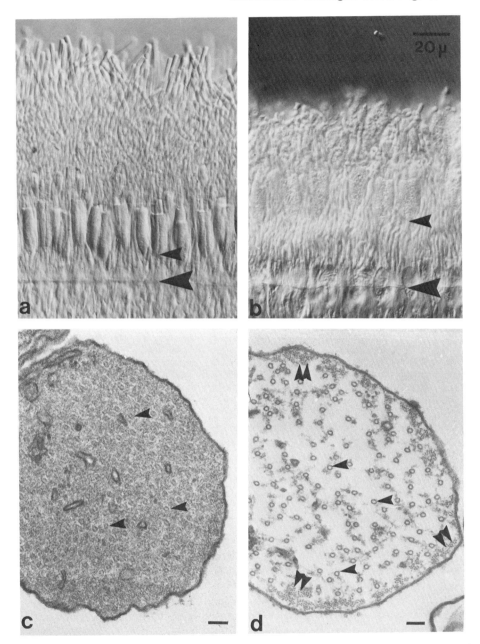

Fig. 11–4. Detergent-lysed motile models of teleost retinal cones. **a,b:** Normarski optics illustrate t_0 half-retina fixed before lysis (a) and another half-retina from the same fish fixed after 3 min lysis in 1% Brij-58 followed by 15 min in detergent-free, elongation-reactivation medium containing 0.1M PIPES buffer, pH 6.9, 1 mM MgATP, 1 mM free Mg^{2+}, 10^{-8} M Ca^{2+}, and 1 mM cyclic adenosine monophosphate (cAMP; b). Cone myoids have elongated 15–20 μm (arrowheads). Bar = 20 μm. (Reproduced from Gilson et al., 1986, with permission of the publisher.) **c,d:** Electron micrographs illustrate cone myoids fixed before (c) and after (d) lysis with Brij-58 in contraction-reactivation medium as described above but containing no cAMP and 10^{-5} M Ca^{2+}. The myoid was contracting at the time of fixation. The cytoplasm is highly extracted, but the microtubules (single arrowheads) and bundles of actin filaments (double arrowheads) are still present. Bar = 0.1 μm.

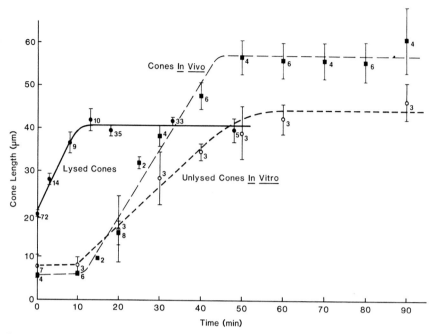

Fig. 11–5. Rates of elongation observed for reactivated cone elongation in lysed models, for cone elongation in unlysed retinas in vitro, and for cone elongation in vivo. For cone models, reactivation medium was as described for Figure 11–4b. Cone elongation was induced in unlysed retinas in vitro by incubation in Ringer's solution containing 2.5 mM dibutryl-cAMP plus 0.1 mM isobutylmethylxanthine and in vivo by exposing the fish to darkness. Rates were calculated using linear regression on the mean values for each time point. Elongation rates were 2.0 μm/min (r = 0.99), 0.9 μm/min (r = 0.99), and 1.6 μm/min (r = 0.97), respectively. (Reproduced from Gilson et al., 1986, with permission of the publisher.)

fushi et al., 1986; Opresko and Brokaw, 1983; Morisawa and Okuno, 1982; Lindemann et al., 1983; Tash and Means, 1982, 1983; Bonini et al., 1986; Sanderson et al., 1985). In teleost cones, as in sperm flagella (Morofushi et al., 1986; Opresko and Brokaw, 1983; Morisawa and Okuno, 1982; Lindemann et al., 1983; Tash and Means, 1982, 1983), cAMP appears to be required only transiently for an activation step. In teleost cone models, transient exposure (3 min) to cAMP is sufficient to induce the full elongation response, most of which occurs subsequent to cAMP removal. This last observation suggests that in cones, as in sperm, an early cAMP-dependent phosphorylation step is sufficient to activate and sustain microtubule-dependent movement and that in the cone model phosphatases do not inactivate

this phosphorylation, at least not in the 10 min of active elongation after cAMP removal.

ATP appears to be required both for a regulatory process, entailing cAMP-dependent phosphorylation, and also for some cAMP-independent process. If ATP is deleted from the reactivation medium either in the initial cAMP-dependent 3-min step or in the subsequent cAMP-independent step (15 min), reactivated elongation is strongly inhibited. The last cAMP-independent, ATP-requiring process is a likely candidate for a component of the force-producing mechanism.

Evidence for Microtubule Sliding in Cone Elongation

The cytoplasmic microtubules of the teleost cone, including those of the motile myoid region, are all oriented with uniform polarity (Troutt and Burnside, 1987) (Fig. 11–3). Microtubule decoration by hooks of exogenous tubulin (cf. Heidemann and McIntosh, 1980) indicate that virtually all of the cone's cytoplasmic microtubules are oriented with their plus ends toward the synapse and their minus ends toward the base of the outer segment (i.e., toward the basal body of the connecting cilium of the outer segment; Figs. 11–3, 11–6) (Troutt and Burnside, 1987). These observations imply that any microtubule sliding occurring as cones elongate would be between microtubules of parallel orientation, as is the case in cilia and flagella (Euteneuer and McIntosh, 1981; Sale and Satir, 1977). In contrast, mitotic spindle elongation has been proposed to involve sliding between cytoplasmic microtubules of opposite polarity, in the region of overlap between half-spindles from each spindle pole (cf. Cande, Chapter 28).

The extent of microtubule assembly occurring during cone elongation appears to be species specific. In the two fish species examined, the total length of microtubules in the cone myoid has been approximated by multiplying the average number of microtubules observed in myoid cross section by the length of the myoid at different stages of elongation (Warren and Burnside, 1978; Burnside, 1987). In the blue-striped grunt, elongation of cones from 5 to 25 μm is not accompanied by appreciable net microtubule assembly; rather, there appears to be a redistribution of numerous short microtubules during elongation (Warren and Burnside, 1978). On the other hand, the much greater elongation (5 to 95 μm) of the green sunfish cone myoid was accompanied by a 10-fold increase in total microtubule length (Fig. 11–6) (Burnside, 1987). All of this net assembly occurs in the first half of the elongation process (5–50 μm), while the elongation from 50 to 95 μm occurs with no net increase in total microtubule length (Fig. 11–7). These observations suggest that, at least in the last stages, elongation can occur in the absence of *net* microtubule assembly. Thus, in the green sunfish, microtubule-

dependent elongation may entail two distinct components: an assembly component necessary to produce more microtubule machinery for the extensive length changes that occur and another separate, force-producing component. Although both may be active simultaneously, they may be separable processes. Nonetheless, these observations do not rule out the possibility that assembly produces force in the first stages of elongation.

Results with lysed cell models argue against a crucial role for microtubule assembly in force production for cone elongation. If force production for cone elongation is provided by microtubule assembly, then one might expect the rate of assembly-driven elongation to be lower in lysed cone models than in intact cells, since dilution of tubulin after lysis would tend to disfavor assembly. However, reactivated elongation proceeds for 10 min at rates corresponding to the fastest rates ever observed in vivo (2.0 μm/min; Fig. 11–5). Furthermore, the extent of reactivated elongation achieved in lysed cone models is not reduced by the presence of 10^{-3} M colchicine in the reactivation medium throughout the incubation (L.L. Troutt and B. Burnside, unpublished observations). These short (18-min) colchicine incubation times slightly reduce microtubule counts in cone myoid cross sections. This resistance to colchicine disruption for short incubation times suggests that the myoid microtubules in the models are relatively stable and undergo little turnover during reactivated elongation and that microtubules are probably not disassembling at some site and reassembling at others to maintain constant microtubule length.

Lateral associations between microtubules during reactivated elongation further suggest that microtubule sliding plays a role in cone elongation (Fig. 11–6). When lysed cone models are fixed during reactivated elongation, cross sections of the cone myoids reveal rows of up to eight closely spaced microtubules (palisades; Fig. 11–6). These palisades are not observed in lysed cone models that were either contracting

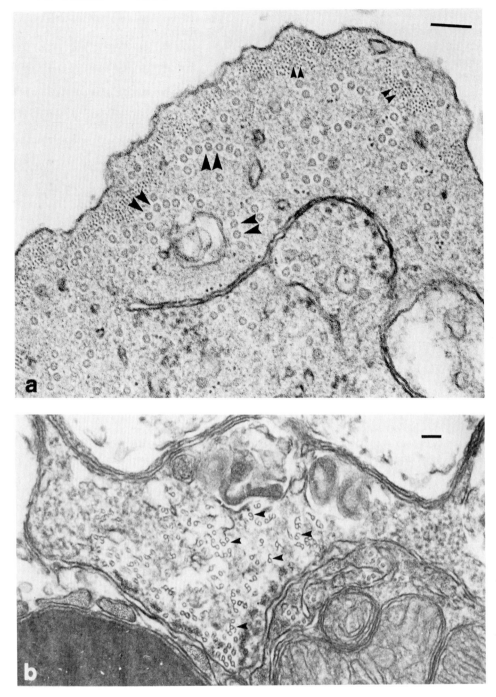

Fig. 11–6. Cross sections of cone myoids. **a:** Myoid fixed during reactivated elongation in a cone model prepared as described for Figure 11–4b. In contrast to the random distribution of microtubules in cross sections of contracting cone models (Fig. 11–4d), microtubules in the elongating myoids are laterally associated to form pairs, rows, and palisades (double arrowheads). Bar = 0.1 μm. (Reproduced from Burnside and Dearry, 1986, with permission of the publisher.) **b:** Myoids fixed after decoration with hooks of exogenous tubulin to determine microtubule polarity orientation. Virtually all hooks (arrowheads) curve in the clockwise direction when the section is viewed looking toward the outer segment, thus indicating that the minus ends of the microtubules lie toward the outer segment. Bar = 0.1 μm. (Reproduced from Burnside, 1987, with permission of the author.)

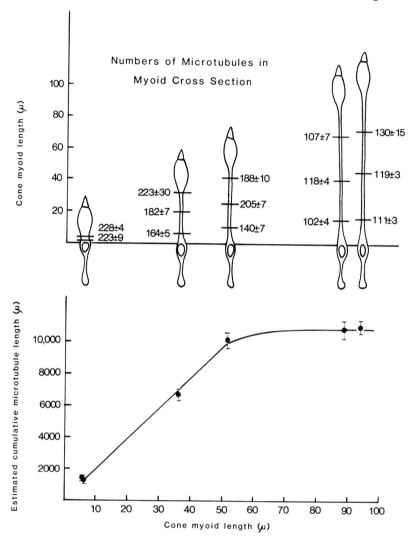

Fig. 11–7. Changes in cumulative myoid microtubule length with change in myoid length in green sunfish cones. After perfusion fixation, retinal pieces were sectioned parallel to the cone axis to determine myoid length and then rotated to obtain transverse sections of the same areas. **Top:** Numbers of microtubules counted in cross section (mean ± SEM) are indicated for different levels of the cone myoid (20 cones were used for each measurement). **Bottom:** Cumulative microtubule length was estimated by multiplying mean cone myoid length by mean number of microtubules per cone myoid in cross section (all three levels combined). The cones in the upper figure correspond to the points on the graph in the lower figure. The first half of elongation is accompanied by assembly, while the last half takes place in the absence of net microtubule assembly. (Reproduced from Burnside, 1987, with permission of the author.)

(Fig. 11–4) or not elongating (in the absence of ATP or cAMP). Intermicrotubule distance in these cone palisades (7.5 ± 0.3 nm, N = 50) is substantially less than that observed between flagellar doublets in rigor (17–18 nm; cf. Zanetti et al., 1979). Similar microtubule palisades were observed when ciliary dynein was added to isolated mitotic spindles or twice-recycled microtubules at relatively low dynein/tubulin ratios (cf. Figs. 1, 4, 5 in Haimo and Fenton, 1984).

Characterization of the Motor for Cone Elongation

Since microtubule sliding was strongly implicated in cone elongation, we set out to determine whether microtubule sliding in cones had properties similar to those observed in cilia and flagella. First, we tested whether reactivated cone elongation would be inhibited by agents that have been shown to inhibit the ATPase activity of flagellar and ciliary dyneins (cf. Warner and Mitchell, 1980; Penningroth, 1986). These inhibitors include vanadate, erythro-9[3-(2-hydroxynonyl)]adenine (EHNA), and N-ethylmaleimide (NEM). Though none of these inhibitors are truly specific for dynein ATPase, other motility-related motors, such as myosin and kinesin, do show sensitivities to these agents that differ from those of dynein (cf. Table 11–1 and Penningroth, 1986).

Vanadate has been shown to inhibit a variety of enzymes of nucleotide and phosphate metabolism, probably by acting as a structural analog of phosphate (cf. Nechay, 1984; Warner and Mitchell, 1980; Penningroth, 1986; Penningroth, Chapter 12). Enzymes inhibited by vanadate include dynein ATPase, myosin ATPase, plasma membrane ion pumps, phosphatases, and kinases. Vanadate ion (VO_3^-) is reduced by glutathione and the catecholamine norepinephrine to vanadyl ion (VO_2^+), which is not inhibitory. Inhibition of dynein ATPase by vanadate is very rapid, requiring milliseconds, and inhibition is effective at low concentrations in the μM range. Vanadate inhibition of myosin ATPase is much slower (minutes to hours) and requires much higher concentrations (mM range). Vanadate inhibition of dynein ATPase is reversed by dilution because the inhibitory complex readily dissociates, but inhibition is not reversed by increased ATP, since vanadate acts as a noncompetitive inhibitor of dynein ATPase.

Vanadate inhibits reactivated cone elonga-tion in a manner similar to its inhibition of dynein ATPase (Gilson et al., 1987) but with some differences. Vanadate completely blocks reactivated cone elongation at concentrations ≥ 10 μM, and even 1 μM vanadate partially inhibits. Inhibition proved to be reversible; cone models elongated after vanadate was washed out and replaced with fresh ATP medium. Vanadate inhibition was prevented by simultaneous incubation with 2.5 mM norepinephrine, and it was reversed by adding norepinephrine to the incubation medium after 10 min. Consistent with the noncompetitive inhibition of dynein ATPase (cf. Warner and Mitchell, 1980), vanadate inhibition of cone elongation was not reversed by increasing the ATP concentration as high as 4 mM. Vanadate specifically inhibited the cAMP-independent component of the ATP requirement for cone elongation. When added after the initial 3-min cAMP-dependent step, 10 μM vanadate was equally as effective as was deleting ATP in preventing the subsequent cAMP-independent phase of reactivated cone elongation. Thus vanadate blocks the cAMP-independent process we consider to be a likely candidate for the force-producing mechanism.

Recent studies suggest that vanadate might also inhibit microtubule assembly (Kirazov and Weiss, 1986). However, inhibition of assembly requires higher concentrations of vanadate (100–700 μM) than are required to inhibit dynein and cone elongation. Thus it seems unlikely that vanadate is acting by inhibiting microtubule assembly in lysed cone models.

Vanadate inhibition was also found to be specific for cone elongation, as vanadate at 100 μM had no effect on actin-dependent reactivated cone contraction. This insensitivity of contraction to vanadate is consistent with the reported slower rate of inhibition of myosin ATPase by vanadate (minutes to hours) and with the weak binding of myosin to vanadate and ADP (K_d in the mM range) (cf. Penningroth, 1986).

Reactivated cone elongation was completely blocked by 1 or 5 mM NEM (Gilson et al., 1987). This sensitivity to millimolar concentrations of NEM resembles that of motility-coupled dynein ATPase and axonemal sliding (Warner and Mitchell, 1980) and contrasts with that of kinesin, which is not inhibited by 5 mM NEM (Vale, Chapter 18).

As expected, the nonhydrolyzable ATP analog adenylyl imidodiphosphate (AMP-PNP) did not support reactivated cone elongation when substituted for ATP (Gilson et al., 1987). However, when cone models were incubated in equimolar concentrations of MgATP and AMP-PNP (0.5 mM), AMP-PNP did not block activation by MgATP. This behavior resembles that of dynein ATPase and contrasts with that of kinesin, in which AMP-PNP interferes with MgATP utilization by the ATPase (Penningroth, Chapter 12; Vale, Chapter 18).

EHNA was first shown to be an inhibitor of protein carboxymethylation (Scheaffer and Schwender, 1974) and was later shown to arrest the motility of spermatozoa because of an inhibition of axonemal dynein ATPase activity (Bouchard et al., 1981; Penningroth, 1986). EHNA appeared to be relatively specific for dynein ATPase, having little effect on several other ATP-metabolizing enzymes such as myosin and kinesin (Bouchard et al., 1981; Penningroth, 1986; Vale, Chapter 18). At first there was much interest in using EHNA as a probe to detect dynein-dependent motility of cytoplasmic microtubules, since, unlike vanadate, it would cross the plasma membrane. It has been used as a probe for the possible involvement of dynein-like ATPases in chromosome movement in mitosis (Cande, 1982), particle transport in chromatophores (Clark and Rosenbaum, 1982; Beckerle and Porter, 1982), and organelle movements in axons (Goldberg, 1982; Forman et al., 1983b). However, interpretation of such studies is complicated by identified effects of EHNA on processes other than dynein activity, including the inhibition of protein carboxymethylation (Bouchard et al., 1981), effects on actin-based motility (Schliwa et al., 1984a), and binding to hydrophobic sites (Penningroth, 1986). Thus EHNA cannot be

considered a specific inhibitor of dynein ATPase or a diagnostic reagent for identifying dynein-based motility. Nonetheless, it provides one with a list of criteria that can be used to try to characterize the mechanisms responsible for motile processes (Table 11-1).

EHNA acts as an effective and reversible blocker of reactivated cone elongation: In media containing 0.1 mM MgATP, 0.5 mM EHNA completely blocks reactivated cone elongation (Gilson et al., 1987). Inhibition of cone movement by EHNA is reversed by increasing the ATP concentration or by dilution. Since cone elongation does not require actin-dependent processes (it is cytochalasin insensitive; Gilson et al., 1986), it seems unlikely that EHNA inhibition is mediated by an effect on the cone's actin system. Indeed, EHNA does not even inhibit actin-dependent reactivated cone *contraction* in lysed cell models, presumably because the actin machinery is already assembled before lysis and exposure to EHNA (Gilson et al., 1987). The reversal of EHNA inhibition of cone elongation by increased ATP concentrations is consistent with observed effects of EHNA on flagellar dynein and with its action as a mixed competitive inhibitor of dynein ATPase (Penningroth, 1986; Chapter 12). This reversal of EHNA inhibition of cone elongation by 1 mM ATP may explain our finding that 0.5 mM EHNA fails to block elongation in intact cones of cultured retinas; even at 5 mM EHNA, only partial inhibition is obtained, and this concentration is likely to produce cytotoxicity (Penningroth, 1986). Since the ratio of EHNA to ATP is crucial to EHNA inhibition, 0.5 mM EHNA might be expected to be ineffective in the cytoplasm of intact cones in which ATP levels are in the millimolar range.

In addition to its effects on ATPases, EHNA is a potent inhibitor of protein carboxylation, a process thought to be involved in repair or elimination of deamination-damaged proteins (Aswad and Johnson, 1987). EHNA increases the intracellular concentration of S-adenosyl-L-homocysteine through inhibition of adenosine deaminase,

TABLE 11–1. Properties of Microtubule-Associated ATPases and Microtubule-Dependent Processes

	ATP specificity	Inhibition by vanadate at <20 µM	Inhibition by NEM at 1–5 mM	Inhibition by EHNA at 0.5 mM	Inhibition by adenosine at 0.5 mM	Inhibition by S-homo-L-cysteine at 100–0.5 mM	Direction movement regarding microtubule polarity	References
Microtubule-associated ATPases								
Ciliary and flagellar dynein	ATP	+	+	+	±	−	Toward the minus end	Sale and Satir (1977), Warner and Mitchell (1980), Penningroth 1986; Penningroth (Volume 1, Chapter 12)
Cytoplasmic dynein-like ATPases	ATP	+	+	+				Pratt (Chapter 8), Penningroth, (Volume 1, Chapter 12), Paschal et al. (1987a)
Kinesins anterograde motors	ATP, GTP UTP, ITP, LTP	−	−	−			Toward the plus end	Vale et al. (1985a–c), Vale (Chapter 18), Penningroth (Volume 1, Chapter 12), Kuznetsov and Gelfand (1986)
Retrograde motors	ATP?	+	+	+			Toward the minus end	Vale et al. (1985c)

Motile processes

Motile processes						Proposed mechanism	References
Motility in flagellar ciliary axonemes	ATP	+	+	+	−	Sliding of parallel microtubules	Penningroth (Volume 1, Chapter 12), Tash and Means (1983)
Reactivated pigment aggregation in chromatophores	ATP	±	+	+	−	Toward the minus end	Beckerle and Porter (1982), Clark and Rosenbaum (1984), Ogawa et al. (1987)
Reactivated elongation of PTK, mitotic spindle models	ATP	+	+	+	+	Sliding of antiparallel microtubules	Cande (1982), Cande (Chapter 28)
Elongation of diatom spindle models	ATP	+	+	−		Sliding of antiparallel microtubules	Cande (Chapter 28)
Reactivated elongation of teleost cone models	ATP	+	+	+	+	Sliding of parallel microtubules	Gilson et al. (1986, 1987)
Reactivated contraction in teleost cone models	ATP	−	+	−	+		Porrello and Burnside (1984), Gilson et al. (1987)
Reactivated microtubule sliding and organelle movements in projections of *Reticulomyra*	ATP	−	+	−		Toward the plus and minus ends; sliding of parallel microtubules	Koonce et al. (1987), Koonce and Schliwa (1986), Euteneuer (Chapter 10)

184   **Burnside**

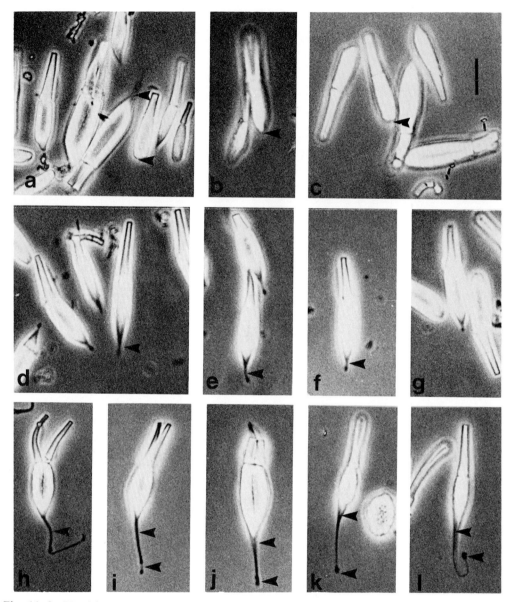

Fig. 11–8. Distal fragments of cones containing cone inner and outer segments (CIS-COS). CIS-COS were obtained by the following procedure: 1) Green sunfish were left in darkness for 2 hr prior to dissection to allow cone myoids to become sufficiently long and delicate so that they readily break when the retina is dissected away from the RPE, leaving the cone's inner and outer segments attached to the RPE pieces; 2) CIS-COS were then detached from the RPE by 2 min treatment with papain (0.1 unit/ml) followed by washes and mechanical agitation (t_0, **a–c**). CIS-COS were then cultured for 1 hr in Ringer's (**d–g**) solution or in Ringer's plus 1 μM forskolin (**h–l**). Myoids of forskolin-treated CIS-COS elongate to lengths as great as 25 μm. Thus CIS-COS contain all the necessary regulatory and force-producing machinery to produce myoid elongation; contributions from the perinuclear region of the cone are not required. Arrowheads indicate myoids. Bar = 10 μm.

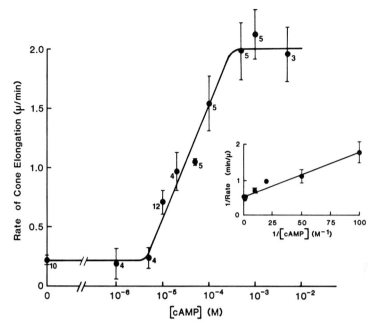

Fig. 11–9. The effect of cAMP concentration on the rate of reactivated elongation in lysed cone models. The maximum rate of elongation (2.0 μm/min) was observed at cAMP concentrations of >0.5 mM. The cAMP concentration required to obtain the half-maximum rate of cone elongation was calculated to be 23 μM. Elongation media contained 1 mM MgATP and 10^{-8} M free Ca^{2+}. (Reproduced from Gilson et al., 1986, with permission of the publisher.)

thereby leading to inhibition of protein carboxymethylase (Bouchard et al., 1981). To investigate whether the EHNA block of reactivated cone elongation was a result of inhibiting protein carboxymethylase, we tested three other inhibitors of this enzyme: adenosine (0.5 mM), cycloleucine (10 mM), and S-adenosyl-L-homocysteine (0.5 mM). All three blocked cone elongation in lysed cell models but only at concentrations that were orders of magnitude higher than required for inhibition of protein carboxylation. Also the inhibitory effects of these agents on cone elongation were reversed by increasing the MgATP concentration to 1 mM, just as was observed with EHNA.

These results illustrate the difficulties inherent in using EHNA as a probe for dynein-like activity. These studies clearly do *not* provide a simple case for specific EHNA inhibition of cone dynein-like ATPase. A comparison of effects of carboxymethylation inhibitors in several cell types is illustrated

in Table 11–1. In its sensitivity to adenosine, cone elongation resembles reactivated spindle elongation in cultured PtK_1 cells (Cande, 1982), but differs from flagellar motility, since dynein ATPase activity and flagellar beat are not inhibited by adenosine (Bouchard et al., 1981). Inhibitory effects of EHNA on fast axonal transport (Ekstrom and Kanje, 1984; Forman et al., 1983b) and on actin assembly (Schliwa et al., 1984a) were not reproduced by inhibitors of carboxymethylation.

The properties of several examples of microtubule dependent-motility and microtubule dependent ATPase activity are listed in Table 11–1. As just described, cone elongation is both vanadate and EHNA sensitive. In *Reticulomyxa* both intracellular vessicle transport along microtubules and microtubule sliding are insensitive to EHNA and require higher concentrations of vanadate (25–100 μM) to produce inhibition (Koonce and Schliwa, 1986a; Koonce et al.,

1987; Euteneuer et al., Chapter 10). In the diatom, spindle elongation is sensitive to vanadate but not to EHNA (Cande, Chapter 28). In axons, high concentrations of vanadate block saltatory organelle movement in both directions, but EHNA was more effective in inhibiting retrograde than orthograde transport (Forman et al., 1983a,b). The variability in the responses in different cell types, along with the well characterized differences between kinesins and cytoplasmic dynein-like ATPases (Vale, Chapter 18; Pratt, Chapter 8) strongly suggest that we may expect to find more than one "microtubule motor" in different cell types and that we are at the beginning of a most interesting period of research in microtubule-dependent motility. The next few years will reveal whether there are either only a few basic classes of microtubule motors (e.g., kinesins and dynein-like ATPases) or several new classes, as yet uncharacterized, and also whether motors used for particle transport like kinesin can also be used for intermicrotubule sliding.

Regulation of Motility in Teleost Cones

Lysed cone models have made it possible to characterize the intracellular conditions that direct a cone either to elongate or to contract. Cone models can be induced to undergo either ATP-dependent elongation or ATP-dependent contraction simply by varying the concentrations of Ca^{2+} and cAMP in the reactivation media (Porrello and Burnside, 1984; Gilson et al., 1986). Elongation is induced by media containing high cAMP ($\geq 10^{-6}$ M) and low Ca^{2+} ($\leq 10^{-7}$ M) concentrations; contraction is induced by media containing high Ca^{2+} ($> 10^{-7}$ M) and low cAMP ($< 10^{-6}$ M) concentrations.

Effects of agents that increase cAMP levels in unlysed, intact cones corroborate our results with lysed cell models and suggest that the models faithfully reflect in vivo regulatory mechanisms. In intraocular injection and retinal organ culture experiments, forskolin and dibutyryl cAMP induce dose-dependent increases in cone elongation (Burnside and Ackland, 1984; Burnside et al., 1982a; Burnside and Basinger, 1983). Forskolin also produces myoid elongation in fragments of cones containing only inner and outer segments (Fig. 11–8), so cones are affected directly. These various observations imply that, in vivo, onset of darkness is accompanied by increased levels of intracellular cAMP, at least in the cone myoid. This suggestion is consistent with the observation that retinal cAMP levels are higher in the dark than in the light in green sunfish and in several other species (cf. Burnside et al., 1982a).

In cone models, the rate of reactivated elongation is proportional to the cAMP concentration between 5 and 500 μM, with half-maximal rate occurring at approximately 23 μM (Fig. 11–9) (Gilson et al., 1986). Similar dose-dependent effects of cAMP have been observed on beat frequency in epithelial cell cilia (Nelson and Wright, 1974; Sanderson et al., 1985) and in demembranated *Paramecium* cilia (Bonini et al., 1986), but not in sperm flagellar axonemes, where cAMP appears to be required for activation of motility but does not influence beat frequency (Lindemann et al., 1983; Morisawa and Okuno, 1982; Opresko and Brokaw, 1983; Tash and Means, 1982, 1983; Tash et al., 1986).

The ability of cAMP to activate motility in lysed cone models and in demembranated ciliary and flagellar axonemes suggests that cAMP is acting on some intracellular component of the motile or regulatory machinery rather than on modulating ion fluxes across the plasma membrane. In dog, bovine, and sea urchin sperm, a component present in detergent extracts of flagella has been shown to confer cAMP dependence on motility (cf. Tash et al., 1986; Ishiguro et al., 1982; Brandt and Hoskins, 1980). Recently Tash et al. (1986) presented evidence that cAMP-dependent phosphorylation of axokinin, a soluble 56 kDa factor, appears to be sufficient to produce motility in isolated axonemes of dog flagella.

Soluble factors may play a similar role in regulating cone elongation. Lysed cone models fail to elongate maximally when cAMP is added 30 min after lysis instead of immediately at lysis (Gilson et al., 1986). Other observations suggest that this loss of motility results from the loss of a soluble factor rather than from degradation of the motile machinery. When cones are reactivated in cAMP (1 mM) and low ATP (10 μM), elongation is initiated but proceeds only partially because available ATP is consumed before elongation is completed. If, however, MgATP is replenished after 20 min, the models can still achieve maximal elongation, indicating that the elongation machinery is still functional 30 min after lysis. Thus the loss of capacity to elongate after 30 min incubation in the absence of cAMP could result from the gradual loss of a soluble factor that like the 56 kDa axokinin, is required for cAMP activation. Tash et al. (1986) have also identified a 56 kDa protein in dog retina that, when phosphorylated by cAMP-dependent protein kinase, activates motility of demembranated dog sperm. Thus there may be a component of the regulatory mechanism by which cAMP activates microtubule-dependent motility that is conserved in both sperm and photoreceptors.

Detergent-insoluble components of the sperm flagellar axoneme have also been shown to participate in cAMP regulation of motility. Murofushi et al. (1986) have found that in sea urchin sperm a KCl extract of demembranated axonemes can confer cAMP dependence to motility activation. In *Ciona* sperm flagellar axonemes cAMP enhances labeled phosphate incorporation into several proteins, including those migrating in the M_r range of dynein heavy chain components (Opresko and Brokaw, 1983). Similar bands were found to be phosphorylated during activation of motility in vivo. Since we have recently been able to obtain pure preparations of elongating cone inner-outer segment preparations (CIS-COS), which can elongate after detachment (Fig. 11–8), it will now be possible to compare the patterns of protein phosphorylation found in cone cytoskeletons during elongation in intact cells to those induced by cAMP.

Reactivated cone elongation is strongly inhibited by Ca^{2+} (Gilson et al., 1986). Ca^{2+} produces concentration-dependent inhibition of elongation rate, with complete inhibition being observed at 10^{-5} M Ca^{2+}. This resembles the dose-dependent effect of Ca^{2+} on beat frequency in ciliate cilia (cf. Naitoh and Kaneko, 1972, 1973), but contrasts with the lack of effect of Ca^{2+} on activation and polarity of sliding in flagellar axonemes (Gibbons and Gibbons, 1972; Walter and Satir, 1979; Zanetti et al., 1979). Other studies show that Ca^{2+} inhibition of reactivated cone elongation does not result from activating a competing contraction, a possibility that should be considered since maximal contraction occurs at the same free Ca^{2+} concentration as Ca^{2+} inhibition of elongation (Porrello and Burnside, 1984). Even when lysed cones models are treated with sufficient cytochalasin D to disrupt actin filaments and thus block the cone's ability to contract, Ca^{2+} nonetheless inhibits cone elongation (Gilson et al., 1986). Thus Ca^{2+} appears to act directly on the microtubule-dependent mechanism to inhibit elongation.

Calmodulin may mediate Ca^{2+} inhibition of cone elongation, since the calmodulin inhibitor trifluoperazine (10 μM) abolishes the Ca^{2+} effect (Gilson et al., 1986). Calmodulin has also been proposed to mediate Ca^{2+} inhibition of microtubule-based motility in the ciliary arrest response of freshwater mussel gill lateral cells (Reed and Satir, 1980; Reed et al., 1982).

Comparison of calmodulin requirements for inhibition of reactivated cone elongation to those previously described for calmodulin action in reactivated cone contraction (Porrello and Burnside, 1984) suggests that two separate pools of calmodulin are employed for activating contraction and inhibiting elongation. Ca^{2+} blocks elongation only if it is present at the time of lysis (first 3 min); subsequent addition is ineffective unless exogenous calmodulin is also added. This observation further indicates that calmodulin is required for Ca^{2+} inhibition and suggests that the relevant cone calmodulin is soluble and gradually lost from the models after lysis. In contracting models, on the other hand, the calmodulin required for activation of movement does not appear to be lost after lysis; even after 90 min, Ca^{2+} addition induces maximal contraction in the lysed cone models.

One possible mechanism of Ca^{2+} inhibition of cone elongation is by disruption of microtubules. Ca^{2+} has been shown to favor microtubule disassembly in brain tubulin preparations in vitro (cf. Margolis, 1983), in lysed and permeabilized cells (Schliwa et al., 1981), in isolated mitotic spindles (Salmon and Segall, 1980), and when injected into cells (Keihart, 1981). However, Ca^{2+} inhibition of cone elongation does not result from disruption of cone myoid microtubules; they are still present in equivalent numbers in lysed cell models that have been incubated 18–30 min in 10^{-5} M Ca^{2+} (Fig. 11–4) (Porrello and Burnside, 1984). The myoid microtubules of the lysed cone models appear to be Ca^{2+} stable, like the subpopulation of Ca^{2+}-stable microtubules identified in brain tubulin preparations (cf. Margolis, 1983). Thus the effect of Ca^{2+} on cone movement resembles that in some cilia and flagella in which Ca^{2+} influences movement without breaking down microtubules (cf. Naitoh and Kaneko, 1972, 1973; Mogami and Takahashi, 1983; Sanderson et al., 1985; Gibbons and Gibbons, 1980).

Together our findings indicate that there is an antagonism between cAMP and Ca^{2+} in the regulation of cone movement, with cAMP producing activation and Ca^{2+} producing inhibition of microtubule-dependent elongation. This antagonism between cAMP activation and Ca^{2+} inhibition has also been suggested for regulation of ciliary motility in *Paramecium* and *Mytilus* gill cilia (Sanderson et al., 1985; Bonini et al., 1986).

CONCLUSIONS

This chapter outlines our studies of the teleost cone as a framework for investigating the mechanisms of metazoan cell elongation. Several of the characteristics of teleost cone elongation resemble those of ciliary and flagellar axonemal motility and suggest that cone elongation is produced by microtubule sliding: 1) Reactivated elongation can occur in the absence of microtubule assembly; 2) regular lateral associations between cone myoid microtubules are observed during reactivated cone elongation but not during contraction or when the cones are not moving; 3) inhibitor sensitivities of reactivated cone elongation closely resemble those of ciliary dyneins and cytoplasmic dynein-like ATPases; and 4) regulation of cone motility by cAMP activation and Ca^{2+} inhibition has features in common with regulation of flagellar and ciliary motility in several species. These observations argue that cone elongation is effected by microtubule sliding and that this sliding is powered by a microtubule motor similar to dynein.

It is now possible to proceed further with our dissection of cone elongation mechanisms. We have been able to obtain distal fragments of cones (CIS-COS) that are highly enriched in the motile machinery responsible for elongation and that will elongate in response to agents that elevate cAMP (Fig. 11–8) and contract in response to dopamine (Dearry and Burnside, 1986). The CIS-COS comprise only 30% of the cone's volume, yet they contain all the necessary components for producing 15–20 μm of myoid elongation as well as contraction. In future studies this preparation should make more detailed biochemical characterization of the cytoskeletal machinery possible and also enable us to look into the molecular mechanisms of cAMP and Ca^{2+} regulation of motility in this cell.

In the teleost retinal cone, the uniquely convenient deployment of actin- and microtubule-dependent processes into temporally discrete events has made it possible to describe in considerable detail the regulatory and force-producing mechanisms of microtubule-dependent cell shape change in a metazoan cell, without ambiguities introduced by simultaneous activity of actin-dependent processes. Similarly, the actin-dependent process can be studied without interference from microtubule-dependent processes. In addition, this temporal separation of motile events has enabled us to compare the physiological constraints of microtubule- and actin-dependent cell shape change in the same cell and thus hopefully obtain some clues to how cells might coordinate activities of their actin- and microtubule machinery for morphogenetic events. More complex cell shape changes, such as those seen in developing neurons or cultured cells, are likely to entail more complex interplays of these and perhaps other cytoskeletal and motile processes. Our results suggest that specific second-messenger conditions similar to those described here for cones, particularly if produced locally within the cell, could provide spatial and temporal regulation of actin-dependent contractile and microtubule-dependent extensive forces and thereby contribute to determining a particular cell shape. Such localized second-messenger conditions might be produced, for example, by contact of the cell with other cells, by interaction with recognized molecules in the extracellular matrix, by synaptic input, or by gradients of substances that are recognized by surface receptors.

Bibliography 2, Chapters 7–11

Abe, S., and S. Uno (1984) Nuclear elongation of dissociated newt spermatids in vitro and their nuclear shortening by antimicrotubule agents. Exp. Cell Res. 154:243–255.

Adams, R.J. (1982) Organelle movement in axons depends on ATP. Nature 297:327–329.

Allen, C., and G.G. Borisy (1974) Structural polarity and directional growth of microtubules from axonemes of *Chlamydomonas*. J. Mol. Biol. 90:381–401.

Allen, R.D. (1975) Evidence for firm linkages between microtubules and membrane-bounded vesicles. J. Cell Biol. 64:497–503.

Allen, R.D., N.S. Allen, and J. Travis (1981) Video-enhanced contrast, differential interference contrast (AVEC-DIC) microscopy: A new method capable of analyzing microtubule-related motility in the reticulopodial network of *Allogromia laticollaris*. Cell Motil. 1:292–302.

Allen, R.D., J. Metuzals, I. Tasaki, S.T. Brady, and S.P. Gilbert (1982) Fast axonal transport in squid giant axon. Science 218:1127–1129.

Allen, R.D., D.G. Weiss, J.H. Hayden, T.D. Brown, H. Fujiwake, and M. Simpson (1985) Gliding movement of and bidirectional movement along single native microtubules from the squid axoplasm: Evidence for an active role of microtubules in cytoplasmic transport. J. Cell Biol. 100:1736–1752.

Amos, L.A. (1987) Kinesin from pig brain studied by electron microscopy. J. Cell Sci. 87:105–111.

Asai, D.J. (1986) An antiserum to the sea urchin 20S egg dynein reacts with embryonic ciliary dynein but it does not react with the mitotic apparatus. Dev. Biol. 118:416–424.

Asai, D.J., R.J. Leslie, and L. Wilson (1986) Dynein-like cytoplasmic microtubule translocators. Ann. N.Y. Acad. Sci. 466:275–291.

Asai, D.J., and L. Wilson (1982) Egg and flagellar dyneins compared using polyclonal and monoclonal antibodies to dynein. J. Cell Biol. 95:329a.

Asai, D.J., and L.S. Wilson (1985) A latent activity dynein-like cytoplasmic magnesium adenosine triphosphatase. J. Biol. Chem. 260:699–702.

Aswad, D.W., and B.A. Johnson (1987) The unusual substrate specificity of eukaryotic protein carboxyl methyltransferases. Trends Biochem. Sci. 12:155–158.

Auclair, W., and B.W. Seigel (1966) Cilia regeneration in the sea urchin embryo: Evidence for a pool of ciliary proteins. Science 154:913–915.

Bagnara, J.T., and M.E. Hadley (1973) Chromatophores and Color Change. The Comparative Physiology of Animal Pigmentation. Englewood Cliffs, NJ: Prentice-Hall.

Ballowitz, E. (1914) Über die Pigmentstromung in den Farbstoffzellen und die Kanälchenstruktur des Protoplasmas. Pflügers Arch. ges. Physiol. 157:165–210.

Barra, H.S., C.A. Arce, J.A. Rodriguez, and R. Caputto (1974) Some common properties of the protein that incorporates tyrosine as a single unit in microtubule proteins. Biochem. Biophys. Res. Commun. 60:1384–1390.

Beckerle, M.C., and K.R. Porter (1982) Inhibitors of dynein activity block intracellular transport in erythrophores. Nature 295:701–703.

Bell, C.W. (1983) The molecular weight of dynein heavy chains. J. Submicrosc. Cytol. 15:201–202.

Bell, C.W., C. Fraser, W.S. Sale, W.J.Y. Tang, and I.R. Gibbons (1982) Preparation and purification of dynein. Methods Cell Biol. 24:373–397.

Bell, C.W., and I.R. Gibbons (1982) Structure of dynein 1 outer arms in sea urchin sperm flagella. II. Analysis by proteolytic cleavage. J. Biol. Chem. 257:516–522.

Bikle, D., L.G. Tilney, and K.R. Porter (1966) Microtubules and pigment migration in the melanophores of *Fundulus heteroclitus* L. Protoplasma 61:322–345.

Binder, L.I., W.L. Dentler, and J.L. Rosenbaum (1975) Assembly of chick brain tubulin onto flagellar axonemes of *Chlamydomonas* and sea urchin sperm. Proc. Natl. Acad. Sci. USA 72:1122–1126.

Birkenmeier, C.S., D.M. Bodine, E.A. Repasky, D.M. Helfman, S.H. Hughes, and J. E. Barker (1985) Remarkable homology among the internal repeats of erythroid and non-erythroid spectrin. Proc. Natl. Acad. Sci. USA 82:5671–5675.

Bloodgood, R.A. (1975) Biochemical analysis of axostyle motility. Cytobios 14:101–120.

Bonini, N.M., M.C. Gustin, and D.L. Nelson (1986) Regulation of ciliary motility by membrane potential in *Paramecium*: A role for cyclic AMP. Cell Motil. Cytoskeleton 6:256–272.

Bouchard, P., S.M. Penningroth, A. Cheung, C. Gagnon, and C.W. Bardin (1981) Erythro-9-[3-(2-hydroxynonyl)]adenine is an inhibitor of sperm motility that blocks dynein ATPase and protein carboxymethylase activities. Proc. Natl. Acad. Sci. USA 78:1033–1036.

Brady, S.T. (1985) A novel brain ATPase with properties expected for the axonal transport motor. Nature 317:73–75.

Brady, S.T. (1987) Fast axonal transport in isolated axoplasm from the squid giant axon. In R.S. Smith and M.A. Bisby (eds): Axonal Transport. New York: Alan R. Liss, Inc., pp. 113–137.

Brady, S.T., R.J. Lasek, and R.D. Allen (1982) Fast axonal transport in extruded axoplasm from the squid giant axon. Science 218:1129–1131.

Brady, S.T., R.J. Lasek, and R.D. Allen (1985) Video microscopy of fast axonal transport in extruded axoplasm: A new model for study of molecular mechanisms. Cell Motil. 5:81–101.

Brandt, H., and D.D. Hoskins (1980) A cAMP-dependent phosphorylated motility protein in bovine epididymal sperm. J. Biol. Chem. 255:982–987.

Brokaw, C.J. (1982) Activation and reactivation of *Ciona* sperm. Cell Motil. Suppl. 1:185–189.

Burns, R.G., and T.D. Pollard (1974) A dynein-like protein from brain. FEBS Lett. 40:274–280.

Burnside, B. (1971) Microtubules and microfilaments in newt neurulation. Dev. Biol. 26:416–441.

Burnside, B. (1976) Microtubules and actin filaments in teleost visual cone elongation and contraction. J. Supramol. Struct. 5:257–275.

Burnside, B. (1988) Photoreceptor contraction and elongation: Calcium and cyclic adenosine 3',5'-monophosphate regulation of actin- and microtubule-dependent changes in cell shape. In R.L. Lasek (ed): Intrinsic Determinants of Neuronal Form and Function. pp. 323–359.

Burnside, B., and N. Ackland (1984) Effects of circadian rhythm and cAMP on retinomotor movements in the green sunfish *Lepomis cyanellus*. Invest. Ophthalmol. Vis. Sci. 25:539–545.

Burnside, B., R. Adler, and P. O'Connor (1983) Retinomotor pigment migration in the teleost retinal pigment epithelium. I. Roles for actin and microtubules in pigment granule transport and cone movement. Invest. Ophthalmol. Vis. Sci. 24:1–15.

Burnside, B., and S. Basinger (1983) Retinomotor pigment migration in the teleost retinal pigment epithelium. II. Cyclic-3',5'-adenosine monophosphate induction of dark-adaptive movement in vitro. Invest. Ophthalmol. Visual Sci. 24:16–23.

Burnside, B., and A. Dearry (1986) Cell motility in the retina. In R. Adler and D. Farber (eds): The Retina: A Model for Cell Biology Studies, Part 1. pp. 151–206.

Burnside, B., M. Evans, R.T. Fletcher, and G.J. Chader (1982a) Induction of dark–adaptive retinomotor movement (cell elongation) in teleost retinal cones by cyclic adenosine 3',5'-monophosphate. J. Gen. Physiol. 79:759–774.

Burnside, B., and B. Nagle (1983) Retinomotor movements of photoreceptors and retinal pigment epithelium: Mechanisms and regulation. In N. Osborne and G. Chader (eds): Progress in Visual Research, vol. 2. Oxford: Pergamon, pp. 67–109.

Burnside, B., B. Smith, M. Nagata, and K. Porrello (1982b) Reactivation of contraction in detergent-lysed teleost retinal cones. J. Cell Biol. 92:199–206.

Burton, P.R., and J.L. Paige (1981) Polarity of axonal microtubules in the olfactory nerve of the frog. Proc. Natl. Acad. Sci. USA 78:3269–3273.

Byers, B., and K.R. Porter (1964) Oriented microtubules in elongating cells of the developing lens rudiment after induction. Proc. Natl. Acad. Sci. USA 52:1091–1099.

Cande, W.Z. (1982) Inhibition of spindle elongation in permeabilized mitotic cells by erythro-9-[3-(2-hydroxynonyl)]adenine. Nature 295: 700–701.

Cande, W.Z., and K.L. McDonald (1985) In vitro reactivation of anaphase spindle elongation using isolated diatom spindles. Nature 316:168–170.

Cande, W.Z., and K.L. McDonald (1986) Physiological and ultrastructural analysis of elongating mitotic spindles reactivated in vitro. J. Cell Biol. 103:593–604.

Cande, W.Z., and S.M. Wolniak (1978) Chromosome movement in lysed mitotic cells is inhibited by vanadate. J. Cell Biol. 79:573–580.

Chitwood, B.G., and M.B. Chitwood (1974) Introduction to Nematology.

Baltimore: University Park Press.Clark, T.G., and J.L. Rosenbaum (1982) Pigment particle translocation in detergent-permeabilized melanophores of Fundulus heteroclitus. Proc. Natl. Acad. Sci. USA 79:4655–4659.

Cleveland, D.W. (1987) The multitubulin hypothesis revisited: What have we learned? J. Cell Biol. 104:381–383.

Cleveland, D.W., M.A. Lopata, R. McDonald, N.J. Cowan, and M.W. Kirschner (1980) Number and evolutionary conservation of α- and β-tubulin and cytoplasmic β- and γ-actin genes using specific cloned cDNA probes. Cell 20:95–105.

Cohn, S.A., A. Ingold, and J.M. Scholey (1987) Correlations between the ATPase and microtubule translocating activities of sea urchin egg kinesin. Nature 328:160–163.

Collins, C.A., and R.B. Vallee (1986a) Effect of ionic strength on microtubule related proteins in sea urchin egg cytosol: evidence for multiple forms of cytoplasmic dynein and for tubulin/MAP oligomers. J. Cell Biol. 103:408a.

Collins, C.A., and R.B. Vallee (1986b) A microtubule-activated ATPase from sea urchin eggs, distinct from cytoplasmic dynein and kinesin. Proc. Natl. Acad. Sci. USA 83:4799–4803.

Davenport, C.B. (1895) Studies in morphogenesis. IV. A preliminary catalogue of the processes concerned in ontogeny. Bull. Museum Comp. Zool. Harvard 27:171–199.

Dearry, A., and B. Burnside (1986) Dopaminergic regulation of cone retinomotor movement in teleost retinas. I. Induction of cone contraction is mediated by D2 receptors. J. Neurochem. 46:1006–1021.

Dentler, W.D., M.M. Pratt, and R.E. Stephens (1980) Microtubule-membrane interactions in cilia II. Photochemical cross-linking of bridge structures and the identification of a membrane-associated dynein-like ATPase. J. Cell Biol. 84:381–403.

Dinenberg, A.S., J.R. McIntosh, and J.M. Scholey (1986) Studies on sea urchin egg cytoplasmic ATPases of possible significance for microtubule functions. Ann. N.Y. Acad. Sci. 466:431–435.

Dujardin, F. (1835) Recherches sur les organismes inferieurs. Ann. Sci. Nat. 4:238–377.

Dustin, P. (1984) Microtubules. New York: Springer-Verlag.

Ekstrom, P., and M. Kanje (1984) Inhibition of fast axonal transport by erythro-9-[3-(2-hydroxynonyl)]adenine. J. Neurochem. 43:1342–1345.

Euteneuer, U., Koonce, M.P., Pfister, K.K. and M. Schliwa (1988). An ATPase with properties expected for the organelle motor of the giant amoeba Reticulomyxa. Nature 332:176–178.

Euteneuer, U., and J.R. McIntosh (1980) Polarity of midbody and phragmoplast microtubules. J. Cell Biol. 87:509–515.

Euteneuer, U., and J.R. McIntosh (1981) Structural polarity of some motility-related microtubules. Proc. Natl. Acad. Sci. USA 78:372–376.

Euteneur, U., and J.R. McIntosh (1981) Structural polarity of kinetochore microtubules in PtK1 cells. J. Cell Biol. 89:338–345.

Flemming, W. (1878) Beitrage zur kenntniss der zelle und ihrer lebenserscheinungen, Theil II. Archiv. Mikrosk. Anat. 18:151–259.

Foltz, K.R., and D.J. Asai (1988) Ionic strength-dependent isoforms of sea urchin egg dynein. J. Biol. Chem. 263:2878–2883.

Forman, D.S. (1982) Vanadate inhibits saltatory organelle movement in a permeabilized cell model. Exp. Cell Res. 141:139–147.

Forman, D.S., K.J. Brown, and D.R. Livengood (1983a) Fast axonal transport in permeabilized lobster giant axons is inhibited by vanadate. J. Neurosci. 3:1279–1288.

Forman, D.S., K.J. Brown, and M.E. Promersberger (1983b) Selective inhibition of retrograde axonal transport by erythro-9-[3-(2-hydroxynonyl)]adenine. Brain Res. 272:194–197.

Fox, L.A., and W.S. Sale (1987) Direction of force generated by the inner row of dynein arms on flagellar microtubules. J. Cell Biol. 105:1781–1787.

Freed, J.J., and M.M. Lebowitz (1970) The association of a class of saltatory movements with microtubules in cultured cells. J. Cell Biol. 45:334–354.

Garbers, D.A., and G.S. Kopf (1980) The regulation of spermatozoa by calcium and cyclic nucleotides. Adv. Cyclic Nucleotide Res. 13:251–306.

Gaskin, F., S.B. Kramer, C.R. Canton, R. Adelstein, and M.L. Shelanski (1974) A dynein-like protein associated with neurotubules. FEBS Lett. 40:281–286.

Gibbons, B.H. (1985) Reactivation of sperm flagella: Properties of microtubule-mediated motility. Methods Cell Biol. 25:253–271.

Gibbons, B.H., and I.R. Gibbons (1972) Flagellar movement and adenosine triphosphatase activity in sea urchin sperm extracted with Triton X-100. J. Cell Biol. 54:75–97.

Gibbons, B.H., and I.R. Gibbons (1973) Effects of partial extraction of dynein arms on the movement of reactivated sea urchin sperm. J. Cell Sci. 13:337–357.

Gibbons, B.H., and I.R. Gibbons (1979) Relationship between the latent adenosine triphosphatase state of dynein 1 and its ability to recombine functionally with KCl-extracted sea urchin sperm flagella. J. Biol. Chem. 254:197–201.

Gibbons, B.H., and I.R. Gibbons (1980) Calcium-induced quiescence in reactivated sea urchin sperm. J. Cell Biol. 84:13–27.

Gibbons, B.H., and I.R. Gibbons (1987) Vanadate sensitized cleavage of dynein heavy chains by 365 nm irradiation of demembranated sperm flagella and its effect on the flagellar motility. J. Biol. Chem. 262:8354–8359.

Gibbons, I.R. (1965) Chemical dissection of the cilia. Arch. Biol. (Liege) 76:317–352.

Gibbons, I.R. (1981) Cilia and flagella of eukaryotes. J. Cell Biol. 91:107s–124s.

Gibbons, I.R. (1982) Introduction: Dynein ATPases. Cell Motil. Suppl. 1:87–93.

Gibbons, I.R., M.P. Cosson, J.A. Evans, B.H. Gibbons, B. Houck, K.H. Martinson, W.S. Sale, and W.J.Y. Tang (1978) Potent inhibition of dynein adenosinetriphosphatase and of the motility of cilia and sperm flagella by vanadate. Proc. Natl. Acad. Sci. USA 75:2220–2224.

Gibbons, I.R., and E. Fronk (1972) Some properties of bound and soluble dynein from sea urchin sperm flagella. J. Cell Biol. 54:365–381.

Gibbons, I.R., and E. Fronk (1979) A latent adenosine triphosphatase form of dynein 1 from sea urchin sperm flagella. J. Biol. Chem. 254:187–196.

Gibbons, I.R., E. Fronk, B.H. Gibbons, and K. Ogawa (1976) Multiple forms of dynein in sea urchin sperm flagella. in Cell Motility (R. Goldman, T. Pollard, and J. Rosenbaum, eds) Cold Spring Harbor Laboratory, Cold Spring Harbor, NY, 915–932.

Gibbons, I.R., A. Lee-Eiford, G. Mocz, C.A. Phillipson, W.J.Y. Tang, and B.H. Gibbons (1987) Photosensitized cleavage of dynein heavy chains. J. Biol. Chem. 262:2780–2786.

Gibbons, I.R., and A.J. Rowe (1965) Dynein: A protein with adenosine triphosphatase activity. Science 149:424–425.

Gilbert, S.P., R.D. Allen, and R.D. Sloboda (1985) Translocation of vesicles from squid axoplasm on flagellar microtubules. Nature 315:245–248.

Gilbert, S.P., and R.D. Sloboda (1986) Identification of a MAP2-like ATP-binding protein associated with axoplasmic vesicles that translocate on isolated microtubules. J. Cell Biol. 103:947–956.

Gilson, C.A., N. Ackland, and B. Burnside (1986) Regulation of reactivated elongation in lysed cell models of teleost retinal cones by cAMP and calcium. J. Cell Biol. 102:1047–1059.

Goldberg, D.J. (1982) Microinjection into an identified axon to study the mechanism of fast axonal transport. Proc. Natl. Acad. Sci. USA 79:4818–4822.

Goldstein, L.S.B., R.A. Laymon, and J.R. McIntosh (1986) A microtubule-associated protein in Drosophila melanogaster: Identification, characterization and isolation of cloning sequences. J. Cell Biol. 102:2076–2087.

Goodenough, U.W., B. Gebhart, V. Mermall, D.R. Mitchell, and J.E. Heuser (1987) High-pressure liquid chromatography fractionation of Chlamydomonas dynein extracts and characterization of inner-arm dynein subunits. J. Mol. Biol. 194:481–494.

Goodenough, U.W., and J.E. Heuser (1984) Structural comparison of purified dynein proteins with in situ dynein arms. J. Mol. Biol. 180:1083–1118.

Gorbsky, G.J., P.J. Sammak, and G.G. Borisy (1987) Chromosomes move poleward in anaphase along stationary microtubules that coordinately disassemble from their kinetochore ends. J. Cell Biol. 104:9–18.

Grafstein, B., and D.S. Forman (1980) Intracellular transport in neurons. Physiol. Rev. 60:1167–1283.

Gunderson, G.G., M.H. Kalnoski, and J.C. Bulinski (1984) Distinct populations of microtubules: Tyrosinated and non-tyrosinated α-tubulin are distributed differently in vitro. Cell 38:779–789.

Gunderson, G.G., S. Khawaja, and J.C. Bulinski (1987) Postpolymerization detyrosination of alpha-tubulin: A mechanism for subcellular differentiation of microtubules. J. Cell Biol. 105:251–264.

Haimo, L.T. (1982) Dynein decoration of microtubules—determination of polarity. Methods Cell Biol. 24:189–206.

Haimo, L.T., and R.D. Fenton (1984) Microtubule crossbridging by Chlamydomonas dynein. Cell Motil. 4:371–385.

Haimo, L.T., B.R. Telzer, and J.L. Rosenbaum (1979) Dynein binds to and crossbridges cytoplasmic microtubules. Proc. Natl. Acad. Sci. USA 76:5759–5763.

Hammerschlag, R., and J.A. Bobinski (1981) Ca^{2+} or Mg^{2+} stimulated ATPase activity in bullfrog spinal nerve: Relation to Ca^{2+} requirements for fast axonal transport. J. Neurochem. 36:1114–1121.

Harrington, W.F., and M.E. Rogers (1984) Myosin. Annu. Rev. Biochem. 53:35–74.

Hayden, J.H., and R.D. Allen (1984) Detection of single microtubules in living cells: Particle transport can occur in both directions along the same microtubule. J. Cell Biol. 99:1785–1793.

Heidemann, S.R., J.M. Landers, and M.A. Hamborg (1981) Polarity orientation of axonal microtubules. J. Cell Biol. 91:661–665.

Heideman, S.R., and J.R. McIntosh (1980) Visualization of the structural polarity of microtubules. Nature 286:517–519.

Heuser, J.E. (1987) Different structural states of a microtubule cross-linking molecule, captured by quick-freezing motile axostyles in protozoa. J. Cell Biol. 103:2209–2227.

Hill, T.L. (1981) Microfilament or microtubule assembly or disassembly against a force. Proc. Natl. Acad. Sci. USA 78:5613–5617.

Hirokawa, N., R. Takemura, and S.I. Hisanaga (1985) Cytoskeletal architecture of isolated mitotic spindle with special reference to microtubule-associated proteins and cytoplasmic dynein. J. Cell Biol. 101:1858–1870.

Hisanaga, S., and N. Hirokawa (1987) Substructure of sea urchin cytoplasmic dynein. J. Mol. Biol. 195:919–927.

Hisanaga, S., and M.M. Pratt (1984) Calmodulin interaction with cytoplasmic and flagellar dynein: Calcium-dependent binding and stimulation of adenosinetriphosphatase activity. Biochemistry 23:3032–3037.

Hisanaga, S., and H. Sakai (1983) Cytoplasmic dynein of the sea urchin egg. II. Purification, characterization, and interactions with microtubules and Ca^{2+}-calmodulin. J. Biochem. 93:87–98.

Hisanaga, S., and H. Sakai (1986) Purification of cytoplasmic dynein from sea urchin eggs. Methods Enzymol. 134:337–351.

Hisanaga, S.I., and H. Sakai (1980) Cytoplasmic dynein of the sea urchin egg. I. Partial purification and characterization. Dev. Growth Differ. 22:373–384.

Hoffmann-Berling, H. (1954) Adenosintriphosphat als Betriebsstoff von Zellbewegungen. Biochim. Biophys. Acta 14:182–194.

Hollenbeck, P.J., and K. Chapman (1986) A novel microtubule-associated protein from mammalian nerve shows ATP-sensitive binding to microtubules. J. Cell Biol. 103:1539–1545.

Hollenbeck, P.J., F. Suprynowicz, and W.Z. Cande (1984) Cytoplasmic dynein-like ATPase cross-links microtubules in an ATP-sensitive manner. J. Cell Biol. 99:1251–1258.

Huang, B., and D. Mazia (1975) Microtubules and filaments in ciliate contractility. In S. Inoué and R.E. Stephens (eds): Molecules and Cell Movement. New York: Raven Press, pp. 389–409.

Huang, B., and D.R. Pitelka (1973) The contractile process in the ciliate, *Stentor coeruleus*. I. The role of microtubules and filaments. J. Cell Biol. 57:704–728.

Huxley, H.E. (1969) Mechanism of muscular contraction. Science 164:1356–1361.

Hyams, J.S., and H. Stebbings (1981) Microtubule associated cytoplasmic transport. In K. Roberts and J.S. Hyams (eds): Microtubules. New York: Academic Press, pp. 487–530.

Inoué, S. (1981a) Video image processing greatly enhances contrast, quality and speed in polarization-based microscopy. J. Cell Biol. 89:346–356.

Inoué, S. (1981b) Cell division and the mitotic spindle. J. Cell Biol. 91:131s–147s.

Inoué, S., and H. Sato (1967) Cell motility by labile association of molecules. The nature of mitotic spindle fibers and their role in chromosome movement. J. Gen. Physiol. Suppl. 50:259–292.

Ishiguro, K., H. Murofushi, and H. Sakai (1982) Evidence that cAMP-dependent protein kinase and a protein factor are involved in reactivation of Triton X-100 models of sea urchin and starfish spermatozoa. J. Cell Biol. 92:777–782.

Johnson, K.A. (1985) Pathway of the microtubule-dynein ATPase and the structure of dynein. Annu. Rev. Biophys. Biophys. Chem. 14:161–188.

Johnson, K.A., M.E. Porter, and T. Shimizu (1984) Mechanism of force production for microtubule-dependent movements. J. Cell Biol. 99:132s–136s.

Johnson, K.A., and J.S. Wall (1983) Structure and molecular weight of the dynein ATPase. J. Cell Biol. 96:669–678.

Kachar, B., J.P. Albanesi, H. Fujisaki, and E.D. Korn (1987) Extensive purification from *Acanthamoeba castellanii* of a microtubule-dependent translocator with microtubule-activated ATPase activity. J. Biol. Chem. 262:16180–16185.

Kamimura, S., and K. Takahashi (1981) Direct measurement of the force of microtubule sliding in flagella. Nature 293:566–568.

Karfunkel, P. (1971) The role of microtubules and microfilaments in neurulation in *Xenopus*. Dev. Biol. 25:30–56.

Khan, M.A., and S. Ochs (1974) Magnesium activated ATPase in mammalian nerve. Brain Res. 81:413–426.

Kiehart, D.P. (1981) Studies on the in vivo sensitivity of spindle microtubules to calcium ions and evidence for a vesicular calcium-sequestering system. J. Cell Biol. 88:604–617.

Kiehart, D.P., I. Mabuchi, and S. Inoué (1982) Evidence that myosin does not contribute to force production in chromosome movement. J. Cell Biol. 94:165–178.

Kimura, I. (1977) Ciliary dynein from sea urchin embryos. J. Biochem. (Tokyo) 81:715–720.

Kirazov, E.P., and D.G. Weiss (1986) Effects of vanadate on the assembly and disassembly of purified tubulin. Cell Motil. Cytoskeleton 6:314–323.

Kirschner, M.W., and T.J. Mitchison (1986) Beyond self assembly: From microtubules to morphogenesis. Cell 45:329–342.

Kobayashi, Y., K. Ogawa, and H. Mohri (1978) Evidence that the Mg^{2+}-ATPase in the cortical layer of sea urchin egg is dynein. Exp. Cell Res. 114:285–292.

Koonce, M.P., U. Euteneur, K.L. McDonald, D. Menzel, and M. Schliwa (1986) Cytoskeletal architecture and motility in a giant freshwater amoeba, *Reticulomyxa*. Cell Motil. Cytoskeleton 6:521–533.

Koonce, M.P., and M. Schliwa (1985) Bidirectional organelle transport can occur in cell processes that contain single microtubules. J. Cell Biol. 100:322–326.

Koonce, M.P., and M. Schliwa (1986a) Directionality of organelle movements in *Reticulomyxa* may be mediated by phosphorylation. J. Cell Biol. 103:275a.

Koonce, M.P., and M. Schliwa (1986b) Reactivation of organelle movements along the cytoskeletal framework of a giant freshwater amoeba. J. Cell Biol. 103:605–612.

Koonce, M.P., J. Tong, U. Euteneur, and M. Schliwa (1987) Active sliding between cytoplasmic microtubules. Nature 328:737–739.

Koshland, D.E., T.J. Mitchison, and M.W. Kirschner (1988) Polewards chromosome movement driven by microtubule depolymerization in vitro. Nature 331:499–504.

Kuznetsov, S.A., and V.I. Gelfand (1986) Bovine brain kinesin is a microtubule-activated ATPase. Proc. Natl. Acad. Sci. USA 83:8530–8534.

Laemmli, U.K. (1970) Cleavage of structural proteins during the assembly of the head of bacteriophage T4. Nature 227:680–685.

Lasek, R.J., and S.T. Brady (1985) Attachment of transported vesicles to microtubules in axoplasm is facilitated by AMP-PNP. Nature 316:645–647.

Lee-Eiford, A., R.A. Ow, and I.R. Gibbons (1986) Specific cleavage of dynein heavy chains by ultraviolet irradiation in the presence of ATP and vanadate. J. Biol. Chem. 261:2337–2342.

Leslie, R.J., R.B. Hird, and L. Wilson (1986) Characterization of mitotic cytoskeletons. J. Cell Biol. 103:411a.

l'Hernault, S., and J.L. Rosenbaum (1985) *Chlamydomonas* α-tubulin is post-translationally modified by acetylation on the epsilon amino group of a lysine. Biochemistry 24:473–478.

Lindemann, C.B., M. Lipton, and R. Shlafer (1983) The interaction of cAMP with modeled bull sperm. Cell Motil. 3:199–210.

Luck, D.J.L. (1984) Genetic and biochemical dissection of the eukaryotic flagellum. J. Cell Biol. 98:789–794.

Lye, R.J., M.E. Porter, J.M. Scholey, and J.R. McIntosh (1987) Identification of a microtubule-based cytoplasmic motor in the nematode *Caenorhabditis elegans*. Cell 51:305–318.

Lynch, T.J., J.D. Taylor, and T.T. Tchen (1986) Regulation of pigment organelle translocation. I. Phosphorylation of the organelle-associated protein p57. J. Biol. Chem. 261:4204–4211.

Lynch, T.J., B. Wu, J.D. Taylor, and T.T. Tchen (1986b) Regulation of pigment organelle translocation. II. Participation of a cAMP-dependent protein kinase. J. Biol. Chem. 261:4212–4216.

Mabuchi, I. (1973) ATPase in the cortical layer of sea urchin egg. Its properties and interaction with cortical protein. Biochim. Biophys. Acta 297:317–332.

Mabuchi, I., and M. Okuno (1977) Effect of myosin antibody on division of starfish blastomeres. J. Cell Biol. 74:251–263.

Mabuchi, I., and T. Shimizu (1974) Electrophoretic studies on dyneins from *Tetrahymena* cilia. J. Biochem. (Tokyo) 76:991–999.

Margolis, R.L. (1983) Calcium and microtubules. In W. Cheung (ed): Calcium and Cell Function. New York: Academic Press, pp. 313–335.

Matsuoka, T., and Y. Shigenaka (1985) Mechanism of cell elongation in *Blepharisma japonicum*, with special reference to the role of cytoplasmic microtubules. Cytobios 42:215–226.

Mazia, D. (1965) Mitosis. J. Cell Biol. 25:1–167.

Mazia, D., R.R. Chaffee, and R. Iverson (1961) Adenosine triphosphatase in the mitotic apparatus. Proc. Natl. Acad. Sci. USA 47:788–790.

McIntosh, J.R. (1973) The axostyle *Saccinobaculus*. II. Motion of the microtubule bundle and a structural comparison of straight and bent axostyles. J. Cell Biol. 56:324–339.

McIntosh, J.R., P.K. Hepler, and U. Van Wie (1969) Model for mitosis. Nature 224:658–663.

McIntosh, J.R., and K.R. Porter (1967) Microtubules in the spermatids of the domestic fowl. J. Cell Biol. 35:153–173.

Miki, T. (1963a) The ATPase activity of the mitotic apparatus of the sea urchin egg. Exp. Cell Res. 29:92–101.

Miki, T. (1963b) ATPase activity of the egg cortex during the first cleavage of sea urchin eggs. Exp. Cell Res. 33:575–578.

Miki, T. (1964) ATPase staining of sea urchin eggs during the first cleavage. Embryologia 8:158–165.

Miller, R.H., and R.J. Lasek (1985) Cross-bridges mediate anterograde and retrograde vesicle transport along microtubules in squid axoplasm. J. Cell Biol. 101:2181–2193.

Mitchell, D.R., and F.D. Warner (1981) Binding of 21S ATPase to microtubules: Effects of ionic conditions and substrate analogs. J. Biol. Chem. 23:12535- 12544.

Mitchison, T.J., and M.W. Kirschner (1985) Properties of the kinetochore in vitro. II. Microtubule capture and ATP dependent translocation. J. Cell Biol. 101:766–777.

Mogami, Y., and K. Takahashi (1983) Calcium and microtubule sliding in ciliary axonemes isolated from *Paramecium caudatum*. J. Cell Sci. 61:107–121.

Mohri, H., T. Mohri, I. Mabuchi, I. Yazaki, H. Sakai, and K. Ogawa (1976) Localization of dynein in sea urchin eggs during cleavage. Dev. Growth Differ. 18:391–398.

Mooseker, M.S., and L.G. Tilney (1973) Isolation and reactivation of the axostyle. J. Cell Biol. 56:13–26.

Morisawa, M., and M. Okuno (1982) Cyclic AMP induces maturation of trout sperm axoneme to initiate motility. Nature 295:703–704.

Murofushi, H., K. Ishiguro, and H. Sakai (1982) Involvement of cyclic AMP-dependent protein kinase and a protein factor in the regulation of the motility of sea urchin and starfish spermatozoa. In H. Sakai, H. Mohri, and G.G. Borisy (eds): Biological Functions of Microtubules and Related Structures. Tokyo: Academic Press, pp. 163–176.

Murofushi, H., K. Ishiguro, D. Takahashi, J. Ikeda, and H. Sakai (1986) Regulation of sperm flagellar movement by protein phosphorylation and dephosphorylation. Cell Motil. Cytoskeleton 6:83–88.

Murphy, D.B., R.R. Hiebsch, and K.T. Wallis (1983a) Identity and origin of the ATPase activity associated with neuronal microtubules. I. The ATPase activity is associated with membrane vesicles. J. Cell Biol. 96:1298–1305.

Murphy, D.B., K.T. Wallis, and R.B. Hiebsch (1983b) Identity and origin of the ATPase activity associated with neuronal microtubules. II. Identification of a 50,000 dalton polypeptide with ATPase activity similar to F-1 ATPase from mitochondria. J. Cell Biol. 96:1306–1315.

Naitoh, Y., and H. Kaneko (1972) Reactivated Triton-extracted models of *Paramecium*: Modification of ciliary movement by calcium ions. Science 176:523–524.

Naitoh, Y., and H. Kaneko (1973) Control of ciliary activities by adenosine triphosphate and divalent cations in triton-extracted models of *Paramecium caudatum*. J. Exp. Biol. 58:657–676.

Nasr, A., and P. Satir (1985) Alloaffinity filtration: A general approach to the purification of dynein and dynein like molecules. Anal. Biochem. 151:97-108.

Nauss, R.N. (1949) *Reticulomyxa* filosa gen. et sp. nov., a new primitive plasmodium. Bull. Torrey Bot. Club 76:161–173.

Nechay, B.R. (1984) Mechanisms of action of vanadium. Ann. Rev. Pharmacol. Toxicol. 24:501–524.

Neighbors, B.W., R.C. Williams, and J.R. McIntosh (1988) Localization of kinesin in cultured cells. J. Cell Biol. 106:1193–1204.

Nelson, D.J., and E.M. Wright (1974) The distribution, activity, and function of the cilia in the frog brain. J. Physiol. 243:63–78.

Nelson, G.A., T.M. Roberts, and S. Ward (1982) *Caenorhabditis elegans* spermatozoan locomotion: Ameboid movement with almost no actin. J. Cell Biol. 92:121–131.

Nicklas, R.B. (1982) Measurements of mitotic spindle forces. J. Cell Biol. 95:302a.

Nicklas, R.B. (1975) Chromosome movement: Current models and experiments on living cells. In S. Inoué and R.E. Stephens (eds): Molecules and Cell Movement. New York: Raven Press, pp. 97–117.

Oberdorf, J.A., J.F. Head, and B. Kaminer (1986) Calcium uptake and release by isolated cortices and microsomes from the unfertilized egg of the sea urchin *Strongylocentrotus droebachiensis*. J. Cell Biol. 102:2205–2210.

Ogawa, K., D.J. Asai, and C.J. Brokaw (1977) Properties of an antiserum against native dynein 1 from sea urchin sperm flagella. J. Cell Biol. 73:182–192.

Ogawa, K., H. Hosoya, E. Yokota, T. Kobayashi, Y. Wakamatsu, K. Ozato, S. Negishi, and M. Obika (1987) Melanoma dynein: Evidence that dynein is a general "motor" for microtubule-associated cell motilities. Euro. J. Cell Biol. 43:3–9.

Ogawa, K., and H. Mohri (1975) Preparation of antiserum against a tryptic fragment (fragment A) of dynein and an immunological approach to the subunit composition of dynein. J. Biol. Chem. 250:6476–6483.

Okagaki, T., and R. Kamiya (1986) Microtubule sliding in mutant *Chlamydomonas* axonemes devoid of outer or inner dynein arms. J. Cell Biol. 103:1895–1902.

Olmsted, J.B. (1981) Affinity purification of antibodies from diazotized paper blots of heterogeneous protein samples. J. Biol. Chem. 256:11955–11957.

Opresko, L.K., and C.J. Brokaw (1983) cAMP-dependent phosphorylation associated with activation of motility of *Ciona* sperm flagella. Gamete Res. 8:201–218.

Pallini, V., C. Mencarelli, L. Bracci, M. Contorni, P. Ruggiero, A. Tiezzi, and R. Manetti (1983) Cytoplasmic nucleoside-triphosphatases similar to axonemal dynein occur widely in different cell types. J. Submicrosc. Cytol. 15:229-235.

Papasozomenos, S.C., L. Antilio-Gambetti, and P. Gambetti (1981) Reorganization of axoplasmic organelles following iminodipropionitrile administration. J. Cell Biol. 91:866–871.

Paschal, B.M., S.M. King, A.G. Moss, C.A. Collins, R.B. Vallee, and G.B. Witman (1987a) Isolated flagellar dynein translocates brain microtubules in vitro. Nature 330:672–674.

Paschal, B.M., H.S. Shpetner, and R.B. Vallee (1987b) MAP 1C is a microtubule-activated ATPase which translocates microtubules in vitro and has dynein-like properties. J. Cell Biol. 105:1273–1282.

Paschal, B.M., and R.B. Vallee (1987) Retrograde transport by the microtubule-associated protein MAP 1C. Nature 330:181–183.

Penningroth, S.M. (1986) Erythro-9-[3-(2-hydroxynonyl)]adenine and vanadate as probes for microtubule-based cytoskeletal mechanochemistry. Methods Enzymol. 134:477–487.

Penningroth, S.M., A. Cheung, P. Bouchard, C. Gagnon, and C.W. Bardin (1982) Dynein ATPase is inhibited selectively in vitro by erythro-9-[3-(2-hydroxynonyl)]adenine. Biochem. Biophys. Res. Commun. 104:234–240.

Penningroth, S.M., P. Rose, A. Cheung, D.D. Peterson, D.Q. Rothacker, and P. Bershak (1985) An EHNA-sensitive ATPase in unfertilized sea urchin eggs. Cell Motil. 5:61–75.

Pfister, K.K., R.B. Fay, and G.B. Witman (1982) Purification and polypeptide composition of dynein ATPases from *Chlamydomonas* flagella. Cell Motil. 2:525–547.

Piperno, G. (1984) Monoclonal antibodies to dynein subunits reveal the existence of cytoplasmic antigens in sea urchin eggs. J. Cell Biol. 98:1842-1850.

Piperno, G., M. LeDizet, and X. Chang (1987) Microtubules containing acetylated α-tubulin in mammalian cells in culture. J. Cell Biol. 104:289–302.

Piperno, G., and D.J.L. Luck (1979) Axonemal adenosine triphosphatases from flagella of *Chlamydomonas reinhardtii*. J. Biol. Chem. 254:3084–3090.

Piperno, G., and D.J.L. Luck (1981) Inner arm dyneins from flagella of *Chlamydomonas reinhardtii*. Cell 27:331–340.

Porrello, K., and B. Burnside (1984) Regulation of reactivated contraction in *Teleost* retinal cone models by calcium and cyclic adenosine monophosphate. J. Cell Biol. 98:2230–2238.

Porrello, K., W.Z. Cande, and B. Burnside (1983) N-Ethylmaleimide modified subfragment-1 and heavy meromyosin inhibit reactivated contraction in motile models of retinal cones. J. Cell Biol. 96:449–454.

Porter, K.R. (1966) Cytoplasmic microtubules and their functions. In G.E.W. Wolstenholme (ed): Ciba Foundation Symposium on Principles of Biomolecular Organization. London: Churchill.

Porter, M.E., P.M. Grissom, C.M. Pfarr, and J.R. McIntosh (1987a) Vanadate-sensitized UV cleavage as a probe for dynein-like peptides. J. Cell Biol. 105:33a.

Porter, M.E., P.M. Grissom, J.M. Scholey, E.D. Salmon, and J.R. McIntosh (1987b) Immunological and biochemical analyses on the distribution of cytoplasmic dynein and dynein-like polypeptides in sea urchin eggs. J. Cell Biol. (in press).

Porter, M.E., P.M. Grissom, J.M. Scholey, E.D. Salmon, and J.R. McIntosh (1988) Dynein isoforms in sea urchin eggs. J. Biol. Chem. 263:6759–6771.

Porter, M.E., T.S. Hays, P.M. Grissom, M.T. Fuller, and J.R. McIntosh (1987c) Characterization of a high molecular weight, ATP sensitive, microtubule-associated polypeptide from *Drosophila* embryos. J. Cell Biol. 105:121a.

Porter, M.E., and K.A. Johnson (1983) Characterization of the ATP-sensitive binding of *Tetrahymena* 30S dynein to bovine brain microtubules. J. Biol. Chem. 258:6575–6581.

Porter, M.E., J.M. Scholey, D.L. Stemple, G.P.A. Vigers, R.D. Vale, M.P. Sheetz, and J.R. McIntosh (1987d) Characterization of the microtubule movement produced by sea urchin egg kinesin. J. Biol. Chem. 262:2794–2802.

Pratt, M.M. (1980) The identification of a dynein-like ATPase in unfertilized sea urchin eggs. Dev. Biol. 74:364–378.

Pratt, M.M. (1984) ATPases in mitotic spindles. Int. Rev. Cytol. 87:83–105.

Pratt, M.M. (1986a) Homology of egg and flagellar dynein. Comparison of ATP-binding sites and primary structure. J. Biol. Chem. 261:956–964.

Pratt, M.M. (1986b) Purification of cytoplasmic dynein from *Strongylocentrotus* sea urchin eggs. Methods Enzymol. 104:325–337.

Pratt, M.M. (1986c) Stable complexes of axoplasmic vesicles and microtubules: Protein composition and ATPase activity. J. Cell Biol. 103:957–968.

Pratt, M.M., N.R. Barton, A. Betancourt, C.L. Hammond, and B. Schroeder (1986) An antibody against cytoplasmic dynein labels vesicular organelles. J. Cell Biol. 103:108a.

Pratt, M.M., S. Hisanaga, and D.A. Begg (1984) An improved purification method for cytoplasmic dynein. J. Cell Biochem. 26:19–33.

Pratt, M.M., T. Otter, and E.D. Salmon (1980) Dynein-like Mg^{2+}-ATPase in mitotic spindles isolated from sea urchin embryos (*Strongylocentrotus droebachiensis*). J. Cell Biol. 86:738–745.

Pratt, M.M., and R.E. Stephens (1978) Dynein synthesis in sea urchin embryos. J. Cell Biol. 79:300a.

Pryer, N.K., P. Wadsworth, and E.D. Salmon (1986) Polarized microtubule gliding and particle saltations produced by soluble factors from sea urchin eggs and embryos. Cell Motil. Cytoskeleton 6:537–548.

Rebhun, L.I. (1963) Saltatory particle movements and their relation to the mitotic apparatus. In L. Levine (ed): The Cell in Mitosis. New York: Academic Press, pp. 67–103.

Rebhun, L.I. (1972) Polarized intracellular particle transport: Saltatory movements and cytoplasmic streaming. Int. Rev. Cytol. 32:93–137.

Reed, W., S. Lebduska, and P. Satir (1982) Effects of trifluoperazine upon the calcium-dependent ciliary arrest response of freshwater mussel gill lateral cells. Cell Motil. 2:405–427.

Reed, W., and P. Satir (1980) Calmodulin in mussel gill epithelial cells: Roles in ciliary arrest. Ann. N.Y. Acad. Sci. 356:319–345.

Rothwell, S.W., W.A. Grasser, and D.B. Murphy (1985) Direct observation of microtubule treadmilling by electron microscopy. J. Cell Biol. 101:1637–1642.

Rozdzial, M.M., and L.T. Haimo (1986a) Bidirectional pigment granule movements of melanophores are regulated by protein phosphorylation and dephosphorylation. Cell 47:1061–1070.

Rozdzial, M.M., and L.T. Haimo (1986b) Reactivated melanophore motility: Differential regulation and nucleotide requirements of bidirectional pigment granule transport. J. Cell Biol. 103:2755–2764.

Sakai, H., I. Mabuchi, S. Shimoda, R. Kuriyama, K. Ogawa, and H. Mohri (1976) Induction of chromosome motion in the glycerol-isolated mitotic apparatus: Nucleotide specificity and effects of anti-dynein and myosin sera on the motion. Dev. Growth Differ. 18:211–219.

Sakai, H., H. Mohri, and G.G. Borisy (1982) Biological Functions of Microtubules and Related Structures. New York: Academic Press.

Sale, R.D., T.S. Reese, and M.P. Sheetz (1985) Identification of a novel force generating protein (kinesin) involved in microtubule-based motility. Cell 41:39–50.

Sale, W.S. (1985) Study of the properties of MgATP-induced stationary bends in demembranated sea urchin sperm. Cell Motil. 5:209–224.

Sale, W.S., U.W. Goodenough, and J.E. Heuser (1985) The substructure of isolated and in situ outer dynein arms of sea urchin sperm flagella. J. Cell Biol. 101:1400–1412.

Sale, W.S., and P. Satir (1977) Direction of active sliding of microtubules in *Tetrahymena* cilia. Proc. Natl. Acad. Sci. USA 74:2045–2049.

Salmon, E.D., and R.R. Segall (1980) Calcium labile mitotic spindles isolated from sea urchin eggs (*Lytechinus variegatus*). J. Cell Biol. 86:355–365.

Sanderson, M.J., E.R. Dirksen, and P. Satir (1985) The antagonistic effects of 5-hydroxytryptamine and methylxanthine on the gill cilia of *Mytilus edulis*. Cell Motil. 5:293–309.

Satir, P. (1968) Studies on cilia. III. Further studies on the cilium tip and a "sliding filament" model of ciliary motility. J. Cell Biol. 39:77–94.

Satir, P. (1982) Approaches to potential sliding mechanisms of cytoplasmic microtubules. Cold Spring Harbor Symposia on Quantitative Biology 46:285-292.

Scheaffer, H.J., and L.F. Schwender (1974) Enzyme inhibitors. 26. Bridging hydrophobic and hydrophylic regions of adenosine deaminase with some 9-(2-hydroxy-3-alkyl)adenines. J. Med. Chem. 17:6–8.

Schliwa, M. (1984) Mechanisms of intracellular organelle transport. Cell Muscle Motil. 5:1–82.

Schliwa, M., and U. Euteneuer (1983) Comparative ultrastructure and physiology of chromatophores, with emphasis on changes associated with intracellular transport. Am. Zool. 23:479–494.

Schliwa, M., U. Euteneuer, J.C. Bulinski, and J.G. Izant (1981) Calcium lability of cytoplasmic microtubules and its modulation by microtubule associated proteins. Proc. Natl. Acad. Sci. USA 78:1037–1041.

Schliwa, M., R.M. Ezzell, and U. Euteneuer (1984a) Erythro-9-[3-(2-hydroxynonyl)]adenine is an effective inhibitor of cell motility and actin assembly. Proc. Natl. Acad. Sci. USA 81:6044–6048.

Schliwa, M., K.L. McDonald, M.P. Koonce, and U. Euteneuer (1984b) *Reticulomyxa*, a new model system for the study of intracellular organelle transport. J. Cell Biol. 99:239a.

Schliwa, M., and J. van Blerkom (1981) Structural interaction of cytoskeletal components. J. Cell Biol. 90:222–235.

Schnapp, B.J., and T.S. Reese (1982) Cytoplasmic structure in rapid-frozen axons. J. Cell Biol. 94:667–679.

Schnapp, B.J., and T.S. Reese (1986) New Developments in Understanding Axonal Transport. Trends in Neurosc. 9:155–162.

Schnapp, B.J., R.D. Vale, M.P. Sheetz, and T.S. Reese (1985) Single microtubules from squid axoplasm support bidirectional movement of organelles. Cell 40:455–462.

Scholey, J.M., B. Neighbors, J.R. McIntosh, and E.D. Salmon (1984) Isolation of microtubules and a dynein-like Mg^{2+}-ATPase from unfertilized sea urchin eggs. J. Biol. Chem. 259:6516–6525.

Scholey, J.M., M.E. Porter, P.M. Grissom, and J.R. McIntosh (1985) Identification of kinesin in sea urchin eggs, and evidence for its localization in the mitotic spindle. Nature 318:483–486.

Shecket, G., and R.J. Lasek (1982) Mg^{2+}- or Ca^{2+}-activated ATPase in squid giant fiber axoplasm. J. Neurochem. 38:827–832.

Shimizu, T. (1981) Steady-state kinetic study of vanadate-induced inhibition of ciliary dynein adenosinetriphosphatase activity from *Tetrahymena*. Biochemistry 20:4347–4354.

Shimizu, T., and K.A. Johnson (1983) Kinetic evidence for multiple dynein ATPase sites. J. Biol. Chem. 258:13841–13846.

Snyder, J.A., and J.R. McIntosh (1976) Biochemistry and physiology of microtubules. Ann. Rev. Biochem. 45:699–720.

Stearns, M.E., and R. Ochs (1982) A functional in vitro model for studies of intracellular motility in digitonin-permeabilized erythrophores. J. Cell Biol. 94:727–739.

Stephens, R.E. (1972) Studies on the development of the sea urchin *Strongylocentrotus droebachiensis*. III. Embryonic synthesis of ciliary proteins. Biol. Bull. 142:489–504.

Stephens, R.E. (1977) Differential protein synthesis and utilization during cilia formation in sea urchin embryos. Dev. Biol. 61:311–329.

Stephens, R.E., and K.T. Edds (1976) Microtubules: Structure, chemistry, and function. Physiol. Rev. 56:709–777.

Summers, K.E., and I.R. Gibbons (1971) Adenosine triphosphate-induced sliding of tubules in trypsin treated flagella of sea urchin sperm. Proc. Natl. Acad. Sci. USA 68:3092–3096.

Tang, W.J.Y., C.W. Bell, W.S. Sale, and I.R. Gibbons (1982) Structure of the dynein-1 outer arm in sea urchin sperm flagella. I. Analysis by separation of subunits. J. Biol. Chem. 257:508–515.

Tash, J.S., H. Hidaka, and A.R. Means (1986) Axokinin phosphorylation by cAMP-dependent protein kinase is sufficient for activation of sperm flagellar motility. J. Cell Biol. 103:649–655.

Tash, J.S., and A. Means (1982) Regulation of protein phosphorylation and motility of sperm by cyclic adenosine monophosphate and calcium. Biol. Reprod. 26:745–763.

Tash, J.S., and A.R. Means (1983) Cyclic adenosine 3',5'-monophosphate, calcium, and protein phosphorylation in flagellar motility. Biol. Reprod. 28:75–104.

Telzer, B.R., and L.T. Haimo (1981) Decoration of spindle microtubules with dynein: evidence for uniform polarity. J. Cell Biol. 89:373–378.

Terasaki, M., and K. Fujiwara (1986) Microtubules and the endoplasmic reticulum are highly interdependent structures. J. Cell Biol. 103:1557–1568.

Travis, J.L., J.F. Keneally, and R.D. Allen (1983) Studies on the motility of *Foraminifera*. II. The dynamic cytoskeleton of the reticulopodial network of *Allogoromia laticollaris*. Proc. Natl. Acad. Sci. USA 97:1668–1676.

Troutt, L.L., and B. Burnside (1986) Polarity of microtubules in teleost cones. J. Cell Biol. 103:558a.

Troutt, L.L., and B. Burnside (1988) Microtubule polarity and distribution in teleost photoreceptors. J. Neurosci. 8:2371–2380.

Tsukita, S., and H. Ishikawa (1981) The movement of membranous organelles in axons. Electron microscopic identification of anterogradely and retrogradely transported organelles. J. Cell Biol. 84:513–530.

Vale, R.D., T.S. Reese, and M.P. Sheetz (1985a) Identification of a novel force-generating protein, kinesin, involved in microtubule-based motility. Cell 42:39–50.

Vale, R.D., B.J. Schnapp, T. Mitchison, E. Steuer, T.S. Reese, and M.P. Sheetz (1985b) Different axoplasmic proteins generate movement in opposite directions along microtubules in vitro. Cell 43:623–632.

Vale, R.D., B.J. Schnapp, T.S. Reese, and M.P. Sheetz (1985c) Movement of organelles along filaments dissociated from the axoplasm of the squid giant axon. Cell 40:449–454.

Vale, R.D., B.J. Schnapp, T.S. Reese, and M.P. Sheetz (1985d) Organelle, bead, and microtubule translocations promoted by soluble factors from the squid giant axon. Cell 40:559–569.

Vale, R.D., and Y.Y. Toyoshima (1988) Rotation and translocation of microtubules in vitro induced by dyneins from *Tetrahymena* cilia. Cell 52:459–469.

Vallee, R.B. (1982) A taxol-dependent procedure for the isolation of microtubules and microtubule-associated proteins (MAPs). J. Cell Biol. 92:435–442.

Vallee, R.B., and G.S. Bloom (1983) Isolation of sea urchin egg microtubules with taxol and identification of mitotic spindle associated proteins with monoclonal antibodies. Proc. Natl. Acad. Sci. USA 80:6259–6263.

Vallee, R.B., G.S. Bloom, and F.C. Luca (1986) Differential structure and distribution of the high molecular weight brain microtubule-associated proteins MAP-1 and MAP-2. Ann. N.Y. Acad. Sci. 466:134–144.

Vallee, R.B., B.M. Paschal, H.S. Shpetner, and J.S. Wall (1987) Structural evidence for the identification of the brain cytosolic microtubule associated protein MAP 1C as dynein. J. Cell Biol. 105:125a.

Vallee, R.B., J.S. Wall, B.P. Paschal, and H.S. Shpetner (1988) Microbule-associated protein IC from brain is a two-headed cytosolic dynein. Nature 332:561–563.

Walter, M.F., and P. Satir (1978) Calcium control of ciliary arrest in mussel gill cells. J. Cell Biol. 79:110–120.

Walter, M.F., and P. Satir (1979) Calcium does not inhibit active sliding of microtubules from mussel gill cilia. Nature 278:69–70.

Ward, S., N. Thomson, J.G. White, and S. Brenner (1975) Electron microscopic reconstruction of the anterior anatomy of the nematode *Caenorhabditis elegans*. J. Comp. Neurol. 160:313–338.

Warner, F.D., and J.H. McIlvain (1982) Binding stoichiometry of 21S dynein to A and B subfiber microtubules. Cell Motil. 2:429–443.

Warner, F.D., and D.R. Mitchell (1980) Dynein: The mechanochemical coupling adenosine triphosphatase of microtubule-based sliding filament mechanisms. Int. Rev. Cytol. 66:1–43.

Warren, R.H. (1974) Microtubular organization in elongating myogenic cells. J. Cell Biol. 63:550–566.

Warren, R.H., and B. Burnside (1978) Microtubules in cone myoid elongation in the teleost retina. J. Cell Biol. 78:247–259.

Weisenberg, R., and E.W. Taylor (1968) Studies on ATPase activity of sea urchin eggs and the isolated mitotic apparatus. Exp. Cell Res. 53:372–384.

Williams, B.D., D.R. Mitchell, and J.L. Rosenbaum (1986a) Molecular cloning and expression of flagellar radial spoke and dynein genes of *Chlamydomonas*. J. Cell Biol. 103:1–11.

Williams, R.C., and H.W. Deitrich (1979) Separation of tubulin from microtubule associated proteins on phosphocellulose. Accompanying alterations in concentrations of buffer components. Biochemistry 18:2499–2503.

Witman, G.B., K.A. Johnson, K.K. Pfister, and J.S. Wall (1983e) Fine structure and molecular weight of the outer arm dyneins of *Chlamydomonas*. J. Submicrosc. Cytol. 15:193–197.

Woodrum, D.T., and R.W. Linck (1980) Structural basis of motility in the microtubular axostyle: Implications for cytoplasmic microtubule structure and function. J. Cell Biol. 87:404–414.

Yano, Y., and T. Miki-Noumura (1980) Sliding velocity between outer doublet microtubules of sea-urchin sperm axonemes. J. Cell Sci. 44:169–186.

Yano, Y., and T. Miki-Noumura (1981) Recovery of sliding ability in arm-depleted axonemes after recombination with extracted dynein 1. J. Cell Sci. 48:223–239.

Yoshida, T., A. Ito, and K. Izutsu (1985) Association of anti-dynein 1 cross reactive antigen with the mitotic spindle of mammalian cells. Cell Struct. Function 10:245–258.

Zanetti, N.C., D.R. Mitchell, and F.D. Warner (1979) Effects of divalent cations on dynein crossbridging and ciliary microtubule sliding. J. Cell Biol. 80:573–588.

Zieve, G.W., and J.R. McIntosh (1981) A probe for flagellar dynein in the mammalian mitotic apparatus. J. Cell Sci. 48:241–257.

Zimmerman, A.M., and A. Forer (1981) Mitosis and Cytokinesis. New York: Academic Press.

The Dynein ATPases, Part 2: Microtubule Accessory Proteins and the Generation of Force

Edited by Roger D. Sloboda

PERSPECTIVE
Dynamic Behavior of Microtubules and Accessory Proteins

Roger D. Sloboda

Department of Biological Sciences, Dartmouth College, Hanover, New Hampshire 03755

INTRODUCTION

Microtubules and their associated proteins (microtubule-associated proteins, or MAPs; see Sloboda et al., 1975) are involved in several important cell motility processes, including mitosis and intracellular particle transport. In addition, microtubules play a structural role in, for example, the development and maintenance of cell form. The molecular basis for the motile and structural functions of microtubules appears to depend not only on the spatial and temporal organization of microtubules within the cell but also on the interaction of these microtubules with important accessory proteins (MAPs). One aspect central to understanding all examples of microtubule function is that microtubules are polar structures. For example, the subunit for assembly of a microtubule is the protein tubulin, which exists under native conditions as a heterodimer composed of one α- and one β-tubulin subunit. The subunit is thus asymmetric, and therefore the microtubules produced by such asymmetric subunits are themselves asymmetric; the subunit lattice thus has an inherent polarity.

Indeed, it has been shown by a number of elegant in vitro experiments that the two ends of a microtubule are kinetically distinct (Allen and Borisy, 1974; Binder et al., 1975; Margolis and Wilson, 1978; Bergen and Borisy, 1980; Mitchison and Kirschner, 1984b). Under certain conditions in vitro a net addition of subunits occurs at one end (the head, or plus end) while a net loss of subunits occurs at the other (the tail, or minus) end. Such experiments thus predicted that microtubule-containing organelles in vivo would have a characteristic structural polarity; for example, an organelle might contain all parallel microtubules, or specific combinations of parallel and antiparallel microtubules might occur in another. In fact, this has been confirmed in cells by the use of polarity-revealing probes—composed of tubulin (Heidemann and McIntosh, 1980) or dynein (Telzer and Haimo, 1981)—that appear as hooks on microtubules when viewed in cross section. The directionality of the hooks (clock- or counterclockwise) thus reveals the underlying directionality of the microtubule subunit lattice. Using such approaches, for example, it has been determined that >90% of the microtubules in a half-spindle of the mitotic apparatus have the same polarity (Telzer and Haimo, 1981), with the plus ends of all microtubules oriented distal to the pole (Euteneuer and McIntosh, 1981b). Yet in the central region of the spindle, where the microtubules from each half-spindle intermingle, the microtubules are oriented antiparallel. Using similar approaches, it has been determined that 96% of the microtubules of the axon have the same polarity, with their plus ends distal to the cell body (Heidemann et al., 1981).

With respect to the microtubule assembly and disassembly that occurs during mitosis and the microtubule-based motility characteristic of the axon, the above brief synopsis raises certain questions about models of microtubule-based motility and stability formulated to describe both phenomena. For example, as McIntosh (1977) and Borisy (1978) have argued, the direction in which a microtubule assembles (by the addition of subunits to the minus or plus ends, i.e., proximal or distal to an organizing center) and the intrinsic structural polarity of the microtubule thus produced (due to the asymmetric nature of the subunits) are two properties that can occur essentially independent of one another. This concept has guided the design of recent experiments aimed at determining the site(s) of subunit incorporation and loss in living cells, particularly those engaged in mitosis. Similarly, because bidirectional transport on microtubules occurs in the axon (for an extensive review of this literature, see Grafstein and Forman, 1980) the finding of uniform polarity of microtubules in these cell extensions has necessitated a re-evaluation of certain models of motility in which directionality of movement is based on antiparallel microtubules.

This section will discuss two specific areas of microtubule-based motility: that associated with microtubule assembly and disassembly and that involved in the movement of membrane-bound organelles in the axon. Because controlled microtubule assembly and disassembly occurs during mitosis, studies on the mitotic apparatus provide the framework

for the design of experiments aimed at understanding microtubule dynamics from an assembly–disassembly point of view. By contrast, because the microtubules of the axon are stable, this system is used as a model for understanding MAP–microtubule interactions and how they relate to particle motility. This introduction will now provide a brief overview of pertinent background information designed for the non-specialist to aid understanding of the experimental approaches currently being taken in each of these areas. More specific details on each subject can be found in the introductory sections of the chapters that follow in this section.

DYNAMICS OF MICROTUBULE ASSEMBLY AND DISASSEMBLY

To understand the mechanism of microtubule assembly and disassembly in cells in general and in the mitotic apparatus in particular, methods have been developed to study the process in living cells actively assembling and disassembling microtubules. Previous data from in vivo and in vitro experiments led to the development of three models to describe microtubule subunit addition and loss. The first model, based on observations with dividing cells using the polarization microscope (Inoué and Sato, 1967; Inoué and Ritter, 1975) proposed that subunit exchange took place throughout the entire length of the microtubule. In this situation, the rate of subunit addition or loss would be a function of the subunit concentration and would be independent of the number of microtubule ends, because addition or loss of subunits could take place throughout the entire length of the microtubule.

Two related models counter the above hypothesis. These are based on in vitro data initially obtained from experiments in which the rate of assembly was observed to depend not only on the subunit concentration but also on the number of microtubules, specifically the number of microtubule ends (Johnson and Borisy, 1975, 1977). For example, at a given subunit concentration it was observed that assembly or disassembly proceeded at a greater rate as the number of microtubule ends was increased, for example, by breaking the microtubules into smaller pieces, even though the total mass of assembled polymer remained constant. Conversely, if the number of ends remained constant, the rate of assembly increased as a function of the subunit concentration. Using morphological observations in which subunits were observed to grow off identifiable microtubule seeds, it was observed that at high protein concentrations subunits would add preferentially to one end with respect to the other of a given microtubule (Allen and Borisy, 1974; Binder et al., 1975). When the kinetics of this biased addition were examined in detail (Margolis and Wilson, 1978; Bergen and Borisy, 1980), it was noted that subunit addition and loss actually occurred at both ends of the microtubule; at steady state, net addition occurred at one (the plus end) and net loss from the other (the minus end). Because subunits in effect work their way through the microtubule from the head to the tail, these observations have led to the hypothesis of assembly and disassembly known as *treadmilling*.

Such head to tail polymerization, first noted for polymers of actin by Wegner (1976), is a consequence of the hydrolysis of bound guanine nucleotide that accompanies subunit addition (Jacobs et al., 1974; Weisenberg et al., 1976). However, when a subunit is removed the bound nucleotide is not rephosphorylated; thus, a true chemical equilibrium does not exist between subunits and polymer, resulting in a situation initially described for actin in which it was noted that the filaments simultaneously elongated from one end and shortened from the other (Wegner, 1976). Kirschner (1980) argued convincingly that microtubule treadmilling was an in vitro manifestation of a mechanism (i.e., nucleotide hydrolysis accompanying subunit addition) that, under conditions existing in the cell, serves three purposes: 1) to stabilize anchored filaments, 2) to remove microtubule fragments selectively by depolymerization, and 3) to suppress sponta-

neous, non-nucleated microtubule assembly. The prediction from such an argument is that the majority of cellular microtubules should have their minus ends embedded in an organizing center where they are presumably unable to exchange subunits at the minus end. Hence microtubule growth and therefore stability is thus controlled by the rate constants governing addition and loss of subunits from the plus end. This prediction has been upheld from directionality experiments in which microtubules in a number of systems (Euteneuer and McIntosh, 1980, 1981a,b) have been shown to radiate from an organizing center—for example, the centrosome or mitotic spindle pole—in which their minus ends are embedded, thus leaving the plus ends free in the cytoplasm.

These considerations, plus further in vitro experimentation (Hill and Carlier, 1983; Mitchison and Kirschner, 1984a; Carlier et al., 1984) have recently led to the third hypothesis of subunit addition and loss, called *dynamic instability* (Mitchison and Kirschner, 1984b). This model is based in part on the assumption that nucleotide hydrolysis occurs not coincident with subunit addition but rather at some finite time after subunit incorporation into the growing end of the microtubule. A cap of subunits containing guanosine triphosphate (GTP) therefore exists at the growing end, while those subunits internal to the cap have hydrolyzed their bound nucleotide and thus contain guanosine diphosphate (GDP). The length of the plus end GTP cap increases with subunit concentration. Thus, subunits are gained during a growing phase stabilized by the GTP cap and are lost from the *same* end during a shrinking phase, which can be initiated at some finite time after the cap is lost, i.e., when all the bound GTP is eventually hydrolyzed to GDP. A given population of microtubules can thus be subdivided into two groups, those that are growing and those that are shrinking, a fact that has been observed experimentally in real time in vitro (Horio and Hotani, 1986).

Hypotheses concerning the mechanism of microtubule turnover during interphase and mitosis have been proposed based on each of the previous models of subunit addition and loss, and together these have provided the framework for the design of many experiments. Obviously, one can make certain predictions about the mechanism of subunit addition and loss in vivo based on the tenets of each model, but these predictions can only be tested directly in the living cell. To do this, methods to identify newly incorporated subunits in vivo have been developed; two approaches have been used in this regard, both variations on the technique of fluorescent analog cytochemistry (for reviews, see Kreis and Birchmeier, 1982; Wang et al., 1982a,b). In one approach, a fluorescent analog of tubulin is synthesized and microinjected into living cells, and then the cells are viewed with fluorescence optics (Keith et al., 1981; Wadsworth and Sloboda, 1983). As an alternative to provide greater sensitivity, at an appropriate time after injection of the fluorescent analog the cells are fixed and processed for indirect immunofluorescence using primary antibodies specific for the group bound to the injected tubulin analog. Both approaches have their advantages: The former allows for continuous observation of the cell after injection, while the latter provides much greater sensitivity and resolution. Several variations on these approaches, for example, fluorescence recovery after photobleaching (Salmon et al., 1984), have also been employed to understand the mechanism of microtubule turnover dynamics in living cells. The results of such approaches and the relationship between microtubule turnover and cellular morphogenesis have been reviewed recently by Kirschner and Mitchison (1986). In this volume, the reader is directed to Sammak (Chapter 20), which provides a comprehensive analysis of these approaches and how they are being used to study microtubule dynamics in the living cell.

MAPS, MICROTUBULES, AND INTRACELLULAR PARTICLE MOTILITY

Microtubule-dependent intracellular particle motility is a fundamental characteristic of all living cells, and one particularly advantageous model system that lends itself to experimentation is the particle motility that occurs in the axon. Movements of materials in the axon can be grouped into various classes (for review, see Brady and Lasek, 1982) based on the identity of the substances moving, the direction of movement, and the speed at which the components move. Based on these characteristics, movement in the axon can be grouped into three classes: 1) fast axoplasmic transport, which occurs in the orthograde (toward the synapse) and retrograde (toward the cell body) directions at rates from 200 to 400 mm/day and involves the movement of membrane-bound vesicular organelles; 2) intermediate orthograde transport, which occurs at rates from 15 to 50 mm/day and involves the movement of mitochondria and myosin-like proteins; and 3) slow orthograde transport, which has two components: slow component A (SC_A), moving at a rate of 0.2–1 mm/day, and composed of elements of the microtubule-neurofilament network of the axon, and SC_B, moving at a rate of 2–4 mm/day and composed of soluble enzymes and components of the microfilament network of the axon. Much information has been obtained over the past few years concerning the molecular mechanism of fast axoplasmic transport, and now information concerning slow transport is starting to be obtained (Weisenberg et al., 1987).

Because all the microtubules of the axon are oriented with their plus ends distal to the cell body, microtubule polarity itself cannot specify the direction of motion induced by a single motive force-generating complex. Thus, with respect to the bidirectional fast transport of vesicular organelles in axoplasm, it is not surprising that at least two classes of motor proteins (Vale et al., 1985b) have been identified. Movement of material in the axon is therefore determined not by varying microtubule orientation but rather by the existence of different motor proteins that generate force in one direction or the other relative to the underlying tubulin subunit lattice. These motor proteins have certain MAP-like characteristics, including the ability to bind to the tubulin subunit lattice (Vale et al., 1985a; Paschal et al., 1987a,b; Gilbert and Sloboda, 1988) and to stimulate microtubule assembly (Do et al., 1988). The discovery of these two classes of proteins was made possible by recent developments in video microscopy (Allen et al., 1981, 1985; Allen and Allen, 1983; Inoué, 1981a), which allowed for the subsequent development of in vitro model systems (Gilbert et al., 1985; Vale et al., 1985c; Pryer et al., 1986) in which the protein and ionic requirements and the directionality of microtubule-based motility could be assayed and established.

These motive force-generating accessory proteins currently fall into two classes: One class is represented by proteins of relatively high subunit M_r ($\sim$300 kDa) that are similar in many respects to the cytoplasmic form of dynein (Pratt, 1980; Gilbert and Sloboda, 1986, 1988; Paschal et al., 1987a,b; Lye et al., 1987). This class is most likely responsible for movement of membrane-bound vesicles in the retrograde direction, i.e., from the plus to the minus end of the microtubule (Paschal and Vallee, 1987a,b). The second class is represented by kinesin ($\sim$120 kDa), a protein that can induce movement in the orthograde direction, i.e., from the minus to the plus end of the microtubule (Vale et al., 1985a; Brady, 1985; Pryer et al., 1986; Porter et al., 1987a,b; Scholey et al., 1987).

Currently, considerable research in this area is directed toward an understanding of the control of directionality of particle movement in the axon. For example, it is not yet clear whether all membrane-bound vesicles contain both classes of proteins with only one component active at any given time or whether a vesicle is ticketed in one direction by having specific receptors for one or the other class of motility proteins. Additionally, the quaternary structure of the active form of the motor complex in vivo has not yet been established. Research in the field currently centers on such problems.

Characterization of Microtubule-Associated Protein (MAP) 1C as the Motor for Retrograde Organelle Transport and Its Identification as Dynein

Richard B. Vallee, Bryce M. Paschal, and Howard S. Shpetner

Cell Biology Group, Worcester Foundation for Experimental Biology, Shrewsbury, Massachusetts 01545

INTRODUCTION

Almost from the time of the discovery of flagellar dynein over 20 years ago it has been speculated that a cytoplasmic counterpart to this enzyme might exist that could account for motility associated with cytoplasmic microtubules. An enzymatic activity with dynein-like properties was, in fact, detected in sea urchin eggs soon after the flagellar enzyme had been identified (Weisenberg and Taylor, 1968). The function of this enzyme has been debated ever since (Pratt, 1980), because the egg is known to stockpile precursors both for cytoplasmic microtubules (see Vallee and Bloom, 1983) and for cilia that are formed in the blastula stage of embryonic development (Auclair and Siegel, 1966).

In the early 1970s it became possible to purify microtubules from brain cytosol. A class of high-M_r microtubule-associated proteins (MAPs) with electrophoretic mobilities close to that of the axonemal dynein heavy chains was found. These proteins were at first suspected to be cytoplasmic equivalents of dynein and were reported to have a corresponding ATPase activity (Burns and Pollard, 1974). However, the activity could be separated from microtubules and from the MAPs, which was in contradiction with the behavior expected for dynein (Gaskin et al., 1974; Murphy et al., 1983).

In our laboratory we found that the high-M_r MAPs were complex in composition and showed dramatic variation in relative abundance under different preparative conditions (Vallee, 1982; Bloom et al., 1984, 1985). We described five distinct proteins and termed them MAP 1A, MAP 1B, MAP 1C, MAP 2A, and MAP 2B (Bloom et al., 1984). Several of these appear to be highly elongated fibers extending from the microtubule surface (Voter and Erickson, 1982), and they probably play an important role in construction of the cytoskeleton (Hirokawa et al., 1985).

MAP 1C was the least prominent of the

five MAPs under standard microtubule purification procedures, but there were early indications that it was structurally distinct from the others (Bloom et al., 1984). We now know it to be an abundant protein that binds to microtubules in a nucleotide-sensitive fashion. Apparently, it has been routinely discarded using standard microtubule purification procedures that involve addition of adenosine triphosphate (ATP) or guanosine triphosphate (GTP) during the microtubule assembly steps. We have purified MAP 1C, taking advantage of its nucleotide-sensitive microtubule binding, and find that it is a new form of dynein involved in microtubule-associated motility in the cytoplasm.

PURIFICATION OF MAP 1C AS A MICROTUBULE-ACTIVATED ATPASE

MAP 1C was first identified in brain microtubule preparations in the course of our work on the chymotryptic fragmentation of MAP 2 (Vallee, 1980). MAP 1C was a trace component of brain microtubules that resisted chymotryptic digestion under conditions that degraded the other MAPs extensively. We subsequently found MAP 1C at somewhat higher levels in preparations of microtubules from bovine white matter (Bloom et al., 1984). We first suspected that MAP 1C might have catalytic properties during a search for microtubule-activated ATPase activity in brain. Such an activity had been observed in cytosolic extracts of sea urchin eggs and in purified egg microtubules as well (Collins and Vallee, 1986a,b). The activity was distinct from both egg dynein (Pratt, 1980) and egg kinesin (Cohn et al., 1987). However, it was difficult to purify, and its function remained enigmatic.

No equivalent activity was detected in cytosolic extracts of brain tissue, possibly because of a much higher level of ATPase activity (C.A. Collins, unpublished observations). However, we did detect microtubule-activated ATPase activity in brain microtubules prepared by a modification of our standard procedures. The microtubules

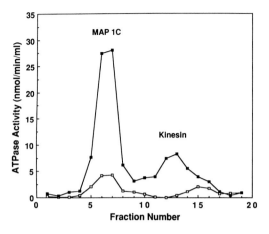

Fig. 13–1. Sucrose density gradient analysis of microtubule-activated ATPases in brain tissue. Microtubules were prepared according to Paschal et al. (1987a), but without the GTP extraction step that is used to remove kinesin. The microtubules were extracted with ATP as described and subjected to sucrose density gradient centrifugation. The fractions were assayed for ATPase activity with (■) or without (□) added microtubules (Paschal et al., 1987a). Two peaks of activity can be seen, one associated with the position of MAP 1C (20S) and the other with kinesin (~10S).

were purified using taxol (Vallee, 1982), but omitting the usual addition of GTP during the microtubule assembly step (Paschal et al., 1987a), which had been a carry-over from earlier microtubule purification procedures. The microtubules were subsequently extracted with ATP to identify MAPs that might bind to microtubules in an ATP-sensitive manner. The ATP-extracted MAPs were then further fractionated by a number of methods.

Fractionation of the ATP-extracted material by sucrose density gradient centrifugation is shown in Figure 13–1. ATPase activity was observed in two peaks, one at 20S and the other toward the top of the gradient. Addition of taxol-stabilized microtubules markedly stimulated the ATPase activity in the 20S peak. Electrophoretic analysis revealed that this activity was associated with a protein whose mobility corresponded to the position of MAP 1C. Kinesin was detected at 10S (Paschal et al., 1987a), which corresponds to the position of a smaller peak of microtubule-stimulated ATPase activity (Fig. 13–1; cf. Kuznetsov and Gelfand, 1986).

The level of kinesin varied from experiment to experiment. To minimize its contribution to the total ATPase and motility activities in the preparation, a step was incorporated to remove it from the microtubules before extracting MAP 1C. We found that kinesin could be extracted from partially purified microtubules using GTP. MAP 1C, however, remained bound to the microtubules. This occurred despite the observation that addition of GTP to cytosolic extracts greatly reduced the yield of MAP 1C (Paschal et al., 1987a). This apparent contradiction presumably arises from the presence of nucleoside diphosphokinase activity in cytosol, but not in the partially purified microtubules. This activity would result in the production of ATP from GTP and adenosine diphosphate (ADP) in the cytosolic extract, but not in the microtubule preparation (Paschal et al., 1987a; Shpetner et al., 1987; 1988). The preparative procedure now in use involves 1) purification of microtubules in the absence of nucleotide, 2) GTP extraction of kinesin, 3) ATP extraction of MAP 1C, and 4) sucrose density gradient centrifugation of the MAP 1C (Paschal et al., 1987a).

A sample of purified MAP 1C is shown in Figure 13–2. In addition to the high-M_r electrophoretic species, a number of additional bands are evident. These were found to copurify with MAP 1C to constant stoichiometry, and we believe that together the several polypeptides are integral components of a multisubunit protein complex (Paschal et al., 1987a; see below).

MAP 1C IS CAPABLE OF RETROGRADE FORCE PRODUCTION

The enzymatic and microtubule-binding properties of MAP 1C strongly suggested that it might play a role in microtubule-associated motility. To assay for force-

MAP 1C

410

74

59
57
55
53

Fig. 13–2. Electrophoresis of MAP 1C purified by ATP extraction of microtubules followed by sucrose density gradient centrifugation (Paschal et al., 1987a). M_rs of subunits are indicated in kilodaltons. (Reproduced from Paschal et al., 1987a, with permission of the publisher.)

producing activity, the protein was adsorbed onto a glass coverslip, and microtubules were applied in the presence of ATP (Allen et al., 1985; Vale et al., 1985). The microtubules were observed to glide in a continuous, unidirectional manner with an average rate of 1.25 μm/sec at room temperature (Paschal et al., 1987a). This rate was about three- to fourfold faster than microtubules gliding on kinesin-coated coverslips.

To determine the direction of force production along microtubules by MAP 1C, *Chlamydomonas* flagellar axonemes were

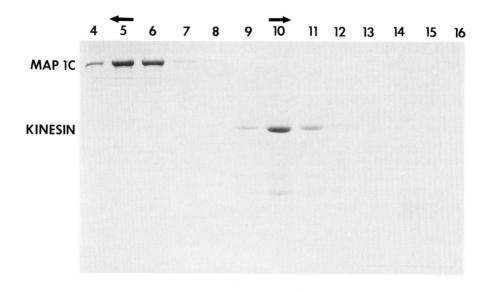

Fig. 13–3. Opposite direction of force production for MAP 1C and kinesin. In this experiment, MAP 1C and kinesin were obtained from the same microtubule preparation using a modification of the standard kinesin purification procedure involving AMP-PNP–induced binding (Paschal and Vallee, 1987b). We found that MAP 1C was a substantial contaminant in our kinesin preparations. The two proteins could be successfully separated by sucrose density gradient centrifugation, shown here by gel electrophoresis of the gradient fractions (Laemmli, 1970; 7% acrylamide, Coomassie blue stain). *Chlamydomonas* axonemes that were applied to MAP 1C-coated coverslips glided toward their frayed ends, corresponding to the retrograde direction of force production. Axonemes applied to kinesin-coated coverslips glided in the opposite direction. The arrows indicate that MAP 1C and kinesin were assayed from the same preparation and found to produce force in opposite directions.

used in the gliding assay (Paschal and Vallee, 1987b). The axonemes fray at their distal (plus) ends during isolation, providing a convenient marker for polarity that could be readily observed in the light microscope.

As a control in these studies, we purified kinesin as well as MAP 1C (Fig. 13–3). Kinesin produced force in the direction corresponding to anterograde organelle transport in the cell; i.e., the axonemes glided with their frayed (plus) ends trailing. In contrast to this behavior, the axonemes glided with their frayed ends leading when applied to coverslips coated with MAP 1C. This direction of force production corresponds to that observed for both inner and outer arm flagellar dynein in the axoneme

(Sale and Satir, 1977; Fox and Sale, 1987), one of many pieces of evidence identifying MAP 1C as a soluble form of the axonemal enzyme (see below).

Of equal importance, the observed direction of force production corresponds to that for retrograde organelle transport in the cell (Paschal and Vallee, 1987b) which, for a variety of reasons, is the most likely role for MAP 1C. Most simply, there are no other obvious roles for a retrograde motor in neuronal tissue. While MAP 1C could be responsible for force production between adjacent neuronal microtubules, the known role for dynein in the axoneme, there is no evidence for a similar interaction between neuronal microtubules. We have also de-

TABLE 13–1. Pharmacology of MAP 1C

Treatment	Concentration	Motility	ATPase activity (%)
Control		+	100
EHNA[a]	1 mM	−	76
EHNA[b]	1 mM	−	15
Vanadate	10 μM	±	44
Vanadate	50 μM	−	18
Vanadate	100 μM	−	18
NEM	0.1 mM	−	73
NEM	1.0 mM	−	33
KCl	200 mM	−	25
Azide	2 mM	+	100
Ouabain	0.05 mg/ml	+	118
Triton X-100	0.2%	+	90

EHNA, Erythro-9[3-2-(hydroxynonyl)]adenine; NEM, N-ethyl-maleimide. Data are from Paschal and Vallee (1987a,b), and Shpetner et al. (1987; 1988). ATPase data refer to microtubule-activated state, with the exception of EHNA at high salt concentration.
[a]Assayed in 0.05 M KCl.
[b]Assayed in 0.62 M KCl.

tected high levels of MAP 1C in tissues such as liver (Collins and Vallee, unpublished results). In cells from these tissues microtubules are probably not organized into the uniformly parallel arrays characteristic of neurons and glial cells. Hence a role for MAP 1C in force production between microtubules is even more difficult to imagine than in neurons. In addition to these arguments, the pharmacology of MAP 1C is consistent with that of retrograde axonal transport, as discussed below.

It is interesting to note that the rate of microtubule gliding on MAP 1C-coated coverslips is slower than that for microtubules gliding on purified sea urchin flagellar outer arm dynein (~4 μm/sec; Paschal et al., 1987d). This may indicate a difference in the force-producing properties of axonemal and non-axonemal forms of dynein, although species differences may also be involved.

MODULATION OF MAP 1C ACTIVITY

A number of important variables have been identified affecting the level of MAP 1C ATPase activity, the most basic being the presence of microtubules. Total activation of the MAP 1C ATPase at saturating microtubule concentrations was as high as sevenfold, half-maximal saturation occurring at

0.2 mg/ml microtubules and saturation at ~1 mg/ml (Shpetner et al., 1987; 1988). Tubulin dimers were ineffective in activating the ATPase. Activation was strongly dependent on ionic strength and was abolished at elevated levels of KCl (Table 13–1).

Inhibitors of dynein ATPases also inhibited MAP 1C. Both the microtubule-activated and basal ATPase activities of MAP 1C were sensitive to vanadate. The K_i for the microtubule-activated ATPase was 5–10 μM. This value was in the range reported for sea urchin egg dyneins (Pratt et al., 1980; Penningroth et al., 1985) and higher than that for axonemal dyneins (Gibbons et al., 1978; Kobayashi et al., 1978), though data on microtubule-activated forms of these enzymes are not available for comparison. MAP 1C and axonemal and egg dynein are all more sensitive to vanadate than are kinesin (Cohn et al., 1987) or the 10S sea urchin microtubule-activated ATPase described by Collins and Vallee (1986a,b). MAP 1C was sensitive to low levels of N-ethyl-maleimide (NEM), which is also the case for ciliary and flagellar dyneins, but different from kinesin.

The effect of erythro-9-[3](2-hydroxynonyl)]adenine (EHNA) on MAP 1C is of interest in that this inhibitor was reported to be relatively specific for dyneins (Penningroth et al., 1982). EHNA inhibited MAP 1C

TABLE 13–2. Substrate Specificity of MAP 1C

Nucleotide	Supports motility[a]	Hydrolyzed	Microtubule-activated Hydrolysis[a]
ATP	−	−	−
MgATP	+	+	+
CaATP	+	+	+
MgGTP	−	+	−
MgCTP	−	+	−
MgTTP	−	+	−
MgITP	−	nd	nd
MgUTP	−	nd	nd

Data are compiled from Paschal and Vallee (1987b) and Shpetner et al. (1987; 1988). All nucleotides were assayed at levels up to 5 mM. nd, not determined. GTP failed to dissociate rigor complexes of MAP 1C and microtubules (Paschal et al., 1987a; Shpetner et al., 1987; 1988), consistent with its failure to support motility and for its hydrolysis not to be activated by microtubules. The effect of the other nucleotides on rigor complexes has not been tested.
[a]Slight (≤ 1.3-fold) stimulation of GTPase, CTPase, and TTPase activities were seen.

motility completely (Table 13–1; Paschal and Vallee, 1987b). However, it showed less of an effect on both the microtubule-activated and basal ATPase activities under the standard low-ionic-strength conditions used for the ATPase assays (Shpetner et al., 1987; 1988). Under the higher-ionic-strength conditions used routinely for flagellar and ciliary dynein ATPase assays, EHNA inhibited most of the MAP 1C ATPase activity. Thus, this agent does affect MAP 1C as expected for a dynein. However, we do not fully understand the difference in relative sensitivities of the ATPase and motility activities at low ionic strength.

It should be pointed out that EHNA has been reported to inhibit organelle motility (Beckerle and Porter, 1982) and mitotic motility (Cande, 1982). Of particular interest, it inhibited retrograde but not anterograde organelle transport in detergent-permeabilized axons (Forman et al., 1983). Thus, inhibition of MAP 1C-mediated motility by EHNA is consistent with a role in retrograde organelle motility (see above; Paschal and Vallee, 1987b).

Among a variety of nucleotides tested, only ATP supported MAP 1C-mediated motility (Table 13–2; Paschal and Vallee, 1987b). In this sense the substrate specificity of MAP 1C is comparable to that of axonemal dyneins, and different from kine-

sin, which can use ATP, GTP, and ITP (Porter et al., 1987a,b). The kinesin ATPase was also more active with Ca^{2+} than with Mg^{2+} (Kuznetsov and Gelfand, 1986) in contrast to MAP 1C (Shpetner et al., 1987; 1988) and other forms of dynein, which can hydrolyze $Ca^{2+}ATP$ but prefer $Mg^{2+}ATP$ as substrate.

A feature that distinguishes MAP 1C from other dyneins is that it can hydrolyze a variety of nucleotides at high rates, though these reactions do not seem to be coupled to force production (Table 13–2; Shpetner et al., 1987; 1988). Thus, GTP, CTP, and TTP were hydrolyzed by MAP 1C more rapidly than was ATP; however, GTP, CTP, and TTP failed to support microtubule gliding, hydrolysis was not substantially activated by microtubules, and GTP failed to dissociate rigor complexes of MAP 1C and microtubules. (CTP and TTP have not yet been tested for this property.) This aspect of the enzymology of MAP 1C seems so far to be unique and is proving to be useful in distinguishing it from other forms of dynein. Both the motility properties and the microtubule-activated ATPase activity of MAP 1C were inhibited by other MAPs, namely, MAP 2 and tau (Paschal and Vallee, 1987b). The effect of these MAPs on the ATPase activity in particular is most readily explained by competition with MAP 1C for binding sites on the microtubule lattice. This is a novel form

TABLE 13–3. Calculated Mass of MAP 1C From Subunit Composition

Polypeptide M_r ($\times$ 10^3)	Mass ratio	Molar ratio	Proposed No. of subunits	Total M_r ($\times$ 10^3)
410 (MAP 1C)	1.00	2.0	2	820
74	0.28	3.1	3	222
59	0.05	0.6	1	59
57	0.05	0.7	1	57
55	0.07	1.0	1	55
53	0.08	1.2	1	53
Total				1,266

Mass data based on gel densitometry are taken from Paschal et al. (1987a). They are recalculated using an M_r of 410 kDa for the MAP 1C heavy chains, which is derived from the sum of the M_rs of the vanadate cleavage fragments (Paschal et al., 1987a). Two heavy chains for MAP 1C are assumed, corresponding to the two heads observed by scanning transmission electron microscopy and the two heavy chains seen by sodium dodecyl sulfate-urea gel electrophoresis (Vallee et al., 1987, 1988). (Reproduced from Vallee et al., 1988, with permission of the publisher.)

of regulation and suggests one way in which the activity of MAP 1C can be modulated in the cell.

STRUCTURAL IDENTIFICATION OF MAP 1C AS DYNEIN

At an early stage in our characterization of MAP 1C, a number of biochemical features were noted that are reminiscent of ciliary and flagellar dynein. These included the electrophoretic mobility of the MAP 1C heavy chain, the native sedimentation coefficient (20S), and the ATP-dependent binding to microtubules (Table 13–4). While this evidence was consistent with MAP 1C being related to dynein, it still left open the possibility that MAP 1C was a totally new enzyme with some dynein-like properties. Underscoring this prospect were the differences in MAP 1C and the known dyneins (Table 13–4), especially the greater sensitivity of MAP 1C to activation by microtubules, the higher rates of hydrolysis of GTP, CTP, and TTP, and the different subunit compositions.

Scanning transmission electron microscopy (STEM) was used to analyze MAP 1C because of its noteworthy success in establishing the structure of axonemal dyneins (Johnson and Wall, 1983; Witman et al., 1983). Unstained, freeze-dried specimens

TABLE 13–4. Comparison of MAP 1C With Axonemal Dyneins

Properties identifying MAP 1C as dynein
1. Sedimentation coefficient = 20S
2. Heavy chain M_r = 410,000
3. Morphology (two heads with associated stalks and base)
4. Total particle mass = 1.2 mDa
5. Head diameter = 13.4 nm; mass = 327 mDa
6. Subunit composition (two heavy chains, three intermediate chains)
7. Susceptibility to cleavage by UV light in presence of vanadate
8. Location of ATPase site in middle of heavy chain polypeptides
9. Sensitivity to vanadate, EHNA, and NEM
10. Divalent cation preference (Mg^{2+} > Ca^{2+})
11. Direction of force production (retrograde; or minus to plus end of microtubule)

Properties distinguishing MAP 1C from ciliary and flagellar dynein
1. Activation of ATPase by low levels of microtubules
2. High hydrolysis rate for CTP, GTP, and TTP
3. Intermediate and light chain composition

were particularly useful in that they provided morphological information, and their mass could also be determined. The particles were also examined by negative-stain electron microscopy. MAP 1C was observed as a two-headed particle in both unstained (Fig. 13–4; Vallee et al., 1987, 1988) and

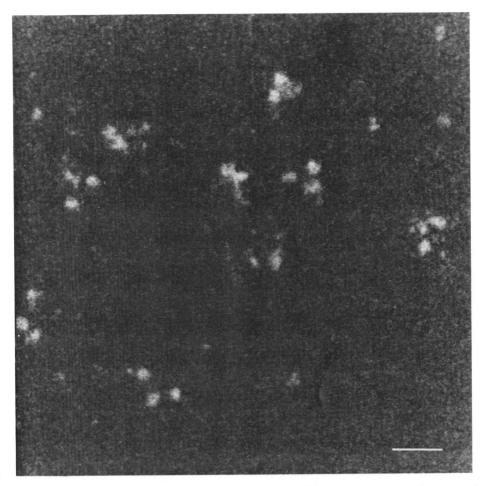

Fig. 13–4. Scanning transmission electron microscope image of MAP 1C. A field of unstained, unfixed calf brain MAP 1C particles purified by ATP extraction of microtubules followed by sucrose density gradient centrifugation. Conditions are according to Vallee et al. (1988). A variety of conformations can be seen, typical of the range of views observed with axonemal dyneins. All particles have at least two distinct globular domains, or heads. A third, variable domain can also be seen. In some cases (as in particle at lower left) the third domain is indistinguishable from the other two, and the particle appears to be three-headed. However, in all such cases, the mass of these particles was indistinguishable from those that were clearly two-headed (Vallee et al., 1988). Bar = 50 nm.

negatively stained preparations. It was, in fact, indistinguishable in morphology from the two-headed 18S *Chlamydomonas* flagellar outer arm dynein particle as viewed by STEM (Witman et al., 1983), as well as the two-headed sea urchin flagellar outer arm 21S dynein as seen in freeze-dried, rotary-shadowed preparations (Sale et al., 1985).

The mass of MAP 1C was 1.16 mDa for unfixed preparations and 1.26 mDa for fixed preparations (Vallee et al., 1988). These values were much lower than was the value obtained by STEM for the three-headed *Tetrahymena* outer arm dynein (1.95 mDa; Johnson and Wall, 1983). They were, however, closely comparable to those obtained by STEM for the outer arm 18S *Chlamydomonas* subunit (1.22 mDa; Witman et al.,

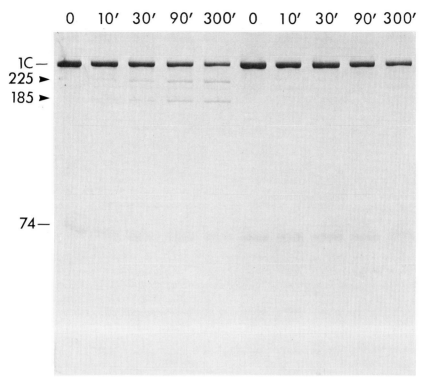

Fig. 13–5. Vanadate-mediated ultraviolet (UV) photocleavage of MAP 1C. Purified MAP 1C was exposed to UV light for a series of times in the presence of ATP and the presence **(left five lanes)** or absence **(right five lanes)** of vanadate. Two fragments were produced in the presence of vanadate. M_rs are indicated in kilodaltons. (Reproduced from Paschal et al., 1987a, with permission of the publisher.)

1983) and by physiochemical means for the sea urchin flagellar outer arm particle (1.25 mDa; Gibbons and Fronk, 1979). Because the sedimentation coefficients of MAP 1C and the two-headed axonemal dyneins are similar, the mass data imply that the frictional coefficients and, therefore, the shape of these molecules in solution are comparable as well. The diameter and mass (327 kDa) of the MAP 1C heads was also determined by STEM (d = 13.4 nm; m = 325 kDa). These values are close to those reported for two- and three-headed axonemal dyneins (Johnson and Wall, 1983; Witman et al., 1983; Sale et al., 1985), though the mass of the MAP 1C heads was somewhat lower than that for the other molecules (~375–400 kDa). We do not know if this implies a significant structural difference or, rather,

reflects some uncertainty in determining the boundary of the heads for the mass analysis.

Based on the direct identification of MAP 1C as dynein by STEM, we were encouraged to look for additional dynein properties. It had been reported that axonemal dyneins could be cleaved, apparently within their active sites, by exposure to ultraviolet (UV) light in the presence of vanadate (Lee-Eiford et al., 1986; Gibbons et al., 1987; King and Witman, 1987). This occurs for MAP 1C as well (Fig. 13–5). Both V1 and V2 cleavage sites were seen (Paschal et al., 1987a; Kravit and Vallee, 1987), and the sizes of the fragments were similar to those generated from axonemal dyneins. The photoaffinity analog of ATP, 8-azido-ATP, also labels the MAP 1C heavy chains (Kravit and Vallee, 1987). These data indicate that, as for axonemal dyneins, the ATPase site(s) of MAP 1C are located in the heavy chains. In addition, the size of the photocleavage fragments places the active site at virtually the same position within the MAP 1C heavy chains as in the heavy chains of axonemal dyneins. This suggests that MAP 1C is probably related to axonemal dyneins at the primary sequence level as well as at higher levels of structural order. Thus, while it is not certain whether vanadate-mediated photocleavage alone can serve to identify new forms of dynein, this method has provided valuable insight into the structure of MAP 1C.

Based on the structure of other two-headed dyneins and on our data on MAP 1C, we envision MAP 1C to be organized as shown in Figure 13–6. The diagram shows a total of nine polypeptide components (Table 13–3). While other two-headed dyneins have been found to obtain two heavy chains, this was not evident from the electrophoretic gels used to resolve the brain MAPs (Paschal et al., 1987a). However, when analyzed under conditions designed to resolve α and β heavy chain subunits from sea urchin outer arm dynein, MAP 1C was also seen as two distinct α and β species (Vallee et al., 1987, 1988). Based on this observation, the mass of MAP 1C can be calculated from its subunits and compared with the mass determined by STEM. Assuming two heavy chains and the mass ratio of the other polypeptides to the high-M_r species, we obtain a value of 3 for the number of 74 kDa chains (Table 13–3; Fig. 13–7). This is also the number of intermediate chains for sea urchin outer arm dynein (Fig. 13–7) and *Tetrahymena* dynein (Johnson and Wall, 1983) and suggests that the three copies of the 74 kDa species may be related to the intermediate chains of the other dyneins. We note that the 74 kDa species generally appears somewhat diffuse on electrophoretic gels and will even split into two or three bands under some conditions (Kravit and Vallee, unpublished observations).

Finally, each of the other chains in the 50–60 kDa range calculates to close to one copy per MAP 1C particle. While we con-

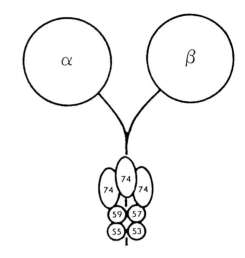

Fig. 13–6. Schematic diagram of MAP 1C molecule. The two heavy chains (Vallee et al., 1988) are designated α and β following the nomenclature used for axonemal dyneins (Witman and Pfister, 1984). Based on evidence from axonemal dyneins (Johnson and Wall, 1983; Witman et al., 1983; Goodenough and Heuser, 1984; Sale et al., 1985), the heavy chains are proposed to extend through both the head and stalk regions. The three 74 kDa chains of MAP 1C (Paschal et al., 1987a) may correspond to the three intermediate chains of *Tetrahymena* ciliary (Porter and Johnson, 1983) and sea urchin flagellar (see Fig. 13–7) outer arm dyneins. They are placed at the base of the molecule to account for the mass of this region (Johnson, 1985; Goodenough and Heuser, 1984; Vallee et al., 1988). The location of the 53–59 kDa MAP 1C subunits (Paschal et al., 1987a) is unknown and is assigned arbitrarily to the base. The heads are thought to be responsible for ATP-dependent microtubule binding and force production (Johnson, 1985). Thus, the base is the likely locus for interaction of MAP 1C with a membranous organelle.

sider it reasonable to expect that the lower two of these species could be residual tubulin, two polyclonal and one monoclonal anti-tubulin antibodies failed to react with these bands (Paschal et al., 1987a). This suggests that they are novel subunits of MAP 1C, not found in axonemal dyneins (Fig. 13–7). Calculation of the mass of MAP 1C from its subunit composition yielded a value of 1.27 mDa (Table 13–3). This is in excellent agreement with the mass determined by

COMPARISON OF
DYNEIN SUBUNITS

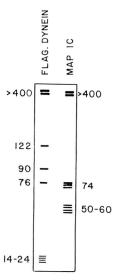

Fig. 13–7. Schematic diagram of electrophoretic components of MAP 1C **(right)** (Paschal et al., 1987a; Vallee et al., 1988) and sea urchin flagellar outer arm dynein **(left)** (Bell et al., 1979). MAP 1C, like the flagellar dynein, has two heavy chains and three polypeptides in the intermediate-chain M_r range. However, the electrophoretic mobility of the intermediate chains is very different in the two molecules. In addition, we have not observed MAP 1C to contain the 14–24 kDa light chains characteristic of the flagellar dyneins, and the 50–60 kDa polypeptides of MAP 1C have not been found associated with flagellar dyneins. Thus, while the two molecules appear to have the same basic structure, there are marked differences in their subunits which could be responsible for differences in function (see Fig. 13–8). M_rs indicated in kilodaltons.

STEM and serves as strong support for the general model shown in Figure 13–6.

DIFFERENCES IN SUBUNIT COMPOSITION MAY SPECIFY DIFFERENCES IN DYNEIN FUNCTION

Table 13–4 summarizes the properties of MAP 1C that identify it as a form of dynein. It also lists the most distinctive differences from ciliary and flagellar dyneins thus far detected. It is not yet certain whether all of these represent inherent differences or whether some will prove to reflect differences in the preparative histories of the different molecules or the assay conditions used. There appears to be a major functional difference between MAP 1C and axonemal dyneins that may be reflected in the observed compositional differences (Paschal et al., 1987a; Vallee et al., 1987, 1988). Axonemal dyneins contain an ATP-sensitive as well as an ATP-insensitive binding site for microtubules that together produce the shearing force between microtubules responsible for axonemal bending. We have no clear evidence that MAP 1C contains an ATP-insensitive binding site, and we believe it unlikely that such a site will be found. Instead, in view of its possible role in retrograde organelle transport (see above), it should contain a binding site for vesicular organelles.

How can a molecule designed for a specific role in microtubule–microtubule sliding in the axoneme be adapted to an additional role in microtubule–organelle interactions? Part of the explanation for this adaptability may already be in hand in the subunit composition of MAP 1C versus other forms of dynein. Figure 13–7 is a schematic diagram of the subunits of MAP 1C in comparison with those of sea urchin flagellar dynein. Phylogenetically, this is the most closely related axonemal dynein to be characterized extensively. The flagellar molecule contains three intermediate chains of M_rs 76,000, 90,000, and 122,000. MAP 1C also appears to contain three intermediate chains, although all are clustered at M_r 74,000. There seems to be no obvious correlate in axonemal dyneins of the four MAP 1C chains in the M_r 50,000–60,000 range. On the other hand, the light chains found in axonemal dynein preparations have not been observed in preparations of MAP 1C.

While it is possible that the differences in subunit composition merely reflect evolutionary changes in the dynein molecule, we believe that this is unlikely in that there are marked similarities in intermediate chain composition between axonemal dyneins ob-

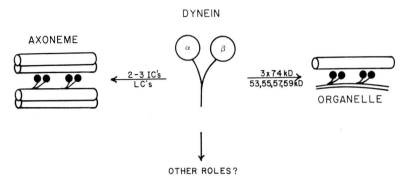

Fig. 13–8. Schematic diagram showing how dynein could be adapted to a role in axonemal or organelle motility. **Left:** Axonemal outer doublet microtubules are shown, with two-headed dynein molecules mediating their interaction. **Right:** MAP 1C shown in its proposed role, mediating the motile action of cellular organelles with microtubules. The two forms of dynein are shown assembled with different complements of intermediate- and low-M_r subunits, indicated by their M_rs. Some or all of these could be involved in specifying the particular role of the dynein molecule in the cell. It is not known whether the α and β heavy chains represent the same or different gene products in the two forms of dynein. Conceivably, dynein participates in even additional roles, as suggested by the arrow at bottom. IC, intermediate chain; LC, light chain.

tained from protozoa, echinoderms, and even mammals (Johnson, 1985; Hastie et al., 1986). In fact, ciliary dynein from pig contains apparent intermediate chains (M_rs 67,000 and 81,000; Hastie et al., 1986) that are closer in size to those of distantly related axonemal dyneins than to those of MAP 1C obtained from calf brain. This suggests that subunit composition may distinguish functional classes of dyneins and may, quite conceivably, help to specify their function.

The location of the intermediate and light chains in axonemal dyneins is unknown and remains an important question. It has been suggested that these chains may be associated with the base of the structure, to account for the mass of this region (Johnson, 1985) as well as its substructure (Goodenough and Heuser, 1984). This would place the dynein subunits in the appropriate part of the molecule to play a role in microtubule or organelle binding (Figs. 13–7, 13–8). We suggest, therefore, that one important function of the MAP 1C subunits may be to mediate the interaction of the molecule with

membranous organelles. It is also worth speculating that MAP 1C could be adapted, perhaps by an additional set of subunits, to other cellular binding sites. Thus, if MAP 1C were associated with the kinetochore, it would produce force in the proper direction to drag chromosomes toward the poles of the mitotic spindle. It will be of interest to search for MAP 1C in the mitotic spindle to evaluate this possibility. Thus, dynein, first identified in flagella and cilia, appears to be adaptable to more than one cellular role. Understanding the full range of dynein functional activity should remain a question of intense interest for further work.

A NOTE ON NOMENCLATURE

Given the extensive evidence that we have obtained for the similarity of MAP 1C to the ciliary and flagellar dyneins, we have chosen to refer to MAP 1C simply as "dynein" (Vallee et al., 1988; Shpetner et al., 1988).

Microtubule–Associated Proteins and Intracellular Particle Motility

Roger D. Sloboda and Susan P. Gilbert

Department of Biological Sciences, Dartmouth College, Hanover, New Hampshire 03755 (R.D.S.); Department of Molecular and Cell Biology, Pennsylvania State University, University Park, Pennsylvania 16802 (S.P.G.)

INTRODUCTION

Neural tissue is a particularly rich source of tubulin, the subunit protein of microtubules, because the axons and dendrites of neurons contain numerous microtubules. Thus, such tissue is extremely amenable to the study of microtubule-based motility for both biochemical and morphological reasons. This is particularly true of axons that contain numerous microtubules oriented with their long axes parallel to the long axis of these cytoplasmic extensions.

When experiments were originally begun to characterize biochemically microtubules assembled in vitro from brain homogenates using procedures originally described by Weisenberg (1972), it was noticed in several laboratories that, in addition to tubulin, a number of other proteins, characterized in part by their relative molecular masses, co-purified with tubulin during the in vitro assembly reaction. The term *microtubule-associated proteins* (MAPs) was originally coined by Sloboda et al. (1975) to refer to a class of high-M_r proteins that copurified with tubulin at a constant stoichiometric ratio during many cycles of the in vitro assembly/

disassembly reaction. Originally, two high-M_r (>250 kDa) proteins, MAP 1 and MAP 2, were identified, that can be readily visualized in the electron microscope as side arm projections having a distinct spatial periodicity extending from the wall of the microtubule (Dentler et al., 1975; Amos, 1977; Kim et al., 1979; Jensen and Smaill, 1986). However, recent experiments have shown that MAPs 1 and 2 are actually more complex, and currently five high-M_r MAPs are recognized (MAP 1A,1B, and 1C and MAPs 2A and 2B), based on relative migrations in sodium dodecyl sulfate (SDS) gels, specific cross reactivity with one or more classes of monoclonal antibodies, and peptide mapping (Kim et al., 1979; Bloom et al., 1984; Hermann et al., 1985; see for a more extensive review, Olmsted, 1986).

In addition to these high-M_r MAPs, another group of brain MAPs, the tau polypeptides, also binds to microtubules assembled in vitro and has properties similar to those of the high-M_r MAPs. For example, both classes of MAPs stimulate microtubule assembly in vitro (Murphy and Borisy, 1975; Sloboda et al., 1976; Cleveland et al., 1977) by binding to the subunit lattice of assembled microtubules after the tubulin assembly reaction has taken place (Sloboda and Rosenbaum, 1979), thereby stabilizing the resulting polymer by reducing the rate of disassembly (Murphy et al., 1977), and both classes of MAPs can be localized by immunofluorescence techniques coincident with microtubules in situ (for review, see Olmsted, 1986). Thus, the currently accepted functional definition of a microtubule-associated protein is a molecule that binds stoichiometrically to microtubules and promotes microtubule assembly (Sloboda and Rosenbaum, 1982). As will be pointed out later, however, recent advances in the study of microtubule-based motility have led to the identification of proteins that only behave as MAPs under certain buffer conditions. Thus, the precise definition of a MAP is becoming less definitive.

MICROTUBULES AND MOTILITY IN AXONS

Neurons provide an important model system for the study of microtubule-dependent, directed intracellular particle transport, a fundamental process characteristic of all cells. Early experiments by Weiss and Hiscoe (1948) first demonstrated the existence of such transport, termed intially by these authors *axoplasmic flow;* in their experiments a nerve was ligated, and it was noticed that a swelling occurred on the side of the ligation proximal to the cell body. When the ligation was removed, the accumulated material again began flowing toward the distal region of the axon. The need for such axoplasmic transport is now clear: Because the axon lacks synthetic capacity, all the material required for the maintenance and correct function of the axon (e.g., synaptic vesicles, tubulin, and so forth) must be synthesized in the cell body and transported down the length of the axon.

The components that are moving in the axon have been identified by a number of experiments in which radioactive precursors have been injected into a cell body or ganglion, and at various times after injection the axon has been removed and the relative amount of radioactivity determined as a function of both the time after injection and the distance from the injection site in the cell body (for an extremely comprehensive review of this literature, see Grafstein and Forman, 1980). Moreover, if after such a labeling experiment the segments of axon are analyzed by SDS-polyacrylamide gel electrophoresis and the radioactively labeled proteins determined by autoradiography (Willard et al., 1974), the identity of the components and the speed with which they are transported can be determined. Thus, five classes of transport based on velocities and direction of movement within the axon have been identified in this manner (for review, see Brady and Lasek, 1982). One of these components, the rapid, bidirectional movement of membranous organelles, is referred to as *fast axonal transport* and occurs at rates of from 200 to 400 mm per day (1–5 μm/sec). Experiments aimed at understanding the molecular basis of this transport, which is microtubule dependent, will be considered in following sections.

Several lines of investigation initially suggested that fast axoplasmic transport was a microtubule-dependent phenomenon: Antimitotic drugs such as colchicine (Dahlstrom, 1971; Banks and Till, 1975) or manipulations such as locally applied cold blocks, which cause microtubule depolymerization, stop transport (Tsukita and Ishikawa, 1980; Miller and Lasek, 1985). Similarly, axons treated with the drug IDPN (Papasozomenos et al., 1982, 1985) rearrange their cytoskeletal components such that neurofilaments, which are normally intermingled with microtubules, take up an annular, circumferential position with respect to the microtubules that occupy the central region in axons treated with IDPN. Motility continues only in the area of the axon occupied by the microtubules. Thus, such indirect evidence suggested (although it did not conclusively prove) that fast transport of membranous elements in axons was a microtubule-dependent phenomenon. The unequivocal proof of this assumption, and the beginning of work on the identification of the motive force-generating molecules involved, came rapidly after recent developments in the area of video microscopy. These developments were important because they enabled investigators to visualize with the light microscope the movement of individual axoplasmic vesicles on their transport filaments and to manipulate experimentally the transport system using in vitro model systems.

VIDEO MICROSCOPY AND PARTICLE MOTILITY IN AXONS

Recent approaches—based on earlier work in which video technology and digital image processing (Inoué, 1981a; Walter and Berns, 1981; Allen and Allen, 1983) were coupled to high-resolution differential interference contrast (DIC) microscopes—have enabled the direct observation of particle motility in axoplasm (For further technical information on video microscopy in general see Inoué, 1986, for an excellent, comprehensive treatment of this topic). The use of a video camera and a digital image processor accomplishes several things that render "visible" subcellular organelles such as microtubules that were heretofore not visible by conventional light microscopy alone (see Fig. 14–1). In this approach, increased visual contrast is achieved first by using relatively high-bias retardation settings when the microscope is operated in the DIC mode and second by using a video system that can reduce image background brightness by means of an offset voltage operating through a DC restoration circuit in the video camera (Inoué, 1981; Allen et al., 1981). Such increases in optical and electronic amplification of the specimen result in much greater image contrast. However, lens defects and dirt on the optical interfaces are also enhanced by this procedure, but these problems can be corrected by digital image processing techniques, as described below.

The use of the computer allows an out of focus image (Fig. 14–1b) of lens imperfections, dirt, and so forth (called *mottle* by

Allen and Allen [1983]) to be subtracted from each successive frame of the in focus image, resulting in a much clearer view of the specimen plane (Fig. 14–1c). Finally, the contrast can be enhanced further by processing routines that expand the relative gray scale of the image being recorded by the camera. The final result of these manipulations is a crisp image having adequate contrast (Fig. 14–1d). Also, video microscopy and image processing are particularly amenable to the study of directed particle transport because of the frame averaging capability of the computer. In this mode, a number of frames can be averaged before display on the video monitor. This results in an image in which random movement caused by Brownian motion is lost, while the observation of directed movement and thus particle translocation is enhanced.

However, it should be noted that while video-enhanced microscopy renders *visible* particles such as a microtubule, whose diameter (25 nm) is considerably below the limit of resolution (~200 nm) of the light microscope, the technique does not *resolve* them. For example, eight microtubules positioned side by side would appear to be the same size as a single microtubule using this technique. Thus, alternative approaches such as immunofluorescence or electron microscopy must be employed in conjuction with video microscopy for the unequivocal identification of subcellular particles and the filaments along which they are moving (see, for example, Hayden et al., 1983; Hayden and Allen, 1984; Schnapp et al., 1985).

When video-enhanced microscopy was applied to the study of particle motility in the squid giant axon (Allen et al., 1982) the extensive transport previously suggested by biochemical studies was observed clearly for the first time in the form of bidirectional movements of membrane-bound organelles. In fact, particles were observed to translocate on single filaments in both directions in the axon (Allen et al., 1982) or in isolated axoplasm (Brady et al., 1982), although the limitations of the technique mentioned above did not allow these investigators to

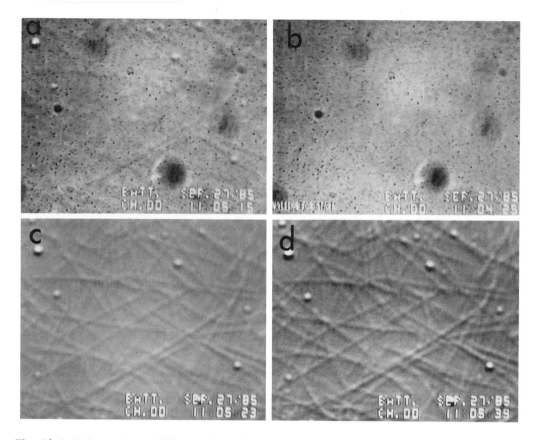

Fig. 14–1. Video enhanced-differential interfence contrast microscopy of in vitro assembled brain microtubules. These images were obtained using a Nikon Optiphot microscope equipped with a ×100/1.35 numerical aperture (NA) planapochromatic objective and an achromatic-aplanatic condenser (1.35 NA); illumination was provided by a 100-W mercury arc lamp. The image was projected from the microscope using a ×10–20 eyepiece at a zoom setting of ×16 and was focused onto the image plane of a Hamamatsu C-1000 chalnicon camera. The video camera and microscope were joined by a Zeiss adaptor having a projection lens of 63 mm. Analog and digital enhancement of raw video images from the chalnicon was performed by a Photonics C1966 image processor and recorded in real time on 3/4" video tape using a SONY VO2610 recorder. **a:** Raw image transmitted to the recorder by the video camera. Microtubules can barely be detected under these conditions because their image is impaired by the extensive mottle (see Allen and Allen, 1983) that results from the superimposition of dirt, lens imperfections, and so forth present at the numerous optical interfaces in the light path from lamp to camera. **b:** Out of focus view of the specimen. The mottle remains in focus, and it is this image that is stored in one of the frame memories of the image processor. **c:** Processed image of the same field shown in a. To obtain this view, the processor has been instructed to subtract the out of focus image (shown in b) of the mottle from each succeeding frame of the in focus image before displaying the result on the monitor. **d:** Enhanced image of the same field. Here, electronic contrast has been added to the specimen in addition to subtraction of the background mottle. To obtain these images from the videotape, micrographs were photographed directly from the monitor through a Ronchi rule onto 35-mm Kodak Plus-X film, which was developed in Microdol-X.

determine the composition of the transport filaments. For example, the sizes of the filaments in axoplasm (microtubules, inter- mediate filaments, and microfilaments) coupled to the resolution limits of the light microscope meant that the observed single filaments on which transport appeared to occur could actually have been one or more of these three cytoskeletal components in various combinations. To identify biochemically the substrate for such organelle transport, Hayden et al. (1983) and Hayden and Allen (1984) performed rigorous correlative light, immunofluorescent, and electron microscopic experiments on particle transport in frog keratocytes and demonstrated unequivocally that in these cells the observed single transport filaments were individual microtubules. Using a similar approach employing light and electron microscopy, Schnapp et al. (1985) demonstrated that the single filaments involved in particle transport in axons were also single microtubules.

Thus, from the brief overview cited above the importance of video microscopy in these studies is clear. However, it should be pointed out that the power of video microscopy reaches further than simply allowing observation of particle movements in living cells or in lysed cell models. Perhaps the greater contribution of video microscopy is that it has allowed for the development of in vitro assays (Gilbert and Sloboda, 1984; Gilbert et al., 1985; Vale et al., 1985a) that are enabling the identification, isolation, and characterization of the molecules involved in various types of intracellular particle motility. For example, video microscopy is currently being used in motility assays that are based on 1) movement of purified, membrane-bound vesicles on MAP-free microtubules (Gilbert and Sloboda, 1986); 2) movement on MAP-free microtubules of polystyrene microspheres coated with motility-promoting proteins (Vale et al., 1985c); and 3) gliding of MAP-free microtubules along a glass substrate coated with a microtubule-based motility-promoting factor (Allen et al., 1985; Vale et al., 1985c). Using any of these assays allows investigators to assess not only the presence or absence of motility but also, and perhaps more importantly, the directionality of movement with respect to the polarity of the microtubule substrate being used (see, for example, Gilbert et al., 1985; Vale et al.,

1985b; Pryer et al., 1986; Porter et al., 1987b).

MICROTUBULE-DEPENDENT INTRACELLULAR PARTICLE MOTILITY

One important characteristic of the microtubule-based fast transport system of the axon is that the microtubules along which membranous organelles travel are all oriented unidirectionally in the axon (Heidemann et al., 1981). Specifically, the microtubules all have their plus (or head) ends distal to the cell body. Thus, any model that attempts to describe microtubule-based motility in axons must explain how membrane-bound vesicles can move bidirectionally on a polarized and thus unidirectional substrate.

The giant axon of the squid *Loligo pealei* has been an important preparation for the study of the molecular basis of such directed organelle transport because 4–8 μl of axoplasm can be mechanically extruded away from the surrounding plasma membrane and glial sheath (Bear et al., 1937; Lasek, 1974). Thus, axoplasm can be obtained free of contaminating vesiculated plasma membrane, which would normally be produced under experimental conditions in which, for example, brain tissue is homogenized in buffer in a tissue grinder. The use of extruded axoplasm thus greatly simplifies the isolation and biochemical characterization of intracellular membranous organelles. Moreover, the extruded preparation remains metabolically active for hours, accessible to surrounding solutions for experimentation, and the organelle motility can be observed directly using video-enhanced differential interference contrast microscopy (Brady et al., 1982, 1985). These characteristics of the axoplasm from the squid *L. pealei* have enhanced the analysis of the relationship between moving organelles and cytoskeletal transport filaments. Using this system, we have been able to identify a high-M_r component of axoplasm that is associated with membrane-bound vesicles yet also shares characteristics in common with both MAPs 1 and 2 from vertebrate brain.

RESULTS AND DISCUSSION

Gilbert and Sloboda (1984) developed a procedure in which axoplasmic vesicles could be isolated from axoplasm and labeled with a fluorescent molecule (in this case rhodamine-conjugated octadecanol, a hydrophobic compound that labels the lipid bilayer). When these labeled vesicles were inserted by microinjection into another axon, the fluorescent vesicles began moving bidirectionally in the host axoplasm. The movement of the inserted vesicles was similar to endogenous transport by several criteria. The movement was strictly adenosine triphosphate (ATP) dependent and occurred at rates similar to endogenous transport. In addition, if the fluorescent vesicles were trypsinized prior to microinjection, they failed to move in the host axoplasm. These experiments showed that vesicles could be isolated in a native state and that the vesicles carried on their surfaces certain proteins—either receptors for a microtubule-based motive force-generating molecule or the force-generating molecule itself. To distinguish between these two possibilities, the following series of experiments was performed.

A reconstituted model system was developed to define and to characterize the MAP-dependent, organelle–cytoskeletal interactions that occur during fast axonal transport. The reconstituted system (Gilbert et al., 1985) contains two components: membrane-bound vesicles isolated from the squid giant axon and MAP-free microtubules composed solely of α and β tubulin. In this assay, different organelles were observed to move bidirectionally on a single microtubule, and all organelles moved at the same rate, approximately 2 μm/sec. An important feature of the system was revealed by these in vitro experiments, namely, that the vesicle population alone contained the necessary motive force-generating molecules needed to effect movement on a microtubule substrate and furthermore that the microtubule itself did not specify directionality of movement because a given microtubule was observed to support movement in both directions.

The fact that ATP-dependent transport of isolated axoplasmic vesicles on purified microtubules was observed (Gilbert and Sloboda, 1985) indicated that the ATP-binding proteins essential for vesicle motility were present on the vesicles. Because one characteristic of a key polypeptide important in the transport process would be the ability to bind ATP, experiments were next performed to identify the ATP-binding proteins of the vesicle preparation. Prior to the identification of the important ATP-binding polypeptides, a procedure was first developed to obtain axoplasmic vesicles free of soluble proteins using combinations of sucrose gradient centrifugation and molecular sieve chromatography. Vesicles so isolated were then observed to translocate on isolated, MAP-free microtubules in an ATP-dependent manner, indicating that after purification the vesicles still contained the necessary motive force-generating polypeptides (Gilbert and Sloboda, 1986). By using radioactive labeling techniques employing a photoaffinity analog of ATP (α ^{32}P-8-azido-adenosine-5′-triphosphate), the ATP-binding proteins of the vesicle preparation were labeled. The protein composition of the vesicles was then determined by SDS-polyacrylamide gel electrophoresis (PAGE), and the labeled ATP-binding polypeptides could then be identified by autoradiography of the resulting SDS gels.

Such experiments identified a high-M_r (292 kDa) polypeptide present on the vesicle surface that specifically bound ATP (Gilbert and Sloboda, 1986). Moreover, this ATP-binding protein could be recognized by antibodies directed against porcine brain (MAP 2). Because the 292 kDa polypeptide associates with vesicles both in vitro and in vivo (See Fig. 14–4, below) we have named the protein *vesikin* (Gilbert and Sloboda, 1988; Do et al., 1988). Vesikin can be isolated in association with vesicles that translocate on isolated microtubules as described above or with microtubules assembled in vitro from homogenates of squid optic lobe (Fig. 14–2, lane c), depending on the buffer conditions employed. Furthermore, if in vi-

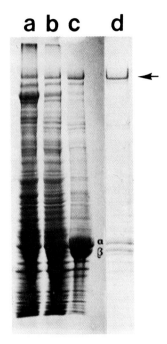

a b c   d

Fig. 14–2. SDS-polyacrylamide gel (4–10% acrylamide, 12–48% urea) stained with Coomassie blue demonstrating the ATP-dependent release of vesikin (arrow) from taxol-stabilized microtubules. **Lane a:** Soluble proteins obtained by centrifugation of a squid optic lobe homogenate at 30,000g for 30 min. **Lane b:** Supernatant obtained after centrifugation of the material shown in lane a at 200,000g for 75 min. **Lane c:** Microtubules induced to assemble from the solution shown in lane b after the addition of taxol to 40 μM (Vallee, 1982) and then collected by centrifugation. **Lane d:** Soluble vesikin (arrow) released from the microtubules shown in lane c by resuspension of the microtubule pellet in buffer containing 10 mM MgATP, incubation at room temperature for 10 min, and then centrifugation to remove the still assembled microtubules. Vesikin can be further purified from this ATP-released supernatant by column chromatography as described in Gilbert and Sloboda (1988). The α and β- subunits of tubulin are identified.

tro assembled microtubules, containing vesikin as a MAP, are resuspended in the presence of ATP, vesikin dissociates from the microtubules (Fig. 14–2, cf. lanes c and d). These are unique characteristics and indicate that, in the absence of ATP, vesikin behaves according to the classic definition of a MAP (Sloboda and Rosenbaum, 1982), while in the presence of ATP it dissociates from microtubules and associates with vesicles, causing them to translocate on MAP-free microtubules. Thus, vesikin has a microtubule-binding site that is ATP sensitive and a vesicle-binding domain that is not.

Vesikin can be purified to electrophoretic homogeneity by taking advantage of its other MAP 2-like characteristic (Fellous et al., 1977; Kim et al., 1979) of stability to extreme temperature. When solutions of microtubules containing MAP 2 or vesikin are boiled in the presence of high salt and dithiothreitol (DTT), all proteins precipitate except for these high-M_r proteins. Using this approach, vesikin can be purified to homogeneity (Fig. 14–3, lane d). We have raised polyclonal antibodies to vesikin and have isolated affinity-purified vesikin antibodies from our antiserum using the heat-purified protein bound to Sepharose as an immunoadsorbant. The characterization and specificity of these affinity-purified vesikin antibodies have been reported in detail elsewhere (Gilbert and Sloboda, submitted).

When affinity-purified vesikin antibodies are used in conjunction with a monoclonal antibody to β tubulin in double-label immunofluorescence experiments with dissociated squid axoplasm, results of the type shown in Figure 14–4 are obtained. Video-enhanced DIC microscopy (Fig. 14–4a) shows numerous membrane-bound vesicles (arrows), some of which are in contact with linear elements identified by indirect immunofluorescence (Fig. 14–4b) as microtubules. In the same field for comparison, the subcellular distribution of vesikin is shown in Figure 14–4c. It is clear that the fluorescent pattern is punctate rather than linear, demonstrating that vesikin and tubulin do not have the same distribution in axoplasm. Rather, the punctate staining of the vesikin antibodies is coincident with globular structures evident in the corresponding DIC image, which are presumed to be membrane-bound vesicles. However, this can only be confirmed conclusively by immunoelectron microscopy, and these experiments are cur-

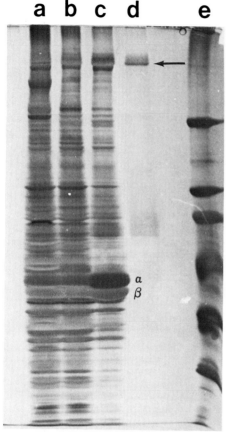

Fig. 14–3. SDS-polyacrylamide gel (5–10% acrylamide, 12–48% urea) stained with silver nitrate demonstrating the heat stability of squid vesikin. **Lane a:** Soluble proteins obtained by centrifugation of a squid optic lobe homogenate at 30,000g for 30 min. **Lane b:** Supernatant obtained after centrifugation of the material shown in lane a at 200,000g for 75 min. **Lane c:** Taxol-stabolized microtubules assembled from the material in lane b, as described in Figure 2. **Lane d:** To obtain heat-stable vesikin (arrow), the microtubules in lane c (containing vesikin as a MAP) were adjusted to 1 mM dithioerythritol and 0.75M NaCl and heated to 100°C in a boiling water bath for 5 min followed by centrifugation to remove precipitated material. Vesikin remains soluble under these conditions and therefore does not sediment. **Lane e:** M_r standards of 205, 116, 97, 66, 45, and 29 kDa (top to bottom). The arrow identifies vesikin, which can be easily recognized by its characteristic yellow color after silver staining, a result confirmed by immunoblotting. The α and β subunits of tubulin are also identified. Complete details of these procedures have been given by Gilbert and Sloboda (1988) and Do et al. (1988).

rently in progress. What is clear, however, from the data in Figure 14–4 is that vesikin is not microtubule associated in situ. Thus the protein only behaves as a MAP under certain conditions in vitro.

Two further results suggest that vesikin is responsible for motility of vesicles on isolated microtubules: 1) Vesikin antibodies stop vesicle transport in a concentration-dependent manner when added to extruded axoplasm. Antibodies to tubulin or (BSA) have no effect on motility when either are added to extruded axoplasm at equivalent concentrations. 2) When purified vesikin is added to polystyrene beads, it confers upon the beads the ability to translocate on isolated microtubules (Gilbert and Sloboda, 1988). In addition, Pratt (1986) has demonstrated that vesikin is a significant component of microtubule–vesicle complexes that can be isolated from squid axoplasm. However, we have not yet been able to demonstrate that vesikin can induce movement in a microtubule gliding assay.

The similarity in antigenic determinants (Gilbert and Sloboda, submitted) and in heat stability (Gilbert and Sloboda, 1988) between vesikin and vertebrate brain MAP 2 led us next to re-examine the behavior of brain MAPs under buffer conditions that promote motility and thus the dissociation of the squid MAP from microtubules (Do et al., 1988). In these experiments, the effect of ATP on the behavior of chick brain MAPs was assessed by first polymerizing brain microtubules with MAPs and then extracting the MAP-containing brain microtubules with varying concentrations of MgATP. Solubilized and microtubule-associated MAPs are then easily separated by a centrifugation step. Based on the data shown in Figure 14–2 and on the fact that antibodies to MAP 2 cross react with vesikin (Gilbert and Sloboda, 1986), it was expected that in the presence of ATP, MAP 2 would dissociate in a manner similar to the dissociation of vesikin. Surprisingly, MAP 2 remained tightly bound under these conditions, while MAP 1 readily dissociated (Do et al., 1988). An analogous behavior of a high-M_r MAP has been noted by Hollenbeck and Chapman

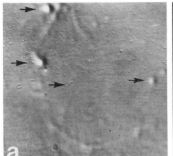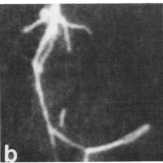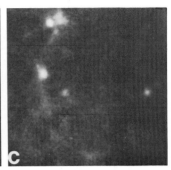

Fig. 14–4. Double-label immunofluorescence using a monoclonal antibody to tubulin and an affinity purified polyclonal antibody to vesikin. **a:** DIC micrograph showing microtubules and vesicles (arrows) in an area of extruded axoplasm from the squid giant axon. **b:** Fluorescent image of the area shown in panel a obtained using a monoclonal antibody to tubulin followed by fluorescein-labeled secondary antibodies. The microtubule distribution is readily apparant in this image. **c:** Fluorescent image of the same area shown in panels a and b obtained using a polyclonal antibody to vesikin followed by rhodamine-labeled secondary antibodies. Labeling in this image is punctate rather than linear and is restricted to areas that correspond to spherical vesicle-like particles evident in the DIC image of a. Complete details of the characterization of the antibodies has been given by Gilbert and Sloboda (1988).

(1986) in experiments using microtubules isolated from bovine spinal nerve roots. Also, MAP 1C has been shown to have ATPase activity and to promote microtubule gliding (Paschal et al., 1987a,b; Paschal and Vallee, 1987a,b). Using another characteristic for comparison, vesikin can stimulate the assembly of purified chick brain tubulin (Do et al., 1988) in a manner similar to that previously reported for other MAPs (Cleveland et al., 1977; see also Sloboda and Rosenbaum, 1982), including brain MAP 1 and MAP 2 (Sloboda et al., 1976; Murphy et al., 1977; Sloboda and Rosenbaum, 1979).

Finally, MAP 1C (Paschal et al., 1987a,b) and a high-M_r protein from *Caenorhabditis elegans* (Lye et al., 1987), but not vesikin (Gilbert and Sloboda; submitted) undergo vanadate-sensitive cleavage in the presence of UV light, a distinct characteristic of dynein (Lee-Eiford et al., 1986). Thus, these high-M_r microtubule-dependent motility proteins appear to represent a class of cytoplasmic dyneins that have evolved specifically to power microtubule-based intracellular particle motility. With respect to vesikin and vertebrate brain MAPs it is thus apparent that vesikin shares certain characteristics in

common with both MAPs 1 and 2, as outlined above. This may indicate that the squid polypeptide represents an early phylogenetic precursor that has evolved into present-day MAPs 1 and 2, each of which has retained one or more of the characteristics of vesikin. Modern techniques of molecular biology will be required to determine the similarities and differences between the various MAPs, and examples of such experimental approaches can be found in the chapter by Goldstein (Chapter 15).

The data summarized above demonstrate that a high-M_r MAP from squid neural tissue is involved in the microtubule-dependent motility that is characteristic of fast axoplasmic transport. On the one hand, this protein can behave in the classic definition of a MAP and bind to in vitro assembled brain microtubules and stimulate the assembly of purified brain tubulin. On the other hand, brain MAPs 1 and 2 are similar to vesikin in that MAP 2 and vesikin are heat stable, while MAP 1 and vesikin exhibit ATP-dependent binding to assembled microtubules. However, just as there are other classes of MAPs characterized by their tissue specificity or M_r (see Olmsted, 1986), there appears to be at least one other lower M_r class of motive force-generating protein (kinesin) that can behave as a MAP under certain buffer conditions. This class will be mentioned briefly below, as well as in greater detail in other papers in this volume.

OTHER EXAMPLES OF MICROTUBULE-BASED MOTILITY PROTEINS

Using extruded axoplasm, Lasek and Brady (1985) reported that when the nonhydrolyzable analog of ATP, adenylyl imidodiphosphate (AMP-PNP), was added to squid axoplasm, stable complexes formed between microtubules and axoplasmic vesicles. This observation allowed Brady (1985) and Vale et al. (1985a) to identify a protein component of these complexes that is involved in microtubule-based motility. The protein isolated from squid neural tissue has a subunit M_r of 116 kDa and has been named *kinesin* (Vale et al., 1985a). A similar protein has been isolated from mammalian brain (Brady, 1985) and from sea urchin eggs (Scholey et al., 1985a,b). Kinesin from any source can promote the movement of polystyrene beads along purified microtubules or the gliding movement of microtubules along a glass surface in an ATP-dependent manner (Vale et al., 1985a,c; Porter et al., 1987a,b). The 116 kDa subunit of kinesin binds ATP (Gilbert and Sloboda, 1986) and has an ATPase activity of approximately 0.06–0.08 μmole min^{-1}mg^{-1} (Kuznetsov and Gelfand, 1986), similar to that of vesikin (Gilbert and Sloboda, 1988). Thus, kinesin represents another class of MAP that binds to microtubules but only under certain buffer conditions, in this case those imposed by the presence of AMP-PNP.

Using oriented microtubule substrates, it has been shown that kinesin induces movement unidirectionally with respect to the microtubule subunit lattice. That is, kinesin moves beads on microtubules (or microtubules relative to the glass slide in a gliding assay) from the minus to the plus end of the microtubule, i.e., in the orthograde direction with respect to the axon. Indeed, if a kinesin antibody is used to immunoprecipitate kinesin from an axoplasmic homogenate, a factor remains soluble that can promote bead movement in the opposite (i.e., retrograde) direction (Vale et al., 1985b). Presumably, vesikin or a MAP 1C-like component is the squid retrograde factor, but unequivocal proof of this requires data describing the directionality of movement induced by vesikin, and these experiments are in progress.

ACKNOWLEDGMENTS

This work was supported by the NSF (BNS-85-03597) and the Muscular Dystrophy Association of America and the authors gratefully acknowledge support from both of these sources. Most of this work was carried out at the Marine Biological Laboratory in Woods Hole, MA 02543; the facilities and support personnel at the MBL are also gratefully acknowledged.

What Can Genetics and Molecular Biology Tell Us About Microtubule-Associated Proteins and Motors?

Lawrence S.B. Goldstein

Department of Cellular and Developmental Biology, Harvard University, Cambridge, Massachusetts 02138

INTRODUCTION

Microtubules are ubiquitous organelles that participate in a wide variety of cellular processes, including mitosis, cellular motility, vesicle transport, and cytomorphogenesis. While the basic protein subunit of microtubules, tubulin, is highly conserved evolutionarily, the structure, interactions, and behavior of microtubules are as varied as the processes in which they participate. For example, a simple survey of biological systems reveals recognizable microtubules participating in structures and processes ranging from the highly stable and well organized microtubules of the eukaryotic flagellum to the highly dynamic and less precisely organized microtubules of the mitotic spindle. Between these two extremes we find the well-organized cross-linked microtubules of the neuronal process and the beautifully elaborated arrays of the interphase cultured cell.

How can a seemingly uniform protein form these various and diverse structures? Two types of explanation have been proposed to answer this fundamental problem. The first suggests that alterations in the tubulin molecule itself, either in its primary sequence or by covalent modification, can modulate or regulate the form and structure of microtubule systems (Fulton and Simpson, 1976; Cleveland, 1987). The second (not necessarily exclusive) explanation for the diversity of microtubule structure and function is that the accessory proteins, either singly or in concert, confer the requisite variability (Vallee et al., 1984b; Wiche, 1985; Solomon, 1986). Eloquent and informative discussions of alterations in the tubulin molecule may be found elsewhere in this volume and in the primary literature (e.g., Cleveland, 1987); these issues will not be discussed further here. Instead, I will deal with the second source of variation, namely, the non-tubulin components of microtubules. In this discussion, I will briefly address the nature of the accessory proteins, their possible in vivo functions, and their role in conferring variation on microtubule functions. I will then focus on how genetic and molecular approaches can be used to understand these interesting proteins and on how these approaches can be used to address the issues raised above.

This discussion is organized into four parts. First, I discuss the possible identity and functions of the accessory proteins as developed by cell biological and biochemical experimentation. Second, I discuss the contributions that genetic and molecular biological analysis can make to our understanding of accessory protein function. Third, I describe recent work from my laboratory that provides examples of these types of approaches and that is beginning to supply these types of understanding. Fourth and finally, I look at two technical innovations that are currently being developed that will contribute to our understanding of accessory proteins in the near future.

A BRIEF REVIEW OF MICROTUBULE-ASSOCIATED PROTEINS

Simple examination of the processes in which microtubules participate has suggested the need for at least three classes (not necessarily distinct) of accessory proteins. First, because cells precisely control the timing and localization of assembly and disassembly of microtubules, there may exist a class of accessory protein that plays a role in the control of these processes. Second, the observation that microtubules can be cross linked to one another, or to other filament systems in vivo, suggests the need for accessory proteins that comprise these cross links; these proteins may also play a role in the formation of organized microtubule assemblies. Third, the observation of bidirectional microtubule-dependent movements in cells, most notably vesicle transport, axonal transport, and mitosis, implies the existence of accessory proteins that generate force for movements within the cell.

In recent years, two major classes of mol-

ecules that are strong candidates to execute many of the above functions have been identified. These two classes are the microtubule-associated proteins (MAPs) and the microtubule motors. MAPs are a diverse class of molecules whose members may play roles in the regulation of assembly of microtubules and the mediation of their interactions (Olmsted, 1986). Microtubule motors, such as kinesin and dynein, may function in the movement of vesicles, the transport of materials within axons, the positioning and development of intracellular organelles, the generation of mitotic forces (Vale, 1987), and, in the case of dynein, in flagellar movement. In the discussion of MAPs and motors below, I will focus on non-axonemal microtubules and will primarily confine my comments to pointing out those areas in which important questions remain unanswered. Because MAPs and motors have both been effectively and recently reviewed by Olmsted (1986) and Vale (1987), respectively, I will in general direct the reader to these sources for primary references and for detailed information.

MAPs

As a class, MAPs are a diverse collection of proteins whose members range in size from M_r 350,000 (e.g., MAP 1A; Bloom et al., 1984) to M_r 32,000 (e.g., a MAP identified in nematode embryos; Aamodt and Culotti, 1986). Despite their great variation in size, MAPs have a surprisingly uniform set of properties. Specifically, they all bind microtubules in vitro, and, when examined, they alter the equilibrium between monomeric and polymeric tubulin. In addition, localization experiments have indicated that MAPs are primarily localized along the walls of cellular microtubules (though MAP 1A may be a constituent of kinetochores and centrosomes). Finally, based on solution behavior, most MAPs that have been studied have highly asymmetric morphologies.

What might be the in vivo functions of members of this diverse class of molecules? Certainly, for molecules with morphologies comparable to those of MAP 1 and MAP 2, i.e., an arm jutting from the microtubule (Kim et al., 1979; Vallee and Davis, 1983), a primary role in mediating microtubule interactions in cellular structures seems likely (though an additional role in assembly regulation remains a possibility). A function is less apparent for molecules, such as MAP 4 and chartin, whose structures are either unknown or unlikely to be that of a large molecular bridge. Perhaps these are molecules that participate in assembly regulation or in mediating interactions with other cross-bridge molecules, motors, or enzymatic factors that regulate microtubule behavior. While it is not readily apparent how a molecule that is located along the walls of a microtubule could participate in regulation of microtubule assembly, which may be a process that occurs primarily at microtubule ends, it is possible that these molecules could participate in an end-mediated process by responding to factors that act at the ends.

While the preceding discussion describes some ideas about the functions MAPs may have in cells, it is unclear how these basic cellular roles of regulation of assembly, or interaction, can be translated to the generation of microtubule diversity. Although no simple answer to this question yet exists (indeed, its broader forms are the essence of the problem of cytomorphogenesis), some suggestions have been proposed. For example, a MAP could contribute to the generation of a specialized array of microtubules by being present only in certain cells because of selective expression, alternative splicing, or covalent modification. It could then confer a cell-specific interaction or property, such as stability, to those microtubules with which it interacts. Possible examples of this mechanism may be provided by chartins and MAPs in neural tissues (e.g., Duerr et al., 1981; Izant and McIntosh, 1980). Alternatively, a cross-bridge MAP could contribute to the generation of a specialized array by first binding to a localized region or specialized structure in a cell and then recruiting or accumulating microtubules by binding. In this case, microtubule organization would

be regulated by the availability of a MAP-binding domain that is not on the microtubule. A possible example of this mechanism may be provided by the avian erythrocyte marginal band (Swan and Solomon, 1984). Finally, a MAP could function by marking a group of microtubules for modification or by regulating the accessibility of the tubulin in a microtubule to modifying enzymes, motors, or other molecules that mediate interactions.

A final issue that has emerged from the study of MAPs concerns how these various molecules are related to one another. For example, how are apparently similar MAPs from different organisms related? The most trenchant postulation of this problem comes from the MAP 4 type of molecules. In almost every cell type or organism yet examined, a MAP or group of MAPs with M_rs 200,000–220,000 has been identified (Olmsted, 1986; Gard and Kirschner, 1987). Frequently, these molecules possess similar properties, e.g., microtubule binding, stimulation of microtubule assembly, intracellular distribution, and thermostability. Unfortunately, definitive evidence either establishing or eliminating the relatedness of the members of this group of MAPs is lacking. In general, antibody probes specific for any one of the molecules is species or class limited in its cross-reactivity properties. Hence, until some common probe recognizes more than one of these molecules, we do not know if there are one, two, or fifty M_r 200,000-type MAPs. The consequence, of course, is that data garnered for any one of these cannot be applied confidently to another, and we cannot know to what extent structural or functional diversity is generated by utilizing different members of this class in different cell types. While this problem is most extreme for the MAP 4 type of molecules, it is possible that the other classes of MAPs are similar in this regard, because information on the presence and nature of several MAPs in different species is still lacking. Hence, the extent and nature of diversity within any one class and its potential for conferring functional diversity are still unknown.

An issue related to the problem of variation within a group concerns the question of whether the existing MAPs are members of a protein superfamily, perhaps possessing similar structural motifs. For example, it is important to know whether there are relationships between molecules in different classes such that different MAPs share a common microtubule-binding domain. Such information might resolve whether different MAPs, which compete for in vitro binding to the same microtubules (discussed by Olmsted, 1986), do so by competing for a common site on the microtubule or by simply sterically inhibiting one another. This information is not only important for understanding how MAPs have evolved but is also necessary for designing probes to find new MAPs. With the imminent availability of structural and sequence information about several molecules, this question should soon be answered.

Motors

The other major class of accessory proteins consists of proteins that generate microtubule-dependent forces or movements, that is, microtubule "motors." The original and best-understood members of this class are the axonemal or ciliary dyneins, for which considerable information is available (Gibbons, 1981; Johnson, 1985). These molecules are of very high M_r, have complex subunit composition, possess adenosine triphosphatase (ATPase) activity, and can generate sliding-displacement forces between axonemal microtubules. Until recently, the axonemal dyneins were the only microtubule force generators known. However, as is often the case, the advent of a new assay system (in vitro microtubule motility; Brady et al., 1982) resulted in the identification of new proteins, including kinesin and cytoplasmic dynein (Vale et al., 1985a; Paschal et al., 1987b; Koonce et al., 1987; Lye et al., 1987). Since other chapters of this volume specifically address the chemistry and in vitro behavior of these various molecules, I will primarily restrict my comments to issues that remain outstanding.

One of the major remaining issues about motors concerns their in vivo functions. Biochemical analyses have revealed the intellectually pleasing result that the intrinsic structural polarity of the microtubule is mirrored by structurally and chemically distinct motors (kinesin and cytoplasmic dynein), which can generate forces in different directions (Vale, 1987; Paschal and Vallee, 1987a,b). However, these studies have not produced direct evidence as to the in vivo functions in which these different classes of motors participate. Nonetheless, consideration of in vitro properties, direction of movement, intracellular localization, and tissue of origin have suggested a variety of functions associated with these motors (Vale et al., 1986; Vale, 1987). For example, the neural origin, activity, and direction of movement of kinesin have suggested that it plays a central role in anterograde axonal transport. Its subsequent identification in non-neural sources (Scholey et al., 1985a; Kachar et al., 1987; Saxton 1988) and its reported intracellular localization have suggested roles in mitosis and in vesicle transport during interphase. Based on similar logic, cytoplasmic dynein has been suggested to be involved in retrograde axonal transport, other types of vesicle transport, and microtubule reorganizations (Paschal et al., 1987a,b). Recent data on the distribution of the endoplasmic reticulum in cells (Terasaki et al., 1986) and on the ability of actively motile microtubule fractions to generate organized arrays of membrane in vitro (Dabora and Sheetz, 1987) suggest a role for motors in the development and placement of intracellular organelles. Finally, motors may play a role in conferring diversity on microtubule function by interacting with different receptors on materials that are transported, by positioning the microtubules themselves in specialized arrays, or by regulating the anchoring of microtubules in arrays. As with MAPs, motors may respond to diversity of tubulin types in microtubules or to MAP composition itself.

An additional important issue concerning motors is how many are there and how diverse will they be? It is interesting in this regard to recall the remarkable complexity and diversity of dyneins in flagella of which up to six distinct species may exist (Piperno, 1987). Given that the most abundant and stable molecules are likely to be the first identified, it seems likely that many motors remain to be found, particularly motors that are cell cycle, organelle, or tissue specific. Such new motors may function in various subsets of the many microtubule-related movements and structures found within cells. Our challenge is to identify and to understand these molecules.

Issues Remaining

In summary, a consideration of cell biological, biochemical, and physiological investigations reveals several unanswered questions about MAPs and motors. What do MAPs and motors do in vivo? How do these molecules contribute to the generation of diversity of microtubule structure and function? How do these molecules execute their functions and with what other proteins do they interact? How are these molecules related to one another? Finally, what other molecules remain to be found, and how will we find and understand them? In the next section I describe how classical genetics and molecular biology may contribute to answering these questions.

WHAT WILL GENETICS AND MOLECULAR BIOLOGY CONTRIBUTE TO AN UNDERSTANDING OF MAPS AND MOTORS?

In this section I examine the contributions that genetics and molecular biology are likely to make to an understanding of the in vivo functions of MAPs and motors. For purposes of discussion, I distinguish between three "levels" of understanding: the protein chemical level, the cellular level, and, for multicellular eukaryotes, the developmental level. I will examine the questions posed about MAPs and motors at each of these three levels in turn, and I will describe aspects of each that can be addressed advantageously with genetic and molecular biological methods. In this discussion, I concentrate on the generation and analysis of mutant forms of these already defined proteins. It should be noted, however, that other genetic approaches may identify previously unidentified MAPs and motors, as well as provide other important information. For example, analysis of mutations directly affecting cell division, mutants resistant to drugs that disturb microtubules, and analysis of second-site suppressor mutations (discussed below) have been and will continue to be informative (e.g., Cabral et al., 1984; Morris et al., 1984; Thomas et al., 1984; Smith et al., 1985). My emphasis here is on genetic and molecular approaches that will be useful both for already defined proteins and for those that are yet to be found.

THE PROTEIN CHEMICAL LEVEL

Understanding a MAP or motor at the protein chemical level is important in evaluating and constraining models of function and in allowing genetics and directed mutagenesis to be conducted and interpreted. For example, information about the primary, secondary, and tertiary structure of the protein is extremely valuable for understanding where domains are located, how they might interact, and whether different protein species are formed by alternative RNA processing. It is also important to determine which residues contribute to various aspects of in vitro and in vivo functions, e.g., microtubule or nucleotide binding. Finally, it is useful to know how a protein's function is regulated, with what other proteins it interacts, and what residues are involved in the interactions. These questions can all be addressed with molecular and genetic methods.

Basic aspects of protein structure can be determined by sequencing the gene encoding a protein. The sequence immediately reveals primary structure and provides the potential to inquire about secondary and tertiary structures (an example from the MAP field is given by Lee et al., 1988). Although secondary and tertiary structures are generally difficult to predict from sequence, the ever-expanding array of proteins that have been sequenced, and whose structures have been solved, are likely to be useful materials for comparison. For example, it might be possible to draw some general conclusions about the secondary or tertiary structure of a MAP or a motor if its sequence is found to be highly similar (homologous?) to a protein whose three-dimensional structure has been determined.

Isolated genes encoding a MAP or motor can also be used to identify and to analyze alternative forms of a protein produced from a single gene. For example, one gene could produce different proteins in different cells, at various times of the cell cycle, or could produce different proteins that are used in disparate structures within one cell. These possibilities can be explored by using isolated genes in Northern hybridization analysis of mRNA or in nuclease protection analysis (Berk and Sharp, 1977) to determine whether different mRNAs are made from the same gene. If multiple mRNAs are found, sequence analysis can be used to determine whether amino acid sequences differ in the alternative forms, as has been found for tau protein (Lee et al., 1988). In favorable cases, antibodies could then be produced against regions specific for each form of the protein and then used to determine the distribution and expression of the various protein species.

In vitro mutagenesis of defined regions of a gene can provide considerable information about the functional domains of the encoded protein. For example, particular mutations can be introduced into a gene, and the resultant mutant proteins can be tested for properties such as microtubule binding and nucleotide response. In addition, for a motor protein, it is also conceivable to alter affinities for substrates or, potentially, the flexibility of domains thought to change conformation during mechanochemical steps and then to assay their ability to generate force. Similar strategies can be used to test which residues are involved in regulating the activity of a protein, e.g., if phosphorylation of a specific residue is thought to be important, that residue can be changed and the activity of the protein assayed.

To mutagenize specific functional residues, it is first necessary to identify which residues participate in which activities. The most rapid way to obtain this information is to generate alterations in various regions of the cloned gene and then to test the resulting protein in a simple and rapid in vitro assay system. Initially, it is most practical to generate insertion or deletion mutations in various regions, because the site of mutation can be mapped easily without sequencing; deletions can be generated with exonucleases or restriction enzymes, and insertions can be generated using oligonucleotides (e.g., Barany, 1985). The products of normal and mutant genes can be produced in three ways: by expression in *Escherichia coli* or in some other organism (e.g., baculovirus; Smith et al., 1983), by transcription and translation in vitro, or by expression in the organism from which the protein was originally isolated. The expressed protein can then be tested for the property of interest, e.g., microtubule binding. Examination of the behavior of deletion and insertion mutations will give a preliminary indication of the functional regions of the protein. However, it is essential to confirm these results with more difficult to produce single-site mutations (see, for example, Botstein and Shortle, 1985), because deletions and insertions of one part of a protein could have a deleterious effect on the folding or conformation of an adjacent region. Taken together, the results obtained with single-site mutations, insertions, and deletions will elucidate the relationship between the primary sequence and defined functional domains of a MAP or motor protein.

Finally, in the cases of MAPs and motors that interact with other proteins, identification of these proteins will be important for understanding the function of the interaction. Several strategies can be used to identify such interacting proteins. For example, there are genetic strategies such as allele-specific second-site suppression and second-site non-complementation, as well as biochemical strategies such as gel overlay analysis.

Allele-specific second-site suppression is a method in which mutations are identified that rescue or suppress the phenotype resulting from mutations in a gene already under study. In some cases, mutations in the new gene rescue the phenotype of the old mutation because the two genes encode interacting proteins. The first mutation abolishes the interaction, and the second mutation restores it by virtue of a compensating change. For example, mutations in one bacteriophage P2 capsid protein can compensate for changes in another (Jarvik and Botstein, 1975). In other cases, the new mutations bypass the requirement for the first gene product, e.g., *sup1* and *sup4* in *Chlamydomonas* (Huang et al., 1982). Examples of the use of this strategy in the microtubule system are given by Cabral et al. (1984), Morris et al. (1984), and Thomas et al. (1984) in which second-site suppressors of tubulin mutations were used to identify other tubulin genes and possibly genes encoding accessory proteins.

Second-site non-complementation (Fuller, 1986) is a relatively new method that may allow identification of genes encoding proteins that interact with another, already identified protein. The basis of this method springs from the observation that some mutations in distinct genes, encoding interacting polypeptides, fail to complement genetically. In theory, this property may turn out to be general, and will provide an additional method suitable for identification of genes encoding polypeptides that interact with MAPs or motors.

Other strategies for identifying interacting proteins are biochemical or molecular in nature and include the identification of interacting proteins with gel overlay assays or affinity columns (e.g., Otto, 1986). In either case, rare proteins or fragments of proteins that would otherwise be difficult to prepare can readily be used as probes if a clone that can be expressed in *E. coli* is available. Once interacting proteins are identified, deletion and point mutagenesis can be used to identify residues involved in the interaction.

In summary, analysis of a MAP or motor at the protein chemical level by analyzing its gene can give us much useful information about its structure and function. In particular, specific functional domains and residues can be identified, analyzed, and manipulated. Ultimately, one hopes that at least in some cases this type of molecular information will be combined with three-dimensional structures obtained by using X-ray crystallography. The resulting view of a protein not only will allow an understanding of its behavior but also will be essential for evaluating its function in cellular processes.

The Cellular Level

There are several aspects of MAP or motor function that are important to understand at the cellular level. First and foremost, it is important to know the in vivo role of the protein, i.e., in what cellular processes does the protein participate, and what functions does it carry out? At a deeper level, it is essential to understand whether all of the cellular processes in which a protein functions require all of its potential interactions. For example, complete loss of a MAP could affect all cellular microtubules and all filament systems and organelles with which it interacts. Alternatively, alterations in only one binding domain might affect placement of one type of organelle and have no effect on other filament systems or on general aspects of microtubule organization. Finally, it is imperative to consider the important question of whether a protein is essential for cellular viability or is involved only in developmental events (see below) and hence would result in organismal but not cell lethality when missing.

The most straightforward way of assessing the cellular functions of a protein is to remove the protein from the cell, either by mutation or by anti-sense inhibition of expression (Izant and Weintraub, 1985; Melton, 1985). Examination of the resulting cellular phenotype then allows determination of the processes for which a protein is required, and whether the protein is essential for cellular viability. For initial evaluation of gene product function by using mutants, it is important to know whether a mutation is "null" (no remaining function) or whether it is one in which function is reduced or altered. Similarly, for anti-sense inhibition, the level to which expression of a gene product has been reduced must be determined. Once a baseline phenotype for complete loss of function is established, it becomes appropriate to analyze mutations that alter activity less drastically. For example, mutations that interfere only with regulation of a protein or that interfere with one specified interprotein interaction may be informative. These ends can be accomplished by recovery and analysis of mutants generated in vivo, or preferably in defined residues in vitro, followed by reintroduction of mutant DNA into a genetic background in which no functional copies of the gene are present. Study of these mutant organisms then reveals how different regions of the protein are involved in executing its function, which interactions are required for function in which cellular processes, and how the residues required for in vitro functions contribute to in vivo processes.

In the specific cases of MAPs and motors, these types of analyses will allow many questions to be addressed. For example, in the case of a MAP, the question of whether the protein is involved in regulation of assembly or interaction can be addressed by removing the protein and observing whether defects in microtubule assembly or organization result. Similarly, for a protein thought to function as a cross bridge, it is possible to alter independently the region thought to interact with the microtubule or the region thought to interact with another structure or filament system. Evaluation of the resulting phenotypes will allow assessment of whether the presumed cross bridge also has a role in the regulation of assembly and of what function the cross bridge plays in cellular processes and microtubule organization. In the case of a motor protein, regions essential to force generation can be mutated, and the roles that movement plays in various cellular processes can be examined.

Of particular value in investigations of cellular function is a system wherein gene replacement can be accomplished so that one can look at the consequences of using an altered protein without the complication of normal protein being present. In fungi, recombinational replacement of a wild-type gene by its mutant counterpart is possible. In multicellular eukaryotes, such as *Drosophila melanogaster,* a more complex methodology is needed because recombinational replacement is not yet possible. In *D. melanogaster,* a mutant version of a gene is introduced into a wild-type genome using P-element transformation (Spradling and Rubin, 1982; Rubin and Spradling, 1982). Following an appropriate genetic crossing scheme, this mutant gene can be introduced into an animal that is homozygous for a null mutation (null mutations are usually maintained as heterozygotes with a wild-type version of the same gene), thus allowing examination of the effects resulting from the engineered mutant protein in an animal that carries no normal gene product.

Finally, it may ultimately be possible to execute a "pseudo gene-replacement" experiment by transforming cell lines that express anti-sense RNA under inducible control, with mutant genes refractory to anti-sense inhibition. For example, if the normal 5' untranslated region of a gene is used as the target sequence for anti-sense inhibition, a mutant version whose 5' untranslated region was different, and hence insensitive to inhibition, could be introduced and expressed in a cell.

The various manipulations that I have discussed will allow the function of a protein in cellular processes to be determined. In addition, some understanding of the function of specific interactions of MAPs or motors with other proteins can be obtained by selectively inactivating defined regions of a MAP or motor. As information about a protein's cellular role emerges, the contribution of its function to development and morphogenesis can begin to be determined.

The Developmental Level

There are several aspects of a protein's function that are important to elucidate at a developmental level. For example, it is essential to understand the contribution of a defined protein, and the cellular subsystem of which it is a constituent, to specific cytomorphogenetic events. This type of understanding can be obtained by functionally dissecting a protein's developmental role in a manner similar to its dissection biochemically or cellularly, i.e., by generating and studying mutants. As with analysis of cellular or biochemical functions, it may also be possible to alter different forms of a protein selectively (e.g., those resulting from differentially spliced mRNAs) so that contributions of a specific form to specific tissues or structures can be evaluated.

These types of investigation are likely to illuminate the functions of proteins that are not essential for cellular viability by virtue of either specialized function or functional redundancy, but are necessary for the development and differentiation of the adult organism. For example, intermediate filaments and spectrin seem to play no role in the economy of a cultured cell, yet these proteins must have some important function in view of their evolutionary conservation and ubiquity. Plausible functions for these proteins include roles in development and other processes unique to multicellular systems (Mangeat and Burridge, 1984; Klymkowsky, 1981). Hence, mutations in such functions are likely to be viable in most cells and tissues during development, but lethal at crucial points during development of an organism. As a result, loss of function of such a protein will probably be non-lethal in cell culture when anti-sense inhibition is used or when homozygous cells are generated in a heterozygous mutant organism via mitotic recombination. An example from among MAPs and motors would be a protein needed specifically for the elaboration of the highly organized axonal microtubule arrays. In this case, mutants would lead to disturbances in development of the nervous system, but in no other cells.

Functions essential for development but not cell viability can be profitably studied with the use of temperature-sensitive mutations in which functions at various stages of development can be probed by shifting temperatures. Alternatively, mitotic recombination can be used in *D. melanogaster* (Becker, 1976) in which case specific tissues and structures are mutant and are examined in the context of a wild-type background (Fig. 15–1). Finally, it may be possible to inhibit gene expression inducibly with anti-sense RNA in cell-lines that undergo morphogenesis in vitro.

One concern about studying most of the mutant changes I have discussed is that they should be lethal and, hence, will lead to death of an organism such as *D. melanogaster* (or other multicellular eukaryotes, e.g., *Caenorhabditis elegans*) during development. However, since higher eukaryotes such as *D. melanogaster* are diploid, stocks of lethal mutations are maintained heterozygous with a wild-type copy. Homozygous mutation-bearing animals can be generated by appropriate crosses and can be recognized with the aid of morphological marker mutations. In addition, because the development of *D. melanogaster* (or *C. elegans*) is so well understood and occurs in isolation away from the confines of the maternal organism, the time and nature of lethality can be used to infer function. In particular, temperature shifts of temperature-sensitive mutations, or generation of homozygous mutant cells in a heterozygous background via mitotic recombination, allow a gene product to be selectively removed at various times and in various defined cells during development. In addition, even gene products that have essential functions early in development can be studied later in development because of the likely maternal contributions of most cytoskeletal proteins to early development. Because of these maternal contributions, lethal MAP or motor mutants are likely to survive until a point in development at which maternal product is exhausted and there is a critical requirement for the gene product. While such phenomena might lead

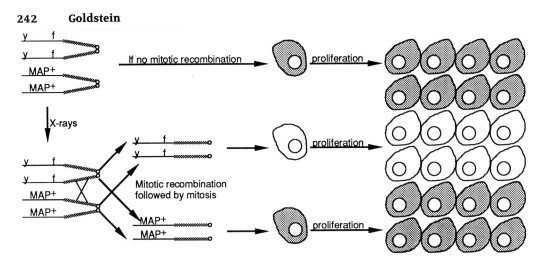

Fig. 15–1. Diagram of how mitotic recombination can be used to generate a subset of cells completely lacking MAP expression. An organism that is homozygous for a lethal mutant that disrupts MAP expression but survives by virtue of a wild-type (duplicate) copy of a transformed MAP gene on the X chromosome is used as the starting genotype in the upper left. y, Mutation that causes yellow body color; f, mutation that causes forked bristles; MAP$^+$, wild-type, duplicate copy of MAP gene. For clarity, only the X chromosomes are shown; the lethal MAP mutant resides elsewhere in the genome. This organism also has the homolog of the chromosome carrying the normal copy of the MAP gene marked with mutants that affect the color and bristle morphology on the adult body. In the absence of any experimental intervention, all cells in this organism will have normal body color and normal bristle morphology and will express normal MAP protein. Cells with these properties are shaded. If the organism is treated with X-rays during its development, a fraction of its cells will undergo the event diagrammed at the bottom, where a mitotic recombination event occurs. Following the next mitosis, cells with the diagrammed constitution can result. The lower mitotic product of this event will give rise to cells that have normal body color, normal bristle morphology, and normal MAP protein. These cells are indistinguishable from descendants of cells in which no mitotic recombination event has occurred. The upper daughter cell, however, will give rise to descendant adult cells that have mutant body color (yellow) and mutant bristle morphology (forked) and lack MAP protein (unshaded cells). If the MAP is not essential for proliferation, then the group of cells diagrammed at the right will result. In this group of cells, most are normal, but those that lack MAP protein will have distinguishable color and bristle morphology and can be examined for the effects of lacking this protein in different regions of the animal.

to an inability to study early events in mutants, they need not. In the case of *D. melanogaster,* early events such as gastrulation and cellularization can be explored with germ-line mitotic recombination to generate homozygous mutant germ cells in an otherwise heterozygous female (e.g., Jimenez and Campos-Ortega, 1982). Early embryos that result from such germ cells will thus completely lack maternal wild-type product and can be analyzed for phenotype.

Thus, by using a combination of genetic analysis and molecular analysis, a protein's role in developmental events such as tissue morphogenesis and embryonic rearrange-

ments can be established. In particular, analysis using mitotic recombination and temperature-sensitive mutations will allow events in specified tissues and cell types to be studied. These investigations, coupled with the use of site-directed mutants, will enable us to reveal with great precision the role of a MAP or motor in various developmental events.

SUMMARY AND PERSPECTIVE

The preceding discussion has described analyses of MAPs and motors at the protein chemical, cellular, and developmental levels.

While these levels of understanding were treated as distinct, they are in fact highly interrelated. For example, an understanding of a protein's structure provides useful information for probing the protein's cellular and developmental roles. Similarly, observation of unanticipated defects in cellular or developmental events can give clues as to the types of interaction or regulation to look for in a protein's structure. Hence, an interdisciplinary approach, weighted toward genetic and molecular analysis in a suitably manipulable system, can provide profound understanding of the structure and function, at various levels, of a MAP or a motor. In the next section, I discuss specific examples that have begun to achieve these goals for one MAP and one motor in *D. melanogaster.*

EXAMPLES FROM *D. MELANOGASTER*

My laboratory has been working to elucidate the in vivo functions of MAPs and motors using genetic and molecular biological investigations of *D. melanogaster.* We conduct our investigations in this organism because we can address questions about MAPs and motors at all three levels of understanding, i.e., the protein chemical, the cellular, and the developmental levels. The features of the biology of this organism that allow these issues to be studied include the availability of well studied cellular and developmental systems from this organism. For example, established and defined cell culture lines are available, as is an advanced understanding of its development, including its neural development, and numerous defined cellular and tissue shape changes. In addition, there are excellent models of cellular systems in the intact organism, e.g., the syncitial and cellular blastoderm, as well as exceptional classical and molecular genetics. These features, when added to the small genome size and the seemingly complete conservation and availability of cytoskeletal proteins found in vertebrate systems (e.g. Tobin et al., 1980; Rozek and Davidson, 1983; Bernstein et al., 1983; Falkenthal et al., 1984; Raff, 1984; Kiehart and Feghali, 1986;

Dubreuil et al., 1987; Byers et al., 1987), have convinced us and others that studies of *D. melanogaster* will be an important element in solving the in vivo functions of various cytoskeletal proteins.

Work from various laboratories has demonstrated that tubulin, tubulin genes, and microtubule systems very similar to those of vertebrate systems exist in *D. melanogaster* (Raff, 1984; Karr and Alberts, 1986). Recent analyses have demonstrated that *D. melanogaster* also probably has MAPs, kinesin, axonemal dynein, and cytoplasmic dynein with properties similar to those in vertebrates (Goldstein et al., 1982, 1986; Porter et al., 1987a; Saxton et al., 1988). For example, recent work in cultured cells and in embryos from this organism has identified two different molecules with properties very similar to members of the MAP 4 group and kinesin, respectively (Goldstein et al., 1986; Saxton 1988). In addition, a variety of other uncharacterized and heterogeneous putative MAPs have been observed in these preparations. In the discussion below, I focus on work on the 205 K MAP and kinesin, since these molecules have been studied most intensively.

The molecule from *D. melanogaster* that is similar to vertebrate MAP 4 has a mobility on gels corresponding to M_r 205,000. It shares with MAP 4 the properties of thermostability, binding to microtubules, size, complexity (as demonstrated by the presence of several similar-sized cross-reacting species), and intracellular distribution on spindle and cytoplasmic microtubules (as demonstrated by staining with specific antibodies). In addition, high levels of the *Drosophila* protein have been identified in various cell types, including neural tissue. As described earlier, this molecule may be a member of a group (family) of related molecules, including the HeLa 210 K MAP, the sea urchin 205 K MAP, the X MAP from *Xenopus,* and the diatom 205 K protein (Olmsted, 1986; Gard and Kirschner, 1987; Wordeman and Cande, 1987). Interestingly, two different antibodies raised against the *D. melanogaster* 205 K MAP cross react with a

250 K species found only in cell homogenates. This cross reactivity behavior is very similar to the behavior of antibodies directed against the HeLa 210 K MAP and MAP 4. As yet, no cross reactivity of *D. melanogaster* and vertebrate materials has been observed, although four new antisera recently generated have not yet been tested (M. Gorman and L.S.B. Goldstein, unpublished data). In the near future, sequence data and/or antibodies directed against specified functional regions (e.g., the microtubule-binding domain) will reveal which molecules in this collection, if any, are truly related.

Kinesin from *D. melanogaster* has properties very similar to that of other kinesins. It generates microtubule-dependent movement with the same polarity as do other kinesins, binds to microtubules in the presence of AMP-PNP, releases in ATP, has a microtubule-stimulated ATPase activity, and cross reacts with kinesin antibodies generated in squid and sea urchin (Saxton 1988). *Drosophila* kinesin also behaves as a protein complex when isolated, a behavior it shares with other kinesins. *Drosophila* kinesin appears to have a major or heavy chain component with a subunit M_r of 115,000–120,000, which is intermediate between squid and sea urchin kinesin, and putative light chains in the M_r 60,000–80,000 range. Intracellular localization studies with specific antibodies are still preliminary, but the fibrous staining of spindles seen in sea urchin has not been observed in *Drosophila* (W.M. Saxton and E.C. Raff, personal communication). Instead, in preliminary studies, staining of spindle poles during mitosis has been observed. Further experiments on kinesin distribution are underway.

To begin structural and functional dissection of the 205 K MAP and kinesin, we isolated and began analysis of their genes by using both molecular and in vivo genetic analysis. We started this work by using specific antibodies recognizing each protein to isolate their genes from λgt11 expression libraries. The 205 K MAP gene was isolated from a genomic expression library (Goldstein et al., 1986); kinesin was isolated from a head cDNA library (Yang et al., 1988). Verification of the identity of these genes is discussed elsewhere, but is based on structural, functional, and immunological criteria. Analysis of genomic organization has revealed that the 205 K MAP gene is a single copy gene that maps at polytene chromosome position 100F on chromosome 3 (Goldstein et al., 1986). The kinesin gene we have isolated is derived from polytene chromosome position 53A on chromosome 2. However, this gene also appears to have homology to other sequences in the genome (Yang et al., 1988). The identity and location of the sequences related to kinesin are unknown, although Southern hybridization experiments suggest that the related sequences are homologous to all regions of the kinesin gene we have isolated (H.B. MacDonald and L.S.B. Goldstein, unpublished results). Analysis of these related sequences is underway; the results will let us determine whether these are other kinesins, other motors, or genes related for reasons other than function.

Our analysis of the structure of both genes is still in its early stages. However, current data suggest that both genes appear to have a simple structure, each with one large intron. In the case of the 205 K MAP, we have observed alternate-sized transcripts during development (R.A. Laymon and L.S.B. Goldstein, unpublished results), although cultured cells have only a single (obvious) transcript. In addition, recent analysis of cDNA clones for the 205 K MAP has indicated the existence of at least two different messages that differ in the 3′ end and at least three types that vary internally within the protein-coding region (L.S.B. Goldstein, unpublished results). These findings raise the interesting possibility that there may exist tissue-specific or cell cycle-specific forms of the 205 K MAP. We may soon be able to test this possibility genetically or immunologically by raising antibodies against unique portions of the variant proteins.

With the availability of isolated genes for each protein and knowledge of the physical location of each gene, we have been able to initiate two different types of in vivo functional analysis. The first type is anti-sense RNA analysis in cultured cells. This work utilizes the isolated sequences expressed in "anti-sense" orientation from inducible promoter vectors that we have recently developed (Bunch et al., 1988). This work is in its early stages and will not be discussed further other than to point out that if successful, analysis of the phenotype of cell lines that conditionally lack 205 K MAP or kinesin will be a valuable adjunct in our studies of MAP and motor function. The second type of analysis is classical genetic analysis in the intact organism. In outline, this method begins with a genetic (physical) map position (Fig. 15–2). Then, by using classical genetic manipulations and mutagenesis, deletions are generated that are viable when they are heterozygous with a normal chromosome and that remove the gene of interest and a few adjacent genes. Following mutagenesis and appropriate crossing schemes, one can recover all recessive lethal, visible, and sterile mutations that are mutant when heterozygous with the deletion but not with a normal chromosome. After classification of mutants into complementation groups, the complementation group that identifies the MAP or kinesin gene is identified. The identification is preferably done by determining which gene has its wild-type function supplied by the cloned DNA so that a system for in vitro mutagenesis and transformation is immediately established. Alternative methods for determining which complementation group contains mutations in a cloned gene include denaturing gradient electrophoresis to map single base changes (Fischer and Lerman, 1983) and identification of rearrangement alleles that have alterations in coding sequences that are visible in Southern blots.

This type of analysis has been initiated for both the 205 K MAP and kinesin. In the case of kinesin, generation of deletions has recently begun (W.M. Saxton and E.C. Raff, personal communication). In the case of the 205 K MAP, the work has reached a more advanced stage (A.J. Pereira, E. Tanaka, and L.S.B. Goldstein, unpublished results). Thus far, we have been able to generate small deletions that remove the 205 K MAP gene and are viable as heterozygotes. Using one of these deletions, we recovered mutations that are lethal or subviable when homozygous and that are likely to be lesions in the 205 K MAP gene. Verification of the identity of these mutations is currently underway using transformation with a cloned 205 K MAP gene and denaturing gradient gel electrophoresis. Examination of the phenotypes caused by these mutations will allow us to address the in vivo functions of the 205 K MAP, as well as the relationship of its structure and binding domains to its function. In particular, we will be able to determine if the 205 K MAP plays a role in the generation of various microtubule systems in the organism, e.g., mitotic spindle and cytoplasmic systems, and whether or not all microtubule systems in the organism require this protein. Once P-element transformation and rescue of 205 K MAP mutants are established, we will have constituted a system in which defined changes in the protein and its functional domains can be studied by altering the gene and reintroducing it into organisms with a mutant genotype.

We have also begun using isolated 205 K MAP and kinesin DNA to investigate the structure of these proteins and to relate their sequences to defined functional regions. We have been using two approaches to accomplish these goals. First, we have been working to produce functional proteins, particularly kinesin, in *E. coli*. This will allow us to make defined changes in the molecule and to assess their effects on movement, thus allowing us to begin dissecting the contribution of various regions of the molecule to mechanochemistry. This is especially important for kinesin with which, if possible, we would like to be able to produce actively motile protein from a source that lacks potentially complicating protein cofactors. A second system we have been using to evaluate the structure of the 205 K MAP and kinesin is an in vitro synthesis system. In this

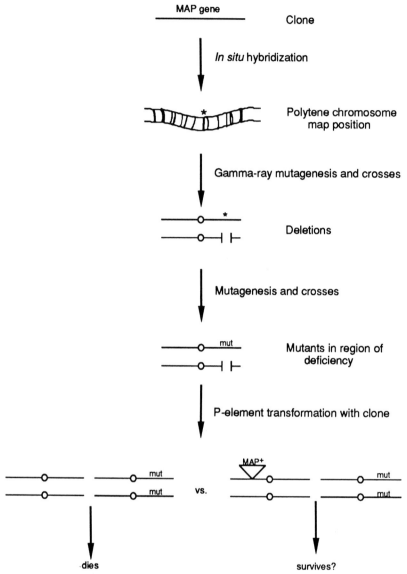

Fig. 15–2. Flow chart of how an isolated MAP (or motor) gene can be used to develop specific mutants in *D. melanogaster*. A clone that has been isolated can be used for in situ hybridization to polytene chromosomes. The resulting map position, indicated by the asterisk, can then be used to initiate classical genetic analysis of the gene. Following γ-ray mutagenesis and appropriate crossing schemes with marker mutants, deletions that remove the gene of interest can be recovered. These deletions would of course be lethal when homozygous, but can be maintained in organisms in which the deletion is heterozygous with a normal chromosome. The deletions that are recovered can then be used in a further series of mutagenesis and crossing schemes to recover mutations that map in the region defined by the boundaries of the deleted region. Thus, mutants that map in the region defined by the deletion are expressed when heterozygous with the deletion, but not when heterozygous with a normal chromosome. This defining characteristic can be used to recover mutants specifically in one region of the genome. In general, since the region defined by a deletion usually contains more than one gene, mutants in more than just the gene of interest are recovered. Therefore, mutants that alter the initial MAP or motor gene can be identified by virtue of their ability to be rescued by a transformed copy of the gene that was originally cloned, in this case a MAP.

system, RNA is synthesized in vitro from cloned DNA (situated adjacent to a promoter for which a specific RNA polymerase may be purchased). The resulting RNA is then translated in vitro in a reticulocyte translation system supplemented with ^{35}S-methionine. The resulting protein is the only radiolabeled protein present, although there are also non-radioactive proteins present in the reticulocyte lysate (Fig. 15–3). The radiolabeled protein can then be tested for relevant in vitro activities such as microtubule binding and its modulation by nucleotide. Using this system we have shown that 205 K MAP synthesized in vitro from cloned DNA can bind to microtubules. This result suggests that deletion analysis of the cloned gene (I. Irminger-Finger and L.S.B. Goldstein, unpublished results) will allow us to map the microtubule-binding region.

Using the in vitro synthesis system, we have preliminarily identified the nucleotide and microtubule-binding regions of kinesin. We first showed that kinesin synthesized in vitro binds to microtubules in the presence of AMP-PNP, but not ATP (Yang et al., 1988; see also Fig. 15–3). This result suggests that the single major polypeptide component of kinesin possesses both the microtubule-binding domain and the nucleotide-binding domain, although it is formally possible that small amounts of essential polypeptide cofactors, such as light chains, are present in the reticulocyte lysate. In the case of kinesin, we have gone on to generate deletions that remove varying extents of the molecule at either the amino or carboxy end. These deletions have all been tested for nucleotide-modulated microtubule binding, with the results shown in Figure 15–4 (J. Yang and L.S.B. Goldstein, unpublished results). As can be seen, both the microtubule-binding activity and the nucleotide response activity map in the amino end of the molecule. Further work on mutations that are not as potentially catastrophic for protein-folding as are deletions is necessary to confirm these results. Sequence analysis of kinesin in the region suggested to be responsible for response to nucleotide reveals a short sequence that is very similar to the nucleotide-binding region (Walker et al., 1982; Fry et al., 1986) of other well-known nucleotide-binding proteins such as recA, myosin, and adenylate kinase (Fig. 15–5; J. Yang, R.A. Laymon, and L.S.B. Goldstein, unpublished results). We will soon be testing the importance of this specific region by in vitro mutagenesis with oligonucleotides.

It is interesting that a fragment of kinesin that is only one-half the length of the intact protein has normal activity. This result suggests that the carboxy end may have some other function, perhaps unrelated to force generation. An interesting test of this idea will be to examine the truncated molecule for motility activity, if the *E. coli* motility system proves to be successful, and to examine the carboxy end carefully in overlay experiments for binding activity to other proteins.

Thus, these experiments on deleted proteins have already told us much about the organization of the kinesin molecule, have raised several interesting and testable questions about its functional regions, and should soon provide additional information on the structure of the 205 K MAP. It is hoped that comparison of the sequences of these molecules with each other, and with other MAPs, in the microtubule-binding regions will reveal consensus features of the structure of this functionally important domain. The final link will come from phenotypic analysis of organisms or cells that lack or have altered 205 K MAP and kinesin. Integration of these various types of information will generate an understanding not only of the cellular and developmental functions of these proteins but also the relation of their structure to their functions.

WHAT COMES NEXT?

There are two technical innovations currently being developed that I think may contribute to our understanding of MAP and motor function in the next several years. The first relies on inducible overexpression of a normal protein or mutant derivatives, e.g., a

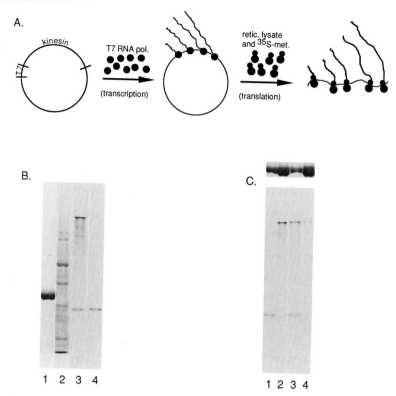

Fig. 15–3. In vitro transcription and translation of a cloned kinesin gene can be used to study the properties of the protein encoded by the clone. **A:** A cloned kinesin gene is placed into a plasmid vector adjacent to a promoter that is specifically used by T7 RNA polymerase. Following transcription with this RNA polymerase, the resulting RNA can be used in in vitro translation in a rabbit reticulocyte lysate. The resulting protein is labeled with ^{35}S-methionine. **B:** An example of the type of data that result following electrophoresis on an SDS-polyacrylamide gel. **Lane 1:** Coomassie blue-stained preparation of tubulin used in the binding experiment shown in C. **Lane 2:** Coomassie blue-stained sample of rabbit reticulocyte lysate showing the numerous unlabeled proteins that are present in the lysate and therefore in all experiments using in vitro translated protein. **Lane 3:** Autoradiograph of results obtained by translating in vitro transcribed kinesin RNA. Note the intense band near the top of the gel, which is newly synthesized, radiolabeled kinesin. **Lane 4:** Autoradiograph of results obtained when no RNA is added to the reticulocyte lysate. No band corresponding to kinesin is seen, and in general no proteins are labeled, with the exception of a single low-M_r species near the bottom of the gel. **C:** An experiment examining the ability of in vitro translated kinesin to bind microtubules. **Top:** Coomassie blue-stained image of the fate of the tubulin in the experiment. **Bottom:** Autoradiograph that follows the fate of the radiolabeled kinesin. **Lanes 1, 2:** Supernatant (lane 1) and pellet (lane 2) fractions obtained when radiolabeled kinesin, microtubules, and AMP-PNP are mixed and subjected to differential centrifugation; most of the kinesin sediments with the microtubules, while a small amount remains in the supernatant. **Lanes 3, 4:** Supernatant (lane 3) and pellet (lane 4) obtained when a mixture of microtubules, ATP, and kinesin is subjected to differential centrifugation; most kinesin fails to bind microtubules under these conditions and hence remains in the supernatant fraction.

protein with only one of its binding sites still functional. This approach has been most recently, and eloquently, articulated by Herskowitz (1987) and used to advantage by Albers and Fuchs (1987) in their studies of keratin. For example, these methods can be used to test, in vivo, the hypothesis that a specific MAP participates in the regulation of microtubule assembly by conditionally overexpressing the protein and to assess the

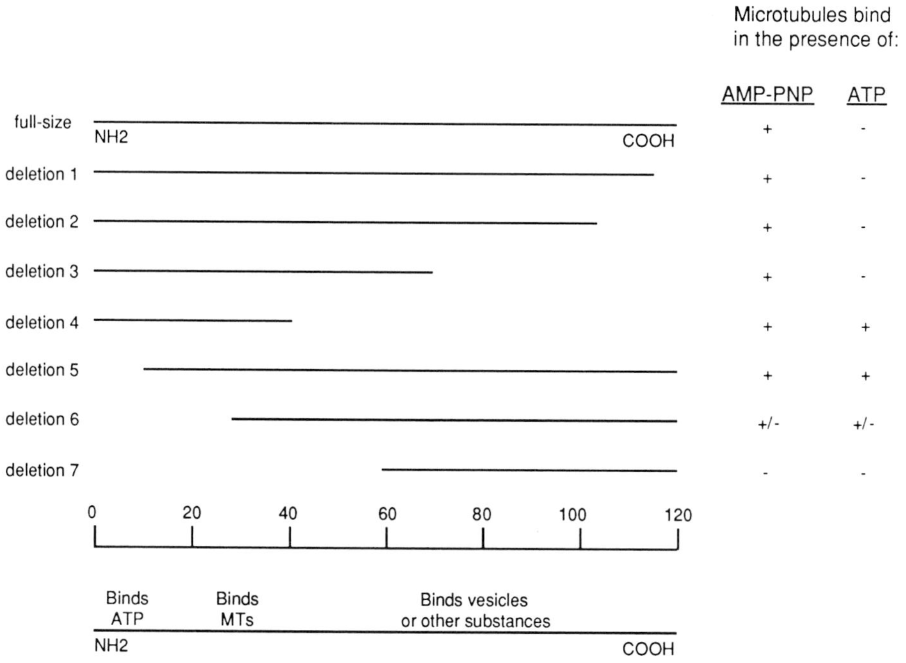

Microtubules bind
in the presence of:

Fig. 15–4. Summary of properties of in vitro expressed kinesin proteins that lack various regions because of deletions in their genes. The ability of these truncated kinesins to bind microtubules in the presence and absence of ATP or AMP-PNP is indicated at the right. $+$, Binds; $-$, does not bind; $+/-$, variable behavior. Interpretation of these data leads to the proposed model of the kinesin protein shown at the bottom. A region in the extreme amino terminus is needed for response to nucleotide (e.g., deletion 5), and also, as shown in Figure 15–5, has a consensus ATP-binding sequence. A region a bit further toward the carboxy terminus is needed for binding to microtubules; deletions that lack this region (e.g., deletion 7) or break near it (e.g., deletion 6) do not bind microtubules normally. Finally, a very large region of the molecule at the carboxy terminus is not needed for binding to microtubules or response to nucleotide, e.g., deletion 3. By elimination this region is proposed to be involved in mediating the interactions with other substances, e.g., vesicles, filaments, organelles, and so forth. The behavior of deletion 4 is problematic and may indicate that more than one region is needed for response to nucleotide or that interruption of a region between the endpoints of deletions 3 and 4 interferes with folding and therefore proper function of the amino-terminal domain.

```
Adenylate kinase  K I I F V V G G P G S G K G T Q C E K I V
RecA-protein        R I V E I Y G P E S S G K T T L T L Q V I
Nematode myosin   S M L I T - G E S G A G K T E N T K K V I
Kinesin             G T I F A Y G Q T S S G K T H T M E G V I
```

Fig. 15–5. Comparison of the kinesin sequence around residue 100 to the sequence of the region around the nucleotide-binding region of myosin, recA protein, and adenylate kinase (Walker et al., 1982). Residues shared between kinesin and any one of the other three proteins are underlined. As can be seen, several of the residues, in particular those that are invariant in many other ATPases and nucleotide-binding proteins (Walker et al., 1982) are shared with kinesin.

effects on microtubule polymerization in vivo. Alternatively, in the case of a cross-bridge protein, while overexpression might not lead to a readily interpretable phenotype, overexpression of a single functional domain might (Fig. 15–6). Thus, in the hypothetical case of a protein that links microtubules to another cellular element such as intermediate filaments, overexpression of either the microtubule-binding do-

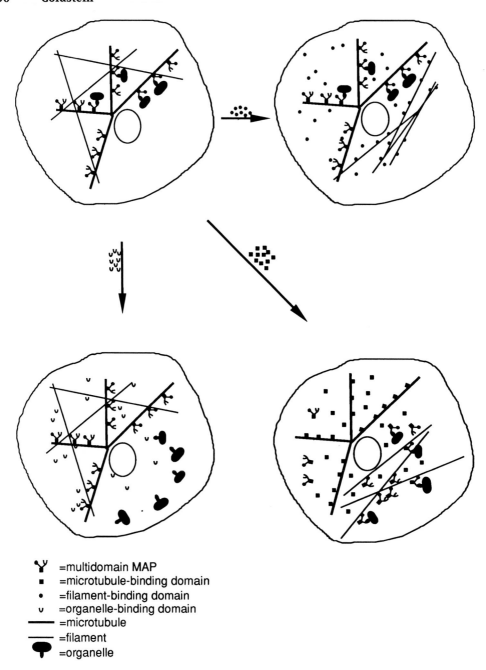

Fig. 15–6. Hypothetical example of experiments in which single domains of a multidomain, cross-bridge MAP are overexpressed in a cell. **Upper left:** A cell is diagrammed in which a multidomain MAP links microtubules to other cellular filaments and organelles. **Upper right:** The possible consequences of overproducing just the filament-binding domain. Selective disruption of the filaments relative to the microtubules might be observed without disturbances in the organization of the microtubules or organelles. **Lower left:** The potential consequences of overproducing the organelle-binding domain. The distribution of the organelles, but not the microtubules or filaments, is perturbed. **Lower right:** The possible consequences of overproducing the microtubule-binding domain. Both organelles and filaments would now be unable to interact with microtubules, and hence their distribution would be altered.

main or the intermediate filament-binding domain might lead to readily observable and equivalent disruptions of the organization of these two filament systems, in particular in relation to one another (Fig. 15–6). If the fragment that is overexpressed is fused to a protein that can be followed with specific antibodies, e.g., substance P or β-galactosidase, the fragment's behavior in the cell can also be followed, perhaps leading to inference of the existence of other, unknown binding domains (for an analogous localization experiment with MAP 2, see Bloom and Vallee, 1983).

A second set of approaches that are being developed for use with microtubule proteins includes new strategies for the identification of novel proteins. Two possibilities are or will soon be available. The first relies on screening by reduced stringency hybridization to a single, known gene to look for other similar genes. The second uses sequence information about several members of a class of proteins to define sequence motifs that are shared, e.g., microtubule-binding regions or nucleotide-binding regions. Screening of libraries, in particular with pairs of such distinct motifs, may allow recovery of new genes that have any pair of properties chosen for screening. This approach has recently been used to identify new protein kinase genes (Hanks, 1987). The advantage of such approaches is that while classical biochemistry is frequently limited by the abundance of proteins, by their stability, or by the availability of appropriate assays to identify new proteins, screening by homology to existing genes can bypass the requirements of stability and abundance. For example, since all genes will be present at roughly similar abundances in genomic libraries, rare gene products can be easily found when screening such libraries, especially in organisms with compact genomes. Such strategies, coupled with screening of expression libraries for clones that encode proteins that bind a protein such as tubulin, should ultimately lead to the identification of new types of proteins in these very interesting protein families. Application of genetic and molecular analysis of these new proteins can then be used to dissect their functions.

CONCLUSIONS

I have discussed several aspects of the physiology and function of MAPs and motors. In particular, I have focused on questions that can be addressed with the powerful tools of genetics and molecular biology. While I have given some examples of the types of experiments that are being done and are potentially valuable, other types of experiments will become possible as the technology continues its rapid development. As the number of clones, structural information, and mutants proliferate, an understanding of the in vivo functions of MAPs and motors should rapidly be attained.

ACKNOWLEDGMENTS

I thank C. Holm, T. Bunch, I. Irminger-Finger, J.R. McIntosh, A.J. Pereira, and R. Sloboda for critical reading of this manuscript; the members of my laboratory for the informative discussions and experiments that led to this Chapter; and J. Yang for help in preparing Figure 15–3. Particular thanks are due my collaborators W.M. Saxton and E.C. Raff for the communication of unpublished data. The work from my laboratory was supported by NIH grants GM35252 and GM29301.

Mechanism of Generation and Turnover of the Microtubule Network in Living Cells

Paul J. Sammak, Bohdan J. Soltys, and Gary G. Borisy

Laboratory of Molecular Biology, University of Wisconsin, Madison, Wisconsin 53706

Cell motility and polarity are fundamental aspects of such diverse multicellular processes as embryonic development, wound healing and organ regeneration, movement of cells of the lymph system, and the formation of metastases by malignantly transformed cells (Trinkaus, 1984). On the level of single cells, directed locomotion and polarized movements within the cell depend on the cytoskeleton and on microtubules in particular (Schliwa, 1986; Goldman et al., 1976). Directed locomotion depends on microtubules, since they play a role in establishing the leading lamellum and in maintaining a vectorial cell morphology (Vasiliev and Gelfand, 1976; Gotlieb et al., 1981). Polarized cytoplasmic organization is also microtubule dependent. Many intracellular vesicles are transported along microtubules (Allen et al., 1982; Vale et al., 1985c), and the cytoplasmic distribution and movement of membranous organelles including the golgi, lysosomes, the endoplasmic reticulum, and some endocytic and secretory vesicles require a functional microtubule network (Kupfer et al., 1982; Wehland and Willingham, 1983; Teresaki et al., 1986; Her-

man and Albertini, 1984; Tooze and Burke, 1987). Since a functional microtubule network is required for maintenance of cell polarity and the coordination of cell locomotion, understanding the mechanisms governing the generation of the microtubule network is important for elucidating cell morphogenesis.

The microtubule network is generated in three phases: formation, turnover, and stabilization; the final cellular distribution depends on controlling factors at each phase of construction. The first phase is the formation of nascent polymer from nucleation sites. The centrosome is the primary site of nucleating factors in the cell, but this is not the case in all cell types (Osborn and Weber, 1976; Gorbsky and Borisy, 1985; Bré et al., 1987). As the distribution of nucleating sites is changed, the distribution of microtubules changes as well (Karsenti et al., 1984; Tassin et al., 1985). The number of nucleating sites in the cell might help to determine the polymer mass and the number of microtubules (Kirschner and Mitchison, 1986). The second phase is the turnover or the redistribution of pre-existing microtubules. The microtubule network is not static, but in fact is in a dynamic equilibrium with subunits (Inoué and Sato, 1967). Once a network is formed it must be reformed as the cell changes morphology. In this review, we examine different possible mechanisms of microtubule turnover. Determining which mechanisms operate is important, as each model suggests different means of regulating cytoplasmic architecture. The third phase is the stabilization of functional microtubules. Microtubules could be stabilized by interaction with microtubule-associated proteins (Vallee et al., 1984a), and stable arrays are associated with post-translational modifications of tubulin (Webster et al. 1987a,b,c; Schulze et al., 1987). In addition, specific microtubule patterns might be produced by the selective stabilization of microtubules. Selected microtubules might be capped by binding their ends with specific sites at, say, the advancing edge of a cell or at kinetochores. The remaining, unbound microtubules would be disassembled in preference to the bound ones (Kirschner and Mitchison, 1986).

Of fundamental importance to all modes of controlling microtubule patterns is the mechanism of assembling tubulin subunits into microtubules. Three models have been proposed for subunit exchange with polymer in vivo: subunit intercalation, treadmilling, and dynamic instability. Subunits might intercalate into the wall of a pre-existing microtubule (model 1). This proposal originated from polarized light microscopic studies that showed that the form birefringence of mitotic spindles in vivo could be accounted for by first order molecular reactions, $A \rightleftharpoons B$ (for review, see Inoué, 1981b); that is, the rate of polymer (B) assembly dependend on the concentration of subunits (A) and not on the number of microtubules ends. This suggested that microtubule ends were unimportant to assembly and that subunits might incorporate along the length of the polymer.

However, in vitro polymerization of microtubules was determined to be second order, $A + B \rightleftharpoons B$ (Johnson and Borisy,

1977); that is, the rate of assembly depended on the number of microtubule ends as well as on the subunit concentration. This suggested that subunits assemble only by elongation onto microtubule ends. Subsequent in vitro studies demonstrated that there were two mechanisms of end-dependent subunit assembly. One mechanism was treadmilling (model 2) (Margolis and Wilson, 1978; Bergen and Borisy, 1980; Farrell et al., 1987) in which net subunit gain is at the plus end and loss at the minus end. The other was dynamic instability (model 3) (Mitchison and Kirschner, 1984a,b), in which subunits are gained during a growing phase and are lost from the same end during a subsequent shrinking phase. Microtubules could catastrophically disassemble during a shrinking phase (Kristofferson et al., 1986), that is, disassemble to completion, or they could persist through several rounds of growing and shrinking before disappearing (Horio and Hotani, 1986; Walker et al., 1987). Both treadmilling and dynamic instability have been theoretically modeled (Hill and Kirschner, 1982; Chen and Hill, 1985), and microtubule length changes could be accounted for by stochastic conversions between the growing and the shrinking phases.

Subunit intercalation is an equilibrium model; that is, the subunit–polymer balance is primarily determined by external thermodynamic conditions and is reversible at each step. Treadmilling and dynamic instability are steady-state models; that is, instead of the constraints of equilibrium thermodynamics, the final monomer–polymer balance depends on the irreversible input of energy and on a constant subunit flux into polymer. This subunit flux is accompanied by energy input, because polymer assembly is followed by hydrolysis of guanosine triphosphate (GTP) on tubulin. Generally, under physiological conditions, GTP–tubulin assembles and guanosine diphosphate (GDP)-tubulin disassembles (Carlier and Pantaloni, 1981; Carlier et al., 1987). With treadmilling, there is net addition of GTP-tubulin at one end and loss of GDP-tubulin at the other. With dynamic instability, microtubules in the grow-

UNIFORM
EXCHANGE

TREADMILLING

DYNAMIC
INSTABILITY

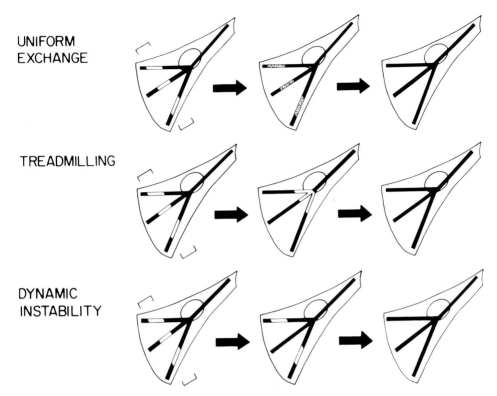

Fig. 16–1. Three models for the incorporation of subunits into microtubules in fibroblasts. With subunit intercalation, subunits uniformly exchange along the length of the microtubule. Marks placed on microtubules would gradually fade as new, unlabeled subunits incorporated into the marked domain. With treadmilling, subunits are added at the distal ends and are lost at the other ends near the cell center. Marks placed on microtubules would move centripetally and be lost at the cell center. With dynamic instability, subunits add at the distal ends during a growing phase and are lost at the same end during a shrinking phase. Marks placed on microtubules would be lost one by one as microtubules individually shrank and were replaced with new, unmarked microtubules. (Reproduced from Sammak et al., 1987, with permission of the publisher.)

ing phase might consist primarily of GTP-tubulin and those in the shrinking phase might consist of GDP-tubulin. The conversion of a microtubule end from growing to shrinking might depend on a balance between the rates of addition of new GTP-tubulin and hydrolysis of previously added subunits to GDP-tubulin, although this has not yet been conclusively demonstrated. In principle, if the rate of subunit addition is faster than hydrolysis, a cap of GTP-tubulin would accumulate at the ends of microtubules and promote stability. If hydrolysis is faster than the rate of GTP-tubulin addition, the ends would lose their GTP-tubulin cap

and the growing microtubule would convert to a shrinking one (Mitchison and Kirschner, 1984b). Although steady-state mechanisms are energy demanding, the benefit to the cell is the ability to modify the thermodynamics of assembly and control the quantity and distribution of polymer.

Each of these models suggest different means of turning over the microtubule network in living cells. This is illustrated in Figure 16–1 where microtubules are marked and replacement is monitored by observing loss of the mark as turnover occurs. Uniform subunit intercalation provides a rapid way of regenerating microtubules along their

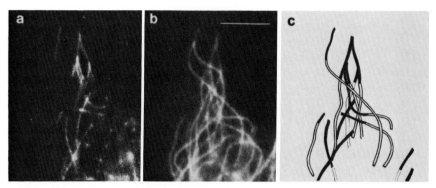

Fig. 16–2. Tubulin was derivatized with the chromophore fluorescein and microinjected into human fibroblasts. The cells were fixed 14 min after the injection and were immunostained with an antifluorescein antibody that improved sensitivity. Fluorescein-tubulin assembled into microtubule domains that were found at the ends of microtubules throughout the cell and at the centrosome. This supports the end-dependent assembly models treadmilling and dynamic instability and is contrary to the subunit intercalation model. Bar = 5 μm. (Reproduced from Soltys and Borisy, 1985, with permission of the publisher.)

length. This model predicts that the mark would simultaneously fade among all microtubules without movement of the mark. Treadmilling suggests that polymer is pulled centripetally, since subunits add at the plus ends (the cell periphery) and fall off at the minus ends (the cell center). This model suggests that marks would not fade and would move toward the cell center. Dynamic instability suggests that microtubules would individually shorten from the cell periphery toward the center. This model suggests that marks would not fade or move but would instead be replaced one by one as microtubules disassembled past the mark and subsequently regrew.

Several experiments have been performed in living cells to determine the pattern of subunit exchange with polymer. In some experiments, cells were microinjected with fluorescein-labeled tubulin and then marked by photobleaching the chromophore. The mark rapidly faded as fluorescence redistributed into mitotic spindles and interphase networks (Salmon et al., 1984; Saxton et al., 1984). These results supported subunit intercalation but did not conclusively exclude other models, since the behavior of individual microtubules was not seen; microtubules could have treadmilled asynchronously or

could have grown and shrunk one by one and redistributed fluorescence into the bleached zone. These experiments provided good temporal information about turnover of the network as a whole, but provided limited spatial information.

Complementary studies have been performed that provided good spatial resolution and detected individual microtubules, but provided limited temporal information. Labeled tubulin was microinjected into cells that were subsequently immunostained to detect newly assembled microtubules (Soltys and Borisy, 1985; Schulze and Kirschner, 1986; Webster et al., 1987a). The results of these experiments showed that microtubules were marked with labeled domains throughout the cell and that all domains were at the ends of microtubules or were at the centrosome (Fig. 16–2). This result was contrary to the predictions of subunit intercalation, which supposed uniform exchange of subunits along the length and seems especially consistent with dynamic instability.

Although pulse labeling of ends and centrosomes has been taken to support dynamic instability uniquely (Schulze and Kirschner, 1986; Mitchison and Kirschner, 1986), labeled ends and centrosomes are predicted by treadmilling as well. Figures 16–3 and

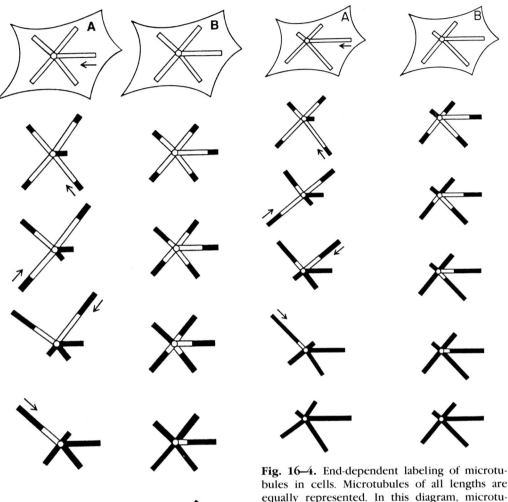

Fig. 16–3. End-dependent labeling of microtubules in cells. Microtubules are all assumed to be the same length. In this illustration, microtubules are pulse labeled, and the pattern of incorporation is shown for dynamic instability **(A)** and treadmilling **(B).** Unlabeled microtubules (open lines) elongate, and new growth includes the label (filled lines). With treadmilling, new growth occurs only at the distal ends and label is constrained to an annulus that widens centripetally over time. With dynamic instability, new growth occurs at the distal ends of microtubules and from the centrosome as unlabeled microtubules disassemble (arrows) back to the cell center and regrow. Over time, labeled domains are randomly distributed throughout the cell.

Fig. 16–4. End-dependent labeling of microtubules in cells. Microtubules of all lengths are equally represented. In this diagram, microtubules are pulse labeled and illustrated as in Figure 16–3. The uniform length distribution shown here is more representative of the actual distribution in cells and could be maintained at steady state, unlike the equal length distribution shown in Figure 16–3. With dynamic instability **(A),** labeled domains (arrows) are found throughout the cell. With treadmilling **(B),** new growth is at distal ends, as in Figure 16–3, but now labeled domains are also found throughout the cell. The pattern at any one time point is similar for both models of microtubule growth. The two models can only be distinguished if the pattern of label is known at two time points, and the changes between the two patterns can be determined.

16–4 illustrate this point. In Figure 16–3, a cell with microtubules all the same length is illustrated, and with this distribution the two models can be distinguished. Microtubules were pulse labeled, and the subsequent changes are shown. With treadmilling, microtubules would be labeled in an annular pattern that would widen centripetally as microtubules disassemble at the cell center. With dynamic instability, microtubules would be labeled in the periphery as they grew and at the center as they disassembled and were replaced by new growth.

However, the patterns that develop for the two models depend strongly on the distribution of microtubule lengths. Figure 16–4 shows two cells that have the microtubule length distribution that was produced by dynamic instability in Figure 16–3. This pattern, in which microtubules of different lengths are equally represented, is more representative of the actual distribution in interphase cells (Soltys and Borisy, 1985; Schulze and Kirschner, 1986; Webster et al., 1987). For this distribution, the pattern at any one time point does not distinguish the two models. Newly labeled domains are produced throughout the cell by both models, since microtubule ends are found throughout the cell. The models are distinguishable only if the change in the microtubule distribution is observed over time. The pulse-labeling studies did not distinguish between treadmilling and dynamic instability because the position of microtubule ends was known only at the time that cells were fixed and movement on a given microtubule could not be assayed. The position of the ends at the time of injection cannot be inferred from the length of the labeled domain unless it is assumed that microtubules were stationary during the time interval between injection and fixation. But this assumption begs the argument because it precludes one outcome, namely, that microtubules treadmill. Dynamic instability cannot be confirmed by pulse labeling unless treadmilling is known not to occur.

A test that would distinguish between these models requires an observation of temporal changes of labeled domains in a single cell at a spatial resolution sufficient to detect individual microtubules. This was the aim of experiments in which interphase cells were microinjected with fluorescein-labeled tubulin. Microtubules were marked by photobleaching and subsequently observed after fixation and immunostaining (Sammak et al., 1987). In this experiment the location of the marked microtubule domains was specified by the time of photobleaching, and the replacement of these marked domains was determined at a subsequent time point, the time of fixation. Figure 16–5 shows the pattern in a cell with partial replacement of marked microtubule domains. Figure 16–5a shows double exposure, phase contrast, and direct fluorescence at the time of photobleaching. Figure 16–5b,c shows, 16.5 min later, the antifluorescein and antitubulin immunofluorescence, respectively, at the time of fixation. Reverse contrast enlargements are shown in Figure 16–5d,e, and an interpretive diagram is shown in Figure 16–5f. New, fluorescent microtubules coexist with microtubules that retain the photobleached mark. In this cell and others, the marked microtubules did not treadmill toward the cell center and disappear, but instead were replaced one by one by unmarked fluorescent microtubules. These results contradict the predictions of both subunit intercalation and treadmilling and support dynamic instability.

Unexpectedly, the time course for replacement of microtubules was much faster at the periphery of the cell than it was toward the cell center (Sammak et al., 1987). Figure 16–6 shows that the degree of microtubule replacement at 10 min was a strong function of distance from the leading edge. If microtubules disassembled catastrophically, there would be no positional dependence of the time required for loss of marked domains. This suggested an alternative, that microtubules did not disassemble to completion, but instead had a significant chance of regrowing before shrinking completely. This tempered disassembly would predict that long microtubules with marked domains near the cell center would be relatively protected, since disassembly would proceed from the plus ends in toward the cell center, and regrowth would be possible

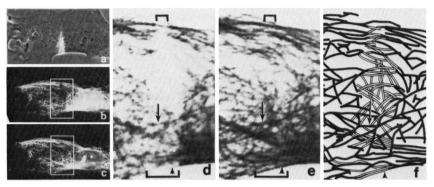

Fig. 16–5. Loss of marked domains over time caused by microtubule turnover. Human fibroblasts were microinjected with fluorescein-labeled tubulin, and cells were cooled and rewarmed to disassemble all microtubules and reassemble them from a pool of subunits with a constant molar fraction of labeled tubulin. Cells were allowed to return to steady state, and then microtubules were marked by photobleaching. Cells were subsequently fixed and immunostained to increase the signal from unbleached chromophore. This figure shows the pattern in a cell with incomplete replacement of marked microtubule domains. **a:** Double exposure, phase contrast, and direct fluorescence at the time of photobleaching. **b,c:** After 16.5 min, the antifluorescein and antitubulin immunofluorescence respectively, at the time of fixation. **d,e:** Reverse contrast enlargements. **f:** Interpretive diagram. New, fluorescent microtubules (arrows in d, e, and f) coexist with microtubules that retain the photo-bleached mark (arrowheads in d, e, and f). In this experiment the location of the marked microtubule domains was known at the time of photobleaching, and the replacement of these marked domains was determined at a subsequent time point, the time of fixation. In this cell, the marked microtubules do not treadmill toward the cell center and disappear, but instead are replaced one by one by unmarked fluorescent microtubules. These results contradict the predictions of subunit intercalation and treadmilling and support dynamic instability. Width of panel d is 8.5 μm. (Reproduced from Sammak et al., 1987, with permission of the publisher.)

before centrally located marks were lost. Another formal possibility is that shorter microtubules were more stable and longer ones more labile. Short, stable microtubules would mean it would take longer for all marks at the cell center to be lost. However, this suggestion still could not explain how catastrophic disassembly could remove all peripheral marks at 10 min while all central marks were retained. While shorter, more stable microtubules and tempered disassembly are both compatible with a gradient of turnover rates, catastrophic disassembly is not. Both suggestions could contribute to a gradient, and both are subject to direct testing.

Although a direct test of the role that stabilized microtubules play in producing the gradient has not yet been performed, there are stable subpopulations that have long turnover times. A stable subpopulation of microtubules could be produced by inter-action with a unique set of stabilizing microtubule-associated proteins (Vallee et al., 1984a) or by post-translational modifica-tions involving phosphate, tyrosine, or ace-tate (Gard and Kirschner, 1985; Wehland and Weber, 1987; Piperno et al., 1987). A subset of shorter, detyrosinated microtu-bules was centrally located in some cell types (Gundersen et al., 1984), and these microtubules were indeed more stable than others (Webster et al., 1987c) However, detyrosinated microtubules were absent from the fibroblast type used in our photo-bleaching experiments (Sammak et al., 1987; Webster et al., 1987a). These fibroblasts did contain short, long-lived, acetylated micro-tubule domains scattered throughout the cytoplasm (Webster et al., 1987b). However, many detyrosinated and acetylated microtu-bules were so long lived that they could not

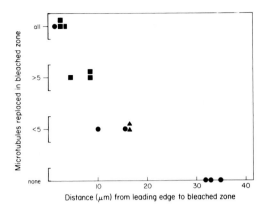

Fig. 16–6. The rate of replacement of microtubule domains depends on the distance from the cell periphery. Cells were microinjected with fluorescein-tubulin and photobleached as described in Figure 16–5. The degree of replacement of marked domains in the bleached zone by new, fluorescent domains was determined by categorizing each cell as containing only marked domains, mostly marked domains (no more than five fluorescent domains), few marked domains (more than five fluorescent domains), or no detectable marked domains. At 10 min after photobleaching, several cells were categorized for the degree of microtubule domain replacement as a function of the distance of the bleached zone from the leading edge of the cell. The symbols ●, ▲, and ■ refer to different experiments. By 10 min, all marked domains near the periphery had been replaced, and near the cell center no marked domains had been replaced. This suggests that as microtubules disassemble from their distal ends toward the cell center, they do not disassemble to completion; instead they disassemble only part way. This tempered disassembly could account for the radial gradient of turnover rates and the one by one nature of microtubule domain replacement. (Redrawn from selected data in Sammak et al., 1987.)

have participated in what photobleaching measured as the bulk turnover of the network (Webster et al., 1987b,c; Schulze et al., 1987). The role that tubulin modifications play in the formation and turnover of microtubules remains unknown, but it is clear that these modifications are associated with stable networks. Whether modifications are a cause or an effect of stability has yet to be determined. Nevertheless, differential stabi-

lization of microtubules is likely to play an important part in the regulation of dynamics, especially in long-lived networks such as those of neuronal cells (Lim et al., 1987).

A direct test of dynamic instability has been performed by observation of length changes of individual fluorescent microtubules in the lamellum of living fibroblasts. Xrhodamine–labeled tubulin was microinjected into cells, and microtubule movements were observed with a low-light video camera and digital image processor (Sammak and Borisy, 1988a). Microtubules underwent rounds of shortening and growing and moved laterally (Sammak and Borisy, 1988b). This is illustrated in Figure 16–7 in which fluorescent microtubules were marked by photobleaching and subsequent length changes were recorded. Microtubules were not broken by the irradiation as determined by antitubulin immunofluorescence after photobleaching (Sammak and Borisy, 1988a). The end of microtubule 1 shrank and then grew with respect to its marked domain, microtubule 2 grew, and microtubule 3 grew and then shrank. In each case, the distance between the microtubule end and the mark decreased or increased, and we concluded that the microtubule length excursions were due to addition and loss of subunits at the plus end. This showed directly that the site of assembly and disassembly is at the plus ends, and, therefore, dynamic instability is a property of microtubules in living cells.

This experiment also provided a direct test of treadmilling and subunit intercalation. If microtubules had asynchronously disassembled at the minus end and treadmilled one by one, or moved by a sliding mechanism (see Koonce et al., 1987), then the mark should have moved in parallel with the microtubule plus end. This was not observed. If subunits had intercalated into microtubule walls, the bleached marks should have faded as microtubules grew. This also was not observed. These observations showed that rapid microtubule length changes were due to plus end subunit addition and loss and that treadmilling and sub-

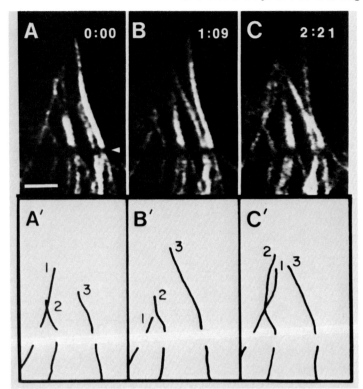

Fig. 16–7. Microtubules in living cells undergo rounds of growing and shortening by subunit addition and loss at the plus end. Cells were injected with X-rhodamine–tubulin, and video micrographs were taken with a low-light camera and a digital image processor. A reference mark (arrowhead in a) was produced across the microtubules by photobleaching the chromophore. Antitubulin immunofluorescence of cells bleached with the same energy showed microtubules were not broken by the bleaching. a–c: Aligned so that the bleach zone (and hence the microtubules) were in the reference frame. a′–c′: Made from tracings of panels a–c, and only microtubules with unambiguous ends are illustrated. The end of microtubule 1 shrank and then grew with respect to its bleached domain, microtubule 2 grew, and microtubule 3 grew and then shrank. Length changes were due to gain and loss of subunits distal to the bleached domain on each microtubule. Dynamic instability accounted for these observations, whereas subunit intercalation and treadmilling did not. Bar = 3 μm. (Reproduced from Sammak and Borisy, 1988a, with permission of the publisher.)

unit intercalation do not account for the turnover of microtubules in vivo.

The direct observations of microtubules also provided a direct test of the tempered nature of microtubule disassembly: Between 50 and 80% of the shortening excursions observed were subsequently followed by growing excursions, and, conversely, 20 to 50% were catastrophic (Sammak and Borisy, 1988a). We found that tempered instability accounted for the rapid turnover in the cell periphery, since the half-times for turnover as determined by direct observation agreed

with those determined by photobleaching near the leading edge. However, since the replacement of microtubules in the center of living cells has not yet been observed directly, the mechanism of turnover there awaits further analysis.

Direct observations of peripheral microtubules, combined with the photobleaching experiments, provided a picture of the turnover of microtubules in locomoting fibroblasts (Fig. 16–8). In Figure 16–8, microtubules initially present are represented as dashed lines, and new polymer is repre-

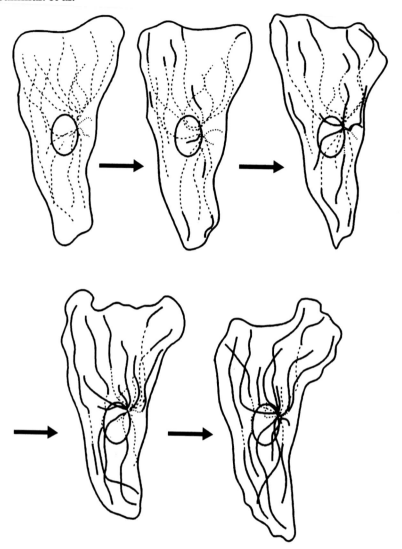

Fig. 16–8. Diagram of microtubule turnover in human fibroblasts. This figure illustrates the incorporation of newly labeled subunits (solid lines) into pre-existing microtubules (dashed lines). This diagram is a composite of information from the photobleaching experiments and from the direct observation of microtubule length excursions. The time interval between illustrations of the cell progressively increases to show nearly equal fractions of turnover per time interval; turnover is an exponential process. Labeled microtubules are formed by elongation from pre-existing ends and by shortening and regrowth of new polymer. Microtubule domains at the periphery of the cell are rapidly turned over by frequent, short-length excursions, and domains in the cell center are more slowly turned over by less frequent, long excursions.

sented as solid lines. The frequent, short excursions produce rapid turnover of the microtubule domains in the lamellum, whereas the less frequent, long excursions are responsible for the slower turnover of microtubule domains in the center of the cell.

Could the excursions in vivo simply be random thermal fluctuations and not an expression of dynamic instability? The average length excursion in the experiments in vivo was about 5 μm (Sammak and Borisy, 1988a), and this value is bounded by an in vitro measurement of 2.4 μm (Horio and Hotani, 1986) and a theoretical estimate of 20 μm (Mitchison and Kirschner, 1984b; Chen ahd Hill, 1985). Calculations show that these excursions were too fast to be thermally induced. Oosawa and Asakura (1975) have developed an expression for diffusive exchange of subunits into polymer. From this expression and a dissociation rate constant of 154 sec^{-1} (Karr et al., 1980), we calculate that the half-time for diffusive exchange of 5 μm (the average excursion) would be 25 days and not 0.5 min as observed.

How do the rates and duration of the excursions in vivo compare with the original formulation of dynamic instability? In the original formulation, dynamic instability was characterized by two phases: slow growth and fast shrinking with infrequent conversions between them (Mitchison and Kirschner, 1984b). In the shrinking phase, microtubules disassembled catastrophically. Similar to the original formulation, growth in vivo was slower than shrinking and microtubules spent more time growing than shrinking (Sammak and Borisy, 1988a). However, interconversion between the two phases was fairly common, occurring about one per minute per microtubule. In the shrinking phase, disassembly was tempered. In our formulation, microtubules infrequently disappear not because they infrequently shrink but because shrinking microtubules frequently reconvert to the growing phase.

Is there a GTP-tubulin cap on microtubules growing in vivo? This remains untested, but if the maximum rate of hydrolysis in vivo is similar to the in vitro value of 40 sec^{-1} or 2 μm/min (Carlier et al., 1987), then the average rate of growth of 3.5 μm/min and the average growing excursion of 5.3 μm in vivo (Sammak and Borisy, 1988a) mean that a substantial cap of GTP-tubulin exists on most microtubules in fibroblast lamellum.

What is the biological significance of tempered instability? One possible function is that it provides a mechanism for accelerating the pace of turnover in the cell periphery. An active locomoting cell is constantly changing morphology as the lamellum undergoes cycles of protrusion and withdrawal. Since microtubule ends regrow before shortening to the cell center, the peripheral microtubules could be efficiently rearranged without the added energy cost of disassembling the complete network. The effect of tempered disassembly is to produce a greater plasticity of the peripheral microtubules. This could explain how the network rearranges quickly as cells reorient their advancing lamella (Kupfer et al., 1982; Abercrombie, 1980).

What are the implications of dynamic instability for microtubule-dependent organelle translocation? Organelles would be expected to stop when the microtubule on which they were translocating disassembled. Tempered instability suggests that individual microtubules in the periphery of the cell are short-lived as they undergo rounds of growing and shrinking, while microtubules in the cell center are long-lived. Therefore, organelles in the cell center could move long distances before they ran out of microtubule track, whereas organelles in the periphery would be able to move only short distances before they fell off. This effect could produce two domains in the cell, a central domain where transport is common and a peripheral domain where transport is less efficient. Observations of organelle movement in fibroblasts support a two-domain structure within the cytoplasm (Bridgeman et al., 1986). Organelle transport in the central region of fibroblasts was observed to be continuous whereas transport in the lamellum was intermittent (on short tracks). The formation of two domains could be due in part to the density of the cytomatrix. The peripheral actin matrix could act like a molecular sieve and exclude movement of larger organelles (Luby-Phelps et al., 1987) or periodically break organelle–microtubule junctions (Bridgeman et al., 1986) Tempered instability and matrix sieving might both cause organelle transport to be different in the peripheral and central domains of the cytoplasm.

Is the tempered mode of dynamic instability a universal mechanism of microtubule turnover? The question can be evaluated only after observations of dynamics in additional cell types. To date, tempered microtubule excursions similar to the ones seen in fibroblasts have also been seen in a few cell types, including pig kidney epithelial cells, goldfish xanthophores, and goldfish scale keratinocytes (Sammak, Lim, Gorbsky, and Borisy, unpublished observations). Even if tempered dynamic instability is a fundamental pattern of microtubule formation and redistribution, it seems likely that this mechanism would be modulated to achieve different purposes. Turnover varies throughout the cell cycle and is fastest at mitosis (Saxton et al., 1984). Different cell types, such as neuronal cells, have notably slower turnover (Lim et al., 1987; Sammak et al., 1988c and submitted for publication). Determinations of the in vivo elongation rates and excursion lengths in different biological situations will provide a basis for evaluating the regulation of microtubule dynamics.

Microtubule dynamics could be altered by changing the various rate constants for subunit exchange with polymer; for example, the rates of growing and shrinking could be changed, the probability of conversion from growing to shrinking could be changed, or the probability of conversion from shrinking to growing could be changed. First, the rate constants for growth and shrinking could be altered. This could accelerate or reduce the rate of turnover without changing the fundamental patterns of rearrangement or could dramatically alter the balance between subunit and polymer mass in the cell at steady state. Second, rate constants for converting shrinking microtubules into growing ones could be altered. Increasing the probability of conversion from shrinking to growing would promote tempered disassembly,

which would produce longer, more stable microtubules. Decreasing the probability of conversions would promote catastrophic instability, which would produce shorter, unstable microtubules. A change from tempered to catastrophic disassembly might take place as interphase cells enter mitosis and long microtubules are replaced by short spindle microtubules. Third, rate constants for converting growing microtubules into shrinking ones could be altered. Increasing the probability of conversion of growing microtubules into shrinking ones would produce shorter microtubules and rapid turnover as found in mitotic cells. Decreasing the probability of conversions would produce longer microtubules with slower turnover, as found when cells exit mitosis and return to interphase or in stationary cells.

The conversion frequencies and the elongation rates provide a formal framework for the elucidation of effects that perturb microtubule dynamics. The conversion frequencies might be sensitive to the activity of microtubule-associated proteins, the concentration of GTP- and GDP-tubulin in the cell, and, possibly, the presence of post-translational modifications of tubulin. Dramatic changes in the distribution and stability of microtubules could be produced by subtle variations of the conversions between the shrinking and growing phases. It seems likely that these conversion rates are points of control of the formation and distribution of microtubules and that their regulation by the cell is important to the generation of specific biological form.

ACKNOWLEDGMENTS

We thank Leslie Compere, Steve Limbach, and Jeannene Krone for expert illustration; John Peloquin for preparation of X-rhodamine–tubulin; and Drs. Dan Webster and Soo Siang Lim for critically reading the manuscript. This work was supported by NIH grant GM25062.

Bibliography 3, Chapters 12-16

Aamodt, E., and J. Culotti (1986) Microtubules and microtubule-associated proteins from the nematode *Caenorhabditis elegans*: Periodic cross-links connect microtubules in vitro. J. Cell Biol. 103:23–31.

Abercrombie, M. (1980) The crawling movement of metazoan cells. Proc. R. Soc. Lond. [Biol.] 207:129–147.

Albers, K., and E. Fuchs (1987) The expression of mutant epidermal keratin complementary DNA transfected in simple epithelial and squamous cell carcinoma lines. J. Cell Biol. 105:791–806.

Allen, C., and G.G. Borisy (1974) Structural polarity and directional growth of microtubules of *Chlamydomonas* flagella. J. Mol. Biol. 90:381–402.

Allen, R.D., and N.S. Allen (1983) Video-enhanced microscopy with a computer frame memory. J. Microsc. 129:3–17.

Allen, R.D., N.S. Allen, and J.L. Travis (1981) Video-enhanced contrast, differential interference contrast (AVEC-DIC) microscopy: A new method capable of analyzing microtubule-related motility in the reticulopodial network of *Allogromia laticollaris*. Cell Motil. 1:291–302.

Allen, R.D., J. Metuzals, I. Tasaki, S.T. Brady, and S.P. Gilbert (1982) Fast axonal transport in squid giant axon. Science 218:1127–1129.

Allen, R.D., D.G. Weiss, J.H. Hayden, D.T. Brown, H. Fujiwake, and M. Simpson (1985) Gliding movement of and bidirectional transport along single native microtubules from squid axoplasm: Evidence for an active role of microtubules in cytoplasmic transport. J. Cell Biol. 100:1736–1752.

Amos, L.A. (1977) Arrangement of high molecular weight associated proteins on purified mammalian brain microtubules. J. Cell Biol. 72:642–654.

Auclair, W., and B.W. Siegel (1966) Cilia regeneration in the sea urchin embryo: Evidence for a pool of ciliary proteins. Science 154:913–915.

Banks, P., and R. Till (1975) A correlation between the effects of anti-mitotic drugs on microtubule assembly in vitro and the inhibition of axonal transport in noradrenergic neurones. J. Physiol. 252:283–294.

Barany, F. (1985) Single-stranded hexameric linkers a system for in-phase insertion mutagenesis and protein engineering. Gene 37:111–124.

Bear, R.S., F.O. Schmitt, and J.Z. Young (1937) Investigations on the protein constituents of nerve axoplasm. Proc. R. Soc. Lond. [Biol.] 123:520–529.

Becker, H.J. (1976) Mitotic Recombination. In M. Ashburner and E. Novitski (eds): The Genetics and Biology of *Drosophila*. Orlando, FL: Academic Press, pp. 1019–1087.

Beckerle, M.C., and K.R. Porter (1982) Inhibitors of dynein activity block intracellular transport in erythrophores. Nature 295:701–703.

Bell, C.W., E. Fronk, and I.R. Gibbons (1979) Polypeptide subunits of dynein 1 from sea urchin sperm flagella. J. Supramol. Struct. 11:311–317.

Bergen, L.G., and G.G. Borisy (1980) Head-to-tail polymerization of microtubules in vitro. Electron microscope analysis of seeded assembly. J. Cell Biol. 84:141–150.

Berk, A.J., and P.A. Sharp (1977) Sizing and mapping of early adenovirus mRNAs by gel electrophoresis of S1 endonuclease digested hybrids. Cell 12:721–732.

Bernstein, S.I., K. Mogami, J.J. Donady, and C.P. Emerson, Jr. (1983) *Drosophila* muscle myosin heavy chain is encoded by a single gene in a cluster of muscle mutations. Nature 302:393–397.

Binder, L.I., W.L. Dentler, and J.L. Rosenbaum (1975) Assembly of chick brain tubulin onto flagellar microtubules from *Chlamydomonas* and sea urchin sperm. Proc. Natl. Acad. Sci. USA 72:1122–1126.

Bloom, G.S., F.C. Luca, and R.B. Vallee (1984) Widespread cellular distribution of MAP 1A (microtubule-associated protein 1A) in the mitotic spindle and on interphase microtubules. J. Cell Biol. 98:331–340.

Bloom, G.S., F.C. Luca, and R.B. Vallee (1985) Microtubule-associated protein 1B: Identification of a major component of the neuronal cytoskeleton. Proc. Natl. Acad. Sci. USA 82:5404–5408.

Bloom, G.S., T.A. Schoenfeld, and R.B. Vallee (1984) Widespread distribution of the major polypeptide component of MAP 1 (microtubule-associated protein 1) in the nervous system. J. Cell Biol. 98:320–330.

Bloom, G.S., and R.B. Vallee (1983) Association of microtubule-associated protein 2 (MAP2) with microtubules and intermediate filaments in cultured brain cells. J. Cell Biol. 96:1523–1531.

Borisy, G.G. (1978) Polarity of microtubules of the mitotic spindle. J. Mol. Biol. 124:565–570.

Botstein, D., and D. Shortle (1985) Strategies and applications of in vitro mutagenesis. Science 229:1193–1201.

Brady, S.T. (1985) A novel brain ATPase with properties expected for the fast axonal transport motor. Nature 317:73–75.

Brady, S.T., and R.J. Lasek (1982) Axonal transport: A cell-biological method for studying proteins that associate with the cytoskeleton. Methods Cell Biol. 25:365–398.

Brady, S.T., R.J. Lasek, and R.D. Allen (1982) Fast axonal transport in extruded axoplasm from squid giant axon. Science 218:1129–1131.

Brady, S.T., R.J. Lasek, and R.D. Allen (1985) Video microscopy of fast axonal transport in extruded axoplasm: A new model for study of molecular mechanisms. Cell Motil. 5:81–101.

Bré, M.H., T.E. Kreis, and E. Karsenti (1987) Control of microtubule nucleation and stability in Madin-Darby canine kidney cells: The occurrence of noncentrosomal, stable detyrosinated microtubules. J. Cell Biol. 105:1283–1296.

Bridgeman, P.C., B. Kachar, and T.S. Reese (1986) The structure of cytoplasm in directly frozen cultured cells. II. Cytoplasmic domains associated with organelle movement. J. Cell Biol. 102:1510–1521.

Bunch, T.A., Y. Grinblat, and L.S.B. Goldstein (1988) Characterization and use of the *Drosophila* metallothionein promoter in cultured *Drosophila melanogaster* cells. Nucleic Acids Res. 16:1043–1061.

Burns, R., and T. Pollard (1974) A dynein-like protein from brain. FEBS Lett. 40:274–280.

Byers, T.J., R. Dubreuil, D. Branton, D.P. Kiehart, and L.S.B. Goldstein (1987) *Drosophila* spectrin II. Conserved features of the alpha-subunit are revealed by analysis of cDNA clones and fusion proteins. J. Cell Biol. 105:2103–2110.

Cabral, F., M. Schibler, R. Kuriyama, I. Abraham, C. Whitfield, C. McClurkin, S. Mackensen, and M.M. Gottesman (1984) Genetic analysis of microtubule function in CHO cells. In G.G. Borisy, D.W. Cleveland, and D.B. Murphy (eds): Molecular Biology of the Cytoskeleton. Cold Spring Harbor, New York: Cold Spring Harbor Laboratory, pp. 305–317.

Cande, W.Z. (1982) Inhibition of spindle elongation in permeabilized mitotic cells by erythro-9-[3-(2-hydroxynonyl)] adenine. Nature 295:700–701.

Carlier, M.F., D. Didry, and D. Pantaloni (1987) Microtubule elongation and guanosine 5'-triphosphate hydrolysis. Role of guanine nucleotides in microtubule dynamics. Biochemistry 26:4428–4437.

Carlier, M.F., T.L. Hill, and Y.D. Chen (1984) Interference of GTP hydrolysis in the mechanism of microtubule assembly: An experimental study. Proc. Natl. Acad. Sci. USA 81:771–775.

Carlier, M.F., and D. Pantaloni (1981) Kinetic analysis of guanosine 5'-triphosphate hydrolysis associated with tubulin polymerization. Biochemistry 20:1918–1924.

Chen, Y., and T.L. Hill (1985) Theoretical treatment of microtubules disappearing in solution. Proc. Natl. Acad. Sci. USA 82:4127–4131.

Cleveland, D.W. (1987) The multitubulin hypothesis revisited: What have we learned? J. Cell Biol. 104:381–383.

Cleveland, D.W., S.Y. Hwo, and M.W. Kirschner (1977) Purification of tau, a microtubule-associated protein that induces assembly of microtubules from purified tubulin. J. Mol. Biol. 116:207–225.

Cohn, S.A., A.L. Ingold, and J.M. Scholey (1987) Correlation between the ATPase and microtubule translocating activities of sea urchin egg kinesin. Nature 328:160–163.

Collins, C.A., and R.B. Vallee (1986a) Characterization of the sea urchin egg microtubule-activated ATPase. J. Cell Sci. (Suppl. 5) 197–204.

Collins, C.A., and R.B. Vallee (1986b) A microtubule-activated ATPase in sea urchin eggs distinct from cytoplasmic dynein and kinesin. Proc. Natl. Acad. Sci. USA 83:4799–4803.

Dabora, S.L., and M.P. Sheetz (1987) Microtubule dependent formation of a tubulovesicular network with characteristics of the endoplasmic reticulum from cultured cell extracts. J. Cell Biol. 105:89a.

Dahlstrom, A. (1971) Effects of vinblastine and colchicine on monoamine-containing neurons of the rat, with special regard to the axoplasmic transport of amine granules. Acta Neuropathol. Suppl. 5:226–237.

Dentler, W.L., S. Granett, and J.L. Rosenbaum (1975) Ultrastructural localization of the high molecular weight proteins associated with in vitro assembled brain microtubules. J. Cell Biol. 65:237–241.

Do, C.V., E.B. Sears, S.P. Gilbert, and R.D. Sloboda (1988) Vesikin, a vesicle-associated ATPase from squid axoplasm and optic lobe, has characteristics in common with vertebrate brain MAP 1 and MAP 2. Cell Motil. Cytoskel. 10:246–254.

Dubreuil, R., T.J. Byers, D. Branton, L.S.B. Goldstein, and D.P. Kiehart (1987) Drosophila spectrin I. Characterization of the purified protein. J. Cell Biol. 105:2095–2102.

Duerr, A., D. Pallas, and F. Solomon (1981) Molecular analysis of cytoplasmic microtubules in situ: Identification of both widespread and specific proteins. Cell 24:203–211.

Euteneuer, U., and J.R. McIntosh (1980) Polarity of mid-body and phragmoplast microtubules. J. Cell Biol. 87:509–515.

Euteneuer, U., and J.R. McIntosh (1981a) Structural polarity of kinetochore microtubules in PtK1 cells. J. Cell Biol. 89:338–345.

Euteneuer, U., and J.R. McIntosh (1981b) Polarity of some motility related microtubules. Proc. Natl. Acad. Sci. USA 78:372–376.

Falkenthal, S., V. Parker, W. Mattox, and N. Davidson (1984) Drosophila melanogaster has only one myosin alkali light-chain gene which encodes a protein with considerable amino acid sequence homology to chicken myosin alkali light chains. Mol. Cell Biol. 4:956–965.

Farrell, K.W., M.A. Jordan, H.P. Miller, and L. Wilson (1987) Phase dynamics at microtubule ends: The coexistence of microtubule length changes and treadmilling. J. Cell Biol. 104:1035–1046.

Fellous, A., J. Francon, A.M. Lennon, and J. Nunez (1977) Microtubule assembly in vitro. Eur. J. Biochem. 78:167–174.

Fischer, S., and L. Lerman (1983) DNA fragments differing by single base-pair substitutions are separated in denaturing gradient gels: Correspondence with melting theory. Proc. Natl. Acad. Sci. USA 80:1579–1583.

Forman, D.S., K.J. Brown, and M.E. Promersberger (1983) Selective inhibition of retrograde axonal transport by erythro-9-[3-(2-hydroxynonyl)]adenine. Brain Res. 272:194–197.

Fox, L.A., and W.S. Sale (1987) Direction of force generated by the inner row of dynein arms on flagellar microtubules. J. Cell Biol. 105:1781–1787.

Fry, D.C., S.A. Kuby, and A.S. Mildvan (1986) ATP-binding site of adenylate kinase: Mechanistic implications of its homology with ras-encoded p21, F1-ATPase, and other nucleotide-binding proteins. Proc. Natl. Acad. Sci. USA 83:907–911.

Fuller, M.T. (1986) Genetic analysis of spermatogenesis in Drosophila: The role of the testis-specific β-tubulin and interacting genes in cellular morphogenesis. In J.G. Gall (ed): Gametogenesis and the Early Embryo. New York: Alan R. Liss, Inc., pp. 19–42.

Fulton, C., and P. Simpson (1976) Selective synthesis and utilization of flagellar tubulin. The multitubulin hypothesis. In R. Goldman, T. Pollard, and J.L. Rosenbaum (eds): Cell Motility, Book C. Cold Spring Harbor, New York: Cold Spring Harbor Laboratory, pp. 987–1005.

Gard, D.L., and M.W. Kirschner (1985) A polymerization-dependent increase in phosphorylation of β-tubulin accompanies differentiation of a mouse neuroblastoma cell line. J. Cell Biol. 100:764–774.

Gard, D.L., and M.W. Kirschner (1987) A microtubule-associated protein from Xenopus eggs that specifically promotes assembly at the plus-end. J. Cell Biol. 105:2203–2215.

Gaskin, F., S.B. Kramer, C.R. Cantor, R. Adelstein, and M.L. Shelanski (1974) A dynein-like protein associated with neurotubules. FEBS Lett. 40:281–286.

Gibbons, I.R. (1981) Cilia and flagella of eukaryotes. J. Cell Biol. 91:107s–124s.

Gibbons, I.R., M.P. Cosson, J.A. Evans, B.H. Gibbons, B. Houck, K.H. Martinson, W.S. Sale, and W.J.Y. Tang (1978) Potent inhibition of dynein adenosine triphosphatase and of the motility of cilia and sperm flagella by vanadate. Proc. Natl. Acad. Sci. USA 75:2220–2224.

Gibbons, I.R., and E. Fronk (1979) A latent adenosine triphosphatase form of dynein 1 from sea urchin sperm flagella. J. Biol. Chem. 254:187–196.

Gibbons, I.R., A. Lee-Eiford, G. Mocz, C.A. Phillipson, W.J.Y. Tang, and B.H. Gibbons (1987) Photosensitized cleavage of dynein heavy chains. J. Biol. Chem. 262:2780–2786.

Gilbert, S.P., R.D. Allen, and R.D. Sloboda (1985) Translocation of vesicles from squid axoplasm on flagellar microtubules. Nature 315:245–248.

Gilbert, S.P., and R.D. Sloboda (1984) Bidirectional transport of fluorescently labeled vesicles introduced into extruded axoplasm of squid *Loligo pealei*. J. Cell Biol. 99:445–452.

Gilbert, S.P., and R.D. Sloboda (1986) Identification of a MAP2-like ATP binding protein associated with axoplasmic vesicles that translocate on isolated microtubules. J. Cell Biol. 103:947–956.

Goldman, R., T.D. Pollard, and J. Rosenbaum (1976) Cell Motility Books A, B & C. Cold Spring Harbor, New York: Cold Spring Harbor Laboratory.

Goldstein, L.S.B., R.W. Hardy, and D.L. Lindsley (1982) Structural genes on the Y chromosome of *Drosophila melanogaster*. Proc. Natl. Acad Sci. USA 79:7405–7409.

Goldstein, L.S.B., R.A. Laymon, and J.R. McIntosh (1986) A microtubule-associated protein in *Drosophila melanogaster*: Identification, characterization, and isolation of coding sequences. J. Cell Biol. 102:2076–2087.

Goodenough, U.W., and J.H. Heuser (1984) Structural comparison of purified dynein proteins with in situ dynein arms. J. Mol. Biol. 180:1083–1118.

Gorbsky, G.J., and G.G. Borisy (1985) Microtubule distribution in cultured cells and intact tissues: Improved immunolabeling resolution through the use of reversible embedment cytochemistry. Proc. Natl. Acad. Sci. USA 82:6889–6893.

Gottlieb, A.I., L.M. May, L. Subrahmanyan, and V.I. Kalnins (1981) Distribution of microtubule organizing centers in migrating sheets of endothelial cells. J. Cell Biol. 91:539–594.

Grafstein, B., and D.S. Forman (1980) Intracellular transport in neurons. Physiol. Rev. 60:1167–1283.

Gundersen, G.G., M.H. Kalnoski, and J.C. Bulinski (1984) Distinct populations of microtubules: Tyrosinated and non-tyrosinated α-tubulin are distributed differently in vivo. Cell 38:779–989.

Hanks, S.K. (1987) Homology probing: Identification of cDNA clones encoding members of the protein-serine kinase family. Proc. Natl. Acad. Sci. USA 84:388–392.

Hastie, A.T., D.T. Dicker, S.T. Hingley, F. Kueppers, M.L. Higgins, and G. Weinbaum (1986) Isolation of cilia from porcine tracheal epithelium and extraction of dynein arms. Cell Motil. Cytoskeleton 6:25–34.

Hayden, J.H., and R.D. Allen (1984) Detection of single microtubules in living cells: Particle transport can occur in both directions along the same microtubule. J. Cell Biol. 99:1785–1793.

Hayden, J.H., R.D. Allen, and R.D. Goldman (1983) Cytoplasmic transport in keratocytes: Direct visualization of particle translocation along microtubules. Cell Motil. 3:1–19.

Heidemann, S.R., J.M. Landers, and M.A. Hamborg (1981) Polarity orientation of axonal microtubules. J. Cell Biol. 91:661–665.

Heidemann, S.R., and J.R. McIntosh (1980) Visualization of the structural polarity of microtubules. Nature 286:517–519.

Herman, B., and D.F. Albertini (1984) A time lapse video intensification analysis of cytoplasmic organelle movements during endosome translocation. J. Cell Biol. 98:565–576.

Hermann, H., R. Pytella, J. Dalton, and G. Wiche (1984) Structural homology of microtubule-associated proteins 1 and 2 demonstrated by peptide mapping and immunoreactivity. J. Biol. Chem. 259:612–617.

Herskowitz, I. (1987) Functional inactivation of genes by dominant negative mutations. Nature 329:219–222.

Hill, T.L., and M.F. Carlier (1983) Steady-state theory of the interference of GTP hydrolysis in the mechanism of microtubule assembly. Proc. Natl. Acad. Sci. USA 80:7234–7238.

Hill, T.L., and M.W. Kirschner (1982) Bioenergetics and kinetics of microtubule and actin filament assembly-disassembly. Int. Rev. Cytol. 78:1–123.

Hirokawa, N., G.S. Bloom, and R.B. Vallee (1985) Cytoskeletal architecture and immunocytochemical localization of microtubule-associated proteins in regions of axons associated with rapid axonal transport: The β,β'-iminodipropionitrile-intoxicated axon as a model system. J. Cell Biol. 101:227–239.

Hollenbeck, P.J., and K. Chapman (1986) A novel microtubule-associated protein from mammalian nerve shows ATP-sensitive binding to microtubules. J. Cell Biol. 103:1539–1545.

Horio, H., and H. Hotani (1986) Visualization of the dynamic instability of individual microtubules by dark-field microscopy. Nature 321:605–607.

Huang, B., Z. Ramanis, and D.J.L. Luck (1982) Suppressor mutations in *Chlamydomonas reinhardtii* reveal a regulatory mechanism for flagellar function. Cell 42:115–124.

Inoué, S. (1981a) Video image processing greatly enhances contrast, quality, and speed in polarization-based microscopy. J. Cell Biol. 89:346–356.

Inoué, S. (1981b) Cell division and the mitotic spindle. J. Cell Biol. 91:131s–147s.

Inoué, S. (1986) Video Microscopy. New York: Plenum Press.

Inoué, S., and H. Ritter (1975) Dynamics of mitotic spindle organization and function. In S. Inoué and R.E. Stephens (eds): Molecules and Cell Movement. New York: Raven Press, pp. 3–30.

Inoué, S., and H.J. Sato (1967) Cell motility by labile association of molecules. J. Gen. Physiol. 50:259–292.

Izant, J., and J. McIntosh (1980) Microtubule-associated proteins: A monoclonal antibody to MAP2 binds to differentiated neurons. Proc. Natl. Acad. Sci. USA 77:4741–4745.

Izant, J., and H. Weintraub (1985) Constitutive and conditional suppression of exogenous and endogenous genes by anti-sense RNA. Science 229:345–352.

Jacobs, M., H. Smith, and E.W. Taylor (1974) Tubulin: Nucleotide binding and enzymatic activity. J. Mol. Biol. 89:455–468.

Jarvik, J., and D. Botstein (1975) Condition-lethal mutations that suppress genetic defects in morphogenesis by altering structural proteins. Proc. Natl. Acad. Sci. USA 72:2738–2742.

Jensen, C.G., and B.H. Smaill (1986) Analysis of the spatial organization of microtubule-associated proteins. J. Cell Biol. 103:559–569.

Jiminez, F.G., and J.A. Campos-Ortega (1982) Maternal effects of zygotic mutants affecting early neurogenesis in *Drosophila*. Wilhelm Roux Arch. 191:191–201.

Johnson, K.A. (1985) Pathway of the microtubule-dynein ATPase and the structure of dynein: a comparison with actomyosin. Annu. Rev. Biophys. Biophys. Chem. 14:161–188.

Johnson, K.A., and G.G. Borisy (1975) The equilibrium assembly of microtubules in vitro. In S. Inoué and R.E. Stephens (eds): Molecules and Cell Movement. New York: Raven Press, pp. 119–139.

Johnson, K.A., and G.G. Borisy (1977) Kinetic analysis of microtubule self-assembly in vitro. J. Mol. Biol. 117:1–31.

Johnson, K.A., and J.S. Wall (1983) Structure and molecular weight of the dynein ATPase. J. Cell Biol. 96:669–678.

Kachar, B., J.P. Albanesi, H. Fujisaki, and E.D. Korn (1987) Extensive purification from *Acanthamoeba castellanii* of a microtubule-dependent translocator with microtubule-activated magnesium ATPase activity. J. Biol. Chem. 262:16180–16185.

Karr, T., and B. Alberts (1986) Organization of the cytoskeleton in early *Drosophila* embryos. J. Cell Biol. 102:1494–1509.

Karr, T.L., D. Kristofferson, and D.L. Purich (1980) Mechanism of microtubule depolymerization. J. Biol. Chem. 225:8560–8566.

Karsenti, E., S. Kobayashi, T.J. Mitchison, and M.W. Kirschner (1984) Role of the centrosome in organizing the interphase microtubule array: Properties of cytoplasts containing or lacking centrosomes. J. Cell Biol. 98:1763–1776.

Keith, C.H., J.R. Feramisco, and M. Shelanski (1981) Direct visualization of fluorescein-labeled microtubules in vitro and in microinjected fibroblasts. J. Cell Biol. 88:234–240.

Kiehart, D.P., and R. Feghali (1986) Cytoplasmic myosin from *Drosophila melanogaster*. J. Cell Biol. 103:1517–1525.

Kim, H., L.I. Binder, and J.L. Rosenbaum (1979) The periodic association of MAP 2 with brain microtubules in vitro. J. Cell Biol. 80:266–276.

King, S.M., and G.B. Witman (1987) Structure of the α and β heavy chains of the outer arm dynein from *Chlamydomonas* flagella. J. Biol. Chem. 262:17596–17604.

Kirschner, M.W. (1980) Implications of treadmilling for the stability of actin and tubulin polymer in vivo. J. Cell Biol. 86:330–334.

Kirschner, M.W., and T.J. Mitchison (1986) Beyond self-assembly: From microtubules to morphogenesis. Cell 45:329–342.

Klymkowsky, M. (1981) Intermediate filaments on 3T3 cells collapse after intracellular injection of a monoclonal anti-intermediate filament antibody. Nature 291:249–251.

Kobayashi, T., T. Martensen, J. Nath, and M. Flavin (1978) Inhibition of dynein ATPase by vanadate, and its possible use as a probe for the role of dynein in cytoplasmic motility. Biochem. Biophys. Res. Commun. 81:1313–1318.

Koonce, M.P., J. Tong, U. Euteneuer, and M. Schliwa (1987) Active sliding between cytoplasmic microtubules. Nature 328:737–739.

Kravit, N.G., and R.B. Vallee (1987) ATP photoaffinity labelling and UV/vanadate induced photocleavage of MAP 1C, a brain cytosolic microtubule-associated protein with similarities to dynein. J. Cell Biol. 105:125a.

Kreis, T., and W. Birchmeier (1982) Microinjection of fluorescently labeled proteins into living cells with emphasis on cytoskeletal proteins. Int. Rev. Cytol. 75:209.

Kristofferson, D., T.J. Mitchison, and M.W. Kirschner (1986) Direct observation of steady-state microtubule dynamics. J. Cell Biol. 102:1007–1019.

Kupfer, A., D. Louvard, and S.J. Singer (1982) Polarization of the Golgi apparatus and the microtubule-organizing center in cultured fibroblasts at the edge of an experimental wound. Proc. Natl. Acad. Sci. USA 79:2603–2607.

Kuznetsov, S.A., and V.I. Gelfand (1986) Bovine brain kinesin is a microtubule-activated ATPase. Proc. Natl. Acad. Sci. USA 83:8530–8534.

Laemmli, U.K. (1970) Cleavage of structural proteins during assembly of the head of bacteriophage T4. Nature (London) 227:680–685.

Lasek, R.J. (1974) Biochemistry of the squid giant axon. In J.M. Arnold, W.C. Summers, and D.L. Gilbert (eds): A Guide to the Laboratory Use of the Squid. Woods Hole, MA: Marine Biological Laboratory, pp. 69–74.

Lasek, R.J., and S.T. Brady (1985) Attachment of transported vesicles to microtubules in axoplasm is facilitated by AMP-PNP. Nature 316:645- 647.

Lee, G., N. Cowan, and M. Kirschner (1988) The primary structure and heterogeneity of tau protein from mouse brain. Science 239:285- 288.

Lee-Eiford, A., R.A. Ow, and I.R. Gibbons (1986) Specific cleavage of the dynein heavy chains by ultraviolet irradiation in the presence of ATP and vanadate. J. Biol. Chem. 261:2337–2342.

Lim, S.S., P.J. Sammak, and G.G. Borisy (1987) Sites of assembly and differential stability of neuronal microtubules. J. Cell Biol. 105:30a.

Luby-Phelps, K., P.E. Castle, D.L. Taylor, and F. Lanni (1987) Hindered diffusion of inert tracer particles in the cytoplasm of mouse 3T3 cells. Proc. Natl. Acad. Sci. USA 84:4901–4913.

Lye, R.J., M.E. Porter, J.M. Scholey, and J.R. McIntosh (1987) Identification of a microtubule-based cytoplasmic motor in the nematode *Caenorhabditis elegans*. Cell 51:309–318.

Mangeat, P., and K. Burridge (1984) Immunoprecipitation of nonerythrocyte spectrin within live cells following microinjection of specific antibodies: Relation to cytoskeletal structures. J. Cell Biol. 98:1363–1377.

Margolis, R.L., and L. Wilson (1978) Opposite-end assembly and disassembly of microtubules at steady state in vitro. Cell 13:1–8.

McIntosh, J.R. (1977) Mitosis in vitro: Isolates and models of the mitotic apparatus. In M. Little, N. Paweletz, C. Petzelt, and D. Ponstingl, D. Schroeter, and H.-P. Zimmerman (eds): Mitosis Facts and Questions. Berlin: Springer-Verlag, pp. 167–184.

Melton, D. (1985) Injected antisense RNAs specifically block messenger RNA translation in vivo. Proc. Natl. Acad. Sci. USA 82:144–148.

Miller, R.H., and R.J. Lasek (1985) Cross-bridges mediate anterograde and retrograde vesicle transport along microtubules in squid axoplasm. J. Cell Biol. 101:2181–2193.

Mitchison, T.J., and M.W. Kirschner (1984a) Microtubule assembly nucleated by isolated centrosomes. Nature 312:232–237.

Mitchison, T.J., and M.W. Kirschner (1984b) Dynamic instability of microtubule growth. Nature 312:237–242.

Mitchison, T.J., and M.W. Kirschner (1986) Sites of assembly and disassembly in the mitotic spindle. Cell 45:515–527.

Morris, N.R., J.A. Weatherbee, J. Gambino, and L.G. Bergen (1984) Tubulins of *Aspergillus nidulans:* Genetics, biochemistry, and function. In G.G. Borisy, D.W. Cleveland, and D.B. Murphy (eds): Molecular Biology of the Cytoskeleton. Cold Spring Harbor, New York: Cold Spring Harbor Laboratory, pp. 211–222.

Murphy, D.B., and G.G. Borisy (1975) Association of high molecular weight proteins with microtubules and their role in microtubule assembly in vitro. Proc. Natl. Acad. Sci. USA 72:2696–2700.

Murphy, D.B., K.A. Johnson, and G.G. Borisy (1977) Role of tubulin-associated protein in microtubule nucleation and elongation. J. Mol. Biol. 117:33–52.

Murphy, D.B., K.T. Wallis, and R.R. Hiebsch (1983) Identity and origin of the ATPase activity associated with neuronal microtubules. II. Identification of a 50,000 dalton polypeptide with ATPase activity similar to F-1 ATPase from mitochondria. J. Cell Biol. 96:1306–1315.

Olmsted, J.B. (1986) Microtubule associated proteins. Annu. Rev. Cell Biol. 2:421–457.

Omoto, C.K., and K.A. Johnson (1986) Activation of the dynein adenosine triphosphatase by microtubules. Biochemistry 25:419–427.

Oosawa, F., and S. Asakura (1975) Thermodynamics of the Polymerization of Protein. London: Academic Press.

Osborn, M., and K. Weber (1976) Cytoplasmic microtubules in tissue culture cells appear to grow from an organizing structure towards the plasma membrane. Proc. Natl. Acad. Sci. USA 73:867–871.

Otto, J.J. (1986) Gel overlay methods for detecting specific protein-protein interactions. Methods Enzymol. 134:555–560.

Papasozomenos, S.C., L.I. Binder, P.K. Bender, and M.R. Payne (1985) Microtubule-associated protein 2 (MAP 2) within axons of spinal motor neurons: Associations with microtubules and neurofilaments in normal and β, β'-iminodipropionitrile-treated axons. J. Cell Biol. 100:74–85.

Papasozomenos, S.C., M. Yoon, R. Crane, L. Autilio-Gambetti, and P. Gambetti (1982) Redistribution of proteins of fast axonal transport following administration of β,β'-iminodipropionitrile: A quantitative autoradiographic study. J. Cell Biol. 95:672–675.

Paschal, B.M., S.M. King, A.G. Moss, C.A. Collins, R.B. Vallee, and G.B. Witman (1987a) Isolated flagellar outer arm dynein translocates brain microtubules in vitro. Nature 330:672–674.

Paschal, B.M., H.S. Shpetner, and R.B. Vallee (1987b) MAP 1C is a microtubule-activated ATPase which translocates microtubules in vitro and has dynein-like properties. J. Cell Biol. 105:1273–1282.

Paschal, B.M., and R.B. Vallee (1987a) Characterization of the in vitro motility properties of MAP 1C, a dynein-related protein from brain tissue. J. Cell Biol. 105:125a.

Paschal, B.M., and R.B. Vallee (1987b) Retrograde transport by the microtubule-associated protein MAP 1C. Nature 330:181–183.

Penningroth, S.M., A. Cheung, P. Bouchard, C. Gagnon, and C.W. Bardin (1982) Dynein ATPase is inhibited selectively in vitro by erythro-9-[3-(2-hydroxynonyl)]adenine. Biochem. Biophys. Res. Commun. 104:234–240.

Penningroth, S.M., P. Rose, A. Cheung, D.D. Peterson, D.Q. Rothacker, and P. Bershak (1985) An EHNA-sensitive ATPase in unfertilized sea urchin eggs. Cell Motil. 5:61–75.

Piperno, G. (1987) Isolation of a sixth dynein subunit adenosine triphosphatase of *Chlamydomonas* axonemes. J. Cell Biol. 106:133–140.

Piperno, G., M. LeDizet, and X. Chang (1987) Microtubules containing acetylated α-tubulin in mammalian cells in culture. J. Cell Biol. 104:289–302.

Porter, M.E., T.S. Hays, P.M. Grissom, M.T. Fuller, and J.R. McIntosh (1987a) Characterization of a high molecular weight, ATP sensitive, microtubule-associated polypeptide from *Drosophila* embryos. J. Cell Biol. 105:121a.

Porter, M.E., and K.A. Johnson (1983) Transient state kinetic analysis of the ATP-induced dissociation of the dynein-microtubule complex. J. Biol. Chem. 258:6582–6587.

Porter, M.E., J.M. Scholey, D.L. Stemple, G.P.A. Vigers, R.D. Vale, M.P. Sheetz, and J.R. McIntosh (1987b) Characterization of the microtubule movement produced by sea urchin egg kinesin. J. Biol. Chem. 262:2794–2802.

Pratt, M.M. (1980) The identification of a dynein ATPase in unfertilized sea urchin eggs. Dev. Biol. 74:364–378.

Pratt, M.M. (1986) Stable complexes of axoplasmic vesicles and microtubules: Protein composition and ATPase activity. J. Cell Biol. 103:956–968.

Pratt, M.M., T. Otter, and E.D. Salmon (1980) Dynein-like Mg^{2+}-ATPase in mitotic spindles isolated from sea urchin embryos (*Strongylocentrotus droebachiensis*). J. Cell Biol. 86:738–745.

Pryer, N.K., P. Wadsworth, and E.D. Salmon (1986) Polarized microtubule gliding and particle saltations produced by soluble factors from sea urchin eggs and embryos. Cell Motil. Cytoskeleton 6:537–548.

Raff, E.C. (1984) Genetics of microtubule systems. J. Cell Biol. 99:1–10.

Rozek, C.E., and N. Davidson (1983) *Drosophila* has one myosin heavy-chain gene with three developmentally regulated transcripts. Cell 32:23–34.

Rubin, G.M., and A.C. Spradling (1982) Genetic transformation of Drosophila with transposable element vectors. Science 218:348–353.

Sale, W.S., U.W. Goodenough, and J.E. Heuser (1985) The substructure of isolated and in situ outer dynein arms of sea urchin sperm flagella. J. Cell Biol. 101:1400–1412.

Sale, W.S., and P. Satir (1977) Direction of active sliding of microtubules in *Tetrahymena* cilia. Proc. Natl. Acad. Sci. USA 74:2045–2059.

Salmon, E.D., R.J. Leslie, W.M. Saxton, M.L. Karow, and J.R. McIntosh (1984) Spindle microtubule dynamics in sea urchin embryos: Analysis using a fluorescein-labeled tubulin and measurements of fluorescence redistribution after laser photobleaching. J. Cell Biol. 99:2165–2174.

Sammak, P.J., and G.G. Borisy (1988a) Detection of single fluorescent microtubules and methods for determining their dynamics in living cells. Cell Motil. Cytoskel. 10:237–245.

Sammak, P.J., and G.G. Borisy (1988b) Microtubule dynamics: direct observation of fluorescent microtubules in living cells. Nature 332:724–726.

Sammak, P.J., G.J. Gorbsky, and G.G. Borisy (1987) Microtubule dynamics in vivo: A test of mechanisms of turnover. J. Cell Biol. 104:395–405.

Sammak, P.J., S.S. Lim, and G.G. Borisy (1988) Microtubule assembly sites and transport of the cytoskeleton in PC-12 cells. Cell Motil. Cytoskeleton 10:346.

Saxton, W.M. (1988) *Drosophila* kinesin: Characterization of microtubule motility and ATPase. Proc. Natl. Acad. Sci. USA 85:1109–1113.

Saxton, W.M., D.L. Semple, R.J. Leslie, E.D. Salmon, M. Zavortink, and J.R. McIntosh (1984) Tubulin dynamics in cultured mammalian cells. J. Cell Biol. 99:2175–2186.

Schliwa, M. (1986) The Cytoskeleton. New York: Springer-Verlag.

Schnapp, B.J., R.D. Vale, M.P. Sheetz, and T.S. Reese (1985) Single microtubules from squid axoplasm support bidirectional movement of organelles. Cell 40:455–462.

Scholey, J.M., M.E. Porter, P.M. Grissom, and J.R. McIntosh (1985) Identification of kinesin in sea urchin eggs and evidence for its localization in the mitotic spindle. Nature 318:483–486.

Schulze, E., D. Asai, J.C. Bulinski, and M.W. Kirschner (1987) Posttranslational modification and microtubule stability. J. Cell Biol. 105:2167–2177.

Schulze, E., and M.W. Kirschner (1986) Microtubule dynamics in interphase cells. J. Cell Biol. 102:1020–1031.

Shpetner, H.S., B.P. Paschal, and R.B. Vallee (1987) Characterization of the microtubule-associated protein 1C (MAP 1C) ATPase: Microtubule-activation and dynein-like properties. J. Cell Biol. 105:126a.

Shpetner, H.S., B.P. Paschal, and R.B. Vallee (1988) Characterization of the microtubule-activated ATPase of brain cytoplasmic dynein. J. Cell Biol. 107:1001–1009.

Sloboda, R.D., W.L. Dentler, and J.L. Rosenbaum (1976) Microtubule-associated proteins and the stimulation of tubulin assembly in vitro. Biochemistry 15:4497–4505.

Sloboda, R.D., and J.L. Rosenbaum (1979) Decoration and stabilization of intact, smooth-walled microtubules with microtubule-associated proteins. Biochemistry 18:48–55.

Sloboda, R.D., and J.L. Rosenbaum (1982) Purification and assay of microtubule-associated proteins. Methods. Enzymol. 85.

Sloboda, R.D., S.A. Rudolph, J.L. Rosenbaum, and P. Greengard (1975) Cyclic AMP-dependent endogenous phosphorylation of a microtubule-associated protein. Proc. Natl. Acad. Sci. USA 72:177–181.

Smith, D.A., B.S. Baker, and M. Gatti (1985) Mutations in genes encoding essential mitotic functions in Drosophila melanogaster. Genetics 110:647-670.

Smith, G., M. Summers, and M. Fraser (1983) Production of human β-interferon in insect cells with a baculovirus expression vector. Mol. Cell Biol. 3:2156-2165.

Solomon, F. (1986) What might MAPs do? Results of an in situ analysis. Ann. N.Y. Acad. Sci. 466:322–327.

Soltys, B.J., and G.G. Borisy (1985) Polymerization of tubulin in vivo: Direct evidence for assembly onto microtubule ends and from centrosomes. J. Cell Biol. 100:1682–1689.

Spradling, A.C., and G.M. Rubin (1982) Transposition of cloned P elements into Drosophila germ line chromosomes. Science 218:341–347.

Swan, J., and F. Solomon (1984) Reformation of the marginal band of avian erythrocytes in vitro using calf-brain tubulin: Peripheral determinants of microtubule form. J. Cell Biol. 99:2108–2113.

Tassin, A.M., B. Maro, and M. Bornens (1985) Fate of microtubule-organizing centers during myogenesis in vitro. J. Cell Biol. 100:35–46.

Telzer, B.R., and L.T. Haimo (1981) Decoration of spindle microtubules with dynein: Evidence for uniform polarity. J. Cell Biol. 89:373–378.

Teresaki, M., L.B. Chen, and K. Fujiwara (1986) Microtubules and the endoplasmic reticulum are highly interdependent structures. J. Cell Biol. 103:1557–1568.

Thomas, J.H., P. Novick, and D. Botstein (1984) Genetics of the yeast cytoskeleton. In G.G. Borisy, D.W. Cleveland, and D.B. Murphy (eds): Molecular Biology of the Cytoskeleton. Cold Spring Harbor, New York: Cold Spring Harbor Laboratory, pp. 153–174.

Tobin, S.L., E. Zulauf, F. Sanchez, E.A. Craig, and B.J. McCarthy (1980) Multiple actin-related sequences in the Drosophila melanogaster genome. Cell 19:121–131.

Tooze, J., and B. Burke (1987) Accumulation of adrenocorticotropin secretory granules in the midbody of telophase AtT20 cells: Evidence that secretory granules move anterogradely along microtubules. J. Cell Biol. 104:1047–1057.

Trinkaus, J.P. (1984) Cells into Organs: The Forces That Shape the Embryo. Englewood, NJ: Prentice Hall.

Tsukita, S., and H. Ishikawa (1980) The movement of organelles in axons. Electron microscopic identification of anterogradely and retrogradely transported organelles. J. Cell Biol. 84:513–530.

Vale, R.D. (1987) Intracellular transport using microtubule-based motors. Annu. Rev. Cell Biol. 3:347–378.

Vale, R.D., T.S. Reese, and M.P. Sheetz (1985a) Identification of a novel force- generating protein, kinesin, involved in microtubule-based motility. Cell 42:39–50.

Vale, R.D., B.J. Schnapp, T.J. Mitchison, E. Steuer, T.S. Reese, and M.P. Sheetz (1985b) Different axoplasmic proteins generate movement in opposite directions along microtubules in vitro. Cell 43:623–632.

Vale, R.D., B.J. Schnapp, T.S. Reese, and M.P. Sheetz (1985c) Movement of organelles along filaments dissociated from the axoplasm of the squid giant axon. Cell 40:449–454.

Vale, R.D., B.J. Schnapp, T.S. Reese, and M.P. Sheetz (1985d) Organelle, bead, and microtubule translocations promoted by soluble factors from the squid giant axon. Cell 40:559–569.

Vale, R.D., J.M. Scholey, and M.P. Sheetz (1986) Kinesin: Biological roles for a new microtubule-based motor. Trends Biochem. Sci. 11:464–468.

Vallee, R.B. (1980) Structure and phosphorylation of microtubule-associated protein 2 (MAP 2). Proc. Natl. Acad. Sci. USA 77:3206–3210.

Vallee, R.B. (1982) A taxol-dependent procedure of the isolation of microtubules and microtubule-associated proteins (MAPs). J. Cell Biol. 92:435–442.

Vallee, R.B., and G.S. Bloom (1983) Isolation of sea urchin egg microtubules with taxol and identification of mitotic spindle microtubule-associated proteins with monoclonal antibodies. Proc. Natl. Acad. Sci. USA 80:6259–6263.

Vallee, R.B., G.S. Bloom, and F.C. Luca (1984a) Differential cellular and subcellular distribution of microtubule-associated proteins. In G.G. Borisy, D.W. Cleveland, and D.B. Murphy (ed): Molecular Biology of the Cytoskeleton. Cold Spring Harbor, New York: Cold Spring Harbor Laboratory, pp. 111–130.

Vallee, R.B., G.S. Bloom, and W.E. Theurkauf (1984b) Microtubule-associated protein subunits of the cytomatrix. J. Cell Biol. 99:39s-44s.

Vallee, R.B., and S.D. Davis (1983) Low molecular weight microtubule-associated proteins are light chains of microtubule-associated protein 1 (MAP 1). Proc. Natl. Acad. Sci. USA 80:1342–1346.

Vallee, R.B., B.P. Paschal, H.S. Shpetner, and J.S. Wall (1987) Structural evidence for the identification of the brain cytosolic microtubule-associated protein MAP 1C as dynein. J. Cell Biol. 105:125a.

Vallee, R.B., J.S. Wall, B.P. Paschal, and H.S. Shpetner (1988) Microtubule-associated protein 1C from brain is a two-headed cytosolic dynein. Nature 332:561–563.

Vasiliev, J.M., and I.M. Gelfand (1976) Effects of colcemid on morphogenetic processes and locomotion of fibroblasts. In R. Goldman, T. Pollard, and J.L. Rosenbaum (eds): Cell Motility, Book C. Cold Spring Harbor, New York: Cold Spring Harbor Laboratory, pp. 279–304.

Voter, W.A., and H.P. Erickson (1982) Electron microscopy of MAP 2 (microtubule-associated protein 2). J. Ultrastruct. Res. 80:374–382.

Wadsworth, P., and R.D. Sloboda (1983) Microinjection of fluorescent tubulin into dividing sea urchin cells. J. Cell Biol. 97:1249–1254.

Walker, J.E., M. Saraste, M.J. Runswick, and N.J. Gay (1982) Distantly related sequences in the α and β subunits of ATP synthase, myosin, kinases and other ATP-requiring enzymes and a common nucleotide binding fold. EMBO J. 1:945- 951.

Walker, R.A., E.T. O'Brien, N.K. Pryer, M. Soboeiro, W.A. Voter, H.P. Erickson, and E.D. Salmon (1987) Calculation of transition frequencies for individual microtubules exhibiting dynamic instability behavior. J. Cell Biol. 105:29a.

Walter, R., and M. Berns (1981) Computer enhanced video microscopy: Digitally processed microscopic images can be produced in real time. Proc. Natl. Acad. Sci. USA 78:6927–6931.

Wang, K., J. Feramisco, and J. Ash (1982a) Fluorescent localization of contractile proteins in tissue culture cells. Methods Enzymol. 85:514–562.

Wang, Y.L., J.M. Heiple, and D.L. Taylor (1982b) Fluorescent analog cytochemistry of contractile proteins. Methods Cell Biol. 25:1–11.

Webster, D.R., G.G. Gundersen, J.C. Bulinski, and G.G. Borisy (1987a) Assembly and turnover of detyrosinated tubulin in vivo. J. Cell Biol. 105:265–276.

Webster, D.R., G.G. Gundersen, J.C. Bulinski, and G.G. Borisy (1987b) Differential turnover of tyrosinated and detyrosinated microtubules. Proc. Natl. Acad. Sci. USA 84:9040–9044.

Webster, D.R., G. Piperno, and G.G. Borisy (1987c) Acetylated microtubule domains turn over slowly. J. Cell Biol. 105:120a.

Wegner, A. (1976) Head-to-tail polymerization of actin. J. Mol. Biol. 108:138–150.

Wehland, J., and J. Weber (1987) Turnover of the carboxy-terminal tyrosine of α-tubulin and means of reaching elevated levels of detyrosination in living cells. J. Cell Sci. 88:185–203.

Wehland, J., and M.C. Willingham (1983) A rat monoclonal antibody reacting specifically with the tyrosylated form of α-tubulin. II. Effects on cell movement, organization of microtubules, and intermediate filaments, and arrangement of golgi elements. J. Cell Biol. 97:1476–1490.

Weisenberg, R.C. (1972) Microtubule formation in vitro in solutions containing low calcium concentration. Science 177:1104–1105.

Weisenberg, R.C., W.J. Deery, and P.J. Dickinson (1976) Tubulin-nucleotide interactions during the polymerization and depolymerization of microtubules. Biochemistry 15:4248–4254.

Weisenberg, R.C., J. Flynn, B. Gao, S. Awodi, F. Skee, S.R. Goodman, and B.M. Riederer (1987) Microtubule gelation-contraction: Essential components and relation to slow axonal transport. Science 238:1119–1122.

Weisenberg, R.C., and E.D. Taylor (1968) Studies of ATPase activity of sea urchin eggs and the isolated mitotic apparatus. Exp. Cell Res. 53:372–384.

Weiss, P., and H.B. Hiscoe (1948) Experiments on the mechanism of nerve growth. J. Exp. Zool. 107:315–395.

Wiche, G. (1985) High molecular weight microtubule-associated proteins (MAPS): A ubiquitous family of cytoskeletal connecting links. Trends Biochem. Sci. 10:67–70.

Willard, M., W.M. Cowan, and P.R. Vagelos (1974) The polypeptide composition of intra-axonally transported proteins: Evidence for four transport velocities. Proc. Natl. Acad. Sci. USA 71:2183–2187.

Witman, G.B., K.A. Johnson, K.K. Pfister, and J.S. Wall (1983) Fine structure and molecular weight of the outer arm dyneins of *Chlamydomonas*. J. Submicrosc. Cytol. 15:193–197.

Witman, G.B., and K.K. Pfister (1984) Subfractionation of *Chlamydomonas* 18S dynein into unique subunits containing ATPase activity. J. Biol. Chem. 259:12072–12080.

Wordeman, L., and W.Z. Cande (1987) Reactivation of spindle elongation in vitro is correlated with the phosphorylation of a 205 kd spindle-associated protein. Cell 50:535–543.

Yang, J.T., W.M. Saxton, and L.S.B. Goldstein (1988) Isolation and characterization of the gene encoding the heavy chain of *Drosophila* kinesin. Proc. Natl. Acad. Sci. USA 85:1864–1868.

SECTION
4

Kinesin ATPases and Cytoplasmic Particle Translocation

Edited by Michael P. Sheetz

PERSPECTIVE
Kinesin Structure and Function

Michael P. Sheetz

*Department of Cell Biology and Physiology, Washington University School of Medicine,
St. Louis, Missouri 63110*

INTRODUCTION

Kinesin is a microtubule-dependent motor (Vale et al., 1985c) found primarily free in solution within the cytoplasm of virtually all cells (for reviews, see Vale et al., 1986b; Sheetz, 1987). There are many cellular functions in which kinesin-mediated forces could be important (see Vale, 1987). Since the earliest days of light microscopy, observations of cytoplasm have revealed that organelles actively move along linear paths in a manner that we now know is indicative of microtubule-dependent organelle transport. Recent experiments suggest that microtubule-dependent transport is required for fast axonal transport (both anterograde and retrograde) (Schnapp et al., 1985; Allen et al., 1985; see also Chapters 14, 19, and 21), the spreading of endoplasmic reticulum (Terasaki et al., 1986; Lee and Chen, 1988; Dabora and Sheetz, 1988b), regulated secretory processes (Lacy et al., 1975), and events in mitosis (reviewed in Section 5 of this volume). This review discusses one of the two major types of known microtubule-dependent motors, kinesin, in terms of its structure and its function within cytoplasm.

The kinesins are defined as microtubule-dependent motors that move anionic beads or glass toward the plus ends of microtubules and bind to microtubules strongly in the presence of AMP-PNP. The kinesins that have been purified to date all appear to have heavy chains of 90–135 kDa, a native molecular weight of 300–400 kDa, and light chains of 55–80 kDa, although there are some differences in the light chain composition (Vale et al., 1985c; Kuznetsov and Gelfand, 1986; Bloom, Chapter 21; Scholey, Chapter 20). The stoichiometry of the light and heavy chains has been measured to be 1:2 (Vale et al., 1985c) or 2:2 (light:heavy) (Kuznetsov et al., 1988; Bloom, Chapter 21) for bovine kinesin by densitometry of gels. For squid kinesin, the ratio was 1:2 as measured by both densitometry (Vale et al., 1985c) and quantitative amino acid analysis (Sheetz et al., unpublished results). The consensus is that kinesin is a dimer of the heavy chains, and the light chains that copurify with the heavy chains may be variable.

Kinesin appears to be a long, thin molecule not unlike myosin (Amos, 1987; T. Reese, personal communication; Steuer et al., in preparation). This is consistent with its low sedimentation coefficient (9.5S)

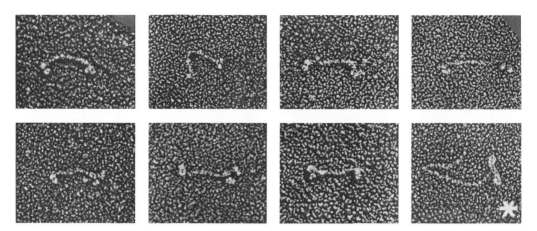

Fig. 17–1. Gallery of selected chicken embryo fibroblast and brain kinesin molecules, chosen for clarity of platinum replication, illustrating the asymmetric and dimeric nature of the molecule as described in the text. Micrographs were kindly prepared by Dr. John Heuser, Washington University School of Medicine, by the technique of molecular adsorption to mica flakes followed by liquid helium quick freezing and freeze etching of the flakes (Heuser, 1983)(Magnification 200,000 ×).

(Scholey, Chapter 20; Porter et al., 1987; Kuznetsov et al., 1988; Sheetz, 1987; Bloom, Chapter 21). In platinum replicas, such as are shown in Figure 17–1, kinesin molecules isolated from chick brain or embryonic fibroblasts measure 70–80 nm in length and 3–4 nm in width (roughly equivalent to the width of the α-helical coiled coil of the myosin tail). In addition, the molecules expand at either end into relatively globular domains. The general configuration of chick brain kinesin seems to be universal (Amos, 1987; T. Reese, personal communication). Replicas of freeze-dried chick kinesin also reveal several additional structural features not previously noted (Fig. 17–1). These will be described in detail in a forthcoming report (Steuer, Sheetz, Goodenough, and Heuser, in preparation) but are summarized in Figure 17–2. Briefly, the two ends of the molecule appear to be slightly different from each other. One end is always clearly divided into two small globular domains (6 nm diameter) that invariably lie side by side (Fig. 17–2). These look like small versions of the two heads of myosin (shown at the same magnification in the last panel of Figure 17–1 for comparison). Thus we will henceforth call these terminal domains kinesin's

"heads." The other end of the kinesin molecule looks more like the feathered tail of an arrow, measuring 6 nm by 10–12 nm or more. This end is also separated into two domains, but those domains are usually less distinct. The morphology of this region is variable because the two domains lie in different positions relative to the thin shaft of the molecule. In any case, the bipartite nature of both ends of kinesin supports the above-mentioned evidence that the native molecule is dimeric. Furthermore, the difference between the two ends suggests that the molecule is a parallel dimer like myosin. Finally, in more than 50% of the kinesins that adsorb to mica, a distinct bend occurs in the thin shaft of the molecule at a point slightly closer to the "feathered" end than to the smaller, more distinctly bipartite globular end. The angle of this bend varies from barely perceptible (0°) to nearly 180°, in which case the two ends of the molecule become closely apposed. Work is in progress to determine which end of the molecule attaches to microtubules and which to membranes.

Our understanding of the functional domains of the kinesin molecule is presently incomplete. Proteolysis studies have identi-

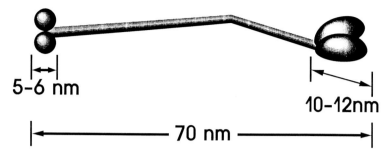

5-6 nm

10-12nm

70 nm

Fig. 17–2. Diagram of the morphology of a kinesin molecule taken from the views in figure 17–1.

fied a 60 kDa fragment of the heavy chain that will bind to microtubules in an adenosine triphosphate (ATP)-dependent manner (Vale and Reese, 1986). Similarly, molecular cloning studies have revealed that approximately 60 kDa of the N-terminal domain when expressed in a reticulocyte system will bind to microtubules in an ATP-dependent manner (Goldstein, Chapter 15). This is similar to the myosin heavy chain, which has an N-terminal actin-binding domain and releases from actin with ATP. An ATP binding site has also been found on the kinesin heavy chain by photolabeling with both 8-azido-ATP (Gilbert and Sloboda, 1986) and ATP (Penningroth et al., 1987). In addition, the sequence of *Drosophila* kinesin shows a consensus ATP binding site near the amino terminus of the heavy chain (see Goldstein, Chapter 15). Although ATP-dependent binding of the kinesin heavy chain from reticulocyte lysate transcripts to microtubules was observed, the expressed heavy chains have not yet moved beads or microtubules in a standard motility assay. The role of the light chains in kinesin function has not been determined. If we carry the analogy to myosin further, then the light chains may play important accessory roles in kinesin function.

KINESIN FUNCTIONS

Kinesin's role in the fast axonal transport of organelles was suggested by a number of experiments (reviewed in Sheetz, 1987; Vale, 1987; Schroer, Chapter 19; Bloom, Chapter 21). Since similar organelle movements on microtubules have been observed in nearly all cells, it is likely that kinesin is a general motor for organelle movements toward the plus ends of microtubules. Evidence that cytoplasmic dynein is the motor for organelle movements toward the minus ends of microtubules has recently been obtained (Schroer et al., 1988b), which addresses the question of how organelles move in the opposite direction. The fact that kinesin and dynein appear to be the motors for the plus end- and minus end-directed movements of organelles, respectively, need not imply that the purified organelles and motors alone form the motile complex (Vale et al., 1985b). Indeed recent studies indicate that an organelle activated for movement must interact with the motor (either kinesin or cytoplasmic dynein) and an accessory factor(s) for movement to occur (Schroer et al., 1988a,b). The major questions now focus on the nature of the accessory factor(s) and the site on the vesicle that selects for the plus end- or minus end-directed organelle motor complex.

Other functions that may also involve kinesin are the spreading of the endoplasmic reticulum (ER) and some of the movements in mitosis. Recent in vitro studies of the formation of tubulovesicular networks (see Fig. 17–3) have demonstrated that network formation involves the movement of membrane strands on microtubules (Dabora and Sheetz, 1988b) in a manner similar to ER movements in vivo (Lee and Chen, 1988). These membranes can be labeled with ER markers and not markers for the plasma membrane, Golgi membranes, or mitochon-

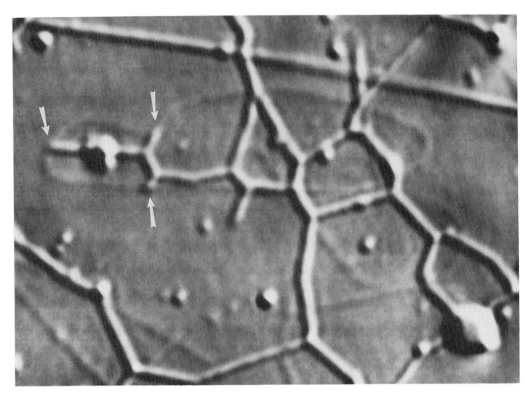

Fig. 17–3. Video micrograph of the endoplasmic reticulum network spread upon microtubules in vitro (see Dabora and Sheetz, 1988b, for details). The higher-contrast membrane tubules typically form trigonal branch points, and often the tubules end at apparent attachment sites on microtubules (arrows). The membrane strands move out from bulbous membrane aggregates with time and branch and fuse to form the final networks. The network and microtubules were visualized by video-enhanced differential interference contrast optics as described by Schnapp (1986)(Magnification 5,000×).

dria. Analysis of the formation of the in vitro ER networks suggests that a microtubule-dependent motor is involved in the process, which we have described as microtubule-dependent tethering. The exact nature of the motor complex that moves the membrane tubules is not known, although kinesin has been implicated. The network forms in the presence of 20 μM vanadate, which will block minus end-directed spherical organelle movements in the same system (Dabora and Sheetz, 1988a), whereas 100 μm of vanadate is required to inhibit kinesin movements (Vale et al., 1985c) and the formation of the network. In addition, after mitosis, the ER spreads to the periphery or toward the plus ends of the microtubules, which is the direction of kinesin movement (Lee and Chen, 1988). Another function that could possibly be powered by kinesin involves the separation of centrioles in anaphase A during mitosis (see Vale et al., 1986b). Kinesin has been found attached to the spindle matrix, where it would move the centrosomes apart by walking toward the plus ends of the spindle microtubules (Leslie et al., 1987).

The amount of soluble kinesin within cells is certainly sufficient to power the normal amounts of organelle transport seen. In neurons, kinesin is a relatively abundant protein, with cytoplasmic concentrations in excess of 100 μg/ml, and there are at least 500-fold extra copies over vesicles in an axoplasmic homogenate (Schroer et al., 1988a). As

TABLE 17-1. ATPase Activities and Bead Velocities of Kinesins

Source	ATPase[a]		V (μm/sec.)	Reference
	− MTs	+ MTs		
Bovine brain	<10	n.d.	0.41 ± 0.05	Vale et al., 1985a
Bovine brain	60–80	2,100[b]	n.d.	Kuznetsov and Gelfand, 1986
Bovine brain	10	157 ± 38	n.d.	Bloom et al., 1988
Bovine brain	2	14	n.d.	Penningroth et al., 1987
Sea urchin egg	2	39	0.47 ± 0.05	Cohn et al., 1987
Drosophila	17	106	0.9	Saxton et al., 1988
Acanthamoeba	10	3,300[b]	3.3 ± 0.3	Kachar et al., 1987

[a]ATPase activities are all expressed in nmoles/min/mg protein. MT, microtubules.
[b]Measured with 10 μM of tubulin dimer assembled into microtubules.

might be expected, kinesin is richest in neural tissue, where the number of cellular processes (axons and dendrites) and the concentration of microtubules are greatest. Because it is primarily a soluble protein, it is available for binding to ligands that are activated to move.

WHAT DOES ATPASE ACTIVITY WITHOUT LIGAND MEAN?

The typical motile complex for kinesin contains a ligand (vesicle or other object to be moved), kinesin, and a microtubule. In vitro measurements of the ATPase activity of kinesin have recently shown an activation with microtubules (see Table 17–1), but these studies have not included any ligand being moved. Under the ionic conditions used to measure ATPase activity (see references in Table 17–1), there is likely to be some microtubule–microtubule sliding and microtubule sliding on the glass of the tube but very little other directed motility. Myosin's actin-activated ATPase activity has been a paradigm for the studies of a microtubule-activated ATPase; however, myosin in its bipolar form needs no additional ligand. Bipolar myosin filaments will move on actin directly to cause superprecipitation in vitro or contraction in vivo. In the case of kinesin, motility is normally observed with kinesin and a ligand, which can be substituted by an anionic surface such as latex beads or glass. The observed ATPase activities in the presence of microtubules alone may represent only a small fraction of the ATPase of the

normal motility complex of ligand, kinesin and microtubule. There is indeed preliminary evidence (Scholey and Schnapp, unpublished results) that the addition of anionic beads greatly increases the microtubule-activated ATPase activity of kinesin. The very low ATPase activities of some kinesin preparations (Scholey, Chapter 20; Penningroth et al., 1987) may be the result of only partial activation in the absence of ligand. The high ATPase activities in other preparations without ligand are puzzling in that an unregulated kinesin would waste significant amounts of energy.

REGULATION OF KINESIN

Estimates of the proportion of kinesin that is soluble in brain and fibroblasts ranges from 60% to 80% of the total kinesin (Sheetz et al., unpublished results; Hollenbeck and Bray, unpublished results). Because it is largely soluble and is in the presence of microtubules, which could activate its ATPase activity, there is concern that kinesin could hydrolyze a significant fraction of the cell's ATP in a wasteful process. This problem is particularly evident for some preparations of bovine brain and *Acanthamoeba* kinesin, which have a microtubule-activated ATPase activity of at least 2 μmoles/mg/min. From the estimated kinesin concentration in neural tissue of 50–100 μg/ml, the ATP hydrolysis rate would be about 1 mM ATP per 5–10 min. This is obviously a very high rate of ATP loss and is unlikely to occur. It is more likely that a regulatory factor or factors prevents kinesin from rapidly hydrolyzing ATP. One possibility is that the cellular microtubules are coated with microtubule-associated proteins (MAPs) and that those MAPs prevent kinesin from interacting with the microtubules. Microtubules present in dissociated axoplasm (Allen et al., 1985; Vale et al., 1985a), sea urchin extracts (Pryer et al., 1986), and fibroblast lysates (Dabora and Sheetz, 1988a) will all support organelle and kinesin-coated bead movements, making it unlikely that regulation is through coating of microtubules. Another possibility is that kinesin-associated proteins (see Schroer, Chapter 19) in cytoplasm block ATP hydrolysis by blocking kinesin binding to microtubules. The proteins present in cytoplasm clearly do not prevent the binding of kinesin to microtubules in AMP-PNP or the subsequent ATP-dependent release of kinesin from microtubules, because that is the normal method of kinesin purification. A third possibility is that kinesin normally has a low microtubule-activated ATPase activity unless it is bound to an active vesicle. This could explain the low microtubule-activated ATPase activities of kinesin (Scholey, Chapter 10; Penningroth et al., 1987), which are insufficient to power movements at the observed rates unless we postulate either an unreasonably large step distance or an unreasonably large number of kinesins in the active motor complex (Scholey, Chapter 20). If kinesin had a much higher ATPase activity when it was fully activated, then a few molecules could power movements at the observed rates. More information is needed on the kinesin ATPase cycle and how it is regulated in the soluble form of kinesin before we can resolve whether ATP hydrolysis uncoupled from movement commonly occurs.

Recent observations of the reactivation of microtubule gliding on glass after an AMP-PNP block suggest that there is a strong cooperativity between multiple ATP binding sites on the kinesin molecule (Schnapp et al., 1986). Because kinesin is a dimer, it is possible that the site on one head influences the other site on the other head by some unknown allosteric mechanism, or a mechanical interaction could be postulated. The concept of one head pulling the other off was considered previously for myosin (Botts et al., 1972), and it is particularly attractive for kinesin. It could explain some of the characteristics of kinesin movement on microtubules at the nanometer level.

NANOMETER-SCALE MEASUREMENTS OF KINESIN MOTIONS

To understand the mechanism of kinesin movement on microtubules, it would be useful to follow the movement of single molecules at the molecular level. Movements of single myosins have been inferred from the contraction of many sarcomeres in series, but the basic motile complex of the many sarcomeres contains many myosins. In the case of kinesin, a few molecules can move a bead that can be visualized in the light microscope, and it is conceivable that the movements of single kinesins can be derived from the movements of individual beads. Recently, we have devised a method of measuring the displacements of submicrometer particles with a precision of 1–2 nm in the light microscope at normal video rates of 30 Hz (Gelles et al., 1988). This technique makes it possible to measure the details of the molecular displacements in two dimensions resulting from the translocation of beads or organelles driven by microtubule-dependent motors. The detailed analysis of kinesin-coated bead movements has revealed many important characteristics of the motor itself that belie the mechanism of kinesin movement (Fig. 17–4) and clearly can be used to differentiate kinesin movements from those of cytoplasmic dynein (Steuer et al., in preparation). When kinesin-coated bead movements are tracked (see Fig. 17–4), we normally find that the beads follow a very narrow path, which indicates that the beads are following the track of single protofilaments. If the bead moves circumferentially from one protofilament to another, it would be displaced by over 40 nm in the perpendicular dimension. In the

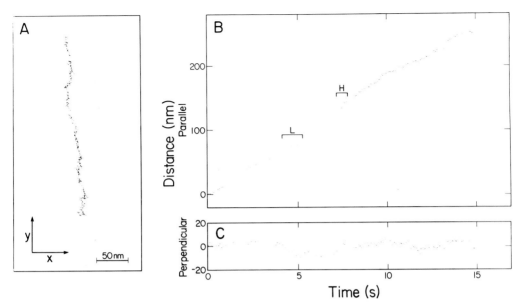

Fig. 17–4. Plots of the movements of kinesin-coated beads upon microtubules (taken from Gelles et al., 1988) in the presence of 10 μM ATP. In **A**, the x and y positions are plotted for a 17-sec interval. After determining the microtubule position by a linear least-squares fit of the points, the parallel (**B**) and perpendicular (**C**) displacements are plotted vs. time. For the entire record in B, the mean parallel velocity is 16.1 nm/sec (3% of maximal velocity). L and H are two segments with mean velocities of 8.2 and 36.2 nm/sec, respectively.

normal kinesin bead movements, the off-axis displacements are less than 20 nm (Fig. 17–4C). Thus, a diagnostic feature of kinesin-dependent bead movements is that they track along the paths of single protofilaments, and studies are underway to determine if plus end-directed organelles move in a similar manner.

At physiological ATP concentrations, kinesin-coated beads move at a maximal velocity of 0.5 μm/sec. Under such conditions, analysis of the axial motion shows that there are periods of markedly different instantaneous velocities (Fig. 17–4B), which suggests that there are differences in the number or character of the kinesin molecules moving the beads with time.

One of the potential uses of this technology is to measure the basic step or motile event of a single kinesin molecule. Because the kinesin molecules are stepping along the microtubule at frequencies of 50–250 steps/sec (assuming that kinesin moves by steps

of 2–10 nm in length) and the video framing rate is 30 frames/sec, it is impossible to measure individual steps at those velocities. We have, therefore, slowed the motion to 2–5 nm/sec by lowering the ATP concentration, which allows us now to measure single steps if there are such. The movement of kinesin-coated beads at these velocities involves rapid jumps followed by stationary periods as well as gradual movements (Gelles et al., 1988). The jumps are of a characteristic distance of 4 nm. Further studies are underway to determine if the 4-nm steps correspond to the average displacement of kinesin per ATP hydrolysis cycle or only to characteristic stopping points of the kinesins on the microtubule lattice (which has a spacing of 4 nm per tubulin subunit).

MECHANISMS OF KINESIN MOVEMENT

The structural characteristics of kinesin (see Fig. 17–2, derived from Fig. 17–1) and the motion behavior of kinesin-coated beads at the nanometer level (Gelles et al., 1988) suggest working models for the mechanism of kinesin movement. To consider such models, it is important to know the minimum number of kinesins required for moving a bead or organelle. A major difference between kinesin and myosin is that typically few kinesin molecules are involved in moving objects, whereas many myosins in bipolar filaments are involved in most myosin movements. The minimum number of kinesins required for movement is not currently known, but the number of cross bridges between vesicles and microtubules is often as low as one and is certainly less than five (Miller and Lasek, 1985; Kachar et al., 1987). This point is critical to any model of the mechanism of kinesin movement.

For the remainder of this discussion, therefore, we will simply assume that a single kinesin is sufficient for movement. Implicit in the assumption that one kinesin with its two heads can move an object is the fact that one head must be attached to a microtubule at all times. If both heads were off simultaneously, the object would diffuse away from the microtubule, and no productive movement would occur. There are two ways in which a head could remain attached for the majority of the time. The first is for the heads to have a very short off time relative to the time in the attached state. This possibility is not very attractive because there is always a reasonable probability that both heads would be off, whereas we often observe the organelles moving for 20 μm or more along a single microtubule without falling off. To put this in mathematical terms, we can assume a step size similar to that of myosin (i.e., 8 nm or the spacing a tubulin dimer), which would mean 2,500 steps before both heads were off. Then we can calculate the percentage of the step time in the off state to be ~2% (we assume that the probability of both heads being off is simply the square of the probability of one head being off). The time for the step would be 4 msec, since the rate of movement is typically 2 μm/sec, which would put the

time for the off state at about 0.08 msec. Although it may be possible to complete the off cycle in 0.08 msec, the behavior of myosin, which typically has an off state lifetime of about 40 msec, is radically different. The other possible way of maintaining one attached head at all times is to make its release conditional on the binding of the other head, i.e., movement would occur in a hand-over-hand fashion. This possibility provides an explanation for the cooperativity between ATP binding sites on kinesin (Schnapp et al., 1986). With the capabilities now available for analyzing the structure of the molecule and the characteristics of the molecular movements, it is possible to devise tests of various models of the mechanism of kinesin movement.

SUMMARY

Within the past 4 years, a novel type of microtubule-dependent motor, kinesin, has been isolated and characterized from a wide variety of organisms and tissues. When viewed in the electron microscope, kinesin appears as a rod of about 70 nm in length, with two small globular domains at one end and two larger domains at the other. There are many similarities between dimeric kinesin and dimeric myosin. Although we do not fully understand the functions of kinesin, it has been shown to have a role in the transport of organelles and is implicated as the motor for endoplasmic reticulum network formation and for the spindle elongation in anaphase A. Because kinesin is primarily found in a soluble phase in cytoplasm, it is available to attach to ligands in all parts of the cell. Ligand binding may be an important component in the activation of kinesin ATPase activity within cells, and much more information is needed to understand the regulation of kinesin-dependent motility. Detailed motion analysis studies have revealed that kinesin moves beads along the paths of single protofilaments of a microtubule, and at low ATP concentrations it periodically stops at 4 nm intervals along the microtubule. We are now in a position to test different models of kinesin movement and bring together the structural and enzymatic studies to understand the mechanisms of kinesin-induced movements in vivo.

ACKNOWLEDGMENTS

The author thanks S. Dabora, J. Gelles, and T. Schroer for their helpful comments. This work was supported by NIH grants GM-36277 and NS23345.

In Vitro Motility Assays for Kinesin and Dynein

Ronald D. Vale and Yoko Yano Toyoshima

Cell Biology Program, Department of Pharmacology, University of California, San Francisco, California 94143; Department of Biology, Ochanomizu University, Ohtsuka, Tokyo 112, Japan

INTRODUCTION

Microtubules are involved in various forms of intracellular motility in eukaryotic cells. Two examples of microtubule-based motility that have been extensively studied are the beating of cilia and flagella (Gibbons, 1981) and the transport of intracellular vesicles along microtubules (Vale, 1987). Although the molecular mechanisms for these movements are far from completely understood, two force-generating proteins, dynein and kinesin, that appear to play important roles in these processes have been purified. Dynein, isolated over 20 years ago by Gibbons and Rowe (1965), is responsible for ciliary and flagellar movement. This protein is stably attached to the A subfiber of outer doublet microtubules and interacts with the B subfiber of adjacent outer doublet microtubules in a cyclic manner that produces sliding of the two outer doublets relative to one another. Cytoplasmic forms of dynein have also been identified, which may be involved in organelle transport as well as mitosis (Pratt, 1984; Paschal et al., 1987a). Kinesin, a more recently purified microtubule motility protein (Vale et al., 1985c),

has also been implicated as a motor for organelle transport (Vale et al., 1986a) and mitosis (Scholey et al., 1985). The biochemical properties of dynein (Johnson, 1985) and kinesin (Vale, 1987) are described in recent reviews as well as in other chapters in this volume.

Both kinesin (Kuznetsov and Gelfand, 1986; Cohn et al., 1987) and dynein (Omoto and Johnson, 1986) are microtubule-activated adenosine triphosphatases (ATPases). The manner in which the energy of ATP hydrolysis is converted into movement, however, is not understood. To examine such questions, one must have suitable systems for examining motility. Reactivated models utilizing detergent-extracted axonemes (Gibbons, 1981) or transport of isolated organelles along purified microtubules (Vale, 1987) have been developed. In addition to the motility-inducing proteins, however, there are additional proteins on the axoneme or organelle that may modulate or influence motility. For elucidating the basic mechanism of kinesin- and dynein-induced movement, simpler assay systems are required, preferably ones involving only the purified force-generating proteins and puri-

Cell Movement, Volume 2: Kinesin,
Dynein, and Microtubule Dynamics, pages 287–294
© 1989 Alan R. Liss, Inc.

fied microtubules. In this article, we describe quantitative motility assays that utilize purified kinesin or dynein and microtubules. Motility assays similar to the ones described here have also been developed for myosin (Kron and Spudich, 1986).

KINESIN MOTILITY ASSAYS

Unlike the case with myosin and dynein, assays for kinesin-induced movement were developed prior to the purification of the protein. The discovery of kinesin emerged from observations made during experiments attempting to reconstitute movement of isolated organelles from squid axoplasm along purified microtubules. In addition to observing organelle movement along the in vitro polymerized microtubules, it was found unexpectedly that high-speed supernatants from squid axoplasm induce movement of microtubules on glass and movement of carboxylated latex beads along the surface of microtubules (Vale et al., 1985b) (Figs. 18–1, 18–2). These findings suggested that axons contain a soluble motor protein that binds to negatively charged surfaces and generates a translocating force on the microtubule. Microtubule movement along glass provided a powerful assay for the fractionation and purification of the force-generating enzyme (kinesin) that elicited these movements (Vale et al., 1985c). Purified kinesin induces microtubule movement on glass and bead movement on microtubules similar to movement in crude axoplasmic supernatants. Hence, these assays can be used to study the motile properties of the purified protein. The following section describes these assays in greater detail.

Microtubule Movement on Glass

Microtubule translocation along glass surfaces requires only purified kinesin, ATP, and microtubules. The microtubules are observed in their native state and in real time using either dark-field (Horio and Hotani, 1986) or differential interference contrast (DIC) light microscopy (Allen, 1985). Images are projected onto targets of either a Newvicon (for DIC) or a silicon-intensified

(for dark-field) camera, and movement is recorded using either 3/4-inch U-matic or 1/2-inch VHS tape recorders. Computerized image processing is useful for improving the contrast and quality of images but is not essential for visualizing microtubules, particularly if dark-field microscopy is used. For a complete description of video microscopy, the reader is referred to a recent book and reviews (Inoué, 1986; Schnapp, 1986). Computer programs are also available for measuring and analyzing velocities of moving objects (see, e.g., Sheetz et al., 1986a).

In the standard assay, microtubules (50

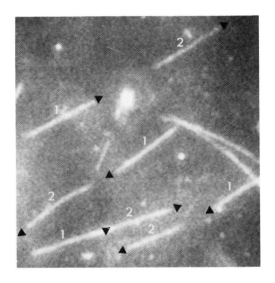

Fig. 18–1. Movement of bovine brain microtubules over a glass surface coated with 22S (outer arm) dynein from tetrahymena cilia. Microtubules were visualized by light microscopy using dark field illumination and movement was recorded using a SIT video camera. This figure was prepared by photographing two video frames 30 sec. apart onto the same 35mm negative. For more information on these experiments, see Vale and Toyoshima (1988). Microtubule movement induced by kinesin adsorbed onto the glass is similar, but occurs at slower rates (0.5μm/sec; Vale et al., 1985b,c).

Kinesin is currently being prepared by microtubule affinity and gel filtration chromatography (Vale et al., 1985c). Concentrations of kinesin greater than 15 μg/ml are necessary for observing motility. The microtubules used to assay motility are free of microtubule-associated proteins (MAPs) and are stabilized with taxol to prevent their depolymerization. Microtubules can be obtained from a variety of sources. Squid kinesin, for example, moves *Tetrahymena* axonemes and bovine or squid microtubules all at approximately the same rate.

The surface coating of the coverslip is an important factor for obtaining kinesin-induced movement (Table 18–1). Untreated glass coverslips are the best surfaces yet tested for kinesin motility. Formvar- and carbon-coated glass also supported movement but to a lesser extent than untreated coverslips. Nitrocellulose (collodion)-treated glass, which has been used successfully in a motility assay with myosin subfragment 1 (Toyoshima et al., 1987), did not support kinesin motility.

Movement of microtubules along kinesin-coated glass coverslips is generally smooth and unidirectional. Although kinesin is presumably randomly oriented on the glass, unidirectional movement occurs because kinesin produces force in only one direction along the microtubule lattice. Hence, only those kinesin molecules that are oriented properly with respect to the correct axis of the microtubule will be capable of producing force. Occasionally, long microtubules follow curved paths (see Fig. 7 in Vale et al., 1985b), as if following a path of kinesin molecules with different orientations.

In some instances, the leading segment of the microtubule becomes stuck or blocked on the coverslip while the trailing region of the microtubule continues to move. The forward propulsion from the rear causes the middle of the microtubule to buckle, a phenomenon termed "fishtailing" by Allen and his colleagues (1985). Although the kinesin-derived force is capable of producing a substantial bend in microtubules, which are normally straight and rigid in solution, the

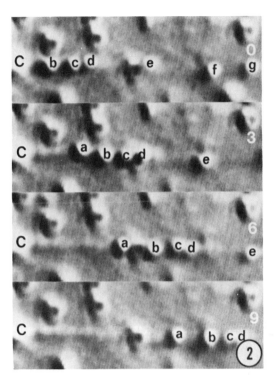

Fig. 18–2. Kinesin-induced movement of carboxylated latex beads along centrosomal microtubules. This figure shows a microtubule polymerized from a centrosome (c); the plus end of the microtubule is free and pointing towards the right, and the minus end is anchored to the centrosome. Beads (a–g) are shown moving along the microtubule towards the plus end. Bead a binds to the microtubule from the solution between the first and second panels. Seconds elapsed are indicated in the upper right of each panel. (Reproduced from Vale et al., 1985d, with permission of the publisher.)

μg/ml), ATP (1 mM), and kinesin are combined in a 10–15-μl aliquot and placed between a glass slide and coverslip. Alternatively, kinesin can be adsorbed onto a glass slide in a flow chamber, followed by removal of unbound kinesin by exchange with buffer. When microtubules are subsequently added in the presence of ATP, they bind to kinesin molecules on the glass and translocate along the surface. This latter method avoids microtubule aggregation in solution, which often occurs in the presence of free kinesin.

TABLE 18–1. Motility Assays for HMM-Myosin, Kinesin, and 14S Dynein Using Different Surfaces*

Surface	Motility protein		
	HMM-myosin	14S dynein	Kinesin
Glass	−	+ + +	+ + +
Formvar	−	−	−
Formvar + carbon	+ + +	+ + +	+
Collodion	+ + +	−	−
Collodion + carbon	+ +	+ +	−
Batvar	−	−	−
Triafor	−	−	−
Alucian blue	−	−	−

*Surface coatings on glass coverslips were prepared by the following procedures. Collodion (1% in amylacetate) was spread over a water surface by applying one or two drops in a 10-cm-diameter petri dish filled with water. After 15 min, a 22 × 22-mm coverslip was floated on the surface, then removed and air dried. Triafol (04.% in ethyl acetate), Formvar (0.5% in chloroform), or Batvar (1% in chloroform) was applied by dipping a glass slide directly into these solutions and then drying the slide in air. Film was removed from one side of the slide by cutting the edge with a razor and floating the film in water. The film was then picked up onto a 22 × 22-mm glass coverslip. Alucian blue (1% in water) was applied directly to the glass coverslip, then rinsed in distilled water and air dried. Carbon was deposited directly onto Formvar or collodion using an evaporator. Motility assays for HMM-myosin (Toyoshima et al., 1987), 14S dynein from *Tetrahymena* (Vale and Toyoshima, 1988), and squid kinesin (Vale et al., 1985c) are described elsewhere. Motility was scored as follows: + + +, continuous movement, essentially all microtubules are moving; + +, each field has some microtubules moving, but movement is more infrequent and is discontinuous; +, only occasional movements of microtubules are observed over a period of 10 min of observation; −, no movement observed.

microtubules do not break apart as has been observed with actin filaments moving along myosin-coated coverslips (Kron and Spudich, 1986).

The velocity of kinesin-induced microtubule movement is 0.5–0.6 μm/sec (Fig. 18–3). Kinesin requires Mg and a nucleotide, preferably ATP, to produce movement; ATP in the absence of Mg functions as a competitive inhibitor (Schnapp et al., 1986; Cohn et al., 1987). The K_m for movement is ~ 50–75 μm ATP (Schnapp et al., 1986; Porter et al., 1987), a value significantly higher than the K_m reported for kinesin ATPase activity (10 μm) (Kuznetsov and Gelfand, 1986). Myosin also displays a fivefold higher K_m for motility than for ATPase activity (Kron and Spudich, 1986). Since both kinesin (Scholey, Chapter 20; Vale, 1987) and myosin (Cooke, 1986) form rigor complexes with microtubules or actin filaments in the absence of ATP, the slower velocity of movement observed at low ATP concentrations may be the result of a drag force produced when an increasing proportion of motility proteins are bound in a rigor state. Similarly, AMP-PNP, which induces a rigor-like binding state between kinesin and microtubules, decreases the velocity of kinesin-induced microtubule movement (Schnapp et al., 1986).

Movement of Carboxylated Latex Beads

Kinesin also attaches to carboxylated latex beads and translocates the beads towards the plus ends of microtubules (Fig. 18–2). The velocities of kinesin-driven bead and microtubule movements are approximately the same (0.5 μm/sec). When examined under the microscope, beads in Brownian motion in solution bind to microtubules and translocate for several micrometers before dissociating. This behavior is similar to that of axoplasmic organelles that move along microtubules (Vale et al., 1985a). Recent motion analysis by Gelles et al. (1988) indicates that beads translocate along a single protofilament track of the microtubule.

The surface charge on the bead is also important for motility. Of a variety of beads

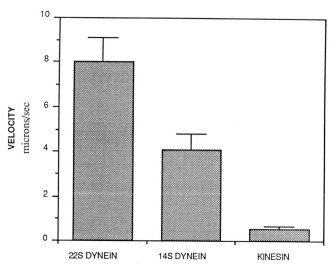

Fig. 18–3. Velocities of microtubule movement along glass induced by squid kinesin, 14S dynein, and 22S dynein in the presence of 1 mM MgATP. Detailed descriptions of velocity measurements for kinesin (Vale et al., 1985c; Porter et al., 1987; Schnapp et al., 1986; Cohn et al., 1987) and dynein (Vale and Toyoshima, 1988) are provided elsewhere. This figure shows the mean velocity and standard deviation for at least 25 microtubules that were moving continuously along the glass.

tested, only carboxylated and methylmethacrylate beads undergo movement (Table 18–2). Similar results were obtained by Adams and Bray (1983), who found that carboxylated beads, but not beads derivatized with amino groups, are transported towards the nerve terminal when injected into axons.

MOTILITY ASSAYS FOR AXONEMAL DYNEIN

Axoneme Model Systems

Summers and Gibbons (1971) demonstrated that outer doublets of trypsinized axonemes slide past one another at rates of 10–14 μm/sec after addition of ATP. The sliding is unidirectional, and the direction of sliding indicates that dynein moves towards the minus ends of microtubules (Sale and Satir, 1977). This assay provides a simplified model for investigating the mechanism of ciliary force generation. Isolated, detergent-extracted axonemes also undergo propagated wave-like beating upon addition of ATP (Gibbons and Gibbons, 1972; Naitoh and Kaneko, 1972), and such systems provide a means of examining how outer doublet microtubule sliding is converted into a propagated wave.

A variety of evidence illustrates that dyneins are involved in the ciliary movements described above; however, motility of purified dynein has been demonstrated only indirectly. Purified 21S dynein from sea urchin sperm flagella, for example, rebinds to salt-extracted axonemes and increases beat frequency (Gibbons and Gibbons, 1976, 1979) or the velocity of outer doublet sliding (Yano and Miki-Noumura, 1981). One difficulty of such assays, however, is that motility occurs without adding extracted dynein, a finding that indicates that residual motility proteins, which are not extracted by salt, contribute to movement in the axoneme. Measurement of beat frequency as an indication of dynein force is also complicated, since other regulatory or structural proteins in axonemes may be involved in this phenomenon. Outer doublet sliding is probably a more direct measurement of dynein force generation; however, long-term observations of movement are not possible,

Bead	Movement
Polystyrene	−
Polystyrene-NH$_2$	−
Polystyrene-OH	−
Butadiene	−
Polystyrene-COOH	+
Polymethylmethacrylate	+

*A variety of different beads were obtained from Polysciences, Inc., and tested for motility along microtubules in the presence of kinesin. + Indicates directed movement of the beads along microtubules; − indicates no movement.

since outer doublet sliding terminates when one outer doublet extends past the adjacent outer doublet, which occurs after 1–5 sec depending on the length of the axoneme.

Microtubule Movement on Glass

For learning about the molecular properties of dynein-based motility, an assay that uses purified dynein and microtubules is required. Because of recent successes of attaching kinesin (Vale et al., 1985b,c) and myosin (Kron and Spudich, 1986) to glass coverslips in a manner that preserves the motile activity of at least some of the molecules, we attempted to perform a similar assay with ciliary dynein. A detailed description of these experiments is reported elsewhere (Vale and Toyoshima, 1988).

Tetrahymena was selected as a source of ciliary dynein, since dynein can be prepared in milligram quantities by a simple purification procedure of high-salt extraction followed by sucrose density gradient centrifugation (Johnson, 1986). Fractions containing the triple-headed, outer arm 22S dynein and the single-headed 14S dynein were tested for motility using the assays already described for kinesin. Microtubules prepared from bovine brain phosphocellulose tubulin were used in these assays.

Microtubules translocated along the surface of the glass when 22S or 14S dyneins were attached to the glass coverslip. As with kinesin, untreated glass was the most effective surface tested for movement (Table 18–1). Fractions containing 14S dynein induced smooth and continuous microtubule movement at a mean velocity of 3–4 μm/sec (Fig. 18–3). Movement induced by 22S dynein, on the other hand, tended to be more discontinuous. Small microtubules < 5 μm often moved rapidly, then would slow down or stop completely and then accelerate again. Short (4μm) reverse movements were sometimes seen. Velocities during times of continuous movement were ~8 μm/sec (Fig. 18–3), although in more recent experiments we have observed velocities as high as 12 μm/sec. The velocity of microtubule movement with 22S dynein was dependent on protein concentration. At high concentrations of 22S dynein (0.5–1 mg/ml during a 2-min adsorption onto the glass), little or no microtubule movement occurred; maximal velocities were generally obtained at protein concentrations of 100 μg/ml. The discontinuous microtubule movement and inhibition at high 22S dynein concentrations may be due to ATP-insensitive (A subfiber) binding which could produce a drag force on movement. The velocity of microtubule movement with 14S dynein, in contrast, was not diminished at high protein concentrations.

A variety of inhibitors of the dynein ATPase were tested for their effects on 22S- and 14S-induced motility. Vanadate (1 μm) and erythro-9 [3-(2-hydroxynonyl)] adenine (EHNA; 1 mM), two of the most potent inhibitors of the dynein ATPase, both inhibited 22S and 14S dynein motility (Table 18–3). EHNA, however, reduced the velocity of movement by 70% but did not completely block movement. Neither 1 μm vanadate nor 1 mM EHNA has an effect on kinesin-induced motility. Furthermore, the alkylating reagent N-ethylmaleimide (NEM; 1 mM), which inhibits dynein motility, does not affect kinesin-induced movement.

We have also used the in vitro motility assay to determine the direction of dynein-induced movement. From electron microscopic examination of outer doublets engaged in sliding, Sale and Satir (1977) concluded that outer arm dynein produces movement of the adjacent outer doublets

TABLE 18–3. Inhibition of Kinesin and Dynein Motility*

Agent	Motor protein		
	Kinesin	14S dynein	22S dynein
NEM (1 mM)	94	—	—
Vanadate (1 μm)	105	—	—
EHNA (1 mM)	104	27	35

*Microtubule movement on glass was tested in the presence of the indicated agents and 1 mM ATP. The numbers indicate the percent of the velocity of microtubule movement in the absence of an added agent. A dash indicates no movement.

towards the tip of the axoneme, which indicates that dynein itself moves towards the minus end of microtubules. We have determined the polarity of movement of purified 22S and 14S dynein using the in vitro motility assay. Since it is not possible to distinguish minus and plus ends of microtubules by light microscopy, axonemes from *Tetrahymena* were used to nucleate assembly of bovine brain tubulin under conditions that preferentially promote tubulin growth from the plus ends (see Vale and Toyoshima, 1988). When applied to coverslips containing bound 22S or 14S dynein, microtubules polymerized from axonemes always moved with their plus ends leading in the direction of movement. Thus both 22S and 14S dynein produce force in the direction predicted from the outer doublet sliding experiments of Sale and Satir. This direction is opposite to that of kinesin-induced movement along a microtubule (Table 18–4).

A surprising result that emerged from the polarity studies is that 14S dynein induces rotation of the microtubule during forward translocation (Vale and Toyoshima, 1988). Many of the *Tetrahymena* axonemes used in the polarity assay are slightly curved, which provides an asymmetric marker. During microtubule translocation in the presence of 14S dynein, the curved end of the trailing axonemes was observed rotating about the longitudinal axis. The direction of rotation is clockwise when viewed from the minus end of rotating axoneme. Rotation requires forward movement of the microtubule, and the microtubule and attached axoneme rotate once for every 0.5 μm of forward movement. Rotation of microtubule–axoneme com-

TABLE 18–4. Polarity of Kinesin and Dynein Movement*

Motility protein	Direction of movement
Kinesin	Plus end
14S dynein	Minus end
22S dynein	Minus end

*Polarity is defined as the direction of movement along a microtubule of the surface containing the bound motor proteins. In the case of kinesin, the polarity was identified by movement of kinesin-coated carboxylated beads along microtubules grown from centrosomes in vitro (Vale et al., 1985d). For dynein, polarity was identified by observing the direction of movement of microtubules polymerized from the plus ends of axonemes along dynein-coated glass coverslips (Vale and Toyoshima, 1988).

plexes is not observed in presence of 22S dynein.

PROSPECTS FOR FUTURE INVESTIGATIONS
Dynein-Based Motility

Microtubule movement on glass provides a simple motility assay for dynein. This assay is an improvement over existing methods in that 1) it requires only pure dynein and microtubules, 2) it provides quantitative velocity information, and 3) it is rapid and requires very small quantities of protein. We (Vale and Toyoshima, unpublished observations) and Paschal et al. (1987b) also have found that dynein prepared from sea urchin sperm flagella is capable of producing microtubule movement across glass coverslips. Lye et al. (1987) and Paschal et al. (1987a) have also shown that cytoplasmic dynein-like molecules generate microtubule movement along a glass coverslip. Collectively, these findings suggest that this motility assay can be used to examine the properties of many different types of dyneins.

The motility assay has also provided the opportunity to make a functional comparison between 22S and 14S dyneins. The biochemical relationship between 14S and 22S dynein has not been conclusively established. Antibodies raised against 22S dynein heavy chains cross react with 14S dynein heavy chains, indicating that they contain similar epitopes (Nishino and Watanabe, 1977); however, the heavy chains of 14S and 22S dynein migrate differently on urea gels and 5% polyacrylamide gels, indicating that they are not identical (Toyoshima, 1987). Furthermore, it is unlikely that 14S is derived from 22S by proteolysis, since a constant ratio of 22S to 14S is obtained in biochemical preparations regardless of whether protease inhibitors are present (Mabuchi and Shimizu, 1974; Vale and Toyoshima, unpublished observations). We have also found that 14S and 22S dynein have different motile properties when tested in a variety of different buffer conditions, suggesting that 14S dynein is a distinct motility protein from 22S dynein.

An unexpected finding of our motility studies is that 14S dynein induces microtubule rotation in addition to translocation. This result suggests that this motility protein is capable of generating torque, which has not been described for other ATP-hydrolyzing force-generating proteins. This result also raises interest in the role of 14S dynein in the cilia. One intriguing possibility is that 14S dynein is involved in the rotation of central-pair microtubules that has been described in several types of cilia (Omoto and Kung, 1980; Hosokawa and Miki-Noumura, 1987). The biochemical and enzymatic properties of 14S dynein, however, have not been as well characterized as 22S dynein, and the location of 14S dynein in the axoneme also has not been conclusively

ascertained. Thus further characterization of this dynein is required to understand how 14S dynein-induced torque is utilized in the axoneme.

The in vitro assay will also provide an important new tool for investigating the structural domains of dynein responsible for producing motility. Outer arm dynein is a remarkably complex protein consisting of several types of polypeptides and has a native molecular weight between 1.2 and 2 × 10^6 Da. The roles of the various polypeptides in dynein force generation are poorly defined. We have found recently that the single-headed β/IC subunit of sea urchin sperm flagellar dynein induces microtubule movement in vitro. We are also beginning to define further domains involved in motility by preparing proteolytic fragments of 22S dynein and studying their behavior in the in vitro motility assay.

Mechanism of Microtubule-Based Force Generation

The simple in vitro motility assays for kinesin and dynein provide new opportunities for examining how force is generated along microtubules. Although the ATPase activities of dynein and kinesin have been characterized, there are many basic questions regarding how these proteins produce movement that remain unanswered. For example, 1) How many kinesin or dynein molecules are required to produce microtubule movement? and 2) What is the quantum step size in a single kinesin or dynein cycle? Although the answers to these questions are not in hand, they are approachable using in vitro motility assays in which microtubule movement is induced by relatively small numbers of molecules. Furthermore, little is known of how kinesin- and dynein-based motility is regulated. The in vitro motility assays could be used to test for factors or post-translational modifications of kinesin or dynein that affect motility.

Role of Kinesin and Kinesin-Associated Proteins in Organelle Transport

Trina A. Schroer and Michael P. Sheetz

*Department of Cell Biology and Physiology, Washington University School of Medicine,
St. Louis, Missouri 63110*

INTRODUCTION

The phenomenon of ATP-dependent intracellular organelle transport has been observed in many types of cells (for reviews, see Schliwa, 1984; Grafstein and Forman, 1980; Schwartz, 1979). The involvement of microtubules in fast axonal transport, pigment granule migration in chromatophores, and organelle movements in cultured cells was first deduced by the sensitivity of these processes to microtubule inhibitors. Recently, elegant microscopic studies have directly demonstrated that organelles move along microtubules and, moreover, that organelles can be translocated in opposite directions on the same microtubule (Allen et al., 1985; Koonce and Schliwa, 1985; Schnapp et al., 1985). In this chapter, we discuss the role of kinesin and other microtubule-based motors in organelle motility.

Organelles move in two directions along microtubules in nerve cell dendrites and axons, processes of cultured cells, and the arms of chromatophores. Microtubules have an intrinsic polarity that can be determined experimentally by measuring the rate of polymerization at the two ends (Bergen and Borisy, 1980; Mitchison and Kirschner, 1984; Pryer et al., 1986) or by the pattern of decoration with proteins (Heidemann and McIntosh, 1979; Haimo et al., 1979). In most cells, microtubules are oriented with their minus ends near the cell center and the plus ends at the periphery (Euteneuer and McIntosh, 1981). Movement of organelles outward to the periphery of the cell (toward the plus end of microtubules) is functionally the same as anterograde axonal transport in neurons. Likewise, movement in the opposite direction, from the cell periphery back to the cell center (toward the minus end of microtubules), is equivalent to retrograde axonal transport. For simplicity, we will use the terms plus end-directed and minus end-directed transport in a general sense here. Cellular microtubules support bidirectional organelle movements, and it is likely that different motors serve to power plus end-directed and minus end-directed translocation. Neither motor has been identified; however, two well characterized, soluble ATPases are obvious candidates. Kinesin promotes plus end-directed motility (Vale et al., 1985d; Porter et al., 1987; see other chapters in this section), and dynein promotes minus end-directed movement (Sale and Satir, 1977; Paschal and Vallee, 1987; see also Volume 1 in this series). We will discuss the evidence that kinesin and cytoplasmic dynein (a homolog of flagellar dynein; Paschal et al., 1987b; Pratt, 1986a) are organelle motors and will present evidence that proteins associated with kinesin are necessary for organelle translocation events in neurons.

ORGANELLE MOTILITY IN VITRO: EXPERIMENTAL APPROACHES

Organelle translocation can be directly assayed only by light microscopic observation. Phase-contrast microscopy is used to examine organelle motility in highly flattened cells (e.g., fibroblasts) or cells containing large, phase-dense, motile organelles (e.g., chromatophores). Observation of motility of small, phase-neutral organelles in rounded cells (e.g., other cultured cells and neuronal axons and dendrites) requires differential interference contrast (DIC) optics. The recent development of video-enhanced microscopy (Allen et al., 1981; Allen and Allen, 1983; Inoué, 1981; Schnapp, 1986) has allowed the direct observation of very small organelles in essentially any cell type and is used in much of the work discussed here. Another major methodological advance has been the use of in vitro approaches for the study of organelle motility. An in vitro motility system can be as simple as a whole cell that has been made experimentally accessible by detergent or a microinjection needle. Other studies examine the motility of exogenous particles that are added to whole cells. Organelle motility can also be completely reconstituted from isolated components.

Organelle Motility in Whole Cells

The effects of drugs and other reagents on organelle motility in live, intact cells cannot be assessed because the plasma membrane is an effective permeability barrier that prevents the entry of most large and charged molecules into the cytoplasm. To use these agents in studies of the mechanism of organelle translocation, it is necessary to bypass this barrier. Nonpermeable macromolecules may be introduced into cytoplasm by microinjection, or the plasma membrane can be gently permeabilized with certain detergents (e.g., Brij 58, saponin, and digitonin). Both approaches yield cells that retain normal levels of organelle motility into which pharmacological agents and enzymes are readily introduced. Forman and coworkers have shown that organelle translocation in detergent-permeabilized fibroblasts (Forman, 1982) and axons (Forman et al., 1983a) is inhibited by vanadate ion, an inhibitor of dynein and other ATPases (see below). Pigment granule migration in microinjected or detergent-permeabilized chromatophores is also vanadate-sensitive (Beckerle and Porter, 1982, Clark and Rosenbaum, 1982; Stearns and Ochs, 1982).

Rodzdial and Haimo (1986a,b) have used permeabilized chromatophores to examine the mechanism of directionality switching of pigment granule migration. Their results indicate that cyclic adenosine monophosphate (cAMP)-dependent phosphorylation of a 57,000 M_r protein is required for the dispersion of pigment granules (plus end-directed movement), whereas dephosphorylation of the same protein occurs during minus end-directed pigment granule aggregation. In *Reticulomyxa* (a freshwater amoeba), cAMP-dependent phosphorylation appears to cause minus end-directed organelle motility, and dephosphorylation causes the complete detachment of organelles from microtubules (Koonce and Schliwa, 1986a). Although the specific results are different in these two studies, it is tempting to speculate that a cycle of phosphorylation and dephosphorylation is a general mechanism for controlling the directionality of organelle movement.

Motility of Exogenous Particles in Cytoplasm

In vitro studies have demonstrated the motility of particles introduced by microinjection into living cytoplasm. Plastic beads were microinjected into axons (Adams and

Bray, 1983), fibroblasts (Beckerle, 1984), or sea urchin eggs (Wadsworth, 1987) and in all cases were observed to be translocated at the same velocity as endogenous organelles. Curiously, beads moved in different directions (exclusively plus end-directed, exclusively minus end-directed, or in both directions) in the different cell types. The observed direction preference is likely a reflection of biochemical characteristics of different motor proteins that allow the plus end-directed and minus end-directed motors to bind nonspecifically with different affinities to plastic beads.

Membranous organelles that were fluorescently labeled to distinguish them from endogenous organelles have also been introduced into axonal cytoplasm (Gilbert and Sloboda, 1984; Schroer et al., 1985). In both studies, the fluorescent organelles were translocated in the expected direction; axoplasmic organelles moved bidirectionally (Gilbert and Sloboda, 1984), and purified synaptic vesicles moved preferentially toward the synapse, i.e., toward the plus end of microtubules (Schroer et al., 1985). Organelles that had been treated with proteases no longer moved. These data suggest that motors bind to protease-sensitive membrane receptors to produce movement in a particular direction and will not bind to organelles in the absence of the appropriate receptor.

Organelle Motility in Reconstituted Systems

A third, more powerful approach to the study of organelle translocation is the development of a reconstituted system. The advantage of an in vitro assay is that individual components can be manipulated separately and added back to the assay to assess the effects of manipulation. In vitro motility assays have been developed using crude cytoplasmic extracts, subfractions of extracts, or purified proteins and organelles. The substrate for motility is endogenous microtubules (native or taxol-stabilized), exogenous microtubules (reconstituted from depolymerized tubulin), or axonemes that have been isolated from flagella. Axo-

nemes have the advantage of obvious morphological polarity, since they will regrow individual microtubules preferentially from the plus end in the presence of depolymerized tubulin (Bergen and Borisy, 1980). Microtubules of a known polarity (plus end-free) that have been polymerized from purified centrosomes (Mitchison and Kirschner, 1984) can also be used to determine the direction of movement observed in a motility assay. The moving particles in a reconstituted assay are endogenous organelles, exogenously added organelles, or inert particles such as latex beads. The most important component of the assay is the motor, which is present in unfractionated cytoplasm, in a clarified cytoplasmic extract, or as a partially purified or pure protein fraction. These three components can be used in any combination in a motility assay.

In one type of in vitro motility assay, the three necessary components, microtubules, organelles, and motors, are present in a crude cytoplasmic extract. This assay system was used successfully by Pryer and coworkers (1986) to examine organelle motility activity in a low-speed supernatant prepared from sea urchin eggs. They observed that organelles were translocated in both directions on aggregates of endogenous, taxol-stabilized microtubules. Microtubules were also observed to glide across the glass surface, an indication of the presence of kinesin in the supernatant (see below).

A similar motility assay using extracts of cultured fibroblasts was developed recently in our laboratory (Dabora and Sheetz, 1988a). A low-speed supernatant fraction is the source of organelles, motors, and microtubules (induced to polymerize with taxol and guanosine triphosphate; GTP). Upon the addition of ATP, organelles are translocated on microtubules, and microtubules writhe on the glass surface. The organelles move bidirectionally, but most (80–90%) are minus end-directed. The fibroblast extract also promotes the formation and motility along microtubules of a network of membrane tubules containing elements of endoplasmic reticulum (Dabora and Sheetz, 1988b). This dynamic network grows slowly along microtubules from membrane aggregates, forming branches where microtubules intersect. Membrane tubule formation and movement occur at a velocity similar to that of organelle translocation. This novel type of motility has profound implications for the structure and dynamics of endoplasmic reticulum (ER) and other intracellular membrane networks. The pharmacological sensitivities of organelle movement in chick embryo fibroblasts (CEF) are discussed below.

Cytoplasm isolated from the squid giant axon is the most extensively characterized source of organelle motility assay components. Both simple and completely reconstituted organelle motility assays have been performed using components of squid axoplasm. The movement of small organelles (50–80 nm in diameter) was first observed in intact axons (Allen et al., 1982) and in extruded axoplasm (Brady et al., 1982) using video-enhanced DIC microscopy. The investigators also noted that organelles moved along filaments (later shown to be microtubules) that had separated from the edges of the bulk axoplasm (Allen et al., 1983, 1985; Lasek and Brady, 1985). Vale and coworkers extended these studies by completely dispersing axoplasm using perfusion (1985a) or homogenization (1985b). Homogenized axoplasm was separated into an organelle fraction and a soluble fraction (S2 supernatant) that contained motor activity. Addition of axoplasmic organelles, S2 supernatant, and ATP to purified microtubules isolated from squid brain resulted in bidirectional organelle movement along the microtubules. If plastic beads were added, they were translocated as well. The microtubules themselves crawled on the glass coverslip, and, using microtubule motility as an assay, Vale and coworkers (1985c) purified kinesin from S2 supernatant. Purified kinesin powers bead movement toward the plus end of microtubules exclusively. If kinesin is removed from S2 supernatant using a monoclonal antibody, the remaining supernatant supports only minus end-directed

TABLE 19–1. Properties of Squid Optic Lobe Kinesin*

Molecular weight	300 kDa
Subunit composition	Two of 110 kDa
	Two of 65–70 kDa
$S_{20,w}$	9.6
ATPase	MT-activated (sea urchin egg and bovine brain kinesin)
	K_m (ATP) = 10 μM
Motor activities	Moves microtubules on glass
	Moves anionic beads on microtubules
	Stimulates organelle movement (see text)
	K_m (ATP) = 85 μM

*References: Vale et al., 1985c; Schnapp et al., unpublished observations; Sheetz, unpublished observations; Bloom et al., 1988.

movement of beads on microtubules (Vale et al., 1985d). These results clearly indicate that axoplasm contains two different soluble motors that power the movement of beads in opposite directions on microtubules.

ORGANELLE MOTOR CANDIDATES: KINESIN, CYTOPLASMIC DYNEIN, AND HIGH-M_r MICROTUBULE-ASSOCIATED PROTEINS (MAPs)

Any microtubule-based motor may be an organelle translocator. Since kinesin and dynein are plus end-directed and minus end-directed microtubule-dependent motors, these two proteins might provide for bidirectional organelle motility in vivo.

Known Features of the Microtubule-Based Motors Kinesin and Dynein

Biochemical properties. The major component of kinesin is a polypeptide that ranges from 90,000 to 135,000 M_r in different species (see Vale et al., 1986b, for review). Kinesin is present in complexes of roughly 300,000 M_r and sediments at 9.5S in sucrose gradients (see Table 19–1 for characteristics of squid kinesin; see also Porter et al., 1987; and Bloom et al., Chapter 21). Dynein is a larger protein, characterized by at least one high-M_r polypeptide (M_r ~400,000) and is present in solution as

TABLE 19–2. Effects of Inhibitors on Motor Activities*

Motor	Na$_3$VO$_4$		NEM	
	20 μM	100 μM	2 mM	5 mM
Motor				
Flagellar dynein[a]	−	−	−	−	−
Cytoplasmic dynein[b]	−	± to +	−	−	−
Kinesin[c]	−	+	−	+	−
Retrograde factor[d]	−	−	−	−	−
Organelle motility				
Squid axoplasm[e]	−	+	−	−	−
Lobster axons[f]	ND	+	−	ND	ND
Cultured fibroblasts[g]	ND	+	−	ND	ND

*The table summarizes the inhibitory effects of pharmacological agents on ATPase and motor activity. Flagellar dynein activity was measured as ATPase and motility; cytoplasmic dynein activity was measured as ATPase; kinesin activity was measured as microtubule motility; retrograde factor activity was measured as bead translocation activity. − Indicates that motility or ATPase activity was not observed; + indicates that a high level of motility or ATPase activity (50% of control) persisted after drug treatment; ± indicates that motility or ATPase activity was inhibited by at least 50%; ND, not determined.

[a]Gibbons et al., 1978, Johnson, 1985.
[b]Pratt et al., 1984; Scholey et al., 1984; Asai and Wilson, 1985.
[c]Vale et al., 1985c; Cohn et al., 1987; Porter et al., 1987.
[d]Vale et al., 1985d.
[e]Lasek and Brady, 1985; Vale et al., 1985b; Vale, unpublished.
[f]Forman et al., 1983a.
[g]Forman, 1982.

a 1–2 × 10^6 M$_r$ complex sedimenting at 14S–21S (Johnson, 1985; Paschal et al., 1987a). Both motors bind tightly to microtubules, but with different nucleotide specificities. Kinesin binds strongly in the presence of the nonhydrolyzable ATP analog AMP-PNP, whereas dynein does not. Both bind microtubules strongly in the absence of ATP (Scholey et al., 1984, 1985; Paschal et al., 1987a).

Pharmacological properties. Since dynein-based and kinesin-based motility are driven by ATP hydrolysis, both ATPase activity and the ability of the proteins to promote microtubule-dependent movement can be assayed. Dynein and kinesin have characteristically different sensitivities to the inhibitors N-ethylmaleimide (NEM) and vanadate (see Table 19–2). Kinesin ATPase and microtubule gliding activities are resistant to 2 mM NEM or 20 μM vanadate (but not to 5 mM NEM or 100 μM vanadate; Vale et al., 1985d; Porter et al., 1987; Cohn et al., 1987). In contrast, dynein ATPase and microtubule translocation activities are inhibited by low concentrations of NEM (< 2 mM) and vana-

date (20 μM; Gibbons et al., 1978; Johnson, 1985). Thus resistance to low concentrations of NEM and vanadate can be used as criteria to identify kinesin-driven translocation events. Since a high concentration of vanadate (100 μM) inhibits both kinesin and dynein, it is not surprising that 100 μM vanadate inhibits both directions of organelle movement in all experimental systems in which it has been tested (Forman, 1982; Forman et al., 1983a; Vale et al., 1985d). Vanadate at 20 μM inhibits minus end-directed but not plus end-directed movements of plastic beads on centrosome microtubules (Vale et al., 1985d) and minus end-directed organelle movement in fibroblast extracts (Dabora and Sheetz, 1988a). These results are consistent with kinesin and dynein acting as plus end-directed and minus end-directed motors, respectively. However, organelle translocation in squid axoplasm is completely inhibited by 2 mM NEM (Vale, unpublished observations), suggesting that plus end-directed transport involves both kinesin and an NEM-sensitive factor. Isolated organelles that have been treated with NEM still move when introduced into axoplasm, indicating that NEM is acting on soluble rather than organelle-associated components (Brady and Schroer, 1985).

Role in Organelle Motility

Dynein. Cytoplasmic dynein from sea urchin eggs has been purified and is well characterized biochemically (Hisanaga and Sakai, 1983; Pratt et al., 1984; Scholey et al., 1984). "Dynein-like" ATPases have been identified in sea urchin and in other cell types on the basis of their binding to microtubules, high M_r, pharmacology, or immunological cross reactivity (Pallini et al., 1983; Hollenbeck et al., 1984; Asai and Wilson, 1985; Vale et al., 1985d; Lye et al., 1987; Ogawa et al., 1987). Recently, a "true" cytoplasmic dynein was purified from bovine brain by Paschal and coworkers (1987b). This protein (MAP 1C) has the same high M_r on SDS-PAGE as *Chlamydomonas* axonemal dynein β chain and sediments at 20S in sucrose gradients. MAP 1C also has a microtubule-activated ATPase activity and is susceptible to ultraviolet (UV) photocleavage in the presence of ATP and vanadate, a feature specific to dynein ATPases. Finally, MAP 1C causes microtubule gliding in a direction that would correspond to retrograde transport in axons. Cytoplasmic dynein has not been directly tested for its ability to promote organelle movement in vitro.

The hypothesis that cytoplasmic dynein powers organelle transport is supported by morphological evidence. In chromatophores, dynein is associated with the microtubules that support pigment granule migration (Ogawa et al., 1987). A subfraction of sea urchin egg dynein copurifies with membranous organelles on sucrose gradients and has the same intracellular distribution as organelles in intact cells (Pratt et al., 1986). It is unclear whether, in vivo, cytoplasmic dynein resides on microtubules or on organelles, but in either location it may serve to link organelles and microtubules and power organelle motility.

High-M_r MAPs. High-M_r MAPs other than dynein may also play a role in organelle translocation. Lye et al. (1987) have identified a high-M_r protein ($M_r \cong 400,000$) in *C. elegans* that, like dynein and kinesin, binds to microtubules in the absence of ATP. Like dynein, this protein is cleaved by UV light and vanadate. This protein also promotes ATP-dependent microtubule gliding on glass, although in the same direction as kinesin (see note added in proof). Gilbert and Sloboda (1986; see also Sloboda, Chapter 12) have identified a high-M_r ATP-binding protein in squid axoplasm that is immunologically related to MAP 2, a well charac terized microtubule binding protein. This protein (called *vesikin*) is found in association with organelles that move on microtubules in the absence of additional motor. Vesikin has been shown to have a microtubule-activated ATPase activity (see Sloboda, Chapter 12) and is also a component of stable microtubule–organelle complexes that form between axoplasmic components (Pratt, 1986b). Taken together, these results suggest that vesikin is involved in organelle translocation. Stearns and Binder (1987) have also identified a protein, immunologically related to MAP 2, that may be involved in organelle transport in chromatophores. The high-M_r MAP 2 ($M_r \cong 300,000$) appears to colocalize with pigment granules during aggregation and dispersion. Unlike the *C. elegans* high-M_r MAP, neither the squid nor chromatophore MAP 2-like protein has been demonstrated to cause microtubule (or organelle) motility in a reconstituted system.

Kinesin. Several properties are characteristic of kinesin: binding to microtubules in the presence of AMP-PNP, a molecular weight in the range of 90,000 to 135,000 Da, immunological reactivity with antikinesin antibodies, and, most importantly, the ability to promote plus end-directed, microtubule-dependent movement. Kinesin has proven to be ubiquitous, having been found in every tissue and cell type examined (Saxton et al., 1986; Dabora and Sheetz, 1988a; see Vale et al., 1986a, for review). Kinesin is readily purified from high-speed cytoplasmic supernatants, suggesting that it may exist in a

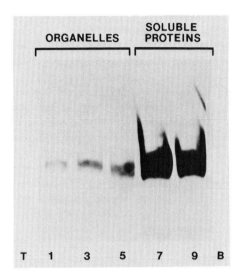

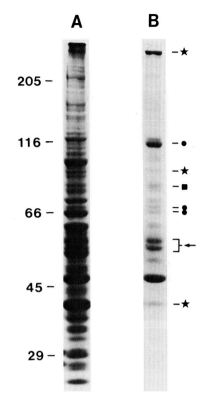

Fig. 19–1. Kinesin copurifies with squid axoplasmic and optic lobe organelles in sucrose gradients. Squid optic lobe organelles were prepared from optic lobe homogenates by flotation in a continuous 15–35% sucrose gradient. (Flotation minimizes contamination of the membrane-containing fractions with soluble proteins.) Fractions are numbered from the top (left, marked T) to bottom (right, marked B). All fractions containing organelles (1, 3, and 5) also contained kinesin as detected by immunoblot using a rabbit antikinesin antibody.

Fig. 19–2. AMP-PNP-dependent microtubule-binding proteins. AMP-PNP-induced microtubule binding proteins from a squid optic lobe supernatant were prepared by binding and ATP-dependent release according to Vale and coworkers (1985c) and analyzed by SDS-PAGE. Positions of M_r markers are shown on the left. The gel was stained with Coomassie blue. **A:** Soluble supernatant (S3). **B:** Proteins released from microtubules by ATP. Kinesin is indicated by dots. Tubulin is marked with an arrow. The 80,000 M_r contaminant of purified kinesin (see text) is marked with a square. Stars indicate kinesin binding proteins (see Fig. 19–4 and text).

soluble form in cells. However, a fraction of total cellular kinesin copurifies with squid optic lobe organelles in sucrose gradients (Fig. 19–1; see also Sheetz et al., 1986b). It is not obvious why a protein that is thought to couple organelles and microtubules should exist free in cytoplasm, and we suspect that the abundance of kinesin in soluble extracts reflects its dynamic interaction with microtubules and organelles.

A critical finding that suggested a method for purifying the organelle motor(s) led to the isolation of kinesin. Lasek and Brady (1985) observed in squid axoplasm that the nonhydrolyzable ATP analog 5′-adenylyimidodiphosphate (AMP-PNP) caused a complete cessation of organelle transport, and moving organelles stopped and accumulated on microtubules. AMP-PNP appeared to induce the formation of a stable complex

between the organelles and microtubules. Organelles remained bound until ATP was added, when they either resumed movement or were released into the surrounding medium. This observation suggested that microtubules could be used as a nucleotide-dependent affinity substrate for purification of organelle motor proteins.

Several proteins, including kinesin, demonstrate AMP-PNP-dependent binding to microtubules (Fig. 19–2) (Vale et al., 1985c;

Brady, 1985b; Scholey et al., 1985). This family of proteins may contain a minus end-directed motor and other components necessary for organelle motility (see below); however, kinesin is the only protein in these preparations that demonstrates well characterized motility and therefore can unequivocally be called a motor.

MOLECULAR MECHANISM OF ORGANELLE TRANSLOCATION

The simplest molecular model for organelle translocation requires three components: a microtubule, an organelle, and a motor protein. Individual organelles move in only one direction, which is determined by the binding of either an plus end-directed or minus end-directed motor to a specific receptor on the organelle. This model can be tested readily by adding purified motors (e.g., kinesin or dynein) to purified organelles and microtubules and assaying for movement.

Role of Kinesin in Organelle Motility

When added to an in vitro organelle motility assay in place of S2 supernatant, purified kinesin stimulated organelle translocation on microtubules, but the extent of stimulation was highly variable (Vale et al., 1985c). This result suggested that kinesin was involved in organelle movement, but it was not clear whether kinesin alone was sufficient for this process. The organelles used in these studies exhibited a low level of motility in the absence of additional motor, suggesting that they had retained some motor activity through the purification (see also Gilbert et al., 1985). These preparations also contained neurofilament proteins that might have interfered in the observation of motility. We have recently developed a more rigorous purification scheme that yields organelles lacking motors and neurofilament contamination. Normal motility is restored when the organelles are reconstituted with S2 supernatant (Schroer et al.,

1988). Kinesin alone does not stimulate translocation of these organelles.

Similar results were obtained when highly purified synaptic vesicles were used in place of squid axoplasmic organelles (Table 19–3). Although the vesicles were not translocated, they demonstrated kinesin-dependent binding to microtubules in the presence of AMP-PNP. These results suggested that kinesin alone can bind to a receptor on organelles but that additional soluble accessory proteins are necessary for organelle motility. Since kinesin alone can drive the movements of plastic beads but not organelles, the soluble accessory proteins may serve to activate kinesin bound to organelles. The fact that moving organelles are translocated three to four times faster than kinesin-driven beads is further evidence that accessory proteins may act to modulate kinesin activity. A working model for the molecular mechanism of organelle translocation is depicted in Figure 19–3. We propose that organelle translocation requires microtubules, organelles (bearing specific motor receptors), and a translocator complex. The organelle translocator complex is composed of a motor protein and a soluble motor accessory protein. Plus end-directed and minus end-directed motors may use the same or different accessory proteins. Organelle translocation depends on the presence of the appropriate accessory protein, whereas bead movement can be driven by purified kinesin alone.

KINESIN BINDING PROTEINS

Kinesin activity is likely to be tightly regulated in vivo, in analogy to other cytoskeleton-based motor systems (myosin and actin, dynein and microtubules). Any protein that modulates kinesin activity must interact physically with kinesin to cause an effect and might therefore be expected to display kinesin binding activity. Kinesin binding proteins may serve to regulate ATPase activity when kinesin is free in cytoplasm and motility when kinesin is associated with organelles and microtubules. Our results suggest that kinesin-dependent organ-

TABLE 19–3. Movement of Different Organelles In Vitro*

Type of organelle	Source of motor	Movement on microtubules	AMP-PNP-dependent binding
Synaptic vesicles			
Electric ray	In axoplasm[a]	+ +	+ +
	Axoplasmic S2	+	ND
	Purified kinesin	−	+ +
Bovine brain	Purified kinesin	−	+
Rat brain	Purified kinesin	−	ND
Squid organelles			
Axoplasmic (untreated)	In axoplasm	+ + +	+ + +
	Axoplasmic S2	+ +	+ + +
	Purified kinesin[b]	+	ND
	No motor[b,c]	±	ND
Optic lobe	Axoplasmic S2	+	+
	Purified kinesin	−	+ +

*The results of our in vitro studies with different organelle preparations are summarized here. Electric ray and bovine and rat synaptic vesicles were purified as previously described (Carlson et al., 1978; Huttner et al., 1983). Axoplasmic organelles were isolated as described in Vale et al. (1985b) or in Schroer et al. (1988). Optic lobe organelles were prepared as described in the legend to Figure 19–1. Organelles and motor-containing supernatants were mixed with purified squid optic lobe microtubules (Vale et al., 1985b), and the amount of organelle movement was determined using video-enhanced DIC microscopy. The binding of organelles to microtubules was induced by the addition of 5 mM AMP-PNP and assayed using video microscopy. − Indicates that organelle movement or binding was not observed; + to + + + indicates the relative amount of movement or binding; ± indicates a + effect in some but not all experiments; ND, not determined.
[a]Schroer et al., 1985.
[b]Vale et al., 1985c.
[c]Schroer et al., 1988.

elle movement is indeed regulated by soluble accessory factors. As a means to identify these accessory factors, kinesin binding proteins must be isolated and their effects on organelle motility assayed in vitro.

Proteins That Copurify With Kinesin

In an early step in the purification of kinesin, AMP-PNP is used to cause a defined subset of soluble proteins, including kinesin, to cosediment with microtubules (Fig. 19–2). These proteins may bind to microtubules independently of kinesin and can be described as AMP-PNP-dependent microtubule-binding proteins. However, kinesin binding proteins may also bind to microtubules indirectly in this step. In an analogous preparation from axoplasm, moving axoplasmic organelles are observed to bind stably

to microtubules (Lasek and Brady, 1985; Schroer, unpublished observations). It is likely that soluble kinesin accessory proteins required for binding and movement are present in the resulting organelle–microtubule complex. However, an AMP-PNP-dependent microtubule binding fraction prepared from optic lobe does not promote organelle motility (Schroer et al., 1988). It is possible that the translocator complex components are too dilute or that the activity is inhibited or absent in optic lobe high-speed supernatants.

Several investigators (Vale et al., 1985c; Kuznetsov and Gelfand, 1986; Porter et al., 1987) have noted tenacious protein contaminants in kinesin preparations isolated from different sources. In particular, an 80,000 M_r protein (Fig. 19–2) routinely copurifies with kinesin and can be separated from it

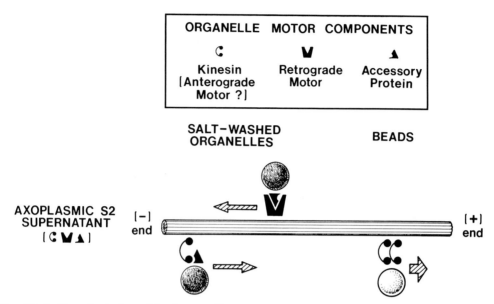

Fig. 19–3. Hypothetical model of organelle transport. Organelles (left side) are translocated. A translocator complex, consisting of a motor protein (kinesin, dumbell; or minus-end-directed motor, V-shape) and a motor accessory protein (triangle), is necessary for organelle movement. For simplicity, we have drawn a single motor accessory protein that binds to both motors. Plastic beads (right) are translocated toward the plus end or minus end of a microtubule in the S2 supernatant and exclusively toward the plus ends by kinesin alone.

only under certain ionic conditions (Vale, unpublished observations). It has not been determined whether the 80,000 M_r protein has a modulatory effect on kinesin-driven motility.

Kinesin Affinity Chromatography

We have also used kinesin affinity chromatography to purify kinesin binding proteins directly. To determine if these proteins modulate kinesin-dependent motility, they can be assayed alone and with kinesin in the organelle motility assay. Kinesin is immobilized on Sepharose resin either directly or by binding to a monoclonal antikinesin IgG on the resin. We have used this approach to identify a number of proteins (Fig. 19–4) in squid optic lobe and axoplasmic extracts that bind tightly to kinesin (Schroer and Sheetz, 1986). Soluble supernatants (containing either no added ATP or 5 mM AMP-PNP) were passed through the kinesin columns and the columns were rinsed extensively. BSA-Sepharose or nonspecific

mouse IgG-Sepharose columns were run in parallel to identify proteins that bound nonspecifically to the resin. Proteins showing AMP-PNP-dependent binding to kinesin (including tubulin, see Fig. 19–4, lane A) were first eluted from the columns with 10 mM ATP and increasing concentrations of KCl. Similar results were obtained with both kinesin resins, and no reproducible differences were noted if binding was done either with no ATP or with 5 mM AMP-PNP. The kinesin binding proteins isolated from the high-speed supernatant from optic lobe S2 (lane A), the same supernatant lacking microtubules and MAPs (S3; lanes B and C), and a detergent lysate of axoplasm (S1A; lane D) are shown in Figure 19–4. In axoplasm, kinesin (circles) appeared to bind to itself under the experimental conditions used. Three proteins (M_rs = 331,000, 93,000, and 40,000, indicated by stars) consistently appeared in the kinesin binding protein fractions from optic lobe and axoplasm. Proteins of the same M_r are also found in the AMP-

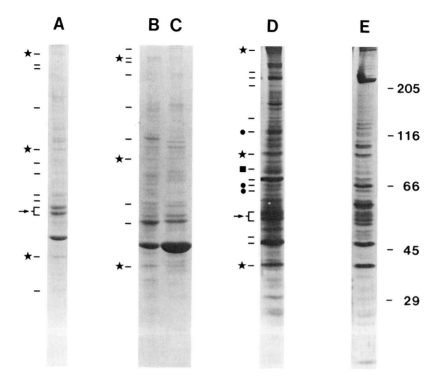

Fig. 19–4. Kinesin-binding proteins in squid optic lobe and axoplasm. Soluble supernatants (Vale et al., 1985c, d) were passed through a kinesin-Sepharose CL4B column, and kinesin binding proteins were eluted with 10 mM ATP and increasing KCl. The eluate fractions were concentrated for analysis by SDS-PAGE. M_r markers are shown on the right. **A:** ATP-eluted kinesin-binding proteins from optic lobe S2 **B:** ATP-eluted kinesin-binding proteins from optic lobe S3 (see Fig. 19–2, lane A, for total polypeptide composition of S3). **C:** KCl-eluted kinesin-binding proteins from S3. **D:** ATP-eluted kinesin-binding proteins from axoplasmic SlA. **E:** Axoplasmic SlA. Lanes A–C were stained with Coomassie blue. Lanes D and E were stained with silver nitrate. Dots (lane D) indicate kinesin, and the square marks the position of the M_r = 80,000 containinant of the kinesin preparation (see Fig. 19–2). Arrows mark the position of tubulin. Hatch marks to the left of lanes A, B, and D mark the positions of proteins that bind specifically to kinesin. Stars mark the positions of the 331,000 M_r, 93,000 M_r, and 40,000 M_r kinesin binding proteins observed in all three supernatants.

PNP-dependent binding fraction (Fig. 19–2, stars).

The optic lobe kinesin binding proteins did not promote organelle motility in the in vitro assay (Schroer, unpublished). In contrast, preliminary evidence (Schroer et al., 1988) suggests that axoplasmic kinesin binding proteins substantially enhance organelle translocation activity. Organelle motor activity cannot be detected in partially purified optic lobe fractions and is only readily available from axoplasm. Until we have further purified the organelle translo-

cator complex, we are limited to studying organelle motility in axoplasmic extracts.

CONCLUSIONS

In vitro assays of organelle motility have provided the means to determine the molecular components involved in organelle translocation. Much of the current evidence suggests a role for the two known microtubule-based motors, dynein and kinesin, in minus end-directed and plus end-directed intracellular organelle movements, respectively. We have recently developed an in vitro assay for organelle translocation using highly purified organelles and microtubules, in which motility is entirely dependent on soluble factors. We have assayed different soluble protein fractions from squid axoplasm and optic lobe for the ability to promote the movement of axoplasmic and foreign organelles. On the basis of our results, we propose that plus end-directed organelle motility requires the activity of a motor complex composed of kinesin and a kinesin accessory protein and that minus end-directed organelle transport utilizes a similar complex. Recent evidence suggests that the motor accessory proteins are indeed kinesin binding proteins. Three kinesin binding proteins have been identified in optic lobe and axoplasm. Any one of these may be the kinesin accessory proteins required for organelle movement. We are currently working to purify further the protein(s) necessary for complete reconstitution of motility in vitro.

ACKNOWLEDGMENTS

We would like to acknowledge the important contributions of Dr. B. J. Schnapp and Dr. T. S. Reese of the NIH at MBL to much of the work described here and the contributions of Dr. Regis B. Kelly and his laboratory to T.A.S. during the early stages of this work. We thank members of the Sheetz laboratory for stimulating discussions and Dr. D. Cotanche for his careful reading of the manuscript. JoAnn Coyle, Rich Fair, and Jane Leighton provided typing assistance. This work was supported by NIH grants to MPS and by a Muscular Dystrophy Association Postdoctoral fellowship and a Grass Foundation fellowship to T.A.S.

NOTE ADDED IN PROOF

The high M_r MAP purified from *C. elegans* (Lye et al., 1987) has been shown to promote minus end-directed translocation and therefore falls in the category of cytoplasmic dyneins (Lye et al., 1988).

We have used the technique of vanadate-mediated UV photocleavage to demonstrate that cytoplasmic dynein is a motor for minus end-directed organelle movement (Schroer et al., 1988).

Biochemical and Motile Properties of Sea Urchin Egg Kinesin: Relationship to the Pathway of the Kinesin-Microtubule ATPase

Jonathan M. Scholey, Stanley A. Cohn, and Amie L. Ingold

Department of Molecular and Cellular Biology, National Jewish Center for Immunology and Respiratory Medicine, Denver, Colorado 80206

INTRODUCTION

Microtubules participate in a wide variety of important cellular activities. Among these are the mediation of cell shape, the organization of the endomembrane system, the directional transport of intracellular components, ciliary and flagellar motility, and mitosis. Kinesin, a mechanochemical protein that drives adenosine triphosphate (ATP)-dependent microtubule movement (Vale et al., 1985a), may play a crucial role in many of these microtubule-based processes.

The eggs and early embryos of echinoderms are particularly well suited for studying the biochemistry and function of microtubules, especially in relation to cell division (Scholey et al., 1988; Vallee and Collins, 1986). The ease of obtaining eggs and inducing synchronized cell divisions facilitates cytological observations of numerous types of motility occurring during early embryogenesis, such as chromosome movement, pronuclear migration, and the directed transport of vesicles or microinjected poly-styrene beads (see, e.g., Inoué, 1981; Hamaguchi et al., 1986; Rebhun, 1960; Harris, 1975). In addition, microtubule-based motility can be studied in cell-free systems prepared from sea urchin eggs and embryos (Pryer et al. 1986), microtubules and their associated proteins can be purified from these cells (Vallee and Bloom, 1983; Scholey et al., 1984, 1985; Collins and Vallee, 1986), and microtubule-based motility can be reconstituted from isolated components (Porter et al., 1987; Cohn et al., 1987).

Kinesin was identified in sea urchin eggs and early embryos (Scholey et al., 1985) on the basis of 1) its 5′-adenylylimidodiphosphate (AMP-PNP)-enhanced cosedimentation with microtubules prepared from cytoplasmic high-speed extract supernatants, 2) the immunological cross reactivity of its major polypeptide component (M_r 130kDa) with the 110 kDa subunit of squid axon kinesin, and 3) its copurification with microtubule translocating activity as observed using video-enhanced differential interference contrast (DIC) light microscopy. Kinesin isolated from sea urchin eggs has a microtubule-activated ATPase activity that generates force for microtubule movement in vitro (Porter et al., 1987; Cohn et al., 1987). Furthermore, light microscopic immunocytochemistry using "blot affinity-purified" polyclonal antibodies (Olmsted, 1986) suggests that kinesin is localized in the mitotic spindle of fixed dividing sea urchin blastomeres, where it may cross link microtubules to a second spindle component (Scholey et al., 1985; Leslie et al., 1987). These observations provide indirect evidence that kinesin generates force for microtubule-associated mitotic movements (Vale et al., 1986a).

Our research is aimed at answering the question "What are the functions and mechanisms of action of kinesin in sea urchin eggs and early embryos; specifically, does kinesin generate force for motility associated with the mitotic spindle?" To address this question, our strategy is 1) to characterize the in vitro motility-inducing properties of sea urchin egg kinesin, 2) to generate probes such as antibodies that interfere with these motility-inducing activities of the molecule, and 3) to microinject such probes into dividing sea urchin blastomeres in order to disrupt the function of kinesin in vivo and observe the consequences.

Here we review our progress in characterizing the in vitro motility-inducing properties of sea urchin egg kinesin using ATPase assays, microtubule binding assays, and video-microscopic motility assays. These assays should not only prove useful in screening for probes that inhibit sea urchin egg kinesin activity but also may provide insights into the molecular mechanisms by which kinesin generates motile force. For example, we find that sea urchin egg kinesin shares three important properties with the other mechanoenzymes, myosin and dynein. These are 1) formation of a bound complex with its cytoskeletal cofactor (microtubules) in the absence of ATP, 2) dissociation of the kinesin–microtubule complex by MgATP, and 3) activation of MgATPase activity by

the cytoskeletal cofactor. In this chapter, we discuss the possibility that these similarities reflect underlying similarities in the mechanochemical pathways of actomyosin, dynein–microtubules, and kinesin–microtubules.

MECHANOCHEMICAL PROTEINS

Four proteins isolated from eukaryotic cells, namely, myosin (Harrington and Rodgers, 1984), "minimyosin" (Pollard and Korn, 1973), dynein (Gibbons, 1981), and kinesin (Vale et al., 1985a), share the property of interacting with cytoskeletal elements (actin or microtubules) and using ATP to generate force. To understand the molecular mechanism of this force transducing process, it is necessary to know the sequence of chemical events that take place as the mechanoenzyme interacts with nucleotides and the cytoskeletal filaments.

On the basis of transient state kinetics, Lymm and Taylor (1971) proposed a model for the reaction pathway of the muscle myosin cross bridge that remains useful for thinking about the mechanism of mechanochemical coupling (Fig. 20–1a). The critical features of the Lymm-Taylor scheme are:

1. In the absence of MgATP, myosin binds very tightly to actin to form a "rigor" complex (AM).
2. Binding of MgATP to myosin causes very rapid dissociation of myosin (M · ATP) from actin.
3. Hydrolysis of MgATP and the release of adenosine diphosphate (ADP) and Pi from myosin occur relatively slowly on the dissociated myosin cross bridge.
4. Rebinding of actin to myosin (M · ADP–Pi) accelerates the dissociation of ADP and Pi from myosin, resulting in the steady-state actin activation of the myosin MgATPase activity.

The Lymm-Taylor reaction scheme probably represents a good approximation of the reaction in dilute protein solutions, although in muscles, where the concentrations of actin and myosin are very high, mass action is thought to drive myosin into the bound

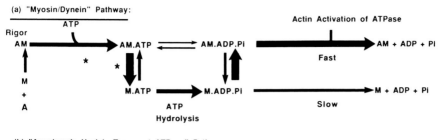

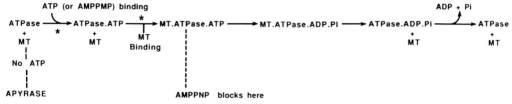

Fig. 20–1. Mechanochemical reaction pathways proposed for myosin/dynein **(a)** and the axoplasmic vesicle transport ATPase **(b)**. Heavy arrows in a represent the Lymm-Taylor scheme. Asterisks denote the reaction steps that Lasek and Brady (1985) propose to be different for the axoplasmic vesicle transport ATPase, where ATP is proposed to bind the ATPase before the ATPase binds microtubules. In contrast, actin (A) binds myosin (M) in the absence of ATP, and ATP binding dissociates myosin from actin.

state, so that ATP hydrolysis by attached myosin cross bridges may be significant (Stein et al., 1979). The bound intermediates AM · ATP and AM · ADP · Pi are then thought to be in rapid equilibrium with the corresponding dissociated cross bridges, M · ATP and M · ADP · Pi, and consequently myosin can detach from one actin and reattach to the next following ATP hydrolysis on the attached cross bridge. The step AM · ADP · Pi → AM is thought to be coupled to movement (see Pollard, 1987, for review). Studies of the interactions between dynein, microtubules, and ATP in solution suggest that dynein may operate by a pathway similar to myosin's (Johnson, 1985).

However, on the basis of their studies on the effects of AMPPNP and apyrase on vesicle transport along microtubules in extruded axoplasm, Lasek and Brady (1985) proposed that the ATPase responsible for vesicle transport operated via a mechanochemical pathway substantially different from those of myosin and dynein (Fig. 20–1b). In apyrase-treated axoplasm, vesicles did not bind to microtubules, suggesting

that, in the absence of ATP, the ATPase and consequently the vesicles do not bind microtubules (Lasek and Brady, 1985). In contrast, axoplasm treated with AMP-PNP contained vesicles that were rigidly bound to microtubules. Lasek and Brady therefore proposed that ATP or AMP-PNP must associate with the ATPase before the ATPase (in the form of ATPase · ATP or ATPase · AMP-PNP) binds to microtubules. The native microtubule-ATPase · ATP intermediate proceeds through the ATP-hydrolysis and product-release steps, whereas addition of AMPPNP results in the formation of a "trapped" microtubule · ATPase · AMP-PNP intermediate, which cannot proceed through the hydrolysis and product-release steps (Fig. 20–1b). Whereas AMPPNP does facilitate kinesin binding to microtubules, and is extremely useful in identifying and purifying kinesins (Vale et al., 1985a; Scholey et al., 1985; Brady, 1985b), in other respects the properties of sea urchin egg kinesin differ from the vesicle transport ATPase studied by Lasek and Brady. We consider the properties of sea urchin egg kinesin in vitro (described in the following sections) to be more consistent with a mechanochemical pathway similar to those of myosin and dynein (Fig. 20–1a) than with the pathway proposed by Lasek and Brady (Fig. 20–1b).

PURIFICATION OF SEA URCHIN EGG KINESIN

To analyze the microtubule-binding, microtubule-translocating, and microtubule-activated MgATPase activities of sea urchin egg kinesin, we purify the protein as follows (Cohn et al., 1988). A high-speed egg extract supernatant is treated with hexokinase plus glucose to reduce the ATP concentration and thereby precipitate actomyosin, which is removed by centrifugation. The supernatant is supplemented with taxol, guanosine triphosphate (GTP), and AMP-PNP to induce the formation of kinesin–microtubule complexes, which are pelleted through a sucrose cushion and then washed in buffer containing ATP plus EDTA. Kinesin cosediments with microtubules, but many other polypeptides are dissociated from microtubules and thereby removed in this EDTA/ATP buffer. Remaining microtubule-associated proteins (MAPs) are extracted from the microtubules by differential centrifugation in MgATP plus 100 mM KCl, and the ATP-extracted MAPs are chromatographed on a Biogel A5M column. Fractions are assayed for microtubule-translocating activity by video microscopy, and the peak fractions are pooled (Fig. 20–2). For some experiments, further purification is accomplished by mixing the pooled kinesin with taxol-stabilized bovine brain microtubules in the presence of ATP and EDTA, which induces binding of kinesin to microtubules. The resulting microtubule–kinesin complexes are pelleted, the pellets are resuspended in MgATP to dissociate kinesin from microtubules, and the mixture is again centrifuged to pellet microtubules, leaving purified kinesin in the supernatant. Contaminating tubulin can be removed using phosphocellulose chromatography. So far, we have detected no significant differences in the activities of the recycled kinesin and the Biogel A5M kinesin peak. Typically, we obtain between 1 and 3 mg Biogel kinesin and ~500 μg "recycled" kinesin from 100 ml high-speed extract supernatant (Table 20–1).

On sodium dodecyl sulfate (SDS)-polyacrylamide gels the major polypeptide component of sea urchin egg kinesin migrates with M_r ~130,000. On the basis of its elution behavior on Biogel A5M columns (Scholey et al., 1985), using the method of Siegel and Monty (1966), we estimate a stokes radius of ~74 Å for egg kinesin. On 5–20% sucrose density gradients, egg kinesin displays a sedimentation coefficient of 9.5S (Porter et al., 1987). We therefore estimate that egg kinesin possesses a solution M_r of 300,000 (Siegel and Monty, 1966), so that native egg kinesin probably consists of at least two 130,000 heavy chains. However, this value must be viewed as being tentative until superior methods for determining molecular weight, such as sedimentation equilibrium analysis, can be used.

Fig. 20–2. Copurification of microtubule-activated MgATPase activity and microtubule translocating activity with the 130 kDa kinesin subunit during Biogel A5M chromatography. Kinesin was prepared from sea urchin egg extracts by AMP-PNP–microtubules affinity binding, "EDTA/ATP washing" of the microtubules-kinesin complexes, i.e., differential centrifugation in 1 mM ATP plus 10 mM EDTA, during which kinesin binds and cosediments with microtubules, followed by MgATP extraction of kinesin from microtubules to yield "ATP MAPs," prior to Biogel chromatography. In **A,** velocities of microtubule gliding (μm/sec) were measured in the presence and absence of ATP, and the -fold dilution at which the motility supported by each fraction stopped was measured as described by Vale et al. (1985a). Fraction 24 contained a low concentration of 130 Kd that was capable of moving a fraction of the microtubules at 0·5–0·6μm/s, but the majority of the microtubules on the coverslip were immotile, resulting in a lower mean velocity for this fraction. − = no motility. The microtubule translocating activities were assayed as described in the legend to Figure 20–3. In **B,** open circles show ATPase activities in the presence of microtubules; and closed circles show ATPase activities in the absence of microtubules. The ATPase activities were assayed as described by Cohn et al. (1987).

A

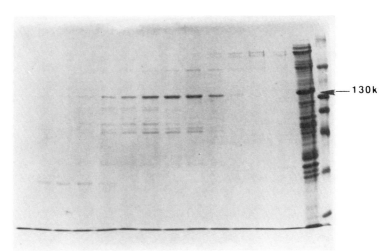

Column Fraction	26	25	24	23	22	21	20	19	18	17	16	15	14		
Motility (+ATP)	-	-	.21	.58	.56	.58	.56	.54	.56	.57	-	-	-		
Motility (-ATP)				.06	.01	.01									
Dilution Factor	-	-	1x	1x	1x	1x	1x	2x	2x	1x	-	-	-		

130k →

B

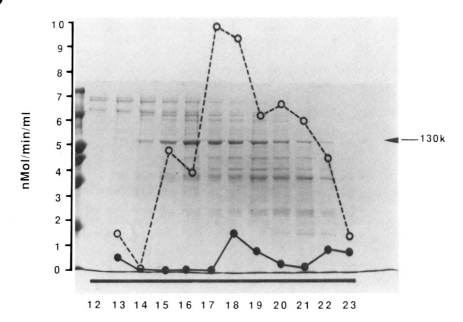

Fraction Number

TABLE 20–1. Purification of Sea Urchin Egg Kinesin*

	ml	mg/ml	Total mg
High-speed egg extract supernatant	100	34	3,400
AMP-PNP–microtubules (washed)	3	18	54
ATP-dissociated MAPs	2.5	5.5	13.8
Biogel A5M kinesin peak	11	0.25	2.8(range 1–3)
Purified EDTA/MgATP-recycled kinesin	3	0.18	0.54

Protein concentrations were determined by the Bradford procedure using the Biorad dye reagent concentrate and γ-globulin standard. Typically, we obtain between 1 and 3 mg kinesin from the Biogel A5M column; we pool a fairly broad peak when material is to be further purified and a narrow peak (three fractions) when the Biogel A5M fractions are used for assays.

Whether native egg kinesin also contains functionally important light chains is an area of interest, since neuronal kinesin contains light chains of M_r ~40–80 kDa (Vale et al., 1985a; Kuznetsov and Gelfand, 1986). Polypeptides of M_r ~110, 90, and 75kDa coelute with the egg kinesin 130,000 heavy chain during Biogel A5M chromatography and rebind to bovine brain microtubules in the absence of ATP or in [AMP-PNP] ≥ [ATP]. However, only the 130 and 75 kDa polypeptides rebind microtubules in EDTA plus ATP. In addition, the 75 kDa polypeptide copurifies with the 130 kDa polypeptide during immunoaffinity chromatography on columns of monoclonal anti-130 kDa IgG. On the basis of gel densitometry, we estimate that there are 0.4–1.0 mole 75 kDa per mole 130 kDa, depending on the preparative method used (unpublished observation). This 75 kDa polypeptide may be a light chain of sea urchin egg kinesin.

TABLE 20–2. Microtubule Binding by Sea Urchin Egg Kinesin*

Experiment	Approximate relative binding (%)
Control	~100
+Apyrase (±ATP)	~100
+0.1 mM ATP	~60
+1 mM ATP	~20
+10 mM ATP	~10
+1 mM ATP + 10 mM AMP-PNP	~100
+1 mM ATP + 10 mM Vi	~70
+1 mM ATP + 10 mM EDTA	~100

*Sea urchin egg kinesin was prepared by Biogel A5M chromatography in ATP-free buffer (Scholey et al., 1985) and was mixed with taxol-stabilized microtubules prepared from bovine brain PC-tubulin, incubated at room temperature and then centrifuged to pellet microtubules. The mixture was incubated with apyrase, ATP, AMP-PNP, vanadate (Vi), or EDTA prior to centrifugation where indicated. The amount of kinesin that bound and cosedimented with the microtubules was determined by SDS-PAGE densitometry of the resulting pellets. Details of the procedures and results will be described elsewhere.

MICROTUBULE-BINDING PROPERTIES OF SEA URCHIN EGG KINESIN

Sedimentation assays reveal that kinesin binds microtubules in the absence of MgATP, but this binding is weakened by MgATP. For example, when sea urchin egg or squid axoplasmic extracts are treated with apyrase, desalted or dialyzed (Scholey et al., 1985; Cohn et al., 1988; Vale et al., 1986b) to remove ATP, the amount of kinesin that cosediments with microtubules increases, whereas MgATP decreases the amount of kinesin that cosediments with microtubules (Vale et al., 1985a, 1986b; Cohn et al., 1988).

We have characterized the binding of Biogel A5M-fractionated egg kinesin to microtubules prepared from bovine brain tubulin using sedimentation assays and gel or blot densitometry (Cohn et al., 1988) (Table 20–2). When kinesin was desalted by gel filtration chromatography or treated with apyrase to remove ATP, we observed essentially complete binding and cosedimentation of kinesin with microtubules, whereas addition of increasing concentrations of MgATP dissociated kinesin from microtubules (Table 20–2: 100 μM MgATP causes approximately half the kinesin to remain soluble).

The formation of a bound complex in the absence of MgATP and dissociation of the complex by addition of MgATP suggest a mechanochemical cycle resembling that of dynein and myosin but are inconsistent with the Lasek-Brady model (Fig. 20–1). Why ATP depletion using apyrase facilitates the attachment of kinesin to microtubules but did not cause axoplasmic vesicles to attach to microtubules in the experiments of Lasek and Brady (1985) is an interesting puzzle. AMP-PNP facilitates attachment of axoplasmic vesicles to microtubules (Lasek and Brady, 1985) and also enhances binding of kinesin to microtubules (Table 20–2) (Vale et al., 1985a; Brady, 1985b; Scholey et al., 1985; Kuznetsov and Gelfand, 1986), whereas vanadate appears to stabilize microtubule binding by kinesin (Scholey et al., 1985; Cohn et al., 1988) (Table 20–2) but did not facilitate attachment of axoplasmic vesicles to microtubules. AMP-PNP and $ADP \cdot Vi$ may both stabilize kinesin–microtubule complexes by forming a $kinesin \cdot ADP \cdot Pi$ analogue that can bind microtubules but from which product release is inhibited (see Fig. 20–5). Addition of excess EDTA to chelate Mg^{2+} also induces binding of sea urchin egg kinesin to microtubules in the presence of ATP (Table 20–2), suggesting that both Mg^{2+} and ATP are required for dissociation, as was originally reported for squid axon kinesin by Vale et al. (1986b).

MICROTUBULE-TRANSLOCATING ACTIVITIES OF SEA URCHIN EGG KINESIN

The basic characteristics of the microtubule movement induced by sea urchin egg kinesin are very similar to those of neuronal kinesin (Vale et al., 1985a,b; Schnapp et al., 1986; Porter et al., 1987). For example, egg kinesin is a unidirectional motor, translocating microtubules over glass with their "minus" ends leading and moving latex beads towards the "plus" ends of microtubules at rates of ~0.5 μm/sec under optimal conditions. Egg kinesin moves individual microtubules and dynein-depleted axonemes at similar velocities (Porter et al., 1987), suggesting that egg kinesin-induced microtubule-movement is load-independent and that the velocity of microtubule movement reflects the underlying enzymatic activity of the kinesin. Microtubule movement is dependent on MgATP, and various nucleotide analogues inhibit microtubule translocation (Porter et al., 1987; Cohn et al., 1987). Kinesin appears to be responsible for much of the microtubule motility observed in crude extracts of sea urchin eggs, although other factors must also contribute to the bidirectional movement observed by Pryer et al. (1986).

Cohn et al. (1987) have described a convenient, inexpensive system for quantitating kinesin-induced microtubule movement, in which the live video signal from a video-enhanced DIC light microscope is combined with the video output from an Amiga 1000 computer. The hand-operated computer mouse controls a cursor, which is superimposed over the image of translocating microtubules enabling the observer to "track" and store positions of the microtubules, with the computer programmed to calculate the velocity for each tracked microtubule (Cohn et al. 1987). Typically, for each preparation, the velocities of 15–30 microtubules are measured, at the end of which the computer prints out a histogram, as shown in Figure 20–3A, with the velocity distribution of microtubules translocated by a preparation of sea urchin egg kinesin.

We are using this system to quantitate the effects of varying solution conditions on the microtubule-translocating activities of sea urchin egg kinesin (see, e.g., Cohn et al. 1987). For example, Figure 20–3 illustrates the effects on microtubule-movement of increasing concentrations of MgATP (Fig. 20–3B) or increasing concentrations of egg kinesin (Fig. 20–3C). In saturating MgATP, microtubules translocate at a relatively constant velocity of ~0.5–0.7 μm/sec, which is independent of the kinesin concentration above a certain critical concentration (usually 20–40 μg/ml Biogel A5M-fractionated

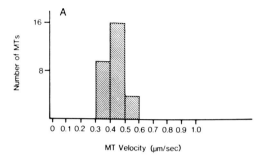

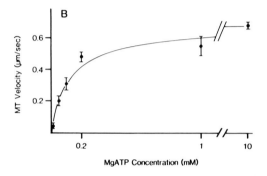

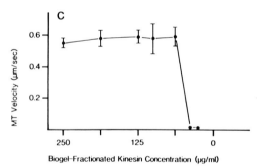

Fig. 20–3. Characterization of the microtubule-translocating activities of sea urchin egg kinesin. **A:** Histogram showing the velocity distribution of microtubules being translocated over a glass coverslip by egg kinesin. Velocities were measured from the live video microscope image by using an interactive video analysis program on an Amiga 1000 computer (Cohn et al., 1987). **B:** The velocity of egg kinesin-induced microtubule-translocation increases in a saturable fashion with the concentration of MgATP. Each data point represents the mean microtubule velocity for 10–30 microtubules, and the error bars represent standard deviations. **C:** Microtubule translocation as a function of relative kinesin concentration. The velocity of microtubule gliding was measured as a function of dilution of a typical pooled Biogel A5M egg kinesin sample. The kinesin solution was diluted with PMEG buffer to the concentrations indicated and allowed to adsorb onto a coverslip for 20 min. All samples had 2.5 mM MgATP added and were assayed as described above.

TABLE 20–3. Microtubule Translocating Properties of Sea Urchin Egg Kinesin*

Maximum velocity of MT movement (V_{max})	0.7 μm/sec
K_{app} for MT movement	120 μM ATP
Polarity of microtubule translocation	Minus end leading

*Microtubule-translocation was analyzed as described by Cohn et al. (1987). The kinetic parameters were obtained from double reciprocal plots of the data in Figure 20–3B. The determination of polarity of egg kinesin-induced motility was described in Vale et al. (1985b) and in Porter et al. (1987).

egg kinesin). Below the critical concentration a sharp decrease is observed in the velocity of microtubule movement (Fig. 20–3C). Similarly, the translocation of beads along actin filament bundles also requires a minimum critical concentration of myosin (Sheetz et al., 1984). Above the critical kinesin concentration, the velocity of microtubule translocation increases in a saturable fashion with increasing [MgATP] (Fig. 20–3B) (Porter et al., 1987). We do not know if there is a critical MgATP concentration below which microtubule movement does not occur, although this hypothetical critical concentration must be less than 10–20 μM. We estimate from double reciprocal plots of the data shown in Figure 20–3B that the maximal velocity of microtubule movement (V_{max}) is ~0.7 μm/sec and that the MgATP concentration required to achieve half V_{max} (K_{app}) is ~120 μM MgATP (Fig. 20–3B; Table 20–3), with the form suggesting that kinesin obeys Michaelis-Menten kinetics for ATP hydrolysis (Fig. 20–3B) (Porter et al., 1987). Very similar curves have been described for the movement of fluorescent actin filaments over myosin adsorbed to glass surfaces (Kron and Spudich, 1986) and for the motility of reactivated demembranated axonemes (Gibbons and Gibbons, 1972). In these cases, motility is coupled to the MgATPase activity of the actomyosin (Eisenberg and Moos, 1968) and microtubule–dynein (Omoto and Johnson, 1986; Warner and McIlvain, 1986) systems, respectively.

TABLE 20–4. Microtubule-Activated MgATPase Activities of Sea Urchin Egg, *Drosophila* Embryo, and Squid Optic Lobe Kinesin*

Assay	Sea urchin	*Drosophila*	Squid
Kinesin	6.7	17.6	15.6
Kinesin + microtubules	55.0	91.9	209.1

*ATPase activities were assayed essentially as described by Cohn et al. (1987) (with minor modifications) at room temperature (23–25° C). Specific activities expressed as nmoles/min/mg. Squid brain kinesin was prepared by Bruce Crise and Bruce Schnapp using monoclonal antibody-affinity chromatography. *Drosophila* (Saxton et al., 1988) and sea urchin kinesins were prepared by microtubule-affinity binding and Biogel A5M chromatography. Typical results are shown after subtracting background activities of microtubules alone from the microtubule-activated MgATPase activities.

MICROTUBULE-ACTIVATED MgATPase ACTIVITY OF SEA URCHIN EGG KINESIN

Kinesin, like dynein and myosin, displays a MgATPase activity that can be activated by its cytoskeletal cofactor, namely, microtubules (Kuznetsov and Gelfand, 1986; Cohn et al., 1987; Saxton et al., 1988) (Table 20–4). For example, sea urchin egg kinesin isolated by Biogel A5M chromatography (Cohn et al., 1987), with or without subsequent purification by EDTA/MgATP recycling, displays a low MgATPase activity (usually < 5 nmoles/min/mg) that is activated severalfold by bovine brain taxol-assembled microtubules, usually to between 40 and 60 nmoles/min/mg at 22–25°C in PMEG buffer (see Cohn et al., 1987, for assay conditions). Microtubule-activated MgATPase activity coelutes with the 130 kDa kinesin heavy chain from Biogel A5M columns (Fig. 20–2). Phosphate is released from ATP at an approximately linear rate for about 1 hr in solutions containing sea urchin egg kinesin and microtubules assembled from purified bovine brain tubulin under our assay conditions (Fig. 20–4). When colchicine is included in the assay in place of taxol to block tubulin polymerization, no activation of the ATPase activity of sea urchin egg kinesin is observed, suggesting that polymerized microtubules are required for activation of ATPase activity (unpublished observation). Under similar assay conditions, kinesins isolated from squid brain, *Drosophila* embryos, and sea urchin eggs all display microtubule-activated MgATPase activity, but the respective rates of microtubule-activated MgATP hydrolysis differ (Table 20–4). The significance of the differences in ATPase activity of these three kinesins is not yet understood.

Kuznetsov and Gelfand (1986) have characterized the kinetic properties of bovine brain kinesin ATPase activity in some detail and report that the ATPase activity obeys simple Michaelis-Menten kinetics when the microtubule concentration is varied in the presence of a constant concentration of MgATP or when the MgATP concentration is varied in the presence of a constant concentration of microtubules (Kuznetsov and Gelfand, 1986; K_m for ATP $\sim$10–12 μM; K_{app} for microtubules $\sim$12–14 μM tubulin). Similarly, linear Lineweaver-Burke plots were obtained when the acto-heavy meromyosin ATPase activity was measured at various ATP or F-actin concentrations (Eisenberg and Moos, 1968).

Different groups of workers have obtained different results when assaying kinesin for ATPase activity (Cohn, 1987), but the reasons for this variability are not understood. For example, in the absence of microtubules, bovine brain kinesin is reported by Kuznetsov and Gelfand (1986) to hydrolyze ATP at rates of $\sim$60–80 nmoles/min/mg, whereas Vale et al. (1985a) and Cohn et al. (1987) report low ATPase activities for neuronal and sea urchin egg kinesins, respectively, in the absence of microtubules. The microtubule-activated MgATPase activity of sea urchin egg kinesin is also reported by Cohn et al. (1987) to be much lower than the analagous value reported by Kuznetsov and Gelfand (1986) for bovine brain kinesin. The conditions used for assaying ATPase activity (for example, the temperature of assay, the ratio of ATP:Mg [Cohn et al., 1987], or the buffer conditions [Kuznetsov and Gelfand, 1986]) and the source of kinesin

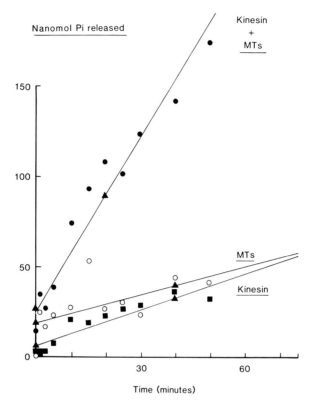

Fig. 20–4. Microtubule activation of kinesin MgATPase activity. Diagram shows the amount of radioactive Pi released from $[\gamma^{32}P]$ MgATP as a function of time in the presence of kinesin alone (squares), microtubules alone (open circles), or kinesin and microtubules (closed circles). Lines represent the best-fit linear regression through the data points as denoted by the triangles. The slopes of these lines represent Pi release rates of 0.71 nMol/min/ml (kinesin alone), 0.6 nMol/min/ml (microtubules alone), and 3.2 nMol/min/ml (kinesin plus microtubules) which correspond to ATPase activities of 9.7 nMol/min/mg for kinesin alone and 35.6 nMol/min/mg for kinesin in the presence of microtubules. ATPase assays were performed as previously described (Cohn et al., 1987).

(Table 20–4) can influence the measured rate of ATP hydrolysis. For example, increasing the assay temperature from 22–25° C to 37° C causes a concomitant increase in the ATPase activity of sea urchin egg kinesin, from < 5 nmoles/min/mg to ~20 nmoles/min/mg in the absence of microtubules (lower than we reported previously) and from 40–60 nmoles/min/mg to 100–120 nmoles/min/mg in the presence of microtubules. Whether other factors, such as the formation of ternary complexes (e.g., vesicle–microtubule–kinesin), interactions between kinesin catalytic sites (Schnapp et al., 1986), uncoupling of ATPase activity from motility

during the preparation of kinesin, or presence or absence of regulatory cofactors, also cause variations in the measured rates of ATP hydrolysis has not yet been investigated.

CORRELATION BETWEEN THE MgATPase AND MICROTUBULE-TRANSLOCATING ACTIVITIES OF SEA URCHIN EGG KINESIN

To understand the physiological relevance of the microtubule-activated MgATPase activity of kinesin, we need to know if ATP hydrolysis is coupled to microtubule-based movement in vitro and in the cell. We have

TABLE 20–5. Inhibitor Concentration for 50% Inhibition of Sea Urchin Egg Kinesin Activity*

Inhibitor	Microtubule-activated ATPase	Microtubule translocation
Na_3VO_4	$420\mu M$	$60\mu M$
AMP-PNP	1mM	$450\mu M$
EDTA	4.5 mM	1.7 mM
Mg-free ATP	5.4 mM	3mM

*The inhibitions of the microtubule-activated Mg ATPase and microtubule-translocating activities were analyzed as described by Cohn et al. (1987). Data are from Cohn et al. (1987).

approached this problem by comparing the effect of a number of inhibitors on the microtubule-translocating and microtubule-activated MgATPase activities of sea urchin egg kinesin and have obtained correlative evidence for coupling between ATP hydrolysis and microtubule movement (Cohn et al., 1987).

Both the microtubule-activated MgATPase and the microtubule-translocating activities of sea urchin egg kinesin are inhibited in a dose-dependent fashion by addition of AMP-PNP, EDTA, Na_3VO_4, or increasing the ratio of ATP to Mg in the assay solutions (Cohn et al. 1987) (Table 20–5). The latter results suggest that MgATP is the native kinesin substrate, although we cannot rule out the possibility that Mg^{2+} plays some other role in addition to acting as a cofactor for the nucleotide (e.g., stabilizing an important structural state of kinesin). Divalent cations are also required for axoneme motility (Gibbons and Gibbons, 1972), and Hayashi (1974) proposes that free ATP is a competitive inhibitor of dynein MgATPase activity. The situation with myosin is more complex. Most myosins possess a high K^+/EDTA-stimulated ATPase activity (Korn, 1978) that is inhibited by Mg^{2+}. The K^+/EDTA ATPase activity of myosin is unrelated to movement and is inhibited by the presence of actin, which binds tightly to myosin in EDTA plus ATP. Actin-activated MgATP hydrolysis (Eisenberg and Moos, 1968), actomyosin super precipitation (Maruyama and Watanabe, 1962), and contraction of skinned skeletal muscle fibers (Gulati and Podolsky, 1981) all occur in excess concentrations of ATP relative to Mg, whereas excess $MgCl_2$ relative to ATP is required for the translocation of skeletal muscle myosin beads along actin filament bundles (Sheetz et al., 1984). Furthermore, the effects of $MgCl_2$ on smooth muscle actomyosin are different from its effects on skeletal muscle myosin (Ikebe et al., 1984).

With all the inhibitors tested (Table 20–5), the concentration of inhibitor required to inhibit motility by 50% was lower than the concentration required to inhibit the ATPase activity by 50%, possibly reflecting differences between the ATPase and motility assays (see Cohn et al., 1987, for discussion). For instance, 1) microtubule translocation over a glass surface requires a minimum critical concentration of active kinesin molecules adsorbed to the coverslip, with the efficacy of the inhibitors in the motility assay being dependent on the kinesin concentration above the critical concentration. Microtubule-activated MgATP hydrolysis, in contrast, probably occurs in solution and is relatively insensitive to the concentration of kinesin. 2) The rigor-like kinesin–microtubule complexes formed by EDTA, Na_3VO_4, and AMP-PNP could mediate strong binding of microtubules to glass surfaces via kinesin "cross bridges," an effect that may amplify the inhibition of microtubule gliding by exerting increasing drag force on the moving microtubules. We are currently analyzing the inhibiton of ATPase and motility-inducing activities of sea urchin egg kinesin in detail to develop a more quantitative understanding of the relationship between these activities.

In summary, three sets of observations suggest that microtubule translocation and ATP hydrolysis are coupled. 1) The ATPase activity is low in the absence of microtubules when no force can be generated, whereas the activity is markedly stimulated by assembled microtubules but not by unpolymerized tubulin. 2) Microtubule translocation and microtubule-activated ATPase exhibit similar requirements for divalent cations (Mg^{2+}) in conjunction with the hydrolyzable nucleotide (ATP). 3) Both assays are sensitive to the same inhibitors.

The similar rates of ATP hydrolysis and movement found with egg kinesin (microtubule-activated ATPase 40–60 nmoles/min/mg; movement of microtubules ~0.5 μm/sec) and with smooth muscle myosin (actin-activated ATPase ~46–51 nmoles/min/mg [Adelstein et al., 1982]; movement of myosin coated beads ~0.15–0.4 μm/sec [Sellers et al., 1985]) suggest that the efficiency of mechanochemical coupling in the microtubule-egg kinesin and acto-smooth muscle myosin systems may be similar. The velocity of myosin-coated bead movement (Sheetz et al., 1984) and the maximum velocity of unloaded shortening of muscles (Barany, 1967) correlate reasonably well with the steady-state actin-activated ATPase activity of the myosin isozyme being studied (although there is a better correlation between the velocity of unloaded muscle shortening and the rate of ADP release from actomyosin, which controls the shortening velocity [Siemankowski et al., 1985]). Whether a similar correlation exists for kinesin isozymes (Table 20–4) is an interesting question that may be relevant to the different rates of microtubule-activated ATPase activities reported by different workers.

RELATIONSHIP OF IN VITRO PROPERTIES OF KINESIN TO ITS MECHANOCHEMICAL CYCLE

The analysis of the mechanochemical properties of kinesin is only just beginning. Nevertheless, a number of observations on the microtubule-binding, microtubule-translocating, and microtubule-activated Mg ATPase activities of kinesins from sea urchin eggs and neural tissues are consistent with the hypothesis that kinesin generates force for movement via a mechanochemical pathway that is basically similar to the other mechanochemical proteins, myosin and dynein. These are:

1. Binding of the mechanochemical protein, kinesin, to its cytoskeletal cofactor, microtubules, in the absence of MgATP.
2. Dissociation of the complex by addition of MgATP.

3. Activation of the ATPase activity of the mechanochemical protein (kinesin) by addition of the cytoskeletal cofactor (microtubules).
4. Coupling between ATP hydrolysis and motility.

In the absence of transient-state kinetic data, the mechanochemical pathway of kinesin is unknown, but the model in Figure 20–5, based on the Lymm-Taylor scheme, can serve as a basis for discussion. In this model, the kinesin–microtubule complex that forms in the absence of ATP (step 1) is dissociated by MgATP (step 2). The ATP is then split (step 3) to ADP plus Pi, allowing microtubules to rebind the K · ADP · Pi intermediate, thereby accelerating product release, which results in the steady-state microtubule activation of MgATPase activity (step 4). We propose that apyrase induces binding by depleting ATP and stabilizing the rigor complex, whereas EDTA chelates Mg away from ATP, leaving Mg-free ATP, which competes with MgATP but is unable to dissociate the rigor complex. We speculate that both AMP-PNP and ADP · vanadate trap the pathway by forming a "microtubule–K–ADP · Pi" analogue from which nucleotide cannot dissociate (step 5).

Although the available steady-state data are consistent with this reaction scheme, proving it will require the identification of the reaction intermediates and a measurement of the rates and sequence of their interconversion using transient-state kinetic analysis (Johnson, 1985). On the basis of available data, however, it is tempting to speculate that the major eukaryotic cell motility systems that are based on interactions between mechanochemical proteins and cytoskeletal elements (actin–myosin, microtubule–dynein, and microtubule–kinesin) all operate via mechanochemical pathways having important common features.

SUMMARY AND CONCLUSIONS

Sea urchin egg kinesin binds to microtubules in an Mg–nucleotide-sensitive fashion,

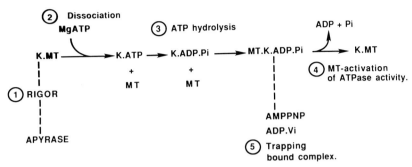

Fig. 5: Tentative Mechanochemical Pathway For Sea Urchin Egg Kinesin.

Fig. 20–5. Tentative model of the mechanochemical cycle of sea urchin egg kinesin. In the absence of nucleotide, kinesin binds to microtubules in a rigor state (step 1), which can be promoted by addition of apyrase. In the presence of Mg–nucleotide, kinesin is released from the microtubules (2). The nucleotide is hydrolyzed (3), and kinesin rebinds to microtubules as the products are released (4), restoring the rigor state. By analogy with actomyosin, microtubules may activate kinesin ATPase activity by accelerating product release. Nucleotide in the absence of Mg^{2+} reversibly competes with Mg–nucleotide to bind kinesin but does not release kinesin from microtubules. Addition of PPPi or EDTA decreases the relative amount of Mg bound to nucleotide, thereby enhancing the binding of kinesin to microtubules. AMP · PNP and ADP·vanadate presumably act by forming a tight microtubule–kinesin–ADP · Pi complex (5), from which products cannot escape.

catalyzes MgATP-dependent unidirectional microtubule motility in vitro, and displays microtubule-activated MgATPase activity. Results of our characterization of these in vitro motility-inducing properties of sea urchin egg kinesin are consistent with the hypothesis that this protein drives microtubule movement via a pathway of mechanochemical coupling analogous to those of myosin and dynein. Although the biological functions of kinesin remain unknown, these in vitro motility-inducing properties, together with the immunocytochemical localization of sea urchin kinesin, make it an attractive candidate for a microtubule-based motor in vivo, where it may mediate the movement of membrane bound organelles, a "spindle matrix," or chromosomes, relative to microtubules. An improved understanding of the in vitro motility-inducing activities of sea urchin egg kinesin should assist us in our efforts to determine the functions and mechanisms of action of kinesin in living sea urchin eggs and early embryos.

ACKNOWLEDGMENTS

Work on sea urchin egg kinesin was initiated when J.M.S. was a postdoctoral fellow in Dick McIntosh's laboratory. J.M.S. is very grateful to Dick for providing a stimulating research environment and for encouraging him to continue this work in his own laboratory. He expresses his thanks to the members of Dick's laboratory who worked with him at various times, in particular Dr. Mary Porter. The ATPase assays performed with *Drosophila* and squid kinesins (Table 20–4) were performed in collaboration with Dr. Bill Saxton and with Drs. Bruce Schnapp and Bruce Crise, respectively. We thank Diana Smith and Drs. Ron Vale, Bruce Schnapp, and Paul D. Wagner for discussions; Dr. Mike Sheetz for discussions and constructive criticism of the manuscript; and Shirley Downs for efficiently preparing the manuscript.

This work was supported by ACS grant BC-530 (J.M.S.), ACS postdoctoral fellowship PF-2925 (S.A.C.), and a March of Dimes Birth Defects Foundation Basil O'Connor Starter Scholar Research award (No. 5; J.M.S.).

Involvement of Microtubules and Kinesin in the Fast Axonal Transport of Membrane-Bounded Organelles

George S. Bloom, Mark C. Wagner, K. Kevin Pfister, Philip L. Leopold, and Scott T. Brady

Department of Cell Biology and Anatomy, University of Texas Southwestern Medical Center, Dallas, Texas 75235

INTRODUCTION: AXONAL TRANSPORT

The transport of proteins from their sites of synthesis to functionally appropriate locations is a task faced by nearly all cells. Neurons, in particular, must move proteins over considerable distances in axons, which may exceed 1 meter in length. Protein synthesis in the neuronal cell is accomplished largely in the perikaryon, although translation may also occur in the proximal dendrites. Because they lack the macromolecular machinery for protein synthesis, axons rely on specialized transport systems for their supply of structural and enzymatic proteins and for the neuropeptides that are released at their terminals.

In this chapter, we review some of the basic principles of axonal transport and focus upon the involvement of microtubules and their constituent proteins, tubulin and the microtubule-associated proteins (MAPs). We conclude by discussing some of the recent developments from our laboratories and from other laboratories regarding the properties of kinesin, a microtubule-activated adenosine triphosphatase (ATPase) that may well serve as a motor for one form of axonal transport.

Rate Classes of Axonal Transport

The best understood feature of protein transport in the axon is that there are two major rate classes in the anterograde direction: fast axonal transport, which takes place at $0.5-5$ μm sec^{-1} and also has a retrograde component, and slow axonal transport, which has a rate about two to three orders of magnitude slower. Several excellent review articles and books addressing these topics have appeared in recent years (Brady, 1985b; Grafstein and Forman, 1980; Smith and Bisby, 1987; Weiss, 1982), and we refer interested readers to those publications for details beyond those presented here.

Multiple, distinct components of both fast and slow transport are known to exist (Lasek and Brady, 1982; Tytell et al., 1981). These components were revealed by injection of radiolabeled amino acids in the vicinity of neuronal cell bodies, such as those found in the mammalian retina, where the amino acids were incorporated into proteins. At varying periods following injection, nerve fibers emanating from those tissues were excised and sliced into segments, which were analyzed sequentially by SDS-PAGE autoradiography to reveal their compositions of newly synthesized proteins. The proteins observed to travel with the fast component of axonal transport generally are associated with membrane-bounded organelles, such as vesicles and mitochondria. Many but not all of the proteins in fast anterograde transport return to the neuronal cell body by retrograde fast transport after having reached the axon terminal.

Slow Axonal Transport

There are two major components of slow axonal transport, and these correspond to the anterograde migration of the cytoskeleton. Microtubules and neurofilaments define "slow component a" (SCa) and move at coherent rates of ~0.2–1 mm per day (Black and Lasek, 1980; Hoffman and Lasek, 1975). Among the major microtubule proteins, both tubulin and the tau MAPs have been detected in SCa (Brady et al., 1984b; Tytell et al., 1984). The rates at which other axonal MAPs migrate has not yet been determined. In the case of neurofilaments, all three of the major subunit proteins have been observed in SCa.

"Slow component b" (SCb) is the faster-moving subclass of slow transport, and actin, the structural subunit of microfilaments, is a conspicuous protein in this group (Black and Lasek, 1979, Willard et al., 1979). Among the other proteins of SCb are presumptive myosin (Willard, 1977), glycolytic enzymes (Brady and Lasek, 1981; Lasek et al., 1984), and clathrin (Garner and Lasek, 1981). A substantial amount of tubulin, presumably in the form of microtubules, has also been observed in SCb in both sensory and motor axons of the sciatic nerve (Oblinger et al., 1987).

Fast Axonal Transport and its Physical Basis

One of the great challenges of cellular neurobiology has been to describe the physical basis of the major rate classes of axonal transport. Currently, the underlying molecular mechanisms for both forms of slow axonal transport remain mysterious, although an in vitro model was proposed recently (Weisenberg et al., 1987). In contrast, substantial progress has been made in understanding fast axonal transport, which corresponds to the translocation of various classes of membrane-bounded organelles along microtubules. Whereas microtubule proteins themselves are transported slowly and unidirectionally through the axon, they serve as tracks along which bidirectional and far more rapid movements of organelles occur.

The direct demonstration that microtubules serve as "highways" for organelle traffic in the axon derives from two relatively recent technical developments: video-enhanced light microscopy (Allen et al., 1981) and a method for extruding axoplasm from the giant axon of the squid (*Loligo pealii*) in a manner that preserves the structural integrity of the axoplasm and its capacity to conduct fast axonal transport (Brady et al., 1982, 1985). When extruded squid axoplasm was first observed by video-enhanced microscopy, the axon was seen to support continuous, bidirectional motility along fibrous elements of membrane-bounded organelles whose sizes were generally below the resolution limit of light microscopy. Larger organelles, such as mitochondria and lysosomes, were also seen to move in both directions along the same set of fibers (Brady et al., 1982, 1985). Comparable observations have since been made in the cytoplasm of numerous kinds of eukaryotic cells. Correlative immunofluorescence (Hayden et al., 1983; Schnapp et al., 1985) and electron (Koonce and Schliwa, 1985; Schnapp et al., 1985) microscopy have revealed that the transport filaments in both neuronal and non-neuronal cells are microtubules. Hence fast axonal transport may be considered to be a special and conveniently studied case of the general phenomenon of organelle transport along microtubules.

Biochemical Requirements and Pharmacological Properties of Fast Axonal Transport

Because extrusion of the cytoplasm from the squid giant axon removes two permeability barriers, the plasma membrane and the glial cell sheath, isolated axoplasm is fully accessible to both low-M_r and high-M_r probes that are soluble in aqueous buffers. Consequently, it has been possible to test systematically the biochemical requirements and pharmacological properties of fast axonal transport by perfusing solutions of known composition into the preparations and monitoring organelle motility by video-enhanced light microscopy. Analogous approaches using detergent-permeabilized preparations of both neuronal (Edmonds and Koenig, 1987; Forman et al., 1983a,b; Hirokawa and Yorifuji, 1986) and non-neuronal (Koonce and Schliwa, 1986a) cells have also been used to characterize organelle motility along microtubules, but these approaches are complicated by the variable extraction of cellular components that may be solubilized by detergents.

A broad variety of probes have been perfused into isolated squid axoplasm, and all that disrupt normal organelle traffic affect both directions of motility indiscriminately (Brady et al., 1984a, 1985; Brady, Pfister, Wagner, and Bloom, submitted; Leopold, Bloom and Brady, manuscript in preparation). Included among the probes that have been examined so far are agents that affect microtubules (taxol and nocodozole), dynein ATPase activity (erythro-9[3-(2-hydroxynonyl)]-adenine [EHNA] and vanadate), protein sulfhydryl groups (N-ethylmaleimide; NEM), divalent cation levels (EGTA, EDTA, and $CaCl_2$), microfilaments (Ca^{2+}, phalloidin, gelsolin, DNAase I, cytochalasin B, and myosin subfragments), and oxidative phosphorylation (DNP and FCCP). Based on the use of these probes, the following conclusions can be

drawn regarding fast axonal transport in the squid.

1. Microtubules are essential.

2. Inhibitors of axonemal dynein suppress organelle transport weakly and only at relatively high (0.5–5 mM) concentrations and do not distinguish anterograde from retrograde movements. There is evidence from other systems, however, that vanadate (Edmonds and Koenig, 1987; Smith, 1987) and EHNA (Forman et al., 1983b) exert a selective inhibition of retrograde particle transport.

3. Modification of free sulfhydryl groups in axoplasm by NEM abolishes organelle motility in both directions.

4. Magnesium is required; although calcium is not essential, levels of calcium high enough to disrupt the axonal cytoskeleton (~10 mM) also inhibit fast transport.

5. Microfilaments, although not required for organelle motility along microtubules, are important for maintaining axoplasmic organization and efficient organelle transport.

6. In the presence of ATP, uncouplers of oxidative phosphorylation inhibit the motility of mitochondria, but not that of other membrane-bounded organelles.

7. None of the pharmacological agents tested to date on isolated squid axons exerts a preferential inhibition of either anterograde or retrograde transport within the limits of detection, although the possibility of two or more distinct motor systems cannot be excluded.

The role of adenine nucleotides in fast axonal transport has been examined in greater detail by perfusion of additional probes into isolated squid axoplasm. Not surprisingly, either ongoing oxidative phosphorylation or exogenous ATP is required for organelle transport (Brady et al., 1982, 1985), suggesting that at least one class of microtubule-associated ATPase serves as motor molecules for fast axonal transport. Further support for this hypothesis was gained from the discovery that 5'-adenylylimidodiphosphate (AMP-PNP), a non-hydrolyzable analogue of ATP, arrests both anterograde and retrograde organelle transport, even in the presence of comparable levels of ATP. Furthermore, treatment with AMP-PNP was found to result in the time-dependent accumulation of membranous organelles along microtubules, even though the organelles were immotile once attached (Lasek and Brady, 1985). A widely accepted interpretation of this observation stipulates that AMP-PNP arrests a normally transient intermediate in the motility cycle of organelles along microtubules by promoting the formation of stable complexes of organelles, microtubules, and motor molecules.

Recently, we examined several other nucleoside triphosphates for their capacity to support. fast axonal transport in isolated squid axoplasm (Leopold, Bloom and Brady, manuscript in preparation). We observed both the peripheries of isolated axons, where microtubules protrude from the main body of the axon and can be detected by light microscopy as distinct fibers, and axon interiors, where cytoskeletal elements and vesicels are too densely packed to permit individual microtubules to be distinguished. Although bidirectional organelle transport was observed on peripheral microtubules, their random orientations relative to the long axes of axons made it impossible to distinguish anterograde from retrograde movements. This ambiguity did not plague our observations of fast transport in axon interiors, however, because axoplasmic polarity was preserved in these regions.

UTP was found to support sustained transport along peripheral microtubules at ~40% normal (ATP) rates and was the best substitute for ATP. GTP, ITP, and CTP, by contrast, were only 20–30% as effective as ATP, and TTP supported transport along the peripheral microtubules only marginally. In the axon interior UTP, GTP, ITP, and CTP were 20–40% as effective as ATP for both anterograde and retrograde transport, but the differences among the four nucleotides were not statistically significant. TTP permitted bidirectional organelle motility in this region at ~15% the normal rates, and ATP-γ-S was completely ineffective at both the periphery of the axon and in the interior. As had been observed for all other probes, none of the nucleotides that we tested preferentially supported anterograde or retrograde transport in squid axoplasm.

BIOCHEMICAL AND PHYSICAL PROPERTIES OF AXONAL MICROTUBULES

To understand the molecular mechanisms that underly fast axonal transport, it is essential to appreciate what proteins are involved and how they are arranged in the axon. Our most extensive knowledge of this subject has been gained from studies of mammalian neuronal tissue.

Protein Composition of Axonal Microtubules in Mammals

Two operationally distinct classes of microtubules, labile and stable, exist in brain. Tubulin and MAPs can be solubilized readily from brain tissue that has been chilled sufficiently to cause extensive depolymerization of labile microtubules. Stable microtubules, in contrast, are highly resistant to extraction by cold or calcium (Brady et al., 1984b). They are abundant in axons and contain a structurally distinct form of α-tubulin (Brady et al., 1984b). It is not presently clear whether enhanced microtubule stability is conferred in vivo by the unusual α-tubulin or by other factors (Margolis et al., 1986; Webb and Wilson, 1980), and it remains to be determined what specialized functions, if any, are served by the stable pool of axonal microtubules.

The microtubule proteins that are readily extractable from brain can be induced to assemble in vitro into microtubules that contain approximately two-thirds tubulin and one-third MAPs. Early studies of these MAPs indicated that the major species fell into two size classes, the high-M_r MAPs of M_r ~300,000–400,000 (Murphy and Borisy, 1975; Sloboda et al., 1975) and the tau proteins of M_r 55,000–62,000 (Weingarten et al., 1975). Subsequent biochemical and immunological work demonstrated that the high-M_r MAPs constitute four distinct families, MAPs 1A, 1B, 1C and 2 (Bloom et al., 1984, 1985). MAPs 1A (Bloom et al., 1984) and 1B (Bloom et al., 1985) are widely distributed in neural tissue, and are abundant in many axons. MAP 2, in contrast, appears to be largely restricted to dendrites and neuronal perikarya (Caceres et al., 1984; De Camilli et al., 1984; Huber and Matus, 1984). The distribution of MAP 1C in the nervous system remains unknown, but recent work has indicated that the protein is a microtubule-activated ATPase, supports gliding of microtubule towards their "plus" ends in vitro, and bears a close physical resemblance to axonemal dynein (Paschal et al., 1987b; Paschal and Vallee, 1987). These findings have led to the suggestion that MAP 1C is a long-sought "cytoplasmic dynein" that functions as a motor for retrograde fast axonal transport in vivo.

The tau proteins are represented by several electrophoretically distinct species that appear to be closely related to one another in primary structure (Drubin et al., 1984; Lee et al., 1988). Monoclonal antibodies specific for tau have indicated that a dephosphorylated form of a phosphorylatable tau epitope is restricted to axons (Binder et al., 1985), whereas another, non-phosphorylatable tau epitope has a more general distribution in the nervous system (Papasozomenos and Binder, 1987). As is the case for all the axonal MAPs mentioned here, the in vivo functions of the tau proteins remain to be determined.

The Organization of Microtubules in the Axon

Electron microscopic studies have yielded a wealth of information regarding how microtubules are arranged in the axon. The long axes of microtubules generally parallel the long axis of the axon in which they reside. The polarity of these microtubules is uniform or nearly so, the fast growing or plus ends being located distal to the perikaryon (Baas et al., 1987; Burton and Paige, 1981; Heidemann et al., 1981; Viancour and For-

man, 1987). Serial sectioning has indicated that, whereas microtubules may extend for a few hundred micrometers or more, individual microtubules do not generally extend the full length of the axon (Bray and Bunge, 1981; Chalfie and Thomson, 1979; Tsukita and Ishikawa, 1981).

Within the axon, microtubules are not randomly organized. Instead, they tend to be clustered in small groups that are thought to represent channels in which fast axonal transport takes place (Lynn et al., 1986; Miller et al., 1987). The detailed ultrastructure of these microtubule domains can be examined more readily in axons from animals that had been treated systemically with β,β'-iminodiproprionitrile (IDPN), a neurotoxic agent that induces the formation of abnormally large microtubule bundles in peripheral axons (Papasozomenos et al., 1981). Observation by quick-freeze, deep-etch electron microscopy of microtubule domains in axons from IDPN-treated rats has revealed the microtubules to be associated with a dense meshwork of straight and anastomosing fine fibers. Comparable images of purified, MAP-containing microtubules and correlative immunofluorescence microscopy of IDPN-treated axons has indicated that the fine fibers correspond, at least in part, to MAPs 1A and 1B (Hirokawa et al., 1985). Immunohistological studies have also demonstrated the presence of actin, presumably in the form of very short filaments, in microtubule-enriched domains of IDPN-treated axons (Papasozomenos and Payne, 1986).

The functional significance of the high-M_r MAPs for fast axonal transport is not clear at this time, although, as was mentioned above, MAP 1C has been proposed to be a retrograde motor protein. A specific role for actin filaments in fast axonal transport is also implied by studies of isolated squid axoplasm perfused with gelsolin and DNAse I (Brady et al., 1984a). The ability of individual axonal microtubules to support transport of membrane-bounded organelles is not impeded by gelsolin, which severs microfilaments. Nevertheless, gelsolin does cause axoplasm to become so disorganized that organelle movement becomes predominantly Brownian, although a few organelles in the axon interior remain attached and translocating along microtubules. These results imply that actin filaments are important for maintaining the structural organization of axoplasm but are not directly involved in organelle motility.

It is reasonable to suppose that motor molecules for fast axonal transport contribute, along with MAPs and actin, to the fine, filamentous structures associated with axonal microtubules in regions where membrane-bounded organelles are located. Several groups have observed organelles linked to microtubules by fine cross bridges in axons and have proposed that the cross bridges represent motor molecules (Ellisman and Porter, 1980; Hirokawa, 1982; Langford et al., 1987; Miller et al., 1987; Schnapp and Reese, 1982; Smith et al., 1977). In the squid giant axon, the length of the cross bridges consistently appears to be between 16 and 18 nm for vesicles travelling in both the anterograde and retrograde directions (Miller and Lasek, 1985).

KINESIN: A MICROTUBULE-ACTIVATED ATPase AND POTENTIAL ORGANELLE TRANSPORT MOTOR

As described above, the establishment of an ATP requirement for fast axonal transport suggested that microtubule-associated ATPases serve as the motors for organelle motility along microtubules. This hypothesis prompted extensive searches for cytoplasmic, dynein-like molecules or novel ATPases that might exhibit in vitro properties consistent with those of a fast axonal transport motor in situ. The net results of these efforts were equivocal for many years.

A major breakthrough in the search for organelle transport motors was provided by the finding that AMP-PNP seems to promote stable binding of motor molecules to microtubules when perfused into preparations of isolated squid axoplasm (Lasek and Brady, 1985). Capitalizing on this discovery, Brady

(1985a) purified microtubule proteins from chick brain cytosol in the presence of AMP-PNP or ATP. Although the two preparations were nearly identical in polypeptide composition, a previously unknown, M_r 130,000 polypeptide was found exclusively in the microtubules prepared in the presence of AMP-PNP. Furthermore, the microtubules purified with AMP-PNP exhibited substantially higher ATPase activity than those isolated from cytosol containing exogenous ATP. These results suggested that the M_r 130,000 polypeptide is a component of a microtubule-associated ATPase that serves as a motor for fast axonal transport in chick brain. Based on these observations, we undertook efforts to purify to homogeneity the protein that comprised the 130,000 dalton polypeptide, to establish whether it possessed ATPase activity, and to characterize its properties further (see below).

Similarly sized polypeptides, whose associations with microtubules are also stabilized by AMP-PNP and which can be partially released from microtubules by treatment with ATP, were detected by a similar approach in squid optic lobe and bovine brain and were partially purified (Vale et al., 1985a). The squid and bovine proteins were named *kinesin*, because they were found to promote ATP-dependent gliding of microtubules relative to inert substrates, such as glass coverslips and latex beads. Curiously, though, these same proteins were reported to be virtually devoid of ATPase activity. As of this writing, microtubules have been purified from numerous additional sources in the presence of AMP-PNP. This ATP analogue stimulates the copurification of polypeptides of ~120 kDa in sources as diverse as sea urchin eggs (Scholey et al., 1985), *Drosophila* (Saxton et al., 1988), and cultured cells (Piazza and Stearns, 1986). Although most of these polypeptides have not yet been extensively characterized, they are all of similar size, AMP-PNP stabilizes their binding to microtubules, and they do not remain firmly bound to microtubules in the presence of ATP. The term *kinesin* has gained widespread acceptance as a name to describe all such proteins, regardless of their source.

Purification of Bovine Brain Kinesin

Our laboratories have been using bovine brain, because of its large size, its abundance of microtubule proteins, and the ease of obtaining fresh tissue, for the purification and characterization of kinesin. We have developed a four-step procedure for obtaining concentrated, highly purified kinesin from this tissue (Bloom et al., 1988; Wagner, Pfister, Brady, and Bloom, manuscript in preparation).

The first step is a modified version of a taxol-dependent procedure to purify MAPs and takes advantage of both ATP and AMP-PNP to modulate the binding to microtubules of kinesin. Microtubules are polymerized in brain cytosol in the presence of ATP and then are centrifuged and discarded. Next, taxol is added to the microtubule-depeleted supernate to promote the assembly of additional tubulin and MAPs. These microtubules are also pelleted and discarded, leaving a supernate of brain cytosol substantially depleted of endogenous tubulin, tau, and high-M_r MAPs but retaining most of its original content of kinesin. Tubulin, taxol, and AMP-PNP are then added to the supernate, and centrifugation is used to collect the microtubules that form. To conclude this initial stage of the kinesin purification procedure, the microtubules are resuspended in buffer containing ATP, and a final centrifugation step is performed. The resulting supernate contains nearly all the kinesin as well as residual levels of other MAPs and tubulin.

Three additional fractionation steps are required to obtain kinesin at an acceptable level of purity. The first of these steps is gel-filtration chromatography. The peak fractions of kinesin from the gel-filtration column are then resolved further by ion-exchange chromatography and, finally, ultra-centrifugation through a sucrose gradient. A summary of the results of each major step of a typical kinesin preparation, as analyzed by SDS-PAGE, is illustrated in Figure 21–1.

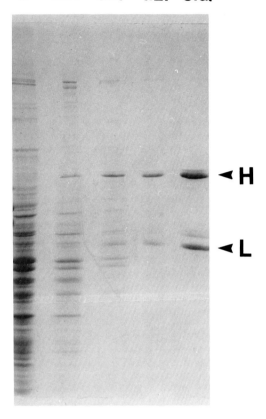

Fig. 21–1. Purification of kinesin from bovine brain. Microtubules were assembled in a cytosolic extract of bovine brain (E) in the presence of ATP. These microtubules, which were enriched in high-M_r and tau MAPs, but not kinesin, were centrifuged and discarded. The microtubule-depleted supernate was then supplemented with purified tubulin, taxol, and AMP-PNP. Microtubules assembled in the extract from the exogenous tubulin and, because of the presence of AMP-PNP, were able to bind endogenous kinesin. The microtubules were collected by centrifugation, resuspended in buffer containing ATP, and centrifuged a final time. Kinesin remained in the supernate (ATP) of the ATP-washed microtubules and was fractionated further by three successive steps: gel-filtration (G.F.) and ion-exchange chromatography (I.E.), and sucrose-gradient ultracentrifugation (S.G.). The pooled, kinesin-containing fractions at each of the final three steps are shown, and all five samples illustrated here are from the same preparation. Arrows indicate the positions of the 124 kDa heavy (H) and 64 kDa light (L) chains of kinesin.

Typical preparations of the kind just described are made from 800 gm brain tissue and yield ~2 mg protein. The bovine brain equivalent of the 130 kDa chick brain polypeptide migrates in SDS-PAGE with an apparent M_r of 124,000. This polypeptide (124k) constitutes more than 60% of the final product, with most of the remainder being a 64 kDa polypeptide (64k). The 124k polypeptide often resolves on SDS-PAGE into two closely spaced bands, the faster migrating of which predominates. Together, the 124k doublet and 64k typically constitute 90–95% of the protein in the final product. We have also frequently observed a minor polypeptide whose electrophoretic mobility is slightly less than that of 64k (see Fig. 21–1). Based on peptide mapping and immunological similarities, the minor polypeptide appears to represent a variant form of 64k.

Native Structure and Physical Properties of Bovine Brain Kinesin

Data obtained from our purification scheme for bovine brain kinesin have been used to determine the quaternary structure of the protein and to characterize some of its physical properties (Bloom et al., 1988). Quantitative densitometry of SDS-polyacrylamide gels was used to determine if any polypeptides copurify to constant stoichiometry with 124k. Although no such polypeptides are readily apparent at early stages, it is evident that 124k and 64k cofractionate at nearly equimolar stoichiometry throughout latter stages of the preparation. These two polypeptides appear to be very distinct structurally by peptide mapping (Fig. 21–2), implying that 64k is not simply a breakdown product of 124k. Measurements of the diffusion (Fig. 21–3) and sedimentation (Fig. 21–4) coefficients of kinesin were made and substituted into the Svedberg equation to calculate a native M_r of ~380,000. Based on these analyses, we have proposed that the bovine brain kinesin molecule contains two 124k heavy chains and two 64k light chains. The mobilities of these polypeptides in SDS-PAGE are not altered when 2-mercapto-

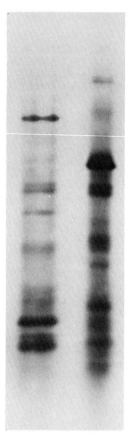

Fig. 21–2. Kinesin heavy and light (L) chains yield dissimilar peptide maps upon limited proteolysis by protease V8. Kinesin was purified as indicated in the legend to Figure 21–1, and the heavy and light chains were resolved by SDS-PAGE. Each kinesin chain was then subjected to limited proteolysis in a second polyacrylamide gel, by protease V8 (Cleveland et al., 1977). Silver staining of the peptide mapping gel revealed dissimilar fragment patterns for the heavy and light chains of kinesin.

ethanol is omitted from the sample buffer (Fig. 21–5), indicating that the quaternary structure of kinesin does not require interchain disulfide bonds.

The Stokes radius of native bovine brain kinesin was found by gel filtration chromatography to be 9.64 ± 0.87 nm. The diffu-

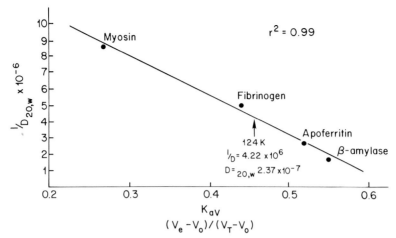

Fig. 21–3. Measurement of the diffusion coefficient ($D_{20,w}$) of kinesin. The retention volumes on a gel filtration column were determined for kinesin (124k) and four proteins of known diffusion coefficients: myosin, fibrinogen, apoferritin, and β-amylase. Retention volumes were expressed as values of $K_{av} = (V_e - V_o)/(V_t - V_o)$, where V_t, V_e, and V_o are the total column volume, retention volume of the protein, and void volume of the column, respectively. A calibration curve for the column, from which the diffusion coefficient of kinesin was measured, was obtained by plotting the reciprocals of the diffusion coefficients of the standards vs. their measured values of K_{av}. Shown here are the results of one experiment. Eight such measurements of the diffusion coefficient of kinesin were made, the average value being $2.24 \pm 0.21 \times 10^{-7}$ cm^2 sec^{-1} (see Table 21–1).

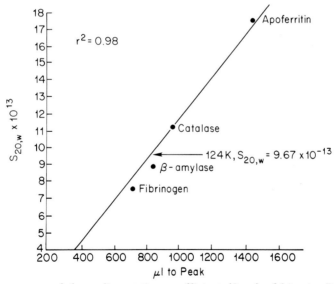

Fig. 21–4. Measurement of the sedimentation coefficient ($S_{20,w}$) of kinesin. Proteins were spun through 2-ml gradients of 5–20% sucrose for 4 hr at 259,000g. The samples included kinesin (124k) and four proteins of known sedimentation coefficients: apoferritin, catalase, β-amylase, and fibrinogen. The sedimentation coefficient of kinesin was determined by comparing the position of its peak in a gradient with the peak positions of the standards (Martin and Ames, 1961). Shown here are the results of one experiment. Six such measurements yielded an average value of $S_{20,w}$ for kinesin of $9.56 \pm 0.34 \times 10^{-13}$ sec (see Table 21–1).

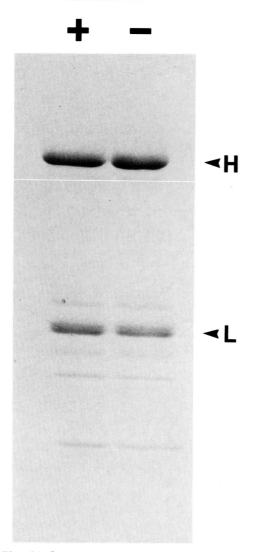

Fig. 21–5. Interchain disulfide bonds do not contribute to the quaternary structure of kinesin. Purified kinesin (as in Figure 21–1, last lane) was analyzed by SDS-PAGE in the presence (+) and absence (−) of 2-mercaptoethanol. The heavy (H) and light (L) chains migrated as M_r 124,000 and 64,000 polypeptides, respectively, whether or not the disulfide reducing agent was present.

sion and hydrodynamic properties of the protein suggest that it is a highly assymetric molecule. Assuming that kinesin has the shape of a prolate ellipsoid, its axial ratio was calculated to be ~20. Recent ultrastructural analysis of purified bovine brain kinesin has

TABLE 21–1. Physical Properties of Bovine Brain Kinesin

Sedimentation coefficient, $S_{20,w} = 9.56 \pm 0.34 \times 10^{-13}$ sec (Six measurements)
Diffusion coefficient, $D_{20,w} = 2.24 \pm 0.21 \times 10^{-7}$ cm^2 sec^{-1} (eight measurements)
Stokes radius = 9.64 $\pm$ 0.87 nm (eight measurements)
Native M_r ~379,000 (possible range 294,000–494,000; eight measurements)
Heavy chain (124k) M_r = 124,000 $\pm$ 2,900 (18 measurements)
Light chain (64k) M_r = 64,000 $\pm$ 1,800 (nine measurements)
Molar ratio of 64k:124k = 1.15 $\pm$ 0.11 (nine measurements)
ATP-binding subunit = 124k
Native structure = $124k_2 64k_2$; no interchain disulfide bonds present
Axial ratio ~20

indicated that it is, indeed, a highly elongated molecule, probably >50 nm long and only 2–5 nm wide (Amos, 1987; Hirokawa, Pfister, Wagner, Brady, and Bloom, manuscript in preparation). A summary of the physical properties we have determined for bovine brain kinesin is given in Table 21–1.

Kinesin is a Microtubule-Activated ATPase

Our original motivation for pursuing studies of kinesin emanated from light microscopic observations of fast axonal transport in isolated squid axoplasm. These studies had implied that ATP-dependent organelle motility involves transient associations of motor molecules with microtubules but that motor molecules could be induced to bind stably to microtubules by AMP-PNP (Lasek and Brady, 1985). Based on this paradigm, we and others reasoned that neuronal ATPases that could be shown to bind stably to mictobules in vitro in the presence of AMP-PNP (but not ATP) would be leading candidates for motor molecules that power fast axonal transport in vivo. It was clear from some of the earliest work on kinesin that AMP-PNP and ATP could be used to promote, respectively, binding and dissociation of the protein from microtubules in vitro (Brady, 1985a; Scholey et al., 1985; Vale et al., 1985d). In contrast, widely divergent results have been reported regarding the ability of isolated kinesin to hydrolyze ATP.

The first evidence that kinesin is, indeed, an ATPase came from studies of isolated, kinesin-enriched chick brain microtubules. These preparations were found to be associated with an ATPase activity that was fourfold greater than that of comparable microtubules lacking kinesin (Brady, 1985a). Nevertheless, ATPase activity was reported to be barely detectable in purer kinesin-containing fractions isolated from squid optic lobe and bovine brain (Vale et al., 1985d). More recently, several groups obtained evidence that an ATPase activity present in kinesin preparations requires microtubules to be activated (Bloom et al., 1988; Cohn et al., 1987; Kuznetsov and Gelfand 1986; Penningroth et al., 1987; Saxton et al., 1988; Wagner et al., 1986; Wagner, Pfister, Brady, and Bloom, manuscript in preparation). Despite the consensus about the presence of an ATPase activity, however, the microtubule-stimulated ATPase activities that were reported vary over more than 2.5 orders of magnitude, ranging from 0.014 to 4.6 μmole min^{-1} mg^{-1}.

To establish definitively whether this ATPase activity is attributable to kinesin itself, we compared the purification properties of the enzymatic activity and kinesin. We found that the microtubule-stimulated ATPase and kinesin do, indeed, cofracionate throughout the gel-filtration, cation exchange and sucrose-gradient steps of our kinesin preparations (Wagner, Pfister, Brady, and Bloom, manuscript in preparation). The basal ATPase activities of the pooled kinesin fractions at each of those three steps remain relatively low, at about 0.01 μmole min^{-1} mg^{-1}. The microtubule-stimulated activity after the sucrose-gradient step is typically about 0.15 μmol min^{-1} mg^{-1}, having risen approximately threefold in specific activity from the gel-filtration step. Hence, microtu-

bules exert an ∼15-fold stimulation of the ATPase activity of bovine brain kinesin purified to virtual homogeneity by our method. A summary of the ATPase activities of kinesin at various stages of a typical preparation in the absence and presence of microtubules is presented in Table 21–2.

The conclusion that the ATPase activity of kinesin is activated by microtubules has been fortified by photoaffinity-labeling experiments of kinesin with ^{32}P-ATP (Bloom et al., 1988; Wagner et al., 1986). In the absence of microtubules, we observed a small but significant amount of label incorporation into the heavy chain of kinesin. When microtubules were present, however, 124k, but not 64k, became heavily labeled. These results indicated that 124k is the ATP-binding subunit polypeptide of kinesin and that turnover of ATP at the active site is enhanced substantially by the presence of microtubules. In a similar study, the kinesin heavy chain was also reported to be the subunit responsible for binding ATP, but stimulation of nucleotide binding by microtubules was not reported (Penningroth et al., 1987).

TABLE 21–2. Coenrichement of Kinesin and a Microtubule-Activated ATPase Activity*

STAGE	ATPase activity (nmole min^{-1} mg^{-1})	
	−MTs	+MTs
Gel filtration	19	56
Ion exchange	14	81
Sucrose gradient	10	123

*Pooled kinesin-containing fractions from the final three purification steps (gel-filtration and ion-exchange chromatography and sucrose-gradient ultracentriguation) were assayed for ATPase activity in the absence (−MTs) and presence (+MTs) of microtubules. Values of the enzymatic activities were epxressed in nmoles ATP hydrolyzed per minute per milligram kinesin-containing fraction. Shown here are the results from successive stages of a single, representative preparation of kinesin. The average ATPase activities for ten kinesin preparations purified through the sucrose gradient step are 10 ± 2 and 157 ± 38 nmoles min^{-1} mg^{-1} in the absence and presence of microtubules, respectively.

Is Kinesin a Motor Protein for Fast Axonal Transport?

The evidence that kinesin is responsible for moving membrane-bounded organelles in axons is currently circumstantial and has been obtained by comparison of the properties of kinesin in vitro with those of motor molecules for fast axonal transport, whatever their identities may be, in situ. For example, microtubule-activated ATPase activity is a property of kinesin that is consistent with the requirements of motor molecules for both ATP and microtubules. AMP-PNP inhibits the enzymatic activity of kinesin (Cohn et al., 1987; Kuznetsov and Gelfand, 1986; Wagner, Pfister, Brady, and Bloom, manuscript in preparation) in the same concentration range in which it reversibly inhibits fast axonal transport (Brady et al., 1985; Lasek and Brady, 1985). AMP-PNP also stabilizes the binding of kinesin to microtubules (Brady, 1985a; Scholey et al., 1985; Vale et al., 1985a), an effect that this nucleotide appears to exert on motor molecules in situ as well (Lasek and Brady, 1985).

We have found that NEM is another reagent that exerts analogous effects on kinesin in vitro and on motors for fast axonal transport in situ (Brady, Pfister, Wagner, and Bloom, submitted). NEM inhibits organelle motility in isolated squid axoplasm in a manner similar to AMP-PNP, but irreversibly. This alkylating reagent, like AMP-PNP, also enables the protein to bind stably to microtubules in the presence of ATP.

Finally, the ability of kinesin to support the translocation of microtubules relative to inert substrates, such as glass coverslips and latex beads (Porter et al., 1987; Vale et al., 1985a), has fueled considerable speculation that the protein is responsible for moving membrane-bounded organelles along axonal microtubles. However, kinesin is not the only brain protein to possess a microtubule-translocating activity. As was mentioned above, MAP 1C is also characterized by this trait and, like kinesin, is a microtubule-activated ATPase (Paschal et al., 1987b; Paschal and Vallee, 1987). Despite these simi-larities, numerous properties distinguish kinesin from MAP 1C. One of the most noteworthy differences is that kinesin causes microtubules to glide towards their minus ends (Vale et al., 1985b), whereas force production by MAP 1C is in the opposite direction (Paschal and Vallee, 1987). Based on the observations that they generate forces unidirectionally in vitro, kinesin and MAP 1C have been proposed to be motor molecules for fast axonal transport in the anterograde (Vale et al., 1985b) and retrograde (Paschal and Vallee, 1987) directions, respectively.

As attractive as those hypotheses may be, a number of important issues need to be resolved before firm conclusions can be made about the functions of kinesin and MAP 1C in the axon. One source of concern is that the biochemical and pharmacological properties of kinesin and MAP 1C in vitro are not consistent with those of membranous organelles moving in fast axonal transport in situ. For example, the nucleotide specificities of the three systems vary significantly. CTP, GTP, ITP, and UTP are relatively poor substrates for supporting bidirectional, fast axonal transport in the squid giant axon, the maximum rates with these nucleotides being only 20–40% those achieved with ATP (Leopold, Bloom, and Brady, manuscript in preparation). By comparison, kinesin has been reported to be capable of hydrolyzing the same nucleotides in vitro at rates 40–85% the rate for ATP (Kuznetsov and Gelfand, 1986), but neither CTP nor UTP supports kinesin-dependent microtubule gliding (Porter et al., 1987). The spectrum of nucleotides capable of being hydrolyzed by MAP 1C has not yet been reported, but whereas ATP supports microtubule gliding in the presence of MAP 1C, several other nucleotides that were tested proved to be unsuccessful (Paschal and Vallee, 1987). Similarly, bidirectional organelle movement in the axon (Brady, Pfister, Bloom, and Brady, submitted) and MAP 1C-dependent microtubule gliding (Paschal and Vallee, 1987) are blocked by submillimolar NEM, but an approximately tenfold higher concentration of NEM is required to inhibit the microtubule translocating activity of kinesin (Porter et al., 1987). These differences among the in vitro properties of MAP 1C and kinesin and organelle transport in the axon suggest that, although microtubule gliding assays have been useful, they are not an accurate model for the process of organelle motility along microtubules in cells. Accordingly, conclusions regarding the in vivo functions of kinesin, MAP 1C and other prospective motor molecules for organelle transport should rest on a broader set of criteria than microtubule gliding assays alone.

The second major reason we are currently reluctant to conclude that kinesin and MAP 1C move membranous organelles in opposite directions along axonal microtubules is the lack of any direct supporting evidence. For example, it remains to be demonstrated that fast axonal transport can be reconstructed in vitro from purified preparations of membranous organelles, microtubules, and kinesin or MAP 1C. Despite the fact that a few antibodies to kinesin have been described (Vale et al., 1985a; Scholey et al., 1985; Saxton et al., 1988), there is still no immunocytochemical evidence that kinesin is, indeed, localized in axons, and none of those antibodies have been reported to inhibit vesicle transport upon microinjection into cells or perfusion into squid axoplasm. The situation regarding MAP 1C is similarly unresolved, because antibodies specific for the protein have not yet been reported. A number of laboratories, including our own, are currently pursuing research designed to fill these gaps in knowledge. Accordingly, some of the current uncertainties regarding the in vivo functions of kinesin and MAP 1C might well be clarified in the foreseeable future.

ACKNOWLEDGMENTS

This work was supported by NIH research grants GM-35364 (G.S.B.), NS-23868 (S.T.B., G.S.B.), and NS-23320 (S.T.B.); NSF biological instrumentation grant DMB-8701164 (G.S.B., S.T.B.); Welch Foundation research grant I-1077 (G.S.B., S.T.B.); and NIH Postdoctoral Fellowship Award GM-10143 (K.K.P.).

NOTE ADDED IN PROOF

We recently obtained direct evidence that kinesin is, indeed, a motor protein for organelle transport along mictotubules. Five new monoclonal antibodies to kinesin were found to stain apparent membrane-bounded organelles in a variety of cultured mammalian cells. One of the antibodies also reacts with the heavy chain of squid kinesin, and stains vesicles and potently retards their motility in isolated giant axons.

Organization of the Axonal Cytoskeleton: Differentiation of the Microtubule and Actin Filament Arrays

Gen Matsumoto, Shoichiro Tsukita, and Takao Arai

*Analogue Information Section, Electrotechnical Laboratory, Tsukuba Science City, Ibaraki 305, Japan (G.M.);
Department of Ultrastructural Research Section, Tokyo Metropolitan Institute of Medical Science,
Honkomagome, Bunkyo-ku, Tokyo 113, Japan (S.T.); Institute of Basic Medical Sciences, University of
Tsukuba, Tsukuba Science City, Ibaraki 305, Japan (T.A.)*

INTRODUCTION

The neuro is a basic element for transmitting and processing information in neural systems and in the brain. Information is received and first processed at multiple sites on the cell body and dendrites of a neuron. The processed information is transferred along the axon, then reprocessed at the terminals to release chemical transmitters. Since neurons can process definite but complicated information, it is now widely accepted that they correspond to microcomputers in the electronic digital-computing system. In the case of neurons, however, the versatility and the variety for their processing ability is extremely high. The synapse is one of the sites responsible for the versatility. Over 50 kinds of functionally different neurons are reported in the cerebrum. This variety may be seen to be tremendously greater when the functions performed within neurons are analyzed in more detail.

Electrical events observed in the neuron are one manifestation associated with neural activities. Opening and closing of ion channels embedded in the nerve membrane are responsible for the electrical activities. However, the fruitfulness of information processing in a neuron can be ascribed not only to the variety of channels and their spatial distribution but also to the dynamic involvement of the cytoskeleton and cytoplasmic elements. The cytoskeleton and cytoplasmic elements may 1) regulate channel functions directly or indirectly through peripheral proteins that bind to channel proteins, 2) regulate the interaction between receptors and channels when they are spatially separated, and/or 3) induce morphological changes in the membrane. Surprisingly, however, compared to the staggering number of electrophysiological studies of channels, investigation of the involvement of the cytoskeletal structures in neuronal activities is quite limited. The first step toward solving this problem is to derive a comprehensive understanding of membrane cytoskeletons

Cell Movement, Volume 2: Kinesin,
Dynein, and Microtubule Dynamics, pages 335–356
© 1989 Alan R. Liss, Inc.

and cytoskeletal-membrane associations in a neuron. The squid giant axon serves as an advantageous model system mainly because of its particularly large size.

Vesicle transport is an essential process in cellular membrane dynamics (Schliwa, 1984). It is particularly refined in neurons that have long cytoplasmic extensions. Axonal transport conveys substances and organelles in both directions, toward the synapse (orthograde direction) and toward the cell body (retrograde direction). The squid giant axon has been particularly useful for studying vesicle transport. The transport of organelles and vesicles continues in the extruded axoplasm of the squid axon for several hours, as long as ATP is available as a source of energy (Brady et al., 1982). Recent studies of vesicle transport of axoplasm isolated from squid giant axons have shown that microtubules are the lineal substrate for vesicle transport. To understand the molecular mechanism of the vesicle transport, one must first understand the structural organization of the motility complex as well as the organization of the total axonal cytoskeleton.

This chapter reviews the present status of the cytoskeletal organization in axons. Particular emphasis is placed on the differences in organization and biochemical characteristics of the "membrane cytoskeleton" and the "transport cytoskeleton." Because the central part of the axoplasm of the squid giant axon can be extruded with a tiny roller, while maintaining the excitability of the axon (Baker et al., 1962; Matsumoto et al., 1984a), the peripheral axoplasm, about 20-μm-thick and containing the membrane cytoskeleton, is especially suited for study in that the cytoskeleton is known to be necessary for the maintenance of the excitability (Matsumoto and Sakai, 1979a,b; Tasaki, 1982).

GENERAL ASPECTS OF CYTOSKELETAL COMPONENTS
Possible Involvement of Cytoskeletons in Neural Activities

Implicit in current concepts of the organization of the cytoskeleton and the cyto-plasmic matrix is the idea that the three major filament systems (actin filaments, microtubules, and 10-nm filaments) are interconnected and dynamically interacting with one another, forming a three-dimensional network inside cells. Dynamic interactions of cytoskeletons with membranes are also thought to be indispensable for membrane activities. The question has naturally arisen of what kinds of dynamic interactions support and regulate the membrane activites and how does the cytoskeleton work in functionally different sites, such as cell bodies, dendrites, axons, and axon terminals. Specific interactions for cytoskeletal–nerve membrane associations have not been clarified except for the putative roles of actin filaments in neurotransmitter release or in the regulation of the number of available receptor sites at postsynaptic membranes (Lynch and Baudry, 1984; Siman et al., 1984). Synapsin I is a neuron-specific phosphoprotein localized in presynaptic terminals, where it is associated with synaptic vesicles (DeCamilli et al., 1984). Synapsin I is thought to play an important role in neural secretion, since membrane excitation induces its phosphorylation (Nestler and Greengard, 1982). This hypothesis was directly tested by pressure-injecting synapsin I purified from bovine brain (Ueda and Greengard, 1977) and calcium/calmodulin-dependent kinase II (McGuinness et al., 1985) into the preterminal digit of the squid giant synapse. These studies demonstrated that synapsin I regulated the availability of synaptic vesicles for release (Llinás et al., 1985). Baines and Bennett (1985) reported that synapsin I was immunologically identical to band 4.1 protein in brain, although Krebs et al. (1986) claimed that synapsin I was structurally, enzymologically, and immunologically distinct from band 4.1. In addition, Perrin et al. (1987) have suggested that the cytoskeletal protein fodrin or calspectrin (brain spectrin) and actin filaments participate in the release mechanism of secretory granules subsequent to their movement towards the cell membrane.

TABLE 22–1. Regional Distribution of Cytoskeletal Proteins and Their Isotypes*

Protein species	Cell bodies and dendrites	Axons	Animal species	References
1. Microtubule-related proteins				
α Tubulin	$\alpha_a + \alpha_b$	α_b	Rat	Cumming et al., 1984
	α_l (Whole brain)	$\alpha_l + \alpha$	Guinea pig	Brady et al., 1984
β Tubulin	β_l (Whole brain)	$\beta_l + \beta_s$		
	$\beta_1 + \beta_2$	β_1 (Stable)	Squid	Arai and Matsumoto,
		$\beta_1{}^*$ (Soluble)		1988c
MAPs	MAP 1A, 1B	MAP 1A, 1B	Rat	Bernhardt and Matus,
	MAP 2	MAP 3		1984
		Tau		Binder et al., 1985
				Bloom et al., 1985
				Huber and Matus, 1984
				Huber et al., 1985
				Morris and Lasek, 1982
	MAP A	MAP A	Squid	Arai and Matsumoto,
	MAP B	Axolinin		1988b,c
	110 kDa			Kobayashi et al., 1986
				Tsukita et al., 1986
2. Microfilament-related proteins				
Actin	—	—		
Fodrin	240/235E	240/235	Mouse	Riederer et al.,
	240/235			1986
	(Small amount only restricted in the cell bodies)			
		Found not only in the cortical but also in the central axoplasm	Squid	Tsukita, Tsukita, Arai, and Matsumoto (in preparation)
255 kDa	Contained	Contained	Squid	Kobayashi et al., 1986
3. Neurofilament-related proteins				
Neurofilament proteins	NF 68	NF 68	Rat	Dahl, 1983
		NF 150		Goldstein et al., 1983
		NF 200		Peng et al., 1986a
	NF 70	NF 160	Chick	Bennett and Condeelis,
	NF 180			1984
	NF 60	NF 60	Squid	Arai and Matsumoto,
		NF 200		1988d
		NF 1		Morris and Lasek, 1982

*Suffices, *a* and *b*, stand for acidic and basic forms of isotypes, respectively. Suffices, *l* and *s,* represent tubulin isomers for labile (equilibrium or soluble) and stable polymers, respectively. See text about β_1, β_2 and $\beta_1{}^*$.

Regional Distribution of Cytoskeletal Components

How different are the cytoskeletal components from one functional region of a neuron to another, for example, from cell body to axon? Several lines of evidence suggest that the regional differences in external shapes of individual neurons can be attributed to dif-ferences in the cytoskeletons underlying the plasma membrane (Drake and Lasek, 1984; Peng et al., 1986a; Cleveland, 1987). The isomers of these cytoskeletal components have also been shown to be regionally different in many neurons (Table 22–1). Neurofilaments are a prominent component of axons but not of dendrites, whereas microtubules are abundant in both axons and dendrites (Wuerker and Kirkpatrick, 1972; Schliwa, 1986). Biochemical and immunological analyses have shown that actin is abundant in both axons and dendrites (Black and Lasek, 1979; Kuczmarski and Rosenbaum, 1979; Willard et al., 1979; Metsuzals and Tasaki, 1978; Morris and Lasek, 1984; Sakai and Matsumoto, 1978; Kobayashi et al., 1986). The proteins associated with the cytoskeletal constituents (actin, tubulin, and neurofilament proteins), such as microtubule-associated proteins (MAPs) and brain spectrin, are also distributed by species and isomers to different regions of axons, cell bodies, and dendrites (Table 22–1). For example, immunological studies have shown that MAP 2 is a component of dendritic microtubules but not of axonal microtubules (Caceres et al., 1984; DeCarmilli et al., 1984; Huber and Matus, 1984; Hirokawa et al., 1985; Papasozomenos et al., 1985; Vallee, 1982), whereas tau protein is enriched in axons relative to the rest of the neuron (Binder et al., 1985; Peng et al., 1986b).

Tubulin isomers are distributed differently between the cell bodies, dendrites, and axons, as summarized in Table 22–1. A survey of brain tubulins from six vertebrates shows the extent of heterogeneity to be similar in all the organisms examined, with at least six isotubulins in the α subunit and 12 in the β subunit (Field et al., 1984; Cleveland, 1987). In some instances, the biochemical and immunological differences between the tubulin isomers correlate with different subcellular locations of microtubules and, therefore, presumably different functions (Schliwa, 1986). In many instances, however, it is not obvious whether the functions of microtubules composed of one type of tubulin isomer are different from those of another type (McKiethan and Rosenbaum, 1984). In particular, recent genetic approaches do not favor functional specialization of individual tubulin isotypes (see review by Cleveland, 1987), although there is an indication that in vivo some functional distinctions among tubulin isotypes must be present (Joshi et al., 1987).

We will show that several types of tubulin isomers are not distributed evenly in a single giant neuron of squid; the forms of tubulin isomers are different not only from the cell bodies to axons but also from the cortical layer of axoplasm to the central part of a single giant axon.

Two major functions of the axon are vesicle transport and impulse conduction. The cytoskeletons related to these functions may be differentiated in squid giant axons because when axoplasm is extruded, the axolemma retains its full excitability, whereas the extruded axoplasm retains its full capability of vesicle transport. The integrity of the cortical axoplasm is important in the maintenance (Metuzals and Tasaki, 1978; Matsumoto and Sakai, 1979a,b; Matsumoto et al., 1979) and generation (Matsumoto et al., 1984a,b, 1985; Matsumoto, 1984) of axonal excitability. It has been found that the subaxolemmal cytoskeleton of the giant axon is highly specialized and differentiated, suggesting that it regulates axonal functions, including electrical excitability (Kobayashi et al., 1986; Tsukita et al., 1986).

COMPONENTS OF THE CORTICAL AXOPLASM

After extrusion, the 20-μm-thick peripheal (cortical) axoplasm remaining under the axolemma of squid giant axon can be compared with the extruded (central) axoplasm by SDS-PAGE (Fig. 22–1). Proteins of squid axoplasm so far identified are almost all related to microtubules, actin filaments, and neurofilaments.

Microtubule-Associated Proteins

Tubulins, MAP A ($\sim$300 kDa), and axolinin (260 kDa) are the most conspicuous MAPs in the cortical layer. The cortical axoplasm is characterized by a particularly large amount of axolinin (Fig. 22–1). Axolinin was originally identified as a protein that might play an important role in maintenance of the excitability of the squid axolemma (Kobayashi and Matsumoto, 1982; Matsumoto et al., 1979, 1983, 1984a,b; Matsumoto

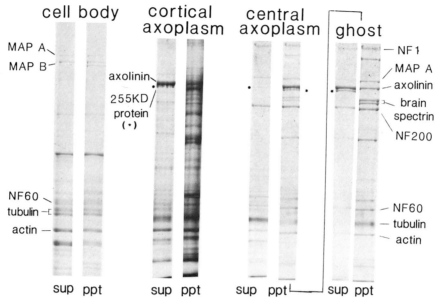

Fig. 22–1. Protein compositions in the axoplasm of the squid giant axon (**right six lanes**) and in the cell bodies of squid stellate ganglia (**left two lanes**). Protein species in the cell body: Squid stellate ganglia are homogenized in a 0.5 M NaCl solution to obtain supernatant (sup) and precipitated (ppt) fractions in the SDS-PAGE (3–12% linear gradient gel) patterns. Protein compositions in the central (or extruded) axoplasm (right four lanes) and in the cortical (or peripheral) axoplasm: "Central axoplasm" shows SDS-PAGE (3–12% linear gradient gel) patterns for supernatant and precipitated components, respectively, which are obtained when the central axoplasm homogenized in 0.1 M MES buffer is centrifuged. The precipitated components are further homogenized in a 0.5 M NaCl solution and centrifuged to devide into supernatant and precipitated components (ghost). "Cortical axoplasm" represents SDS-PAGE (3–12% linear gradient gel) patterns for supernatant and precipitated components of the cortical axoplasm, respectively, when it is homogenized in the 0.5 M NaCl solution and centrifuged. MAPs of MAP A (300 kDa), MAP B (260 kDa), axolinin (260kDa), and tubulin, microfilament-associated proteins of brain spectrin (235 and 240 kDa), 255 kDa protein (*) and actin, and neurofilament components of NF 1 (>400 kDa), NF 200 (200 kDa), and NF 60 (60 kDa) are characterized as described in the text.

and Sakai, 1979a,b; Sakai and Matsumoto, 1978; Sakai et al., 1984, 1985; Murofushi et al., 1983; Arai and Matsumoto, 1988a,b). Axolinin is easily purified from squid axons by its characteristic solubility (soluble in 0.6 M NaCl and insoluble in 0.1 M NaCl) (Kobayashi et al., 1986) and/or its binding to concanavalin A-Sepharose (Murofushi et al., 1983). Axolinin has a rod shape, with a knob at one end, and a contour length of about 100 nm (Fig. 22–2A) (Tsukita et al., 1983b; Kobayashi et al., 1986). It is a particularly unique MAP localized mainly at the cortical axoplasm. Axolinin copurifies with axoplasmic microtubules (Murofushi et al., 1983;

Kobayashi et al., 1986) and can bind to microtubules or tubulin aggregates its tail end (Fig. 22–2C). Unlike other MAPs, however, axolinin does not promote the polymerization of purified tubulin, but it can stimulate bundling of microtubules in vitro in the absence of other MAPs (Murofushi et al., 1983). Axolinin is different from other high-M_r proteins such as erythrocyte spectrin (for review, see Bennett et al., 1986), brain spectrin (Levine and Willard, 1981; Kakiuchi et al., 1982; Glenney et al., 1982), filamin (Wang, 1977), and myosin, as judged from the comparative studies on molecular shapes and weights, immunological cross

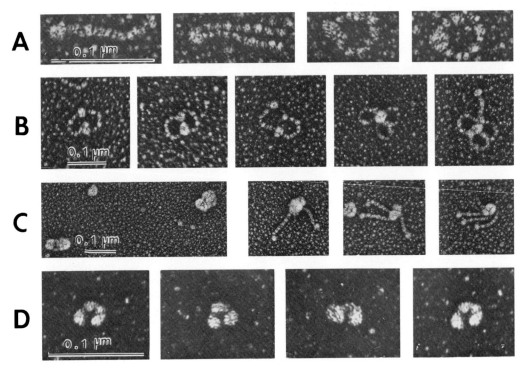

Fig. 22–2. A: Morphology of axolinin molecule in 0.6 M NaCl solution in rotary-shadowed preparations (Kobayashi et al., 1986). The axolinin molecule appears as a straight rod about 105-nm-long, with a globular head at one end. Some molecules are split into two thinner strands and form ring structures. **B:** Morphology of the aggregates of the axolinin molecules in 0.1 M NaCl solution in rotary-shadowed preparations. In 0.1 M NaCl solution, the axolinin molecules form various sizes of aggregates. Two, three, or four molecules form small aggregates by a head-to-tail association between two molecules. **C:** Rotary-shadowing electron micrographs of axolinin–tubulin complexes. Extreme left picture: Purified tubulin forms small aggregates in a 0.6 M NaCl solution containing 50% glycerol. Right three pictures: A mixture of axolinin and purified tubulin in the same condition. Each axolinin molecule is associated with a tubulin aggregate at its tail end, forming spot-like structures. Molecular shape of the 255 kDa protein molecule in 0.1 M NaCl solution. The 255 kDa protein molecule appears as a characteristic horseshoe-shaped structure ~30–35 nm in diameter.

reactivities, and biochemical properties (Kobayashi et al., 1986; Murofushi et al., 1983; Tsukita et al., 1983b, 1986). Axolinin molecules are successively incorporated into aggregates (see below) by head-to-tail association of two molecules (Fig. 22–2B) and is mainly localized in the cortical layer, although some axolinin is found in the central axoplasm (Tsukita et al., 1983b, 1986; Arai and Matsumoto, 1988a,b).

The second MAP or MAP A appears as a faint band near 300 kDa seen in SDS gels of the cortical axoplasm (Fig. 22–1). This protein is similar to the MAP 2-like ATP-binding 292 kDa protein (Gilbert and Sloboda, 1986) and to heat-sensitive 320 kDa MAP (Kobayashi et al., 1986). Although MAP A cross reacts with antiserum to porcine brain MAP 2 (Gilbert and Soloboda, 1986), MAP A is heat-sensitive and cannot be phosphorylated, whereas rat and porcine brain MAP 2 are heat-resistant (Kobayashi et al., 1986) and become phosphorylated (Gilbert and Soloboda, 1986) under the same conditions. Further, monoclonal antibodies against MAP A do not cross react with MAP 2 (Arai and

Matsumoto, 1988c). MAP A is more abundant in the central axoplasm than in the cortical layer (Fig. 22–1), and is also present at the cell bodies (Fig. 22–1, Table 22–1). Therefore, it is difficult simply to compare MAP A of squid neurons with the high-M_r MAPs of mammalian brain, although the high-M_r MAP family of giant axons is rather simple compared with that of mammalian neurons. In the cortical layer, axolinin is a major high-M_r MAP and MAP A is minor, whereas MAP A is major and axolinin is minor in the central axoplasm. Further, cell bodies in squid neurons contain another MAP, which we call MAP B (Fig. 22–1) (Arai and Matsumoto, 1988c). The M_r of MAP B is 260 kDa, exactly the same as that of axolinin, judged from its motility in the SDS-polyacrylamide gel. However, several lines of immunological and biochemical study show that MAP B is definitely different from axolinin. Thus, in the cell bodies, MAPs A and B are two major microtubule-associated proteins different from axolinin (Arai and Matsumoto, 1988a, b, c).

Tubulins are biochemically abundant in both cortical and central axoplasms (Metuzals and Tasaki, 1978; Sakai and Matsumoto, 1978; Matsumoto et al., 1982; Hodge and Adelman, 1983; Metuzals et al., 1983; Kobayashi et al., 1986; Arai and Matsumoto, 1988c). By immunological criteria, using monoclonal antibodies against β tubulins, β tubulins in the cortical layer are of axonal isomer β_1 type, which are also present at the cell bodies, whereas the cell bodies also possess another form, β_2. The central part of the axoplasm has a modified form of β_1 isomers, β_1^* (Table 22–1) (Arai and Matsumoto, 1988c).

Microfilament-Associated Proteins

Actin is also one of the most abundant proteins in axons and exists as both a monomer and a polymer (Metuzals and Tasaki, 1978; Sakai and Matsumoto 1978; Black and Lasek, 1979; Jockusch et al., 1979; Kuczmarski and Rosenbaum, 1979; Willard et al., 1979; Shaw et al., 1981; Morris and Lasek, 1982, 1984; Hirokawa, 1982, 1983; Koba-

yashi et al., 1986; Tsukita et al., 1986). Because actin filaments are rarely observed except in the subaxolemmal space of squid giant axons (Metuzals and Tasaki, 1978; Tsukita et al., 1986), actins and actin-binding proteins in axons have not been extensively studied compared with tubulins and MAPs in spite of the fact that an ATPase-dependent interaction between actin and myosin is postulated to generate the force for the slow axonal transport mechanism (Lasek and Hoffman, 1976; Lasek, 1982).

Brain spectrin (calspectrin or fodrin) is a 1,000 kDa fibrous protein, with subunits of 240 kDa (α) and 235 kDa (β), forming an $(\alpha\beta)_2$ tetrameric complex. The α subunit contains a binding site for calmodulin (Tsukita et al., 1983a); the phosphorylated β subunit contains a binding site for brain ankyrin, a potential membrane-attachment site. Brain protein 4.1 and actin filaments attach to both ends of the bivalent brain spectrin tetramer (for reviews, see Bennett, 1985; Goodman and Zagon, 1984, 1986). Recently, immunohistochemical studies have shown that mammalian brain contains two distinct spectrin subtypes, both of which have subunits of 240 and 235 kDa (Riederer et al., 1986). Brain spectrin (240/235) (nomenclature of Goodman and Zagon, 1984) is located in axons and, to a lesser extent, in cell bodies. This brain spectrin subtype does not react with mammalian red blood cell spectrin antibodies. Brain spectrin (240/235E) (E stands for erythrocyte subtype) is found in neural cell bodies and dendrites but not in axons.

Spectrin of squid giant neurons, which also has subunits of 240 and 235 kDa, is found in both the cortical and the central axoplasm (Morris and Lasek, 1982, 1984; Kobayashi et al., 1986; Gilbert and Sloboda, 1986; Pratt, 1986b; Arai and Matsumoto, 1988c) and, to a lesser extent, in the cell bodies (Fig. 22–1). In the subaxolemmal cytoskeleton of the squid giant axon, electron microscopy shows that a specialized meshwork of of slender strands connects the actin filament clusters to the axolemma (Tskukita et al., 1986). This meshwork resembles the spectrin-actin network underlying the human erythrocyte membrane (Branton et al., 1981; Tsukita et al., 1980, 1981), suggesting that axonal spectrin localizes just beneath the axolemma to constitute part of the meshwork in the microfilament-associated domain of the subaxolemmal cytoskeleton (see below). Axonal spectrin not only is located in the vicinity of the inner surface of the axolemma but also is present in the axoplasmic ghost of the central axoplasm. Furthermore, preliminary immunological studies using monoclonal antibodies against neural spectrin isolated from squid optic lobes show that axonal spectrin has at least two subtypes (Tsukita, Tsukita, Arai, and Matsumoto, unpublished results).

Another actin-binding protein found in squid giant axons is the 255 kDa protein (Kobayashi et al., 1986), which occurs in both the cortical and the central axoplasm (Fig. 22–1). In low-angle rotary-shadowing microscopic images, the 255 kDa molecule has a characteristic horseshoe-shaped structure with diameter of 35 nm (Fig. 22–2D). The 255 kDa proteins in the subaxolemmal cytoskeleton may play a role as a kind of cross linker within the network of microfilaments (see below).

Neurofilament Associated Proteins

Neurofilaments are a prominent component of axons (Table 22–1), where they extend parallel to the long axis. The neurofilament triplet proteins (three polypeptides of 200, 150, and 68 kDa in the case of mammalian axons, and of > 400, 200, and 60 kDa in squid axons) are major constituents of the neurofilaments (Table 22–1) (for review, see Schliwa, 1986). The triplet proteins are not proteolytic fragments of a precursor, and each is translated from different mRNAs (Czosnek et al., 1980). Immunoelectron microscopic observation of the mammalian axon shows that the 68 kDa protein forms the core of the filament, whereas the 200 kDa protein occurs along the periphery of individual filaments as periodic cross linkers (Willard and Simon, 1981; Sharp et al., 1982; Hirokawa et al., 1984). Only the 68

kDa subunit is competent to self-assemble in vitro into morphologically normal neurofilaments. The 150 kDa and the 200 kDa polypeptides are able to copolymerize only if the 68 kDa subunit is also present (Geisler and Weber, 1981; Liem and Hutchinson, 1982; Minami and Sakai 1983; Minami et al., 1984; Geisler et al., 1984, 1985). Neurofilaments in situ can be categorized into two groups according to their level of phosphorylation. Cell bodies and the proximal portions of axons contain non-phosphorylated neurofilaments, whereas the neurofilament triplet proteins in long fibers with compact assemblies are more highly phosphorylated (Sternberger and Sternberger, 1983).

In squid giant axons, the neurofilament triplet is abundant in the central axoplasm and, to a lesser extent, in the cortical layer (Fig. 22–1). This correlates with the morphological observation that neurofilaments are not found in the vicinity of the axolemma, whereas microtubules and microfilaments are associated with the axolemma through their respective specialized meshwork of thin strands (see below). These observations indicate that neurofilaments do not, at least directly, support and regulate membrane activities in squid giant axons. Morris and Lasek (1982) propose that neurofilaments function to conserve cytoskeletal organization, because these polymers are highy stable.

COMPONENTS OF THE CENTRAL AXOPLASM

Stable and Equilibrium Cytoskeletons

The cytoskeleton of the axoplasm extruded from the squid giant axon contains both stable polymers and soluble (or equilibrium) polymers (Morris and Lasek, 1982, 1984). The stable polymers are found after the soluble fraction is extracted in a high-salt solution P (Morris and Lasek, 1982). Morris and Lasek (1982, 1984) refer to the extracted preparation as the "axoplasmic ghost." The insoluble ghost proteins consist of neurofilament proteins of NF 1 (> 400 kDa peptides), NF 200 (200 kDa peptides), and NF 60 (60 kDa peptides); MAPs of tubulins, axolinin, and MAP A; microfilament-associated proteins of actins and brain spectrin; and others. The most conspicuous members of the insoluble proteins are the subunit proteins of neurofilaments. Several proteins, especially tubulin and actin, show both soluble and insoluble forms in axoplasm. Tubulin and actin are detected in significant amounts both in the insoluble ghost and in the salt extract (Morris and Lasek, 1982). The relative proportion of monomeric tubulin and actin in the central part of axoplasm is larger than that of stable (insoluble) and equilibrium (soluble) polymers. As a result, the cytoskeleton in the central part can be regarded as a single system that is interconnected through a large free monomer pool. Equilibrium (soluble) polymers are responsive to changes in the concentration of monomer and decrease in length if the monomer concentration declines (Pollard and Mooseker, 1981; Kirschner and Mitchison, 1986; Schulze and Kirschner, 1987).

Molecular Origins of Polymer Stability

A question arises about the molecular basis for the stability differences found in tubulins and actins. It may be attributed to multiple genes, to posttranslational modification, or to both. As was previously described, recent immunological studies using monoclonal antibodies against β-tubulins have shown that stable β-tubulin, whether it is in the axoplasmic ghost or in the cortical axoplasm, belongs to the subtype β_1, whereas soluble tubulin belongs to subtype β_1^*, the modified form of β_1 (Arai and Matsumoto, 1988c). This localization of heterogeneous tubulin subtypes inside the squid giant axon may, at least in part, be responsible for the different level of stability of tubulin polymers.

Essentially all axolinins remain associated with the stable axonal cytoskeleton when the axoplasm is bathed in a 0.1 M 2-(N-Morpholino) ethanesulfonic acid (MES) so-

lution (Fig. 1) but some of them are soluble both in a 0.5 M NaCl solution (Fig. 1) and in the buffer P (Morris and Lasek, 1982). This is expected since axolinin in vitro is soluble in high-salt solutions (Kobayashi et al., 1986). On the other hand, MAP A is found almost equally in both insoluble and soluble fractions (Fig. 22–1). Axonal (brain) spectrin is essentially contained in the axoplasmic ghost (Morris and Lasek, 1982), as is shown in Figure 22–1. An intriguing question that remains to be answered is whether the subtype of axonal spectrin in the axoplasmic ghost differs from that in the cortical axoplasm.

STRUCTURAL ORGANIZATION OF AXONAL CYTOSKELETON

Conventional Electron Microscopy and Chemical Fixation

A prerequisite of conventional electron microscopy is that samples be chemically fixed and dehydrated before observation. There are some possibilities that chemical fixation could cause artifacts. To minimize the artifact, both cortical axoplasm and extruded axoplasm of squid giant axons are particularly suited for chemically fixing their respective cytoskeletons. Chemical fixative molecules could rapidly and homogeneously diffuse into their cytoplasmic matrices without being blocked by any special obstacles when the extruded axoplasm is directly bathed in the chemical fixative and when the axon after the extrusion is intraaxonally perfused with the fixative. With this advantage, and by the use of tannic acid, the morphology of the subaxolemmal cytoskeleton, especially microtubules and actin filaments, was first well preserved (Tsukita et al., 1986).

Time-Resolved Rapid-Freezing Microscopy

An alternative to chemical fixation is the recently developed rapid-freeze, deep-etch technique (Heuser et al., 1979; Heuser and Salpeter, 1979; Heuser and Kirschner, 1980; Hirokawa and Heuser, 1981; Tsukita et al., 1982; Usukura et al., 1983). This method

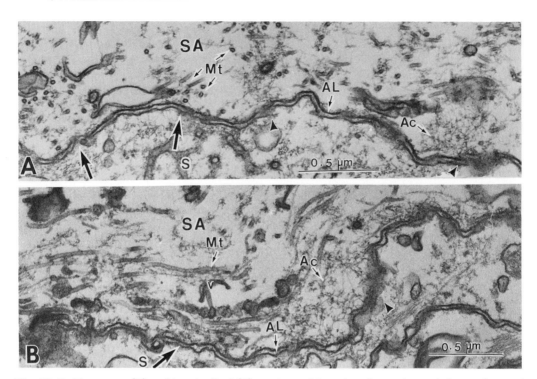

Fig. 22–3. Transverse **(A)** and longitudinal **(B)** sections of the subaxolemmal cytoskeleton of a squid giant axon. The axolemma (AL) of a giant axon is divided into two domains: microtubule-associated (large arrows) and microfilament-associated (arrowheads). Microtubules (Mt) are oriented longitudinally, and some are associated laterally with axolemma. One microtubule runs along the cytoplasmic surface of the axolemma and attaches laterally to the axolemma through slender strands in a side-to-membrane fashion. Microfilaments ~4–5 nm in thickness form spot-like clusters beneath the axolemma. S, schwann cell. SA, subaxolemmal axoplasm.

enables us to observe not only the three-dimensional architecture of cytoskeletal elements at a resolution great enough to pick out macromolecular structures (Heuser and Kirschner, 1980; Hirokawa, 1982; Hirokawa et al., 1985; Tsukita et al., 1982, 1986) but also to observe structural changes associated with the physiological mechanisms at a temporal resolution of 2 msec or better. Studies on the organization of the axonal cytoskeleton have concentrated on the transport axoplasm and have been limited as far as the subaxolemmal cytoskeleton is concerned.

ORGANIZATION OF THE CORTICAL AXOPLASM
Subaxolemmal Microtubules

How is the subaxolemmal cytoskeleton associated with the axolemma? The subaxo-

lemmal cytoskeleton is characterized by parallel bundles of longitudinally oriented microtubules, which appear to be interconnected by slender strands (Endo et al., 1979; Hodge and Adelman, 1980; Matsumoto et al., 1982; Metuzals et al., 1983; Tsukita et al., 1986) (Fig. 22–3). In the transversely cut plane of the squid giant axon, the average density of microtubules at the region nearest the axolemma is over $100/\mu m^2$. This density rapidly decreases toward the interior of the axon to $20/\mu m^2$ (the general characteristics for an intact axon are the same as those for a perfused axon in Fig. 22–4) (Matsumoto et al., 1982, 1983; Metuzals et al., 1983).

These observations indicate that densely packed subaxolemmal microtubules within 3 μm of the inner surface of the axolemma are specially differentiated from other corti-

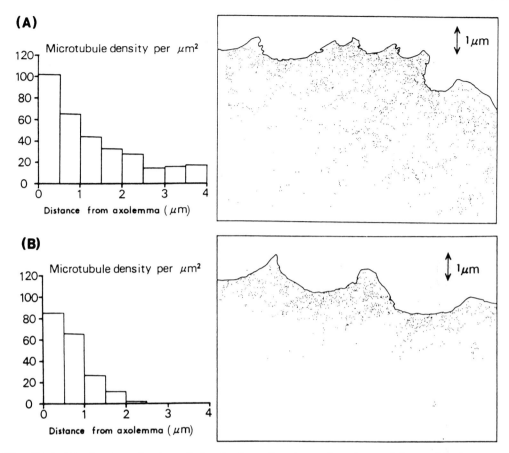

Fig. 22–4. Distribution of microtubules in the subaxolemmal regions of the squid giant axons intraxonally perfused with a physiological buffer that favors the maintenance of membrane excitability **(A)** and after intraaxonal perfusion with the buffer containing 20 mM colchicine for 10 min **(B).** In the control axon, the density of microtubules is $100/\mu m^2$ at the region nearest to the axolemma and rapidly decreases toward the interior of the axon to $20/\mu m^2$ at a distance 3–4 μm from the axolemma. On the other hand, the microtubule density for the colchicine-treated axon is reduced compared with that of the control axon (A). Particularly the microtubules located 2–4 μm from the axolemma are colchicine-sensitive.

cal microtubules present in regions more than 3 μm from the axolemma. This is supported by the observations that the subaxolemmal microtubules are functionally differentiated from other cortical microtubules since the membranous organelles are not transported or are slowly transported along the subaxolemmal microtubules (0–3 μm from the axolemma), whereas they are actively transported on cortical microtubules 3–20 μm away from the axolemma (Arai et al., 1988). The subaxolemmal

microtubules are also stable polymers, judging from the fact that their density is unchanged when the axon, after its axoplasm is extruded, is perfused with a buffer that favors microtubule assembly (Sakai and Matsumoto, 1978; Matsumoto and Sakai, 1979a). Similarly, they are resistant to the colchicine (Fig. 22–4B) or cold treatment (Tsukita, Tsukita, Ichikawa, Arai, and Matsumoto, in preparation). Stabilization and bundling of subaxolemmal microtubules may, in part, result from their relationship to the sur-

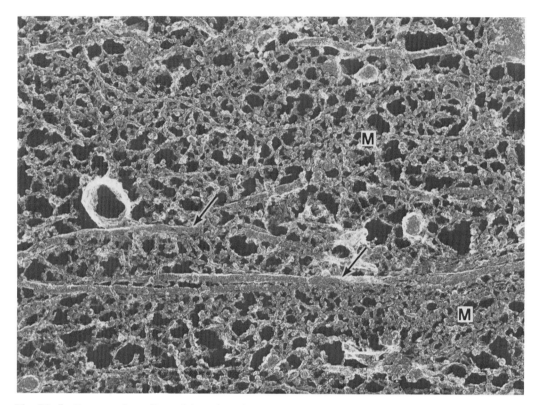

Fig. 22–5. Freeze-etch replicas of the subaxolemmal axoplasm fractured tangentially at a distance ~2 μm from the axolemma. Before the rapid freezing, the specimen was chemically fixed by perfusing the fixative intracellularly. The fixative was washed out with distilled water containing 10% methanol, then the specimen was rapidly frozen. The replica is characterized by the longitudinally oriented microtubules (arrows) embedded in a well developed, three-dimensional fine meshwork (M).

rounding meshwork of axolinin (Tsukita et al., 1986). When the cortical axoplasm of the rapidly frozen giant axon is fractured tangentially at a distance ~2 μm away from the axolemma, the replicas obtained are characterized only by the longitudinally oriented microtubules embedded in a well developed, three-dimensional fine meshwork of the axolinin (Fig. 22–5). The organization contrasts sharply with that of the cytoskeleton of the extruded axoplasm characterized by the longitudinally oriented microtubules and the neurofilament lattice, indicating that the cytoskeleton of the giant axon is specialized into cortical and central portions. Because axolinin induces bundling of microtubules in vitro in the absense of MAPs

(Murofushi et al., 1983), the axolinin meshwork may arrange the subaxolemmal microtubules into groups inasmuch as MAP A is absent in the subaxolemmal region (Arai and Matsumoto, 1988c). In addition, neurofilaments that also run parallel to the microtubules in the subaxolemmal region may support the stability of the cytoskeleton. However, this is insufficient to explain the stability and bundling of microtubules 1 μm or less away from the axolemma, because in these regions the axolinins are less abundant and the density of neurofilaments is extremely low. In this respect, the finer distribution of tubulin isotypes in the cortical axoplasm is interesting, although isotype β_1 is identified in the cortical layer.

Microtubule- and Actin Filament-Associated Domains

The way in which the subaxolemmal cytoskeleton is differentiated to regulate axolemmal activities is central to our understanding of axolemmal function. A partial solution to the problem may reside in the observations that, nearer to the axolemma, the density of microtubules becomes greater (Fig. 22–4A) and that some microtubules run along the cytoplasmic surface of the axolemma and are attached to the axolemma by slender strands (Fig. 22–3) (Tsukita et al., 1986). Furthermore, actin filaments are also associated with the axolemma, tangled with each other and forming spot-like clusters (Fig. 22–3). The actin filaments are seen as large, electron-dense structures when heavy meromyosin of rabbit skeletal muscle is intraaxonally perfused prior to chemical fixation. They are aligned just beneath the axolemma, often in a periodic manner (Tsukita et al., 1986). We expected that decoration with heavy meromyosin would help to define the polarity of the actin filaments. However, most of filaments were detached from the axolemma after the heavy meromyosin treatment, and general disruption of the association between actin filaments and the plasma membrane by heavy meromyosin or S1 decoration is known to occur with other plasma membrane fragments (Goodloe-Holland and Luna, 1984; Bennett and Condeelis, 1984).

The axolemma is divided into a microtubule-associated domain and an actin filament-associated domain. The axolemma is covered over 10% ± 5% of its area with the actin filament-associated domains (Tsukita et al., 1986). The bundles of microtubules associated with the axolemma are excluded from the axolemma near the actin filament-associated domains (Fig. 22–3A). To analyze further the association of the subaxolemmal cytoskeletons with the cytoplasmic surface of the axolemma, replicas were prepared that provide three-dimensional views of the cytoskeletal network underlying the axolemma (Fig. 22–6). When the subaxolemmal cytoskeleton was fractured tangentially just beneath the axolemma, the cytoplasmic surface of both microtubule-associated and microfilament-associated domains of the axolemma was revealed (Fig. 22–3B). The replicas provide three-dimensional views of the well developed cytoskeletal network underlying the axolemma, in which microtubules running along the axolemma and the clusters of actin filaments are easily identified.

In the actin filament-associated domain, the actin filament cluster is a complicated three-dimensional network in which actin filaments are intertangled (Fig. 22–7). Some actin filaments exhibit a ~5-nm period on their surface, which may correspond to the native helical pitch of the filaments (Heuser and Cooke, 1983). Within the network of actin filaments, thin cross-linking strands and globular structures are uniformly distributed (Fig. 22–7b). Some of the globular structures that are 30–35 nm in diameter show a characteristic horseshoe-like appearance, which resembles the molecular shape of the 255 kDa protein (Fig. 22–2D). Occasionally, some microtubules are observed to run into the actin filament clusters and to be intermingled with actin filaments (Fig. 22–7a,b).

A specialized layer of the characteristic meshwork of thin strands occurs between the actin filament clusters and the axolemma (Fig. 22–8). This meshwork is directly attached to the cytoplasmic surface of the axolemma. On the cytoplasmic surface, a number of globular extrusions 5–10 nm in diameter occur, some of which are associated with the meshwork of thin strands. Actin filaments run parallel to this meshwork and associate laterally with it, thus being incorporated into the meshwork itself. Actin filaments in the clusters do not appear to bind to the cytoplasmic surface of the axolemma directly; rather, they associate through a two-dimensional meshwork of thin strands just beneath the axolemma. This meshwork strongly resembles the spectrin–actin network underlying the human erythrocyte membrane (Tsukita et al., 1980,

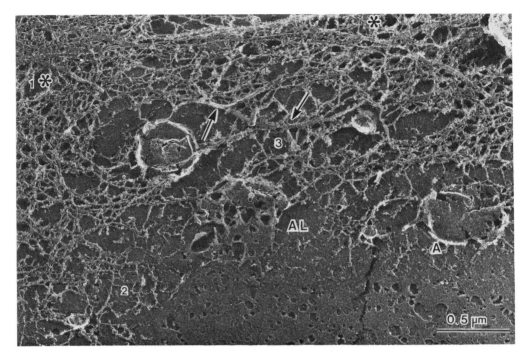

Fig. 22–6. Freeze-etch replicas of the subaxolemmal cytoskeleton tangentially fractured beneath the squid axolemma. The giant axon is intraaxonally fixed using chemical fixatives before rapid freezing. The replicas provide three-dimensional views of the well developed cytoskeletal network underlying the axolemma, in which the microtubules (arrows) gazing along the axolemma (AL) and the clusters of microfilaments (*) are easily identified. Regions 1, 2, and 3 correspond to Figures 22–7, 22–8, and 22–9, respectively.

1981; Branton et al., 1981). Considering that brain spectrin is reported to localize just beneath the axolemma in mammalian axons (Levine and Willard, 1981; Glenney et al., 1982; Kakiuchi et al., 1982; Repasky et al., 1982; Tsukita et al., 1983a), it may well be that the meshwork in the actin filament-associated domains is composed mainly of brain spectrin and actin.

In the microtubule-associated domain among the clusters of microfilaments, the longitudinally oriented microtubules run along and associate with the cytoplasmic surface of the axolemma (Fig. 22–3) and are connected laterally on the cytoplasmic surface by slender strands (Fig. 22–9). Some actin filaments extend out from the neighboring clusters and run closely with the microtubules associated with axolemma,

forming a complicated, coarse network around the microtubules.

In conclusion, the organization of the subaxolemmal cytoskeleton of squid giant axon can be characterized in the following ways (Fig. 22–10). 1) The major constituents are microtubules and actin filaments. 2) Actin filaments appear to be associated with the axolemma through a specialized two dimensional meshwork possibly composed of brain spectrin and actin, forming clusters just beneath the axolemma. 3) Microtubules run parallel to the axolemma and are embedded in a fine meshwork consisting mainly of axolinin. Some microtubules run along the axolemma among clusters of actin filaments and associate laterally with the axolemma through slender connections. 4) The axolemma, therefore, can be divided into actin

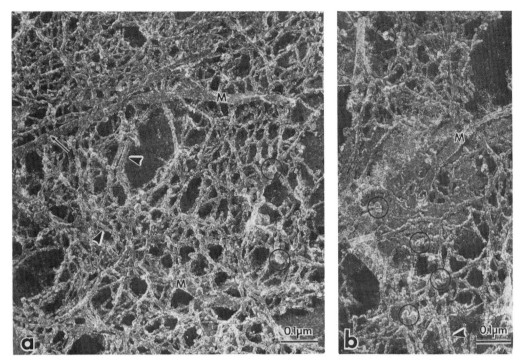

Fig. 22–7. Freeze-etch replicas of microfilament clusters beneath the axolemma. **a** Corresponds to the region 1 in Figure 22–6. Some microfilaments show ~5-nm period on their surface (arrowheads), which may correspond to the helical pitch of actin filament. Microfilaments are intertangled, forming a complicated three-dimensional network, held together by thin cross-linking strands. Globular structures ~30–35 nm in diameter showing a horseshoe-like appearance are circled. Some microtubules (M) are observed to run into the microfilament clusters and to be associated with microfilaments through short, slender strands (arrow).

filament-associated and microtubule-associated regions, which probably respresent two important functional domains.

ORGANIZATION OF THE CENTRAL AXOPLASM

The cytoskeleton of the central or extruded axoplasm is characterized by longitudinally oriented microtubules and neurofilament lattice, which are interconnected by slender strands, as shown in Figure 22–11 (Morris and Lasek, 1982, 1984; Hodge and Adelman, 1983; Metuzals et al., 1983; Tsukita et al., 1986). A comparison of Figures 22–10 and 22–11 (or Fig. 22–12) again supports the idea that the cytoskeleton of the giant

axon is specialized into peripheral and central portions.

Neurofilaments, Microtubules, and Actin Filaments

Morris and Lasek (1982) used electron microscopy to characterize the axoplasmic ghost and compared it to the unextracted form of the extruded axoplasm (extruded directly into fixative). They found that neurofilaments are a prominent feature of axoplasm both before and after extraction. Before extraction, neurofilaments have irregular profiles and interconnect to form a three-dimensional network extending through the axoplasm (Fig. 22–11). After extraction, the cross-linking network is pre-

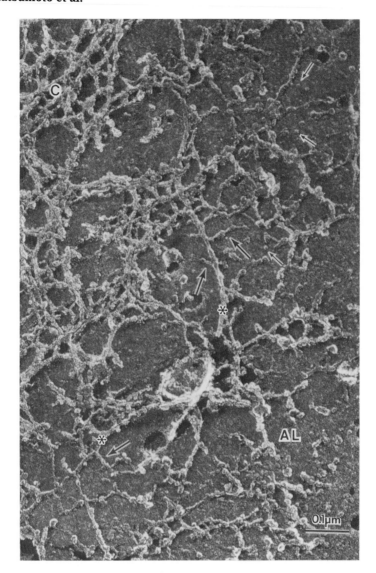

Fig. 22–8. Freeze-etch replica of the specialized layer of thin strand meshwork identified between the microfilament clusters and the axolemma. This image is a high-power electron micrograph from region 2 in Figure 22–6. Note a large number of gloublar extrusions ~5–10 nm in diameter (small arrows) on the cytoplasmic surface of the axolemma (AL), some of which are associated with the meshwork of thin strands (large arrows). Microfilaments (*) run parallel to this meshwork and are associated with thin strands. C, clusters of microfilaments.

served and the neurofilaments in general have smooth profiles. The size of the spaces between adjacent neurofilaments does not appear to change greatly, suggesting that the density of the neurofilament network is unaltered during the loss of the soluble components of axoplasm. Several other ultrastructural features of axoplasm are relatively unchanged after extraction. Mitochondria and smooth endoplasmic reticulum are retained in the insoluble fraction as well as a small number of (stable) microtubules. In

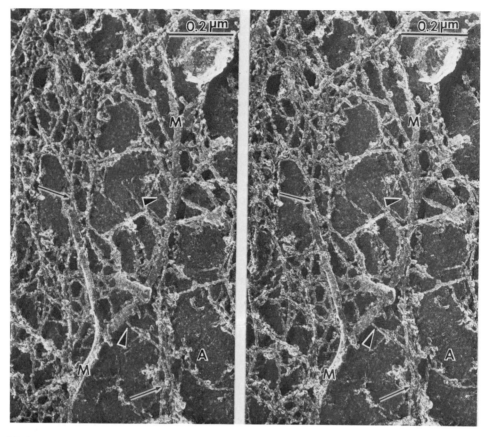

Fig. 22–9. Stereo pair of micrographs of freeze-etch replica of the microtubule-associated domain of the axolemma. This image corresponds to region 3 in Figure 22–6. Two microtubules (M) run along the cytoplasmic surface of the axolemma (A) and connect laterally to the axolemma by slender strands (arrows) extending out from the neighboring clusters (arrowheads) and running closely with the microtubules.

myelinated axons, microtubules appear in groups among the neurofilaments but are encountered much less frequently than neurofilaments (Wuerker and Kirkpatrick, 1972; Smith et al., 1975; Hirokawa, 1982; Schnapp and Reese, 1982; Tsukita et al., 1982). Although this has not been seen in the central axoplasm of the squid giant axon, it is likely that "microtubule territories" (the domains occupied by microtubules) are formed around the stable microtubules. The microtubules either can act as nucleating sites for equilibrium microtubules or, through the meshwork of axolinins, bundle the microtubule into groups (Murofushi et al., 1983).

Thus it can be concluded that stable polymers constituted mainly of neurofilaments and/or stable microtubules maintain the structural pattern within the cytoskeleton.

Actin filaments are difficult to preserve and identify in ultrastructural studies (Lehrer, 1981; Small, 1981; Maupin and Pollard, 1983; McDonald, 1984; Pollard et al., 1984). As a result, the organization of axonal actin has remained unclear, except for some knowledge about the subaxolemmal actin filaments in giant axons. However, there is little doubt of the presence of two kinds of actin filaments in the cortical and central axoplasms, stable and equilibrium (soluble).

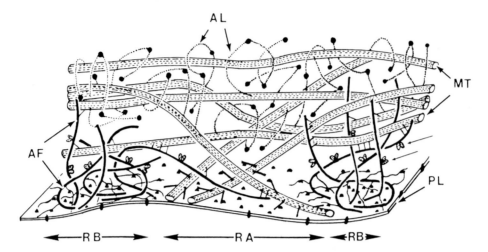

Fig. 22–10. Schematic drawing of the architecture of the subaxolemmal cytoskeleton of a squid giant axon. The plasmalemma (PL) can be divided into two domains, microtubule-associated (RA) and microfilament-associated (RB). The subaxolemmal cytoskeleton is composed mainly of spot-like clusters of microfilaments (AF) and longitudinally oriented microtubules (MT), which are embedded in the fine meshwork consisting mainly of axolinin (AL). The horseshoe-shaped structures (small arrows) on the microfilaments may be the morphological counterparts of the 255 kDa protein. Note three different types of cross linkers between MT and AF **(a)**, MT and PL **(b)**, AF and PL **(c)**.

Furthermore, new evidence indicates a functional association between microtubules and actin filaments in the central axoplasm. Brady et al. (1984a) reported that an actin-associated protein, gelsolin, whose only known function is to sever actin filaments in the presence of micromolar calcium, inhibits fast axonal transport of organelles. This may indicate that microtubules and actin filaments maintain a close association throughout the cytoplasmic network in the central axoplasm. How the morphological relationship reflects the functional association is intriguing and remains to be characterized.

Cross Linkers

The system of cross linkers among neurofilaments, microtubules, and actin filaments appears to determine their spatial relationships. Three populations of cross linkers, each mediating a different-axonal linkage, have been observed in both vertebrate and invertebrate axons, between neurofilaments and neurofilaments, between microtubules and microtubules, and between microtubules and membranous organelles. In addition, linkers are also observed between microtubules and neurofilaments, particularly at the boundaries of the microtubule and neurofilaments territories. To understand the nature of the neurofilament-associated cross linkers in vertebrate axons, in vivo decoration with antibodies against the three major neurofilament polypeptides (200, 150, and 68 kDa) was carried out in conjunction with the rapid-freeze, deep-etch technique. The results indicate that the 200 kDa polypeptide is a component of the cross linkers between neurofilaments, that anti-68 kDa decorates the neurofilament core uniformly but not the cross linkers, and that anti-150 kDa also decorates the core but less uniformly and sometimes spans the bases of the cross linkers (Willard and Simon, 1981; Sharp et al., 1982; Hirokawa et al., 1984). Together with other lines of evidence (Minami and Sakai, 1983; Minami et al., 1984; Geisler et al., 1984, 1985). These results indicate that the 200 kDa protein and possibly the 150 kDa protein may be cross-linking proteins, but they also have structural features in common with the 68 kDa protein.

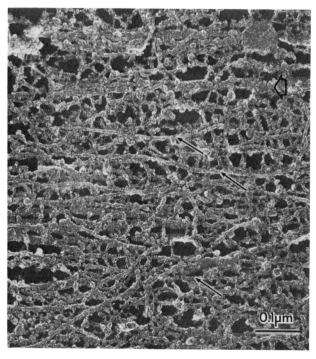

Fig. 22–11. Freeze-etch replica of the extruded axoplasm of a squid giant axon. The axoplasm is chemically fixed and washed with distilled water before freezing. Note that the longitudinally oriented neurofilaments (arrows) are connected with each other by thin strands, resulting in a ladder-like appearance.

This may also hold true for squid neurofilaments, since there are three (> 400, 200, and 60 kDa polypeptides) polypeptide components in the axon, whereas only the 60 kDa polypeptides is found in the cell bodies. This suggests that the 60 kDa polypeptide is a component of the central core of neurofilaments (Arai and Matsumoto, 1988d).

Efforts to explore the identity of the microtubule-associated, cross-linking strands have been made primarily with mammalian neurons (for reviews, see Schliwa, 1986; Hirokawa, 1986). In vertebrate axons, MAP 1A, MAP 1B, and tau are the main components of cross linkers between microtubules (Hirokawa et al., 1985). MAP 1A and MAP 1B are long, flexible molecules. MAP 1A has a 100-nm rod-like structure that forms regularly spaced projections from the microtubule surface to make connections between microtubules (Hirokawa et al., 1985). There

may be two kinds of cross linkers ~20 nm in length protruding from the surface of a microtubule; one kind is the vesicle transport cross linkers and the other may be MAP tau. Projections < 20 nm in length from the microtubule surface generally represent tau proteins, which also cross link microtubules in vertebrate axons (Hirokawa, private communication). Similar cross bridges between microtubules and membranous organelles are frequently observed in frog axons (Hirokawa, 1982) and in squid giant axons (Miller and Lasek, 1985). However, the (< 20 nm) cross bridges found in the squid axon are not MAPs, since they are preferentially located on the organelle surface, whether or not the organelle contacts a microtubule (Miller and Lasek, 1985). The cross linkers apparently remain attached to a microtubule only if they are already bound to a vesicle. The cross linkers may be directly related to the

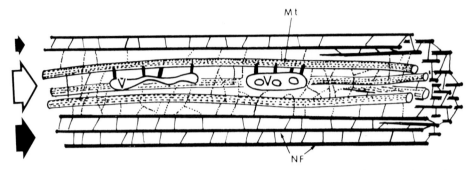

Fig. 22–12. Shematic drawing of the architecture of the cytoskeleton in the central axoplasm of a squid giant axon. Large white arrow, microtubule territory; large black arrow, neurofilament territory; Mt, microtubule; NF, neurofilament; V, transported vesicles. Note the four types of cross-linker strands: 1) between microtubules, 2) between neurofilaments, 3) between microtubule and neurofilament, and 4) between microtubule and vesicle.

translocator proteins that bind reversibly to organelles and to microtubules to generate motive force for vesicle transport (Brady, 1985a; Miller and Lasek, 1985; Vale et al., 1985a,b).

Neurofilaments and microtubules are closely apposed and frequently interconnected by filamentous cross linkers (Ellisman and Porter, 1980; Hirokawa, 1982; Tsukita et al., 1982). Although the amount of MAP 2 in axons is less than the amount of MAP 1 (Vallee, 1982; Binder et al., 1984; Papasozomenos et al., 1985; Hirokawa, 1986), MAP 2 may be, at most, part of the system of cross linkers observed in the microtubule domain of the rat axon (Hirokawa et al., 1985). Treatment of axons with β,β′-imino-dipropionitrile (IDPN) separates microtubules from neurofilaments to form the respective domains, whereas in normal axons they are interspersed. MAPs may have two binding sites, one for microtubules and one for neurofilaments (Runge et al., 1981; Leterrier et al., 1982; Bloom and Vallee, 1983) and may serve to cross link these two cytoplasmic components.

One of the most conspicuous features of the central axoplasm in the squid axon is the presence of brain spectrin in the axoplasmic ghost. Brain spectrin generally has been believed to localize only beneath the plasma membrane of cells (for reviews, see Bennett et al., 1986; Schliwa, 1986). In fact, it is also found in the subaxolemmal cytoskeleton and looks like a constituent protein of the meshwork that connects membrane proteins to the subaxolemmal actin filaments. It is unclear whether the isotype of axonal spectrin in the ghost is the same as that in the subaxolemmal region. The functional and structural roles of central axoplasmic brain spectrin are unknown.

In conclusion, the organization of the cytoskeleton in the central axoplasm can be characterized in the following ways (Fig. 22–12). 1) The cytoskeleton is constituted of longitudinally oriented microtubules and a neurofilament lattice, both of which are interconnected by slender strands. Characterization of the cross linkers between microtubules and neurofilaments, between neurofilaments and neurofilaments, and between microtubules and microtubules is incomplete, although some aspects of the cross linkers have been described for vertebrate axons. 2) The cytoskeleton is constituted of two kinds of chemically different polymers; one kind is stable polymers, such as neurofilaments, stable microtubules, and stable actin filaments; the other is equilibrium (soluble) polymers, such as equilibrium microtubules and equilibrium actin filaments. Stable polymers are essential structures in axonal architecture, whereas microtubules in equilibrium polymers are the prefered substrates for vesicle transport.

These two different polymer populations seem not to be spatially segregated but rather to be distributed homogeneously, although equilibrium microtubules may tend to be arranged into groups around the stable microtubules in some locally limited regions. 3) The organization of the stable and equilibrium actin filaments in the central axoplasm and its functional importance are a complete mystery. Fast axonal transport may require actin filaments in vivo inasmuch as gelsolin inhibits it and brain spectrin is abundant in the axoplasmic ghost constituted of the stable polymers.

FUNCTIONAL RELATIONSHIPS IN THE GIANT AXON

Functional Differentiation of Axonal Cytoskeletons

The two major functions of the axon are axonal transport and impulse conduction. Axonal transport occurs inside the axon; impulse conduction occurs along the surface of the axon. Involvement of the cytoskeleton in transport is obvious, since microtubules now have been demonstrated to be the lineal substrate for fast axonal transport (Allen et al., 1985; Schnapp et al., 1985; Vale et al., 1985a–d) and since microtubules and neurofilaments presumably interact (as a result of cross linking) as a coherent complex in the slow component of transport (Lasek and Hoffman, 1976; Black and Lasek, 1980; Brady et al., 1982). However, the mechanism for the slow component is unresolved (Alvarez and Torres, 1985; Komiya et al., 1986a,b; Lasek, 1982). Recently, a new proposal for the mechanism of the slow transport has been described by Komiya, Tashiro, and Kurokawa (1986a,b). They suggested that the mechanism is in fact the same for both the fast and the slow components and involves microtubules as the substrate. However, slow transport has two basic processes in its mechanism; one is a stationary phase in which neurofilament proteins, tubulins, and actins cannot be transported; the other is a moving phase in which the pro-teins are transported at a rate similar to fast transport. If this mechanism is correct, the problem of the transport cytoskeleton will relate primarily to microtubules. Since the basic process of the transport, that is, the characteristics of the microtubules as the substrate and the translocater proteins such as kinesin, will soon be understood, an intriguing problem will be discovering how transport is regulated in cellular functions, which should eventually lead to further understanding of the cytoskeletal components, their organization, and their functional characteristics.

The *Third* Subclass Cytoskeleton

The architechtural cytoskeleton may be categorized as a static structure or a rigid entity, principally unchangeable by any environmental stimuli. This kind of static architecture may function as nucleating sites that inhibit the random and spontaneous polymerization of soluble polymers in the axon. This may be the case for the axoplasmic ghost constituted of neurofilaments, stable microtubules, and stable actin filaments.

In addition to the transport cytoskeleton and architectural cytoskeleton, the subaxolemmal cytoskeleton represents a third subclass, consisting primarily of stable microtubules and stable actin filaments. The subaxolemmal cytoskeleton is stable to the same extent that the architectural cytoskeleton is, but it can become unstable under certain environmental conditions. A conformational change in cytoskeletal organization could take place within the time range of submilliseconds to several milliseconds and in a spatially limited region to which a specific stimulus is applied. The advantage of a cytoskeleton composed of stable polymers could be the ability of a conformational change to return to the steady-state conformation as soon as the stimulus is removed. The biochemical properties and organization of the subaxolemmal cytoskeleton are fully consistent with the idea that it is a third subclass of cytoskeleton, which may be functional and may play a role in membrane activities. To relate the subaxolemmal cytoskeleton to electrical excitability, much more information is needed about the static interactions between sodium-channel proteins and cytoskeletal proteins and about the conformational change in the subaxolemmal cytoskeleton proposed to accompany an electrical stimulus. Heterogeneous distribution of sodium channels in the squid giant axon could be anticipated inasmuch as the squid axolemma is differentiated into microtubule-associated and actin filament-associated domains. It has been found in frog skeletal muscle that sodium channels are unevenly distributed, whereas the potassium channels are homogeneously distributed. The lateral diffusion coefficient of the sodium channel is three orders of magnitudes less than that expected from its molecular size, suggesting that sodium channels are anchored in the sarcolemma (Almers et al., 1983). Most intriguing is whether the sodium channels are located mainly in the microtubule-associated or in the actin filament-associated domains of the squid giant axon.

CONCLUSIONS

Cytoskeletal arrays in squid giant axons are categorized into three types, according to their functional, biochemical, and structural characteristics. The first subclass is the "transport cytoskeleton" for axonal transport; the second is the "architectural cytoskeleton," an essential structure in axonal architecture; and the third is the subaxolemmal cytoskeleton. The proposed dynamic involvement of the subaxolemmal cytoskeleton in electrical excitability remains to be elucidated.

ACKNOWLEDGMENTS

The authors thank Drs. Sachiko Tsukita (Tokyo Metropolitan Institute of Medical Science), Takaaki Kobayashi (Jikei University, School of Medicine), and Michinori Ichikawa (Electrotechnical Laboratory) for stimulating discussions and for critical reading of the manuscript.

Bibliography 4, Chapters 17–22

Adams, R.J., and D. Bray (1983) Rapid transport of foreign particles microinjected into crab axons. Nature 303:718–720.

Adelstein, R.S., M.D. Pato, J.R. Sellers, P. de Lanerolle, and M.A. Conti (1982) Regulation of contractile proteins by reversible phosphorylation of myosin and myosin kinase. In B.M. Twarog, R.J.C. Levine, and M.M. Dewey (eds): Basic Biology of Muscles: A Comparative Approach. New York: Raven Press, pp. 273–281.

Allen, R.D. (1985) New observations on cell architecture and dynamics by video-enhanced contrast optical microscopy. Annu. Rev. Biophys. Biophys. Chem. 14:265–290.

Allen, R.D., and N.S. Allen (1983) Video-enhanced microscopy with a computer frame memory. J. Microsc. 129:3–17.

Allen, R.D., N.S. Allen, and J.L. Travis (1981) Video-enhanced contrast, differential interference contrast (AVEC-DIC) microscopy: A new method capable of analyzing microtubule-related motility in the reticulopodial network of *Allogromia laticollaris.* Cell Motil. 1:291–302.

Allen, R.D., D.T. Brown, S.P. Gilbert, and H. Fujiwake (1983) Transport of vesicles along filaments dissociated from squid axoplasm. Biol. Bull. 165:523.

Allen, R.D., J. Metuzals, I. Tasaki, S.T. Brady, and S.P. Gilbert (1982) Fast axonal transport in squid giant axon. Science 218:1127–1129.

Allen, R.D., D.G. Weiss, J.H. Hayden, D.T. Brown, H. Fujiwake, and M. Simpson (1985) Gliding movement of and bidirectional transport along single native microtubules from squid axoplasm: Evidence for an active role of microtubules in cytoplasmic transport. J. Cell Biol. 100:1736–1752.

Almers, W., P.R. Stanfield, and W. Stuhmer (1983) Lateral distribution of sodium and potassium channels in frog skeletal muscle: Measurements with a patch-clamp technique. J. Physiol. 336:261–284.

Alvarez, J., and J.C. Torres (1985) Slow axoplasmic transport: A fiction? J. Theor. Biol. 112:627–652.

Amos, L.A. (1987) Kinesin from pig brain studied by electron microscopy. J. Cell Sci. 87:105–111.

Arai, T., M. Ichikawa, and G. Matsumoto (1988) Structural and functional differentiation of microtubules in the squid giant neuron: Functional differentiation of the subaxolemmal microtubules in the squid giant axon. J. Cell Biol. (in press).

Arai, T., and G. Matsumoto (1987) Relation of 400-kD squid neurofilament protein (NF 1) to its 200-kD protein (NF 200) and their subcellular localization in the squid neuron. J. Neurochem. (in press).

Arai, T., and G. Matsumoto (1988a) Axolinin localization in the nervous tissue of squid revealed by monoclonal antibodies against axolinin: cellular and subcellular localization of axolinin in the squid neuron. J. Neurochem. (in press).

Arai, T., and G. Matsumoto (1988b) Structural and functional differentiation of microtubules in the squid giant neuron: Subcellular localization of structurally differentiated microtubules in the squid neurons. J. Neurochem. (in press).

Arai, T., and G. Matsumoto (1988c) Axolinin localization in the nervous tissue of squid revealed by monoclonal antibodies against axolinin: Production and properties of monoclonal antibodies to axolinin. J. Neurochem. (in press).

Asai, D.J., and L. Wilson (1985) A latent activity dynein-like cytoplasmic magnesium adenosine triphosphatase. J. Biol. Chem. 260:699–702.

Baas, P.W., L.A. White, and S.R. Heidemann (1987) Microtubule polarity reversal accompanies regrowth of amputated neurites. Proc. Natl. Acad. Sci. USA 84:5272–5276.

Baines, A.J., and V. Bennett (1985) Synapsin I is a spectrin-binding protein immunologically related to erythrocyte protein 4.1. Nature (London) 315:410-413.

Baker, P.F., A.L. Hodgkin, and T.I. Shaw (1962) Replacement of the axoplasm of giant nerve fibres with artificial solutions. J. Physiol. 164:330–354.

Barany, M. (1967) Correlation between the velocity of unloaded muscle shortening and actomyosin ATPase activity. J. Gen. Physiol. 50:197–216.

Beckerle, M.C. (1984) Microinjected fluorescent polystyrene beads exhibit saltatory motion in tissue culture cells. J. Cell Biol. 98:2126–2132.

Beckerle, M.C., and K.R. Porter (1982) Inhibitors of dynein activity block intracellular transport in erythrophores. Nature 295:701–703.

Bennett, H., and J. Condeelis (1984) Decoration of myosin subfragment-1 disrupts contacts between microfilaments and the cell membrane in isolated Dictyostelium cortices. J. Cell Biol. 99:1434–1440.

Bennett, V. (1985) The membrane skeleton of human erythrocytes and its implications for more complex cells. Annu. Rev. Biochem. 54:273–304.

Bennett, V., C.M. Cohen, S.E. Lux, and J. Palek (1986) Membrane Skeletons and Cytoskeletal-Membrane Associations. New York: Alan R. Liss., Inc.

Bergen, L.G., and G.G. Borisy (1980) Head-to-tail polymerization of microtubules in vitro. J. Cell Biol. 84:141–150.

Binder, L.I., A. Frankfurter, and L.I. Rebhun (1984) A monoclonal antibody to tau-factor localizes predominantly in axons. J. Cell Biol. 99:191a.

Binder, L.I., A. Frankfurter, and L.I. Rebhun (1985) The distribution of tau in the mammalian central nervous system. J. Cell Biol. 101:1371–1378.

Black, M.M., and R.J. Lasek (1979) Axonal transport of actin: Slow component b is the principal source of actin for the axon. Brain Res. 171:401–413.

Black, M.M., and R.J. Lasek (1980) Slow components of axonal transport: Two cytoskeletal networks. J. Cell Biol. 86:616–623.

Bloom, G.S., F.C. Luca, and R.B. Vallee (1985) Microtubule-associated protein 1B: Identification of a major component of the neuronal cytoskeleton. Proc. Natl. Acad. Sci. USA 82:5404–5408.

Bloom, G.S., T.A. Schoenfeld, and R.B. Vallee (1984) Widespread distribution of the major polypeptide component of MAP 1 (microtubule-associated protein 1) in the nervous system. J. Cell Biol. 98:320–330.

Bloom, G.S., and R.B. Vallee (1983) Association of MAP 2 with microtubules and intermediate filaments in cultured brain cells. J. Cell Biol. 96:1523–1531.

Bloom, G.S., M.C. Wagner, K.K. Pfister, and S.T. Brady (1988) Native structure and physical properties of bovine brain kinesin, and identification of the ATP-binding subunit polypeptide. Biochemistry 27:3409–3416.

Botts, J., R. Cooke, C. dosRemedios, J. Duke, R. Mendelson, M.F. Morales, T. Tokiwa, G. Viniegra, and R. Yount (1972) Does a myosin cross-bridge progress arm-over-arm on the actin filament? Cold Spring Harbor Symp. Quant. Biol. 37:195-200.

Brady, S.T. (1985a) A novel brain ATPase with properties expected for the fast axonal transport motor. Nature 317:73–75.

Brady, S.T. (1985b) Axonal transport: Methods and applications. In A. Boulton and G. Baker (eds): Neuromethods I: General Neurochemical Methods. Clifton, New Jersey: Humana Press.

Brady, S.T., and R.J. Lasek (1981) Nerve-specific enolase and creatine phosphokinase in axonal transport: Soluble proteins and the axoplasmic matrix. Cell 23:515–523.

Brady, S.T., R.J. Lasek, and R.D. Allen (1982) Fast axonal transport in extruded axoplasm from squid giant axon. Science 218:1129–1131.

Brady, S.T., R.J. Lasek, and R.D. Allen (1985) Video microscopy of fast axonal transport in extruded axoplasm: A new model for study of molecular mechanisms. Cell Motil. 5:81–101.

Brady, S.T., R.J. Lasek, R.D. Allen, H.L. Yin, and T.P. Stossel (1984a) Gelsolin inhibition of fast axonal transport indicates a requirement for actin microfilaments. Nature 310:56–58.

Brady, S.T., and T.A. Schroer (1985) Axonal transport of NEM-treated fluorescent synaptic vesicles. Trans. Am. Soc. Neurochem. 16:168.

Brady, S.T., M. Tytell, and R.J. Lasek (1984b) Axonal tubulin and axonal microtubules: Biochemical evidence for cold stability. J. Cell Biol. 99:1716–1724.

Branton, D., C.M. Cohen, and J. Tyler (1981) Interaction of cytoskeletal proteins on the human erythrocyte membrane. Cell 24:24–32.

Bray, D., and M. Bunge (1981) Serial analysis of microtubules in cultured rat sensory neurons. J. Neurocytol. 10:589–605.

Burton, P.R., and J.L. Paige (1981) Polarity of axoplasmic microtubules in the olfactory nerve of the frog. Proc. Natl. Acad. Sci. USA 78:3269–3273.

Caceres, A., L.I. Binder, M.R. Payne, P. Bender, L.I. Rebhun, and O. Steward (1984) Differential subcellular localization of tubulin and the microtubule-associated protein MAP 2 in brain tissue as revealed by immunocytochemistry with monoclonal hybridoma antibodies. J. Neurosci. 4:394–410.

Carlson, S.S., J.A. Wagner, and R.B. Kelly (1978) Purification of synaptic vesicles from elasmobranch electric organ and the use of biophysical criteria to demonstrate purity. Biochemistry 17:1188–1199.

Chalfie, M., and J.N. Thomson (1979) Organization of neuronal microtubules in the nematode *Caenorhabditis elegans*. J. Cell Biol. 82:278–289.

Clark, T.G., and J.L. Rosenbaum (1982) Pigment particle translocation in detergent permeabilized melanophores of *Fundulus heteroclitus*. Proc. Natl. Acad. Sci. USA 79:4655–4659.

Cleveland, D.W. (1987) The multitubulin hypothesis revisited: What have we learned? J. Cell Biol. 104:381–383.

Cleveland, D.W., S.G. Fischer, M.W. Kirschner, and U.K. Laemmli (1977) Peptide mapping by limited proteolysis in sodium dodecyl sulfate and analysis by gel electrophoresis. J. Biol. Chem. 252:1102–1106.

Cohn, S.A. (1987) Microtubule activation of kinesin ATPase activity. Nature 326:16–17.

Cohn, S.A., A.L. Ingold, and J.M. Scholey (1987) Correlation between the ATPase and microtubule translocating activities of sea urchin egg kinesin. Nature 328:160–163.

Collins, C.A., and R.B. Vallee (1986) A microtubule-activated ATPase from sea urchin eggs, distinct from cytoplasmic dynein and kinesin. Proc. Natl. Acad. Sci. USA 83:4799–4803.

Cooke, R. (1986) The mechanism of muscle contraction. CRC Crit. Rev. Biochem. 21:53–118.

Cumming, R., R.D. Burgoyne, and N.A. Lytton (1984) Immunocytochemical demonstration of α-tubulin modification during axonal maturation in the cerebellar cortex. J. Cell Biol. 98:347–351.

Czosnek, H., D. Soifer, and H.M. Wisniewski (1980) Studies on the biosynthesis of neurofilament proteins. J. Cell Biol. 85:725–734.

Dabora, S.L., and M.P. Sheetz (1988a) The microtubule dependent formation of a tubulovesicular network with characteristics of the endoplasmic reticulum from cultured cell extracts. Cell 54:27–35.

Dabora, S.L., and M.P. Sheetz (1988b) Cultured cell extracts support organelle movement on microtubules in vitro. Cell Motil. Cytoskel. (in press).

DeCamilli, P., P. Miller, F. Navone, W.D. Theurkauf, and R.B. Vallee (1984) Distribution of microtubule-associated protein 2 (MAP 2) in the nervous system of the rat studied by immunofluorescence. Neuroscience 11:819–846.

Drake, P., and R.J. Lasek (1984) Regional differences in the neuronal cytoskeleton. J. Neurosci. 4:1173–1186.

Drubin, D.G., D. Caput, and M.W. Kirschner (1984) Studies on the expression of the microtubule-associated protein, tau, during mouse brain development, with newly isolated complementary DNA probes. J. Cell Biol. 98:1090–1097.

Edmonds, B., and E. Koenig (1987) Powering of bulk transport (varicosities) and differential sensitives of directional transport in growing axons. Brain Res. 406:288–293.

Eisenberg, E., and C. Moos (1968) The adenosine triphosphate activity of acto-heavy meromyosin. A kinetic analysis of actin activation. Biochemistry 7:1486–1489.

Ellisman, M.H., and K.R. Porter (1980) Microtrabecular structure of the axoplasmic matrix: Visualization of cross-linking structures and their distribution. J. Cell Biol. 87:464–479.

Endo, S., H. Sakai, and G. Matsumoto (1979) Microtubules in squid giant axon. Cell Struct. Function 4:285–293.

Euteneuer, U., and J.R. McIntosh (1981) Polarity of some motility related microtubules. Proc. Natl. Acad. Sci. USA 78:372–376.

Field, D.J., R.A. Collins, and J.C. Lee (1984) Heterogeneity of vertebrate brain tubulins. Proc. Natl. Acad. Sci. USA 81:4041–4045.

Forman, D.S. (1982) Vanadate inhibits saltatory organelle movement in a permeabilized cell model. Exp. Cell Res. 141:139–147.

Forman, D.S., K.J. Brown, and D.R. Livengood (1983a) Fast axonal transport in permeabilized lobster giant axon is inhibited by vanadate. J. Neurosci. 3:1279–1288.

Forman, D.S., K.J. Brown, and M.E. Promersberger (1983b) Selective inhibition of retrograde axonal transport by erythro-9-[3-(2-hydroxynonyl)]adenine. Brain Res. 272:194–197.

Garner, J.A., and R.J. Lasek (1981) Clathrin is ax- onally transported as part of slow component b: the microfilament complex. J. Cell Biol. 88:172–178.

Geisler, N., S. Fischer, J. Vanderkerckhove, U. Plessmann, and K. Weber (1984) Hybrid char- acter of a large neurofilament protein (NF-M): Intermediate filament type sequence followed by a long and acidic carboxy-terminal exten- sion. EMBO J. 3:2701–2706.

Geisler, N., J. Vanderkerckhove, J. van Damme, U. Plessmann, and K. Weber (1985) Protein-chem- ical characterization of NF-H, the largest mam- malian neurofilament component; intermediate filament-type sequences followed by a unique carboxy-terminal extension. EMBO J 4:57–63.

Geisler, N., and K. Weber (1981) Self-assembly in vitro of the 68,000 molecular weight compo- nent of the mammalian neurofilament triplet proteins into intermediate-sized filaments. J. Mol. Biol. 151:565–571.

Gelles, J., B.J. Schnapp, and M.P. Sheetz (1988) Tracking kinesin-driven movements with na- nometre-scale precision. Nature 331:450–453.

Gibbons, B.H., and I.R. Gibbons (1972) Flagellar movement and adenosine triphosphatase activ- ity in sea urchin sperm extracted with Triton X-100. J. Cell Biol. 54:75–97.

Gibbons, B.H., and I.R. Gibbons (1976) Functional recombination of dynein I with demembran- ated sea urchin sperm partially extracted with KCl. Biochem. Biophys. Res. Commun. 73:1– 6.

Gibbons, B.H., and I.R. Gibbons (1979) Relation- ship between the latent adenosine triphospha- tase state of dynein I and its ability to recombine functionally with KCl-extracted sea urchin sperm flagella. J. Biol. Chem. 254:197– 201.

Gibbons, I.R. (1981) Cilia and flagella of eukary- otes. J. Cell Biol. 91:107s–124s.

Gibbons, I.R., M.P. Cosson, J.A. Evans, B.H. Gib- bons, B. Houck, K.H. Martinson, W.S. Sale, and W.-J.Y. Tang (1978) Potent inhibition of dynein adenosine triphosphatase and of the motility of cilia and sperm flagella by vanadate. Proc. Natl. Acad. Sci. USA 75:2220–2224.

Gibbons, I.R., and A.J. Rowe (1965) Dynein: A protein with adenosine triphosphatase activity from cilia. Science 149:424–426.

Gilbert, S.P., R.D. Allen, and R.D. Sloboda (1985) Translocation of vesicles from squid axoplasm on flagellar microtubules. Nature 315:245–248.

Gilbert, S.P., and R.D. Sloboda (1984) Bidirec- tional transport of fluorescently labeled vesi- cles introduced into extruded axoplasm of the squid Loligo pealei. J. Cell Biol. 99:445–452.

Gilbert, S.P., and R.D. Sloboda (1986) Identifica- tion of a MAP 2-like ATP-binding protein asso- ciated with axoplasmic vesicles that translocate on isolated microtubules. J. Cell Biol. 103:947– 956.

Glenney, J.R., P. Glenney, M. Osborn, and K. We- ber (1982) An F-actin- and calmodulin-binding protein from isolated intestinal brush borders has a morphology related to spectrin. Cell 28:843–854.

Goodloe-Holland, C.M., and E.J. Luna (1984) A membrane cytoskeleton from Dictyostelium discoideum. III. Plasma membrane fragments bind predominantly to the sides of actin fila- ments. J. Cell Biol. 99:71–78.

Goodman, S.R., and I.S. Zagon (1984) Brain spec- trin: A review. Brain Res. Bull. 13:813–832.

Goodman, S.R., and I.S. Zagon (1986) The neural cell spectrin skeleton: A review. Am. J. Physiol. 250:C347-C360.

Grafstein, B., and D.S. Forman (1980) Intracellular transport in neurons. Physiol. Rev. 60:1167– 1283.

Gulati, J., and R.J. Podolsky (1981) Isotonic con- traction of skinned muscle fibres on a slow time base. Effects of ionic strength and cal- cium. J. Gen. Physiol. 78:233–257.

Haimo, L.T., B.R. Telzer, and J.L. Rosenbaum (1979) Dynein binds to and crossbridges cyto- plasmic microtubules. Proc. Natl. Acad. Sci. USA 76:5659–5763.

Hamaguchi, M.S., Y. Hamaguchi, and Y. Hiramoto (1986) Microinjected polystyrene beads move along astral rays in sand dollar eggs. Dev. Growth Differ. 28:461–470.

Harrington, W.F., and M.E. Rodgers (1984) Myosin. Ann. Rev. Biochem. 53:35–73.

Harris, P. (1975) The role of membranes in the organization of the mitotic apparatus. Exp. Cell Res. 94:409–425.

Hayashi, M. (1974) Kinetic analysis of axoneme and dynein ATPase from sea urchin sperm. Arch. Biochem. Biophys. 165:288–296.

Hayden, J.H., R.D. Allen, and R.D. Goldman (1983) Cytoplasmic transport in keratocytes: Direct visualization of particle translocation along mi- crotubules. Cell Motil. 3:1–19.

Heidemann, S.R., J.M. Landers, and M.A. Hamborg (1981) Polarity orientation of axonal microtu- bules. J. Cell Biol. 91:661–665.

Heidemann, S.R., and J.R. McIntosh (1979) Visu- alization of the structural polarity of microtu- bules. Nature 286:517–519.

Heuser, J.E. (1983) Procedure for freeze-drying molecules adsorbed to mica flakes. J. Mol. Biol. 169:155–195.

Heuser, J.E., and R. Cooke (1983) Actin-myosin interactions visualized by the quick-freeze, deep-etch replica technique. J. Mol. Biol. 169:97–122.

Heuser, J.E., and M.W. Kirschner (1980) Filament organization revealed in platinum replicas of freeze-dried cytoskeletons. J. Cell Biol. 86:212–234.

Heuser, J.E., T.S. Reese, M.J. Dennis, Y. Jan, L. Jan, and L. Evans (1979) Synaptic vesicle exocytosis captured by quick freezing and correlated with quantal transmitter release. J. Cell Biol. 81:275–300.

Heuser, J.E., and S.R. Salpeter (1979) Organization of acetylcholine receptors in quick-frozen deep-etch, and rotary-replicated *Torpedo* postsynaptic membrane. J. Cell Biol. 82:105–173.

Hirokawa, N. (1982) Cross-linker system between neurofilaments, microtubules, and membranous organelles in frog axons revealed by the quick-freeze, deep-etching method. J. Cell Biol. 94:129–142.

Hirokawa, N. (1983) Membrane specialization and cytoskeletal structures in the synapse and axon revealed by the quick-freeze, deep-etch method. In D.-C. Chang, I. Tasaki, W.J. Adelman, Jr., and H.R. Leuchtag (eds): Structure and Function in Excitable Cells. New York: Plenum Press, pp. 113–141.

Hirokawa, N. (1986) 270K microtubule-associated protein cross-linking with anti-MAP2 IgG in the crayfish peripheral nerve axon. J. Cell Biol. 103:33–39.

Hirokawa, N., G.S. Bloom, and R.B. Vallee (1985) Cytoskeletal architecture and immunocytochemical localization of microtubule-associated proteins in regions of axons associated with rapid axonal transport: The β,β'-iminodipropionitrile-intoxicated axon as a model system. J. Cell Biol. 101:227–239.

Hirokawa, N., M.A. Glicksman, and M.B. Willard (1984) Organization of mammalian neurofilament polypeptides within the neuronal cytoskeleton. J. Cell Biol. 98:1523–1536.

Hirokawa, N., and J.E. Heuser (1981) Quick-freeze, deep-etch visualization of the cytoskeleton beneath surface differentiation of intestinal epithelial cells. J. Cell Biol. 91:399–409.

Hirokawa, N., and H. Yorifuji (1986) Cytoskeletal architecture of reactivated crayfish axons, with special reference to crossbridges among microtubules and between microtubules and membrane organelles. Cell Motil. Cytoskeleton 6:458–468.

Hisanaga, S.I., and H. Sakai (1983) Cytoplasmic dynein of the sea urchin egg. II. Purification, characterization and interactions with microtubules and Ca-calmodulin. J. Biochem. 93:87–98.

Hodge, A.J., and W.J. Adelman (1980) The neuroplasmic network in *Loligo* and *Hermissenda* neurons. J. Ultrastruct. Res. 70:220–241.

Hodge, A.J., and W.J. Adelman (1983) The neuroplasmic lattice. Structural characteristics in vertebrate and invertebrate axons. In D.-C. Chang, I. Tasaki, W.J. Adelman, Jr., and H.R. Leuchtag (eds): Structure and Function in Excitable Cells. New York: Plenum Press, pp. 75–111.

Hoffman, P.N., and R.J. Lasek (1975) The slow component of axonal transport. Identification of the major structural polypeptides of the axon and their generality among mammalian neurons. J. Cell Biol. 66:351–366.

Hollenbeck, P.J., F. Suprynowicz, W.Z. Cande (1984) Cytoplasmic dynein-like ATPase cross-links microtubules in an ATP-sensitive manner. J Cell Biol 99:1251–1258.

Horio, T., and H. Hotani (1986) Visualization of the dynamic instability of individual microtubules by dark-field microscopy. Nature 321:605-607.

Hosokawa, Y., and T. Miki-Noumura (1987) Bending motion of *Chlamydomonas* axonemes after extrusion of central-pair mirotubules. J. Cell Biol. 105:1297–1301.

Huber, G., and A. Matus (1984) Differences in the cellular distributions of two microtubule-associated proteins, MAP 1 and MAP 2, in rat brain. J. Neurosci. 4:151–160.

Huttner, W.B., W. Schiebler, P. Greengard, and P. DeCamilli (1983) Synapsin I (Protein I), a nerve terminal-specific phosphoprotein. III. Its association with synaptic vesicles studied in a highly purified synaptic vesicle preparation. J. Cell Biol. 96:1374–1388.

Ikebe, M., R.J. Barsotti, S. Hinkins, and D.J. Hartshorne (1984) Effects of magnesium chloride on smooth muscle actomyosin adenosine triphosphatase activity, myosin conformation, and tension development in glycerinated smooth muscle fibers. Biochemistry 23:5062–5068.

Inoué, S. (1981a) Video image processing greatly enhances contrast, quality, and speed in polarization-based microscopy. J. Cell Biol. 89:346–356.

Inoué, S. (1981b) Cell division and the mitotic spindle. J. Cell Biol. 91:131S–147S.

Inoué, S. (1986) Video Microscopy. New York: Plenum Press.

Jockusch, H., B.M. Jockusch, and M.M. Burger (1979) Nerve fibers in culture and their interaction with non-neural cells visualized by immunofluorescence. J. Cell Biol. 80:629–641.

Johnson, K.A. (1985) Pathway of the microtubule dynein ATPase and the structure of dynein: A comparison with actomyosin. Annu. Rev. Biophys. Chem. 14:161–188.

Johnson, K.A. (1986) Preparation and properties of dynein from *Tetrahymena* cilia. Methods Enzymol. 134:305–317.

Joshi, H.C., T.J. Hen, and D.W. Cleveland (1987) In vivo coassembly of a divergent β-tubulin subunit (cβ6) into microtubules of different function. J. Cell Biol. 105:2179–2190.

Kachar, B., P.C. Bridgman, and T.S. Reese (1987) Dynamic shape changes of cytoplasmic organelles translocating along microtubules. J. Cell Biol. 105:1267–1271.

Kakiuchi, S., K. Sobue, K. Kanda, K. Morimoto, S. Tsukita, S. Tsukita, H. Ishikawa, and M. Kurokawa (1982) Correlative biochemical and morphological studies of brain calspectin: A spectrin-like calmodulin-binding protein. Biomed. Res. 3:400–410.

Kirschner, M.W., and T.J. Mitchison (1986) Beyond self-assembly: from microtubules to morphogenesis. Cell 45:329–342.

Kobayashi, T., and G. Matsumoto (1982) Tubulin from squid nerve cytoplasm fully retains C-terminus tyrosine. J. Biochem. (Tokyo) 92:647–652.

Kobayashi, T., S. Tsukita, S. Tsukita, Y. Yamamoto, and G. Matsumoto (1986) Subaxolemmal cytoskeleton in squid giant axon. I. Biochemical analysis of microtubules, microfilaments and their associated high-molecular-weight proteins. J. Cell Biol. 102:1699–1709.

Komiya, Y., T. Tashiro, and M. Kurokawa (1986a) Phosphorylation of neurofilament proteins during their axonal transport. Biomed. Res. 7:345-348.

Komiya, Y., T. Tashiro, and M. Kurokawa (1986b) Occurrence of faster migrating neurofilament proteins as revealed by their phosphorylation. Biomed. Res. 7:359–363.

Koonce, M.P., and M. Schliwa (1985) Bidirectional organelle transport can occur in cell processes that contain single microtubules. J. Cell Biol. 100:322–326.

Koonce, M., and M. Schliwa (1986a) Directionality of organelle movements in *Reticulomyxa* may be mediated by phosphorylation. J. Cell Biol. 103:275a.

Koonce, M.P., and M. Schliwa (1986b) Reactivation of organelle movements along the cytoskeletal framework of a giant freshwater ameba. J. Cell Biol. 103:605–612.

Korn, E.D. (1978) Biochemistry of actomyosin-dependent cell motility. Proc. Natl. Acad. Sci. USA 75:588–599.

Krebs, K.E., A.C. Nairn, M. Bähler, W. Schiebler, I.S. Zagon, P. Greengard, and S.R. Goodman (1986) The relationship of erythrocyte protein 4.1 to the neuron specific phosphoprotein synapsin I. J. Cell Biol. 103:542a.

Kron, S.J., and J.A. Spudich (1986) Fluorescent actin filaments move on myosin fixed to a glass surface. Proc. Natl. Acad. Sci. USA 83:6272–6276.

Kuczmarski, E.R., and J.L. Rosenbaum (1979) Studies on the organization and localization of actin and myosin in neurons. J. Cell Biol. 80:356–371.

Kuznetsov, S.A., and V.I. Gelfand (1986) Bovine brain kinesin is a microtubule-activated ATPase. Proc. Natl. Acad. Sci. USA 83:8530–8534.

Kuznetsov, S.A., E.A. Vaisberg, N.A. Shanina, N.N. Magretova, V.Y. Chernyak, and V.I. Gelfand (1988) The quaternary structure of bovine brain kinesin. EMBO J. 7:353–358.

Lacy, P.E., E.H. Finke, and R.C. Codilla (1975) Cinemicrographic studies on β granule movement in monolayer culture of islet cells. Lab. Invest. 33:570–576.

Langford, G.M., R.D. Allen, and D.G. Weiss (1987) Substructure of sidearms on squid axoplasmic vesicles and microtubules visualized by negative contrast electron microscopy. Cell Motil. Cytoskelrton 7:20–30.

Lasek, R.J. (1982) Translocation of the cytoskeleton in neurons and axonal growth. Phil. Trans. R. Soc. London 299:319–327.

Lasek, R.J., and S.T. Brady (1982) The structural hypothesis of axonal transport: two classes of moving elements. In (ed): Axoplasmic Transport. Berlin: Springer-Verlag, pp. 397–405.

Lasek, R.J., and S.T. Brady (1985) Attachment of transported vesicles to microtubules in axoplasm is facilitated by AMP-PNP. Nature (London) 316:645-647.

Lasek, R.J., J.A. Garner, and S.T. Brady (1984) Axonal transport of the cytoplasmic matrix. J. Cell Biol. 99:212s-221s.

Lasek, R.J., and P.N. Hoffman (1976) The neuronal cytoskeleton, axonal transport, and axonal growth. In R. Goldman, T. Pollard, and J. Rosenbaum (eds): Cell Motility, Book C. Cold Spring Harbor: Cold Spring Harbor Lab. Press, pp. 1021–1049.

Lee, C., and L.B. Chen (1988) Behavior of endoplasmic reticulum in living cells. Cell 54:37–46.

Lee, G., N. Cowan, and M.W. Kirschner (1988) The primary structure and heterogeneity of tau protein from mouse brain. Science (Wash. D.C.) 239:285-288.

Lehrer, S.S. (1981) Damage to actin filaments by glutaraldehyde: protection by tropomyosin. J. Cell Biol. 90:459–466.

Leslie, R.J., R.B. Hird, L. Wilson, J.R. McIntosh, and J.M. Scholey (1987) Kinesin is associated with a nonmicrotubule component of sea urchin mitotic spindles. Proc. Natl. Acad. Sci. USA 84:2771–2775.

Leterrier, J.F., R.K.H. Liem, and M.C. Shelanski (1982) Interactions between neurofilaments and microtubule-associated proteins: A possible mechanism for intraorganellar bridging. J. Cell Biol. 95:982–986.

Levine, J., and M. Willard (1981) Fodrin: Axonally-transported polypeptides associated with the internal periphery of many cells. J. Cell Biol. 90:631–643.

Liem, R.K.H., and S.B. Hutchison (1982) Purification of individual components of the neurofilament triplet: Filament assembly from the 70,000 dalton subunit. Biochemistry 21:3221–3226.

Lliñas, R., T.L. McGuinness, C.S. Leonard, M. Sugimori, and P. Greengard (1985) Intraterminal injection of synapsin I or calcium/calmodulin-dependent protein kinase II alters neurotransmitter release at the squid giant synapse. Proc. Natl. Acad. Sci. USA 82:3035–3039.

Lye, R.J., M.E. Porter, J.M. Scholey, and J.R. McIntosh (1987) Identification of a microtubule-based cytoplasmic motor in the nematode *Caenorhabditis elegans*. Cell 51:309–318.

Lymm, R.W., and E.W. Taylor (1971) Mechanism of adenosine triphosphate hydrolysis by actomyosin. Biochemistry 10:4617–4624.

Lynch, G., and M. Baudry (1984) The biochemistry of memory: A new and specific hypothesis. Science 224:1057–1063.

Lynn, M.P., M.B. Atkinson, and A.C. Breuer (1986) Influence of translocation track on the motion of intra-axonally transported organelles in human nerve. Cell Motil. Cytoskeleton 6:339–346.

Mabuchi, I., and T. Shimizu (1974) Electrophoretic studies on dyneins from *Tetrahymena* cilia. J. Biochem. 76:991–999.

Margolis, R.L., C.T. Rauch, and D. Job (1986) Purification and assay of a 145 kDa protein (STOP) with microtubule-stabilizing and motility behavior. Proc. Natl. Acad. Sci. USA 83:639–643.

Martin, R.G., and B.N. Ames (1961) A method for determining the sedimentation behavior of enzymes: Application to protein mixtures. J. Biol. Chem. 236:1372–1379.

Maruyama, K., and S. Watanabe (1962) The role of magnesium in the superprecipitation of myosin B. J. Biol. Chem. 237:3437–3442.

Matsumoto, G. (1984) A proposed membrane model for generation of sodium currents in squid giant axons. J. Theor. Biol. 107:649–666.

Matsumoto, G., M. Ichikawa, and A. Tasaki (1984a) Axonal microtubules necessary for generation of sodium current in squid giant axons. II. Effect of colchicine upon asymmetrical displacement current. J. Memb. Biol. 77:93–99.

Matsumoto, G., M. Ichikawa, A. Tasaki, H. Murofushi, and H. Sakai (1984b) Axonal microtubules necessary for generation of sodium current in squid giant axons. I. Pharmacological study on sodium current and restoration of sodium current by microtubule proteins and 260K protein. J. Membrane Biol. 77:77–91.

Matsumoto, G., T. Kobayashi, and H. Sakai (1979) Restoration of the excitability of squid giant axon by tubulin-tyrosine ligase and microtubule proteins. J. Biochem. (Tokyo) 86:155–158.

Matsumoto, G., H. Murofushi, S. Endo, T. Kobayashi, and H. Sakai (1983) Tyrosinated tubulin necessary for maintenance of membrane excitability in squid giant axon. In D.-C. Chang, I. Tasaki, W.J. Adelman, Jr., and H.R. Leuchtag (eds): Structure and Function in Excitable Cells. New York: Plenum Press, pp. 471–483.

Matsumoto, G., H. Murofushi, S. Endo, and H. Sakai (1982) Microtubules composed of tyrosinated tubulin are required for membrane excitability in squid giant axon. In H. Sakai, H. Mohri, and G.G. Borisy (eds): Biological Functions of Microtubules and Related Structures. Tokyo: Academic Press, pp. 391–404.

Matsumoto, G., and H. Sakai (1979a) Microtubules inside the plasma membrane of squid giant axons and their possible physiological function. J. Membrane Biol. 50:1–14.

Matsumoto, G., and H. Sakai (1979b) Restoration of membrane excitability of squid giant axons by reagents activating tyrosine-tubulin ligase. J. Membrane Biol. 50:15–22.

Matsumoto, G., M. Urayama, and M. Ichikawa (1985) Modified Hodgkin-Huxley gating kinetics of sodium activation in giant axons of squid (*Doryteuthis bleekeri*). J. Theor. Biol. 112:695–705.

Maupin, P., and T.D. Pollard (1983) Improved preservation and staining of HeLa cell actin filaments, clathrin-coated membranes, and other cytoplasmic structures by tannic acid-glutaraldehyde-saponin fixation. J. Cell Biol. 96:51–62.

McDonald, K. (1984) Osmium-ferricyanide fixation improves microfilament preservation and membrane visualization in a variety of animal cell types. J. Ultrastruct. Res. 86:107–118.

McGuinness, T.L., Y. Lai, and P. Greengard (1985) Ca^{2+}/calmodulin-dependent protein kinase II. Isozymic forms from rat forebrain and cerebellum. J. Biol. Chem. 260:1696–1704.

McKiethan, T.W., and J.L. Rosenbaum (1984) The biochemistry of microtubules. Cell Muscle Motil. 5:255–288.

Metuzals, J., D.F. Clapin, and I. Tasaki (1983) The axolemma-ectoplasm complex of squid giant axon. In D.-C. Chang, I. Tasaki, W.J. Adelman, Jr., and H.R. Leuchtag (eds): Structure and Function in Excitable Cells. New York: Plenum Press, pp. 53–73.

Metuzals, J., and I. Tasaki (1978) Subaxolemmal filamentous network in the giant nerve fiber of the squid (*Loligo pealei L.*) and its possible role in excitability. J. Cell Biol. 78:597–621.

Miller, R.H., and R.J. Lasek (1985) Cross-bridges mediate anterograde and retrograde vesicle transport along microtubules in squid axoplasm. J. Cell Biol. 101:2181–2193.

Miller, R.H., R.J. Lasek, and M.J. Katz (1987) Preferred microtubules for vesicle transport in lobster axons. Science 235:220–222.

Minami, Y., S. Endo, and H. Sakai (1984) Participation of 200K or 150K subunit of neurofilament in construction of the filament core with 70K subunit and promotion of tubulin polymerization by incorporated 200K subunit. J. Biochem. (Tokyo) 96:1481–1490.

Minami, Y., and H. Sakai (1983) Network formation by neurofilament-induced polymerization of tubulin: 200K subunit of neurofilament triplet promotes nucleation of tubulin polymerization and enhances microtubule assembly. J. Biochem. (Tokyo) 94:2023–2033.

Mitchison, T.J., and M.W. Kirschner (1984) Microtubule assembly nucleated by isolated centrosomes. Nature 312:232–236.

Morris, J.R., and R.J. Lasek (1982) Stable polymers of the axonal cytoskeleton: The axoplasmic ghost. J. Cell Biol. 92:192–198.

Morris, J.R., and R.J. Lasek (1984) Monomer-polymer equilibria in the axon: Direct measurement of tubulin and actin as polymer and monomer in axoplasm. J. Cell Biol. 98:2064–2076.

Murofushi, H., Y. Minami, G. Matsumoto, and H. Sakai (1983) Bundling of microtubules in vitro by a high molecular weight protein prepared from the squid axon. J. Biochem. (Tokyo) 93:639–650.

Murphy, D.B., and G.G. Borisy (1975) Association of high molecular weight proteins with microtubules and their role in microtubule assembly in vitro. Proc. Natl. Acad. Sci. USA 72:2696–2700.

Naitoh, Y., and H. Kaneko (1972) Reactivated Triton-extracted models of *Paramecium*: modification of ciliary movement by Ca^{2+} ions. Science 176:523–524.

Nestler, E.J., and P. Greengard (1982) Nerve impulses increase the phosphorylation state of protein I in rabbit superior cervical ganglion. Nature 296:452–454.

Nishino, Y., and Y. Watanabe (1977) Immunological relation between 14S and 30S dynein from cilia of *Tetrahymena pyriformis*. Biochim. Biophys. Acta 490:132–143.

Oblinger, M.M., S.T. Brady, I.G. McQuarrie, and R.J. Lasek (1987) Cytotypic differences in the protein composition of axonally transported cytoskeleton in mammalian neurons. J. Neurosci. 7:453–462.

Ogawa, K., H. Hosoya, E. Yokota, T. Kobayashi, Y. Wakamatsu, K. Ozato, S. Negishi, and M. Obika (1987) Melanoma dynein: Evidence that dynein is a general "motor" for microtubule-associated cell motilities. Eur. J. Cell Biol. 43:3–9.

Olmsted, J.B. (1986) Analysis of cytoskeletal structures using blot-purified monospecific antibodies. Methods Enzymol. 134C: 467–472.

Omoto, C.K., and K.A. Johnson (1986) Activation of dynein adenosinetriphosphatase by microtubules. Biochemistry 25:419–427.

Omoto, C.K., and C. Kung (1980) Rotation and twist of the central-pair microtubules in the cilia of *Paramecium*. J. Cell Biol. 87:33–46.

Pallini, V., C. Mencarelli, L. Bracci, M. Contorni, P. Ruggiero, A. Tiezzi, and R. Manetti (1983) Cytoplasmic nucleoside-triphosphatases similar to axonemal dynein occur widely in different cell types. J. Submicrosc. Cytol. 15:229–235.

Papasozomenos, S.C., L. Autilio-Gambetti, and P. Gambetti (1981) Reorganization of axoplasmic organelles following β,β'-iminodipropionitrile administration. J. Cell Biol. 91:866–871.

Papasozomenos, S.C., and L.I. Binder (1987) Phosphorylation determines two distinct species of tau in the central nervous system. Cell Motil. Cytoskeleton 8:210–226.

Papasozomenos, S.C., L.I. Binder, P.K. Bender, and M.R. Payne (1985) Microtubule-associated protein 2 within axons of spinal motor neurons: Associations with microtubules and neurofilaments in normal and β,β'-iminodipropionitrile-treated axons. J. Cell Biol. 100:74–85.

Papasozomenos, S.C., and M.R. Payne (1986) Actin immunoreactivity localizes with segregated microtubules and membranous organelles and in the subaxolemmal region in the β,β'-iminodipropionitrile axon. J. Neurosci. 6:3483–3491.

Paschal, B.M., S.M. King, A.G. Moss, C.A. Collins, R.B. Vallee, and G.B. Whitman (1987a) Isolated flagellar outer arm dynein translocates brain microtubules in vitro. Nature (London) 330:672–674.

Paschal, B.M., H.S. Shpetner, and R.B. Vallee (1987b) MAP 1C is a microtubule-activated ATP-ase which translocates microtubules in vitro and has dynein-like properties. J. Cell Biol. 105:1273–1282.

Paschal, B.M., and R.B. Vallee (1987) Retrograde transport by the microtubule-associated protein MAP 1C. Nature 330:181–183.

Peng, I., L.I. Binder, and M.M. Black (1986a) Cultured sympathetic neurons contain a variety of microtubule-associated proteins. Brain Res. 361:200-211.

Peng, I., L.I. Binder, and M.M. Black (1986b) Biochemical and immunological analyses of cytoskeletal domains of neurons. J. Cell Biol. 102:252–262.

Penningroth, S.M., P.M. Rose, and D.D. Peterson (1987) Evidence that the 116kDA component of kinesin binds and hydrolyzes ATP. FEBS Lett. 222:204–210.

Perrin, D., K. Langley, and D. Aunis (1987) Anti-α-fodrin inhibits secretion from permeabilized chromaffin cells. Nature 326:498–501.

Piazza, G.A., and M.E. Stearns (1986) Characterization of purified kinesin from cultured human prostatic tumor cells. J. Cell Biol. 103:551a.

Pollard, T.D. (1987) The myosin crossbridge problem. Cell 48:909–910.

Pollard, T.D., and E.D. Korn (1973) *Acanthamoeba* myosin: 1. Isolation from *Acanthamoeba castellanii* of an enzyme similar to muscle myosin. J. Biol. Chem. 248:4682–4690.

Pollard, T.D., and M.S. Mooseker (1981) Direct measurement of actin polymerization rate constants by electron microscopy of actin filaments nucleated by isolated microvillus cores. J. Cell Biol. 88:654–659.

Pollard, T.D., C.S. Selden, and P. Maupin (1984) Interaction of actin filaments with microtubules. J. Cell Biol. 99:33s-37s.

Porter, M.E., J.M. Scholey, D.L. Stemple, G.P.A. Vigers, R.D. Vale, M.P. Sheetz, and J.R. McIntosh (1987) Characterization of the microtubule movement produced by sea urchin egg kinesin. J. Biol. Chem. 262:2794–2802.

Pratt, M.M. (1984) ATPases in mitotic spindles. Int. Rev. Cytol. 87:83–105.

Pratt, M.M. (1986a) Homology of egg and flagellar dynein. J. Biol. Chem. 261:956–964.

Pratt, M.M. (1986b) Stable complexes of axoplasmic vesicles and microtubules: protein composition and ATPase activity. J. Cell Biol. 103:957–968.

Pratt, M.M., N. Barton, A. Betancourt, C. Hammond, and B. Schroeder (1986) An antibody against cytoplasmic dynein labels vesicular organelles. J. Cell Biol. 103:408a.

Pratt, M.M., S. Hisanaga, and D.A. Begg (1984) An improved purification method for cytoplasmic dynein. J. Cell. Biochem. 26:19–33.

Pryer, N.K., P. Wadsworth, and E.D. Salmon (1986) Polarized microtubule gliding and particle saltations produced by soluble factors from sea urchin eggs and embryos. Cell Motil. Cytoskeleton 6:537–548.

Rebhun, L.I. (1960) Aster-associated particles in the cleavage of marine invertebrate eggs. Ann. N.Y. Acad. Sci. 90:357–380.

Repasky, E.A., B.L. Granger, and E. Lazarides (1982) Widespread occurrence of avian spectrin in nonerythroid cells. Cell 29:821–833.

Riederer, B.M., I.S. Zagon, and S.R. Goodman (1986) Brain spectrin (240/235) and brain spectrin (240/235 E): Two distinct spectrin subtypes with different locations within mammalian neural cells. J. Cell Biol. 102:2088-2097.

Rodzdial, M., and L.T. Haimo (1986a) Bidirectional pigment granule movements of melanophores are regulated by protein phosphorylation and dephosphorylation. Cell 47:1061–1070.

Rodzdial, M., and L.T. Haimo (1986b) Reactivated melanophore motility: Differential regulation and nucleotide requirements of bidirectional pigment granule transport. J. Cell Biol. 103:2755–2764.

Runge, M.S., T.M. Laue, D.A. Yphantis, M.R. Lifsics, A. Saito, and M. Altin (1981) ATP-induced formation of an associated complex between microtubules and neurofilaments. Proc. Natl. Acad. Sci. USA 78:1431–1435.

Sakai, H., and G. Matsumoto (1978) Tubulin and other proteins from squid giant axon. J. Biochem. (Tokyo) 83:1413–1422.

Sakai, H., G. Matsumoto, and H. Murofushi (1985) Role of microtubules and axolinin in membrane excitation of the squid giant axon. Adv. Biophys. 19:43–89.

Sakai, H., H. Murofushi, and G. Matsumoto (1984) High molecular weight proteins of nerve cells inducing cross-linking or bundling of cytoskeletal proteins. Zool. Sci. 1:16–28.

Sale, W.S., and P. Satir (1977) The direction of active sliding of microtubules in *Tetrahymena* cilia. Proc. Natl. Acad. Sci. USA 74:2045–2049.

Saxton, W.M., M.E. Porter, S.A. Cohn, J.M. Scholey, E.C. Raff, and J.R. McIntosh (1988) *Drosophila* kinesin: characterization of microtubule motility and ATPase. Proc. Natl. Acad. Sci. USA 85:1109–1113.

Saxton, W.M., J. Yang, M.E. Porter, J.M. Scholey, L.S.B. Goldstein, and J.R. McIntosh (1986) Isolation and characterization of kinesin from Drosophila. J. Cell Biol. 103:550a.

Schliwa, M. (1982) Chromatophores: Their use in understanding microtubule-dependent intracellular transport. Methods Cell Biol. 25:285–312.

Schliwa, M. (1984) Mechanisms of intracellular organelle transport. Cell Muscle Motil. 5:1–82.

Schliwa, M. (1986) The Cytoskeleton. An Introductory Survey. Vienna: Springer-Verlag. pp. 1–326.

Schnapp, B.J. (1986) Viewing single microtubules by video light microscopy. Meth. Enzymol. 134:561–573.

Schnapp, B.J., S. Khan, M.P. Sheetz, R.D. Vale, and T.S. Reese (1986) Kinesin-driven microtubule sliding involves interacting nucleotide binding sites. J. Cell Biol. 103:551a.

Schnapp, B.J., and T.S. Reese (1982) Cytoplasmic structure in rapid-frozen axon. J. Cell Biol. 94:667–679.

Schnapp, B.J., R.D. Vale, M.P. Sheetz, and T.S. Reese (1985) Single microtubules from squid axoplasm support bidirectional movement of organelles. Cell 40:455–462.

Scholey J.M., B. Neighbors, J.R. McIntosh, E.D. Salmon (1984): Isolation of microtubules and a dynein-like ATPase from unfertilized sea urchin eggs. J Biol Chem 259:6516–6525.

Scholey, J.M., M.E. Porter, P.M. Grissom, and J.R. McIntosh (1985) Identification of kinesin in sea urchin eggs, and evidence for its localization in the mitotic spindle. Nature 318:483–486.

Scholey, J.M., M.E. Porter, R.J. Lye, and J.R. McIntosh (1989) Cytoplasmic microtubule associated motors. In G. Schatten and H. Schatten (eds): The Cell Biology of Fertilization. New York: Academic Press, pp. 139–163.

Schroer, T.A., S.T. Brady, and R.B. Kelly (1985) Fast axonal transport of foreign synaptic vesicles in squid axoplasm. J. Cell Biol. 101:568–572.

Schroer, T.A., B.J. Schnapp, T.S. Reese, and M.P. Sheetz (1988) The role of kinesin and other soluble proteins in organelle movement along microtubules. J. Cell Biol. (in press).

Schroer, T.A., and M.P. Sheetz (1986) Identification of kinesin binding proteins in squid brain. J. Cell Biol. 103:553a.

Schulze, E., and M.W. Kirschner (1987) Dynamic and stable populations of microtubules in cells. J. Cell Biol. 104:277–288.

Schwartz, J.H. (1979) Axonal transport: Components, mechanisms and specificity. Annu. Rev. Neurosci. 2:467–504.

Sellers, J.R., J.A. Spudich, and M.P. Sheetz (1985) Light chain phosphorylation regulates the movement of smooth muscle myosin on actin filaments. J. Cell Biol. 101:1897–1902.

Sharp, G.A., G. Shaw, and K. Weber (1982) Immunoelectronmicroscopical localization of the three neurofilament triplet proteins along neurofilaments of cultured dorsal root ganglion neurons. Exp. Cell Res. 137:403–413.

Shaw, G., M. Osborn, and K. Weber (1981) Arrangement of neurofilaments, microtubules, and microfilament-associated proteins in cultured dorsal root ganglia cells. Eur. J. Cell Biol. 24:20–27.

Sheetz, M.P. (1987) What are the functions of kinesin? Bioessays 6:165–170.

Sheetz, M.P., S.M. Block, and J.A. Spudich (1986a) Myosin movement in vitro: A quantitative assay using oriented actin cables from Nitella. Methods Enzymol. 134:531–544.

Sheetz, M.P., R. Chasan, and J.A. Spudich (1984) ATP-dependent movement of myosin in vitro: Characterization of a quantitative assay. J. Cell Biol. 99:1867–1871.

Sheetz, M.P., R.D. Vale, B.J. Schnapp, T.A. Schroer, and T.S. Reese (1986b) Vesicle movements and microtubule-based motors. J. Cell Sci. Suppl. 5:181–188.

Siegel, L.M., and K.J. Monty (1966) Determination of molecular weights and frictional coefficients of proteins in impure systems by use of gel filtration and density gradient centrifugation. Application to crude preparations of sulfite and hydroxylamine reductase. Biochim. Biophys. Acta 112:346–362.

Siemankowski, R.F., M.O. Wiseman, and H.D. White (1985) ADP disassociation from actomyosin subfragment 1 is sufficiently slow to limit the unloaded shortening velocity in vertebrate muscle. Proc. Natl. Acad. Sci. USA 82:658–662.

Siman, R., M. Baudry, and G. Lynch (1984) Brain fodrin: Substrate for calpain I, an endogenous calcium-activated protease. Proc. Natl. Acad. Sci. USA 81:3572–3576.

Sloboda, R.D., S.A. Rudolph, J.L. Rosenbaum, and P. Greengard (1975) Cyclic AMP-dependent endogenous phosphorylation of a microtubule-associated protein. Proc. Natl. Acad Sci. USA 72:177–181.

Small, T.V. (1981) Organization of actin in the leading edge of cultured cells. J. Cell Biol. 91:695–705.

Smith, D.S., U. Jarlfors, and B.F. Cameron (1975) Morphological evidence for the participation of microtubules in axonal transport. Ann. N.Y. Acad. Sci. 253:472–506.

Smith, D.S., U. Jarlfors, and M.L. Cayer (1977) Structural cross-bridges between microtubules and mitochondria in central axons of an insect (Periplaneta americana). J. Cell Sci. 27:255–272.

Smith, R.S. (1987) Control of the direction of rapid axonal transport in vertebrates. In R.S. Smith and M.A. Bisby (eds): Axonal Transport (Neurology and Neurobiology, vol. 25). New York: Alan R. Liss, Inc., pp. 139–154.

Smith, R.S., and M.A. Bisby (eds) (1987) Axonal Transport (Neurology and Neurobiology, volume 25). New York: Alan R. Liss, Inc.

Stearns, M.E., and L.I. Binder (1987) Evidence that MAP 2 may be involved in pigment granule transport in squirrel fish erythrophores. Cell Motil. Cytoskeleton 7:221–234.

Stearns, M.E., and R.L. Ochs (1982) A functional in vitro model for studies of intracellular motility in digitonin-permeabilized erythrophores. J. Cell Biol. 94:727–739.

Stein, L.A., R.P. Schwartz, P.B. Chock, and E. Eisenberg (1979) Mechanism of actomyosin adenosine triphosphatase. Evidence that adenosine triphosphate hydrolysis can occur without dissociation of the actomyosin complex. Biochemistry 18:3895–3909.

Sternberger, L.A., and N.H. Sternberger (1983) Monoclonal antibodies distinguish phosphorylated and nonphosphorylated forms of neurofilaments in situ. Proc. Natl. Acad. Sci. USA 80:6126–6130.

Summers, K.E., and I.R. Gibbons (1971) Adenosine triphosphate-induced sliding of tubules in trypsin-treated flagella of sea urchin sperm. Proc. Natl. Acad. Sci USA 68:3092–3096.

Tasaki, I. (1982) Physiology and Electrochemistry of Nerve Fibers. New York: Academic Press.

Terasaki, M., L.B. Chen, and K. Fujiwara (1986) Microtubules and the endoplasmic reticulum are highly interdependent structures. J. Cell Biol. 103:1557–1568.

Toyoshima, Y.Y. (1987) Chymotryptic digestion of *Tetrahymena* 22S dynein. I. Decomposition of three-headed 22S dynein to one- and two-headed particles. J. Cell Biol. 105:887–895.

Toyoshima, Y.Y., S.J. Kron, E.M. McNallay, K.R. Niebling, C. Toyoshima, and J.A. Spudich (1987) Myosin subfragment 1 is sufficient to move actin filaments in vitro. Nature 328:536–539.

Tsukita, S., and H. Ishikawa (1981) The cytoskeleton in myelinated axons: A serial section study. Biomed. Res. 2:424–437.

Tsukita, S., S. Tsukita, and H. Ishikawa (1980) Cytoskeletal network underlying the human erythrocyte membrane. Thin-section electron microscopy. J. Cell Biol. 85:567–576.

Tsukita, S., S. Tsukita, H. Ishikawa, M. Kurokawa, M. Morimoto, K. Sobue, and S. Kakiuchi (1983a) Binding sites of calmodulin and actin on the brain spectrin, calspectin. J. Cell Biol. 97:574–578.

Tsukita, S., S. Tsukita, H. Ishikawa, S. Sato, and M. Nakao (1981) Electron microscopic study of reassociation of spectrin and actin with the human erythrocyte membrane. J. Cell Biol. 90:70–77.

Tsukita, S., S. Tsukita, T. Kobayashi, and G. Matsumoto (1983b) A high molecular weight protein in axoplasm underlying excitable membrane of squid giant axon. Biomed. Res. 4:615–618.

Tsukita, S., S. Tsukita, T. Kobayashi, and G. Matsumoto (1986) Subaxolemmal cytoskeleton in squid giant axon. II. Morphological identification of microtubule- and microfilament-associated domains of axolemma. J. Cell Biol. 102:1710–1725.

Tsukita, S., J. Usukura, S. Tsukita, and H. Ishikawa (1982) The cytoskeleton in myelinated axons: A freeze-etch replica study. Neuroscience 7:2135–2147.

Tytell, M., M.M. Black, J.A. Garner, and R.J. Lasek (1981) Axonal transport: Each major rate component reflects the movement of distinct macromolecular complexes. Science 214:179–181.

Tytell, M., S.T. Brady, and R.J. Lasek (1984) Axonal transport of a subclass of tau proteins: Evidence for the regional differentiation of microtubules in neurons. Proc. Natl. Acad. Sci. USA 81:1570–1574.

Ueda, T., and P. Greengard (1977) Adenosine 3',5'-monophosphate-regulated phosphoprotein system of neuronal membranes. I. Solubilization, purification, and some properties of an endogenous phosphoprotein. J. Biol. Chem. 252:5155–5163.

Usukura, J., H. Akahori, H. Takahashi, and E. Yamada (1983) An improved device for rapid freezing using liquid helium. J. Electron Microsc. 32:180–185.

Vale, R.D. (1987) Intracellular transport using microtubule-based motors. Annu. Rev. Cell Biol. 3:347–378.

Vale, R.D., and T.S. Reese (1986) Proteolytic fragments of kinesin with microtubule binding activity. J. Cell Biol. 103:552a.

Vale, R.D., T.S. Reese, and M.P. Sheetz (1985a) Identification of a novel force-generating protein, kinesin, involved in microtubule-based motility. Cell 42:39–50.

Vale, R.D., B.J. Schnapp, T.J. Mitchison, E. Steuer, T.S. Reese, and M.P. Sheetz (1985b) Different axoplasmic proteins generate movement in opposite directions along microtubules in vitro. Cell 43:623–632.

Vale, R.D., B.J. Schnapp, T.S. Reese, and M.P. Sheetz (1985c) Movement of organelles along filaments dissociated from the axoplasm of the squid giant axon. Cell 40:449–454.

Vale, R.D., B.J. Schnapp, T.S. Reese, and M.P. Sheetz (1985d) Organelle, bead, and microtubule translocations promoted by soluble factors from the squid giant axon. Cell 40:559–569.

Vale, R.D., B.J. Schnapp, M.P. Sheetz, and T.S. Reese (1986a) Nucleotide and divalent cation dependent binding of kinesin to microtubules. J. Cell Biol. 103:552a.

Vale, R.D., J.M. Scholey, and M.P. Sheetz (1986b) Kinesin: Possible roles for a new microtubule motor. Trends Biochem. Sci. 11:464–468.

Vale, R.D., and Y.Y. Toyoshima (1988) Rotation and translocation of microtubules in vitro induced by dyneins from *Tetrahymena* cilia. Cell 52:459–469.

Vallee, R.B. (1982) A taxol-dependent procedure for the isolation of microtubules and microtubule-associated proteins (MAPs). J. Cell Biol. 92:435–442.

Vallee, R.B., and G.S. Bloom (1983) Isolation of sea urchin egg microtubules with taxol and identification of mitotic spindle microtubule-associated proteins with monoclonal antibodies. Proc. Natl. Acad. Sci. USA 80:6259–6263.

Vallee, R.B., and C.A. Collins (1986) Purification of microtubules and MAPs from sea urchin eggs and cultured mammalian cells using taxol. Methods Enzymol. 134 c:116–127.

Viancour, T.A., and D.S. Forman (1987) Polarity orientations of microtubules in squid and lobster axons. J. Neurocytol. 16:69–75.

Wadsworth, P. (1987) Microinjected carboxylated beads move predominantly poleward in sea urchin eggs. Cell Motil. Cytoskeleton 8:293–301.

Wagner, M.C., G.S. Bloom, and S.T. Brady (1986) Purification and physical characterization of an apparent motor for fast axonal transport. J. Cell Biol. 103:551a.

Wang, K. (1977) Filamin, a new high-molecular-weight protein found in smooth muscle and non-muscle cells. Purification and properties of chicken gizzard filamin. Biochemistry 16:1857–1865.

Warner, F.D., and J.H. McIlvain (1986) Kinetic properties of microtubule activated 13S and 21S dynein ATPase. J. Cell Sci. 83:251–267.

Webb, B.C., and L. Wilson (1980) Cold-stable microtubules from brain. Biochemistry 19:1993–2001.

Weingarten, M.D., A.H. Lockwood, S.-Y. Hwo, and M.W. Kirschner (1975) A protein factor essential for microtubule assembly. Proc. Natl. Acad. Sci. USA 72:1858–1862.

Weisenberg, R.C., J. Flynn, B. Gao, S. Awodi, F. Skee, S.R. Goodman, and B.M. Reiderer (1987) Microtubule gelation-contraction: Essential components and relation to slow axonal transport. Science 238:1119–1122.

Weiss, D.G. (1982) Axoplasmic Transport. Berlin: Springer-Verlag.

Willard, M. (1977) The identification of two intra-axonally transported polypeptides resembling myosin in some respects in the rabbit visual system. J. Cell Biol. 75:1–11.

Willard, M., and C. Simon (1981) Antibody decoration of neurofilaments. J. Cell Biol. 89:198–205.

Willard, M.M., M. Wiseman, J. Levine, and P. Skene (1979) The axonal transport of actin in rabbit retinal ganglion cells. J. Cell Biol. 81:581–591.

Wuerker, R.B., and J.B. Kirkpatrick (1972) Neuronal microtubules, neurofilaments, and microfilaments. Int. Rev. Cytol. 33:45–75.

Yano, Y., and T. Miki-Noumura (1981) Recovery of sliding ability in arm-depleted flagellar axonemes after recombination with extracted dynein. J. Cell Sci. 48:223–239.

SECTION

5

Microtubule Movements During Mitosis

Edited by J. Richard McIntosh

PERSPECTIVE
Dynamic Behavior of
Mitotic Microtubules

J. Richard McIntosh, Guy P.A. Vigers, and Thomas S. Hays

*Department of Molecular, Cellular and Developmental Biology, University of Colorado,
Boulder, Colorado 80309*

INTRODUCTION

Chromosome Dynamics Are Related to Microtubule Dynamics

The essential result of mitosis is the organized segregation of the duplicate chromosomes into two identical sets. This process is absolutely dependent on the presence of microtubules (MTs) (for review, see Bajer and Mole-Bajer, 1972; Inoué, 1981; McIntosh, 1985). Chromosomes move on and with MTs, so the arrangements and rearrangements of MTs are certainly significant for chromosome motion and may well be a causal agent for mitotic motions. An improved understanding of chromosome segregation is therefore dependent on an understanding of the movements of spindle MTs. The chapters in this section summarize much of what is known about the arrangement of spindle MTs, the patterns of their assembly and disassembly, and their motions during mitosis.

The Multiple Facets of Microtubule Dynamics

There are two general aspects to spindle MT dynamics. Microtubules undergo changes in their arrangements as a result of two factors: 1) the assembly and disassembly of tubulin and its associated proteins and 2) the translocation of MTs without a change in their length. Each aspect of MT behavior probably contributes to chromosome motion. It will become clear in the following essays that neither aspect of mitotic MT dynamics is understood in detail, but enough is now known to lay out an overview of spindle MT behavior and to relate its principal features to the major events of chromosome movement.

Tubulin assembly dynamics are related to microtubule structure. MTs possess an intrinsic structural polarity as a result of the head-to-tail assembly of the asymmetric tubulin molecules from which they are made (Amos and Klug, 1974). The two ends of an MT are therefore different. The end

Cell Movement, Volume 2: Kinesin,
Dynein, and Microtubule Dynamics, pages 371–382
© 1989 Alan R. Liss, Inc.

called *plus* has higher rate constants for both assembly and disassembly than does the opposite, or *minus,* MT end (Allen and Borisy, 1974). Under most conditions, then, one end of an MT either adds or loses subunits faster than does the other, resulting in a relative motion of the two ends of the MT. This kind of motion will be called *assembly movement.* Assembly movements of MTs can be both fast and complex because of "dynamic instability," a behavior that results from tubulin polymers existing in either an elongating or a shortening state (Carlier et al., 1984). The rate of elongation is many times slower than the rate of shortening, so at steady state many more MTs are elongating than are shortening (Mitchison and Kirschner, 1984a,b). In MTs formed from pure tubulin, the plus end changes back and forth between elongating and shortening states more frequently than does the minus end, but brain MT-associated proteins (MAPs) reduce the frequency of these transitions, promoting plus end growth (Horio and Hotani, 1986; E.D. Salmon, personal communication).

Microtubule translocations are also related to microtubule structure. The structural polarity of MTs is also evident in the movement of these polymers along their axes as a result of enzymes like dynein and kinesin. Such motions will be called *motor movements,* and they can be divided into two kinds on the basis of their direction of action relative to an MT's structural polarity. A plus motor, like kinesin, moves over the MT surface toward its plus end. If the kinesin molecule is bound to something much larger than the MT with which it is interacting, then the MT will respond to kinesin's activity by moving relative to the big object with its plus end trailing (for review see Sheetz, Chapter 17). Dynein is a minus motor and works in the opposite direction (Sale, Volume 1, Chapter 7; Vallee et al., Chapter 13; Lye et al., Chapter 9). Coupling between the structural and the movement polarities of MTs is probably a result of the geometry of the bonds between the ATPase in question and the MT surface, but the details of these interactions remain to be discovered.

Experiments on organelle motility in vivo confirm that movements relative to MTs are dependent on MT polarity. Pigment granules move in chromatophores on radial arrays of MTs whose plus ends are distal to the centrosome (Euteneuer and McIntosh, 1981a). One stimulus promotes the inward movement of granules, another the outward. When an arm extending from a chromatophore is cut free from the rest of the cell and stimulated for inward movement, the granules in the cell fragment move in different directions, depending on the time since the arm was cut off (McNiven et al., 1984). However, movement direction relative to MT polarity remains invariant, suggesting that MT polarity in vivo is tightly linked to the movements that occur along these polymers.

Methods For Watching Microtubule Dynamics

The polymerization and/or movement of individual MTs are readily visualized in vitro by using the light microscope (LM) together with any of several high-contrast optical systems, such as polarization, differential interference contrast, or fluorescence optics. These methods depend on the spatial isolation of one MT from its neighbors; because the LM cannot resolve objects as small as an MT, it merely allows them to be detected. Since spindle MTs are bunched closely together, their individual movements are impossible to distinguish in the LM, and other descriptive tools are required. The electron microscope (EM) was the first to be used for this purpose, since it has ample resolution to define the walls of single MTs, but MT dynamics are not directly visible with this instrument. Motions must be inferred from the comparison of cells fixed at different times. Since the spindles of two cells generally differ in their details, this method is imperfect. The possiblity of fixation artifact adds further insecurity to the EM-dependent motion data, but, nonetheless, some useful and probably accurate observations have been made this way, as will be described in the following chapters.

An ideal method for following MT movements in vivo would allow the investigator to place a visible but nondisruptive tag on particular MTs and then follow the position of the tag with the LM. The first effort in this direction was the use of a microbeam of ultraviolet light to irradiate a small region of the spindle, reducing its birefringent retardation (Inoué, 1964). Fine-structure studies of areas of reduced birefringence suggest that MTs dissolve in the region irradiated (Leslie and Pickett-Heaps, 1983). Because the MTs under study are damaged, this method is not ideal, but it does mark one region of the spindle in a way that can be followed in live material (e.g., Forer, 1965). More recently, several investigators have made tubulin labeled with a detectable tag, injected it into living cells, and followed the movement of the tag. Fluorescent tubulin can be watched directly in the LM, either immediately following microinjection or as its fluorescence redistributes after photobleaching. Other probes, such as biotinylated tublin, can be detected after fixation by using a secondary tag visible in either the LM or the EM. All such "analog cytochemistry" depends for its validity on the fidelity with which the labeled tubulin mimics the behavior of endogenous tubulin.

In this minireview we will outline the evidence for different aspects of spindle MT dynamics and focus attention on the mitotic phenomena that accompany them. The practical problem that pervades the work covered, and hence the review itself, is that mitotic MTs assemble, disassemble, and move all at once in different parts of the same cell. The phenomenology is therefore quite complex and exceedingly difficult to analyze experimentally. For example, it is hard to speak about MT motor movements without also discussing the sites of tubulin addition and loss. We will therefore treat the different aspects of MT dynamics together, suggesting ways in which they may be interdependent and relating them when possible to the movements of the chromosomes.

MICROTUBULE AND CHROMOSOME DYNAMICS DURING PROMETAPHASE AND METAPHASE

Microtubule Assembly During Prometaphase

The assembly of MTs during prometaphase is largely a growth of polymers initiated by the two spindle poles. The MTs that form are oriented with their plus ends distal to the sites of polymer initiation (Bergen et al., 1980; Euteneuer and McIntosh, 1981b). The geometry and dynamics of this process are discussed by McIntosh (Chapter 25). In overview, the result of all the polymerization activity is the formation of two interacting arrays of MTs emanating from the poles and invading the space occupied by the chromosomes. The chromosomes cannot escape interacting with some of these MTs. The chromosomes may also initiate MTs in the vicinity of their kinetochores; certainly they can do so in vitro (Telzer et al., 1975; Mitchison and Kirschner, 1985a) and during recovery from drug inhibition of MT assembly in vivo (Witt et al., 1980; DeBrabander et al., 1981b). Observations on chromosome attachment to spindle MTs during recovery from cold treatment, on the other hand, suggest that kinetochores capture the plus ends of MTs that were initiated by the centrosomes (Rieder and Borisy, 1981). Whether kinetochore initiation of MTs is an important aspect of normal spindle formation remains to be determined.

Chromosome Interaction With Prometaphase Microtubules

Chromosome–MT interactions in vivo. Chromosomes will bind at their kinetochores to the MTs that grow from centrosomes. Early during prometaphase kinetochores seem to interact with the lateral surfaces of MTs (Roos, 1973a,b), but in most cells the number of MTs and their lack of spatial organization make it difficult to determine what is going on. In diatoms the situation is somewhat simplified, because prometaphase MTs are of two distinguishable classes: those that interdigitate at the spindle equator and those that do not. Some of the latter probably interact with kinetochores, as indicated by the observation that one locus on a chromosome will move sharply in or out from the pole along a linear track, as if pulled by forces that act along the pole-associated MTs. This erratic behavior continues until another locus on the same chromosome, presumably the sister kinetochore, interacts with the oppsoite pole, whereupon the chromosome takes up a stable position near the spindle equator (Tippit et al., 1980a; Pickett-Heaps et al., 1982). Likewise, in mammalian cells with comparatively few chromosomes, such as the PtK line from the rat kangaroo, one can see that chromosomes that interact initially with a single pole move transiently toward that pole, as in the diatom (Roos, 1973a,b; Rieder et al., 1986). Subsequently, each chromosome usually interacts with both poles, and its congression ensues.

Analysis of chromosome–MT interactions. In mammals and most other eukaryotes the prometaphase kinetochores soon become attached to the plus ends of MTs, at least some of which have their minus ends located at the spindle poles (Euteneuer and McIntosh, 1981b). The large number of MTs that grow from the mitotic poles of many organisms may be sufficient to pepper the kinetochore with the plus ends of pole-associated MTs, accounting for the observed association in a simple way (e.g., Kirschner and Mitchison, 1986). On the other hand, the movements of specific chromosomal loci over the lateral surfaces of pole-associated MTs, as in diatoms, may be a general mechanism that contributes to the ability of kinetochores to find the pole-distal ends of pole-associated MTs. The latter mechanism would depend on MT-associated motor activity and suggests that kinetochores have such activities bound to them. Indeed, Mitchison and Kirschner (1985b) have presented evidence that isolated chromosomes display adenosine triphosphate (ATP)-dependent movement over the lateral surfaces of MTs, translocating toward the MT plus ends.

The attachment of a kinetochore to MTs from a single pole appears to be intrinsically unstable until the sister kinetochore becomes attached to the opposite pole. Such behavior is evident in the movements of diatom chromosomes during their initial movements on pole-associated MTs, and it has been studied experimentally in grasshopper spermatocytes (Nicklas and Koch, 1969). An experimentally applied tension that opposes the pole-directed force acting at one kinetochore makes the chromosome's attachment to its spindle fiber more stable. Normally such tension is supplied by the spindle's action on the sister kinetochore. The mechanism by which tension promotes strength of attachment is not known.

Chromosome orientation to face the poles. The chromosomes of essentially all organisms come to lie with one kinetochore facing each pole, rotating as if the poles were pulling on the kinetochores, drawing them as near as possible. In some organisms the coupling between sister kinetochores is not rigid, and during prometaphase a chromosome with attachments to both poles becomes stretched across the equator, as if each kinetochore was being attracted to the pole it faces (Hughes-Schrader, 1943). Indeed, a significant body of experimental work using microneedles to reposition large chromosomes in meiotic cells has shown that there are persistent, pole-directed forces resulting from interactions between chromosomes and pole-associated MTs (for review, see Nicklas, 1986). It is not yet clear whether this pole-directed force requires the kinetochores to be associated with plus MT ends or whether, as might be suggested from LM observations of chromosomes in living diatoms (Pickett-Heaps et al., 1982), a lateral interaction between MTs and kinetochores will suffice. There is an important enigma here, because kinetochores seem to move back and forth along pole-associated MTs, ultimately becoming attached to their pole-*distal* ends, yet on average the kinetochores are pulled *toward* the poles. Such behavior implies that more than one motor is acting on each chromosome during prometaphase.

Chromosome congression to the spindle equator. The motion of a prometaphase chromosome is erratic, but the net result of its many movements is a congression to the spindle equator, producing the metaphase configuration. Because chromosomes are generally attached to both poles at the time they congress, their motions usually require the lengthening of one kinetochore MT bundle while its sister shortens. It has been proposed that assembly movements of the kinetochore MTs cause the congression of the chromosomes (Dietz, 1958), but experimental work indicates that metaphase is more likely to be the result of a balance of forces. Two short kinetochore MT bundles will balance the action of a long one, and quantification of the relative bundle lengths suggests that the pole-directed force acting on a chromatid is proportional to the distance between its kinetochore and the pole it faces (Hays et al., 1982).

Laser microsurgery has been used to ablate portions of a single kinetochore, and the subsequent readjustment of chromosome position shows that one short kinetochore fiber containing a normal number of MTs will balance the action of a longer fiber that contains the few MTs that remain attached to a damaged kinetochore (Hays and Salmon, 1988). The numbers of kinetochore MTs and the positions of the chromosomes after microsurgery have been used to evaluate a model that attributes to each kinetochore MT the generation of a pole-directed force proportional to its length. In such a model the force on each kinetochore (F_i) is proportional to the number of MTs attached (N_i) and the distance from the kinetochore to the pole it faces (L_i). Thus, $F_i = N_i L_i$. Data from Hays and Salmon (1988) fit this model with a correlation coefficient of 0.96. Such a model is suggestive of "plus motor" activity interacting with the kinetochore MTs to generate a net force that is proportional to the total number of motors working and hence to the total contour length of the MTs attached to a given kinetochore.

The tight coupling between chromosome mechanics and MT dynamics.
While the problem of establishing the metaphase chromosome positions is neatly solved with this hypothesis, the idea must be expanded to address the question of MT growth and shortening as the chromosomes connected to both poles move back and forth on the spindle. This problem can be solved in principle by the assertion that the pole-directed forces generate a compression in the kinetochore MTs and thereby destabilize them at the pole (for review, see Hill and Kirschner, 1982). When a chromosome is asymmetrically placed on the spindle, the longer bundle of kinetochore MTs should be destabilized by compression, while the shorter MT bundle connected to the sister kinetochore should be stabilized by a net stretch that would promote its growth.

Such an idea is supported by two recent observations. The processes of cultured neurons are under a destabilizing compression, caused at least in part by the actin component of the cytoskeleton. When this force is released, the neuronal MTs become more stable (Joshi et al., 1987). When grasshopper spermatocyte spindles are placed under an artificial compression applied by a microneedle, the amount of spindle polymer, as visualized with polarization optics, decreases. The release of compression is accompanied by spindle regrowth (Hays, 1985). An analogous compression on spindle MTs could result from the plus motor activity suggested above because the longer a spindle MT, the greater the surface available for plus motor activity and the greater its compression near the pole, hence the greater its tendency to disassemble there.

It has been suggested that the spindle contains a contractile matrix attached to both the poles and the kinetochores (e.g., Pickett-Heaps, 1986). Such a matrix could readily provide the pole-directed forces that are directly proportional to the distances between kinetochores and poles (Hays et al., 1982). The resulting compressions and extensions in the kinetochore MTs could induce polymer stabilization and destabilization, as described above, and thus promote MT growth and shortening during prometaphase. A closer look at the model suggests, however, that it does not fit the data of Hays and Salmon (1988) without additional assumptions. If the MTs do not contribute to the pole-directed forces acting on the kinetochores, then ablating the kinetochore and reducing the number of kinetochore MTs should have no effect on chromosome position, but it does. One must assume that the amount of contractile matrix attached to each kinetochore is proportional to the kinetochore surface area left unablated. A contractile matrix that pervades the kinetochore MT bundle would fit the data of Hays et al. as well as the plus motor model.

The force balance model based on plus motors makes a strong prediction about the sites of subunit loss from the kintochore MTs, a nice example of the intimate relationship between two kinds of spindle MT dynamics. Such models are discussed with some detail by McIntosh (Chapter 25) and by Mitchison (Chapter 26). Briefly, when a prometaphase kinetochore fiber is shortening, it is hypothetically being pulled toward the pole it faces by interactions between the plus motors anchored to the spindle and the kinetochore-associated MTs. Subunit loss would therefore be expected at the polar end of the kinetochore MTs. When a kinetochore fiber is elongating, however, it could add subunits at either the pole or the kinetochore.

There is some evidence that during late prometaphase kinetochore fibers add tubulin at the kinetochore and lose it at the pole. Biotinylated tubulin has been injected into metaphase cells, and EM of cells fixed after various times of incubation postinjection suggests that exogenous subunits are added in the vicinity of the kinetochore (Mitchison et al., 1986). Over the course of a few minutes, the length of MT showing incorporation of labeled tubulin increases, so one might infer the existence of a comparable loss of subunits at the spindle poles. This result has been confirmed using fluorescein-labeled tubulin and antifluorescein to improve the visibility of the label (Wise et al., 1986). A record of the congression movements that occurred between injection and fixation appears to exclude the possibility that tubulin is added at the kinetochore simply in response to erratic chromosomal congression. We infer that kinetochore MTs are engaged in a head-to-tail assembly during prometaphase and metaphase, treadmilling slowly to the poles, as suggested by Margolis et al. (1978). As Mitchison (Chapter 26) points out, however, there are other legitimate interpretations of the observations, and it is hard to draw strong conclusions about sites of MT subunit loss from the data presently available.

Interaction Of Prometaphase Microtubules With the Spindle Poles

The observations described above draw attention to the nature of the attachment of MTs to the spindle pole. If MTs treadmill toward the poles, they must be able to lose subunits there while maintaining a mechanical attachment. The recent identification by immunofluorescence of kinesin as a component of the mammalian and amphibian spindle poles suggests a mechanical model for this phenomenon (Fig. 23–1; Neighbors et al., 1988). Kinesin is a plus motor, so if it were bound to a matrix associated with the pole, and if it moved over MTs as it does in vitro, then it should pull the spindle MTs toward the poles, promoting the treadmilling motion described above.

Kinesin localization has also been studied in the spindles of sea urchin embryos (Scholey et al., 1985; Scholey, Chapter 20). Here kinesin is distributed throughout the spindle, showing the localization characteristic for any MT-associated protein. The differences between kinesin localizations in spindles of different cell types are hard to interpret. It is unlikely that they are due to differences in the antibodies used, because a broadly cross-reacting antibody to squid kinesin (courtesy of M. Sheetz, Washington University, St. Louis, MO) was used to supplement both studies, and it confirmed the patterns described. The differences may be accurate representations of biological varia-

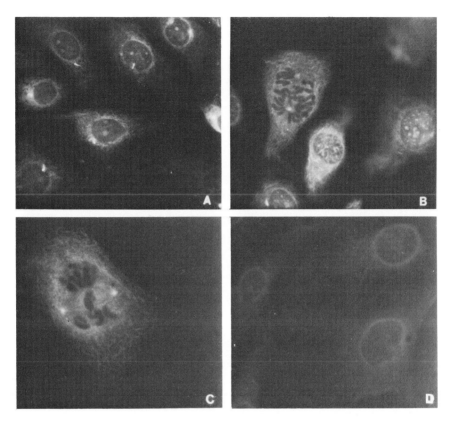

Fig. 23–1. Cultured mammalian cells, strain PtK$_1$, stained by indirect immunofluorescence to reveal the localization of kinesin. **A–C:** Cells in interphase, prometaphase, and metaphase, respectively. **D:** Control preparation stained with preimmune serum at the same dilution.

tion, they may represent fixation differences, or they may reflect special properties of particular spindles, such as the plethora of vesicles that pervades the sea urchin spindle. Either localization of kinesin could accomplish the function suggested for it here.

Prometaphase Physiology Of Monopolar Spindles

Chromosome behavior on monopolar spindles. Part of the complexity of prometaphase chromosome behavior is doubtless due to the bipolarity of both the normal spindle and the spindle attachment sites on chromosomes. A different view of prometaphase has been gained by looking at chromosome motions on monopolar spindles, which can be generated experimentally in several ways. If all the spindle's action on

kinetochores were working to pull them toward the pole they faced, then chromosomes associated with a monopolar spindle should all come to lie close to the centrosome. Mazia et al. (1981), Bajer (1982), and Rieder et al. (1986) have shown that chromosomes associated with monopoles lie at a distance from the pole that approximates that seen in a normal metaphase spindle. Either the pole-directed forces developed by these spindles are different from those of a bipolar spindle, or there is a force developed in monopolar spindles that is directed away from the centrosome (or both).

Laser microsurgery can be used to sever a chromosome arm from its centromere, and the resulting acentric fragment moves slowly away from the center of a monopolar spindle (Rieder et al., 1986). This motion reveals the action of forces originally described by Ostergren (1950) and called *elimination forces.* Such forces have generally been thought to be weak. Certainly they produce slow movements, but their magnitude has not yet been measured. It is nonetheless surprising that they are able to counterbalance the pole-directed forces, which appear to be strong during prometaphase micromanipulation experiments and which have been shown to be strong during anaphase (Nicklas, 1983). Since Nicklas has demonstrated that a stable chromosomal attachment to a biopolar spindle requires tension, it is plausible that the elimination forces seen on monopoles do not provide the requisite opposition to the pole-directed forces acting at the kinetochores. As a result, the chromosomes on monopoles may never really attach to the spindle and never experience the normal magnitude of the prometaphase pole-directed force.

An alternative model for prometaphase. Models for prometaphase congression can be constructed on the basis of elimination forces and the idea that kinetochore fibers develop a position-independent, pole-directed force as a result of the special properties of the kinetochore's interactions with MT plus ends. (For a different view of kinetochore action, see Mitchison, Chapter 26.) Suppose that the kinetochore promotes the disassembly of the MTs attached to it, pulling the chromatid to the pole, as discussed below in the section on anaphase. During prometaphase, when the sister chromatids are still attached to one another, the net force resulting from these actions on sister kinetochores should be approximately zero. In addition, however, the chromosome would be subject to elimination forces acting from both poles. The hypothesis that each elimination force field falls off with distance would make the spindle equator the locus of points at which a chromosome should experience zero net force, as discussed by Salmon (Chapter 27).

The model for prometaphase congression based on position-dependent elimination forces is qualitatively successful, but when based on physically plausible assumptions about the elimination forces, it does not account very well for the linearity described by Hays and Salmon (1988) in the relationship between chromosome position and the net force acting on a chromosome. The data from laser microsurgery (Hays and Salmon 1988) fit the elimination force model described by Salmon (Chapter 27) with a correlation coefficient of 0.89. If the elimination force is made linear with distance from a pole, falling to zero at the opposite pole, the correlation coefficient is only 0.85. (The same value is obtained with a model based on an MT-eating kinetochore and an elastic matrix whose force-production is not proportional to kinetochore area.) The differences between the fit to the data by the plus motor model ($F_i = N_i L_i$) and the others is certainly not sufficient to exclude the latter models, but it does whet our interest in models that could develop congression forces that are proportional to both the number and the length of the MTs in a kinetochore fiber.

MICROTUBULE DYNAMICS DURING ANAPHASE

Microtubule Behavior During Chromosome Motion to the Poles (Anaphase A)

Many MTs shorten during anaphase A. As the chromosomes approach the poles during early anaphase, the kinetochore-associated MTs disassemble. Many other spindle MTs also depolymerize at this time, decreasing the number of MTs seen in most spindle cross sections (e.g., McIntosh and Landis, 1971). Three-dimensional reconstructions of spindle MTs made by EM of serial sections at different times in anaphase show that many of the MTs that run from the poles to the region of the chromosomes get shorter as the chromosomes approach the poles (Tippit et al., 1980b, 1984; McIntosh et al., 1985). In addition, there is an overall decrease in MT number, consistent with the idea that as the MTs disassemble, the short ones disappear.

The spindle MTs that shorten during anaphase A lose subunits mostly at their pole-distal ends. Four independent lines of evidence suggest that the majority of the MT disassembly that accompanies chromosome to pole motion occurs at the MT plus ends, even for those MTs that are associated with a kinetochore. 1) The distribution of birefringence along a spindle fiber is often irregular, and during anaphase A the irregularities are at rest with respect to the pole; the chromosome appears to move over a static fiber (Schaap and Forer, 1984). 2) Biotinylated tubulin injected into a metaphase cell shows some specific incorporation into the MTs in the immediate vicinity of the kinetochore, as cited above. This label disappears during anaphase, suggesting that the pole-distal portion of the kinetochore fiber is disassembled as a chromosome approaches the pole (Mitchison et al., 1986). 3) After fluorescein-labeled tubulin has been microinjected and allowed to equilibrate with a spindle in vivo, and after a part of the fluorescence between chromosomes and poles has been bleached to mark the MTs during early anaphase, the moving chromosomes appear to approach the bleach mark while the mark stays approximately at rest with respect to the poles (Gorbsky et al., 1987a,b). 4) Spermatocytes of the grasshopper can be cultured in their tissue liquids under oil and mechanically demembranated without perturbing anaphase. A microneedle can then be used to cut the spindle between the chromosomes and poles, cleanly severing the MTs in this region. Some of the chromosomes in this truncated spindle continue to move toward the cut without thrusting their kinetochore-associated MTs poleward beyond the cut, suggesting that the pole is irrelevant for the mechanisms of anaphase A (Nicklas, 1987b). In sum, these results suggest that 1) the motors for anaphase A reside at or near the chromosome and 2) during chromosome to pole motion, kinetochore MTs disassemble at or near the kinetochores.

It is important to recognize that this evidence does not exclude the possibility of some subunit disassembly at the poles. The evidence from spindle birefringence cited above is an indirect visualization of spindle MTs, and its interpretation may be confused by the presence of birefringent objects other than the spindle MTs. Neither the experiment based on injection of biotinylated tubulin nor the spindle truncation addresses the question of subunit loss at the poles. The photobleach experiment should provide clear evidence on the issue, but work published by 1987 lacks good markers for the position of the spindle poles at the time of photobleaching, so movement of the bleach mark relative to the poles is hard to measure. A second generation of these experiments has recently been published (Gorbsky et al., 1988). In one experiment, the bleach mark was so close to the pole that its lack of movement is difficult to interpret, and in another, the bleach mark disappeared. Thus we cannot yet exclude the possibility of some MT subunit loss during anaphase at places other than the kinetochores.

The kinetochore is an active agent in anaphase A. The kinetochore, or factors associated with it, appears on current evidence to be much more active in mitosis than was previously thought (Nicklas, 1987a). Prometaphase kinetochores appear to move both ways on MTs (Tippit et al., 1980a), and isolated chromosomes move toward the MT plus end (Mitchison and Kirschner, 1985b). On current evidence, however, kinesin is not a kinetochore protein (Fig. 23–1; Scholey et al., 1985; Neighbors et al., 1988).

Several models for anaphase kinetochore action can be distinguished (Mitchison, Chapter 26), but all of them must encompass the roles of binding to the plus ends of MTs and staying bound to these ends as tubulin subunits are lost. One class of model sees MT disassembly itself as the force-producing agent during anaphase A, while the other posits the existence of a minus motor at the kinetochore to provide the substantial force a chromosome can receive from the spindle (Nicklas, 1983). Hirokawa and his collaborators have examined the localization of a dynein antigen in spindles from sea urchin eggs. It appears to be associated with spindle MTs during both metaphase and anaphase, but it is not localized at the kinetochore (Hirokawa, Chapter 24; Hisanaga et al., 1987). Further, dynein is a minus motor (Lye, Chapter 9), so it is unlikely to account for all the MT translocations of mitosis.

The localization of dynein in spindles has been quite controversial. Some antibodies to dynein have shown clear evidence for spindle localization (e.g., Mohri et al., 1976), while others have not (e.g., Zieve and McIntosh, 1981). One source of this disagreement is probably the difficulty of purifying dynein, so the antibodies used have not necessarily been raised against pure antigen. A second problem may be that dynein is a large protein that displays many epitopes. A given antiserum may recognize only a subset of these, so if some dynein epitopes are blocked during immunolocalization, different antibodies could give different results. There may also be dynein-related proteins that share some but not all epitopes with the antigens used. Further, there appear to be at least two distinct dynein-like proteins in sea urchin eggs, and these may have quite different cellular roles and localizations (Porter et al., 1988). Finally, there may be true variation between different biological systems. Nonetheless, there is some impressive evidence for dynein localized in spindles from sea urchin eggs (e.g., Hirokawa, Chapter 24).

No one has yet obtained functional evidence for the involvement of any known motor in chromosome movement, and until such evidence is available, we must be very open-minded about the molecules that transduce chemical energy into the mechanical work for MT and chromosome movement. For example, Collins and Vallee (1986) have identified a 10S, MT-stimulated ATPase activity in extracts of sea urchin eggs. The enzyme has not been purified, so there is not yet information about its ability to work as an MT-dependent motor, its chemistry, or its role in cells. As new MT-dependent motors are discovered, it will be important to ask

whether any of them is associated with spindle MTs or kinetochores. It will also be important to investigate more thoroughly the capacity of kinetochores to stabilize MTs initiated by centrosomes (Kirschner and Mitchison, 1986). Both the mechanical and the assembly roles of kinetochores defined here seem likely to be of real significance for mitosis.

Microtubule Behavior During Spindle Elongation (Anaphase B)

Some of the MTs that do not associate with kinetochores remain stable during anaphase. One might imagine that the MT disassembly associated with anaphase A would lead to a shrinkage of the spindle rather than to chromosome movement toward the poles, yet the poles of an anaphase spindle not only keep their separation as the chromosomes draw near but they also usually move apart. Both the stability and the elongation of the spindle is probably a result of the framework constructed from the MTs that pass the chromosomes and interdigitate near the spindle equator. Certainly a severing of this interpolar bundle in diatoms during metaphase leads to the collapse of the interpolar distance (Leslie and Pickett-Heaps, 1983), suggesting that this MT system bears a compressive force probably imposed by the reaction to the pole-directed forces acting on the chromosomes. Structural studies on a cellular slime mold (McIntosh et al., 1985), on algae (McDonald et al., 1979; Tippit et al., 1983), and on a fungus (Tippit et al., 1984) show that there is a population of long MTs that interdigitate during metaphase, anaphase, and telophase. This population is of approximately constant number, and in any given cell type it probably represents the same MTs sampled at different times during mitosis. The interdigitating MTs are stabilized against the disassembly characteristic of all other spindle fibers, presumably by the interaction of their pole-distal ends (McDonald et al., 1979). In most organisms the interdigitating MTs actually elongate during anaphase B.

Microtubules that elongate during anaphase B probably add subunits at thier pole-distal ends. Several lines of evidence, discussed below by McIntosh (Chapter 25) and by Cande (Chapter 28), show that during anaphase some tubulin subunits are added at the pole-distal ends of the interdigitating spindle MTs. No evidence yet available excludes some polymerization at the pole-proximal end as well, but studies of tubulin assembly sites at other stages of the cell cycle have thus far failed to find any pole-proximal addition of MT subunits.

Stable, interdigitating microtubules can slide apart during anaphase B. Fine structural studies on several species of diatom have shown that the extent of MT interdigitation at the spindle equator decreases during anaphase (for review, see Pickett-Heaps and Tippit, 1978). The length of the interdigitating MTs is either constant or growing during this time, so the decrease in MT overlap is unlikely to be due to tubulin disassembly. The decrease occurs as the spindle poles move apart, so the interpolar bundle appears to be functioning like a muscle working backward.

In diatoms the spindle elongation of anaphase B can be reactivated in vitro (Cande and McDonald, 1985). Analysis of the elongation process suggests that it is at least in part a relative sliding of antiparallel MTs mediated by a motor molecule that shares some properties with dynein but is in other ways unique (for review, see Cande, Chapter 28). A sliding apart of the interdigitating MTs rationalizes the otherwise enigmatic addition of tubulin at the pole-distal ends of MTs, permitting MT polymerization to augment the anaphase separation of spindle poles. MT elongation at the pole-distal ends should simply increase the extent of MT overlap near the spindle equator, but when this polymerization is coupled to a sliding action, it permits the interdigitating MTs to slide farther and thereby to increase the elongation of the spindle. Once again we see that spindle MT assembly–disassembly is intimately linked with MT movements during the complex motions of mitosis.

Coupling of spindle elongation to chromosome motion. The MT motions that accompany spindle elongation are not directly coupled to the chromosomes, and one can ask whether they have any impact on chromosome segregation. Two kinds of mechanical coupling are probably important for conveying to the chromosomes the MT motions being generated elsewhere in the spindle: 1) If kinetochore MTs are bound to the pole, e.g., by the kinesin–matrix system postulated above, then an outward movement of the poles will be conveyed through the kinetochore MTs to the chromosomes; and 2) in spindles without structured poles (either the acentrosomal spindles of higher plants or animal spindles subject to experimental truncation), the motions of nonchromosomal MTs that occur during spindle elongation may be coupled to motions of the kinetochore MTs by bridges that connect the two kinds of MTs (McIntosh et al., 1969). Such bridges have been identified structurally by EM (Hepler et al., 1970; Hirokawa, Chapter 24) and mechanically by the behavior of meiotic spindle fibers subjected to micromanipulation (Nicklas et al., 1982). The chemical nature of these bridges remains to be identified.

Some spindle elongation may be better described as nuclear movement. In the fungus *Fusarium,* anaphase spindle elongation is by about a factor of five, and it continues after the daughter nuclei are well established. In this cell a severing of the interzone spindle fibers with a laser microbeam increases the speed at which the two poles separate (Aist and Berns, 1981). These workers have suggested that spindle elongation results from a pulling on the spindle poles by motors working on the aster MTs that project out from the spindle toward the cell cortex. This explanation is unlikely to pertain to anaphase B in diatoms, because diatom spindle elongation will occur without an aster in vivo and without a matrix with which an aster might interact in vitro (Cande, Chapter 28). MT behavior during spindle elongation may have to be considered in two parts—anaphase B mediated by the spindle and anaphase C mediated by an aster—but such a distinction should await more evidence for a motor that resides outside the spindle.

CONCLUSIONS

MT dynamics are of fundamental significance for the motions of chromosomes during mitosis. The salient aspects of these dynamics are the assembly and disassembly of pole-associated MTs, the coupling of these MTs to the kinetochores, the generation of pole-directed forces acting at the kinetochores (contributing to the bipolar orientation of the chromosomes), the development of a balance of forces on the chromosomes that leads them to congress to the spindle equator, the pulling of the chromosomes toward the poles during anaphase as the majority of the spindle MTs disassemble, and the pushing apart of the poles as the remaining MTs elongate and slide past one another. In most of these aspects of spindle MT dynamics, assembly–disassembly is interwoven with MT movement to make a machine that is hard to understand but marvelously effective in its action. Students of the spindle have a fair way to go in understanding the subtleties of this intriguing organelle, but it is pleasing to see how much progress has been made in the last few years. We expect that the near future will be equally productive.

ACKNOWLEDGMENTS

The work from our laboratory that is described here was supported by grant GM36663 from the NIH and by grant BC498 from the ACS. G.V. and T.H. are supported by postdoctoral fellowships from NATO and from the NIH.

Cytoskeletal Architecture of the Mitotic Spindle

Nobutaka Hirokawa

Department of Anatomy and Cell Biology, University of Tokyo School of Medicine, Hongo, Tokyo 113, Japan

INTRODUCTION

Mitosis is a very important aspect of cell reproduction and involves a dynamic rearrangement of the cytoskeleton. It is well established that mitosis is based on the assembly and disassembly of microtubules. Mitosis includes two main motilities based on microtubules: chromosome movement to the poles and spindle elongation. These dynamic phenomena have attracted much interest, and a number of structural, biochemical, and physiological studies have been undertaken to study the mechanisms of these movements. Although abundant and valuable data have been accumulated from different approaches, we do not yet fully understand mitotic mechanisms.

Because mitosis is based on the dynamic reorganization of cytoskeletal elements, some data important for understanding the process have come from structural studies: serial thin-section electron microscopy (Brinkley and Cartwright, 1971; McIntosh and Landis, 1971), high-voltage electron microscopy (McIntosh et al., 1975a,b), immunocytochemistry (DeBrabander et al., 1981a,b), and studies of microtubule polarity (Euteneuer and McIntosh, 1981a,b; Tel-

zer and Haimo, 1981). Based on these data, several attractive hypotheses have been proposed to account for the mechanisms of spindle motilities, such as a sliding-filament model (McIntosh et al., 1969), a zipper mechanism (Bajer, 1973), and force production by microtubule assembly–disassembly (Inoué and Sato, 1967). In this chapter I will review some of the findings on spindle architecture, especially the cytoskeletal architecture of mitotic spindles, and summarize our recent studies using quick-freeze, deep-etch electron microscopy, a technique that has provided resolution high enough to identify macromolecular structures (Heuser and Salpeter, 1979; Hirokawa and Heuser, 1981). The main focus of the chapter is on the spindles of sea urchin eggs and mammalian cells. For more extensive reviews, including mitotic spindles of both plants and animals, the reader is referred to Fuge (1978), McIntosh et al. (1975a,b), and Bajer and Mole-Bajer (1972).

REVIEW OF SPINDLE STRUCTURE
Basic Elements of the Mitotic Spindle

The mitotic apparatus of higher eukaryotes is composed mainly of the bipolar spindle and the centrosome-aster complexes. Its basic elements consist of microtubules, spindle matrix, the kinetochores (associated with condensed chromosomes), and the centrosomes. These elements are described in the following sections.

Microtubules

Microtubules form the frameworks of mitotic spindles. Three distinct groups of spindle microtubules are recognized: 1) polar microtubules, 2) kinetochore microtubules, and 3) astral microtubules. The polar microtubules originate from the spindle poles, the kinetochore microtubules are associated with condensed chromosomes, and the astral microtubules radiate from the centrospheres.

Organization of microtubules. The centrosomes and astral microtubules are formed in the cytoplasm prior to spindle assembly. The spindle microtubules appear at the time the nuclear envelope becomes fragmented. In early prometaphase microtubules are observed to run through the openings of nuclear envelope and then become connected with chromosomes. It is possible that these microtubules grow from the centrosomes and become connected with chromosomes, but because the kinetochores have been shown to function as nucleating sites for microtubule polymerization, it is more likely that the microtubules connected with chromosomes grow from the kinetochores (Roos, 1973a,b). During prometaphase polar and kinetochore microtubules accumulate, while astral microtubules disassemble.

Chromosome orientation is accompanied by a gradual increase in kinetochore and polar microtubules. Polar microtubules appear to influence the poleward orientation of the kinetochore microtubules during early spindle formation. Kinetochore microtubules gradually become arranged parallel to each other and to the long axis of the spindle during metaphase, when all the chromosomes have become arranged at the equator.

Extensive studies have been carried out to analyze the distribution and arrangement of kinetochore microtubules and polar microtubules during metaphase. The main approaches have been counting and measuring microtubules in serial sections perpendicular to the spindle axis and high-voltage electron microscopy (McIntosh et al., 1975a,b). Polar microtubules originate from one pole region and end either in the proximal half-spindle, in the equatorial region, or in the distal half-spindle, depending on their different lengths. Therefore, a certain number of polar microtubules overlap in the middle of the spindle (McIntosh et al., 1975a,b). Because of the presence of kinetochore microtubules the number of microtubules is maximum in the two half-spindles (1,600 to 2,700 microtubules/section), whereas it is lower at the equator (600 to 1,000 microtubules/section) (Brinkley and Cartwright, 1971, 1975). Microtubules decrease in number toward the poles. There is controversy about whether all the kinetochore microtubules reach into the polar region.

At anaphase chromosomes become separated into sister chromatids that move toward the poles (anaphase A), and the spindle elongates (anaphase B). During this stage the number of microtubules at the equator increases, while the concentration of microtubules in the half-spindle decreases. This is mainly because of the formation of stem bodies in the equator and the decomposition of kinetochore microtubules in the half-spindle. As mentioned above, some of the polar microtubules are overlapping in the middle of the spindle between sister chromatids. This overlapping of polar microtubules is important to account for possible sliding of microtubules at anaphase B. The ratio of the number of microtubules in a half-spindle to that in the interzone and to that in the other half-spindle should be 1:2:1, while actually it is 1:1.5:1 (Brinkley and Cartwright, 1971; McIntosh and Landis, 1971). Therefore, it has been suggested that the zone of overlap is "sloppy" (McIntosh et al., 1975a,b).

Polarity of microtubules. The polarity of kinetochore and polar microtubules is important for understanding the mechanisms of motility at anaphase A and anaphase B. Two approaches have so far demonstrated it clearly. One used the assembly of hook-shaped sheets of tubulin onto the walls of spindle microtubules (Euteneuer and McIntosh, 1981a,b), while the other used the decoration of spindle microtubules with axonemal dynein (Telzer and Haimo, 1981). Both showed that the kinetochore and polar microtubules in a half-spindle possess the same polarity, with their plus ends located distal to the pole.

Molecular Structure of Spindle Microtubules and Associated Elements

The spindle microtubules themselves are 25 nm in diameter. They are composed of 13 protofilaments and appear to be similar to other microtubules in the cytoplasm in many cell types (Tilney et al., 1973). However, from thin-section electron microscopy it has been recognized that a low-density, fine, filamentous material coats the walls and is dispersed between the microtubules of sea urchin egg spindles (Salmon and Segall, 1980; Salmon, 1982). Further, the overlapping ends of polar microtubules are connected by numerous cross bridges and embedded in an electro-opaque matrix in anaphase mammalian spindles (Brinkley and Cartwright, 1971; McIntosh and Landis, 1971; Roos, 1973a,b). Lateral arms have been reported to connect microtubule surfaces with the membranes of mitochondria or of vesicles, with the diffuse spindle matrix material, and with the extrakinetochore surface of chromosomes. These arms appear to be identical to the intertubular cross bridges that connect the microtubules aligned parallel with one another.

The chemical natures of the structures associated with microtubules are unknown. Some of them could be composed of microtubule-associated proteins (MAPs) and/or motor molecules. Several spindle MAPs have been described: 210 kDa, and 125 kDa in HeLa cells (Bulinski and Borisy, 1979; Bulinski et al., 1980) and 37, 78, 80, 150,

and 200 kDa in sea urchin eggs (Keller and Rebhun, 1982; Scholey et al., 1984; Vallee and Bloom, 1983). Motor molecules, such as a cytoplasmic, dynein-like ATPase (Pratt, 1980; Pratt et al., 1980; Hisanaga and Sakai, 1983) and kinesin (for review, see Scholey et al., Chapter 20; Leslie et al., 1987; Porter et al., 1987) have been isolated from sea urchin eggs. Although these MAPs and motor molecules are localized in fixed spindles, the distribution of these molecules in vivo has not yet been characterized. In the following section I will describe our attempts to localize some of these molecules in the mitotic spindle of sea urchin eggs.

ARCHITECTURE OF MITOTIC SPINDLE COMPONENTS

Cytoskeletal Architecture of Spindle Microtubules and Associated Elements

Structural studies of spindles by quick-freeze, deep-etch electron microscopy. We studied the cytoskeletal architecture of the mitotic apparatus isolated from sea urchin eggs using quick-freeze, deep-etch electron microscopy (Hirokawa et al., 1985b). This method revealed an extensive, three-dimensional network of straight and branching cross bridges between spindle microtubules (Fig. 24–1). In addition, the surfaces of the spindle microtubules (MTs) were covered with at least two kinds of granules, smaller ones and larger ones. The smaller granules had a dome-like shape and looked like buttons (Fig. 24–1). The surface of many spindle microtubules was covered with these button-like structures, which were uniform in shape and size (8–9 nm in diameter) and often appeared to be hexagonally packed. These microtubule buttons frequently provided bases for cross bridges between adjacent microtubules (Fig. 24–2).

Analysis of components isolated from mitotic spindles. These button-like structures were removed from the surfaces of microtubules by high salt (0.6 M NaCl) extraction. To study the chemical nature of

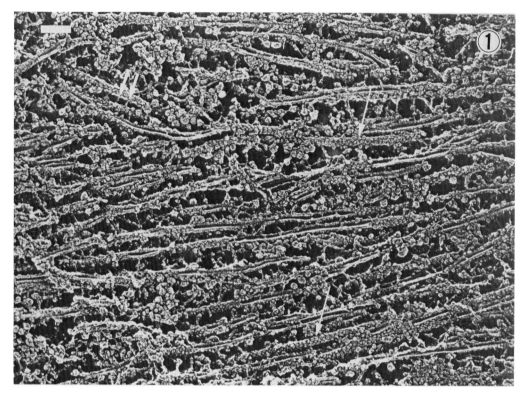

Fig. 24–1. Low-magnification view of an isolated metaphase mitotic spindle of the sea urchin egg processed by the quick-freeze, deep-etch electron microscopy. This electron micrograph shows extensive cross bridges between parallel arrays of numerous spindle microtubules. The cross bridges consist of a short, straight type (short arrows) and a longer, straight or branching type. Clusters of globular substances varying in sizes are attached to the cross bridges. The surface of microtubules was covered by hexagonally packed small granules (8–9 nm in diameter; long arrows) and occasional larger granules (11–26 nm in diameter). Bar = 0.1 μm. (Reproduced from Hirokawa et al., 1985b, with permission of the publisher.)

the structures, MAPs were analyzed. MAPs isolated from mitotic spindles were composed mainly of a 75 kDa protein and some proteins of high M_r (250 and 245 kDa) (Fig. 24–3). These MAPs and tubulin were polymerized in vitro and examined by quick-freeze, deep-etch electron microscopy. The surfaces of such microtubules were entirely covered with the same hexagonally packed round buttons (Fig. 24–4). Short cross bridges and some longer cross bridges were also observed. Once again, high-salt treatment (0.6 M NaCl) extracted both the 75 kDa protein and high-M_r proteins and removed both the microtubule buttons and

most of the cross bridges from the surfaces of the microtubules (Fig. 24–4).

The 75 kDa protein was further purified from sea urchin egg microtubule proteins through gel filtration chromatography. The purified 75 kDa protein enhanced the polymerization of porcine brain tubulin, but was not heat stable and did not bind to calmodulin in the presence of calcium, as demonstrated by calmodulin affinity column chromatography (Hirokawa and Hisanaga, 1987). Rotary shadowing of the freeze-etched 75 kDa protein adsorbed on mica revealed the protein to be a spherical molecule (~9 nm in diameter; Fig. 24–5).

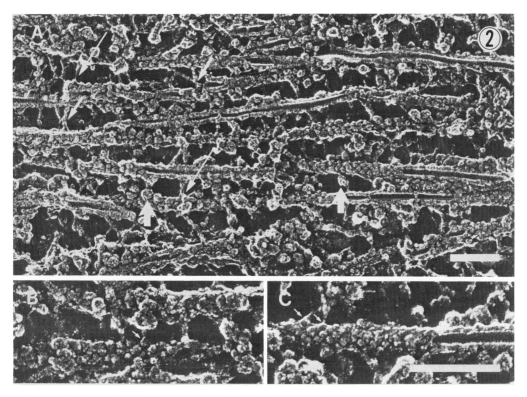

Fig. 24–2. A: High-magnification view of spindle microtubules. The surface of microtubules is decorated by hexagonally packed microtubule buttons (8–9 nm) and occasional large, spherical granules (thick arrows), from which fine tails sometimes extended to adjacent microtubules. Long and thin arrows point to straight cross bridges, and short arrows indicate branching cross bridges. **B,C:** Higher magnification views showing the relationships between microtubule buttons and cross bridges. Arrows point to small granules where cross bridges terminate. Bar = 0.1 μm. (Reproduced from Hirokawa et al., 1985b, with permission of the publisher.)

Quick-freeze, deep-etch electron microscopy revealed that the surfaces of microtubules polymerized with 75 kDa were entirely covered with hexagonally packed, round, button-like structures that were quite uniform in shape and size (~9 nm) (Fig. 24–6) and similar to the buttons observed on microtubules of mitotic spindles in vivo or microtubules isolated from mitotic spindles (Figs. 24–1, 24–2, 24–4, and 24–5). Hence, we concluded that the microtubule buttons in vivo consist of a unique 75 kDa MAP we have called *buttonin* and that some of the cross bridges in vivo could belong to high-M_r MAPs (Hirokawa and Hisanaga, 1987).

Arrangement of buttonin on microtubules. The microtubule buttons were aligned at an angle of 11° to a line perpendicular to the axes of the microtubules. The lateral, center-to-center spacing between adjacent buttons was 15 nm. The characteristic striations observed on the inner walls of the microtubules were three start helices and were separated by ~4 nm. They were also arranged at an angle of 11° to the horizontal axes of the microtubules. Because these striations probably reflect the arrangement of tubulin monomers, we suppose that buttonin is arranged in a close relationship to the tubulin lattice. The center-to-center distance between adjacent buttons aligned at

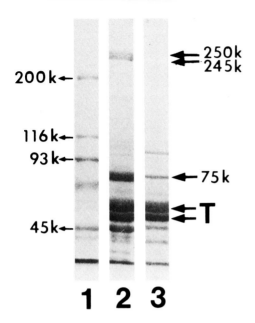

Fig. 24–3. Microtubules and MAPs prepared from isolated mitotic apparatus by the taxol/salt method. **Lane 1:** Molecular maker; **lane 2:** pellet of microtubules and MAPs; **lane 3:** tubulin-containing pellet after incubation in assembly buffer containing taxol and 0.6 M NaCl. Microtubule pellet prepared from isolated mitotic apparatus by taxol contains a large amount of 75 kDa protein and some high-M_r proteins (250 and 245 kDa) (lane 2). After extraction with high salt, the 75 kDa protein and the high-M_r proteins were released prominently from the microtubule pellet (lane 3). A 43 kDa protein is probably actin, which contaminated the preparation and is also found in SDS gels of all the previous studies. T, tubulin. (Reproduced from Hirokawa et al., 1985b, with permission of the publisher.)

an angle of 11° to the horizontal axes of the microtubules was ~15 nm (the distance between oblique striations on the inner surface was ~4 nm), and the buttons were 8–9 nm in diameter. Therefore, it is reasonable to assume that each button associates mainly with two tubulin monomers (α–β or β–α) and tends to span two immediately adjacent protofilaments. Thus, a single button is related to about three tubulin dimers. Because microtubule buttons cover the surface of spindle microtubules and because

buttonin stimulates the polymerization of tubulin, we suppose that buttonin may play an important role in spindle formation by stabilizing spindle microtubules.

The arrangement and significance of large spindle MAPs. Larger granules, 11–26 nm in diameter, were also on occasion associated with the surfaces of microtubules in mitotic spindles (Hirokawa et al., 1985b) (Figs. 24–1, 24–2). Fine sidearms sometimes connected the larger granule to adjacent microtubules (Fig. 24–2). Several of the hypotheses proposed to account for the mechanism of anaphase chromosome movement and spindle elongation have been based on dynein-like molecules. Recently the involvement of dynein-like ATPase in this process has been suggested by physiological and biochemical studies (Mohri et al., 1976; Sakai et al., 1976). Using the isolated mitotic apparatus or permeabilized PtK$_1$ cell model, chromosome movement or spindle elongation has been induced by adenosine triphosphate (ATP) and inhibited by vanadate, erythro-9-(3-[2-hydroxynonyl])adenine (Cande, 1982a,b), or antibodies to flagellar dynein (Sakai et al., 1976). In addition, a dynein-like ATPase has been isolated from sea urchin egg cytoplasm or mitotic spindles and characterized biochemically (Weisenberg and Taylor, 1968; Pratt, 1980; Pratt et al., 1980; Hisanaga and Sakai, 1983; Scholey et al., 1984). This dynein-like ATPase caused extensive parallel bundling of MAP-free microtubules. Negative-stain electron microscopy of these bundled microtubules revealed that they were arranged in parallel networks with extensive close lateral association (Hollenback et al., 1984). Furthermore, monoclonal antibodies (McAb) to flagellar dynein cross reacted specifically with cytoplasmic dynein and stained mitotic spindles of sea urchin eggs by immunofluorescent microscopic studies (Hisanaga et al., 1987) (Figs. 24–7, 24–8).

Localization of cytoplasmic dynein ATPase in the mitotic spindle has been investigated by electron microscopic immunocytochemistry with a McAb against sea urchin sperm flagellar 21S dynein and colloidal gold-labeled second antibody (Hirokawa et al., 1985a,b). Immunogold particles were closely associated with spindle microtubules (Fig. 24–9). Seventy-six percent of these were within 50 nm, and 55% were within 20 nm from the surface of the microtubules. These gold particles were sporadically found on both polar and kinetochore microtubules of half-spindles at both metaphase and anaphase (Fig. 24–9; Hirokawa et al., 1985a,b). These data indicate that cytoplasmic dynein is attached to the microtubules in sea urchin mitotic spindles.

Structure of large spindle MAPs. We have studied the substructure of a cytoplasmic, dynein-like molecule isolated from sea urchin eggs and visualized with the quick-freeze, deep-etch technique (Hisanaga and Hirokawa, 1987) (Figs. 24–10, 24–11). The molecule consisted of a head and a stem. The head was pear-shaped (16 × 11 nm; Fig. 24–10) and a little smaller than the pear-shaped head of 21S dynein (18 × 14 nm; Goodenough and Heuser, 1984). The form of the stem was irregular, and its apparent length varied from 0 to 32 nm. Binding of cytoplasmic dynein to brain microtubule in the solution was observed by negative staining and that in the precipitate was examined by the quick-freeze, deep-etch method as well. Both methods revealed the presence of two kinds of microtubules, one fully decorated and the other without decoration. Cytoplasmic dynein bound to microtubule also appeared as a globular particle (Fig. 24–12). Considering the sporadic distribution, the proximity to microtubules, and the molecular structures seen, dynein could comprise at least some of the large granules observed on microtubules in vivo by the quick-freeze, deep-etch technique (Figs. 24–1, 24–2; Hirokawa et al., 1985b). The data also suggest that dynein and cross bridges between microtubules could be an important part of the machinery of chromosome movement.

Spindle Matrix

General structure of spindle matrix. Thin-section electron microscopy (EM) has revealed ill-defined, electron-dense material, ribosomes, particles, and occasionally membrane vesicles in the intertubular spindle matrix (Roos, 1973a,b; Harris, 1975). Because the assembly and disassembly of microtubules are important processes for mitosis, tubulin dimers must also be present in the intertubular space during a large part of mitosis. These tubulin dimers may contribute to the background density observed by thin-section EM. In sea urchin eggs, particles 20 nm in diameter adhere to the finely filamentous material between spindle microtubules (Salmon and Segall, 1980; Salmon, 1982). The particles, sparsely dispersed along the central spindle microtubules, occur in much higher concentrations in the centrosome–centriole complex, forming large clumps along the aster microtubules in the region distal from the centrosome–centriole complex. These particle complexes appear to correspond with the globular material seen in light micrographs of the isolated spindles. Some of these particles may correspond to the larger granules (11–26 nm in diameter) associated with spindle microtubules observed by quick-freeze, deep-etch. Therefore, some of them may be cytoplasmic dynein, while the nature of most of the particles is not yet known. It has been postulated that some of these particles are ribosomes or some other complex of ribonucleic protein (Salmon, 1982).

Actin-like filaments.. There are several reports that identify actin filaments in glycerinated spindles, using heavy meromyosin (HMM) (Hinckley and Telser, 1974; Sanger, 1975). The 6- to 7-nm-thick filaments are found between, and are laterally associated with, those single-spindle microtubules that are resistant to extraction with glycerol. Roos observed microfilaments in the cytoplasm of dividing PtK$_1$ cells and occasionally between poorly preserved mitotic chromosomes, but never associated with kinetochores or kinetochore microtubules. These fibers are not, however, pole to pole oriented. They seem instead to radiate from the chromatin surfaces in all directions. Recently Maupin and Pollard (1986) examined HeLa cell spindles using an improved fixa-

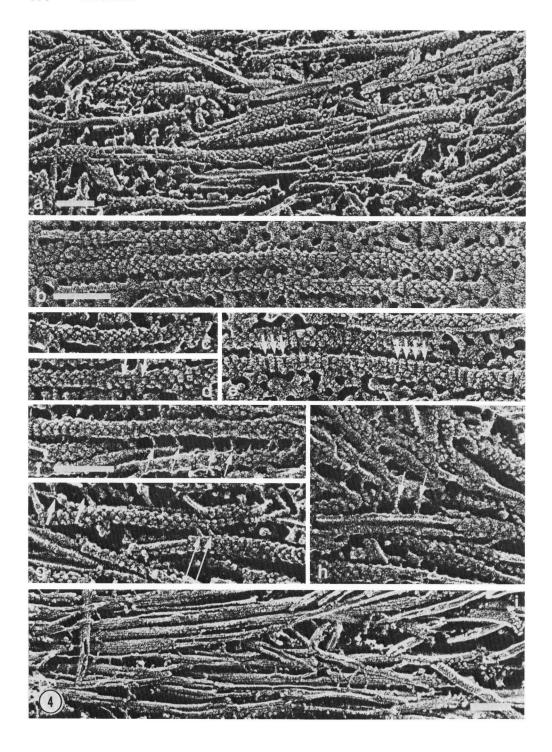

tion method. They found a large number (400 to 1,000/μm^2) of very short filaments in the mitotic spindle. These appear identical to actin filaments in other parts of these cells, but the chemical nature of the short filaments was not examined. Therefore, some of the cross bridges between spindle microtubules observed with the quick-freeze, deep-etch method may be composed of actin oligomers. It has not, however, been settled whether actin-like filaments are actually present in mitotic spindle in vivo.

Kinetochore

The kinetochore, which can function as a nucleating site for microtubules, is a specialized region of the chromosome where spindle microtubules attach at their ends. In many different kinds of eukaryotes, including mammals, the kinetochore is composed of three plate-like layers 0.3–0.6 μm in diameter. The layer proximal to the chromosome is intimately associated with chromatin and displays some electron density similar to that of the chromosome. The distal layer is 30–50 nm thick and is less dense than chromatin (Comings and Okada, 1971; Roos, 1973a,b). Between the proximal and distal layers is a low-density layer. In sea urchin eggs no specialized structures, such as the trilaminar region, are observed at the kinetochore. The chemical nature of kinetochores is now beginning to be characterized. 18 kDa and 80 kDa proteins have been identified as components of the kinetochores from HeLa metaphase chromosomes (Valodivia and Brinkley, 1986), but further studies will be necessary to understand the molecular architecture of the kinetochores.

Centrosphere

The centrosphere is assembled around two centrioles prior to the appearance of a spindle in the cytoplasm. It is composed of granules, a dense material associated with the centrioles, vesicles, and numerous microtubules radiating from and surrounding the centrioles and the granular material. Centrospheres have been shown to function as microtubule organizing centers. Especially in sea urchin eggs, we can recognize numerous clusters of granules in the centrosphere region (Fig. 24–13). This granular material is thought to correspond to microtubule organizing sites (Endo et al., 1983). A 51 kDa protein has been isolated from sea urchin centrospheres. It has microtubule nucleating activity and is supposed to be a component of the granular material from the centrosphere regions (Toriyama et al., 1985).

CONCLUSIONS

Overall Organization of Spindle Microtubules

Kinetochore and polar microtubules in a half-spindle possess the same polarity with

---

Fig. 24–4. Quick-freeze, deep-etch electron micrographs of microtubules and MAPs prepared from isolated mitotic apparatus by the taxol/salt method. a to h are taken from the sample in lane 2 and i is taken from the sample in lane 3 in Fig. 24–3. **a:** Low-magnification view. The surface of microtubules is entirely covered with hexagonally packed microtubule buttons. **b–e:** High-magnification views of microtubules processed by shallow etching. The surfaces of microtubules are just barely exposed from the ice. The hexagonally packed buttons are well observed in b and c. In d, hints of a boundary between adjacent protofilaments are found (arrows). In e, because the knife sometimes removes some granules, regular (14-nm) stripes aligned at an angle of ~11° relative to the horizontal axis of microtubules were observed (arrows). **f–h:** Higher-magnification views of deep-etched samples to display cross bridges associated with microtubules. In f, short, straight cross bridges connect adjacent microtubules (arrows). In g, some longer cross bridges (long arrows) and short cross bridges are observed. Short cross bridges appear to terminate on the small granules (short arrows). Right-handed helical stripes are found on the inner surface of microtubules. In h, short cross bridges (arrows) link adjacent microtubule buttons, and cross bridges are removed from the surface of microtubules. Bars = 0.1 μm. (Reproduced from Hirokawa et al., 1985b, with permission of the publisher.)

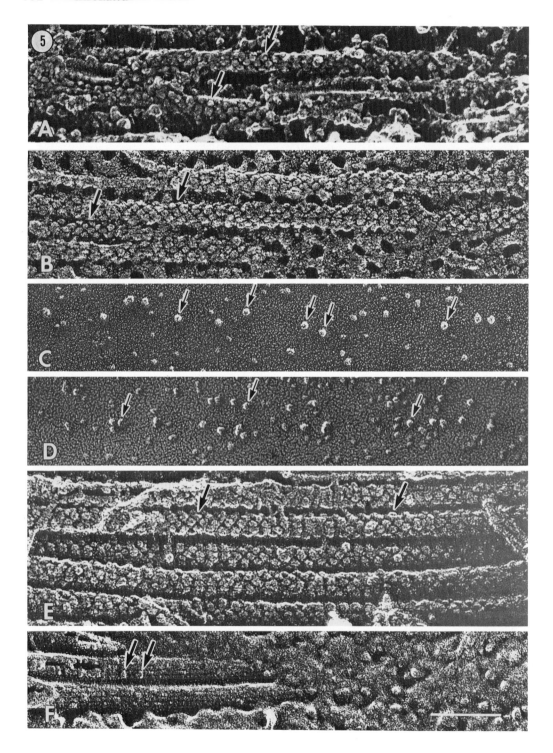

at the spindle equator. This structural con- their plus ends located distal to the pole. Polar microtubules from each pole overlap figuration supports an idea that sliding between antiparallel microtubules could occur when the spindle elongates at anaphase. In this case cross bridges between polar microtubules at the overlapping zone could be motor molecules.

MAPs of the Spindle

Spindle microtubules in at least some species are associated with specialized granular structures. Extensive cross bridges are also present between spindle microtubules. In sea urchin eggs the 75 kDa MAP buttonin covers the surfaces of spindle microtubules, forming a hexagonally packed coat. These structures enhance the polymerization of tubulin, so they may play an important role in spindle formation and in the stabilization of spindle microtubules. The cross bridges between spindle microtubules could be composed in part of high-M_r MAPs.

Cytoplasmic Dynein of Sea Urchin Eggs

A dynein-like molecule from these cells possesses a tadpole form, consisting of a single head and a stem. Based on the immunocytochemical data and the molecular structures visualized by quick-freeze, deep-etch, it is likely that some of the larger granules associated with spindle microtubules are cytoplasmic dynein. This molecule may be involved in force-production for spindle motility, but further study will be necessary to understand its function clearly.

Structure of the Spindle Poles

In the centrosomal region, there are characteristic clusters of granules that could function as microtubule organizing centers.

ACKNOWLEDGMENTS

I thank Dr. S. Hisanaga for allowing me to use some of his figures. I thank Ms. Y. Kawasaki for her secretarial assistance and Mr. Y. Fukuda for his photographic expertise. This work was supported by a Grant in Aid for Scientific Research from the Japanese Ministry of Education.

Fig. 24–5. A: Quick-frozen, deep-etched spindle microtubules in isolated mitotic apparatus. Microtubules are covered with microtubule buttons (arrows) that tend to be packed hexagonally. **B:** Quick-frozen, deep-etched microtubule proteins that were isolated from mitotic spindles and polymerized in vitro. Surfaces of microtubules are decorated with microtubule buttons (arrows). **C,D:** Quick-frozen, deep-etched, low-angle rotary-shadowed buttonin (75 kDa) adsorbed on mica. Most spherical molecules (arrows) are ~9 nm in diameter, while smaller ones also exist. These spherical molecules are similar in shape and size to those on the microtubules polymerized with buttonin (75 KD; E and F) and also to the microtubule buttons observed on spindle microtubules (A) or microtubule proteins polymerized in vitro (B). **E,F:** Quick-frozen, deep-etched microtubules polymerized with buttonin (75 kDa) MAP. In E (75 kDa/tubulin = 1) the entire surface of the microtubules is covered with spherical buttons (~9 nm in diameter) that are packed hexagonally (arrows). In F (75 kDa/tubulin = 1/29), microtubule buttons are observed sporadically on the surfaces of microtubules (arrows). In this case (F), microtubules were polymerized in the presence of taxol (10 μM). Bar = 0.1 μm. (Reproduced from Hirokawa and Hisanaga, 1987, with permission of the publisher.)

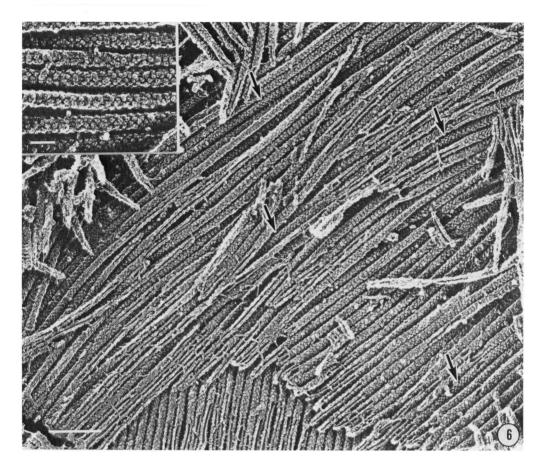

Fig. 24–6. A quick-freeze, deep-etch view of the pellet of porcine brain tubulin polymerized with buttonin (75 kDa) (tubulin/75 kDa = 1). Numerous microtubules are formed. The surfaces of microtubules are mostly covered with round, button-shaped molecules that tend to be packed hexagonally (arrows). Bar = 0.1 μm. **Inset:** A higher magnification of microtubules covered with 75 kDa MAP. Bar 0.1 = μm. (Reproduced from Hirokawa and Hisanaga, 1987, with permission of the publisher.)

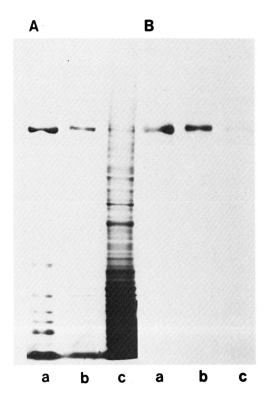

Fig. 24–7. The reaction of a monoclonal antibody against sea urchin flagellar 21S dynein (D57) with cytoplasmic and flagellar dyneins. An SDS-polyacrylamide gel **(A)** and its immunoblot **(B)** were prepared by means of *Hemicentrotus pulcherrimus* sperm flagellar 21S dynein **(a)**, purified cytoplasmic dynein **(b)**, and a crude extract of unfertilized sea urchin eggs **(c)**. Electrophoresis was performed on a 3–7.5% polyacrylamide gradient gel. B is the autoradiogram showing the binding of D57 to flagellar and cytoplasmic dynein heavy chains. (Reproduced from Hisanaga et al., 1987, with permission of the publisher.)

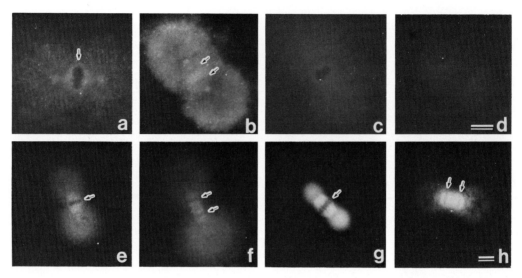

Fig. 24–8. Indirect immunofluorescent staining of isolated mitotic apparatus. Mitotic apparatus isolated from prometaphase **(a,c)** metaphase **(d)**, and anaphase **(b)** sea urchin eggs of H. pulcherrimus and those from metaphase **(e)**, early-anaphase **(g)**, and midanaphase **(f,h)** eggs of *P. depressus* are shown. Mitotic apparatuses in a, b, e, and f were stained with D57; that in c with D57 absorbed with H. pulcherrimus sperm axonemes; that in d with P3U1 culture medium, and those in g and h with antitubulin. Astral regions of anaphase mitotic apparatus (h) were largely removed during the immunofluorescent procedure. Arrows indicate chromosomes. Bar = 10 μm. (Reproduced from Hisanaga et al., 1987, with permission of the publisher.)

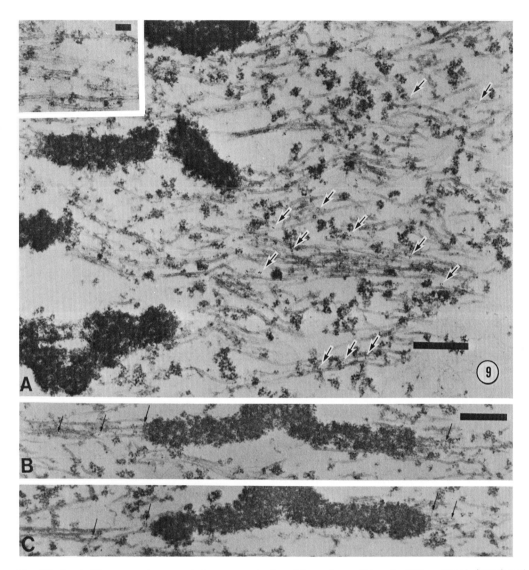

Fig. 24–9. A: Electron microscopic immunocytochemistry using antidynein ATPase McAb (D57) and gold-labeled antimouse IgG. Gold particles (5 nm in diameter) tend to be localized close to the spindle microtubules in the early anaphase. Bar = 0.5 μm; ×38,000 **Inset:** Higher magnification. Bar = 0.1 μm. **B,C:** Semiserial sections showing a chromosome and kinetochore microtubules in early anaphase stained with D57. Gold particles are associated with kinetochore microtubules (arrows). Bar 0.5 = μm. (Reproduced from Hirokawa et al., 1985b, with permission of the publisher.)

Fig. 24–10. SDS-polyacrylamide gel electrophoresis of egg cytoplasmic dynein. **(a)** and flagellar 21S dynein **(b)**. Dyneins were electrophoresed according to the method of Laemmli (1970) using 5% polyacrylamide gel. Dynein heavy chains are indicated by the arrowhead. (Reproduced from Hisanaga and Hirokawa, 1987, with permission of the publisher.)

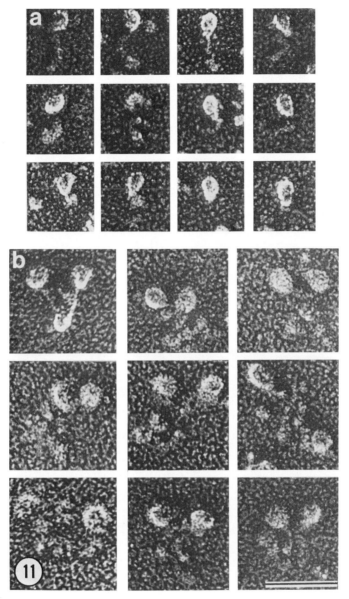

Fig. 24–11. Representative molecules of single-headed cytoplasmic dynein **(a)** and two-headed flagellar 21S dynein **(b)**. Cytoplasmic dynein are composed of a pear-shaped head and an irregular form of stem. Flagellar 21S dyneins were two-headed molecules joining at the stem domain. Bar = 50 nm. (Reproduced from Hisanaga and Hirokawa, 1987, with permission of the publisher.)

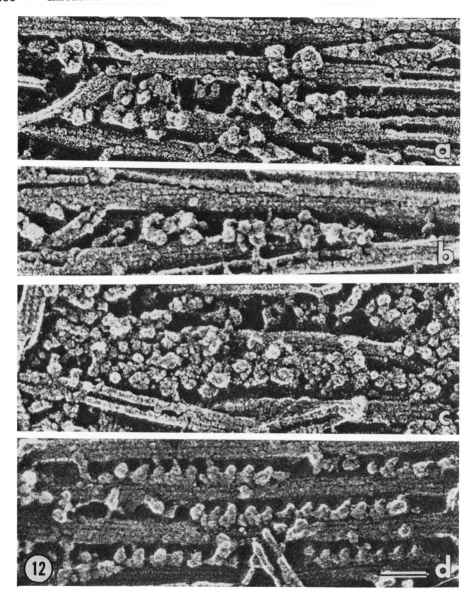

Fig. 24–12. High-magnification views of the binding of dynein to microtubules. Microtubule pellets incubated with cytoplasmic or flagellar 21S dynein were processed for quick freeze, deep etch. **a,b:** The binding of relatively small amounts of cytoplasmic dynein. The predominant form of cytoplasmic dynein bound to microtubules seems to be oligomeric aggregates. **c:** The microtubules fully decorated with dynein particles. **d:** The binding of flagellar 21S dynein (0.22 mg/ml) to microtubules (0.21 mg/ml). Periodic association of 21S dynein is observed clearly. Bar = 50 nm. (Reproduced from Hisanaga and Hirokawa, 1987, with permission of the publisher.)

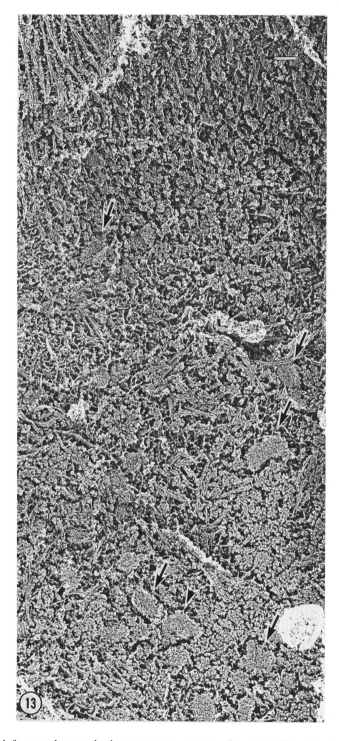

Fig. 24–13. Quick-frozen, deep-etched centrosome region of a sea urchin mitotic spindle. At the upper part of the figure are numerous microtubules emerging from centrosomes. At the lower part the central portion of centrosomes are exposed. Many globular structures 0.2–0.4 μm in diameter, composed of condensed tiny granules (arrows), are observed. Bar = 0.2 μm.

CHAPTER

25

Assembly and Disassembly of Mitotic Spindle Microtubules

J. Richard McIntosh

Department of Molecular, Cellular, and Developmental Biology, University of Colorado, Boulder, Colorado 80309

INTRODUCTION

It has long been recognized that the dynamic nature of the mitotic spindle is intrinsic to its function. The spindle forms as it organizes the chromosomes and disassembles as it accomplishes their segregation. The dynamic properties of the spindle are directly related to the properties of the microtubules (MTs) that comprise it. MT assembly is essential in the formation of the spindle, and further assembly accompanies anaphase spindle elongation. MT disassembly is a concomitant of anaphase chromosome motion to the poles. Further, the well-known lability of spindle MTs, demonstrated by their rapid disappearance in response to various experimental treatments, is in some way necessary for mitotic progression, because spindle action is inhibited by treatments with agents that promote MT stability. For example, glycols (Rebhun et al., 1974) and taxol (for review, see DeBrabander et al., 1986) interfere with tubulin disassembly and prevent normal chromo-

some movement. Mutations that promote MT stability block chromosome segregation (Oakley and Morris, 1981; Ripoll et al., 1985), and some such mutants can be rescued by treatments with drugs that destabilize the spindle (Cabral et al., 1984).

Both published and unpublished information on the assembly and disassembly of MTs during mitosis will be discussed in this chapter. Data on the pathways for MT polymerization and depolymerization will be reviewed, and when possible the relationships between these events and specific aspects of chromosome movement will be described. The factors that may couple MT polymerization and depolymerization to the generation of mitotic forces will also be discussed.

MICROTUBULE ASSEMBLY DURING PROMETAPHASE AND METAPHASE

Morphology of Spindle Microtubule Formation

Microtubules associated with a centrosome. Prophase ends and prometaphase be-

Cell Movement, Volume 2: Kinesin,
Dynein, and Microtubule Dynamics, pages 403–419
© 1989 Alan R. Liss, Inc.

gins when spindle MTs begin to interact with the chromosomes. Mammalian spindle assembly begins with an increase in the number of MTs that each centrosome will initiate (Snyder and McIntosh, 1975). In many cells radially symmetric arrays of MTs begin to grow from the cell's duplicate centrosomes even before the nuclear envelope has broken down (Fig. 25–1A). As the number of MTs in these arrays increases, the average MT length decreases (Fig. 25–1B–D; Saxton et al., 1984; Soltys and Borisy, 1985). Sometimes, however, spindles begin formation with the centrosomes lying too close to form separate asters. These spindles become shaped like small footballs that elongate as the MTs in the region of the spindle grow (Fig. 25–2A–D; McIntosh et al., 1975a,b).

Spindles in many lower eukaryotes grow from centrosomes that are not radially symmetric, e.g., plaque-shaped structures that promote MT growth in a particular direction (for discussions of centrosome diversity, see Heath, 1980; McIntosh, 1983; Mazia, 1984). The resulting spindles often contain a shaft of MTs that runs from plaque to plaque and other MTs that fan out and interact with the chromosomes (for review, see Pickett-Heaps et al., 1982).

The MTs emanating from a centrosome are oriented with their plus (fast-growing) ends distal to the centrosome (Euteneuer and McIntosh, 1981a,b; Haimo and Telzer, 1981), even when the MT array grows from an isolated centrosome (Bergen et al., 1980). We conclude that the centrosome defines the polarity of the MTs it initiates. MTs that grow from a centrosome almost always contain 13 protofilaments, while those that polymerize spontaneously in vitro contain a variable number of protofilaments (Evans et al., 1985), suggesting that the centrosome helps to define the geometry of tubulin assembly as well as the polarity of the resulting MT.

Microtubules associated with kinetochores. Early during prometaphase, MTs can be seen in close association with kinetochores. The geometry of this apposition is variable, including glancing interaction between the lateral surface of an MT and a kinetochore, MTs ending in kinetochores, and everything in between. Such associations occur very early during spindle formation, just as the nuclear envelope begins to disperse or as soon as MTs first appear in the nucleus, so many workers have speculated that kinetochores initiate MTs. Certainly kinetochores can promote MT growth in vitro (Telzer et al., 1975; McGill and Brinkley, 1975; Snyder and McIntosh, 1975), but in most such studies the extent of MT initiation observed is less than that seen with isolated centrosomes, and the arrangement of the resulting kinetochore MTs is less well ordered than that found in cells. Kinetochores can also promote MT growth in vivo when cells are removed from a drug that blocks tubulin assembly and placed under physiological conditions (Witt et al., 1980; DeBrabander et al., 1981a,b). These data are consistent with the hypothesis that kinetochores are MT organizing centers.

Other data are more consistent with the idea that kinetochores become associated with MTs by capturing some of the polymers that are initiated by the centrosomes. The kinetochore-associated MTs formed during normal spindle assembly are oriented with their plus ends proximal to the kinetochore (Euteneuer and McIntosh, 1981a,b; Haimo and Telzer, 1981). This orientation is not

---

Fig. 25–1. Immunolocalizations of tubulin in PtK cells fixed with cold methanol. **A, B:** Prophase, showing the pronounced, aster-like structures that develop when centrosomes are separated before nuclear envelope breakdown. The average MT length seems to shorten as the spindle forms **(C, D),** and the progression of the MTs from approximately radial symmetry to arrangements focused on the chromosomes is evident.

Fig. 25–2. A–D: Preparations as in Figure 25–1. In these cells the centrosomes were close as the spindles began to form, so biradiate symmetry is not seen. Nonetheless, the average MT length shortens, and a normal spindle geometry develops.

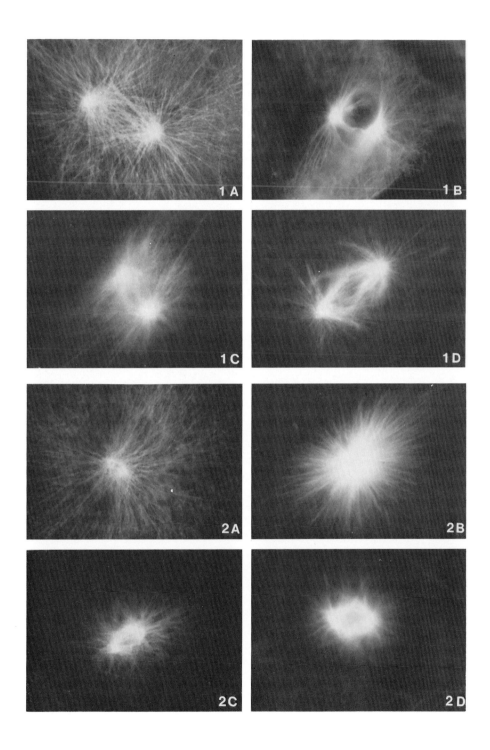

consistent with the idea that kinetochores initiate the MTs to which they become attached, because in all other cases studied the plus end of the MT is distal to the site of its initiation (Euteneuer and McIntosh, 1980, 1981a,b; Euteneuer et al., 1982). Further, during spindle formation in PtK cells that are recovering from a treatment with low temperature, the kinetochore facing a nearby pole attaches to MTs before MTs are seen on the kinetochore facing away from the pole (Rieder and Borisy, 1981). A comparison of the MTs associating with the kinetochores of several chromosomes in the vicinity of one pole suggests that it is not simply proximity to the pole but orientation toward the pole that is significant for kinetochore MT attachment. Further, when sea urchin blastomeres enter mitosis without a centrosome, the chromosomes condense normally but fail to initiate MTs (Sluder and Rieder, 1985). All these facts are consistent with the idea that kinetochores usually become associated with MTs by capturing the plus ends of polymers initiated by the centrosomes.

During normal spindle formation there may be some initiation of MTs at kinetochores. The kinetochore MT bundles of several cell types include short MTs that are kinetochore-associated but are not long enough to reach the pole (e.g., Rieder, 1982; Schibler and Pickett-Heaps, 1987). These might be formed from pole-initiated MTs that break, either under physiological conditions or during preparation for electron microscopy, but they may also be true, kinetochore-initiated MTs. The most recent and thorough study of MT initiation by kinetochores in vitro has shown that MTs do not grow from the well defined plates found on mammalian kinetochores, but from among the fibers of the kinetochore's "corona" (Mitchison and Kirschner, 1985a). The resulting polymers point in almost every direction. Such a tuft of MTs may be transformed by the action of other spindle components into the short but more-ordered MTs that are found in the kinetochore-proximal region of the normal kinetochore fiber.

The function of short kinetochore-associated MTs is obscure; they might even be irrelevant for chromosome movement. Spindle poles in the yeast *Saccharomyces cerevisiae* form connections to the chromosomes with a single MT that appears to run from pole to kinetochore (Peterson and Ris, 1976). Short, kinetochore-associated MTs are therefore not essential for mitosis.

Kinetochore microtubule formation in spindles without structured poles. Kinetochore fibers in the green alga *Oedogonium* contain about 40 MTs, many of which are short and none of which connects with an identifiable structure at the spindle pole (Schibler and Pickett-Heaps, 1987). In this spindle, and in those of all higher plants, there is no well defined pole, so it is not obvious that any MTs run all the way from the pole to a kinetochore at metaphase. Detailed descriptions of spindle formation in such cells suggest, however, that the process of kinetochore fiber formation may be no different in these cells from that in cells with structured poles. The forming spindle in endosperm cells of *Haemanthus katherinae* begins as a sheaf of MTs surrounding the nucleus (for review, see Bajer and Mole-Bajer, 1972). As the nuclear envelope disperses, there is significant initiation of new MTs from two regions that lie on opposite sides of the nucleus, presumably the incipient poles of the spindle (DeMey et al., 1982). Thus the spindles of higher plants behave much like those of animals and lower plants, even though they lack visible structures to mark them. Probably all spindles form connections with chromosomes in essentially the same way, though structural evidence suggests at least subtle variations among the lower eukaryotes (for review, see Heath, 1980).

The predominant path for attachment of chromosomes to the spindle begins with the initiation of many MTs from two foci in the cytoplasm. These MTs grow into the region occupied by the chromosomes, where a subset of them interacts with kinetochores and becomes bound. On current evidence we are inclined to believe that MTs initiated

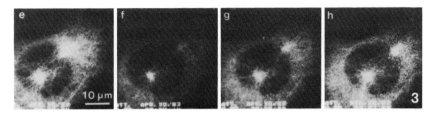

Fig. 25–3. Fluorescence redistribution after photobleaching in a PtK cell microinjected with fluorescent tubulin during interphase and then allowed to equilibrate for about 1 hr. **e:** Two astral arrays are visible in the prophase cell. **f:** Prior photobleaching leaves the cell darker, and the fluorescence in one aster is essentially eliminated. **g,h:** Subsequent fluorescence redistribution is approximately uniform over the aster, suggesting plus end exchange of tubulin subunits. (Reproduced from Saxton et al., 1984, with permission of the publisher.)

at the kinetochore play no significant role in subsequent chromosome movements.

The Pathways Of Spindle Microtubule Assembly

Control of microtubule initiation. The factors that regulate the initiation of spindle MTs by the centrosome are just beginning to be understood. There is a change in the extent of phosphorylation of one or more protein components in the centrosome as the cell goes into mitosis (Vandre et al., 1984). A monoclonal antibody that recognizes these sites of protein phosphorylation will block the initiation of MTs by isolated centrosomes, suggesting a direct relationship between this post-translational modification and the observed increase in the number of MTs initiated (Centouze et al., 1986).

Sites of microtubule subunit addition. MTs growing from interphase centrosomes add subunits at their centrosome-distal ends, both in vitro (Heidemann et al., 1980) and in vivo (Schulze and Kirschner, 1985; Soltys and Borisy, 1985). The site of MT subunit addition during prometaphase has not been determined directly, but it too is probably at the pole-distal ends of the polymers. When fluorescent tubulin is microinjected into living cells, allowed to equilibrate with the pool of endogenous tubulin, then analyzed by laser photobleaching of a small region of the cell's MTs, the geometry of fluorescence redistribution after photobleaching shows

tubulin fluorescence coming back uniformly over the extent of the aster (Saxton et al., 1984). There is not a centrosomal focus of recovery that spreads outward from the center, as one would expect from a pole-proximal addition of MT subunits (Fig. 25–3).

Rates of microtubule assembly. Organized arrays of MTs are visible in vivo with polarization optics. Spindle length as a function of time is probably a direct measure of the rate of growth in the component MTs. Such data from cultured newt cells suggest that spindle MTs elongate at about 1.4 μm/min at 25°C (Taylor, 1959). Comparable rates have been found in diverse types of cells.

PROMETAPHASE AND METAPHASE MICROTUBULE TURNOVER

Spindle microtubules turn over fast.

Three lines of evidence support the assertion that spindle MTs in prometaphase and metaphase turn over surprisingly rapidly. 1) When mitotic cells are subjected to a rapid increase in the cytoplasmic concentration of colchicine or nocodazole, spindle birefringence decreases with a half-time of about 7 sec. These drugs bind well to soluble tubulin but poorly to MTs. The results therefore imply that inactivation of the soluble tubulin pool by drug binding leads to the rapid dissolution of existing polymer (Salmon et al., 1984a). 2) When labeled tubulin is injected into a mitotic cell, the label is visibly incorporated into the spindle within seconds. The process reaches an apparent steady state in less than 1 min (Wadsworth and Sloboda, 1983; Salmon et al., 1984b; Saxton et al., 1984; Mitchison et al., 1986). 3) When fluorescent tubulin is injected into mitotic cells and allowed to equilibrate with the endogenous pool, tubulin turnover in the resulting fluorescent spindle can be studied by following the rate of fluorescence redistribution after photobleaching (FRAP). Half-times for spindle FRAP under physiological conditions are between 15 and 30 sec, suggesting that the spindle MT assembly steady state is highly dynamic (Salmon et al., 1984b; Saxton et al., 1984). Taken together, these data suggest that a spindle at metaphase exists as a balance of rapidly disassembling and reassembling MTs. The turnover of MTs in cultured cells during interphase, however, is about 10 times slower (Saxton et al., 1984).

Pathways for spindle microtubule turnover. Spindle MT turnover is so fast that some of the conventional ideas about protein polymer assembly must be set aside. For example, assuming diffusion-limited rate constants for tubulin disassembly kinetics, a 20-sec turnover half-time by an end exchange mechanism (for review, see Oosawa and Asakura, 1975) would require MTs to be no longer than 0.2 μm (~325 tubulin dimers). There are not many measurements of MT lengths in spindles, but in an early anaphase spindle of *Dictyostelium* (~3 μm pole to pole) the mean MT length is about 1.4 μm (McIntosh et al., 1985). The mean length of a sample of 145 MTs from the 10-μm PtK spindle at metaphase was 2.3 ± 1.4 μm (McIntosh and Vigers, 1987). Apparently MT turnover by end exchange of subunits cannot account for the speed of spindle tubulin FRAP.

Two other plausible mechanisms for spindle tubulin exchange may be excluded with current evidence. A "treadmilling mechanism," based on subunit addition at one MT end and loss at the other (Margolis et al.,

1978), makes the strong prediction that a zone of bleached fluorescence should move as it recovers, but bleached zones recover without movement (Fig. 25–4; Wadsworth and Salmon, 1986a). Treadmilling is therefore not the mechanism of fast tubulin turnover. The observation that microinjected tubulin adds only to the pole-distal ends of centrosome-associated MTs in interphase (see "Sites of Microtubule Subunit Addition," above) suggests that tubulin does not exchange at an appreciable rate with the subunits in the body of an MT; thus "wall exchange" of subunits is not likely to be a pathway for fast tubulin turnover.

The most plausible explanation for fast turnover of spindle MTs is the polymerization mechanism called *dynamic instability.* MTs formed from *pure* tubulin can exist in two states: one favoring assembly and the other disassembly (Carlier et al., 1984). In the assembly state the rate of MT growth is slow compared with the rate for MT shortening during disassembly. At steady state, therefore, most of the MTs are growing while a few are rapidly shortening and occasionally disappearing all together (Mitchison and Kirschner, 1984b). The plus end of an MT is faster than the minus end at both assembly–disassembly and at transitions back and forth between the two states (Horio and Hotani, 1986). In this context, the centrosome-associated MTs of mitosis are thought to be in a highly dynamic state, growing and rapidly disassembling in sequence. Data describing centrosome behavior in vitro predicts that as many as 1,000 new MTs form each minute from one mammalian centrosome (Mitchison and Kirschner, 1984a); thus no MT subunit is far from an end for very long, and the rapid turnover of tubulin is explained (Kirschner and Mitchison, 1986).

A concern about this interpretation of fast MT turnover is that the addition of brain MT-associated proteins (MAPs) to a tubulin assembly mixture reduces the rates of transition between states of assembly and disassembly (Horio and Hotani, 1986). Spindle MTs are known to be decorated with MAPs

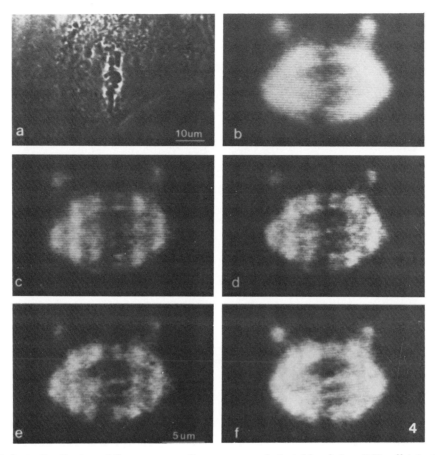

Fig. 25–4. Redistribution of fluorescence after a patterned photobleach in a PtK cell injected with fluorescent tubulin during early prometaphase. **a:** The cell in phase. **b:** The cell in fluorescence optics before bleaching. The two fluorescent dots beside the spindle are ectopic poles. The cell was then bleached for 100 msec with the beam from an argon ion laser passed through a Ronchi ruling and imaged on the cell. **c–f:** Images were taken 3, 27, 47, and 283 sec after photobleaching. Redistribution of fluorescence occurs without motion of the bleach marks. (Unpublished micrographs, courtesy of W. M. Saxton.)

(for review, see Vallee et al., 1984; Sloboda, Chapter 12), and spindle MAPs might slow dynamic instability to the point that it could no longer account for the fast turnover of the spindle MTs. The turnover rates for two MAPs in the spindle have, however, been measured (Olmsted et al., 1988). They show half-times for FRAP of about 20 sec at 37°C, within experimental uncertainty of the rate for tubulin turnover. While at first sight this result would appear to be trivial (of course proteins bound to MTs must turn over as fast as the MTs themselves), an additional result makes the finding interesting. At 25°C, about one-half of the metaphase spindle tubulin turns over very slowly, while MAPs continue to turn over with a half-time of about 20 sec. MAPs in interphase turn over with a half-time of about 75 sec, faster than interphase tubulin but significantly slower than the MAPs of mitosis. Apparently the cell changes the character of the tubulin–MAP bond between interphase and mitosis, so mitotic MTs exchange MAPs about four times as fast as do interphase MTs. This change may go in parallel with a change in the MAP–MT interaction that makes mitotic MAPs less able to suppress the assembly-to-disassembly transitions than are the interphase brain MAPs in vitro. The modifications of MAPs or of tubulin that effect this change are not yet known, but they may well include phosphorylation, given that such post-translational modifications are rife at mitosis onset (Vandre et al., 1984) and that phosphorylation of brain MAPs has been shown to reduce their interaction with tubulin (Jameson et al., 1980).

RESTRUCTURING THE SPINDLE DURING PROMETAPHASE

Microtubule Rearrangements During Spindle Formation

Transformation from a bi-astral to a spindle-shaped morphology. Although many spindles begin as two astral arrays, their structures change as the MTs interact with the chromosomes. The MTs that grow out from one centrosome but point away from the second centrosome (astral MTs) generally shorten, while those that grow toward the chromosomes elongate and/or become more numerous (Figs. 25–1, 25–2). The major exceptions to this generalization are spindles in the blastomeres of early embryos, which appear to contain sufficient tubulin to maintain large asters as the spindle forms. The normal change in MT length distribution may be due to a stabilizing influence of the chromosomes on the MTs initiated by centrosomes (Salmon, 1975). Certainly the detachment of a chromosome from its fiber destabilizes that fiber (Nicklas and Kubai, 1985) and the removal of chromosomes from a spindle decreases the number of MTs it contains (Nicklas and Gordon, 1985). MTs without kinetochore-mediated stabilization may therefore undergo the frequent transitions from assembling to disassembling states that are characteristic of dynamic instability (Kirschner and Mitchison, 1986). Consequently they have a higher probability of disappearing than do kinetochore-associated MTs.

The idea of spindle restructuring by kinetochore-mediated MT stabilization predicts that the number of nonkinetochore MTs per cross-sectional area in the region between the two centrosomes should be the same as that in an aster; only the MTs that are actually associated with kinetochores should be stabilized. No data are available to provide a rigorous test of this prediction, because the number of kinetochore and aster MTs is imperfectly known in most spindles. Nonetheless, immunofluorescence studies of late prometaphase and metaphase spindles provide an overview of the density of MTs, and these do not appear to confirm the prediction (Fig. 25–5). One has the clear impression that some other factor is important in the change from an essentially biradial geometry to the spindle morphology most commonly seen.

An analogous effect is observed in the spindles that form from nearby centrosomes and never pass through the astral stage. In such spindles almost all the MTs that form lie between the two separating centrosomes (Fig. 25–2B, C). One way to account for these morphologies within the context of the idea that kinetochores stabilize MTs is to suppose that kinetochores may exchange the MTs with which they associate. The stabilizing influence of a kinetochore would then be spread over many MTs but would be less marked for any one subset of MTs. Another possibility is that some nonkinetochore factor, such as MT cross bridging, can contribute stability to the MTs that lie in the region between the spindle poles.

Spindle formation without radially symmetric centrosomes. Spindles in the cells of many lower eukaryotes form from two closely positioned centrosomes. No asters develop, in part because the centrosomal MTs begin to interact with chromosomes shortly after their initiation and in part because the centrosomes themselves are not radially symmetric and bias the directions in which MTs are initiated. In such spindles (e.g., those of diatoms, as reviewed by Pickett-Heaps and Tippit

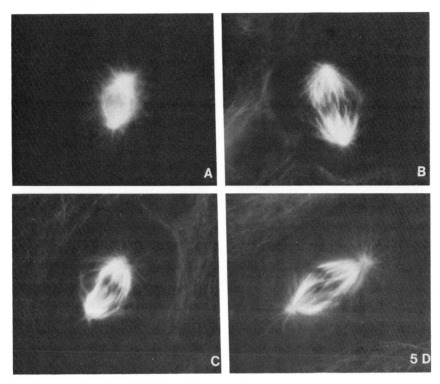

Fig. 25–5. A–D: PtK cells in late prometaphase and metaphase visualized by indirect immunofluorescence with antitubulin. While some astral MTs are seen, their numbers appear to be fewer than the numbers of nonkinetochore MTs in the body of the spindle proper.

[1978]) a shaft of MTs forms between the two centrosomes. This "central spindle" is often very stable and can be isolated without special precautions to stabilize it, even though the MTs that comprise it do not interact with the chromosomes at all (for review, see Cande, Chapter 28). In these spindles it looks as if the interaction between MTs from opposite poles conveys stability to MTs, perhaps even more strongly than does interaction with kinetochores.

Stabilization of nonkinetochore MTs during spindle formation. The factors that impart stability to the nonkinetochore MTs are not yet known with any certainty. It is suggestive, however, that analyses of near-neighbor MT arrangements in the zones where MTs from the two poles interdigitate have shown that the MTs from one pole prefer neighbors from the opposite pole.

Such antiparallel near-neighbors usually lie at a well defined spacing (for a diatom, McDonald et al., 1979; for another alga, Tippit et al., 1983; for a cellular slime mold, McIntosh et al., 1985). These data constitute morphological evidence for a binding between antiparallel spindle MTs. One occasionally sees structurally defined bridges between interdigitating spindle MTs, but the only evidence for true periodic links between MTs in a central spindle has come from the hypermastigote flagellate *Barbulanympha* (Inoué and Ritter, 1975).

The zone of MT interdigitation in most spindles contains a structureless, osmiophilic matrix (e.g., Buck and Tisdale, 1962; McIntosh and Landis, 1971). The matrix is generally found where MTs from opposite poles interdigitate, so it is plausible that the matrix binds specifically to antiparallel MTs and functions to link them into a mechanically continuous framework capable of holding the ends of the spindle apart.

The interpolar MT bundle from mammalian cells in late anaphase and telophase is markedly stable, as measured by its resistance to hydrostatic pressure (for review, see Salmon, 1975) and its slow tubulin FRAP (Saxton and McIntosh, 1987). Such MT bundles have been isolated and subjected to preliminary biochemical analysis (Mullins and McIntosh, 1982). Recently a component of the matrix from isolated spindles was identified by its reaction with a monoclonal antibody (Sellito and Kuriyama, 1988). This antibody recognizes polypeptides of about 95 and 105 kDa on one-dimensional sodium dodecyl sulfate (SDS) gels. Immunolocalization of the corresponding antigen shows that it appears in the vicinity of the spindle equator during prometaphase when the spindle is taking shape. It persists as a fairly broad band near the metaphase plate until after anaphase onset. The antigen is localized only in regions where there are many interdigitating MTs, but there is as yet no chemical information about whether the protein can serve as part of a system for cross linking antiparallel MTs.

The inter-MT matrix may have an impact on the dynamic instability of the MTs it swathes. Certainly there are numerous MAPs that promote MT stability by binding to their surfaces in vitro (for review, see Sloboda, Chapter 12). It is plausible that the matrix confers upon the interdigitating spindle MTs a comparable assembly advantage. If the matrix has the property that it will bind only to those MTs that have an antiparallel neighbor, then it could contribute to the tendency of interdigitating MTs to be more stable than astral MTs. In any case, the spindle geometry that evolves during prometaphase is probably the result of several factors: MT initiation from the centrosomes, centrosome geometry, MT interaction with kinetochores, and MT–MT interaction where the fibers from the two poles meet.

Prometaphase Chromosome Congression to the Spindle Equator

Chromosome congression involves microtubule assembly and disassembly. Chromosome congression is treated elsewhere in this volume (see review by McIntosh, Chapter 23, and Salmon, Chapter 27, and Mitchison, Chapter 26). In the context of MT assembly, the important question is how chromosomes can move toward and away from the spindle equator while they are attached to both poles. Clearly one kinetochore fiber must shorten while the other elongates. Evidence reviewed in Chapter 23 shows that a prometaphase chromosome's behavior is likely to be defined by a balance of forces: A chromosome positioned nearer to one pole than to the other experiences a net force away from the nearby pole. In response, the chromosome moves toward the distant pole, accompanied by an elongation of the fiber running to the near pole and a shortening of the sister fiber. Such behavior is also seen in response to exogenous forces exerted by a microneedle pulling on a chromosome (Nicklas, 1977). How then is the length of kinetochore fibers regulated so one will elongate while its sister shortens in response to the forces that move the chromosome?

Coupling of mitotic forces and microtubule assembly. The most economical model for prometaphase congression posits a direct coupling between the forces that move a chromosome and the polymerization/depolymerization of kinetochore fibers. This is an old idea (McIntosh et al., 1969), one that has been formulated quantitatively (Hill and Kirschner, 1982) and one for which there is some evidence (Hays, 1985). By such an hypothesis, the force that pulls a chromosome closer to a pole compresses the fiber between the chromosome and that pole, destabilizing it and inducing it to depolymerize. The force that pulls the chromosome toward the opposite pole increases the stability of the chromosomal fiber running to the first pole and induces it to elongate. Such words relate force to polymerization in a formal way, but now the fun begins. Where are subunits added to and lost from kinetochore fibers? How are the forces for moving the chromosomes generated? What is the nature of the coupling between force and the tubulin–MT equilibrium? Mitchison (Chapter 26) enumerates several possible solutions to these problems. Here I will point out only that there is now convincing evidence that tubulin adds to kinetochore MTs at or near the chromosome (for review, see McIntosh, Chapter 23). It is less clear, however, where subunits are lost from the same polymers. The answer to this question will help greatly to clarify the mechanism for chromosome congression.

Relationship between microtubule behavior and chromosome congression. The motion of the chromosomes to the spindle equator is a kind of flow. Because MTs are essential for this motion it is of interest to ask whether spindle MTs flow with the chromosomes. Prometaphase MT motions have been studied by tubulin FRAP, and the static behavior of lines bleached across the MTs between chromosomes and poles suggests that the MTs are at rest while the chromosomes move (Wadsworth and Salmon, 1986a). The recovery of fluorescence is so fast, however, that comparatively little time is available in which to follow MT movements. Further, it is not clear at present whether all the MTs in the spindle are behaving in the same way. Electron microscope studies show that as many as one-third, but probably at least one-fourth, of the spindle's MTs in PtK cells are kinetochore associated (McIntosh et al., 1975a,b). Wadsworth and Salmon (1986b) have found a slow component in tubulin FRAP that they interpret as a reflection of kinetochore MT behavior. Their results are consistent with the idea that kinetochore MTs are more stable than other spindle MTs at metaphase.

Spindle MT behavior has also been studied by irradiation with microbeams of ultraviolet light. Brief irradiation with 260-nm light induces local MT disassembly and hence the formation of an "area of reduced birefringence" (ARB). These spindle lesions have

been used as probes for the behavior of spindle MTs. Forer (1965) showed that ARBs made on the spindle fibers of crane fly spermatocytes would migrate slowly to the pole during metaphase, suggesting that the spindle fibers are continuously moving toward the poles. This result is consistent with the results from labeled tubulin injection (e.g., Mitchison, Chapter 26). On the other hand, Leslie and Pickett-Heaps (1983) made ARBs on the central spindles of diatoms; these did not migrate toward the poles. The pole-proximal edge of the lesion moved poleward, as if the plus ends generated by the irradiation were unstable, but the pole-distal (or minus) edge of the ARB stayed put. The behavior of ARBs in spermatocytes has been interpreted as evidence for pole-directed forces acting on the kinetochore MTs and consequently on the kinetochores. It is, however, impossible on current evidence to say for sure what these experiments mean, because one cannot say whether the motion of an ARB is a reflection of MT assembly and disassembly or of MT translocation.

A unified hypothesis for prometaphase spindle fiber behavior. These disparate observations may be assembled into a self-consistent set of ideas. From the behavior of astral MTs during all stages of mitosis, we suppose that MTs that grow from a pole and have their plus ends free are continuously displaying dynamic instability. Such MTs are the most numerous kind of MTs in many spindles and may account for the observations demonstrating fast turnover of spindle MTs. The association of a kinetochore with the plus end of a subset of these MTs may confer a degree of stability on particular polymers, though the MTs bound to kinetochores may exchange, so no specific subset of the spindle MTs is uniquely stabilized (McIntosh and Vigers, 1987). Nonetheless, some kinetochore MTs may now survive long enough to reveal the slow action of an MT-dependent motor, such as kinesin, that may be pulling the spindle MTs toward the poles, forcing them to lose subunits there (McIntosh, Chapter 23). This slow motion could account for the pole-directed forces acting on prometaphase chromosomes, and if the MT-associated motor extends a significant distance into the spindle, it could explain the position dependence of the pole-directed forces. It would also account for the pole-directed movement of ARBs, a phenomenon not seen with tubulin FRAP because the fast turnover of nonkinetochore MTs may mask slow kinetochore fiber treadmilling in the cell types studied so far. Polarization optics yields a stronger signal from MTs that are bundled together, so it would naturally enhance the visibility of kinetochore MTs, and the ARBs in spermatocytes would therefore emphasize the behavior of kinetochore MTs. The behavior of ARBs in diatoms would naturally be different from that in spermatocytes because the MTs studied are from the central spindle and therefore have different properties.

RESTRUCTURING OF THE SPINDLE DURING ANAPHASE

Microtubule Disassembly as Chromosomes Approach the Poles: Anaphase A

Morphology of anaphase microtubule disassembly. During early anaphase, kinetochore MTs disassemble as the chromosomes approach the poles (anaphase A). The rates of normal chromosome movement range from about 0.5 to 5 μm/min, depending on the organism, but in all cases studied, chromosome speed during anaphase is less than that of prometaphase (Rickards, 1975). During anaphase A, chromosome velocity is a direct reflection of the rate of MT disassembly. A chromosome's speed is independent of its proximity to the pole, so spindle MTs shorten at a rate that is independent of their length. Anaphase velocity is independent of chromosome size (Nicklas, 1965), but strongly dependent on temperature; the warmer an insect spermatocyte, the faster its chromosomes move (Ris, 1949; Nicklas, 1979). This is a significant property of anaphase, because elevated temperatures pro-

mote MT stability, and one might think that anaphase A should be slower in warmer cells. When a temperature gradient is established between the poles of a spindle, both sets of chromosomes move at about the same speed: the average of the values expected from the temperatures at the two poles (Nicklas, 1979).

Structural studies of spindles during anaphase demonstrate that many of the spindle MTs disassemble, not just the MTs associated with the kinetochores. In an alga (Tippit et al., 1980a,b), a fungus (Tippit et al., 1984), and a cellular slime mold (McIntosh et al., 1985), three-dimensional reconstructions show that most spindle MTs shorten as anaphase proceeds. Since many MTs are short at anaphase onset, many disappear as anaphase proceeds, and the total spindle MT number decreases. The only MTs excepted are those that interdigitate with counterparts from the opposite pole, as discussed below.

The sites of MT subunit loss may now be inferred from four lines of evidence (McIntosh, Chapter 23); tubulin disassembles at or near kinetichores and probably also at the free ends of the nonkinetochore MTs that are not interdigitating with polymers from the opposite pole. Some loss of subunits at the spindle poles is not excluded by the evidence, but the bulk of MT shortening seems to result from disassembly at the plus ends.

Regulation of anaphase microtubule disassembly. The onset of anaphase appears to be initiated by a pancellular trigger that in at least some cells is independent of the presence of the spindle. In mitotic endosperm blocked with colchicine, all chromosomes separate synchronously into chromatids, even though the lack of a spindle prevents subsequent organized movements of the sisters (for review, see Bajer and Mole-Bajer, 1972). Several lines of evidence suggest that a transient increase in the concentration of free cytosolic calcium is a component of this mitotic trigger. 1) Injection of micromolar calcium induced precocious anaphase onset (Izant, 1983). 2) Injection of calcium chelators to keep cytosolic calcium at a pCa below about 7 retards the onset of anaphase (Izant, 1983). 3) Observations using fluorescent reporters for the concentration of free calcium reveal a transient calcium concentration increase just prior to anaphase onset (Wolniack and Hepler, 1980; Poenie et al., 1986).

Chromatid separation is probably coupled to this calcium transient, but the mechanism is only just beginning to be understood. The "inner centromere protein" sticks strongly to chromosomes throughout metaphase, binding near the centromere where sister chromatids touch (Cooke et al., 1988). This protein loses its tight binding to chromosomes as the chromatids separate at anaphase onset, whereupon it becomes localized near the midregion of the spindle between the separating chromosomes. Calpain 2, a calcium-activated protease, has also been localized on metaphase chromosomes (Schollmeyer, 1988). It too moves to the midregion of the spindle after the onset of anaphase. A plausible model for anaphase onset is that the calcium concentration transient activates calpain 2, which cleaves the inner centromere protein, releasing it from the chromosomes and allowing the separation of chromatids.

Calcium may have other roles in the regulation of chromosome movement. The metaphase spindle contains a significant concentration of calmodulin (Welsh et al., 1979; DeMey et al., 1980). It is bound to the MTs between chromosomes and poles in a calcium-independent manner (Zavortink et al., 1983). Fluorescent calmodulin has been injected into living cells and its turnover measured by FRAP (Stemple et al., 1988). It behaves indistinguishably from the MAPs that have been studied (Olmsted et al., 1988). The calcium concentration transient at anaphase onset may form Ca^{2+}-calmodulin and affect numerous mitotic processes, such as MT disassembly or the activity of a mitotic motor.

A different reporter for calcium, arsinazo III, has been used to study free calcium levels in mitotic cells from plant stamen hairs. Here there is a slow, continual rise in free calcium throughout anaphase (Hepler and Callahan, 1987). Given the ability of injected calcium-calmodulin to destabilize MTs in interphase cells (Keith et al., 1983), Ca^{2+}-calmodulin in the spindle may control MT stability during anaphase A.

An additional factor in MT behavior during anaphase A is the loss of the force balance that acts on chromosomes until the end of metaphase. When the chromatids separate, the forces that caused chromosome congression to the spindle equator are no longer coupled at the centromere, and each chromatid is free to respond by itself. The motions of anaphase A, including the disassembly of the kinetochore MTs, may in part result from this change. For example, the tendency of the kinetochore to dissolve the MTs to which it is attached may have been inhibited during metaphase by the balance of tensions on the sister chromatids. After anaphase onset, this tendency may show up as anaphase A. The poleward treadmilling of kinetochore MTs that seems to occur throughout prometaphase may be dwarfed by the new activity at the pole-distal ends of the MTs.

Microtubule Assembly as the Spindle Elongates: Anaphase B

Some spindle microtubules are stable during anaphase. While most spindle MTs are disassembling and the chromosomes are approaching the poles, some MTs remain stable. These form bundles that continue to span the distance from pole to pole while the rest of the spindle dissolves (Fig. 25–6). The MTs that comprise these bundles are pole-associated polymers that interdigitate with neighbors from the opposite pole. This situation pertains not only in the small, well ordered spindles that have been studied rigorously by electron microscopy (see "Relationship Between Microtubule Behavior and Chromosome Congression," above) but also in the spindles of lily endosperm (Euteneuer et al., 1982), of mammalian cells (McIntosh and Euteneuer, 1984), and presumably of other eukaryotes as well. The

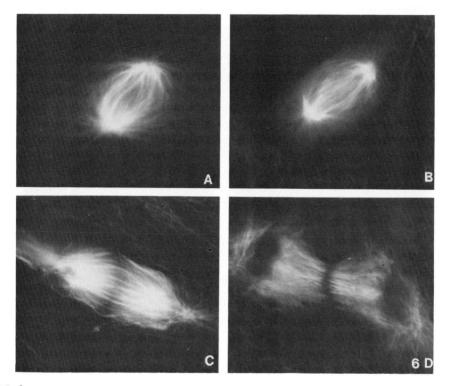

Fig. 25–6. PtK cells in late anaphase and telophase visualized by indirect immunofluorescence with antitubulin. **A–C:** The chromosomes are near the poles. Many of the MTs have shortened, but the bundles of MTs that span the space between the separating chromosomes are evident. **C, D:** There is a less-stained region at the middle of the interchromosomal zone. The lack of staining here is probably due to the masking of tubulin epitopes by the matrix material that pervades this region. Certainly EM shows that MTs run through the region. The bundles of interpolar MTs probably help to keep the spindle poles apart.

extent to which these MTs overlap is highly variable, because their individual lengths are polydisperse (for review, see McIntosh, 1985). Generally, the places where MTs interdigitate are marked by the electron-dense matrix discussed above (see "Stabilization of Nonkinetochore MTs During Spindle Formation," above).

Functions of the stable MTs of anaphase. The stability of these "interpolar MTs" is probably significant for maintaining the space between the poles as the anaphase chromosomes move. Certainly the spindle can exert a significant force on a chromosome, and some aspect of cell structure must support this force to prevent the motion of the poles toward the chromosomes

rather than the other way round. A reasonable range of evidence (for review, see McIntosh, 1985) suggests that the spindle is mechanically autonomous, so one cannot look beyond the poles for this counterforce. The role of supporting the spindle's force-generating system and providing the framework upon which the chromosomes can move apart is probably one of the major functions of the MTs that are stable during anaphase.

A similar role for the stable anaphase MTs is probably important in cells, like those of higher plants, that lack structured poles. A spindle pole is really more a location than a structure: It is the region at each end of the spindle toward which chromosomes move in anaphase. Some cells have visible centrosomes at their poles, and others do not. Nonetheless, during anaphase the chromosomes approach the ends of the spindle, and these ends move apart as the spindle elongates. For the interpolar MT bundles to play a supporting role in spindles without structured poles, they must be coupled to the kinetochore-associated MTs at or near the spindle ends. Such coupling could be provided by bridges between MTs. Indeed, the MTs of the interpolar bundles fan out in the region between chromosomes and poles and commingle with the MTs of the kinetochore bundles (Bajer and Mole-Bajer, 1975; Jensen, 1982), and bridges have been detected between these two classes of MTs (Hepler et al., 1970; Jensen, 1982). The supporting function of the interpolar bundles can therefore be achieved regardless of whether there is a structured pole at the spindle's ends.

The stable spindle microtubules usually elongate during anaphase. Anaphase spindle elongation (anaphase B) generally follows or comes near the end of anaphase A (for review, see Inoué, 1981). In some cells, anaphase B comprises as much as a sixfold elongation of the spindle (e.g., the micronuclei of ciliates; LaFountain and Davison, 1980), so there must be accompanying MT assembly. In other cases, anaphase B is brief and yields only a 10–20% increase in the pole-to-pole distance (e.g., the diatom *Fragilaria*; Tippit et al., 1978). Here more careful examination is required to determine whether MT polymerization or MT movements accompany anaphase B. The results from three-dimensional reconstructions of spindles at various stages of anaphase suggest that the latter kind of anaphase is accomplished with no change in MT length; it is simply a sliding apart of the interdigitating MTs of the interpolar bundle (for review, see Pickett-Heaps and Tippit, 1978). In other diatoms, however, direct measure of MT lengths by electron microscopy (McIntosh et al., 1979) or by immunofluorescence (Masuda and Cande, 1987; for review, see Cande, Chapter 28) shows that the MTs of the interpolar bundle elongate during anaphase

B, even when there is also a sliding of the interdigitating MTs. Anaphase B in most cells probably includes two processes: MT translocation and MT elongation.

Spindle MTs that elongate during anaphase B add subunits at their pole-distal ends and contribute to spindle elongation. Four lines of evidence suggest that the spindle MTs that elongate during anaphase B do so by subunit addition at their plus ends. 1) Fine structural studies of *Dictyostelium* spindles during anaphase B shows that the pole-distal ends of the interdigitating MTs are uneven because some protofilaments extend farther than others (McIntosh et al., 1985). While this morphology could be the result of either assembly or disassembly, the MTs with uneven ends are the ones that elongate, while the MTs that shorten show the usual blunt-end morphology. MT end structure therefore suggests that the plus ends that interdigitate are actively adding subunits during spindle elongation. 2) In some diatoms the interdigitating MTs elongate as they slide, as described above. Diatom spindle elongation in vitro can be augmented by the addition of exogenous tubulin and ATP to the reaction mixture (for review, see Cande, Chapter 28). When the exogenous tubulin is labeled, it is seen to incorporate at the midzone of the spindle, suggesting that normal diatom spindle elongation includes plus end tubulin assembly in association with MT sliding (Masuda and Cande, 1987). 3) Fluorescent tubulin injected into anaphase mammalian cells is incorporated near the equator of the elongating spindle (Fig. 25–7; Saxton and McIntosh, 1987). 4) A fluorescence bleach mark placed at the midzone of the interdigitating MTs in an anaphase mammalian spindle shows a focus of fluorescence recovery where the plus MT ends interdigitate, and bleach marks made on either side of the midzone move slowly away from the equator (Saxton and McIntosh, 1987). In sum, these observations suggest that anaphase B is the result of plus end MT polymerization associated with a relative sliding apart of the two interdigitating half spindles.

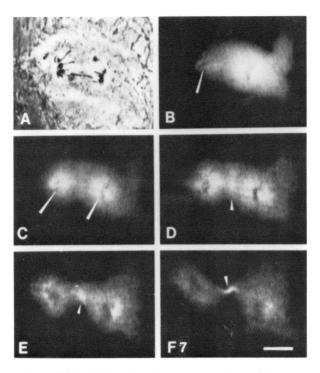

Fig. 25–7. A late anaphase PtK cell, showing the incorporation of fluorescent tubulin. **A:** Phase micrograph just before injection. **B:** Fluorescence micrograph taken 5 sec after injection. Note that the fluorescence has not yet had time to diffuse across the cell. **C–F:** Taken 65, 305, 545, and 845 sec after injection, showing the fast incorporation of tubulin that occurs near the chromosomes (long arrowheads) and the slower incorporation that occurs at the zone of MT overlap near the center of the spindle (short arrowheads). Bar = 10 μm. (Reproduced from Saxton and McIntosh, 1987, with permission of the publisher.)

The osmiophilic matrix that swathes the plus ends of interdigitating, nonkinetochore MTs may include a motor that promotes MT sliding (Cande, Chapter 28). The ATP-dependent sliding of MTs grown from neurotubulin on the plus ends of diatom spindle MTs in vitro certainly supports this view, because the matrix stays approximately immobile at the spindle equator while the newly elongated MTs slide through it (Cande, Chapter 28). The continued separation of the two interdigitating MT families after the poles have fallen from the mammalian spindle in late anaphase is consistent with the view, because it reduces the likelihood that action outside the spindle might pull the interdigitating MTs apart (Saxton and McIntosh, 1987). The matrix material from the zone of MT interdigitation therefore seems to have a role in both the translocation and the assembly of interzone MTs. Its biochemical composition will indeed be interesting to know.

Bundles of interpolar microtubules sometimes become thinner as they elongate. In the spindles of *Barbulanympha* (Inoué and Ritter, 1975), *Dictyostelium* (McIntosh et al., 1985), *Stephanopyxis* (Cande, Chapter 28); *Saccharomyces* (King et al., 1982), and of many other cells, the interpolar MT bundles elongate significantly during late anaphase. As they lengthen the bundles narrow. When electron microscopy has been done, it shows that the number of MTs in the bundle cross section decreases as the remaining MTs elongate. Spindle elongation in these cases thus includes an element of MT disassembly as well as the more obvious elements of assembly. In *Dictyostelium* the distribution of MT lengths varies widely at any one stage of mitosis. On the basis of MT sliding at the zone of interdigitation, accompanied by MT plus end assembly, one can account for the narrowing of the interpolar bundle with a simple model. Assume that the matrix material at the zone of MT interdigitation confers stability upon the MTs whose plus ends it surrounds. Assume that the MTs are sliding out from this region but simultaneously growing by subunit addition at their plus ends. If an MT does not elongate as fast as it slides, then its plus end will be dragged from the region occupied by matrix and lose its assembly advantage. That MT will then disassemble, and its subunits will be available for the further assembly of the MTs whose plus ends are still in the matrix, a process that can continue until the MT bundle becomes very narrow (McIntosh et al., 1985).

CONCLUSIONS

MT assembly and disassembly are essential processes during many phases of mitosis. MTs must form to make the machinery that orients and organizes the chromosomes; MT assembly and disassembly are integral parts of chromosome congression to the metaphase plate; assembly–disassembly is a part of both stages of anaphase. Assembly–disassembly is not, however, the whole story of mitotic motions. Because the interdigitating MTs of the anaphase interpolar bundle slide as well as elongate, and because these MTs add tubulin at their interdigitating ends, one cannot account for anaphase B simply by MT assembly. Some mechanism for MT translocation is also required. The same is probably true for anaphase A, although the only evidence for an MT-related motor during chromosome-to-pole motion is the strong, positive temperature dependence of chromosome speed. Indeed, it is plausible on current evidence that prometaphase also requires a mitotic motor of some kind. In this view, mitotic processes are dependent *both* on MT assembly–disassembly and on the action of MT translocators. As described in the section above on prometaphase, it even seems likely that assembly–disassembly events are in part driven by MT motors. Thus the phenomenology of mitosis is a complex mixture of polymerization and translocation processes. As reviewed above, students of mitosis are making some progress on sorting out the contributions to chromosome movements made by each class of process, but the clarity we seek has certainly not yet been achieved. There are many well defined questions still to be answered, and some valuable tools for their answering are already in hand.

ACKNOWLEDGMENTS

The work described here was supported in part by grants from the NIH (GM33787 and 36663) and from the ACS (BC498). The photomicrographs in Figures 25–1, 25–2, 25–5, and 25–6 were taken by Mark Ladinsky. His skillful help is gratefully acknowledged.

Chromosome Alignment at Mitotic Metaphase: Balanced Forces or Smart Kinetochores?

Timothy J. Mitchison

Department of Pharmacology, University of California, San Francisco, California 94143

INTRODUCTION

The last few years have seen considerable progress toward understanding the structure of the mitotic spindle and the mechanism of mitosis. Studies on dynamic aspects of microtubule organization have begun to reveal the basic mechanical organization of the spindle and thus have begun to lay the groundwork for understanding how the forces that move chromosomes are generated and controlled. Two kinds of experiments have been particularly informative: 1) microinjection of chemically tagged tubulin molecules into living mitotic cells either alone (Mitchison et al., 1986) or in conjunction with photobleaching (Gorbsky et al., 1987a,b; Hamaguchi et al., 1987; Salmon et al., 1984a,b; Saxton et al., 1984; Wadsworth and Salmon, 1985) and 2) studies on the properties of microtubules and chromosomes in vitro (Koshland et al., 1988; Mitchison and Kirschner, 1984a,b, 1985a,b). In this chapter, I will draw on the results of such experiments, including new data from our laboratory, to discuss one important aspect of mitosis: the alignment of paired chromatids at the metaphase plate.

Metaphase in higher animal and plant spindles is a sort of steady state, albeit a dynamic one, at which progress through mitosis pauses, usually for a few minutes, but sometimes for days in the case of meiotic spindles in unfertilized eggs. During prometaphase, chromosomes move continuously and unpredictably toward and away from the spindle poles. Eventually they all end up equidistant between the poles, where they achieve some kind of balance with sister kinetochores attached to opposite poles through kinetochore microtubules. This process of congression gives the metaphase spindle its characteristic shape. It is likely to be significant that chromosomes do not come to a complete rest in the center of the spindle, but rather in most spindles continue to oscillate gently on the spindle axis (Bajer, 1982; Roos, 1976). This steady-state situation is eventually disturbed by some global signal that causes sister chromatids to separate and that may well trigger other events at the same time. Once anaphase is initiated, changes in the spindle proceed smoothly

Cell Movement, Volume 2: Kinesin,
Dynein, and Microtubule Dynamics, pages 421–430
© 1989 Alan R. Liss, Inc.

and predictably: The chromatids move toward the poles, with concomitant shortening of their kinetochore fibers. At some point the poles start to move apart, and eventually the cleavage furrow forms, contracts, and separates the daughter cells.

Many models have been advanced to explain why paired chromatids come to a steady state equidistant between the poles, but these models all postulate that in this position the forces acting on the chromosomes in opposite directions become balanced. The purpose of this chapter is to discuss this hypothesis and to examine an alternative: that metaphase alignment is achieved not simply by a balance of opposite forces, but rather by kinetochores actively controlling chromosome motility on the basis of positional information. To examine and contrast these hypotheses I will briefly review what is currently known about the forces acting on mitotic chromosomes and then discuss which, if any, of these forces might act in a position-sensitive manner, so as to achieve metaphase alignment. The key players in this discussion are the kinetochore and the bundle of microtubules attached to it at their plus ends (Euteneuer and McIntosh, 1981a,b), the kinetochore fiber (Rieder, 1982; Roos, 1973a,b).

KINETOCHORE INTERACTIONS WITH MICROTUBULES IN VITRO

The first suggestion that the connection between microtubule plus ends and the kinetochore was a dynamic one came from in vitro experiments. Labeled microtubule seeds were attached to the kinetochores of isolated chromosomes and, the complexes were incubated with unlabeled subunits, guanosine triphosphate (GTP) and adenosine triphosphate (ATP) (Mitchison and Kirschner, 1985b). Under these conditions polymerization of new subunits onto microtubule ends attached to the kinetochore occurred, with concomitant sliding of the kinetochore toward the plus end of the newly polymerizing lattice. This sliding reaction required ATP. More recently this system was developed to allow analysis of microtubule dynamics at the kinetochore under conditions favoring depolymerization of the lattice (Koshland et al., 1988). This required development of labeled microtubule seeds that could elongate but were resistant to depolymerization, which was achieved by gentle cross linking of biotin-labeled microtubules with ethylene-glycol-bis-succinimidyl-succinate. When such seeds were connected to kinetochores via a segment of labile lattice and the complexes subjected to depolymerizing conditions, they could only disassemble from the kinetochore (plus) end, since the free (minus) end was blocked by the cross linking. Under these conditions depolymerization occurred at the kinetochore end, with a low enough frequency of dissociation that the labeled seed was observed to be reeled in to the kinetochore at a rate that depended on the tendency of the lattice to depolymerize. Interestingly this reaction was completely independent of nucleotide triphosphate and seemed to proceed using only the tendency of the microtubule lattice to depolymerize as an energy source.

Analysis of kinetochore function in vitro suffers the drawback that its relevance to mitosis in vivo cannot be automatically inferred. In particular, it is not yet clear how much force can be generated by either the ATP-dependent plus end-directed motile activities or the depolymerization-dependent minus end-directed motile activities. However, the system does have the advantage of having relatively defined components, and, when considered in conjunction with in vivo and lysed cell experiments, it can provide useful information. Presently it seems likely that the kinetochore is capable of generating poleward force by holding on to a microtubule lattice that is depolymerizing at the attached plus end (for discussions of possible mechanisms for this, see Gorbsky et al., 1987a; Hill, 1985; Koshland et al., 1988). It also seems likely that under some circumstances the kinetochore may also be able to generate away-from-poleward force by an ATP-dependent reaction that could involve a dynein- or kinesin-like ATPase. Given these two opposing capabilities, the questions arise of how they are regulated, which dominates at any particular time in the spindle, and how each contributes to congression. This way of thinking about the kinetochore echoes the earlier ideas of Pickett-Heaps et al. (1982).

KINETOCHORE MICROTUBULE DYNAMICS IN VIVO

The dynamic behavior of kinetochore microtubules has been probed by experiments in which chemically tagged tubulin subunits were introduced into mitotic cells. The fate of these subunits was followed using real-time fluorescence observations together with photobleaching (Gorbsky et al., 1987a; Hamaguchi et al., 1987; Salmon et al., 1984; Saxton et al., 1984; Wadsworth and Salmon, 1985), immunocytochemistry (Mitchison et al., 1986), or a combination of the two techniques (Gorbsky et al., 1987a). The interpretation of these experiments is presently quite controversial, but consensus is being approached on some aspects. Non-kinetochore microtubules rapidly exchange with free subunits, probably by rapid cycles of polymerization and depolymerization resulting from dynamic instability (Mitchison and Kirschner, 1984a,b). Kinetochore microtubules seem to turn over more slowly (Mitchison et al., 1986; Wadsworth and Salmon, 1985), probably in part because of the interaction of their plus ends with the kinetochore (Kirschner and Mitchison, 1986). Microtubule ends attached to the kinetochore are dynamic, as seen in vitro: Subunits are added to microtubule ends at the kinetochore during metaphase (Mitchison et al., 1986) and lost during anaphase (Mitchison et al., 1986). Photobleaching experiments suggest that in tissue culture cells during anaphase, essentially all depolymerization of kinetochore microtubules occurs at the kinetochore (Gorbsky et al., 1987a,b).

To understand congression, it is particularly important to determine the dynamic behavior of kinetochore microtubules during metaphase. The photobleaching approach has thus far been somewhat disappointing in this respect, since rapid microtubule turnover has obscured kinetochore fiber behavior. Some experiments (in tissue culture cells) suggest that kinetochore fibers show no net flux during metaphase (Wadsworth and Salmon, 1985), while others (in sand dollar embryos) show net poleward flux (Hamaguchi et al., 1987). The published electron microscopic data are also non-definitive: Subunit incorporation at the kinetochore gave labeled segments that appeared to elongate with time, which was interpreted as evidence for a poleward flux (Mitchison et al., 1986). I still favor that interpretation, but others cannot be ruled out, as discussed below. In the next section I will introduce new data obtained using the biotin tubulin injection method, which have changed my views on the nature of polymerization at the kinetochore during metaphase. However, these data still do not resolve the issue of poleward flux, a situation we are trying to rectify by further experiments. To distinguish models for congression, it is extremely important to determine whether kinetochore microtubules are dynamic only at kinetochores or at both kinetochores and poles. Unfortunately the evidence to date appears not to be decisive.

KINETOCHORE MICROTUBULE DYNAMICS IN METAPHASE PTK₂ CELLS

In collaboration with Louise Evans, I have been microinjecting biotin-labeled tubulin into metaphase PtK_2 cells, using essentially the same conditions as our earlier study with BSC1 cells (Mitchison et al., 1986). The PtK_2 line has several advantages that compensate for its relatively low rate of division, including a small number of chromosomes (12) and excellent visibility of the spindle when cultured on glass or mylar coverslips. The progress through mitosis has been extensively characterized in this line (Roos, 1973a,b, 1976), and division will occur normally over the temperature range 25–37°C. We used a temperature of 33°C. We also introduced two new methods of visualizing subunit incorporation into microtubules at the kinetochore: 1) semithick section (0.5 μm) electron microscopy using a Phillips electron microscope operated at 300 kV and 2) immunofluorescence using calcium ions in the permeabilization step to remove non-kinetochore microtubules that would otherwise obscure the image. These methods will be characterized in more detail elsewhere.

When cells injected in metaphase were permeabilized and then fixed shortly afterwards while still in metaphase, we obtained images as shown in Figure 26–1a,b and in Figure 26–2a–d. Some kinetochore fibers have incorporated subunits at the kinetochore, while others have not. When it was possible to visualize sister kinetochore fibers we usually observed that one fiber had incorporated label while the sister had not. At later times the fraction of pairs with both sisters labeled increased, and by 4 min all chromosomes had both sister fibers labeled (Figs. 26–1c,d, 2e). At the same time the labeled segments increased in average length, but the length incorporated on opposite sides was usually dissimilar. When fibers were labeled at the kinetochore, the length of labeled segments was similar for the majority of individual microtubules within one fiber, though not identical (Fig. 26–2d,e). When the fiber was unlabeled at the kinetochore, which we define as having a majority of microtubules unlabeled, we often saw one or two microtubules in the fiber that appeared to be completely labeled, as if they had joined the fiber by new polymerization and capture after the injection (Fig. 26–2b,d).

The nature of subunit incorporation at the kinetochore seen in these experiments is basically similar to that in our earlier study, with one important difference. Previously we always saw incorporation at all kinetochores, including sisters, even at the earliest time point. We currently interpret this difference as being due to much slower kinetochore fiber dynamics in the PtK$_2$ cells because of the lower temperature, and per-

haps because of their much larger chromosomes. In particular we think it likely that the PtK$_2$ chromosomes oscillate on the metaphase plate with a much slower periodicity than do BSC1 cells.

Oscillations of chromosomes on the spindle axis have been most thoroughly characterized by Bajer (1982), though they have been noticed by others; such oscillations are probably a universal feature of mitosis, though they are more prevalent in animal than in plant spindles (Bajer and Mole-Bajer, 1972). We have clearly seen such oscillations in PtK$_2$ spindles, both injected and uninjected. The oscillations are rather variable, but typically a paired chromatid leaves the equator, moves 10–30% of the half-spindle length toward one pole, and then returns, the whole excursion taking 1–4 min. The oscillatory behavior is continuous; chromosomes are rarely at rest, and the metaphase plate is in reality an average position rather than a true equilibrium. This behavior is quite typical for animal spindles.

The kinetics of label incorporation at kinetochores shown in Figures 26–1 and 26–2 are consistent with their reflecting at least in part normal chromosome oscillations, with all microtubule dynamics occurring at the kinetochore. In this view, a chromosome like the one in Figure 26–2a–c was moving in the direction of the unlabeled kinetochore between the time of injection and permeabilization. We surmise that it was adding subunits to the elongating fiber at the kinetochore, and losing them from the unlabeled fiber. We are planning to record in detail the movement of a particular chromosome in an injected cell and correlate this with its incorporation behavior to test this hypothesis. Unfortunately we cannot define the depolymerization site. Since the kinetochore has the potential to hold on to depolymerizing microtubules, it may be the most likely candidate.

Polymerization at the trailing kinetochore during movement away from the equator is an attractive hypothesis to explain the early incorporation pattern, but how can we ex-

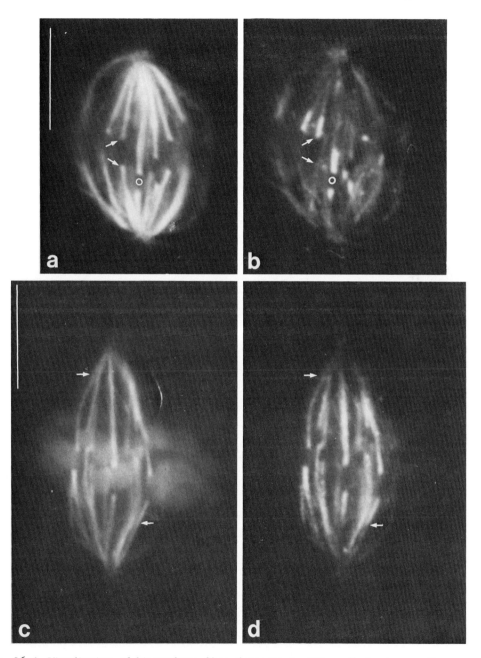

Fig. 26–1. Visualization of kinetochore fiber dynamics in PtK$_2$ cells by immunofluorescence. Metaphase cells on glass coverslips were injected with biotin-labeled tubulin (2 mg/ml in the needle) and incubated at 33°C. They were then permeabilized in the presence of 1 mM calcium ions for 2 min (no spindle shrinkage was observed), fixed, and stained with antitubulin (fluorescein channel; **a,c**) and antibiotin (Texas red channel; **b,d**). This treatment selectively preserves kinetochore fibers and disperses astral microtubules that rapidly incorporate label and would otherwise obscure the kinetochore fibers. The cell shown by double-label in a and b was incubated 67 sec after injection before permeabilizing, and the cell in c and d for 316 sec. The arrows in a and b show sister fibers in which only the upper one has incorporated subunits at the kinetochore, while the circles indicate a chromosome for which both sister fibers have incorporated, but to different extents. The arrows in c and d indicate the boundary between labeled proximal portions of kinetochore fibers and unlabeled poleward portions. Note that the labeled segments are much longer than in a and b. Bars = 10 μm.

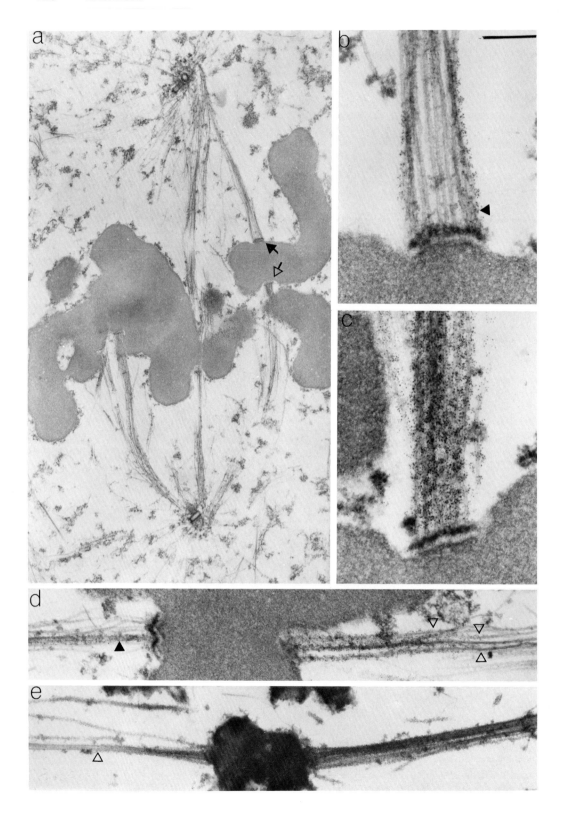

plain the pattern at later times? Since the chromosomes must change direction after a minute or two they will start to polymerize subunits at the previously leading kinetochore, which would lead to both sister fibers becoming labeled (e.g., the pair denoted by a circle in Fig. 1a,b). However, we have to explain why the labeled segments increase in average length with time (Figs. 26–1c,d, 26–2e), eventually leading to labeling of almost all of the spindle (see also Mitchison et al., 1986). Can this be explained invoking dynamics only at the kinetochore end of the fiber? If all depolymerization occurs at the kinetochore of the shortening fiber during movement back to the equator, the previously trailing fiber would tend to lose the labeled subunits it incorporated on the way out. Thus even after long times the label would be confined to an equatorial zone demarked by the maximum extent of the poleward oscillations. The chromosomes in the cell in Figure 26–1c,d were observed after injection, and they did not make excursions as far as the arrows—greater than 60% of half-spindle length. Thus the poleward extension of labeled segments at the kinetochore requires additional explanations. Our previous interpretation was depolymerization at the poleward end of the fiber (Mitchison et al., 1986). However, the new data suggest an alternative possibility: microtubule turnover in the kinetochore fiber.

The appearance of long labeled segments on otherwise unlabeled kinetochores (Fig. 26–2b,d) suggests that new microtubules can continuously attach to kinetochores during metaphase. Since the system is at steady state, this presumably reflects a similar rate of detachment. From our preliminary data we crudely estimate the rate of such turnover to be about one microtubule per kinetochore per minute. This corresponds to less than one-tenth of a microtubule per kinetochore per minute and is thus considerably slower than astral microtubule turnover, which proceeds at least 10 times as fast. We do not yet know if such turnover involves complete depolymerization of the detached microtubule or whether a kinetochore microtubule can detach, shrink part way to the pole, and then regrow with labeled subunits and reattach. The fact that the poleward regions of the kinetochore fibers in Figure 26–1c,d are largely unlabeled, despite the probable occurrence of turnover, suggests the latter possibility. The combination of synchronous polymerization at the kinetochore during oscillations with asynchronous detachment, partial depolymerization, and then regrowth and reattachment could probably explain the kinetics of subunit incorporation into the fiber in this and in our earlier study. Thus we cannot yet unambiguously decide whether kinetochore fibers show any poleward flux during meta-

Fig. 26–2. Visualization of kinetochore fiber dynamics in PtK_2 cells by immuno–electron microscopy. Metaphase cells were injected with biotin-labeled tubulin and visualized essentially as previously described (Mitchison et al., 1986), but we used a lower concentration of biotin tubulin (calcium was not used during permeabilization), and cut thicker sections (0.4 μm) for examination at 300 KeV. Microtubules that incorporated biotin-labeled subunits are visualized by 5-nm gold particles. **a–d:** From the same cell permeabilized 60 sec after injection. **e:** From a cell permeabilized 240 sec after injection. b is the kinetochore indicated in a by the closed arrow, at higher magnification; and c is its sister (open arrow in a) shown from the next section. Note that the lower of the pair has incorporated label while its sister has not. The same is true for the pair in d. The arrowheads in b and d indicate single labeled microtubules terminating at kinetochores with otherwise unlabeled fibers. We interpret this as being due to turn over of kinetochore microtubules (see text). It is interesting that the kinetochore in d appears indented at the site of attachment of the labeled microtubule. The open arrowheads in d and e indicate the transition between the labeled proximal portion and the unlabeled poleward portion of the kinetochore fibers. Bars = a, 2.0 μm; b,c, 0.3 μm; d, 0.5 μm; e, 1.0 μm.

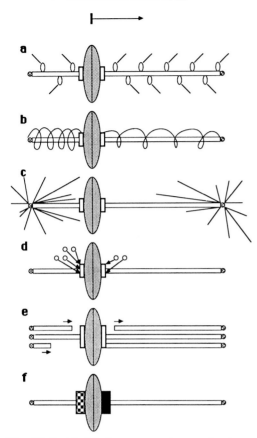

Fig. 26–3. Models for congression mechanisms. The hatched ovals represent paired chromatids displaced from an equatorial position on the metaphase plate, with the arrow at top representing the restorative force. The sister chromatids (boxes) are attached to opposite poles (small hatched circles) by kinetochore microtubules (open bars). **a:** Force-producing molecules (tadpoles) act along the length of kinetochore microtubules, pulling them poleward. **b:** An elastic element is stretched between kinetochores and poles. **c:** Astral microtubules generate a pushing force by an unknown mechanism that repels the chromosome. **d:** The kinetochore on the left experiences a greater microtubule polymerizing potential, shown as an increased concentration of tubulin subunits (open circles). **e:** More microtubules are attached to the kinetochore on the right side, but these have an increased tendency to detach compared to the left side, where the net tendency is to add microtubules. **f:** The two kinetochores are in different functional states, controlled by an internal switch such as phosphorylation state. The left kinetochore is pushing while the right one is pulling.

phase; a different type of study that directly assays flux (or its absence) is required to decide this issue.

MECHANISMS FOR ACHIEVING CONGRESSION

Figure 26–3 is a diagram of six different models for achieving congression. The first four are from the literature or personal communications, and the last two are probably new—although it may be possible that nothing is ever new in the mitosis field, simply more explicit!

Figure 26–3a shows force per unit length. This is perhaps the most widely discussed model, the simplest to imagine in molecular terms, and currently the one with the most experimental support (Hayes et al., 1982). An essential feature of this model is that it integrates force along the whole kinetochore fiber. To achieve congression on its own, the summed force must be capable of moving the whole paired unit and thus also of influencing the rate of depolymerization at the poles. This is the only model that requires depolymerization at the poles during metaphase, and by this criterion is likely to be critically tested in the near future. The profile of restorative force versus displacement from the equator is likely to be smooth for any simple form of this model. Thus it does not predict continued oscillations of chromosomes at metaphase.

Figure 26–3b shows the parallel elastic element. This model achieves congression with dynamics only at the kinetochore. Central to this model is the molecular identity of the elastic element, which has been proposed to be part of the cytomatrix (Pickett-Heaps et al., 1982). Its critical test is likely to come from in vitro attempts to reconstitute chromosome movement in the absence of accessory spindle structures. As in Figure 26–3a, this model predicts smooth congression without oscillations.

Figure 26–3c shows the polar exclusion model. Microtubule asters clearly repel large particles, resulting in an exclusion force that decreases with distance from the pole and could thus achieve congression in partnership with kinetochore-derived poleward force (Rieder et al., 1986). This model depends on astral microtubules and thus has some difficulty explaining congression in plant spindles. These lack astral microtubules and probably also polar exclusion forces, as evidenced by the distribution of chromosome arms, which often lie parallel to the spindle axis and are not pushed out normal to the spindle axis as in animal spindles (Bajer and Mole-Bajer, 1976). Since the balance between poleward and exclusion forces is thought to give rise to the oscillations observed when only one kinetochore is attached to a pole (Rieder et al., 1986), this model may predict an oscillating, rather than a completely balanced, metaphase plate. In this model oscillations could result from transient pushing by single growing microtubules.

Figure 26–3d shows gradient of polymerization potential. Microtubule ends at the kinetochore can add or lose subunits during metaphase; polymerization in conjunction with a plus end-directed ATPase is expected to exert away-from-poleward force (Mitchison and Kirschner, 1985b), while depolymerization exerts poleward force (Hill, 1985; Koshland et al., 1988). Thus a gradient of tubulin subunit concentration in the spindle, high at the poles and low at the equator, would lead to congression. The leftward kinetochore in Figure 26–3d experiences more pushing and less pulling than does its sister because of the higher subunit concentration in its vicinity. Since tubulin subunits diffuse rapidly in cytoplasm (Salmon et al., 1984a,b; Saxton et al., 1984), this model would be more plausible if polymerization potential were controlled by some factor other than actual subunit concentration, such as concentration of a cofactor (calcium, pH, and so forth) or by local covalent modification of microtubule subunits (including MAPs).

Figure 26–3e shows that depolymerization promotes detachment. This novel mechanism depends on the following assumptions. 1) Kinetochore microtubules turn over at an appreciable rate during meta-

phase. 2) Detachment at the kinetochore is promoted by depolymerization occurring there. (This is the case in vitro [Koshland et al., 1988], and detachment is prevalent when depolymerization occurs at the kinetochore during anaphase in vivo [Jensen, 1982].) 3) Poleward force increases with the number of microtubules attached at the kinetochore (supported experimentally; see Hayes et al., 1982). In Figure 26–3e, the chromosome is moving rightward because the kinetochore on that side has more microtubules attached. Microtubule turnover is occurring on both kinetochores, but there is a net tendency to lose them on the depolymerizing side and to gain them on the polymerizing side because of the effect of depolymerization on affinity for ends. This will lead to a reversal of the imbalance in microtubule number, causing the previously trailing kinetochore to start pulling harder and thus for the overall direction to reverse. The rate of reversal, and thus the persistence of movement, would depend greatly on the inherent turnover rate. The net tendency in such a model is an equatorial balance. This model is interesting in that it requires microtubule turnover at the kinetochore, and it requires continuous oscillations to achieve congression and to maintain an equatorial balance, both of which are observed.

Figure 26–3f shows smart kinetochores. This is really a whole class of models in which kinetochores are able to sense their position on the spindle and to use this information to control forces. I term these *smart kinetochores*, since they act as switches to control and harness forces actively that in themselves may be position independent. This is in contrast to all the other models in which kinetochores are elements that simply transduce between forces and polymerization dynamics and are passive with respect to transducing information. As discussed above, in vitro analysis of kinetochore function suggests that they possess two distinct motile activities that differ both in directionality and in the energy source for movement, and thus they presumably utilize different sets of molecules in the kinetochore. It is not yet clear from in vitro studies how these apparently opposing activities are regulated, but I can imagine two extreme possibilities: Both activities may be potentially on at all times, and whether kinetochore microtubules polymerize or depolymerize may be governed by forces external to the kinetochore, generated elsewhere in the spindle. This is the situation implicit in the models shown in Figure 26–3a–e. The alternative is that the functional state of the kinetochore is determined by an internal switch, phosphorylation state, for example. One state would promote only microtubule polymerization at the kinetochore and ATP-dependent away-from-pole motility. The other would promote depolymerization-driven poleward motility. In Figure 26–3f, the dark kinetochore is in a pulling state while the checkered one is in a pushing (or trailing) state. These states alternate during metaphase to achieve congression, and then both kinetochores convert to a pulling state at anaphase. This hypothesis requires the existence of two states of kinetochore function and of some position-sensitive mechanism for interconverting them. Evidence for two states, if they exist, is most likely to come from in vitro studies. The question of how such hypothetical states might be regulated is perhaps too speculative to consider in great depth at present, but in principle any one of the position-sensitive mechanisms in Figure 26–3a–e could act to control the state of a switch rather than to cause congression directly. In particular, the model in Figure 26–3d could be generalized so that the concentration gradient was of some unknown factor affecting kinetochore activity. The model in Figure 26–3a could also receive a new lease of life even in the absence of polar depolymerization if tension along the microtubules was sensed by the kinetochore and translated such that the kinetochore experiencing greater tension switched to the depolymerizing state. This is an interesting possibility in light of classic observations that tension on kinetochore fibers can influence their affinity for microtubule ends (Nicklas, 1971) and thus presumably their chemistry. Since individual kinetochores are either pushing or pulling, this model predicts continuous oscillations at metaphase.

CONCLUSIONS

I have listed six different mechanisms by which paired chromosomes could theoretically achieve congression to an equatorial position in the spindle. This is not an exhaustive list, but it includes all the main categories of models, and I think that the real situation will most likely involve elements from this catalog: from only one model or from several. It is premature to decide between these models, but experiments now in progress or planned are likely to thin the list considerably over the next few years. I am currently particularly interested in distinguishing models involving passive kinetochores from those involving smart ones, since this distinction will profoundly influence our approach to identifying the molecular components involved in kinetochore function. The classic mitosis literature has made clear the versatility and precision of the mitotic apparatus, and recent experiments have all pointed toward kinetochores as the major decision-making loci. Thus I will not be surprised if they turn out to be very smart indeed!

ACKNOWLEDGMENTS

I acknowledge the excellent technical contributions of Louise Evans and her help in preparing the manuscript. I also thank Marc Kirschner for his unflagging support and encouragement. This work was supported by grants from the NIH and from the Howard Hughes Medical Institute.

Metaphase Chromosome Congression and Anaphase Poleward Movement

E.D. Salmon

Department of Biology, University of North Carolina, Chapel Hill, North Carolina 27599

INTRODUCTION

We have described a model for the mechanism of chromosome positioning and transport in mitotic animal cells (Cassimeris et al., 1987a). The model is based on 1) the intrinsic structural polarity of a microtubule and the polarized arrangements of microtubules in the spindle; 2) the rapid dynamic instability of polar microtubule assembly; 3) the bipolarity of the orientation of sister kinetochores in chromosome duplexes before anaphase; 4) the formation of kinetochore fibers by kinetochore capture of the distal plus ends of polar microtubules; 5) the generation of poleward force on the chromosome at sites located only at the kinetochore by a "Pac Man"-type molecular complex located at the microtubule attachment site (this activity pulls the kinetochore poleward while tubulin dissociation and association occur proximal to the kinetochore); and 6) the generation of outward forces on the bulk of the chromosome by polar ejection forces produced by interactions between the dynamic polar microtubules and the chromosome arms.

In this chapter, I develop a simplified mechanistic model based on the above concepts to explain chromosome positioning and poleward movement during metaphase and anaphse in both monopolar and bipolar astral spindles. This model was initially conceived by considering the functional significance of the mechanism for chromosome congression in monopolar spindles. Examples of monopolar spindles at metaphase are shown in Figure 27–1 for a mitotic newt lung epithelial cell and in Figure 27–2 for a meiosis I grasshopper spermatocyte. Analysis of chromosome movement in newt monopolar spindles has provided the following information about chromosome positioning. 1) The positions of the chromosomes are not static, and they oscillate several micrometers toward and away from the pole, while maintaining an average distance from the pole of 10–20 μm (Bajer, 1982; Rieder et al., 1986). 2) Chromosomes are pulled toward the pole by poleward-directed forces acting at the kinetochores that face the pole. 3) Only the kinetochores facing the pole form a kinetochore fiber; their sister kinetochores, which face away from the pole, have no visible kinetochore microtubules and are apparently not functional (Rieder et al., 1986). Thus, there is one poleward force on a chromosome acting

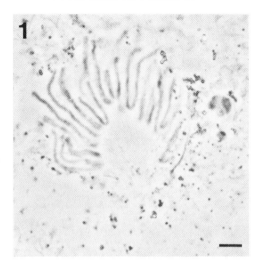

Fig. 27–1. Phase contrast light micrograph of a monopolar spindle in a mitotic newt lung epithelial cell of the newt *Taricha granulosa*. Chromosome arms are aligned parallel to the microtubules. The centrosome at the spindle pole is visible as a dark spot. Bar = 10 μm. (Courtesy of Lynn Cassimeris.)

at one kinetochore. 4) The number of microtubules that end on kinetochores which face the pole are typical of kinetochores in metaphase bipolar spindles, and this number appears to be independent of the distance of the chromosome from the pole (Cassimeris, Rieder, and Salmon, unpublished observations).

It is well established that the spindle fiber attached to a kinetochore exerts a pole-directed force on the chromosome during premetaphase (for review, see Nicklas, 1977). Why then are the chromosomes in monopolar spindles not pulled all the way to the pole? Work with Lynne Cassimeris in my laboratory and collaborative studies with Conly Rieder and associates have shown that in newt cells forces associated with the polar microtubule arrays push the chromosome arms outward away from the pole (Rieder et al., 1985a,b, 1986; Cassimeris et al., 1987b). When chromosome arms, or segments of chromosome arms, are cut free of the kinetochore complex by laser microsurgery, they are transported at several micrometers per minute radially outward (Rieder et al., 1986). Small severed fragments of the chromosome containing the kinetochore complex move up close to the pole (Cassimeris et al., 1987b). Depolymerization of the polar microtubules by cold or nocodazole treatment results in the movement of all the chromosomes to the pole (Rieder et al., 1985; Cassimeris et al., 1987b). After cooling, rewarming the cells results in the reassembly of the polar microtubule arrays and the movement of the chromosomes outward away from the poles.

Thus, there are two distinctly different types of forces that move and position chromosomes in the monopolar spindle: a poleward force acting at the kinetochore and an outward force acting along the length of the chromosome. Chromosome movement and positioning in bipolar spindles potentially involves four forces: antagonistic poleward forces acting at the kinetochores that face opposite spindle poles and antagonistic polar ejection forces acting on the chromosome arms and generated by the oppositely oriented arrays of polar microtubule.

PRINCIPLES AND ASSUMPTIONS OF THE MODEL

The first major assumption of this model is that chromosomes move to a position relative to the spindle poles either in monopolar or normal bipolar spindles, where the result of the forces on the chromosome is zero. There is substantial evidence supporting this assumption (Nicklas, 1977; Ellis and Begg, 1981; Hays, 1985). An excellent example of this principle comes from an analysis by Nicklas (1977) of the repositioning of chromosomes in the first meiotic bipolar spindles of grasshopper spermatocytes following the application of an external poleward force to the chromosome. Prior to experimental intervention, the chromosome was situated at the spindle equator and was attached to opposite poles by kinetochore fibers. An external poleward force was applied to the chromosome by stretching an arm of the chromosome toward one pole with a micro-

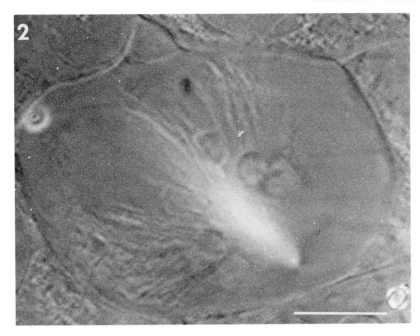

Fig. 27–2. Polarization light micrograph of a monopolar spindle in a meiosis I grasshopper spermatocyte. The compensator was set for bright contrast of the birefringent monopolar spindle. Chromosomes are not birefringent, and they appear in negative contrast. Bar = 10 μm.

needle. This applied poleward force produced movement of the chromosome from an equatorial position toward the pole in the direction of the stretch. If the stretch was maintained, the chromosome moved all the way to the pole. The movement of the chromosome toward one pole was accompanied by the shortening of the kinetochore fiber directed toward that pole and the concurrent lengthening of the opposite kinetochore fiber. When the microneedle was removed, the chromosome moved back to the spindle equator, accompanied by concurrent changes in the lengths of the kinetochore fibers. Chromosome velocity and the concurrent changes in the lengths of the kinetochore fibers occurred at rates typical of natural metaphase and anaphase chromosome movement (0.5–1 μm/min). Velocity was probably limited by the dynamics of assembly and disassembly of the kinetochore fiber microtubules (Salmon, 1975; Salmon and Begg, 1980).

The second major assumption of this model is that the net force on a chromosome is produced by two distinctly different types of forces. Chromosomes are pulled toward a pole by force producers that are located only at the microtubule attachment sites at the kinetochores. We view these force producers like "Pac-Man" complexes, because they can hold onto the end of a microtubule while allowing tubulin association–dissociation reactions to occur (Cassimeris et al., 1987a).

The aggregate strength of the poleward force producers (PF) is assumed to be proportional to the number of kinetochore microtubules:

$$PF = kN, \qquad (1)$$

where N is the number of kinetochore microtubules and k is a constant relating microtubule number to force. There is good evidence to justify this assumption (Hays, 1985). In our current model, k does not depend on distance between chromosome and pole.

In our model, the chromosomes are pushed away or ejected outward from each pole by forces generated through interactions between the polar microtubules and non-kinetochore regions of the chromosome (Rieder et al., 1986). The molecular origins of this outward ejection force (EF) are unknown. It may be produced by the growth of the polar microtubules, which occurs continuously because of their dynamic instability (Cassimeris et al., 1987a). The outward force could also be generated by translocator molecules with the transport polarity of kinesin, which are located on the surface of the chromosome (Rieder et al., 1986). In either case, the total outward force (OF) generated by one polar array of microtubules acting on a chromosome is the integral of EF over the surface of the chromosome arms:

$$OF = \int EF(s)ds, \qquad (2)$$

where EF(s) is the magnitude of EF at position s, acting over the surface S, of the chromosome.

Calculation of OF from Equation 2 is complex, because EF will depend on the local density of microtubules, the orientation of the surface of the chromosome with respect to the axis of the microtubules, and variations in other unknown surface-specific factors, such as kinesin concentration. Structural studies have shown that the density of polar microtubules decreases as a function of the distance from the pole (McIntosh et al., 1985), but detailed information about the distribution of microtubule density is very limited.

The model assumes that the magnitude of the outward force on the chromosome (OF) generated by one polar microtubule array is a decreasing function of the distance of the chromosome from the pole and an increasing function of chromosome size. Thus, when a chromosome initially attaches to microtubules extending form the pole, the

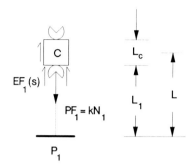

Fig. 27–3. Diagram of the distances and forces associated with a mono-oriented chromosome (C) in a monopolar spindle. The kinetochores are situated at the ends of the chromosome complex, as occurs in meiosis I metaphase. L is the distance from the pole, P_1, to the center of mass of the chromosome; L_1 is the distance from P_1 to the mono-oriented kinetochore; and L_c is the length of the chromosome. PF_1 is the poleward force at the kinetochore facing P_1 as defined by Equation 1 in the text. $EF_1(s)$ is the ejection force at the surface of the chromosome produced by interactions with the polar microtubule array extending from P_1. The cross-sectional perimeter of the chromosome is the perimeter seen by an observer at P_1 looking at C.

chromosome will be pulled toward that pole by the poleward motors at the kinetochore. As the chromosome moves poleward, the strength of the ejection force increases. The chromosome stops moving poleward when OF = PF. Fluctuations in the strength of either PF or OF produces the oscillations in the position of the chromosome toward and away from the pole (Bajer, 1982).

Chromosome position will also depend on the geometry of the spindle and chromosome orientation. In monopolar spindles, chromosome position is produced by the resultant action of one PF force and one OF force, which are oriented in opposite radial directions (Fig. 27–3). In bipolar spindles, chromosome position is produced by one PF force if the chromosome is mono-oriented (one kinetochore fiber; Fig. 27–4) or two oppositely oriented PF forces and two oppositely oriented OF forces if the chromosome is bi-oriented (two kinetochore fibers; Fig. 5). The resultant of the OF forces on the

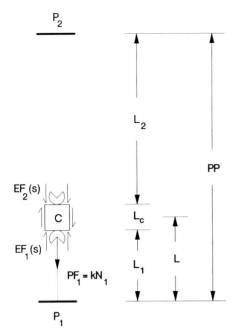

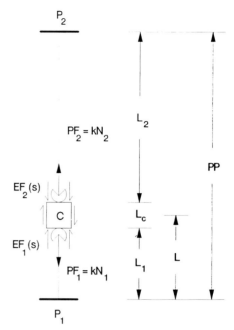

Fig. 27–4. Diagram of the distances and forces associated with a mono-oriented chromosome in a bipolar spindle. P_2 is the second pole, PP is the interpolar length of the spindle, L_2 is the distance of the kinetochore facing P_2 to P_2, and $EF_2(s)$ is the ejection force at the surface of the chromosome generated by interactions with the polar microtubule array extending from P_2. The other parameters are defined in Figure 27–3.

Fig. 27–5. Diagram of the distances and forces associated with a bi-oriented chromosome in a bipolar spindle. PF_2 is the poleward force at the kinetochore facing P_2. The other parameters are defined in Figures 27–3 and 27–4.

chromosome in a bipolar spindle will in general have a vectorial component directed along the spindle interpolar axis and a second component normal to this axis. The normal component pushes the chromosomes to the periphery of the central spindle, a phenomenon commonly observed in animal spindles (Rieder et al., 1986).

A SIMPLIFIED MECHANISTIC MODEL

Further Assumptions

I will demonstrate the *principles* of the above model for metaphase congression and anaphase poleward movement of idealized chromosomes in monopolar and bipolar animal spindles of meiosis I grasshopper spermatocytes, using the following simplifying assumptions.

Each meiotic chromosome complex (e.g., a bivalent) is assumed to be a cylinder with constant cross-sectional perimeter (p) and length (L_c). The kinetochore regions on the chromosome are located at the ends of the cylinder as shown in Figures 27–1 to 27–3. This is similar to the geometric arrangement of kinetochores in the meiotic chromosomes of first meiotic spermatocytes.

The magnitudes of the poleward forces at the kinetochores are calculated from Equation 1. The average number of kinetochore microtubules per kinetochore complex is assumed to be the same for chromosomes in both monopolar and bipolar spindles. It is also assumed that there are no quantitative differences in the values of k between monopolar and bipolar spindles.

The magnitude of the outward force on a chromosome generated by one polar microtubule array is assumed to be proportional to the size of the chromosome and proportional to the reciprocal of the distance of the center of mass of the chromosome from the pole or

$$OF_m(L) = epL_c[1/L], \qquad (3)$$

where L is the distance from the pole, P_1, to the center of mass of the chromosome as defined in Figure 27–3; e is a constant; p is the average cross-sectional perimeter of the chromosome (defined in Fig. 27–3); and L_c is the length of the chromosome.

A similar function may be used to calculate the magnitude of OF on a chromosome within a bipolar spindle with the following assumptions: that the spijndle is symmetrical about the equator; that the magnitude of OF on a chromosome between the poles of a bipolar spindle is the simple difference in the magnitudes calculated by Equation 3 for each polar microtubule array; that the magnitude of the proportionality constant, e, is the same for both monopole and bipolar microtubule arrays; and that the chromosome is situated along the spindle interpolar axis. I neglect the effects of the reduction in OF, which occurs in bipolar spindles because chromosomes are pushed to the periphery of the spindle where the density of microtubules is reduced. Given these assumptions, the value of OF for a chromosome in a bipolar spindle is

$$\begin{aligned} OF_b(L) &= epL_c[(1/L) - 1/(PP - L)] \\ &= epL_c[(PP - 2L)/L(PP - L)], \quad (4) \end{aligned}$$

where PP is the interpolar length of the spindle.

In the following examples, I will calculate the equilibrium positions of the idealized chromosome in terms of the distance, L_1, between the kinetochore facing the pole, P_1, as diagrammed in Figures 27–3 to 27–5. L_1 is given by

$$L_1 = L - L_c/2. \qquad (5)$$

A Mono-Oriented Chromosome in a Monopolar Spindle

Figure 27–3 shows the forces on a chromosome oriented to pole P_1 in a monopolar spindle. PF_1 pulls the chromosome poleward, and OF_m, the integration of EF(s) over the chromosome surface, pushes the chromosome away from the pole. At congression equilibrium, $PF_1 = OF_m$, and from Equations 1, 3, and 5:

$$kN_1 = epL_c[1/(L_1 + L_c/2)], \qquad (6)$$

where N_1 is the number of microtubules at the kinetochore in the monopolar spindle.

The distance of the kinetochore from the pole, L_1, where $PF_1 = OF_m$ is calculated by rearranging Eq 6:

$$L_1 = (e/k)[pL_c/N_1] - L_c/2. \qquad (7)$$

A Mono-Oriented Chromosome in a Bipolar Spindle

The situation I will next consider is shown in Figure 27–4. The chromosome is mono-oriented in a bipolar spindle. It has formed only one kinetochore fiber, which extends from the pole labeled P_1. There is only one PF on the chromosome, but there are two sets of ejection forces acting on the chromosome, which are oriented in opposite directions. At congression equilibrium,

$$PF_1 = kN_1 = OF_b, \qquad (8)$$

where OF_b is given by Equation 4. L_1 at congression equilibrium may be obtained from the solution to a quadratic equation generated from Equations 4, 5, and 8:

$$BL^2 - [2 + BPP]L + PP = 0. \qquad (9)$$

where $B = (k/e)[N_1/pL_c]$, and $L = L_1 + L_c/2$.

A Bi-Oriented Chromosome in a Bipolar Spindle

The forces on a bi-oriented chromosome in a bipolar spindle are shown in Figure 27–5. The net poleward force on the chromosome is the difference between the antagonistic forces generated at oppsoite kinetochores:

$$PF_1 = k(N_1 - N_2), \qquad (10)$$

where N_1 and N_2 are the numbers of kineto-chore microtubules attached to the kineto-chores facing P_1 and P_2, respectively.

At congression equilibrium,

$$k(N_1 - N_2) = OF_b, \qquad (11)$$

where OF_b is calculated from Equation 5. L_1 is calculated from Equation 9 by substituting $(N_1 - N_2)$ for N_1.

PREDICTIONS OF THE MODEL

In the numerical examples presented below, I use values for $PP = 28\ \mu m$, $p = 6\ \mu m$, $L_c = 3.5\ \mu m$ for the average length of the chromosome, and $N_1 = 37$ for the average number of kinetochore microtubules unless the parameter is a dependent variable in the analysis. These values are typical of the first meiosis in the grasshopper spermatocyte (Hays, 1985).

Direct measurements of k and e are unavailable. However, the ratio of (k/e) can be estimated from the value of L_1 in monopole spindles. L_1 for chromosomes in monopoles in living cells depends on the position of the chromosome within the array of microtubules, as seen in Figures 27–1 and 27–2. When the chromosomes are grouped together, microtubule density is highest in the section of the polar microtubule array facing the chromosomes and lower for other regions of the aster. Chromosomes in the higher microtubule density region position further away from the pole than do those in the low microtubule density regions. On average, the chromosomes achieve positions a distance away from the pole that are equivalent to at least one-half the distance between the metaphase plate and the poles in a bipolar spindle (Figs. 27–1, 27–2; Rieder et al., 1986). As a first approximation in the following analysis, I assume that L_1 in a monopolar spindle equals $L_1/2$ for a bi-oriented chromosome in a bipolar spindle. For $PP = 28\ \mu m$ and $L_c = 3.5\ \mu m$, then

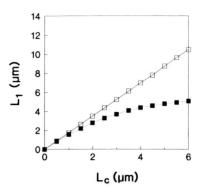

Fig. 27–6. The effects on L_1 of changes in the length, L_c, of a mono-oriented chromosome in a monopolar (open squares) or a bipolar (closed squares) spindle. L_1 was calculated from Equation 7 for the monopolar spindle and from Equation 9 for the bipolar spindle using $PP = 28\ \mu m$, $(k/e) = 0.002$, $N_1 = 37$, and $p = 6\ \mu m$.

$L_1 = 0.5[PP - L_c] = 12.25$ for a bi-oriented chromosome in a bipolar spindle and $L_1 = 6.125$ in the monopolar spindle. The ratio of the proportionality constants, (k/e), is calculated by rearranging Equation 7 as

$$(k/e) = pL_c/[L_1 + L_c/2]N_1. \qquad (12)$$

For $PP = 28\ \mu m$, $L_c = 3.5\ \mu m$, $N_1 = 37$, $p = 6\ \mu m$ and $L_1 = 0.5(PP - L_c) = 6.25$, then $(k/e) = 0.002$. In the numerical examples presented below, I assume this value for (k/e) is the same for monopolar and bipolar spindles.

Effects of Chromosome Size

Figure 27–6 shows the effect of chromosome size, modeled as changes in chromosome length, L_c, on the distance, L_1, of a mono-oriented chromosome from the pole. In both monopolar and bipolar spindles, L_1 is an increasing function of L_c. Chromosomes of equivalent size achieve positions closer to the pole in bipolar spindles in comparison to their position in monopolar spindles. For long chromosomes, changes in chromosome size in bipolar spindles have less effect on position in bipolar spindles compared with monopolar spindles.

In reality, a mono-oriented chromosome

in a bipolar spindle may move even closer to the pole than is predicted from Figure 27–6. In the above analysis, I have neglected the vectorial component of the antagonistic ejection forces, which is normal to the spindle interpolar axis. This resultant force pushes a chromosome out of the central spindle region into peripheral regions of lower microtubule density (Rieder et al., 1986). The lower microtubule density would have a lower magnitude of ejection force associated with it, and the chromosome could move close to the pole before the poleward force at the kinetochore is balanced by the outward ejection forces.

Figure 27–6 predicts that small mono-oriented chromosomes should position much closer to the pole than do longer chromosomes. We have shown that when the bulk of a chromosome arm is cut free of the centromere region of a mono-oriented chromosome using a laser microbeam, the centromere does move up close to the pole (Cassimeris et al., 1987b, Salmon and Rieder, unpublished observations). However, no quantitative position information is yet available.

Effects of the Number of Kinetochore Microtubules

Figure 27–7 shows the effects on L_1 of changes in the number of kinetochore microtubules, N_1, for mono-oriented chromosomes in monopolar or bipolar spindles. Chromosome position in the monopolar spindle is more sensitive to changes in the number of kinetochore microtubules than is the case for the bipolar spindle. In either case, position from the pole decreases as a function of the increase in the number of kinetochore microtubules.

Effects of Differences in the Number of Kinetochore Microtubules in Bi-Oriented Chromosomes

Figure 27–8 plots the change in L_1 as a function of the difference between $N_1 - N_2$ for a bi-oriented chromosome in a bipolar spindle. Figure 27–8 shows that when $N_1 =$

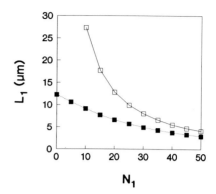

Fig. 27–7. The effects on L_1 of changes in the number of microtubules, N_1, at the kinetochore of a mono-oriented chromosome facing pole, P_1, in a monopolar (open squares) or a bipolar (closed squares) spindle. L_1 was calculated from Equation 7 for the monopolar spindle and from Equation 9 for the bipolar spindle using PP = 28 μm, L_c = 3.5 μm, p = 6 μm, and (k/e) = 0.002.

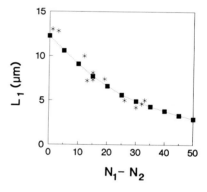

Fig. 27–8. The effects on L_1 of the difference between $N_1 - N_2$ for a bi-oriented chromosome in a bipolar spindle. L_1 was calculated (solid squares) from Equation 9 using PP = 28 μm, L_c = 3.5 μm, p = 6 μm, (k/e) = 0.002, and $N_1 = N_1 - N_2$. The asterisks are data taken from the work of Hays (1985) as described in the text.

N_2, $L_1 = 0.5(PP - L_c) = 12.25$ μm, and the chromosome is at the spindle equator independent of the value of the number of kinetochore microtubules and independent of the strengths of the polar ejection fields, as long as they have symmetrical values about the spindle equator.

Figure 27–8 also shows that the distance, L_1, decreases as $N_1 - N_2$ increases. This result has been found by Hays (1985) for the congression position of meiotic chromosomes in grasshopper spermatocytes when the number of kinetochore microtubules at one kinetochore complex is decreased by laser microsurgery. A focused laser microbeam was used to selectively destroy part of a kinetochore complex in a metaphase chromosome. After irradiation, the chromosome moved away from the spindle equator toward the pole faced by the undamaged kinetochore complex. When the chromosome achieved a new equilibrium position, the cell was fixed, processed for electron microscopy, and the number of microtubules at the opposing kinetochores determined by serial section reconstruction. Independent of position, the undamaged kinetochore had the typical number of kinetochore microtubules. Data measured by Hays (1985, Table 1, Chapter 2) for L_1 as a function of the difference $(N_1 - N_2)$ between the number of microtubules at the undamaged kinetochore (N_1) to the damaged kinetochore (N_2) are also plotted in (Fig. 10).

The simplified model fits the Hays data surprisingly well. This may be fortuitous for several reasons. First, the real data involve chromosomes of different sizes (range 1.4–5.5 μm),. and chromosome size can have a major effect on chromosome position, as shown in Figure 27–6. Second, the simplified model does not consider effects of the orientation of the chromosome surface relative to the orientation of the microtubules in the calculation of OF on the chromosome. For example, if the ejection force is produced by the dynamic instability growth of polar microtubules (Rieder et al., 1986), then the magnitude of the ejection force may be much greater at surfaces of the chromosome facing the pole in comparison to surfaces oriented normal to the direction of microtubule growth. A third reason is the uncertainty in the assumptions I used to simplify the calculations of the values for the constant (k/e). Fourth, I have assumed that the magnitude of OF decreases as the reciprocal of the distance of the chromosome from the pole; it may be some other decreas-

ing function of the distance of the chromosome from the pole. A final reason is that the simplified model does not account for the reduced density of microtubules and, hence, the strength of the ejection force, which occurs at the periphery of the central spindle in a bipolar spindle.

Chromosome Positioning in Anaphse

At the onset of anaphase, the mechanical link between sister chromatids disappears in mitosis or homologous chromosomes in meiosis. Two mono-oriented chromosome complexes are formed, each having one-half the size of the chromosome complex in metaphase. In this numerical example, I assume that the size of the chromosome in anaphase is one-half the 3.5-μm length of the chromosome complex in metaphase, or $L_c/2$, and that the other spindle parameters remain unchanged. At metaphase, a 3.5-μm-long chromosome is positioned 6.125 μm away from the pole for the monopolar spindle (Fig. 27–7) and 12.25 μm from the pole in a bipolar spindle (Fig. 27–8). In anaphase, a mono-oriented chromosome of $L_c = 1.75$ will move to a position where $L_1 = 3$ μm in a monopolar and 2.5 μm in a bipolar spindle (Fig. 27–6). Thus, the majority of the movement of a chromosome to the pole in anaphase may simply be the consequence of the formation of mono-oriented chromosome complexes at the onset of anaphase that are one-half the size of the metaphase chromosome complex. No other changes in kinetochore function or in spindle dynamics may be required. Further poleward movement of the chromosome would occur concurrently with a reduction in the strength of OF produced by several mechanisms: the decrease in the density of polar microtubules, which occurs during anaphase, a reduction in the dynamic growth of the polar microtubules, or an inactivation of microtubule-associated translocators located on the chromosome. Similar arguments can also be made for anaphase in mitotic cells in which the metaphase chromosome splits along its length into two sister chromatids.

CONCLUSIONS

A simplified mechanistic model is presented for the congression of chromosomes at metaphase and the poleward movement of chromosomes in anaphase in animal spindles. The model represents a working hypothesis; it is by no means an established theory. It is based on a force balance mechanism and on two distinctly different types of force producers. One is a poleward force generator at the kinetochore whose strength depends only on the number of kinetochore microtubules (a "Pac-Man" motor). The other is an outward-directed force producer whose strength depends on the density of polar microtubules proximal to the surface of the chromosome arms (polar ejection force). The model evolved from analysis of the mechanism of metaphase chromosome congression in monopolar spindles.

ACKNOWLEDGMENTS

I thank Lynn Cassimeris and Neal Gliksman for their critical thinking and useful discussions about the model developed in this chapter. I also thank Richard Walker for his creative input into the drawings. This work was supported by NIH grant GM24364.

In Vitro Analysis of Anaphase Spindle Elongation

W. Zacheus Cande, Tobias Baskin, Christopher Hogan, Kent L. McDonald, Hirohisa Masuda, and Linda Wordeman

Department of Botany, University of California, Berkeley, California 94720; Department of Molecular, Cellular, and Developmental Biology, University of Colorado, Boulder, Colorado 80309 (K.L.M.)

INTRODUCTION

Anaphase chromosome movement is a complex process that may involve a series of different mechanochemical events (for review, see Inoué, 1981; McIntosh, 1985). In most spindles, chromosomes move poleward as kinetochore-attached microtubules shorten (anaphase A). This is usually accompanied by an increase in spindle length or pole-from-pole separation (anaphase B). During anaphase B, there is a massive rearrangement of microtubules in the spindle midzone, which is often interpreted as being due to the sliding apart of the two half-spindles (McDonald et al., 1977, 1979). Moreover, this process often occurs in association with microtubule polymerization, leading to an increase in the length of half-spindle microtubules. Finally, in some cells, forces generated by interactions between the spindle poles and other cytoplasmic components may act to reposition the spindle within the cell or further increase pole-from-pole separation (anaphase C). Although these events all involve microtubules as the primary cytoskeletal component and may all occur at the same time in any one cell, the mechanisms of force generation for each type of movement may be different (for review, see Inoué, 1981; McIntosh, 1985).

Our understanding of the cellular mechanochemistry of such processes as flagellar beat and fast axoplasmic transport has been aided by the development of in vitro model systems that mimic key elements of cellular movements that occur in vivo. The study of chromosome movement could also be clarified by an in vitro system. Hoffman-Berling (1954) pioneered the use of permeabilized cells for studying chromosome movements in vitro. We have successfully used this approach to describe the physiological requirements for maintenance of anaphase A and B in PtK$_1$ cells after lysis (Cande et al., 1981; Cande, 1982a,b). However, permeabilized cells rival living cells in morphological complexity, and it is difficult to analyze these preparations by conventional biochemical techniques. Alternatively, many attempts have been made to isolate mitotic spindles that move chromosomes, but, with one or two exceptions (for review, Cande, 1986, 1988; Sakai, 1978), isolated spindles are non-functional.

Recently we described a simple procedure for isolating functional spindles from cells of the diatom *Stephanopyxis turris,* using glycerol to stabilize spindle microtubules and filtration and differential centrifugation to purify the spindles free of cytoplasmic contamination (Cande and McDonald, 1985, 1986). After adenosine triphosphate (ATP) addition, the isolated spindles elongate in a life-like manner. Since our isolation medium and preparative procedures are similar to those used for preparation of morphologically intact but non-functional spindles from sea urchin zygotes and mammalian tissue culture cells (Silver et al., 1982; Zieve et al., 1980), retention of function in the diatom preparations probably depends on the unique and highly ordered morphology of the diatom spindle.

We have used isolated diatom spindles to analyze the mechanochemical events responsible for spindle elongation, the role of tubulin polymerization in this process, and the role of protein phosphorylation in regulating this event (Cande and McDonald, 1985, 1986; Masuda and Cande, 1987; McDonald et al., 1986; Wordeman and Cande, 1987). Our analysis of spindle elongation in vitro has lead us to postulate a new theoretical model for the mechanochemical events associated with anaphase B, which is presented in the last section of this chapter.

THE DIATOM CENTRAL SPINDLE: A SYSTEM FOR STUDYING SPINDLE ELONGATION

In the diatom, nature has performed a useful purification of key spindle components by spatially separating the machinery responsible for anaphases A and B. Since the chromosomes and kinetochore microtubules are on the spindle periphery, the movement of chromosomes poleward during anaphase A can occur independently of anaphase B and does not perturb the ordering of microtubules in the central spindle. The central spindle, which is responsible for anaphase B, consists of two sets of microtubules in paracrystalline-like arrays. These originate from the two plate-like spindle poles, interdigitate with one another, and show specific near-neighbor interactions in the zone of microtubule overlap (McDonald et al., 1977, 1979; Pickett-Heaps et al., 1978). The microtubules in each half-spindle are of relatively uniform length so that the microtubule ends distal to the poles are found in a narrow length distribution at the edges of the zone of microtubule overlap. Because of this morphology, the zone of microtubule overlap is visible in the light microscope. Therefore it has been possible to show that, in many diatoms, the overlap zone decreases in extent as the spindle elongates in vivo (Pickett-Heaps et al., 1980).

The spindle in *S. turris* is typical of diatom spindles in its organization (Fig. 28–1). Each half-spindle consists of about 300 microtubules, and the zone of microtubule overlap is about 25% of the total spindle length at the time of isolation (metaphase or early anaphase). Anaphase A occurs before anaphase B in vivo, and during anaphase B the spindle elongates at about 1.7 μm/min to more than double its metaphase length (McDonald et al., 1986). Microtubule growth must make a substantial contribution to the increase in spindle length, since the maximum change in pole-to-pole distance caused by a decrease in the extent of microtubule overlap could not be more than about 25% of the original spindle length.

Spindles of relatively uniform length (characteristically 8 ± 1 μm) are isolated from populations of dividing cells synchronized by day-length manipulations and drug blockage-/reversal (Wordeman et al., 1986). The methods used for isolation are gentle enough so that the arrangement and number of microtubules in isolated spindles is essentially the same as that found in vivo (McDonald et al., 1986). The pole structure is retained during isolation, but membranous components are lost, the chromatin unravels, and the kinetochores become less apparent.

SPINDLE ELONGATION IN VITRO

Spindle reactivation includes at least three different ATP-dependent events: 1) phos-

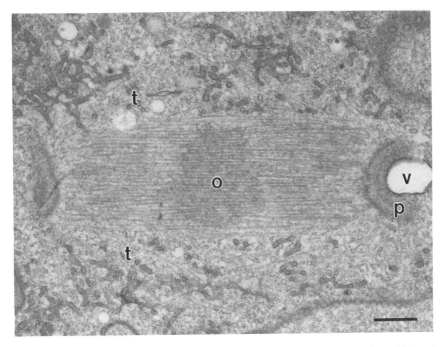

Fig. 28–1. A prometaphase spindle in *Stephanopyxis turris* sinking into the nucleus. This spindle has a distinct zone of microtubule overlap (o). The pole complex (p) is recurved and contains a single vacuole (v). Peripheral microtubules (t) are evident. ×28,500. Bar = 5 μm.

phorylation of spindle-associated proteins by an endogenous spindle-associated kinase (Wordeman and Cande, 1987), 2) separation of the half-spindles leading to an increase in spindle length (Cande and McDonald, 1985), and 3) selective microtubule depolymerization from the overlap zone poleward (Cande and McDonald, 1986). During spindle reactivation visualized with polarization optics and video microscopy, the two half-spindles slide completely apart with a concurrent decrease in the extent and magnitude of birefringence in the overlap zone (Fig. 28–2). Similar structural changes are observed in populations of spindles studied by indirect immunofluorescence. After ATP addition, a prominent gap develops between the two half-spindles. The gap is bridged by only a few microtubules, and the phase dense material that normally delineates the overlap zone has dispersed (Fig. 28–3a–f). Populations of spindles that have gaps are longer than control populations, and those

spindles that do not have gaps are often the shortest ones in the population (Fig. 28–3g,h). Since almost all spindles undergo these structural changes during reactivation, we can study the ultrastructure of individual spindles and the biochemistry in bulk preparations with some assurance that the machinery responsible for anaphase B is present in a typical form and functional state.

Chromatin swelling is not likely to account for elongation seen in vitro. After DNAse I digestion, little chromatin remains attached to the spindle, yet they will still elongate after ATP addition (Fig. 28–3). Spindles prepared and reactivated in spermidine/spermine have condensed chromatin, and after ATP addition these spindles will also elongate and form gaps (McDonald et al., 1986).

At an ultrastructural level the formation of gaps observed in the light microscope is seen as a decrease in number and a rearrangement of microtubules in the overlap

FORCE GENERATION INVOLVES MICROTUBULE SLIDING IN THE ZONE OF MICROTUBULE OVERLAP

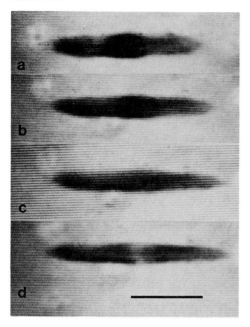

Fig. 28–2. Changes in spindle structure after reactivation as monitored by polarization optics with negative compensation and video microscopy. At 0 min **(a)**, 1 mM ATP is added and a noticeable change occurs in the birefringence of the zone of microtubule overlap at 70 sec **(b)**, 115 sec **(c)**, and 225 sec **(d)** after addition of nucleotide. Bar = 2 μm. (Reproduced from Baskin and Cande, 1988, with permission of the publisher.)

Spindle elongation in vitro is due to the sliding apart of the two half-spindles and a concomitant decrease in the zone of microtubule overlap (Fig. 28–2; Cande and McDonald, 1985). These results can best be interpreted by imagining that the microtubules of one half-spindle push against the microtubules of the other half-spindle, generating sliding forces between them. Our observations are consistent with models of force generation that postulate mechanochemical interactions in the zone of microtubule overlap that generate the forces necessary for anaphase B (Margolis et al., 1978; McDonald et al., 1977, 1979; McIntosh et al., 1969; Nicklas, 1971). Movement apart of the two half-spindles is not likely to be due to the autonomous swimming of each half-spindle, since the extent of spindle elongation is the same as the size of the microtubule overlap zone and since the two half-spindles always remain associated with each other during motility in vitro.

The changes in the distribution of newly incorporated tubulin in the spindle midzone during spindle elongation give further support to our interpretation of the mechanism of force generation (Masuda and Cande, 1987; Matsuda et al., 1988). When spindles are incubated in biotinylated tubulin before ATP addition, labeled tubulin is incorporated into the spindle midzone as two bands that flank the original zone of microtubule overlap (Fig. 28–4). This new tubulin is a marker for the free ends of the original microtubules in each half-spindle. As the spindle elongates, the two bands become one broad band in the spindle midzone. This change can most simply be explained if the newly labeled microtubules of each half-spindle slide over each other toward the center of the overlap zone.

Our observations of anaphase B in vitro are inconsistent with several published models for force generation. Based on observations of spindle elongation by a fungal spindle after laser irradiation, Aist and Berns

zone. After 10 min in the absence of ATP, the number of microtubules in the midzone is the same as in spindles fixed immediately after isolation. After 10 min in nucleotide, however, the number of microtubules in the spindle midzone is reduced to one-sixth the control value (Cande and McDonald, 1986). The changes that are observed in the midzone after different times in ATP are consistent with rearrangements of microtubules caused by the half-spindles sliding apart accompanied by microtubule depolymerization (Cande and McDonald, 1985, 1986). After ATP addition we have found in some spindles a striated fiber and other fibrous elements among the microtubules; but the role of these structures during mitosis is unknown (McDonald et al., 1986).

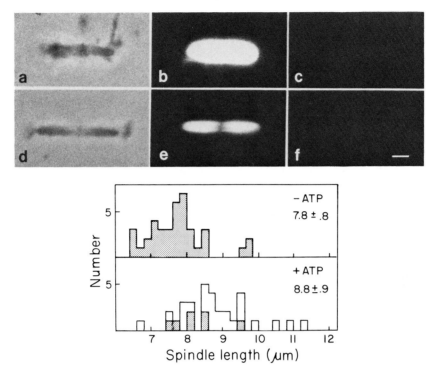

Fig. 28–3. Phase contrast and fluorescent micrographs of isolated spindles treated with DNAse I to remove chromatin before reactivation. **a,d:** Phase contrast micrographs and fluorescent micrographs to show **b,e:** antitubulin distribution and **c,f:** DAPI staining of chromatin. **a–c:** A spindle after incubation for 10 min without ATP. **d–f:** A spindle after 10 min in 1 mM ATP. The pole complexes are still attached to the spindle. The zone of overlap contains phase dense material and is reduced after addition of ATP. Bar = 2 μm. The histogram illustrates the lengths of spindles with and without ATP. Before reactivation, the chromatin was removed from these spindles by digestion with DNAse I. Average spindle lengths (±S.D.) are given in the upper right-hand corner of each panel. Spindles with prominent zones of microtubule overlap are shown as shaded areas, while those with midzone structural alterations (gaps) are not shaded. (Reproduced from McDonald et al., 1986, with permission of the publisher.)

(1981) argued that the spindle poles were pulled apart by cytoplasmic components interacting with astral microtubules. According to this model, the function of the central spindle is to provide a bipolar axis for chromosome separation and to act as a mechanical governor affecting the rate of spindle elongation. Girbardt (1968) and Health et al. (1984) came to similar conclusions after studying mitoses in other fungal spindles. They have suggested that the machinery responsible for the nuclear migration that occurs in many fungal cells also plays a role in pole-from-pole separation. Although a pole-pulling mechanism may play a prominent role during anaphase in fungi as well as in other cell types, it is not responsible for the spindle elongation we observe in vitro. There are no cytoplasmic structures present that could generate force. After isolation, many of these spindles have at least one and often both poles sticking out of the chromatin (Cande and McDonald, 1986; McDonald et al., 1986).

Since spindle elongation in vitro can occur in the absence of tubulin and in drugs that block microtubule assembly (Cande and McDonald, 1986), it is unlikely that microtu-

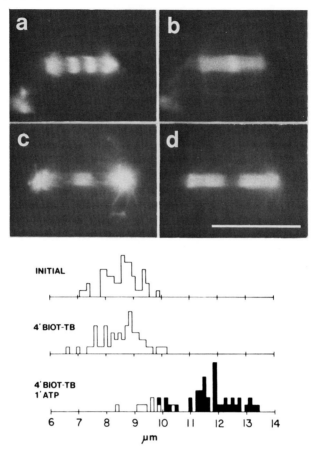

Fig. 28–4. The effect of tubulin on spindle elongation in vitro is shown in immunofluorescence micrographs of spindles double stained with antibiotin **(a,c)** and antiplant tubulin **(b,d)**. The antibiotin recognizes the biotinylated neurotubulin that has been incorporated into the spindle, and the antiplant tubulin only reacts with the diatom tubulin. Isolated spindles display the length distribution shown in the histogram ("initial"; N = 50). Spindles were incubated for 4 min in 20 μM biotinylated tubulin and 20 μM taxol (a,b) and display the length distribution shown ("4'BIOT-TB"; n = 50). After removing the tubulin, 1 mM ATP was added to initiate spindle elongation. Micrographs c and d show the pattern of biotinylated tubulin incorporation (c) and the distribution of original diatom microtubules after 1 min in ATP (d). The histogram "4'BIOT-TB, 1'ATP"; n = 50) shows that spindle elongation has occurred. Average spindle lengths were 8.0 μm (initial), 8.0 μm (no ATP), and 10.7 μm (1 mM ATP). Spindles with one zone of antibiotin staining in the midzone are shown as shaded areas in the histograms.

bule polymerization generates the forces required for anaphase B (Inoué and Sato, 1967; Pickett-Heaps et al., 1986). As shown in Figure 28–4, neurotubulin can be incorporated into the spindle, but this does not lead to spindle elongation unless ATP is present and microtubule sliding in the spindle midzone occurs (Masuda and Cande, 1987).

Finally, it has been suggested that tension generated during spindle formation and released during chromosome-to-pole movement may be responsible for spindle elongation (Snyder et al., 1984). However, this model of force generation cannot explain the spindle elongation we observe in vitro, since spindles increase in length in the absence of chromosome-to-pole movement and after digestion of chromatin by DNAse I treatment (Fig. 28–3).

THE ROLE OF MICROTUBULE POLYMERIZATION DURING SPINDLE ELONGATION

When neurotubulin is incorporated into the midzone of isolated diatom spindles, the extent of spindle elongation is no longer limited to the size of the original overlap zone, and some spindles elongate by three to four times the length of the original overlap (Masuda and Cande, 1987). Neurotubulin is incorporated in aster-like arrays at the spindle poles and as broad bands flanking the zone of microtubule overlap; during spindle reactivation the two bands in the midzone merge into one (Fig. 28–4). In the absence of taxol, biotinylated tubulin is incorporated onto spindle midzone microtubules but not at the poles (Masuda and Cande, 1987). Since these spindles elongate by more than the original overlap zone, tubulin incorporation into the midzone but not the poles is required for the increase in extent of spindle elongation.

Electron microscopy of spindles after elongation in tubulin shows that there are few microtubule fragments in the midzone. The newly incorporated tubulin must be adding onto the ends of the original half-spindle microtubules and not forming new microtubules adjacent to old ones. The distribution and arrangement of newly extended microtubules in the overlap zone after extensive spindle elongation is similar to that seen in control (no ATP, no tubulin) spindles (Masuda et al., 1988). Given the extensive spindle elongation that has occurred, this means that the microtubules of the overlap zone are comprised entirely of neurotubulin and that the original half-spindle tubulin polymer is no longer contained within the overlap zone. This inference is confirmed by Figure 28–4c,d. An antibody that recognizes only diatom tubulin shows that the two original half-spindles are separated by a gap, which is nevertheless spanned by tubulin recognized by neurotubulin-staining antibodies.

The redistribution of biotinylated tubulin during spindle elongation suggests that after tubulin is incorporated onto the ends of pre-existing microtubules at the ends of the overlap zone, the newly formed microtubules slide into and through the spindle midzone. Therefore, the mechanism of force generation is a process that is separate and distinct from tubulin polymerization. The rate of tubulin polymerization and the rate of spindle elongation define the extent of microtubule overlap during anaphase B and how much polymer slides through the overlap zone as the two half-spindles slide apart. We predict that in the presence of an unlimited pool of tubulin subunits and with no physical constraints on the separation of the spindle poles, the central spindle would elongate indefinitely. We suppose that the spindle motor is somehow tethered and confined to the spindle midzone, even as microtubules slide through it.

PHOSPHORYLATION OF SPINDLE-ASSOCIATED PROTEINS

To investigate the role of protein phosphorylation during spindle reactivation, we isolated spindles under conditions that permitted endogenous phosphatase activity (Table 28–1). The resulting spindles were incapable of elongating. The ability to elongate was restored to such spindles by incubating them in low levels of ATPγS, an ATP analog that acts as a phosphate donor for many kinases but does not support spindle motility (Wordeman and Cande, 1987). These experiments demonstrate that preserving the phosphorylated state of spindle proteins is essential for achieving spindle elongation in vitro.

An antibody to thiophosphate groups (Gerhart et al., 1985) has allowed us to visualize directly the distribution of thiophosphorylated proteins in spindles treated with ATPγS. As shown in Figures 28–5 and 28–6, when spindles are incubated in the minimal concentrations of ATPγS required

TABLE 28–1. Effect of Phosphatase Inhibitors on Spindle Reactivation

Treatment (15 min)[a]	Gaps (%)
Ice	47
20°C	13
20°C + 100 μM ATPγS	67
20°C + 40 mM sodium glycerophosphate	31

[a]Mitotic *S. turris* cells were homogenized in a spindle stabilization buffer at pH 7.0, and the crude homogenate was incubated for 15 min in the presence or absence of inhibitors of phosphatase activity. Mitotic nuclei were collected and reactivated in 1 mM ATP for 10 min. Reactivated spindles were scored as those that formed gaps within 10 min. These results indicate that maintaining isolated spindles in a highly phosphorylated state is integral to preserving spindle function in vitro.

to restore function, the spindle overlap zone and, in some spindles, the kinetochores and spindle poles are labeled. The major peptide labeled under these conditions has an apparent molecular weight of 205 kDa (Wordeman and Cande, 1987). At higher concentrations of nucleotide, more proteins become labeled and more structures in the spindle become stained (Fig. 28–5b). However, under these conditions the 205 kDa peptide is still one of the major thiophosphorylated spindle proteins. When spindle microtubules are depolymerized, the 205 kDa protein is released into the supernatant (Wordeman and Cande, 1987). This suggests that the 205 kDa protein may be a MAP. Since spindle reactivation is correlated with phosphorylation of the 205 kDa protein, it is possible that this protein is part of the regulatory machinery or a component of the enzyme complex in the overlap zone that is responsible for generating the forces required for anaphase B.

A variety of studies suggests that the mechanism by which cells regulate their progression through mitosis may involve protein phosphorylation. It has been demonstrated that the level of phosphate incorporation into many proteins increases when cells enter mitosis (Doree et al., 1983; Howlett, 1986; Karsenti et al., 1987), and immunocytochemical studies demonstrate that phosphoproteins are associated with the centrosomes, kinetochores and midbodies of spindles from a variety of cells (Vandre et al., 1986). It is likely that phosphorylation of many of these proteins plays a key role in spindle assembly and in the regulation of spindle mechanochemistry. The phosphorylation of overlap zone proteins we observe in vitro may be an example of such an event.

PHYSIOLOGY OF SPINDLE ELONGATION

In Table 28–2 we have summarized the pharmacology of spindle elongation in isolated diatom central spindles and compared it with conditions that maintain anaphase B in permeabilized PtK$_1$ cells, reactivate flagellar beat, and promote kinesin-based microtubule gliding. Although there are several ATP-dependent processes occurring during spindle reactivation, the pharmacology described in Table 28–1 is associated with the diatom spindle motor rather than a spindle-associated kinase. The phosphorylation of spindle-associated proteins is broader in its nucleotide specificity than spindle elongation, and it is unaffected by vanadate, sulfhydryl reagents, and adenylyl imidodiphosphate (AMP-PNP) (Wordeman and Cande, 1987). Since the physiological requirements for anaphase B are similar in diatom spindles, PtK$_1$ cells, and isolated sea urchin spindles (for review, see Sakai, 1978), analogous mechanochemical systems may be involved in anaphase spindle elongation in many cell types. Based on the pharmacology of spindle reactivation we previously argued that a dynein-like ATPase is involved in anaphase B (Cande, 1982a,b). However, it is more reasonable to assume that the motor responsible for anaphase spindle elongation is unique to the spindle. Although reactivation of the diatom central spindle is similar to reactivation of the axoneme with respect to vanadate inhibition and sulfhydryl reagent sensitivity, it differs in nucleotide specificity, EHNA sensitivity, and inhibition by equimolar mixtures of AMP-PNP and ATP. Kinesin, an ATPase involved in fast axoplasmic transport (Vale et al., 1985), does share

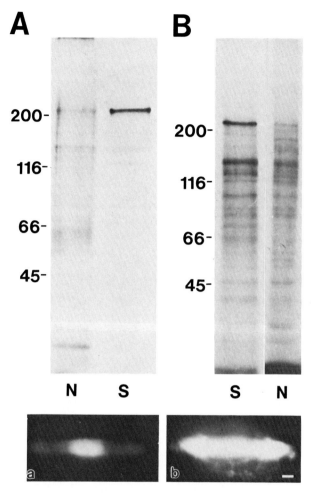

Fig. 28–5. Identification of thiophosphorylated antigens. 1) Mitotic spindles thiophosphorylated with low levels of ATPγS^{35} (10 μm, 5 min) show mainly midzone thiophosphorylation when labeled with an antibody to thiophosphorylated proteins (a). Fluorographs of such spindles that have been depolymerized and analyzed by SDS-PAGE (S) reveal the major thiophosphorylated species to be a 205 kDa polypeptide (A). Indirect immunofluorescence of spindles incubated in high levels of ATPγS^{35} (50 μm, 10 min) show heavy labeling throughout the spindle (b). Many peptides are labeled in extracts of these spindles (B). S, spindle extract; N, pellet after extraction (for methods, see Wordeman and Cande, 1987).

with spindle elongation a low affinity for AMP-PNP, but kinesin-based microtubule gliding is insensitive to vanadate or sulf-hydryl reagents (except at high concentrations) and is not very specific in its nucleotide requirements. Given that spindle elongation involves a unique mechanical event, the sliding apart of antiparallel sets of microtubules, it is plausible to assume that the mechanochemical enzymes responsible for this process are also unique to the spindle.

BEHAVIOR OF OVERLAP ZONE PROTEINS DURING SPINDLE ELONGATION

We have used the thiophosphorylation of spindle midzone proteins (Wordeman and

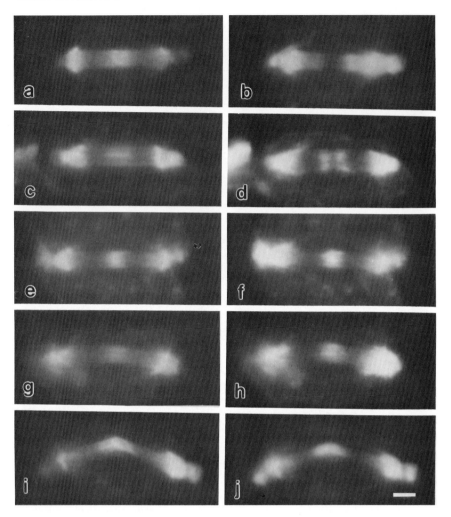

Fig. 28–6. Behavior of phosphorylated midzone antigen during reactivation in the presence of ATP. Mitotic spindles exposed to ATPγS during isolation were incubated for 5 min in exogenous biotinylated tubulin and then reactivated in 1 mM ATP. Spindles were double labeled with fluorescein-conjugated avidin (**b, d, f, h, j**) and an antibody to thiophosphorylated proteins (**a, c, e, g, i**). Spindles before addition of ATP are shown in a and b. In b, the bands of biotinylated tubulin that flank the overlap zone have merged with the staining of the pole-nucleated biotinylated microtubules. Spindles were in 1 mM ATP for 0.5 min (c and d), 1 min (e and f), or 2 min (G–J). Photomicrographs correspond to typical spindles in each population. Notice that newly added biotinylated microtubules move into the midzone and eventually colocalize with the phosphorylated midzone proteins. Bar = 2 μm.

Cande, 1987) to study the changes in distribution of midzone-associated proteins during spindle reactivation. Normally, during spindle reactivation there is a decrease in the extent of microtubule overlap that parallels the increase in spindle length. Under these conditions the zone of thiophosphory-

lation of midzone proteins also decreases, until at gap formation little or no label remains in the spindle midzone (Wordeman, unpublished data; Wordeman et al., manuscript in preparation).

In double-labeling experiments we studied the relative distribution of newly incor-

TABLE 28–2. Pharmacology of Anaphase Spindle Elongation Compared With Other Motile Systems

	Diatom[a]	PtK₁ cell[b]	Flagellar beat[c]	Kinesin-based microtubule gliding[d]
Nucleotide specificity	ATP	ATP > CTP > ITP	ATP	ATP > GTP, ITP
Vanadate inhibition (50% inhibition)	+ (<25 μM)	+ (<25 μM)	+ (<1 μM)	− (>100 μM)
Inhibition by N-ethyl-maleimide (<1 mM)	+	+	+	−
Inhibition by EHNA (~1.5 mM)	−	+	+	−
Inhibition by equimolar mixture of AMP-PNP/ATP	+	+	−	+

EHNA, = erythro-9-[3-(2-hydroxynonyl)]adenine; AMP-PNP, adenylyl imidodiphosphate; ATP, adenosine triphosphate; GTP, guanosine triphosphate; ITP, inosine triphosphate; CTP, cytidine triphosphate.
[a]Cande and McDonald (1986).
[b]Cande (1982a,b).
[c]Gibbons and Gibbons (1972), Gibbons et al. (1978), Bouchard et al. (1981).
[d]Vale et al. (1985).

porated biotinylated tubulin versus thiophosphorylated proteins (Fig. 28–6). As described above, the biotinylated tubulin can be used as a marker for free microtubule ends in the overlap zone. During spindle reactivation the new tubulin, hence the original microtubule ends, move into the midzone, and the two bands of biotinylated tubulin merge into one band (Fig. 28–6). However, the thiophosphorylated overlap zone proteins do not change position or move out of the spindle midzone with the sliding microtubules. This shows that the distribution of some accessory proteins in the spindle midzone is largely unaffected by the mechanical translocation of microtubules, until the terminal stages of spindle elongation when the extent of overlap decreases (Wordeman et al., manuscript in preparation).

A MODEL FOR THE MECHANISM OF ANAPHASE B

Two observations from our analysis of spindle elongation in vitro must be explained by any theoretical model for the mechanism of force generation during anaphase B: 1) spindles elongate because the two half-spindles slide apart and 2) when isolated spindles are incubated in exogenous tubulin, spindles keep elongating, even after the original half-spindles have separated, and the overlap zone has become composed entirely of microtubules whose subunits have been added in vitro. Since these spindles have elongated by the equivalent of three to four times the original overlap zone, interactions between diatom microtubules and neurotubules of opposite polarity, mediated by cross bridges stationed permanently on the diatom microtubules, could not account for the spindle elongation seen. Since there is no exogenous molecular pool to provide motors for the new polymer, the enzyme complexes responsible for the half-spindles sliding apart must behave in a manner radically different from dynein arms in a flagellar exoneme. We have identified two possibilities consistent with our observations. One is that the mechanochemical transducer is a bipolar element with several sites of mechanical interaction, capable of driving microtubules poleward while it remains in the spindle midzone. In the other we assume that the mechanochemical transducer is a unipolar element, like dynein, but that it is bound to a second cytoskeletal element that remains stationary as microtubules slide past it.

If spindle motors can move laterally along a microtubule toward its free, i.e., plus, end, a behavior originally postulated by Margolis et al. (1986) for STOP proteins, then motors will accumulate in the zone of microtubule overlap regardless of the distribution of the original half-spindle microtubules. The motor complex, at a minimum, would have two sites capable of generating mechanical forces: one to move the motor complex toward the free end of the microtubule and another to move an adjacent antiparallel microtubule past it. Each site would alternate in function, since, if both sites work at the same time, they would cancel each other out or release the motor complex from the microtubules. Alternatively, the spindle motor may be the equivalent of a myosin thick filament with many active sites capable of driving microtubules away from the spindle midzone while always remaining in the zone of microtubule overlap. In either case this model is consistent with the morphological studies that demonstrate defined spacings between antiparallel microtubules and cross bridges in the overlap zone (McDonald et al., 1977, 1979).

In our second model we suggest that the spindle motor complexes are permanently bound to another cytoskeletal component that acts as a scaffold to tether motors in the spindle midzone and to give the motors something stable to push against as microtubules move out of the midzone. Like dynein, each motor complex would only need one active site capable of microtubule translocation; however, unlike a dynein cross bridge the other end is not bound to another microtubule but to a midzone cytomatrix that remains in the midzone as the microtubules move away. The 205 kDa thiophosphorylated protein has the postulated behavior of this complex. The osmophilic fuzz that is a prominent feature in electron micrographs of spindle midbodies and zones of microtubule overlap in many cells (see Fig. 28–1) also behaves in this fashion during anaphase and may be a morphological expression of a spindle midzone scaffold.

ACKNOWLEDGMENTS

We thank Douglas Ohm and Barbara Brady for technical assistance. The research summarized in this chapter was supported by NSF grant PCM8408594 and NIH grant GM23238.

Bibliography 5, Chapters 23–28

Aist, J.R., and M.W. Berns (1981) Mechanics of chromosome separation during mitosis in *Fusarium* (*Fungi imperfecti*): New evidence from ultrastructural and laser microbeam experiments. J. Cell Biol. 91:446–458.

Allen, C., and G.G. Borisy (1974) Structural polarity and directional growth of microtubules of *Chlamydomonas* flagella. J. Mol. Biol. 90:381–402.

Amos, L.A., and A. Klug (1974) The arrangement of subunits in flagellar microtubules. J. Cell Sci. 14:523–549.

Bajer, A. (1973) Interaction of microtubules and the mechanism of chromosome movement (Zipper hypothesis). Cytobios 8:139–160.

Bajer, A., and J. Mole-Bajer (1972) Spindle dynamics and chromosome movements. Int. Rev. Cytol., Suppl. 3:1–271.

Bajer, A., and J. Mole-Bajer (1975) Lateral movements in the spindle and the mechanism of mitosis. In S. Inoué and R.E. Stephens (eds): Molecules and Cell Movement. New York: Raven Press, pp. 77–96.

Bajer, A.S. (1982) Functional autonomy of monopolar spindle and evidence for oscillatory movement in mitosis. J. Cell Biol. 93:33–48.

Baskin, T., and W.Z. Cande (1988) Direct observation of mitotic spindle elongation in vitro. Cell Motil. Cytoskeleton 10:210–216.

Bergen, L.G., R. Kuriyama, and G.G. Borisy (1980) Polarity of microtubules nucleated by centrosomes and chromosomes of CHO cells in vitro. J. Cell Biol. 84:151–159.

Bloom, G.S., F.C. Lica, and R.B. Vallee (1984) Widespread cellular distribution of MAP 1A in the mitotic spindle and on interphase microtubules. J. Cell Biol. 98:331–340.

Bouchard, P., A. Cheung, S. Penningroth, C. Gagnon, and C. Bardin (1981) Erythro-9-[3-(2-hydroxyl-3-nonyl)]adenine is an inhibitor of sperm motility that blocks dynein ATPase and protein carboxylase activities. Proc. Natl. Acad. Sci. USA 78:3610–3613.

Brinkley, B.R., and J. Cartwright (1971) Ultrastructural analysis of the mitotic spindle elongation in mammalian cells in vitro. Direct microtubule counts. J. Cell Biol. 50:416–431.

Brinkley, B.R., and J. Cartwright (1975) Cold-labile and cold-stable microtubules in the mitotic spindle of mammalian cells. Ann. N.Y. Acad. Sci. 253:428–439.

Buck, R.C., and J.M. Tisdale (1962) The fine structure of the midbody of the rat erythroblast. J. Cell Biol. 13:109–123.

Bulinski, J.C., and G.G. Borisy (1979) Self-assembly of microtubules in extracts of cultured HeLa cells and the identification of HeLa microtubule-associated proteins. Proc. Natl. Acad. Sci. USA 76:293–297.

Bulinski, J.C., J.A. Rodriguez, and G.G. Borisy (1980) Microtubule-associated proteins from cultured HeLa cells: Analysis of molecular properties and effects on microtubule polymerization. J. Biol. Chem. 255:11570–11576.

Cabral, F., M. Schibler, I. Abraham, C. Witfield, R. Kenyama, C. McClurbin, S. Mackensen, and M.M. Gottesman (1984) Genetic analysis of microtubule functions in CHO cells. In G.G. Borisy, D. Cleveland, and D. Murphy (eds): Molecular Biology of the Cytoskeleton. Cold Spring Harbor, New York: Cold Spring Harbor Laboratory, pp. 305–317.

Cande, W.Z. (1982a) Nucleotide requirements for anaphase chromosome movements in permeabilized mitotic cells: Anaphase B but not anaphase A requiring ATP. Cell 28:15–22.

Cande, W.Z. (1982b) Inhibition of spindle elongation in permeabilized mitotic cells by erythro-9-[3-(2-hydroxynonyl)]adenine. Nature 295: 700–701.

Cande, W.Z. (1986) Reactivation of mitosis in vitro. Trends Biochem. Sci. 11:447–449.

Cande, W.Z. (1988) Mitosis in vitro. In J. Hyams and B.R. Brinkley (eds): Mitosis. London: Academic Press, (in press).

Cande, W.Z., and K.L. McDonald (1985) In vitro reactivation of anaphase spindle elongation using isolated diatom spindles. Nature 316:168–170.

Cande, W.Z., and K.L. McDonald (1986) Physiological and ultrastructural analysis of elongating mitotic spindles reactivated in vitro. J. Cell Biol. 103:593–604.

Cande, W.Z., K. McDonald, and R.L. Meeusen (1981) A permeabilized model for studying cell division: a comparison of anaphase chromosome movement and cleavage furrow constriction in lysed P+K$_1$ cells. J. Cell Biol. 88:618–629.

Carlier, M.F., T. Hill, and Y. Chen (1984) Interference of GTP hydrolysis in the mechanism of microtubule assembly: An experimental study. Proc. Natl. Acad. Sci. USA 81:771–775.

Cassimeris, L.U., C.L. Rieder, and E.D. Salmon (1987a) Monopolar spindles: Microtubule dynamics and chromosome position. J. Cell Biol. 105:205a.

Cassimeris, L.U., R.A. Walker, N.K. Pryer, and E.D. Salmon (1987b) Dynamic instability of microtubules. Bioessays 7:149–154.

Centouze, V.E., D.D. Vandre, and G.G. Borisy (1986) Growth of microtubules on mitotic centrosomes is blocked by MPM-2. J. Cell Biol. 103:412a.

Collins, C.A., and R.B. Vallee (1986) A microtubule-activated ATPase from sea urchin eggs, distinct from cytoplasmic dynein and kinesin. Proc. Natl. Acad. Sci. USA 83:4799–4803.

Comings, D.E., and T.A. Okada (1971) Fine structure of kinetochore in Indian muntjac. Exp. Cell Res. 67:97–110.

Cooke, C.A., M.M.S. Heck, and W.C. Earnshaw (1988) The INCENP antigens: Movement from inner centromere to midbody during mitosis. J. Cell Biol. 105:2053–2068.

DeBrabander, M., J.C. Bulinski, G. Geuens, J. DeMey, and G.G. Borisy (1981a) Immunoelectron microscopic localization of the 210,000 mol. wt. microtubule-associated protein in cultured cells of primates. J. Cell Biol. 91:438–445.

DeBrabander, M., G. Geuens, J. DeMey, and M. Joniau (1981b) Nucleated assembly of mitotic microtubules in living PtK2 cells after release from nocodazole treatment. Cell Motil. 1:469–484.

DeBrabander, M., G. Geuens, R. Nuydens, R. Willebords, F. Aerts, and J. DeMey (1986) Microtubule dynamics during the cell cycle: The effects of taxol and nocodazole on the microtubule system of PtK2 cells at different stages of the mitotic cycle. Int. Rev. Cytol. 101:215–274.

DeMey, J., A.M. Lambert, A.S. Bajer, M. Moeremans, and M. DeBrabander (1982) Visualization of microtubules in interphase and mitotic plant cells of Haemanthus endosperm with the immuno-gold staining method. Proc. Natl. Acad. Sci. USA 79:1898–1902.

DeMey, J., M. Moeremans, G. Geuens, R. Nuydens, H. VanBelle, and M. DeBrabander (1980) Immunocytochemical evidence for the association of calmodulin with microtubules of the mitotic apparatus. In M. DeBrabander and J. DeMey (eds): Microtubules and Microtubule Inhibitors. Amsterdam: Elsevier/North Holland Biochemical, pp. 227–240.

Dietz, R. (1958) Multiple Geshlechtschromosomen bei den Cypriden ostracoden, ihre Evolution und ihr Teilungsvergalten. Chromosoma 9:359–440.

Doree, M., G. Peaucellier, and A. Picard (1983) Activity of the maturation-promoting factor and the extent of protein phosphorylation oscillate simultaneously during meiotic maturation of starfish oocytes. Dev. Biol. 99:489–501.

Ellis, G.W., and D.A. Begg (1981) Chromosome micromanipulation studies. In Mitosis/Cytokinesis. New York: Academic Press, pp. 155–179.

Endo, S., M. Toriyama, and H. Sakai (1983) The mitotic apparatus with unusually many microtubules from sea urchin eggs treated with hexyleneglycol. Dev. Growth Differ. 25:307–314.

Euteneuer, U., W.T. Jackson, and J.R. McIntosh (1982) Polarity of spindle microtubules in Haemanthus endosperm. J. Cell Biol. 94:644–653.

Euteneuer, U., and J.R. McIntosh (1980) Polarity of midbody and phragmoplast microtubules. J. Cell Biol. 87:509–515.

Euteneuer, U., and J.R. McIntosh (1981a) Structural polarity of kinetochore microtubules in PtK1 cells. J. Cell Biol. 89:338–345.

Euteneuer, U., and J.R. McIntosh (1981b) Polarity of some motility related microtubules. Proc. Natl. Acad. Sci. USA 78:372–376.

Evans, L., T.J. Mitchison, and M.W. Kirschner (1985) Influence of the centrosome on the structure of nucleated microtubules. J. Cell Biol. 100:1185–1191.

Forer, A. (1965) Local reduction of spindle fiber birefringence in living *Nephrotoma suturalis* spermatocytes induced by ultraviolet microbeam irradiation. J. Cell Biol. 25:95–117.

Fuge, H. (1977) Ultrastructure of the mitotic spindle. Int. Rev. Cytol. Suppl. 6:1–58.

Gerhart, J., M. Cyert, and M. Kirschner (1985) M-phase promoting factors from eggs of *Xenopus laevis.* Cytobios 43:335–347.

Gibbons, B.H., and I.R. Gibbons (1972) Flagellar movement and adenosine triphosphatase activity in sea urchin sperm extracted with Triton X-100. J. Cell Biol. 54:75–97.

Gibbons, I.R., M.P. Cosson, J.A. Evans, B.H. Gibbons, B. Houck, K.H. Martinson, W.S. Sale, and W.J.Y. Tang (1978) Potent inhibition of dynein adenosine triphosphatase and the motility of cilia and flagella by vanadate. Proc. Natl. Acad. Sci. USA 75:2220–2224.

Girbardt, M. (1968) Ultrastructure and dynamics of the moving nucleus. Symp. Soc. Exp. Biol. 22:249–259.

Goodenough, U., and J.E. Heuser (1984) Structural comparison of purified dynein proteins with in situ dynein arms. J. Mol. Biol. 180:1083–1118.

Gorbsky, G.J., P.J. Sammak, and G.G. Borisy (1987a) Chromosomes move poleward in anaphase along stationary microtubules that coordinately disassemble from their kinetochore ends. J. Cell Biol. 104:9–18.

Gorbsky, G.J., P.J. Sammak, and G.G. Borisy (1987b) Microtubule dynamics and chromosome motion visualized in living anaphase cells. J. Cell Biol. 105:175a.

Gorbsky, G.J., P.J. Sammak, and G.G. Borisy (1988) Microtubule dynamics and chromosome motion visualized in living anaphase cells. J. Cell Biol. 106:1185–1192.

Haimo, L.T., and B.R. Telzer (1981) Dynein-microtubule interactions. ATP-sensitive dynein binding and the structural polarity of mitotic microtubules. Cold Spring Harbor Symp. Quant. Biol. 46:207–218.

Hamaguchi, Y., M. Toriyama, H. Sakai, and Y. Hiramoto (1987) Redistribution of fluorescently labeled tubulin in the mitotic apparatus of sand dollar eggs and the effects of taxol. Cell Struct. Funct. 12:43–52.

Harris, P. (1975) The role of membranes in the organization of the mitotic apparatus. Exp. Cell Res. 94:409–425.

Hays, T.S. (1985) The Force–Balance Mechanism of Chromosome Congression. Thesis. University of North Carolina at Chapel Hill.

Hays, T.S., D. Wise, and E.D. Salmon (1982) Traction force on a kinetochore at metaphase acts as a linear function of kinetochore fiber length. J. Cell Biol. 93:374–382.

Heath, I.B. (1980) Varient mitosis in lower eukaryotes: Indicators of the evolution of mitosis? Int. Rev. Cytol. 64:1–80.

Heath, I.B., K. Rethoret, and P.B. Moens (1984) The ultrastructure of mitotic spindles from conventionally fixed and freeze-substituted nuclei of the fungus *Saprolegnia.* Eur. J. Cell Biol. 35:284–295.

Heidemann, S.R., G.W. Zieve, and J.R. McIntosh (1980) Evidence for microtubule subunit addition to the distal end of mitotic structures in vitro. J. Cell Biol. 87:152–159.

Hepler, P.K., and D.A. Callahan (1987) Free calcium increases during anaphase in stamen hair cells of *Tradescantia.* J. Cell Biol. 105:2137–2143.

Hepler, P.K., J.R. McIntosh, and S.C. Cleland (1970) Intermicrotubule bridges in the mitotic spindle apparatus. J. Cell Biol. 45:438–449.

Heuser, J.E., and S.R. Salpeter (1979) Organization of acetylcholine receptors in quick-frozen, deep-etched, and rotary-replicated *Torpedo* postsynaptic membrane. J. Cell Biol. 82:150–173.

Hill, T.L. (1985) Theoretical problems related to the attachment of microtubules to kinetochores. Proc. Natl. Acad. Sci. USA 82:4404–4408.

Hill, T.L., and M.W. Kirschner (1982) Bioenergetics and kinetics of microtubule and actin filament assembly–disassembly. Int. Rev. Cytol. 78:1–125.

Hinkley, R., and A. Telser (1974) Heavy meromyosin-binding filaments in the mitotic apparatus of mammalian cells. Exp. Cell Res. 86:161–164.

Hirokawa, N. (1982) Cross-linker system between neurofilaments, microtubules, and membrane organelles in frog axons revealed by the quick-freeze, deep-etching method. J. Cell Biol. 94:129–142.

Hirokawa, N., G.S. Bloom, and R.B. Vallee (1985a) Cytoskeletal architecture and immmunocytochemical localization of microtubule-associated proteins in regions of axons associated with rapid axonal transport: The β, β'-imminodipropionitrile-intoxicated axon as a model system. J. Cell Biol. 101:227–239.

Hirokawa, N., and J.E. Heuser (1981) Quick-freeze, deep-etch visualizations of intestinal epithelial cells. J. Cell Biol. 91:339–409.

Hirokawa, N., and S. Hisanaga (1987) "Buttonin," a unique button-shaped microtubule-associated protein (75 KD) that decorates the spindle microtubule surface hexagonally. J. Cell Biol. 104:1553–1561.

Hirokawa, N., R. Takemura, and S. Hisanaga (1985b) Cytoskeletal architecture of isolated mitotic spindle with special reference to MAPs and cytoplasmic dynein. J. Cell Biol. 101:1858–1870.

Hisanaga, S., and N. Hirokawa (1987) Substructure of sea urchin egg cytoplasmic dynein. J. Mol. Biol. 195:919–927.

Hisanaga, S., T. Masaki, H. Sakai, I. Mabuchi, and Y. Hiramoto (1987) Localization of sea urchin egg cytoplasmic dynein in mitotic apparatus studied by using a monoclonal antibody against sea urchin sperm flagellar 21S dynein. Cell Motil. Cytoskeleton 7:97–109.

Hisanaga, S., and H. Sakai (1983) Cytoplasmic dynein of the sea urchin egg. II. Purification, characterization and interactions with microtubules and Ca^{2+}-calmodulin. J. Biochem. 93:87–98.

Hoffman-Berling, H. (1954) Die Bedeutung des Adenosintriophosphate für die Zell und Kernteilungsbewegungen in des Anaphase. Biochem. Biophys. Acta. 15:332–339.

Hollenbeck, P.J., F. Suprynowicz, and W.A. Cande (1984) Cytoplasmic dynein-like ATPase crosslinks microtubules in an ATPase-sensitive manner. J. Cell Biol. 99:1251–1258.

Horio, T., and H. Hotani (1986) Visualization of the dynamic instability of individual microtubules by dark-field microscopy. Nature 321:605- 607.

Howlett, S.K. (1986) A set of proteins showing cell cycle dependent modification in the early mouse embryo. Cell 45:387–396.

Hughes-Schrader, S. (1943) Polarization, kinetochore movements, and bivalent structure in the meiosis of male spermatids. Biol. Bull. 85:265–300.

Inoué, S. (1964) Organization and function of the mitotic spindle. In R.D. Allen and N. Kamiya (eds): Primitive Motile Systems in Cell Biology. New York: Academic Press, pp. 548–598.

Inoué, S. (1981) Cell division and the mitotic spindle. J. Cell Biol. 91:131s–147s.

Inoué, S., and H. Ritter (1975) Dynamics of mitotic spindle organization and function. In S. Inoué and R.E. Stephens (eds): Molecules and Cell Movement. New York: Raven Press, pp. 3–29.

Inoué, S., and H. Sato (1967) Cell motility by labile association of molecules: The nature of mitotic spindle fibers and their role in chromosome movement. J. Gen. Physiol. 50:259–292.

Izant, J.G. (1983) The role of calcium ions during mitosis. Chromosoma 88:1–10.

Jameson, L., T. Frey, B. Zeeberg, F. Dalldorf, and M. Caplow (1980) Inhibition of microtubule assembly by phosphorylation of MAPs. Biochemistry 19:2472-2479.

Jensen, C.G. (1982) Dynamics of spindle microtubule organization: Kinetochore fiber microtubules of plant endosperm. J. Cell Biol. 92:540–558.

Joshi, H.C., V.L. Steel, R.E. Buxbaum, and S.R. Heidemann (1987) Mechanical force alters microtubule assembly in PC 12. J. Cell Biol. 105:320a.

Karsenti, E., R. Bravo, and M. Kirschner (1987) Phosphorylation changes associated with the cell cycle in Xenopus eggs. Dev. Biol. 119:442–453.

Keith, C., M. DiPaola, F.R. Maxfield, and M.L. Shelanski (1983) Microinjection of Ca^{2+}-calmodulin causes a localized depolymerization of microtubules. J. Cell Biol. 97:1918–1924.

Keller, T.C.S., and L.I. Rebhun (1982) Strongylocentrotus purpuratus spindle tubulin. I. Characteristics of its polymerization in vitro. J. Cell Biol. 93:788–796.

King, S.M., J.S. Hyams, and A. Luba (1982) Absence of microtubule sliding and an analysis of spindle function and elongation in isolated mitotic spindles from yeast. J. Cell Biol. 94:341–349.

Kirschner, M.W., and T.J. Mitchison (1986a) Beyond self-assembly: From microtubules to morphogenesis. Cell 45:329–342.

Koshland, D., T.J. Mitchison, and M.W. Kirschner (1988) Chromosome movement driven by microtubule depolymerization in vitro. Nature 331:499–504.

La Fountain, J.R., and L.A. Davison (1980) An analysis of spindle ultrastructure during anaphase of micronuclear division in Tetrahymena. Cell Motil. 1:41–61.

Leslie, R.J., R.B. Hird, L. Wilson, J.R. McIntosh, and J.M. Scholey (1987) Kinesin is associated with a nonmicrotubule component of sea urchin mitotic spindles. Proc. Natl. Acad. Sci. USA 84:2771–2775.

Leslie, R.J., and J.D. Pickett-Heaps (1983) Ultraviolet microbeam irradiations of mitotic diatoms: Investigations of spindle elongation. J. Cell Biol. 96:548–561.

Margolis, R., and L. Wilson (1978) Opposite end assembly and disassembly of microtubules at steady state in vitro. Cell 13:1–8.

Margolis, R.L., C.T. Rauch, and D. Job (1986) Purification and assay of a 145-kda protein (STOP 145) with microtubule-stabilizing and motility behavior. Proc. Natl. Acad. Sci. USA 83:639–643.

Margolis, R.L., L. Wilson, and B.I. Kiefer (1978) Mitotic mechanisms based on intrinsic microtubule behavior. Nature 272:450–452.

Masuda, H., and W.Z. Cande (1987) The role of tubulin polymerization during spindle elongation in vitro. Cell 49:193–202.

Masuda, H., K.L. McDonald, and W.Z. Cande (1988) The mechanism of anaphase spindle elongation: Uncoupling of tubulin incorporation and microtubule sliding during in vitro spindle reactivation. J. Cell Biol. 107, in press.

Maupin, P., and T.D. Pollard (1986) Arrangement of actin filaments and myosin-like filaments in the contractile ring and of actin-like filaments in the mitotic spindle of dividing HeLa cells. J. Ultrastruct. Mol. Res. 94:92–103.

Mazia, D. (1984) Centrosomes and mitotic poles. Exp. Cell Res. 153:1–15.

Mazia, D., N. Paweletz, G. Sludor, and E.M. Finze (1981) Cooperation of kinetochore and pole in establishment of monopolar mitotic apparatus. Proc. Natl. Acad. Sci USA 78:377–381.

McDonald, K.L., M.K. Edwards, and J.R. McIntosh (1979) Cross-sectional structure of the central mitotic spindle of *Diatoma vulgare*. Evidence for specific interactions between antiparallel microtubules. J. Cell Biol. 83:443–461.

McDonald, K.L., K. Pfister, H. Masuda, L. Wordeman, C. Staiger, and W.Z. Cande (1986) Comparison of spindle elongation in vivo and in vitro in *Stephanopyxis turris*. J. Cell Sci. Suppl. 5:205–227.

McDonald, K.L., J.D. Pickett-Heaps, J.R. McIntosh, and D.H. Tippit (1977) On the mechanism of anaphase spindle elongation in *Diatoma vulgare*. J. Cell Biol. 74:377–388.

McGill, M., and B.R. Brinkley (1975) Human chromosomes and centrioles as nucleating sites of the in vitro assembly of microtubules from bovine brain tubulin. J. Cell Biol. 67:189–199.

McIntosh, J.R. (1983) The centrosome as an organizer of the cytoskeleton. Mod. Cell Biol. 2:115–142.

McIntosh, J.R. (1985) Spindle structure and mechanisms of chromosome movement. In V.L. Dellarco, P.E. Voytec, and A. Holleander (eds): Aneuploidy: Etiology and Mechanisms. New York: Plenum Press, pp. 197–229.

McIntosh, J.R., W.Z. Cande, and J.A. Snyder (1975a) Structure and physiology of the mammalian mitotic spindle. In S. Inoué and R.E. Stephens (eds): Molecules and Cell Movement. New York: Raven Press, pp. 31–75.

McIntosh, J.R., W.Z. Cande, J.A. Snyder, and K. Vanderslice (1975b) Studies on the mechanism of mitosis. Ann. N.Y. Acad. Sci. 253:407–427.

McIntosh, J.R., and U. Euteneuer (1984) Tubulin hooks as probes for microtubule polarity. J. Cell Biol. 98:525–533.

McIntosh, J.R., P.K. Hepler, and D.G. VanWie (1969) Model for mitosis. Nature 224:659–663.

McIntosh, J.R., and S.C. Landis (1971) The distribution of spindle microtubules during mitosis in cultured human cells. J. Cell Biol. 49:468–497.

McIntosh, J.R., K.L. McDonald, M.K. Edwards, and B.M. Ross (1979) Three-dimensional structure of the central mitotic spindle of *Diatoma vulgare*. J. Cell Biol. 83:428–442.

McIntosh, J.R., U.P. Roos, B. Neighbors, and K.L. McDonald (1985) Architecture of the microtubule component of mitotic spindles from *Dictyostelium discoideum*. J. Cell Sci. 75:93–129.

McIntosh, J.R., and G.P.A. Vigers (1987) Microtubule dynamics in the mitotic spindle. Proc. EMSA 45:794–797.

McNiven, M.A., M. Wang, and K.R. Porter (1984) Microtubule polarity and direction of pigment transport reverse simultaneously in surgically severed melanophore arms. Cell 37:753–765.

Mitchison, T.J., L. Evans, E. Schulze, and M.W. Kirschner (1986) Sites of microtubule assembly and disassembly in the mitotic spindle. Cell 45:515-527.

Mitchison, T.J., and M.W. Kirschner (1984a) Microtubule assembly nucleated by isolated centrosomes. Nature 312:232–236.

Mitchison, T.J., and M.W. Kirschner (1984b) Dynamic instability of microtubule growth. Nature 312:237–242.

Mitchison, T.J., and M.W. Kirschner (1985a) Properties of the kinetochore in vitro. I. Microtubule nucleation and tubulin binding. J. Cell Biol. 101:755–765.

Mitchison, T.J., and M.W. Kirschner (1985b) Properties of the kinetochore in vitro. II. Microtubule capture and ATP-dependent translocation. J. Cell Biol. 101:766–777.

Mohri, H., T. Mohri, I. Mabuchi, I. Yazuki, H. Sakai, and K. Ogawa (1976) Localization of dynein in sea urchin eggs during cleavage. Dev. Growth Differ. 18:391–398.

Mullins, J.M., and J.R. McIntosh (1982) Isolation and initial characterization of the mammalian midbody. J. Cell Biol. 94:654–661.

Neighbors, B.W., R.C. Williams, and J.R. McIntosh (1988) Localization of kinesin in cultured cells. J. Cell Biol. 106:1193–1204.

Nicklas, R.B. (1965) Chromosome velocity during mitosis as a function of chromosome size and position. J. Cell Biol. 25:119–135.

Nicklas, R.B. (1971) Mitosis. Adv. Cell Biol. 2:225–297.

Nicklas, R.B. (1977) Chromosome movement: Facts and hypothesis. In M. Little, N. Paweletz, C. Petzelt, H. Ponstingl, D. Schroeter, and H.P. Zimmerman (eds): Mitosis Facts and Questions. Berlin: Springer-Verlag, pp. 150–155.

Nicklas, R.B. (1979) Chromosome movement and spindle birefringence in locally heated cells: Interaction versus local control. Chromosoma 74:1–37.

Nicklas, R.B. (1983) Measurement of the force produced by the mitotic spindle in anaphase. J. Cell Biol. 97:542–548.

Nicklas, R.B. (1986) Mitosis in eukaryotic cells: An overview of chromosome distribution. In V.L. Dellarco, P.E. Voytec, and A. Holleander (eds): Aneuploidy: Etiology and Mechanisms. New York: Plenum Press, pp. 183–195.

Nicklas, R.B. (1987a) Chromosomes and kinetochores do more in mitosis than was previously thought. In J.P. Gustafson, R. Appels, and R.J. Kaufman (eds): Chromosome Structure and Function: The Impact of New Concepts. New York: Plenum Press.

Nicklas, R.B. (1987b) Chromosomes move on trunctated spindles. J. Cell Biol. 105:176a.

Nicklas, R.B., and G.W. Gordon (1985) The total length of spindle microtubules depends on the number of chromosomes present. J. Cell Biol. 100:1–7.

Nicklas, R.B., and C.A. Koch (1969) Chromosome micromanipulation. III. Spindle fiber tension and the reorientation of mal-oriented chromosomes. J. Cell Biol. 43:40–56.

Nicklas, R.B., and D.F. Kubai (1985) Microtubules, chromosome movement, and reorientation after chromosomes are detached from the spindle by micromanipulation. Chromosoma 92:313–324.

Nicklas, R.B., D.F. Kubai, and T.S. Hays (1982) Spindle microtubules and their mechanical associations after micromanipulation in anaphase. J. Cell Biol. 95:91–104.

Oakley, B.R., and N.R. Morris (1981) A β-tubulin mutation in Aspergillus nidulans that blocks microtubule function without blocking assembly. Cell 24:837–845.

Oosawa, F., and S. Asakura (1975) Thermodynamics of the Polymerization of Proteins. New York: Academic Press.

Ostergren, G. (1950) Considerations on some elementary features of mitosis. Hereditas 36:1.

Paweletz, N. (1967) Zur funktion des "Fleming-Koerper" bei der Teilung Tierscher Zellen. Naturwissenschaften 54:533–541.

Peterson, J.B., and H. Ris (1976) Electron microscopic study of the spindle and chromosome movement in the yeast Saccharomyces cerevisiae. J. Cell Sci. 22:219–242.

Pickett-Heaps, J.D. (1986) Mitotic mechanisms: An alternative view. Trends Biochem. Sci. 11:504–507.

Pickett-Heaps, J.D., and D.H. Tippit (1978) The diatom spindle in perspective. Cell 14:455–457.

Pickett-Heaps, J.D., D.H. Tippit, S.A. Cohn, and T.P. Spurck (1986) Microtubule dynamics in the spindle: Theoretical aspects of assembly/disassembly reactions in vivo. J. Theor. Biol. 118:153–169.

Pickett-Heaps, J.D., D.H. Tippit, and R. Leslie (1980) Light and electron microscope observations in two large pennate diatoms Hantzschia and Nitzschia. I. Mitosis in vivo. Eur. J. Cell Biol. 21:1–11.

Pickett-Heaps, J.D., D.H. Tippit, and K.R. Porter (1982) Rethinking mitosis. Cell 29:729–744.

Poenie, M., J. Alderton, R. Steinhardt, and R.Y. Tsien (1986) Calcium rises abruptly and briefly throughout the cell at the onset of anaphase. Science 233:886–887.

Porter, M., J.M. Scholey, D.L. Stemple, G.P.A. Vigers, R.D. Vale, M.P. Sheetz, and J.R. McIntosh (1987) Characterization of the microtubule movement produced by sea urchin egg kinesin. J. Biol. Chem. 262:2794–2802.

Porter, M.E., P.M. Grissom, J.M. Scholey, E.D. Salmon, and J.R. McIntosh (1988) Immunological and biochemical analysis on the distribution of cytoplasmic dynein and dynein-like polypeptides in sea urchin eggs. J. Biol. Chem. 263:6759–6771.

Pratt, M.M. (1980) The identification of a dynein ATPase in unfertilized sea urchin eggs. Dev. Biol. 74:364–378.

Pratt, M.M., T. Otter, and E.D. Salmon (1980) Dynein-like Mg-ATPase in mitotic spindles isolated from sea urchin embryos (Strongylocentrotus droebachiensis). J. Cell Biol. 86:738–745.

Rebhun, L.I., M. Mellon, D. Jemiolo, J. Nath, and N. Ivy (1974) Regulation of size and birefringence of the in vivo mitotic apparatus. J. Supramol. Struct. 2:466–485.

Rickards, G.K. (1975) Prophase chromosome movements in living house cricket spermatocytes and this relationship to prometaphase, anaphase and granule movements. Chromosoma 49:407–455.

Rieder, C.L. (1982) The formation, structure, and composition of the mammalian kinetochore and kinetochore fiber. Int. Rev. Cytol. 79:1–58.

Rieder, C.L., and G.G. Borisy (1981) The attachment of kinetochores to the prometaphase spindle in PtK1 cells. Chromosoma 82:693–716.

Rieder, C.L., E.A. Davison, L.C.W. Jensen, and E.D. Salmon (1985) The distal kinetochore is not responsible for the oscillation of monooriented chromosomes in newt lung cells. In M. DeBrabander and J. DeMey (eds): Microtubules and Microtubule Inhibitors. Amsterdam: Elsevier Science Publishers, B.V., pp. 253–260.

Rieder, C.L., E.A. Davison, L.C.W. Jensen, L. Cassimeris, and E.D. Salmon (1986) Oscillatory movements of monooriented chromosomes and their position relative to the spindle pole result from he ejection properties of the aster and half-spindle. J. Cell Biol. 103:581–591.

Ripoll, P., S. Piminelli, M.M. Valdivia, and J. Avila (1985) A cell division mutant of *Drosophila* with a functionally abnormal spindle. Cell 41:907–912.

Ris, H. (1949) The anaphase movement of chromosomes in the spermatocytes of the grasshopper. Biol. Bull. 96:90–105.

Roos, U.P. (1973a) Light and electron microscopy of rat kanagaroo cells in mitosis. I. Formation and breakdown of the mitotic apparatus. Chromosoma 40:43–82.

Roos, U.P. (1973b) Light and electron microscopy of rat kangaroo cells in mitosis. II. Kinetochore structure and function. Chromosoma 41:195–220.

Roos, U.P. (1976) Light and electron microscopy of rat kangaroo cells in mitosis. III. Kinetochore structure and function. Chromosoma 54:363–385.

Sakai, H., I. Mabushi, S. Shimoda, R. Kuriyama, K. Ogawa, and H. Mohri (1976) Induction of chromosome motions in the glycerol-isolated mitotic apparatus: Nucleotide specificity and effects of anti-dynein and myosin sera on the motion. Dev. Growth Differ. 18:211–219.

Salmon, E.D. (1975) Spindle microtubules: Thermodynamics of in vivo assembly and role in chromosome movement. Ann. N.Y. Acad. Sci. 253:383–406.

Salmon, E.D. (1982) Mitotic spindles isolated from sea urchin eggs with EGTA lysis buffer. Methods Cell Biol. 25:69–105.

Salmon, E.D., and D.A. Begg (1980) Functional implications of cold-stable microtubules in kinetochore fibers of insect spermatocytes during anaphase. J. Cell Biol. 85:853–865.

Salmon, E.D., R.J. Leslie, W.M. Saxton, M.L. Karow, and J.R. McIntosh (1984a) Spindle microtubule dynamics in sea urchin embryos. J. Cell Biol. 99:2165–2174.

Salmon, E.D., M. McKeel, and T. Hays (1984b) Rapid rate of tubulin dissociation from microtubules in the mitotic spindle in vivo measured by blocking polymerization with colchicine. J. Cell Biol. 99:1067–1076.

Salmon, E.D., and R.R. Segall (1980) Calcium-labile mitotic spindles isolated from sea urchin eggs (*Lytechinus*). J. Cell Biol. 86:355–365.

Sanger, J.W. (1975) Presence of actin during chromosome movement. Proc. Natl. Acad. Sci. USA 72:2451.

Saxton, W.M., and J.R. McIntosh (1987) Interzone microtubule behavior in late anaphase and telophase spindles. J. Cell Biol. 105:875–886.

Saxton, W.M., D.L. Stemple, R.J. Leslie, E.D. Salmon, M. Zavortink, and J.R. McIntosh (1984) Tubulin dynamics in cultured mammalian cells. J. Cell Biol. 99:2175–2186.

Sellitto, C., and R. Kuriyama (1988) Distribution of a matrix component of the midbody during the cell cycle in Chinese hamster ovary cells. J. Cell Biol. 106:431–439.

Schaap, C.J., and A. Forer (1984) Video digitizer analysis of birefringence along the lengths of single chromosomal spindle fibers. J. Cell Sci. 65:21–40.

Schibler, M., and J.D. Pickett-Heaps (1987) The kinetochore fiber structure in the acentric spindles of the green alga *Oedogonium*. Protoplasma 137:29–44.

Scholey, J.M., B. Neighbors, J.R. McIntosh, and E.D. Salmon (1984) Isolation of microtubules and a dynein-like MgATPase from unfertilized sea urchin eggs. J. Biol. Chem. 259:6516–6525.

Scholey, J.M., M.E. Porter, P.M. Grissom, and J.R. McIntosh (1985) Identification of kinesin in sea urchin eggs and evidence for its localization in the mitotic spindle. Nature 318:483–486.

Schollmeyer, J.V. (1988) Calpain II involvement in mitosis. Science 240:911–913.

Schultz, E., and M. Kirschner (1986) Microtubule dynamics in interphase cells. J. Cell Biol. 102:1020–1031.

Silver, R.B., R.D. Cole, and W.Z. Cande (1980) Isolation of mitotic apparatus- containing vesicles with calcium^{2+}-sequestering activity. Cell 19:505–516.

Sluder, G., and C.L. Rieder (1985) Experimental separation of pronuclei in fertilized sea urchin eggs: Chromosomes do not organize a spindle in the absence of chromosomes. J. Cell Biol. 100:887–903.

Snyder, J.A., R. Golub, and S.P. Berg (1984) Sucrose-induced spindle elongation in mitotic PtK1 cells. Eur. J. Cell Biol. 35:62–69.

Snyder, J.A., and J.R. McIntosh (1975) Initiation and growth of microtubules from mitotic centers in lysed mammalian cells. J. Cell Biol. 67:774–760.

Soltys, B.J., and G.G. Borisy (1985) Polymerization of tubulin in vivo: Direct evidence for assembly onto microtubule ends and from centrosomes. J. Cell Biol. 100:1682–1689.

Stemple, D.L., S.S. Sweet, M.J. Welsh, and J.R. McIntosh (1988) Dynamics of a fluorescent calmodulin analog in the mammalian mitotic spindle at metaphase. Cell Motil. Cytoskeleton 9:231–242.

Taylor, E.W. (1959) Dynamics of spindle formation and its inhibition by chemicals. J. Cell Biol. 6:193–196.

Telzer, B.R., and L.T. Haimo (1981) Decoration of spindle microtubules with dynein: Evidence for uniform polarity. J. Cell Biol. 89:373–378.

Telzer, B.R., M.J. Moses, and J.L. Rosenbaum (1975) Assembly of microtubules onto kinetochores of isolated mitotic chromosomes of HeLa cells. Proc. Natl. Acad. Sci. USA 72:4023–4027.

Tippit, D.H., C.T. Fields, K.L. O'Connell, and J.D. Pickett-Heaps (1984) The organization of microtubules during anaphase and telophase spindle elongation in the rust fungus Puccinia. Eur. J. Cell Biol. 34:34–44.

Tippit, D.H., J.D. Pickett-Heaps, and R. Leslie (1980a) Cell division in two large pennate diatoms. III. A new proposal for kinetochore function during prometaphase. J. Cell Biol. 86:402–416.

Tippit, D.H., L. Pillus, and J.D. Pickett-Heaps (1980b) Organization of spindle microtubules in Ochromonas danica. J. Cell Biol. 87:531–545.

Tippit, D.H., L. Pillus, and J.D. Pickett-Heaps (1983) Near-neighbor analysis of spindle microtubules in the alga Ochromonas. Eur. J. Cell Biol. 30:9–17.

Tippit, D.H., D. Schulz, and J.D. Pickett-Heaps (1978) Analysis of the distribution of spindle microtubules in the diatom Fragilaria. J. Cell Biol. 79:737–763.

Toriyama, M., K. Ohta, S. Endo, and H. Sakai (1985) A protein that constitutes the microtubule-organizing center in sea urchin egg. Cell Struct. Funct. 10:533.

Vale, R.D., T.S. Reese, and M.P. Sheetz (1985) Identification of a novel force-generating protein kinesin involved in microtubule-based motility. Cell 42:32–50.

Vallee, R.B., and G.S. Bloom (1983) Isolation of sea urchin egg microtubules with taxol and identification of mitotic spindle microtubule-associated proteins with monoclonal antibodies. Proc. Natl. Acad. Sci. USA 80:6259–6263.

Vallee, R.B., G.S. Bloom, and W.E. Theurkauf (1984) Microtubule associated proteins: Subunits of the cytoplasmic matrix. J. Cell Biol. 99:38s–44s.

Valodivia, M.M., and B.R. Brinkley (1986) Isolation of a kinetochore-centromere fraction from HeLa metaphase chromosomes. Methods Enzymol. 134:268–280.

Vandre, D.D., F.M. Davis, P.N. Rao, and G.G. Borisy (1984) Phosphoproteins are components of mitotic microtubule organizing center. Proc. Natl. Acad. Sci. USA 81:4439–4443.

Vandre, D.D., F.M. Davis, P.N. Rao, and G.G. Borisy (1986) Distribution of cytoskeletal proteins sharing a conserved phosphorylated epitope. Eur. J. Cell Biol. 41:72–81.

Wadsworth, P., and E.D. Salmon (1986a) Analysis of the treadmilling model during metaphase of mitosis using fluorescence redistribution after photobleaching. J. Cell Biol. 102:1032–1038.

Wadsworth, P., and E.D. Salmon (1986b) Microtubule dynamics in mitotic spindles of living cells. Ann. N.Y. Acad. Sci. 466:580–592.

Wadsworth, P., and R.D. Sloboda (1983) Microinjection of fluorescent tubulin into dividing sea urchin cells. J. Cell Biol. 97:1249–1254.

Warner, F.D., and D.R. Mitchell (1981) Polarity of dynein-microtubule interactions in vitro: Crossbridging between parallel and antiparallel microtubules. J. Cell Biol. 89:35–44.

Weisenberg, R., and W. Taylor (1968) Studies on ATPase activity of sea urchin eggs and the isolated mitotic apparatus. Exp. Cell Res. 53:372–384.

Welsh, M.J., J.R. Dedman, B.R. Brinkley, and A.R. Means (1979) Tubulin and calmodulin. Effects of microtubule and microfilament inhibitors on localization in the mitotic apparatus. J. Cell Biol. 81:624–634.

Wise, D., L.U. Cassimeris, C.L. Rieder, P. Wadsworth, and E.D. Salmon (1986) Incorporation of tubulin into kinetochore microtubules—Relation to chromosome congression. J. Cell Biol. 103:412a.

Witt, P.L., H. Ris, and G.G. Borisy (1980) Origin of kinetochore microtubules in CHO cells. Chromosoma 81:483–505.

Wolniack, S.M., and P.K. Hepler (1980) Detection of the membrane–calcium distribution during mitosis in Haemantus endosperm with chlorotetracyclin. J. Cell Biol. 87:23–32.

Wordeman, L., and W.Z. Cande (1987) Reactivation of spindle elongation in vitro is correlated with the phosphorylation of a 205 kd spindle-associated protein. Cell 50:535–543.

Wordeman, L., K. McDonald, and W.Z. Cande (1986) The distribution of cytoplasmic microtubules through the cell cycle of centric diatom Stephanopyxis turris: Their role in nuclear migration and repositioning the mitotic spindle during cytokinesis. J. Cell Biol. 102:1688–1698.

Zavortink, M., M.L. Welsh, and J.R. McIntosh (1983) The distribution of calmodulin in living mitotic cells. Exp. Cell Res. 149:375–385.

Zieve, G.W., S.R. Heidemann, and J.R. McIntosh (1980) Isolation and partial characterization of a cage of filaments that surrounds the mammalian mitotic spindle. J. Cell Biol. 87:160–169.

Zieve, G.W., and J.R. McIntosh (1981) A probe for flagellar dynein in the mammalian mitotic apparatus. J. Cell Sci. 48:241–257.

Index